Understanding the Business Environment

Visit the *Understanding the Business Environment*, third edition Companion Website at www.pearsoned.co.uk/capon to find valuable **student** learning material including:

- Multiple choice and true/false questions to test your learning
- Weblinks to relevant sites on the web
- An online glossary to explain key terms
- Interactive online flashcards that allow the reader to check definitions against the key terms during revision

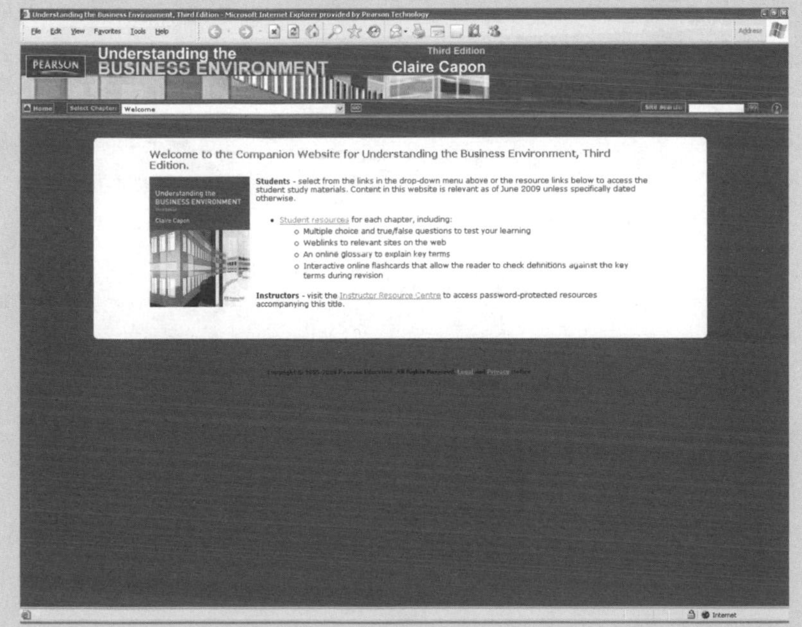

We work with leading authors to develop the strongest educational materials in business, bringing cutting-edge thinking and best learning practice to a global market.

Under a range of well-known imprints, including Financial Times Prentice Hall we craft high-quality print and electronic publications which help readers to understand and apply their content, whether studying or at work.

To find out more about the complete range of our publishing, please visit us on the World Wide Web at:
www.pearsoned.co.uk

Understanding the Business Environment

Inside and Outside the Organisation

Third Edition

Claire Capon
Staffordshire University

An imprint of Pearson Education
Harlow, England • London • New York • Boston • San Francisco • Toronto
Sydney • Tokyo • Singapore • Hong Kong • Seoul • Taipei • New Delhi
Cape Town • Madrid • Mexico City • Amsterdam • Munich • Paris • Milan

Pearson Education Limited

Edinburgh Gate
Harlow
Essex CM20 2JE
England

and Associated Companies throughout the world

Visit us on the World Wide Web at:
www.pearsoned.co.uk

First published 2000
Second edition published 2004
Third edition 2009

ISBN: 978-0-273-70814-8

British Library Cataloguing-in-Publication Data
A catalogue record for this book is available from the British Library

10 9 8 7 6 5 4 3 2 1
13 12 11 10 09

Typeset in 9.5/13 pt Stone Serif by 35
Printed and bound by Ashford Colour Press Ltd. Gosport

The publisher's policy is to use paper manufactured from sustainable forests.

Contents

Supporting resources

Visit **www.pearsoned.co.uk/capon** to find valuable online resources

Companion Website for students

- Multiple choice and true/false questions to test your learning
- Links to relevant sites on the web
- An online glossary to explain key terms
- Interactive online flashcards that allow the reader to check definitions against the key terms during revision

For instructors

- Complete, downloadable Instructor's Manual
- PowerPoint slides that can be downloaded and used for presentations
- Additional FT case studies and questions

Also: The Companion Website provides the following features:

- Search tool to help locate specific items of content
- E-mail results and profile tools to send results of quizzes to instructors
- Online help and support to assist with website usage and troubleshooting

For more information please contact your local Pearson Education sales representative or visit **www.pearsoned.co.uk/capon**

List of case studies

Preface

This third edition of *Understanding Organisational Context* has been renamed as *Understanding the Business Environment* to better reflect the content of the book and the type of modules for which it is suitable. Hence the overall approach of the previous editions has been maintained, while revising and updating the text for this new edition. Facts and figures have been updated, with new data and information being included where it has been appropriate to do so, including a new chapter on managing knowledge and innovation. The chapter on stakeholders now also covers corporate governance, ethics and corporate social responsibility. In addition, each chapter now contains 'Check your understanding' activities throughout each chapter and the full chapter summaries are retained. The chapter objectives have been specifically linked to appropriate activities at the end of each chapter, namely the exit case studies and assignment questions. The short-answer questions remain, the case studies have been updated to provide contemporary material, and the glossary has also been revised.

Overall, the desire remains as it has for the previous two editions, to provide students studying broad-based business modules with a useful and appealing textbook covering both the external and internal environments of organisations, unlike the many business environment textbooks currently on the market.

A *Lecturer's Guide* is available at **www.pearsoned.co.uk/capon** for lecturers adopting this book.

Claire Capon
April 2009

Teaching with this book

This textbook is designed to be used on level 1 modules on courses in business or on courses with a significant element of business in them. Examples of such courses would be BA Business Management, BA Business Administration, HND/HNC Business Studies or courses such as BSc/HND Business and Technology. Additionally this book can be used successfully with postgraduate and post-experience students studying business for the first time.

This book is suitable for modules that examine the environment in which organisations operate. The business environment model, shown at the start of each chapter, summarises all that is covered in this book and provides a useful diagrammatic overview of all that organisations have to consider.

This edition of *Understanding the Business Environment* examines the environment in which organisations operate. Chapter 1 examines why organisations analyse their external environment and how such analysis may be undertaken. Chapter 2 builds on Chapter 1 and explores in great detail the elements that could go to make up the external environment of an organisation. Chapter 3 continues with the theme of the external environment, but considers an extremely important constituent of any organisation's external environment, namely competition.

The inside of organisations and what they consist of is considered in Chapter 4 by looking at organisations as resource converters, which organise or structure themselves to best use the resources and succeed in their external environment. The idea of organisational culture linked to structure is also explored briefly in Chapter 4. Correspondingly, Chapter 5 examines the influence of personal and national culture on doing business and organisational culture in more detail. Chapter 6 covers organisational behaviour by looking at the individual, groups and leadership in organisations.

The four key functions or areas of activity for organisations are covered in Chapters 7–10 (human resource management, marketing, operations management and finance). Human resource (HR) management is examined in Chapter 7, covering the impact of the external environment on the HR function and the recruitment process. Chapter 8 looks at the development of marketing, the discipline as it is today and some marketing tools. Chapter 9 presents an overview of the operations management activities that both manufacturing and service providers will undertake. Chapter 10 covers finance by looking at the key areas of financial management and management accounting, along with financial reporting and financial stakeholders (for more on stakeholders, *see* Chapter 12). Chapter 11 examines knowledge and innovation. Different types of knowledge, innovation and the protection of intellectual property are considered. Chapter 12 is devoted to stakeholders, corporate governance, ethics and corporate social responsibility. The material on stakeholder analysis examines how an organisation can identify and manage those other organisations and people, both external and internal, that may have a role to play in the future of the organisation. The pages on corporate governance provide an overview of good corporate governance and the key roles involved and the remaining material discusses ethics and corporate responsibility in relation to businesses and stakeholders.

Designing a schedule of study

In modules designed to cover both the internal and external environments of organisations, there are several ways in which this book can be used. The most common semester length is 12 weeks and the most obvious programme of study using this book would be to cover one chapter per week. However, there are many possible combinations in which the chapters of this book could be studied during a 12-week teaching semester.

In considering the four key functional areas, tutors may choose to omit one if it is covered elsewhere on the students' course. For example, many business students will cover finance and accounting in a separate module. The extra week could be spent on Chapter 2, 'The composition of the external environment', which is a long chapter. This is illustrated in the design of the schedule of study shown below.

Alternatively, if an area is not covered anywhere else on the first year of a business programme, it may be that more than one week will be spent on it in the business environment module. The example used in the schedule of study shown below is operations management, which takes two weeks.

The remaining weeks of such a module may be used to cover the chapters presenting a variety of topics.

Possible schedule of study for a business environment module

Week 1	Chapter 1	The external environment
Week 2	Chapter 2	The composition of the external environment
Week 3	Chapter 2	The composition of the external environment
Week 4	Chapter 3	The competitive environment
Week 5	Chapter 4	Inside organisations
Week 6	Chapter 5	Culture and organisations
Week 7	Chapter 6	Organisational behaviour
Week 8	Chapter 7	Human resource management
Week 9	Chapter 8	Marketing
Week 10	Chapter 9	Operations management
Week 11	Chapter 9	Operations management
Week 12	Chapter 11	Managing knowledge and innovation

Module delivery

To aid the tutor in delivering business environment modules, a number of features appear in each chapter.

Clear chapter structure

Each chapter has the same layout: the business environment model; entry case study; introduction; main text, including 'Check your understanding' activities throughout; full chapter summary; exit case study and questions linked to the chapter objectives; short-answer questions; assignment questions linked to the chapter objectives; weblinks; further reading; and references.

Business environment model

The business environment model at the start of each chapter shows by shading the areas examined in that particular chapter. This allows readers to see at a glance what is covered in a chapter.

Chapter objectives

Chapter objectives allow tutors to check that they have covered everything they intended with a class and they also allow students to check that they have achieved the knowledge and skills covered by a particular chapter.

Case studies

There are two case studies in each chapter. Most of the case studies are copyright extracts from the *Financial Times* and are reproduced with its kind permission.

The entry case studies provide an example of the topic(s) covered in a chapter and are often referred to in the main text of the chapter by way of a real-life example. Therefore, students should be encouraged to read the entry case study before starting to read the chapter in detail. Students should also be encouraged to refer back to the entry case study, if necessary, when it is discussed or referred to in the main text. The exit case studies have been chosen to allow students to apply the knowledge and skills gained to a real-life situation. In addition, the exit case study and questions are linked to the chapter objectives, which makes it easy for the tutor to write relevant learning outcomes if the case study is to be used for assessed coursework.

Questions at end of chapter

The short-answer questions found at the end of each chapter have several uses. They could constitute a quick testing mechanism with students to see whether they have learned basic facts about a topic. This could be done in the form of an in-class quiz. Alternatively, if the formal examination for the business environment module contains a section of short-answer questions, those provided in the book allow students an opportunity to practise answering short-answer questions. A range of multiple-choice and true/false questions can be found on the accompanying websites at **www.pearsoned.co.uk/capon**.

Finally, it is intended that the assignment questions are used for formal assessed coursework. The normal length of report or essay that a student should be able to produce in response to such questions is around 2000 words.

Lecturer's Guide

A *Lecturer's Guide* is available to lecturers adopting this book and can be found at www.pearsoned.co.uk/capon.

About the author

Claire Capon teaches strategy in the Business School at Staffordshire University. She previously taught in the Business School at Sheffield Hallam University. She has worked as a researcher at Huddersfield Polytechnic, and at UMIST as a researcher in the areas of strategic management and the use of design by SMEs. Claire is also the author of another Financial Times Prentice Hall textbook: *Understanding Strategic Management* (2008).

Guided tour of the book

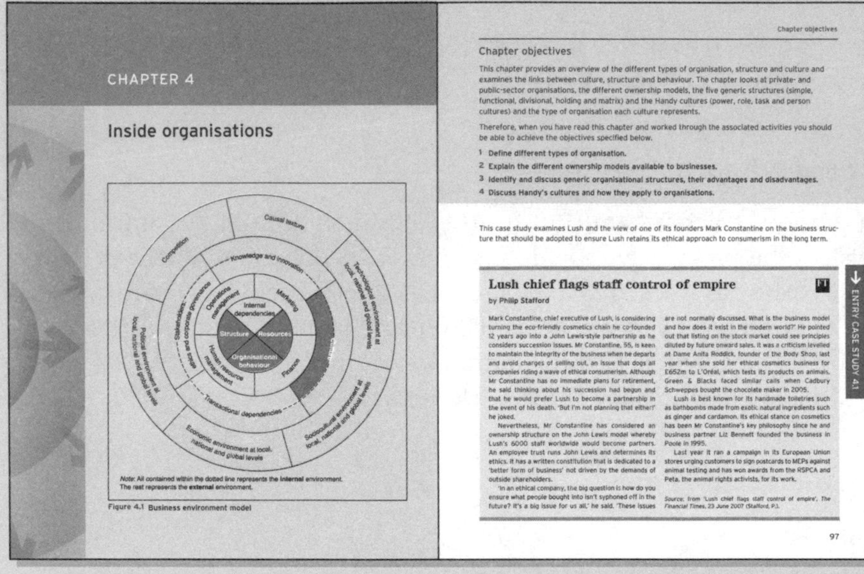

CHAPTER 4

Inside organisations

Note: All contained within the dotted line represents the **internal** environment. The rest represents the **external** environment.

Figure 4.1 Business environment model

Chapter objectives

Chapter objectives

This chapter provides an overview of the different types of organisation, structure and culture and examines the links between culture, structure and behaviour. The chapter looks at private- and public-sector organisations, the different ownership models, the five generic structures (simple, functional, divisional, holding and matrix) and the Handy cultures (power, role, task and person cultures) and the type of organisation each culture represents.

Therefore, when you have read this chapter and worked through the associated activities you should be able to achieve the objectives specified below.

1. **Define different types of organisation.**
2. **Explain the different ownership models available to businesses.**
3. **Identify and discuss generic organisational structures, their advantages and disadvantages.**
4. **Discuss Handy's cultures and how they apply to organisations.**

This case study examines Lush and the view of one of its founders Mark Constantine on the business structure that should be adopted to ensure Lush retains its ethical approach to consumerism in the long term.

ENTRY CASE STUDY 4.1

Lush chief flags staff control of empire

by Philip Stafford

Mark Constantine, chief executive of Lush, is considering turning the eco-friendly cosmetics chain he co-founded 12 years ago into a John Lewis-style partnership as he considers succession issues. Mr Constantine, 55, is keen to maintain the integrity of the business when he departs and avoid charges of selling out, an issue that dogs all companies riding a wave of ethical consumerism. Although Mr Constantine has no immediate plans for retirement, he said thinking about his succession had begun and that he would prefer Lush to become a partnership in the event of his death. 'But I'm not planning that either!' he joked.

Nevertheless, Mr Constantine has considered an ownership structure on the John Lewis model whereby Lush's 6000 staff worldwide would become partners. An employee trust runs John Lewis and determines its ethics. It has a written constitution that is dedicated to a 'better form of business' not driven by the demands of outside shareholders.

'In an ethical company, the big question is how do you ensure what people bought into isn't syphoned off in the future? It's a big issue for us all,' he said. 'These issues are not normally discussed. What is the business model and how does it exist in the modern world?' He pointed out that listing on the stock market could see principles diluted by future onward sales. It was a criticism levelled at Dame Anita Roddick, founder of the Body Shop, last year when she sold her ethical cosmetics business for £652m to L'Oréal, which tests its products on animals. Green & Blacks faced similar calls when Cadbury Schweppes bought the chocolate maker in 2005.

Lush is best known for its handmade toiletries such as bathbombs made from exotic natural ingredients such as ginger and cardamon. Its ethical stance on cosmetics has been Mr Constantine's key philosophy since he and business partner Liz Bennett founded the business in Poole in 1995.

Last year it ran a campaign in its European Union stores urging customers to sign postcards to MEPs against animal testing and has won awards from the RSPCA and Peta, the animal rights activists, for its work.

Source: from 'Lush chief flags staff control of empire', *The Financial Times*, 23 June 2007 (Stafford, P.).

97

Each chapter begins with an **Entry case study** to situate the reader in a real-world context.

Check your understanding boxes throughout each chapter encourage the reader to assess their new knowledge.

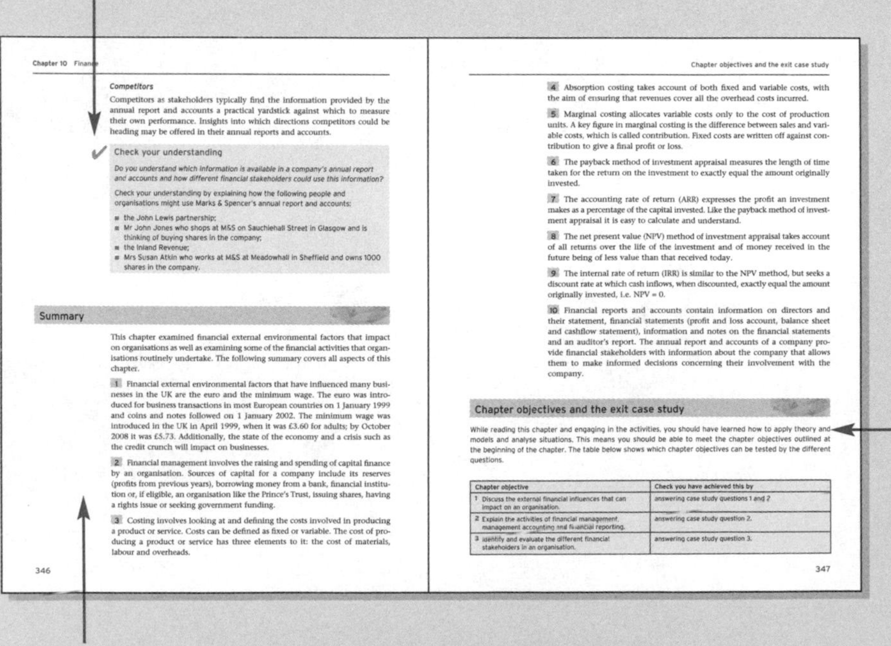

Chapter 10 Finance

Competitors

Competitors as stakeholders typically find the information provided by the annual report and accounts a practical yardstick against which to measure their own performance. Insights into which directions competitors could be heading may be offered in their annual reports and accounts.

Check your understanding

Do you understand which information is available in a company's annual report and accounts and how different financial stakeholders could use this information?

Check your understanding by explaining how the following people and organisations might use Marks & Spencer's annual report and accounts:

- the John Lewis partnership;
- Mr John Jones who shops at M&S on Sauchiehall Street in Glasgow and is thinking of buying shares in the company;
- the Inland Revenue;
- Mrs Susan Atkin who works at M&S at Meadowhall in Sheffield and owns 1000 shares in the company.

Summary

This chapter examined financial external environmental factors that impact on organisations as well as examining some of the financial activities that organisations routinely undertake. The following summary covers all aspects of this chapter.

1 Financial external environmental factors that have influenced many businesses in the UK are the euro and the minimum wage. The euro was introduced for business transactions in most European countries on 1 January 1999 and coins and notes followed on 1 January 2002. The minimum wage was introduced in the UK in April 1999, when it was £3.60 for adults; by October 2008 it was £5.73. Additionally, the state of the economy and a crisis such as the credit crunch will impact on businesses.

2 Financial management involves the raising and spending of capital finance by an organisation. Sources of capital for a company include its reserves (profits from previous years), borrowing money from a bank, financial institution or, if eligible, an organisation like the Prince's Trust, issuing shares, having a rights issue or seeking government funding.

3 Costing involves looking at and defining the costs involved in producing a product or service. Costs can be defined as fixed or variable. The cost of producing a product or service has three elements to it: the cost of materials, labour and overheads.

346

Chapter objectives and the exit case study

4 Absorption costing takes account of both fixed and variable costs, with the aim of ensuring that revenues cover all the overhead costs incurred.

5 Marginal costing allocates variable costs only to the cost of production units. A key figure in marginal costing is the difference between sales and variable costs, which is called contribution. Fixed costs are written off against contribution to give a final profit or loss.

6 The payback method of investment appraisal measures the length of time taken for the return on the investment to exactly equal the amount originally invested.

7 The accounting rate of return (ARR) expresses the profit an investment makes as a percentage of the capital invested. Like the payback method of investment appraisal it is easy to calculate and understand.

8 The net present value (NPV) method of investment appraisal takes account of all returns over the life of the investment and of money received in the future being of less value than that received today.

9 The internal rate of return (IRR) is similar to the NPV method, but seeks a discount rate at which cash inflows, when discounted, exactly equal the amount originally invested, i.e. NPV = 0.

10 Financial reports and accounts contain information on directors and their statement, financial statements (profit and loss account, balance sheet and cashflow statement), information and notes on the financial statements and an auditor's report. The annual report and accounts of a company provide financial stakeholders with information about the company that allows them to make informed decisions concerning their involvement with the company.

Chapter objectives and the exit case study

While reading this chapter and engaging in the activities, you should have learned how to apply theory and models and analyse situations. This means you should be able to meet the chapter objectives outlined at the beginning of the chapter. The table below shows which chapter objectives can be tested by the different questions.

Chapter objective	Check you have achieved this by
1 Discuss the external financial influences that can impact on an organisation.	answering case study questions 1 and 2
2 Explain the activities of financial management, management accounting and financial reporting.	answering case study question 2.
3 Identify and evaluate the different financial stakeholders in an organisation.	answering case study question 3.

347

Specific **Chapter objectives for case studies** enable students to focus on the most important concepts being illustrated.

A **Summary** at the end of each chapter reviews the key themes and ensures that these are understood.

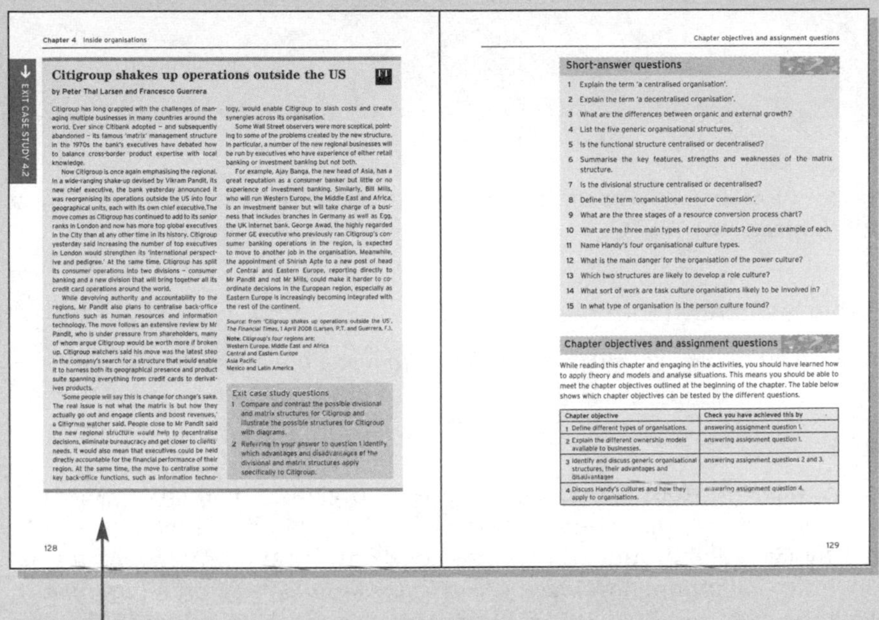

Chapter 4 Inside organisations

EXIT CASE STUDY 4.2

Citigroup shakes up operations outside the US

by Peter Thal Larsen and Francesco Guerrera

Citigroup has long grappled with the challenges of managing multiple businesses in many countries around the world. Ever since Citibank adopted – and subsequently abandoned – its famous 'matrix' management structure in the 1970s the bank's executives have debated how to balance cross-border product expertise with local knowledge.

Now Citigroup is once again emphasising the regional. In a wide-ranging shake-up devised by Vikram Pandit, its new chief executive, the bank yesterday announced it was reorganising its operations outside the US into four geographical units, each with its own chief executive. The move comes as Citigroup has continued to add to its senior ranks in London and now has more top global executives in the City than at any other time in its history. Citigroup yesterday said increasing the number of top executives in London would strengthen its 'international perspective and pedigree.' At the same time, Citigroup has split its consumer operations into two divisions – consumer banking and a new division that will bring together all its credit card operations around the world.

While devolving authority and accountability to the regions, Mr Pandit also plans to centralise back-office functions such as human resources and information technology. The move follows an extensive review by Mr Pandit, who is under pressure from shareholders, many of whom argue Citigroup would be worth more if broken up. Citigroup watchers said his move was the latest step in the company's search for a structure that would enable it to harness both its geographical presence and product suite spanning everything from credit cards to derivatives products.

'Some people will say this is change for change's sake. The real issue is not what the matrix is but how they actually go out and engage clients and boost revenues,' a Citigroup watcher said. People close to Mr Pandit said the new regional structure would help to decentralise decisions, eliminate bureaucracy and get closer to clients' needs. It would also mean that executives could be held directly accountable for the financial performance of their region. At the same time, the move to centralise some key back-office functions, such as information technology, would enable Citigroup to slash costs and create synergies across its organisation.

Some Wall Street observers were more sceptical, pointing to some of the problems created by the new structure. In particular, a number of the new regional businesses will be run by executives who have experience of either retail banking or investment banking but not both.

For example, Ajay Banga, the new head of Asia, has a great reputation as a consumer banker but little or no experience of investment banking. Similarly, Bill Mills, who will run Western Europe, the Middle East and Africa, is an investment banker but will take charge of a business that includes branches in Germany as well as Egg, the UK internet bank. George Awad, the highly regarded former GE executive who previously ran Citigroup's consumer banking operations in the region, is expected to move to another job in the organisation. Meanwhile, the appointment of Shirish Apte to a new post of head of Central and Eastern Europe, reporting directly to Mr Pandit and not Mr Mills, could make it harder to co-ordinate decisions in the European region, especially as Eastern Europe is increasingly becoming integrated with the rest of the continent.

Source: from 'Citigroup shakes up operations outside the US', *The Financial Times*, 1 April 2008 (Larsen, P.T. and Guerrera, F.).

Note: Citigroup's four regions are:
Western Europe, Middle East and Africa
Central and Eastern Europe
Asia Pacific
Mexico and Latin America

Exit case study questions

1 Compare and contrast the possible divisional and matrix structures for Citigroup and illustrate the possible structures for Citigroup with diagrams.
2 Referring to your answer to question 1 identify which advantages and disadvantages of the divisional and matrix structures apply specifically to Citigroup.

128

Chapter objectives and assignment questions

Short-answer questions

1 Explain the term 'a centralised organisation'.
2 Explain the term 'a decentralised organisation'.
3 What are the differences between organic and external growth?
4 List the five generic organisational structures.
5 Is the functional structure centralised or decentralised?
6 Summarise the key features, strengths and weaknesses of the matrix structure.
7 Is the divisional structure centralised or decentralised?
8 Define the term 'organisational resource conversion'.
9 What are the three stages of a resource conversion process chart?
10 What are the three main types of resource inputs? Give one example of each.
11 Name Handy's four organisational culture types.
12 What is the main danger for the organisation of the power culture?
13 Which two structures are likely to develop a role culture?
14 What sort of work are task culture organisations likely to be involved in?
15 In what type of organisation is the person culture found?

Chapter objectives and assignment questions

While reading this chapter and engaging in the activities, you should have learned how to apply theory and models and analyse situations. This means you should be able to meet the chapter objectives outlined at the beginning of the chapter. The table below shows which chapter objectives can be tested by the different questions.

Chapter objective	Check you have achieved this by
1 Define different types of organisations.	answering assignment question 1.
2 Explain the different ownership models available to businesses.	answering assignment question 1.
3 Identify and discuss generic organisational structures, their advantages and disadvantages	answering assignment questions 2 and 3.
4 Discuss Handy's cultures and how they apply to organisations.	answering assignment question 4.

129

An **Exit case study** with questions encourages critical reflection of the issues raised.

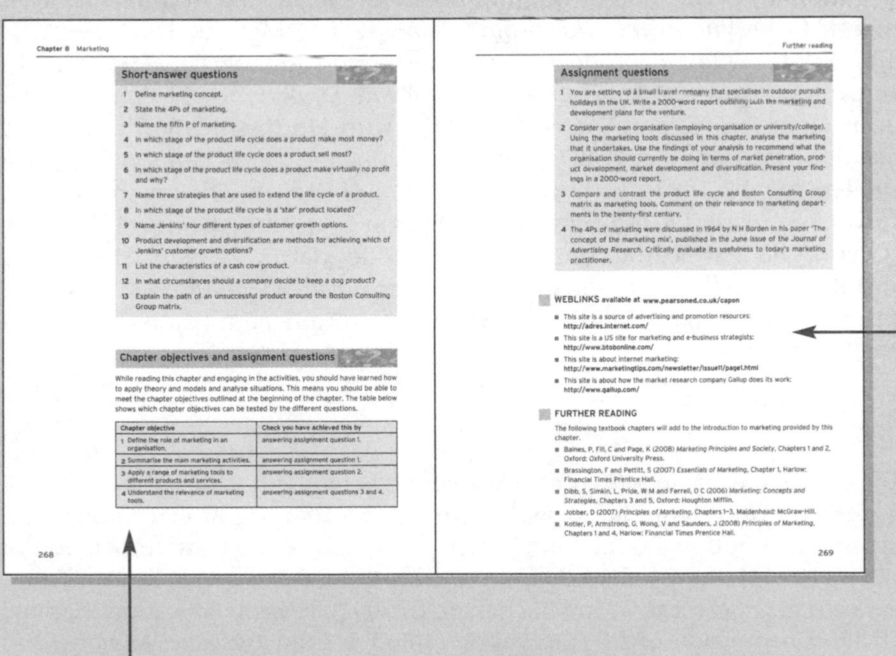

Chapter 8 Marketing

Short-answer questions

1 Define marketing concept.
2 State the 4Ps of marketing.
3 Name the fifth P of marketing.
4 In which stage of the product life cycle does a product make most money?
5 In which stage of the product life cycle does a product sell most?
6 In which stage of the product life cycle does a product make virtually no profit and why?
7 Name three strategies that are used to extend the life cycle of a product.
8 In which stage of the product life cycle is a 'star' product located?
9 Name Jenkins' four different types of customer growth options.
10 Product development and diversification are methods for achieving which of Jenkins' customer growth options?
11 List the characteristics of a cash cow product.
12 In what circumstances should a company decide to keep a dog product?
13 Explain the path of an unsuccessful product around the Boston Consulting Group matrix.

Chapter objectives and assignment questions

While reading this chapter and engaging in the activities, you should have learned how to apply theory and models and analyse situations. This means you should be able to meet the chapter objectives outlined at the beginning of the chapter. The table below shows which chapter objectives can be tested by the different questions.

Chapter objective	Check you have achieved this by
1 Define the role of marketing in an organisation.	answering assignment question 1.
2 Summarise the main marketing activities.	answering assignment question 1.
3 Apply a range of marketing tools to different products and services.	answering assignment question 2.
4 Understand the relevance of marketing tools.	answering assignment questions 3 and 4.

268

Further reading

Assignment questions

1 You are setting up a small travel company that specialises in outdoor pursuits holidays in the UK. Write a 2000-word report outlining both the marketing and development plans for the venture.
2 Consider your own organisation (employing organisation or university/college). Using the marketing tools discussed in this chapter, analyse the marketing that it undertakes. Use the findings of your analysis to recommend what the organisation should currently be doing in terms of market penetration, product development, market development and diversification. Present your findings in a 2000-word report.
3 Compare and contrast the product life cycle and Boston Consulting Group matrix as marketing tools. Comment on their relevance to marketing departments in the twenty-first century.
4 The 4Ps of marketing were discussed in 1964 by N H Borden in his paper 'The concept of the marketing mix', published in the June issue of the *Journal of Advertising Research*. Critically evaluate its usefulness to today's marketing practitioner.

WEBLINKS available at www.pearsoned.co.uk/capon

- This site is a source of advertising and promotion resources: http://adres.internet.com/
- This site is a US site for marketing and e-business strategists: http://www.btobonline.com/
- This site is about internet marketing: http://www.marketingtips.com/newsletter/issue11/page1.html
- This site is about how the market research company Gallup does its work: http://www.gallup.com/

FURTHER READING

The following textbook chapters will add to the introduction to marketing provided by this chapter.

- Baines, P, Fill, C and Page, K (2008) *Marketing Principles and Society*, Chapters 1 and 2, Oxford: Oxford University Press.
- Brassington, F and Pettitt, S (2007) *Essentials of Marketing*, Chapter 1, Harlow: Financial Times Prentice Hall.
- Dibb, S, Simkin, L, Pride, W M and Ferrell, O C (2006) *Marketing: Concepts and Strategies*, Chapters 3 and 5, Oxford: Houghton Mifflin.
- Jobber, D (2007) *Principles of Marketing*, Chapters 1–3, Maidenhead: McGraw-Hill.
- Kotler, P, Armstrong, G, Wong, V and Saunders, J (2008) *Principles of Marketing*, Chapters 1 and 4, Harlow: Financial Times Prentice Hall.

269

Weblinks, Further reading and **References** at the end of each chapter recommend reliable sources for futher research and study.

Assignment questions provides activities for seminar and out-of-class use. These are preceded by **Chapter objectives** to indicate the objectives of these tasks.

Acknowledgements

Thanks go to Matthew Walker and all the other excellent and patient staff at Pearson Education.

Publisher's acknowledgements

We are grateful to the following for permission to reproduce copyright material:

Figures

Figure 3.2 adapted from 'The causal texture of organisational environments', *Human Relations*, 18, pp. 21–32 (Emery, F.E. and Trist, E.L. 1965), copyright © 1965 by (Sage Publications). Reprinted by Permission of SAGE; Figures 3.3 and 3.4 from *Competitive Advantage: Creating and Sustaining Superior Performance*, The Free Press (Porter, M.E. 1985), Reprinted with the permission of The Free Press, a Division of Simon & Schuster, Inc., Copyright © 1985, 1998 by Michael E Porter. All rights reserved; Figures 4.9, 4.10, 4.11 and 4.12 from *Understanding Organizations*, 4 ed., Penguin Books Ltd (Handy, C. 1993), pages 183, 185, 187 and 190. Copyright © Charles Handy, 1976, 1981, 1985, 1993, 1999. Reproduced by permission of Penguin Books Ltd; Figure 5.3 from *International Business: Competing in the Global Marketplace*, 2 ed., McGraw-Hill Education (Hill, C.W.L. 1994), Reproduced with the permission of The McGraw-Hill Companies; Figure 5.4 from *Exploring Corporate Strategy*, 5 ed., Prentice Hall Europe (Johnson, G. and Scholes, K. 1999), with kind permission of Pearson Education, Harlow; Figure 8.7 from *The Customer Centred Strategy*, Prentice Hall (Jenkins, M. 1997), with kind permission of Pearson Education, Harlow; Figure 8.8 from *The Product Portfolio*, The Boston Consulting Group (1970), The BCG Portfolio Matrix from the Product Portfolio Matrix, © 1970, The Boston Consulting Group; Figure 12.3 from *Exploring Corporate Strategy*, 5 ed., Prentice Hall (Johnson, G. and Scholes, K. 1999), with kind permission of Pearson Education, Harlow.

Tables

Table 6.2 adapted from *Makers of Management*, Macmillan (Clutterbuck, D. and Crainer, S. 1990), reproduced with permission of Curtis Brown Group Ltd, London on behalf of David Clutterbuck. Copyright © D. Clutterbuck and S. Crainer, 1990; Table 6.4 adapted from *Organzational Behaviour*, Financial Times Prentice Hall (Huczynski, A. and Buchanan, D. 2001), Pearson Education, Harlow, with kind permission of Dr Huczynski; Table 7.5 from *Personnel Management: HRM in Action*, 3 ed., Prentice Hall (Torrington, D. and Hill, L. 1995), with kind permission of Pearson Education, Harlow; Table 7.7 from People Resourcing, 4 ed., (Taylor, S. 2008) with the permission of the publisher, the Chartered Institute of Personnel and Development, London (www.cipd.co.uk).

Text

Case Study 3.2 from 'The going gets tough for organic', *Guardian*, 14 August 2008 (Saner, E.), Copyright Guardian News & Media Ltd 2008; Case Study 6.1 from 'Nelson Mandela: Global admiration has drawbacks', *Daily Telegraph*, 27 June 2008 (Blair, D.), © Telegraph Media Group Limited 2008.

The Financial Times

Case Study 1.1 from 'Toyota trims output in China as market slows', *The Financial Times*, 29 September 2008 (Soble, J.); Case Study 1.2 from 'Cadbury to cut further 580 jobs', *The Financial Times*, 14 October 2008 (Urry, M.); Case Study 2.1 from 'Nafta drives car production', *The Financial Times*, 16 June 2008 (Lapper, R.); Case Study 2.2 from 'Tui slashes number of holiday packages', *The Financial Times*, 27 November 2008 (Yuk, P.K.); Table 2.20 from UN Population Division Data from 'People, plagues and prosperity', *The Financial Times*, 27 February 2003 (Wolf, M.); Case Study 3.1 from 'Competition watchdog flexes its muscles', *The Financial Times*, 20 August 2008 (Peel, M.); Case Study 4.1 from 'Lush chief flags staff control of empire', *The Financial Times*, 23 June 2007 (Stafford, P.); Case Study 4.2 from 'Citigroup shakes up operations outside the US', *The Financial Times*, 1 April 2008 (Larsen, P.T. and Guerrera, F.); Case Study 5.1 from 'Open culture wins plaudits from staff', *The Financial Times*, 28 May 2008; Case Study 5.2 from 'Mars trades on new healthy image', *The Financial Times*, 30 April 2008 (Wiggins, J.); Case Study 6.2 from 'Final encore for a man of the people', *The Financial Times*, 8 June 2008 (Birchall, J.); Case Study 7.1 from 'Skills shortage hits Russian revival', *The Financial Times*, 17 April 2008 (Wagstyl, S. and Buckley, N.); Case Study 7.2 from 'Recruitment and retention: How to find the best and keep them', *The Financial Times*, 28 May 2008 (Murray, S.); Case Study 8.1 from 'Costa aims to stir a coffee revolution in Russia', *The Financial Times*, 27 March 2008 (Wiggins, J.); Case Study 8.2 from 'Hot times ahead for curry houses', *The Financial Times*, 14 May 2008 (Jacobs, E.); Case Study 9.1 from 'Fingers burnt in a hands-on operation', *The Financial Times*, 20 February 2008 (Sherwood, B.); Case Study 9.2 from 'Ingredients for success on a plate', *The Financial Times*, 26 March 2008 (Marsh, P.); Case Study 10.1 from 'Tesco shrugs off retail clouds', *The Financial Times*, 16 April 2008 (Rigby, E.); Case Study 10.2 from 'Minimum wage increases by 3.8%', *The Financial Times*, 5 March 2008 (Taylor, A.); Case Study 11.1 from 'The brains of the operation', *The Financial Times*, 5 November 2008 (Newing, R.); Case Study 11.2 from 'Help at hand for bringing clients' ideas to market', *The Financial Times*, 14 November 2008 (Stern, S.); Case Study 12.1 from 'Sir Stuart Rose and the thorny issue of corporate governance', *The Financial Times*, 11 March 2008 (Braithwaite, T. and Rigby, E.); Case Study 12.2 from 'No help for charities in Iceland plight', *The Financial Times*, 10 October 2008 (Pickard, J. and Braithwaite, T.).

In some instances we have been unable to trace the owners of copyright material, and we would appreciate any information that would enable us to do so.

CHAPTER 1

The external environment

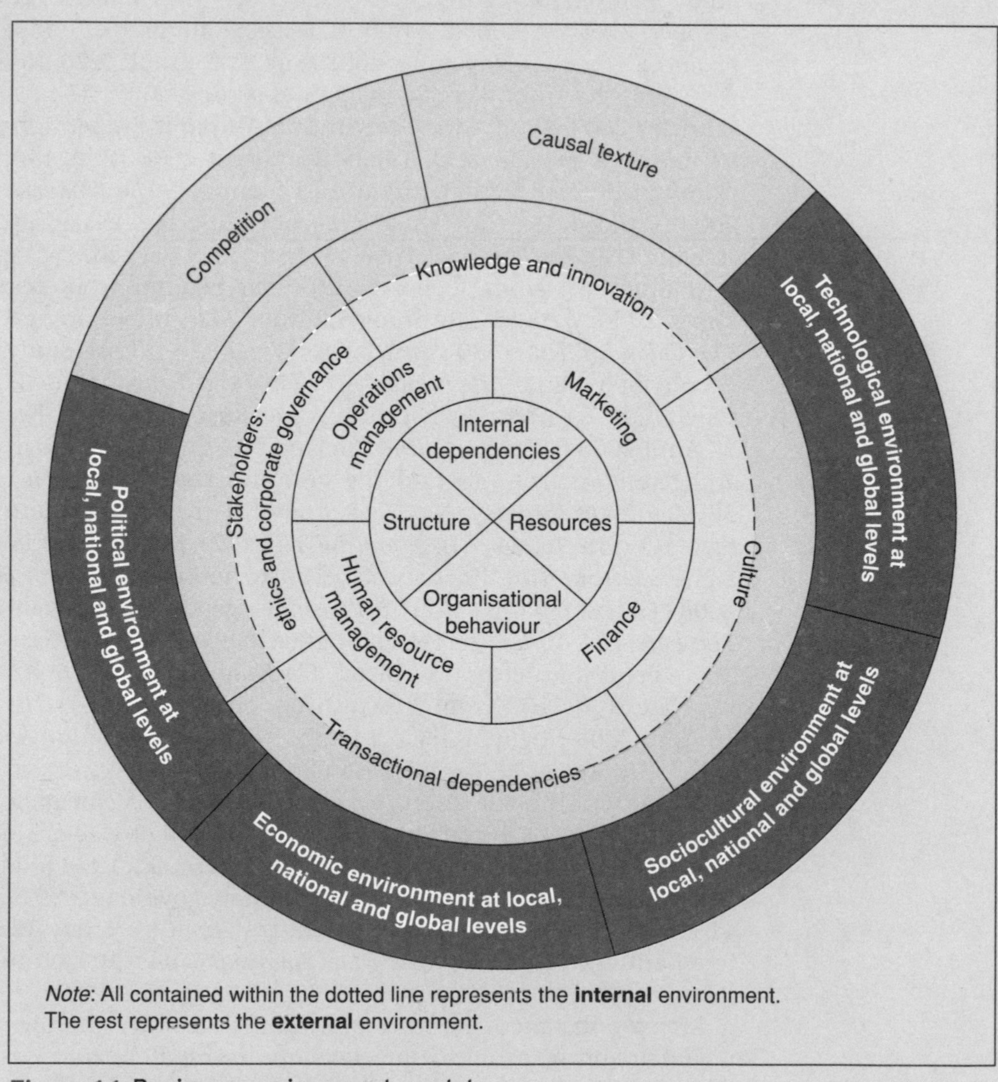

Figure 1.1 Business environment model

Chapter objectives

This chapter aims to provide an introduction to the business environment and its analysis. The idea of both PEST analysis and LoNGPEST analysis are introduced, information sources for such analyses and the process for performing analyses of the external environment are also discussed.

Therefore, when you have read this chapter and worked through the associated activities you should be able to achieve the objectives specified below.

1. **Define PEST and LoNGPEST analysis.**
2. **Identify and discuss relevant sources of information that assist in environmental analysis.**
3. **Explain the process for carrying out a PEST or LoNGPEST analysis.**
4. **Perform PEST and LoNGPEST analyses.**

This case study shows how the economic downturn has had an impact in China as new car sales have declined in the West, Japan and China.

ENTRY CASE STUDY 1.1

Toyota trims output in China as market slows

by Jonathan Soble in Tokyo

A weakening Chinese car market has forced Toyota to curb production in the country and threatened the Japanese carmaker's ambitious sales targets. Toyota and other global carmakers have been counting on a boom in car ownership in China – the world's second-biggest market by volume – to help offset plunging sales in the US.

Demand in western Europe and Japan has also been in decline and Toyota's move will confirm suggestions that the slowdown has now spread to China. Toyota said it had slowed the production line at its Camry plant in Guangzhou, which it operates with local joint venture partner Guangzhou Automotive. 'The market overall is not expanding as quickly as we thought initially. We're making adjustments,' Toyota said, without giving more details.

After growing at a double-digit pace through the first half of the year, overall passenger-car sales in China fell for the first month in more than two years in August, shrinking by 6.2 per cent, according to the national industry association. Analysts on Monday attributed part of the decline in sales to the Beijing Olympics, which forced cars off the road in the Chinese capital and may have kept potential buyers elsewhere at home in front of their televisions. But Toyota's production cut suggests the Japanese carmaker is bracing for a more protracted slowdown in car sales. China's state-subsidised petrol refineries have been allowed to pass some price rises on to drivers while the stock market, a source of much new middle-class wealth, has gone into retreat.

The Japanese carmaker made 450,000 cars in China last year, accounting for most of the cars it sold in the country and making it one of the three largest sellers in China. Toyota's official sales forecasts call for a 40 per cent increase in Chinese sales this year to 700,000 cars. The company left that projection figure unchanged in July when it cut its global sales projection by 3.5 per cent. Toyota's first-quarter net profit fell 28 per cent after a decline in US sales of trucks and sport-utility vehicles. It has cut production in the US and is now retooling plants there to focus on small cars.

Separately, shares in Isuzu Motors, the Japanese light-truck maker, fell to their lowest level in more than three years on Monday after Goldman Sachs cut its rating on the company from 'buy' to 'neutral'. Sales in the US tumbled more than 20 per cent in the first eight months of the year while domestic sales dropped 14 per cent. Isuzu's stock fell 10 per cent to close at ¥291 on Monday.

Source: from 'Toyota trims output in China as market slows', *The Financial Times*, 29 September 2008 (Soble, J.).

Introduction

This chapter introduces the idea of organisations analysing their external environment in order to make sense of the volatile world in which they operate, such that appropriate management and business decisions can be taken. In contemplating the complex and dynamic world in which they operate, organisations have to consider many influences and issues. The entry case study on Toyota illustrates the impact of an economic downturn on a company's operations.

Analysis of the external environment can be done at a broad general level by use of PEST and **LoNGPEST** analyses, which are covered in this chapter and Chapter 2. Further examination of other components of the external environment needs to occur for a full understanding of the external environment to be possible. These other components include competition, competitors, customers and other external stakeholders.

To be able to compete effectively, organisations need to understand who their competitors are and the best way to compete with them. For example the airline Lufthansa has sought to compete with both low-cost carriers in Europe and on longer-haul routes, by understanding very clearly the relationship between costs, price and profits and improving their fleet. Improvements in the cost, price, profit relationship may be achieved by employing cost-cutting strategies and for airlines this can mean ensuring planes are full and being more stringent about charging for excess baggage and even charging for issuing a paper ticket. These approaches are used by airlines to survive in a complex and turbulent environment, caused by a rapidly changing environment, including an economic downturn, increasing fuel prices and changing consumer behaviour which follows several years in which war, terrorism and bankruptcy have impacted on the aviation industry.

Organisations may choose to compete by offering low-priced, good-value products and services, such as Hyundai cars, or by offering a better or luxury product or service at a higher price, such Audi or BMW. We look at the issues of competition in Chapter 3. Equally, the understanding of competitors and their behaviour ties in directly with the need to understand the marketplace, who your customers are, where they are located, and how they can be persuaded to buy the products and services offered by your company rather than those of one of your competitors. This is explored in Chapter 8. For airlines the access customers now have to information on flights and fares via the internet has resulted in airlines having to work harder to compete and make their offering attractive and appealing to customers.

The tool of **PEST analysis** is examined and developed for the purpose of analysing the external environment or outside world. Analysis of the external environment is an ongoing process for organisations that takes the dynamic and changing nature of the external environment seriously.

Hence, in summary, this chapter examines:

- the elements and levels of the external environment faced by organisations;
- the benefits of external environmental analysis;
- the guidelines for undertaking LoNGPEST analysis;
- in brief, the part that competition plays in the organisation's external environment.

The elements and levels of the external environment

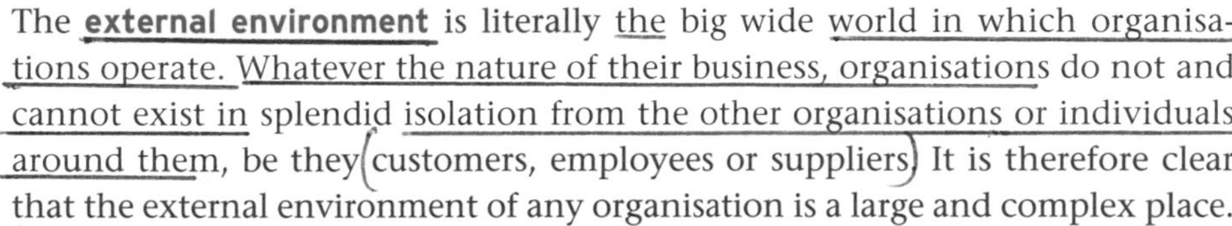

The **external environment** is literally the big wide world in which organisations operate. Whatever the nature of their business, organisations do not and cannot exist in splendid isolation from the other organisations or individuals around them, be they customers, employees or suppliers. It is therefore clear that the external environment of any organisation is a large and complex place.

The term 'environment' in this case refers to much more than the ecological 'green' issues that the word commonly evokes. 'Environment' here is more appropriately interpreted as the external context in which organisations find themselves undertaking their activities. Each organisation has a unique external environment that has unique impacts on the organisation, due to the fact that organisations are located in different places and are involved in different business activities, with different products, services, customers and so on. In addition to this unique context, individual organisations will all have their own distinctive view of the world surrounding them, leading them to interpret what is happening in the external environment correctly or incorrectly, depending on their ability to understand the external forces affecting them. This suggests it is crucial for organisations to undertake external environmental analysis and to aim to get it right.

Careful and accurate analysis of the external environment benefits organisations by providing overall greater understanding and an appreciation of the context in which the organisation operates. The key benefits of external environmental analysis are best realised if it is undertaken on a long-term, ongoing basis. These benefits can be summarised as follows:

- managers in the organisation achieve a greater understanding and appreciation of the external environment, leading to improvement in long-term and strategic planning;
- highlighting of the principal external environmental influences generating change;
- anticipation of threats and opportunities within a timescale of long enough duration to allow responses to be considered.[1]

Check your understanding

Do you understand what is meant by the term 'external environment'?

Check your understanding by explaining what the external environment of an organisation is.

External environments can be defined and analysed using PEST analysis, examining political, economic, sociocultural and technological categories into which external influences on the organisation can be placed.

- *Political* influences on organisations encompass both those with a big and small letter 'p', i.e. politics in the conventional sense, with the rules and regulations imposed by government, as well as the **political influences** on organisations of various trade associations, trade unions and chambers of commerce.
- *Economic* influences on organisations include the impact of banks, stock markets, the world money markets, and trading blocs such as the European Union.
- *Sociocultural* influences on organisations include changes in the age and structure of populations, the manner in which populations behave, and the way in which the culture of a population or country changes and develops.
- *Technological* developments influence the magnitude and rate of change that organisations face, and how this affects their capacity to meet their customers' demands. Technological developments have included the development of increasingly sophisticated computer hardware and software. The development of media and communications technology covers electronics and telecommunications, including use of the internet. The ongoing development of the internet as a way of doing business and accessing information has meant a whole new 'media' which needs to be understood in terms of its potential use and reliability.

Basic analysis of an organisation's external environment can be done by breaking down the external influences on the organisation into the PEST categories and assessing the impact of the individual elements identified in each category.

However, there exists a second dimension to the external environment of organisations. This is the level at which the influences occur. There are three levels that will be considered alongside the PEST categories. The levels are local, national and global (LoNG).

- The *local* level can be said to be the immediate town, city or region in which the organisation operates.
- The *national* level is then the home country in which an organisation identifies its headquarters.
- The *global* level then becomes anything outside the local and national levels.

A company operating in and being influenced by the **global level** of the external environment will be trading in a foreign country, be it right next door or on the other side of the world. A company in this situation is subject not only to the laws and culture of its local and national environments but also to the laws and culture of the foreign country in which it is trading. In addition to national rules and regulations, there are the laws and procedures of both home and host countries specifically governing importing/exporting and foreign direct investment activity to consider.

The literature of international business clearly differentiates the terms 'international' and 'global'. Some of the issues considered here are 'international'; i.e. they are issues that occur between nations. However, the third level will be described as 'global', i.e. affecting all parts of the world in similar and simultaneous ways. This is because many of the issues of globalisation in the twenty-first century increasingly affect the local and national levels of organisations' external environments.

The traditional PEST analysis, then, is a short, one-dimensional view of the external environment. The two-dimensional analysis will be referred to in this text as a LoNG (local, national and global) PEST analysis. A generic LoNGPEST analysis could look like the grid shown in Table 1.1.

The grid represents the view that these external influential elements, whether political, economic, sociocultural or technological, all exist at local, national and global levels. The political, economic and **sociocultural influences** are easily identified at the three different levels. However, it could be argued that all types of technology affect and influence organisations at all levels of the environment.

Table 1.1 Generic LoNGPEST grid

<table>
<tr><th></th><th>Political</th><th>Economic</th><th>Sociocultural</th><th>Technological</th></tr>
<tr><td>Local</td><td>• Local government
• Local offices of national government
• Local associations
– Chambers of commerce
– Business Link</td><td>• Local bank branches
• Local economy</td><td>• Local community
• Social capital</td><td rowspan="3">• Communications technology
– Mobile phones and faxes
– Video conferencing
– Internet and world wide web
• Organisations and the application of technology
– The personal computer
– The banking and financial services industry</td></tr>
<tr><td>National</td><td>• National government
• Devolution for Scotland and Wales
• National bodies
– Employers' bodies
– Employees' bodies</td><td>• Central bank
– Bank of England
• Stock market
– London</td><td>• Demographic change
• Social change</td></tr>
<tr><td>Global</td><td>• Alliances and agreements
– UK and USA
– UK and China
– EU
– Cold War
– CIS
– CBSS
– Eastern Europe
• International bodies
– The Commonwealth
– NATO</td><td>• Trading blocs and bodies
– EU
– EFTA
– OECD
– NAFTA
– ASEAN
• World money markets
• WTO</td><td>• Global demographics
• Cross-cultural issues
– Language
– Behaviour
– Culture shock</td></tr>
</table>

It should be noted that not every organisation will identify strongly influential elements in all four PEST categories at all three levels all the time. However, the possibility should be considered for any organisation when carrying out a LoNGPEST analysis because elements have to be identified before they can be evaluated and discounted.

The next section of this chapter offers some guidelines for use when carrying out external environmental analysis. The grid in Table 1.1 shows the possible different external environmental influences on an organisation. These external environmental influences are discussed in more detail in Chapter 2.

Check your understanding

Do you understand what is meant by LoNGPEST?

Check your understanding by naming one influence from each of the following categories: technology; local/political; national/economic; global/sociocultural.

Performing external environmental analysis

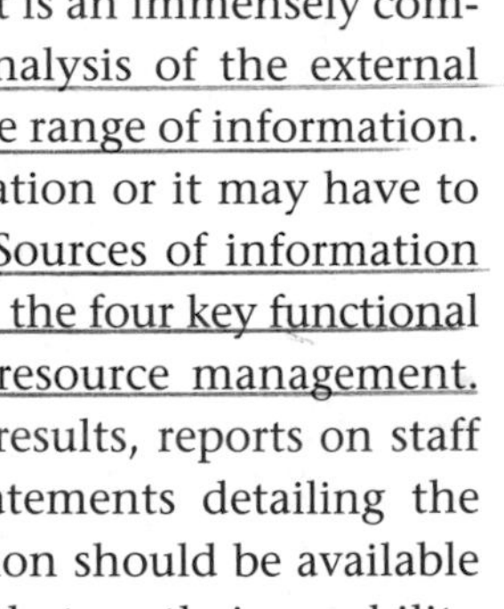

As has been stated previously, the external environment is an immensely complex and dynamic place. Therefore, performing an analysis of the external environment of an organisation requires access to a wide range of information. This information may already exist within the organisation or it may have to be sought, collected and collated from other sources. Sources of information within an organisation will encompass information from the four key functional areas of marketing, production, finance and human resource management. This will include sales reports, customer/client survey results, reports on staff skills and availability, and budgets and cashflow statements detailing the amount and availability of cash. In addition, information should be available on the systems in place in the organisation, including that on their capability and capacity, and efficiency and effectiveness. This type of information provided by internal sources, if it is up to date, will provide details of the resources available to deal with current influences in the external environment and indicate the level of resources needed to respond to possible future influences from the external environment.

External information sources are compiled by organisations other than that undertaking analysis of its external environment. The external information sources most widely available and accessible to everyone are the press, television and radio. In the UK the most familiar press includes the daily and Sunday broadsheet newspapers, which all contain business pages or sections in addition to reporting the general political and economic news. These are The *Independent*, the *Daily Telegraph*, *The Times*, The *Guardian*, the *Financial Times*, the *Sunday Times*, the *Sunday Telegraph*, The *Observer*, and the *Independent on Sunday*. Publications such as *The Economist* and *Management Today* supply more extensive coverage of the economy and the latest developments in the world of trade and commerce than that provided by the daily and Sunday press.

The annual report and accounts of a company also provide a summary of recent activities and may offer clues to or an indication of future activities. The annual report and accounts of publicly quoted companies are readily available from the companies themselves or via their website, so are easily obtainable by competitor companies. Specific information concerning an industry will be available from industry- or trade-specific publications.

Current affairs programmes on radio and television cover economic and political news as well as reporting company and industry news and events. For example, Radio 4's *Today* programme comprises items of economic, political and business news and is broadcast at breakfast time on weekday mornings. In addition, economic, political and business news is reported on television news programmes, for example on ITV and BBC1 at teatime and in the late evening. Daily news broadcasts, such as *Newsnight* on BBC2 and Channel 4 News, are longer news programmes than the broadcasts on BBC1 and ITV and consequently devote more time to economic, political and business news stories.

The internet and electronic information are other sources of information which are widely available in organisations. An immense and extensive amount of information can be found on the internet, although one must be aware of who or which organisation originated the information, as this will affect its reliability and accuracy. Much printed and broadcast material can now be accessed via the internet, and many organisations have their own website.

The other method of accessing information electronically is via the use of subscription databases such as Lexis/Nexis, which gives access to the world's

Table 1.2 Blank grid for LoNGPEST analysis

	Political	Economic	Sociocultural	Technological
Local				
National				
Global				

press. Other subscription databases which can be found in libraries include MINTEL, FAME and journal databases.

There is likely to be an increase in the number of websites available on a subscription-only basis. For example the FT internet archive is now subscription only.

The use of the LoNGPEST framework and information will allow analysis of the external environment of an organisation to be completed. The following guidelines will help in applying the LoNGPEST framework. It is suggested that a blank grid like the one in Table 1.2 is used when carrying out external environmental analysis.

Guidelines for external environmental analysis

1 Identify the influences affecting the organisation.
2 Categorise the influences by using the LoNGPEST grid.
   (a) First, decide whether the influence is political, economic, sociocultural or technological.
   (b) Second, decide whether the influence is local, national or global.
3 Make sure you can explain how and why a particular influence is affecting an organisation. Remember, elements in the external environment do not exist in isolation at any level and can impinge on and influence one another.
4 Select and judge which categories are most important to the company, for example **technological influences** at the global level or **economic influences** at the **national level**.
5 Select key individual influences from the important categories. For example, the important category economic influences at the national level may contain the crucial influence of falling interest rates.
6 Consider the important categories and influences you have identified. Do any of these pose threats or opportunities to which the company must react immediately or in the longer term, when anticipating and planning the future?
7 How should the organisation react to and deal with the opportunities and threats? Do short-term opportunities take priority over long-term threats or vice versa?

Check your understanding

Do you understand the importance of information gathering and its reliability in undertaking external environmental analysis?

Check your understanding by stating where you would search for information on the following types of influence: political, economic, sociocultural and technological.

Summary

This chapter examined the external environment influences (PEST) which impact on organisations and how those factors could also be assessed at the local, national and global levels of the external environment. The following summary covers all aspects of this chapter.

1 Organisations analyse their external environment in an effort to understand what it is that impacts on them. In broad general terms, factors impacting on organisations arise from the PEST factors (political, economic, sociocultural and technological), competition and the marketplace.

2 Undertaking external environmental analysis allows managers to better understand the external environment and hence have an improved idea of how to respond to threats and opportunities in the external environment.

3 Political influences on organisations include legislation and industry regulations. Economic influences include the impact of banks, stock markets and trading blocs. Sociocultural influences cover age, structure and behaviour of populations. The impact of technology is wide-reaching and includes computer hardware, computer software, communications technology and electronic media.

4 The second dimension to PEST analysis is that provided by consideration of the PEST categories at local, national and global levels, giving rise to LoNGPEST. The local level is the immediate town, city or region in which the company operates. The national level is the home country with which the organisation identifies. Hence the global level is anything beyond the local and national levels.

5 Information for performing a PEST or LoNGPEST analysis exists both inside and outside the organisation and takes the form of sales reports, budgets, press articles and TV programmes.

6 The guidelines for performing a LoNGPEST analysis cover identification of factors impacting on the organisation, their categorisation and an assessment of their impact on the organisation and its decision making.

Chapter objectives and the exit case study

While reading this chapter and engaging in the activities, you should have learned how to apply theory and models and analyse situations. The exit case study and the questions which follow will provide an opportunity to assess how well you have met the relevant chapter objectives relating to specific material covered in the chapter.

Chapter objective	Check you have achieved this by
4 Perform PEST and LoNGPEST analyses.	answering case study questions 1 and 2.

EXIT CASE STUDY 1.2

Cadbury to cut further 580 jobs

FT

by Maggie Urry

Cadbury on Tuesday announced a further 580 job cuts as part of a cost saving plan announced last year. The 'vision into action' plan envisaged reducing the group's 50,000 headcount by 7,500. The confectioner said the cuts would generate 'significant' savings in 2009 and the group had announced measures that would capture 60 per cent of the savings it had planned. Todd Stitzer, chief executive, said the other 40 per cent had been identified and would be revealed after consultations with employees. The group was on track to make a mid-teen margin by 2011. Cadbury shares rose 3.6 per cent in opening trading up $17\frac{3}{4}$ at $516\frac{1}{2}$p.

Mr Stitzer said 'affordable treats' such as chocolate, candy and gum, made it resilient if not immune to the worsening economic conditions. 'We operate in a resilient category with a strong business model,' he said, 'our revenue performance remains robust despite the weaker economic background.' Mr Stitzer reconfirmed guidance given with the group's interim profits in July that sales growth would be at the top end of a 4 to 6 per cent range and that margins would rise by 120 basis points, after announcing third quarter revenues up 6 per cent on a like-for-like basis. For the first nine months, revenues were up 7 per cent.

Ken Hanna, finance director who is to leave the group next spring, said that while most of the revenue increase reflected higher prices needed to offset rises in raw material costs, volumes were still expected to be positive for the year. Cocoa prices had risen particularly sharply and the outlook for 2009 was for further increases. The group expected its input prices to rise by 6 to 8 per cent in 2009, with higher cocoa costs the primary cause, up from 5 to 6 per cent in 2008.

Of the job losses, 250 would be achieved by removing a layer of regional management between the seven business units and the head office in the UK. In future the seven units would report directly to Mr Stitzer. Many of these job losses would be senior managers. The other 330 jobs were to go in Australia and New Zealand where the confectionery business would be streamlined, with fewer lines and a plant optimization programme. Mr Stitzer said Cadbury was still reviewing the future of the Australian beverage business where sales fell by 5 per cent in the quarter. He said it was a competitive market but he expected that business to have a reasonable year. The group demerged its American beverages activities in May having previously sold its European drinks business.

Revenues in the UK rose 11 per cent, with the relaunched Wispa bar a particular success. Strong increases were also achieved in South Africa, up 22 per cent, and in Asian emerging markets, up 19 per cent. However, in mainland Europe revenues increased by 4 per cent with weaker performances in France, Spain and northern Europe. In the Americas, revenues were up 7 per cent, but the US gum market slowed while Canada was weak.

Cadbury expects the fall in the pound to increase its revenues for 2008 by 7 per cent and its underlying profits by 12 per cent because of the translation of international results into sterling.

Source: from 'Cadbury to cut further 580 jobs', *The Financial Times*, 14 October 2008 (Urry, M.).

Exit case study questions

1. Using the guidelines for external environmental analysis in this chapter, the information in the Cadbury case study and your own general knowledge, perform a PEST analysis of the external environment faced by Cadbury.
2. Consider your analysis for question 1 and comment on how Cadbury could respond to its external environment.

	POLITICAL	ECONOMIC	SOCIOCULTURAL	TECHNOLOGICAL
LOCAL				
NATIONAL				
GLOBAL				

Short-answer questions

1 Define the term 'external environment'.
2 Explain the term 'LoNGPEST'.
3 Explain the difference between 'international' and 'global'.
4 Name three economic factors which could impact on organisations.
5 Name three political factors which could impact on organisations.
6 Name three sociocultural factors which could impact on organisations.
7 Name three technological factors which could impact on organisations.
8 Name three trading blocs.
9 Where can organisations find the information which will allow them to analyse their external environment?
10 Write down the three key benefits to organisations of undertaking external environmental analysis.

Chapter objectives and assignment questions

While reading this chapter and engaging in the activities, you should have learned how to apply theory and models and analyse situations. This means you should be able to meet the chapter objectives outlined at the beginning of the chapter. The table below shows which chapter objectives can be tested by the different questions.

Chapter objective	Check you have achieved this by
1 Define PEST and LoNGPEST analysis.	answering assignment question 2.
2 Identify and discuss relevant sources of information that assist in environmental analysis.	answering assignment questions 1a, 1b, 2 and 3.
3 Explain the process for carrying out a PEST or LoNGPEST analysis.	answering assignment questions 2 and 3.
4 Perform PEST and LoNGPEST analysis.	answering assignment questions 1a and 1b.

Assignment questions

1 (a) Refer to the section 'Performing external environmental analysis' in this chapter. Identify and collect appropriate information to perform a LoNGPEST analysis of your own college, university or organisation. Your LoNGPEST analysis should contain a completed grid and relevant discussion and explanation.

or

(b) Refer to the section 'Performing external environmental analysis' in this chapter. Identify and collect appropriate information on a public- or private-sector organisation of your choice. Perform a LoNGPEST analysis on your chosen organisation. Your LoNGPEST analysis should contain a completed grid and relevant discussion and explanation.

2 External environmental analysis is an ongoing process for any organisation. Advise an organisation wishing to undertake external environmental analysis for the first time and seeking to set up a system to allow external environmental analysis to take place on an ongoing basis in the future. Present your advice in the form of a 2000-word report.

3 Identify and collect appropriate information from a variety of media sources that show how a particular organisation is evolving. Evaluate and analyse the general usefulness and reliability of the information sources you identify as currently available. Comment on the usefulness of the information to managers within the organisation that is being affected by changes in the external environment. Your answer should take the form of a 2000-word essay.

WEBLINKS available at www.pearsoned.co.uk/capon

The websites for this chapter are for some of the key bodies in the UK impacting on organisations. There are more websites, including those for international and global bodies, at the end of Chapter 2.

- The following website is for British Chambers of Commerce:
  http://www.chamberonline.co.uk
- The following website is for the House of Commons:
  http://www.parliament.uk/about_commons/about_commons.cfm
- The following website is for the Bank of England:
  http://www.bankofengland.co.uk
- The following website is for the London Stock Exchange:
  http://www.londonstockexchange.com/Default.asp
- The following website is for the European Union:
  http://www.europa.eu.int

FURTHER READING

The following book chapters all look at the external environment.

- Johnson, G, Scholes, K and Whittington, R (2008) *Exploring Corporate Strategy*, 8th edn, Chapter 2, Harlow: Financial Times Prentice Hall.
- Lynch, R (2006) *Corporate Strategy*, 4th edn, Chapter 3, Harlow: Financial Times Prentice Hall.
- Palmer, A and Hartley, B (2006) *The Business Environment*, 5th edn, Chapter 1, Maidenhead: McGraw Hill.
- Thompson, J L and Martin, F (2005) *Strategic Management: Awareness, Analysis and Change*, 5th edn, Chapter 4, London: Thomson Learning.
- Worthington, I and Brittion, C (2006) *The Business Environment*, 5th edn, Chapter 1, Harlow: Financial Times Prentice Hall.

REFERENCE

1 Duncan, Peter M and Ginter, W Jack (1990) 'Macro-environmental analysis for strategic management', *Long Range Planning*, 23(6), December.

CHAPTER 2

The composition of the external environment

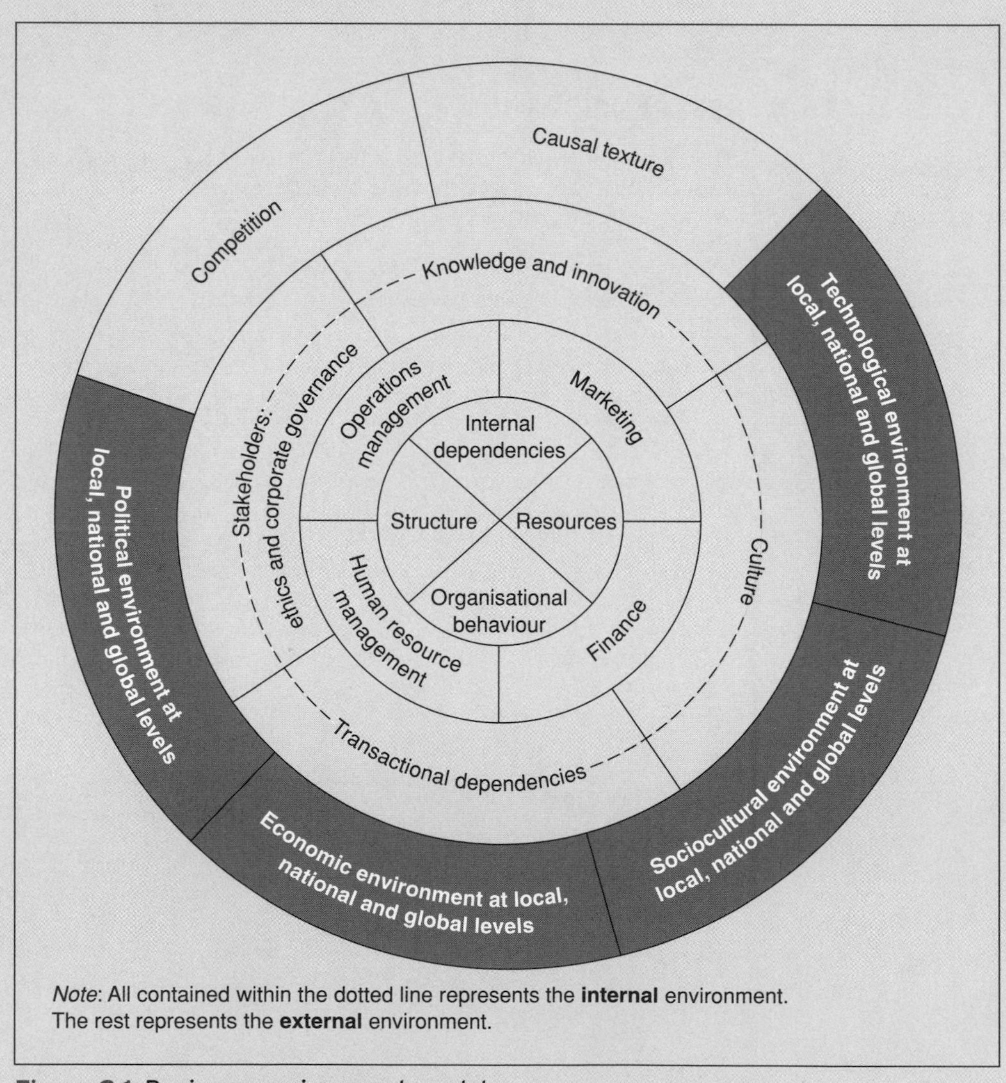

Figure 2.1 Business environment model

Chapter objectives

This chapter aims to define in detail many of the bodies which shape the external environment for organisations at the local, national and global levels. This should allow both PEST analysis and LoNGPEST analysis, which were introduced in Chapter 1, to be performed by thinking more widely and in more detail. Therefore, when you have read this chapter and worked through the associated activities you should be able to achieve the objectives specified below.

1. **Analyse the external environment of an organisation by using PEST and LoNGPEST, drawing conclusions from the analysis.**
2. **Select the most appropriate data and information sources for undertaking analysis of an organisation's external environment.**
3. **Discuss the links between economic and political factors and how this shapes external environments.**

ENTRY CASE STUDY 2.1

Nafta drives car production

by Richard Lapper

At the Volkswagen car plant near the Mexican city of Puebla, the arms of bright orange robots trace precise arcs through the air and gently stamp grey metal car doors into shape. Next door, amid posters urging them to 'take pride in your work', men and women fix dashboards into car bodies that move slowly down an assembly line. The products of these efforts – elegant red, white and lemon-yellow Beetles – stand in formation a few hundred yards away on Avenue B, in another spotlessly clean factory hall. This is the face of Mexico's car industry: efficient, technologically advanced and increasingly oriented to export. Thomas Karig, a vice president at Volkswagen in Mexico, says the decision in 1997 to base world-wide production of the New Beetle at the plant has borne fruit. 'Sales of the model have exceeded forecasts. Mexico is very competitive.'

Volkswagen's success mirrors broader trends. Over the past 20 years, output of new cars has increased fourfold, reaching 1,416,665 units in 2007. Investment has flooded into the sector. Since 2002 more than $10bn has been ploughed into car plants, with a further $6bn–$7bn injected into the booming components business, according to industry figures. The industry as a whole accounts for 13.4 per cent of all manufacturing jobs and, in the component sector alone, employment has more than doubled from 200,000 to 470,000 in the last 10 years. Exports have surged, with 80 per cent of new cars sold abroad, compared with 41 per cent in 1988. Overall, the sector generated $43bn in 2007, an amount that makes it the biggest single earner of foreign exchange.

Carmakers are sourcing more and more of their components from Mexican suppliers, with the industry increasingly concentrated in clusters of manufacturers based in northern and central cities. Nissan, which manufacturers in Aguascalientes and Cuernavaca, now brings in between 60 and 70 per cent of its components from local suppliers, compared with less than half a decade ago. 'We are increasing locally procured parts,' says Shoichi Miyatani, president of the company's Mexican operation. He adds that only the very most advanced state-of-the-art components are brought in from outside. The big driver of all this growth has been the gradual migration of chunks of the once mighty US motor industry south of the Rio Grande in the wake of the North American Free Trade Agreement (Nafta) in 1994. The deal attracted US manufacturers to locate new capacity in Mexico, mainly because wage rates are less than a sixth of their levels north of the border.

The US industry is far from dead. Two years ago Toyota, for example, chose to base a new north American plant in Texas. But all three US majors – General Motors, Chrysler and Ford – have significant operations in Mexico. Nafta helped make the Mexican industry more internationally focused. As Eduardo Solís, president of the Mexican Association of Motor Manufacturers, puts it:

→

'You must manufacture in the dollar zone what you sell in the dollar zone.'

But two other developments have given extra momentum to exports. First, over the past decade Mexico has entered into a string of free-trade agreements with other trading blocs, most notably the European Union, Japan and Mercosur, the South American customs union linking Argentina and Brazil. Second, the decline of the dollar against the euro and yen has helped to boost competitiveness significantly. The peso has appreciated against the greenback, but only marginally, and certainly to a much lesser extent than the currencies of rival production centres such as Brazil. As a result, Mexican carmakers are selling greater volumes to Europe and Asia. Volkswagen sold more than 60 per cent of its output outside the Nafta area. Nissan began exporting its new Tiida model to Europe in 2007 for the first time. 'We exported more than we planned to Europe,' says Mr Miyatani at Nissan.

Export success masks deepening problems in the domestic market. Here, the problem is the scale of imports of second-hand vehicles from the US, sales of which are undercutting domestic demand for new cars. Mexico is obliged by its membership of Nafta to open up to imports of cars made since 1994, with a final deadline due next year. New rules allowing the import of used cars were introduced three years ago and led to a rapid rise in imports, with more than 1m vehicles brought in annually during 2006 and 2007. At the same time, sales of new cars in Mexico itself have gradually fallen, sinking to 288,833 in 2007, the lowest figure since 1998. Smaller, so-called subcompact cars – popular among lower-income families – have been particularly depressed, with that niche seeing a fall of between 15 and 20 per cent. Mr Solís says it is particularly difficult to monitor the safety and emissions standards of these second-hand vehicles. 'In the US, a 10-year-old car is virtually scrap,' he says. 'These cars come in and we don't know where they are.'

Source: from 'Nafta drives car production', *The Financial Times*, 16 June 2008 (Lapper, R.).

Introduction

This chapter follows on directly from Chapter 1 and seeks to examine in much greater detail the generic LoNGPEST model – *see* Table 2.1. The constituent elements of the external environment and their influence on organisations are discussed here. The chapter examines the nature and influence on organisation of politics, economics, society and culture and technology, all at the local, national and global levels.

The political elements of the external environment

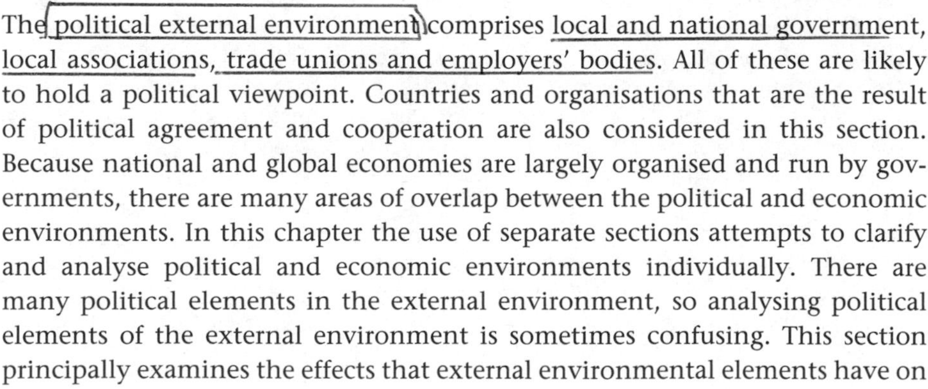

The political external environment comprises local and national government, local associations, trade unions and employers' bodies. All of these are likely to hold a political viewpoint. Countries and organisations that are the result of political agreement and cooperation are also considered in this section. Because national and global economies are largely organised and run by governments, there are many areas of overlap between the political and economic environments. In this chapter the use of separate sections attempts to clarify and analyse political and economic environments individually. There are many political elements in the external environment, so analysing political elements of the external environment is sometimes confusing. This section principally examines the effects that external environmental elements have on

Table 2.1 Generic LoNGPEST grid

	Political	Economic	Sociocultural	Technological
Local	• Local government • Local offices of national government • Local associations – Chambers of commerce – Business Link	• Local bank branches • Local economy	• Local community and social capital	• Mobile phones and faxes • Video conferencing • Internet and world wide web • Manufacturing technology
National	• National government • Devolution for Scotland and Wales • National bodies – Employers' bodies – Employees' bodies	• Central bank – Bank of England • Stock market – London	• Demographic change • Social change – inequality of income – family and household structure	
Global	• Alliances and agreements – UK and US – UK and China – EU – Cold War – CIS – CBSS – Eastern Europe • International bodies – The Commonwealth – NATO	• Trading blocs and bodies – EU – EFTA – OECD – NAFTA – ASEAN • World money markets • WTO	• Global demographics – Europe – Asia – Africa • Cross-cultural issues – Language – Behaviour – Culture shock	

organisations, but inevitably it will become clear that organisations also affect the external environment around them. This is perhaps especially so for employers' organisations, as will be seen later.

The local political environment

At the **local level**, the political elements of the external environment are local government, local offices of national government and local associations – *see* Table 2.2.

Local government

Local government has a significant impact on the businesses within its boundaries. It has responsibilities for regulating private-sector business activity and for directly providing a wide range of services. Some of these responsibilities have a very direct effect on businesses and others a more minimal influence. Local authorities have a statutory responsibility, i.e. they are bound by law to uphold trading standards and environmental health. As such, they hold great powers over all organisations within their area, and have the authority to close them down if severe breaches of law are discovered.

Table 2.2 The local political environment

	Political	Economic	Sociocultural	Technological
Local	• Local government • Local offices of national government • Local associations – Chambers of commerce – Business Link			
National				
Global				

The services provided by the local authority include social services such as care of the elderly, education and services used by private householders and organisations alike, such as refuse collection, street cleaning, transport and planning permission for new buildings or extensions to existing premises. Clearly, a local authority's policies on trade refuse collection, street cleaning and transport to and from the city centre are all going to affect local businesses and shops in the city centre. A congestion charge, such as that introduced in London by Ken Livingstone in early 2003, will be aimed at reducing the amount of traffic in a particular area and is likely to have a detrimental effect on the amount of passing trade for shops in the area. The provision and promotion of effective and cheap public transport, however, ought to go some way to counterbalancing these detrimental effects.

Local government is also responsible for setting and collecting council tax from residents and business rates from commercial organisations. The money raised via council tax and business rates will partially fund the services that local authorities provide, although the main source of funding for local government is money provided by national government. For the purpose of environmental analysis, this illustrates neatly that the levels of the external environment are as interdependent as organisations and their external environments.

It is also important to remember that a local authority is a large public-sector organisation operating in its own external environment. In many UK regions, cities, towns and villages, the local authority is the biggest local employer and the largest organisation. It too has customers and suppliers, and with the introduction of Compulsory Competitive Tendering (CCT) by the Conservative governments of the 1980s, local authorities now also have competitors for the provision of services in the locality where previously they had the monopoly. Here we begin to observe one of the complexities of environmental analysis.

Clearly demonstrated here are the interdependencies between different elements of the environment: one organisation has a complex external environment consisting of other organisations and individuals; it in turn is an element in each of these organisations' individual external environments.

Local offices of national government

As national government has responsibility for the direct provision of many welfare services, the local offices of national government departments play a key role in the lives of local organisations and the local people. There is a local interface between the Department for Work and Pensions, the local offices of the Inland Revenue, and the Department for Education and Skills local Jobcentre Plus service. The current Labour government introduced a review of welfare provision geared towards removing the disincentives to finding work that the welfare system can engender, and towards promoting the opportunities that unemployed people can offer organisations. The 1998 Green Paper 'A New Contract for Welfare' laid out proposals to introduce the first wholescale reform of the welfare state since its introduction in 1945. This has affected organisations in the local environment by providing funding for training and employment of those who are workless through various initiatives under what is called the 'New Deal'.

Local associations

For private-sector organisations in the model, local associations are defined as trade and business associations operating in the geographic vicinity.

Chambers of Commerce

The British Chambers of Commerce are a network of quality accredited chambers of commerce, which are independent, non-profit-making and non-political organisations which are funded via membership subscriptions. British Chambers of Commerce offer business training, and information on a range of issues, such as exporting, suppliers and saving on overheads. At local, regional and national levels the British Chambers of Commerce act to put forward views and opinions on matters affecting their member businesses with a view to influencing local and national government and other decision-making bodies. Chambers of Commerce also offer a powerful voice in terms of comment in the media concerning businesses at the local, regional and national level.

Business Link

Business Links are privately led partnerships between Training and Enterprise Councils, Chambers of Commerce, Enterprise Agencies, local authorities and government. Business Link partnerships are involved in providing advice via a one-stop shop for small and medium-sized businesses. Business Link partnerships operate very much on a regional and local level; for example, in

South Yorkshire, Business Link services are available for Barnsley, Doncaster, Rotherham and Sheffield.

Business Link partnerships generally provide advice and expertise in the areas of raising finance, entering export markets, employee training and managing change. A Business Link partnership aims to provide advice and expertise at a price that small and medium-sized businesses can afford. The partnerships are funded by the Department of Trade and Industry, with the condition that by the fifth year of existence the partnership must be at least 25 per cent self-funding.[1]

The national political environment

The national government and national bodies constitute the national political environment – *see* Table 2.3.

National government

The ways in which the national government manages the economic environment are dealt with under the relevant section below. As a result of the UK's membership of the **European Union (EU)**, the distinction of a national political environment is becoming blurred. Acts that appear on the surface to have been the British Parliament making laws governing British businesses turn out to have originated in Brussels and required all member countries to implement them. Examples of European decisions enacted by the national British government are the fitting of seatbelts to coaches, vans and lorries, adding costs to transport companies; the export ban on British beef in the wake of the BSE

Table 2.3 The national political environment

	Political	Economic	Sociocultural	Technological
Local				
National	• National government • Devolution for Scotland and Wales • National bodies – Employers' bodies – Employees' bodies			
Global				

crisis in the 1990s and its impact on British beef farmers; and the abolition of duty-free goods within the European Union, meaning that tax-free shopping has come to an end except for intercontinental flights.

Examples of the purely national political environment affecting organisational activity are therefore increasingly hard to find, but focus largely on the legislation passed regarding permissible commercial activity, production and service functions and human resource strategies. This latter example is dealt with in Chapter 7, but to give one example, the 1995 Disability Discrimination Act (DDA) made it illegal for organisations not to provide access for disabled workers or customers on their premises. The direct effect of this legislation, which was stronger than anything preceding it, caused many organisations to commission alterations to their existing facilities in order to comply with the new law. The DDA covers equal access to goods, facilities and services, and employment and education.

Although its effects could be said to be largely economic, the national government's political decision making affects most citizens directly through its annual budget. Government has to raise money to provide for its services. It does this via taxation revenue that it uses to pay for publicly funded services such as education, the National Health Service, public transport subsidies, and social and welfare services such as the state pension for those too old to be economically active. Some of the money raised by taxation is distributed via local government and some is distributed and spent directly by national government. This is covered in more detail under the national economic environment, later in this chapter.

Decisions with an economic effect on business may be classified as political when taken by government. One such decision was made in November 1992 by Norman Lamont, then Chancellor of the Exchequer (Finance Minister) in the Conservative government. The pound sterling had been entered into the Exchange Rate Mechanism (ERM), the European Union's mechanism for preparing its member nations' currencies for European Monetary Union (EMU) and eventual merger into a single European Currency Unit (ECU), now better known as the euro. The ERM was designed to bring all its currencies to a level value by setting a range of exchange rate limits beyond which a currency should not be allowed to rise or fall. Norman Lamont took the decision to withdraw the pound from the ERM and hence effectively took Britain out of the first group of countries to enter EMU. The pound was removed from the ERM because its value fell outside the exchange rate range within which it was supposed to remain. However, the decision was also taken for political reasons, as the Conservative party was showing early signs of the internal divisions over European policy that partially led to its defeat in the 1997 elections.

The withdrawal of the pound from the ERM resulted in what the City referred to subsequently as 'Black Wednesday', when there was an immediate 10–15 per cent devaluation of the pound in relation to other currencies. Consequently, businesses in Britain trading with overseas companies were affected. Companies importing goods, components or raw materials into the UK from overseas had to pay more for them. In 1992 the UK economy was depressed and importing companies faced the dilemma of whether to pass the increased costs on to consumers or to absorb the increased cost in whole or in part, via reduced profit margins. On the day the pound was removed from the ERM, Yorkshire Television news reported on a company based in Hull that was facing exactly this dilemma. The company imported high-quality, up-market German kitchens and kitchen appliances, manufactured by companies such as AEG, Siemens and Bosch. In contrast, companies exporting UK manufactured goods found it easier as the lower cost of production made UK goods more price competitive abroad. This partly contributed to the growth of the UK economy in 1993.

From this it can be seen that the link between the national political and economic environments is clear. Politicians are elected by the people and run the economy. In doing so, they decide the economic policy that affects both individuals and organisations operating at the national level of the environment.

Devolution in Scotland and Wales

The Labour government elected on 1 May 1997 had promised in its election manifesto to hold referendums on devolution in both Scotland and Wales. This was duly implemented. In Wales the referendum was held on 18 September 1997 and 50.1 per cent of the electorate turned out to vote, with 50.3 per cent voting for a Welsh Assembly and 49.7 per cent voting against. In Scotland the referendum on 11 September had a turnout of 60.4 per cent, with 74.3 per cent of those who voted supporting the creation of a Scottish Parliament and 63.5 per cent voting to give the Scottish Parliament limited tax-varying powers.[2]

The Scottish Parliament consists of a total of 129 seats, of which 73 are directly elected and 56 allocated to additional members. Directly elected members were elected by a constituency to represent them. The additional members were elected by the electorate voting for a party and the additional seats given to members of the party voted for. The allocation of additional seats is complex but is representative of the voting pattern in the electorate as a whole.[3]

The Scottish Parliament appointed a First Minister, Donald Dewar, who in turn appointed members to and headed the Scottish Executive. The First Minister and Scottish Executive are drawn from the party or group commanding the majority in the Scottish Parliament. The Scottish Parliament is able to pass laws in a number of areas for Scotland, including health, education, local government, housing, economic development, trade, transport, criminal and civil law, courts, prison, police and fire services, animals, the environment, agriculture, food standards, forestry, fisheries, sport and the arts. The Scottish Parliament also has powers to repeal legislation passed at Westminster as far as Scotland is affected.[4]

The Welsh Assembly contains 60 directly elected seats and 40 additional seats. In contrast to the Scottish Parliament, the Welsh Assembly does not have the same powers governing the establishment of legislation and the repeal of Westminster legislation. The areas of responsibility devolved to the Welsh Assembly include economic development, agriculture and food, industry and training, education, local government, health and personal social services, housing, environment, planning, transport and roads, arts and culture, the built heritage and sport and recreation. The Secretary of State for Wales has the power to make secondary legislation in these areas. For example, the Secretary of State for Wales is able to decide the school curriculum in Wales.[5]

National bodies

National bodies represent businesses and employees and present views on employment and trade issues to one another, and to the government and opposition parties. Both employer and employee organisations try to shape and influence events in the external environment for the benefit of their members. Employer and employee national bodies are often closely aligned with the government or a particular political party. Employers' organisations traditionally support the Conservative Party, while the Labour Party is linked financially and in terms of membership to the trade unions. For the Labour Party to achieve victory at the 1997 general election, it was thus crucial for it to have gained support from both sides of the negotiation table.

Employers' bodies

Examples of national employers' bodies include employers' organisations such as the Institute of Directors (IOD) and the Confederation of British Industry (CBI). The IOD was formed in 1903 and its members are individual company directors from large FTSE 100 companies through to smaller entrepreneurial start-up businesses. The IOD provides members with information, advice, training, conferences and publications. In addition the IOD seeks to be an influential organisation in representing the concerns of its members to government and does this via lobbying and the media. The CBI was founded in 1965, bringing together several other industry bodies. Members of the CBI are companies, including both multinationals and small and medium-sized enterprises as well as trade associations and employers' organisations. The CBI seeks to provide UK industry with a forum for developing and influencing policy on a host of areas which impact on business organisations, such as the economy, legislation and technology. Additionally the CBI seeks to encourage efficiency and competitiveness in UK industry and in doing so develop the contribution of UK industry to the economy.

These organisations provide a forum for employers or owners of businesses to put forward their views and be represented on issues affecting businesses, such as the national minimum wage, the euro and the 2008 financial crisis. Both the IOD and CBI frequently use the printed and broadcast media to do this. At the time of the election of the Labour government, in 1997, the CBI was contributing to the minimum wage debate via the media. Labour had made the introduction of a minimum wage in the UK a manifesto pledge, and the CBI was suggesting a minimum wage of £3.50 per hour as an acceptable amount. It pitched this figure between the £4.29 per hour favoured by the Trades Union Congress and the £3.00 per hour suggested by 'certain employers'.[6] The rate at which the minimum wage was initially set was £3.60 for workers aged over 21, and by October 2008 this had risen to £5.73 per hour.

Employees' bodies

In contrast, trade unions are national bodies representing employees. Examples of trade unions are UCU, representing teachers in further and higher education, USDAW, representing shop and distribution workers, and UNISON, representing public-sector employees. Trade unions represent their members in negotiations with employers on issues concerning pay and conditions, whether in the private or public sector. They are linked to the Labour Party, although reforms made to party membership after Labour's 1992 election defeat attempted to reduce the unions' impact and promote the concept of 'one member, one vote'. Most trade unions are affiliated to the Trades Union Congress, which is the largest voluntary organisation and the largest pressure group in the UK. The TUC operates to represent its member unions collectively at a national level.

There has been a steady decline in trade union membership since 1979 and the reasons for this decline include a reduction in the number of jobs in manufacturing industries, which typically had high levels of union membership among employees. This fall in union membership has been consolidated by an increase in the percentage of people working for small companies where it is often more difficult for unions to organise themselves. Additionally, larger numbers of unemployed people or people not working have helped to reduce the level of trade union membership. Finally, under the Conservative administrations led by Margaret Thatcher in the 1980s, trade union membership and the power of the unions were drastically curbed. This occurred as the view taken by the Thatcher governments was that Britain's industrial unrest of the 1970s and the cause of its industrial decline was due to the unions' rise to political power. In contrast, the Employment Relations Act 1999 established a new statutory procedure for recognition of independent trade unions in the workplace, although it did not include the adoption of European-style workers' councils. Union influence, however, is unlikely to rise to previous post-war levels.

The global political environment

Alliances and agreements

The global political environment (*see* Table 2.4) encompasses alliances and agreements between countries that have an effect on the international activities

Table 2.4 The global political environment

	Political	Economic	Sociocultural	Technological
Local				
National				
Global	• Alliances and agreements – UK and USA – UK and China – EU – Cold War – CIS – CBSS – Eastern Europe • International bodies – The Commonwealth – NATO			

that each country's citizens may undertake. Two or more countries may come together to establish independent or semi-independent global bodies to oversee or regulate the conduct of international trade and commerce, as well as to work towards the improvement of social issues, such as health, poverty or human rights.

Alliances and agreements occur between two or more countries for mutual benefit. The countries involved concur to support each other in global politics or in bilateral or multilateral economic activity. In extreme cases, consent may be given to the merger of countries into a single entity, or one country may consent to divide into separate countries to fulfil ideals of cultural identity, national integrity or economic benefit; for example, Czechoslovakia separated in 1993 to become the Czech Republic and Slovakia.

The UK and the US

A good example of an alliance in which two countries concur to support each other is the close and special relationship between the UK and the US. Although there are few formal bilateral treaties, a special relationship exists as a result of the two countries' historical and linguistic ties. In the 1980s the relationship between the UK and the US was personified by the close friendship and mutual support of Conservative Prime Minister Margaret Thatcher and US Republican President Ronald Reagan. Both headed conservative governments in their respective countries and combined radical free-market agendas with strong global politics. This caused some difficulty for President Reagan during the UK–Argentine Falklands War in 1982, as his special relationship with the UK required support of Britain's efforts, while US links with the rest of the American continent precluded actual aggression against Argentina. On a separate occasion in 1986, Margaret Thatcher approved the use of US airbases in the UK to launch bomb attacks against Libya.

The special relationship continues between the UK Prime Minister and the US President. In the 2003 Gulf War to liberate Iraq there was close agreement between the UK and the US, while France and Germany were in less agreement over the decision to go to war without a UN mandate. There had been greater global consensus over the 1991 Gulf War, where international forces, the UK and US among them, liberated Kuwait from Iraqi invasion.

The UK and China

China is extremely important on the global political stage because of its sheer size, geographically, politically and economically. The Chinese market is an important part of Britain's overseas trade, with the UK exporting to China and importing Chinese goods. The return of Hong Kong to China is an example of an agreement at the global level of the external environment, which was designed to promote business stability and minimise political and economic risk for British business in China. On 1 July 1997, the British colony of Hong Kong was handed back to China after 99 years of British rule under the terms of a lease forced from the Chinese at the height of Britain's imperial activity. This was unlike the fate of any of the UK's other colonial possessions, which all left the Empire to become independent countries in the Commonwealth – *see* Table 2.9 in this chapter. Hong Kong, however, had not been independent before the colony was established but had always been part of China, so had to be returned to it at the end of the lease.

The negotiations governing the return of Hong Kong to China were started in the early 1980s by Margaret Thatcher and Deng Xiaoping, China's then paramount leader. In the late 1970s Deng Xiaoping engineered economic reforms in China and allowed the slow development of a more market-based economy, while retaining strict political control over personal liberty. He died on 19 February 1997 prior to the deadline for Hong Kong's return to China, which duly went ahead. China described itself as 'one country – two systems', referring to the promise to continue unchanged for a minimum of 50 years Hong Kong's capitalist free-market economy under Chinese communist rule. This free-market economy has long been the gateway to the Chinese market for foreign businesses and for Chinese exports to the world and so it is greatly in China's interest to maintain the status quo.

China's lack of a democratic political system should not have been a cause for concern, as the British colony had been ruled without recourse to democracy. Nevertheless, following Britain's long-held policy of establishing democratic systems before withdrawing from colonial possessions, the last Governor of Hong Kong, former Conservative politician Chris Patten, attempted to introduce some last-minute democracy to the colony. In the 1990s Hong Kong people were allowed to vote for the first time for a minority of members of Hong Kong's governing body, the Legislative Council (Legco). However, the return of Hong Kong to China in 1997 saw the dismantling of the Legco and the appointment by Beijing of a replacement administration and a new Chief Executive of the Hong Kong Special Administrative Region, Tung Chee-hwa, a wealthy local businessman who had previously been ennobled by the Queen.

The European Union

In 1957 the European Economic Community was established by the Treaty of Rome. There were six founding countries, with a further twenty-one countries joining the European Union by 2007 (*see* Table 2.5). In 2008 the EU describes its aims as being 'peace, prosperity and freedom for its 495 million citizens – in a fairer, safer world'.[7]

The 1997 Treaty of Amsterdam covered new rights for EU subjects concerning issues such as freedom of movement and employment. The Agenda 2000 blueprint presented to the European Parliament in July 1997 allowed the EU to expand eastwards and for former Communist countries of Eastern Europe (*see* Table 2.5) to become members. Enlargement of the EU is viewed as an opportunity to unite Europe and extend and consolidate political stability and economic prosperity more widely. The criteria laid down by the European Council in Copenhagen in 1993 required potential member states to demonstrate democracy, human rights, a functioning market economy, and a commitment to the EU's aims covering political, economic and monetary union. The political and economic conditions of applicant countries have to be judged satisfactory by the EU before it allows their admittance. Negotiations to admit

Table 2.5 European Union member countries

Year of entry	European Union member countries		
1957	• Belgium • Italy	• France • Luxembourg	• Germany • Netherlands
1973	• UK	• Denmark	• Ireland
1981	• Greece		
1986	• Spain	• Portugal	
1995	• Austria	• Finland	• Sweden
2004	• Cyprus • Hungary • Malta • Slovenia	• Czech Republic • Latvia • Poland	• Estonia • Lithuania • Slovakia
2007	• Bulgaria	• Romania	

Source: http://www.europa.eu.int/

Table 2.6 European Union candidate countries

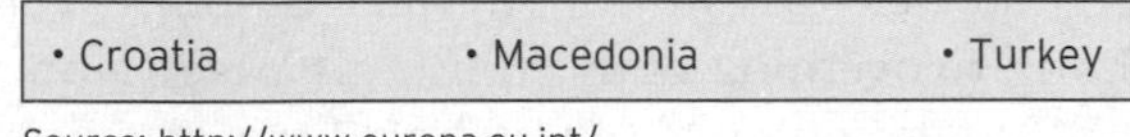

• Croatia	• Macedonia	• Turkey

Source: http://www.europa.eu.int/

new members are complex and examine how the significant differences in economic and social development between member and potential members states can be tackled.[8]

In 2007 there were three countries awaiting admittance to the EU (*see* Table 2.6). Croatia is expected to join by 2012 and Macedonia's negotiations will be lengthy, particularly since the country's elections in the summer of 2008 were not conducted in a sufficiently open and safe manner and violence erupted on the streets. Turkey has now met conditions to be considered as a candidate country, although negotiations will be lengthy and there is no expected date for Turkey's accession to the EU.

The Cold War

World political events result in alliances being created and demolished, hence altering the political map of the world. In order to understand events in the late 1990s, it is essential to consider some political background. After the Second World War (1939–45), the world was plunged into the Cold War, an ideological battle between democratic and Communist political systems backed up by the technology of nuclear warfare, bringing for the first time in history the constant threat of a Third World War that would annihilate millions of civilians and destroy entire countries. The two sides of the Cold War, put simplistically, consisted of the US and Western Europe – with its institutions such as NATO, EFTA and the EU – and the then Soviet Union (USSR or Union of Soviet Socialist Republics) and Eastern Europe, with its equivalent institutions: the Warsaw Pact was the mutual defence treaty signed by Communist countries in the USSR sphere of influence, and Comecon was the alliance of planned economies.

The division of East and West was never more starkly evident than in the division of Germany on its defeat by the victorious Allies into two states: the western, democratic, free-market Federal Republic of Germany (FRG), and the eastern, Communist, **planned economy** of the German Democratic Republic (GDR). The former capital of Berlin, geographically inside the GDR, was itself split into two halves and a wall built down the centre between East and West. The Berlin Wall came to symbolise the Cold War.

The Cold War split was mirrored in the Far East during the Korean War (1950–53), where US forces supported the democratic South Korea against the Chinese-backed Communist north. The country remains divided into two administrations and a state of civil war still exists officially. Similarly, the People's Republic of China (PRC) and the Republic of China on Taiwan both claim to be the legitimate government of China, after a similar civil war whose hostilities ended in 1949, but peace has never been negotiated. The US originally backed the Republic of China, and did not switch allegiances until president Nixon visited the PRC in 1973. In Vietnam, the American-backed south eventually fell to the Communist north after many years of bloody war, uniting the country under a Communist government in the early 1970s.

In Europe in the late 1980s and early 1990s, the geopolitical map altered considerably and unexpectedly as a result of the collapse of strict controls over personal liberty in many Communist-controlled countries. This had begun with the last ever President of the USSR, Mikhail Gorbachev, who introduced policies of *glasnost* (openness) and *perestroika* (economic restructuring) during his term in office. These alterations to the political map provided unprecedented opportunities for trade and commerce and began in the GDR, when the Communist regime lost control over the population and the Berlin Wall was suddenly dismantled in a popular uprising that was not opposed by the police or military forces. By 3 October 1990 East and West Germany had officially reunified under the former FRG's government. As a result of reunification, the German government moved its parliament from Bonn, capital of the FRG, back to Berlin.

Commonwealth of Independent States

The ending of the Cold War resulted in other changes to the geopolitical map of Eastern Europe. During the years 1989–91 the USSR collapsed as the Soviet government in Moscow went the way of the GDR government, and the Soviet Union dissolved the federation into its component independent states, which then came together under the auspices of a looser association called the Commonwealth of Independent States (CIS) – *see* Table 2.7.

Council of Baltic Sea States

The Council of Baltic Sea States (CBSS) was established in March 1992, when the foreign ministers of the member states met in Copenhagen at the invitation of the Danish and German foreign ministers – *see* Table 2.8. The foreign ministers were seeking to strengthen cooperation and coordination between Baltic sea states and viewed the creation of the CBSS as helping to achieve this aim, along with the promotion of democratic and economic development in the region.[9]

Table 2.7 Members of the Commonwealth of Independent States (CIS)

• Armenia	• Azerbaijan	• Belarus
• Georgia	• Kazakhstan	• Kyrgyzstan
• Moldova	• Russia	• Tajikistan
• Turkmenistan	• Ukraine	• Uzbekistan

Source: http://www.cisstat.com

Table 2.8 Members of the Council of Baltic Sea States (CBSS)

• Denmark	• Estonia	• Finland
• Germany	• Iceland	• Latvia
• Lithuania	• Norway	• Poland
• Russia	• Sweden	• European Commission

Source: http://www.battinfo.org/CBSS.htm, 28 April 2000.

Eastern Europe

Countries such as Poland, Hungary, Czechoslovakia, Romania and Yugoslavia all experienced cataclysmic change after the dissolution of the USSR. In geographic terms Poland, Hungary and Romania remained unchanged, in contrast to Czechoslovakia and Yugoslavia, which altered significantly. Czechoslovakia, for reasons of national and economic identity, split into two countries, the Czech Republic and Slovakia. In the 1990s civil war split Yugoslavia into several independent countries: Croatia, Bosnia Herzegovina, the former Yugoslav Republic of Macedonia and Slovenia, with Montenegro and Serbia remaining as a rump Yugoslavian Federation. A multinational peacekeeping force administered Kosovo: geographically a small country between Serbia, Montenegro, Albania and Macedonia.

However, in February 2008 Kosovo's parliament declared independence from Serbia. Russia had backed Serbia and opposed this move by Kosovo. However, countries including Germany, Italy, France, the UK, USA, Turkey and Albania recognised Kosovo as an independent state, while Russia, Cyprus, Romania and Slovakia refused to do likewise. Following Kosovo's declaration of independence the EU took over the administrative roles undertaken by the UN, and NATO continued to provide security in Kosovo.[10,11,12]

In January 2001 Zoran Djindijic was democratically elected as Prime Minister of Serbia, three months after toppling Slobodan Milosevic. Zoran Djindijic pushed for economic reform in Serbia and helped engineer the arrest and extradition of Slobodan Milosevic to the United Nations court in The Hague. Milosevic was tried for war crimes committed during the Balkan wars of the 1990s, dying of a heart attack in 2006, before the end of his trial. However, in March 2003 Zoran Djindijic was assassinated and there followed uncertainty for Serbia. In July 2008, Radovan Karadzic who was practising as an alternative therapist in Belgrade, was captured and taken to the International Court at The Hague to be put on trial for war crimes. Serbia's admission as an EU candidate country will only begin to be considered once headway has been made in capturing Ratko Mladic who is also wanted for war crimes and is thought to be hiding in Serbia.

All these former Eastern bloc countries have seen major changes to their political and economic systems, with elections taking place in many countries and greater opportunities for international trade and commerce becoming available. Some of these opportunities allow Western companies to invest and manufacture in countries such as Poland, Hungary, Slovakia and the Czech Republic; for example, Volkswagen bought Skoda in the Czech Republic and now manufactures Skoda cars which sell successfully all over Europe.

International bodies

The international bodies discussed here are bodies that have a global political influence on the world political order. This is important, as peace and political stability are key elements in allowing a country to have an active economy and stable trade with other countries.

The Commonwealth

The Commonwealth derives from Britain's imperial past and comprises countries from all regions of the world, including Europe, the Pacific, Asia, Africa and the Caribbean. The countries belonging to the Commonwealth are shown in Table 2.9 and range from India, with a population of over 900 million people, to Naura in the Pacific, with 8000 people. The Commonwealth consists of 53 countries, 52 of which are former colonies or protectorates of the UK, the exception being Mozambique, a former Portuguese colony. Mozambique was admitted as a member in November 1995 due to its close association with the Commonwealth in opposing apartheid in South Africa and because it wanted to reap the benefits of membership. Apartheid was the official system of keeping the white minority population in South Africa in a position of power and wealth, while the black and coloured populations had no access to money or political decision making. South Africa withdrew from the Commonwealth in 1961 following pressure from other member countries over apartheid. It was readmitted only in 1994 after the development of a new, democratic and multiracial constitution, with Nelson Mandela, a leading dissident of the old regime, released from imprisonment and elected president in the country's first ever democratic elections.

In contrast, Nigeria was suspended from the Commonwealth in November 1995 after its most recent military coup. The deteriorating relationship between Nigeria and the Commonwealth was caused by the Nigerian military cancelling the presidential elections in 1993 and in November 1995 executing nine minority rights leaders, including the author Ken Saro-Wiwa. The Commonwealth held a summit meeting in November 1995 in New Zealand and acted quickly and forcibly by suspending Nigeria from the Commonwealth.[13,14] Nigeria's suspension from the Commonwealth was finally lifted in April 1999, following the election of a civilian government led by President Olusegun Obasanjo.[15]

In 2002 the Commonwealth was discussing the suspension of Zimbabwe, due to President Mugabe's tyrannical regime, which has devastated its agriculture and economy. However, a few short months later in 2003 Robert Mugabe withdrew Zimbabwe from the Commonwealth.

The examples discussed above illustrate that the Commonwealth is an international body that can, along with other international bodies, affect and

Table 2.9 Members of the Commonwealth

Year of entry	Countries			
1931	• Australia	• Canada	• New Zealand	
1947	• India			
1948	• Sri Lanka			
1957	• Malaysia	• Ghana		
1960	• Nigeria[1]			
1961	• Sierra Leone	• Cyprus	• Tanzania	
1962	• Uganda	• Jamaica	• Trinidad and Tobago	
1963	• Kenya			
1964	• Malawi	• Zambia	• Malta	
1965	• Singapore	• Gambia		
1966	• Lesotho	• Botswana	• Barbados	• Guyana
1968	• Nauru	• Mauritius	• Swaziland	
1970	• Tonga	• Western Samoa		
1972	• Bangladesh			
1973	• The Bahamas			
1974	• Grenada			
1975	• Papua New Guinea			
1976	• Seychelles			
1978	• Solomon Islands	• Tuvalu	• Dominica	
1979	• St Vincent and the Grenadines	• St Lucia	• Kiribati	
1980	• Zimbabwe[2]	Vanuatu		
1981	• Antigua and Barbuda	• Belize		
1982	• Maldives			
1983	• St Kitts and Nevis			
1984	• Brunei			
1989	• Pakistan[3]			
1990	• Namibia			
1994	• South Africa[4]			
1995	• Cameroon	• Mozambique		

Notes:

1 Suspended 1995, rejoined in 1999.
2 Zimbabwe was withdrawn from the Commonwealth by Robert Mugabe in 2003.
3 Rejoined, had withdrawn in 1972.
4 Rejoined, had withdrawn in 1961.

Source: http://www.thecommonwealth.org/about/general/general/1.html

Table 2.10 Members of NATO

Year of entry	Countries		
1949	• Belgium • France • Luxembourg • Portugal	• Canada • Iceland • Netherlands • UK	• Denmark • Italy • Norway • USA
1952	• Turkey	• Greece	
1955	• Germany		
1982	• Spain		
1999	• Czech Republic	• Poland	• Hungary
2004	• Bulgaria • Lithuania • Slovenia	• Estonia • Romania	• Latvia • Slovakia

Source: http://www.nato.int/welcome/home.htm

influence the status of a country with regard to participating in trade and commerce on a global level. Accordingly, the role of the Commonwealth is to further economic and social development, democracy and human rights in its member countries.[16]

The North Atlantic Treaty Organisation

The North Atlantic Treaty Organisation (NATO) was formed in April 1949 and consisted of 12 members, with a further 14 countries joining between 1952 and 2004 – *see* Table 2.10. NATO's primary role is to ensure the security of its member countries and in the first instance this largely involved countering the threat created by the Cold War until that came to an end in 1990/1. Since then NATO has reorganised and restructured to develop security arrangements for the whole of Europe and to allow 'peacekeeping and crisis management tasks undertaken in co-operation with countries which are not members of the Alliance and with other international organisations'.[17] The ending of the Cold War created an opportunity for the expansion of NATO and in July 1997 agreement was reached between member countries to allow the Czech Republic, Poland and Hungary to become members in 1999. This was followed by a second wave of former Eastern bloc countries joining NATO in 2004, including the Baltic States of Estonia, Latvia and Lithuania (*see* Table 2.10).

Check your understanding

Do you understand the impact that political factors in the external environment can have on an organisation like Volkswagen?

Check your understanding by referring to the entry case study, identifying and explaining the political factors which have made it possible for Volkswagen to manufacture in Mexico.

Political and economic links

The alliances and agreements between countries described in the previous section altered the political map and political systems for the countries involved. Alterations to their economic systems also occurred alongside the political changes. In terms of international business, the assessment of political and economic risks is a major factor when deciding which target market and mode of entry would be appropriate in various countries. Comparative analysis of various countries' political and economic stability, potential and future trends enables companies to take a judgement about whether or not to invest in or export to that destination.

Democracy

Democracy is the system of government most recognisable to those born and brought up in the West. Democracy comes from the Greek *demos*, 'the people', and *kratis*, 'power', and describes those systems where the people are able to choose, through a system of voting, those who represent them in the corridors of power and decision making. As it is impossible for every individual in society to be completely free and unfettered by the rules of the state, democratic systems are the mutual agreements under which people are able to live together collectively and yet express a collective opinion on periodic change via fair and proper elections. It would be understandable to think of all Western governments as being equally democratic, yet not each country has the same system. Democratic systems divide broadly into those that have evolved and those that are the product of a sudden and cataclysmic change, e.g. popular revolution. The latter are those that have perhaps the greatest spread of democracy in their institutions.

For example, the UK is called a constitutional monarchy and has a parliamentary system. Despite a 40-year interruption under Oliver Cromwell, the UK's monarchy can be traced back a thousand years. The current system has evolved through a system of concessionary changes to the point where its system of hereditary figurehead monarch, popularly elected House of Commons and mix of hereditary and appointed second chamber, the House of Lords. The House of Lords is used as a blueprint of democratic government and has around 750 peers of which 92 hereditary peers are elected by their colleagues. Countries such as the US, France and Germany, in contrast, have all had occasion to invent their political systems from scratch after revolution or war. These systems are based on written constitutions and codes of conduct, and feature elected government at all levels, including both chambers and head of state (president).

Autocracy

The exact opposite of democracy, autocratic systems are those where one person retains all power in his or her hands. The historical embodiment of autocracy was the absolute monarchy, where the king held all political and economic power. During the Cold War, this lack of democratic process was most keenly observed under Communism, where the people were unable to choose the political party to represent them and had little or no personal liberty (these systems are more appropriately called oligarchies, since they are dominated by a powerful elite).

The free market

Providing in-depth knowledge of economics is not the purpose of this text, but to be able to discuss a variety of political and economic contexts, it is necessary to define different economic systems. The **free market** is that situation in which there is little or no regulation of commercial activity on the part of political entities. In a free market, the market forces of demand and supply will lead to perfect competition, providing all that the people need or want at a price they can afford. If there is no demand for a product or service in a free market, that product will not sell, no matter how cheaply it is priced.

The planned economy

In Communist countries, attempts were made to eradicate the free market and its differences between rich and poor, by planning and orchestrating all economic activity from central government. Thus people were not free to seek whatever job they wished, and organisations could not recruit whoever they wanted. All jobs, housing, production, services and food were organised by the state via its work units, or state-owned organisations. Market forces were denied, as consumers were able to purchase products or services only from the state-owned factories and companies, whether they were good or bad. No decision was left to the individual, no matter how small. Thus individuals' every need was catered for in a basic way, but individualism, innovation and creativity were stifled.

The mixed economy

Most Western economies are a mixture of free and planned economic activity. Where there is no regulation on business, employees and consumers alike are at risk. Regulation in the UK protects employees at work through health and safety and employment protection legislation, while the consumer is protected by the Sale of Goods and Trades Descriptions Acts.

Links between countries' political and economic systems

When considering the global political environment (*see* Table 2.4) or the global economic environment (*see* Table 2.14), it is essential first to know something about the political and economic systems of various countries and regions in the world. Figure 2.2 is a matrix that plots various countries (*see*

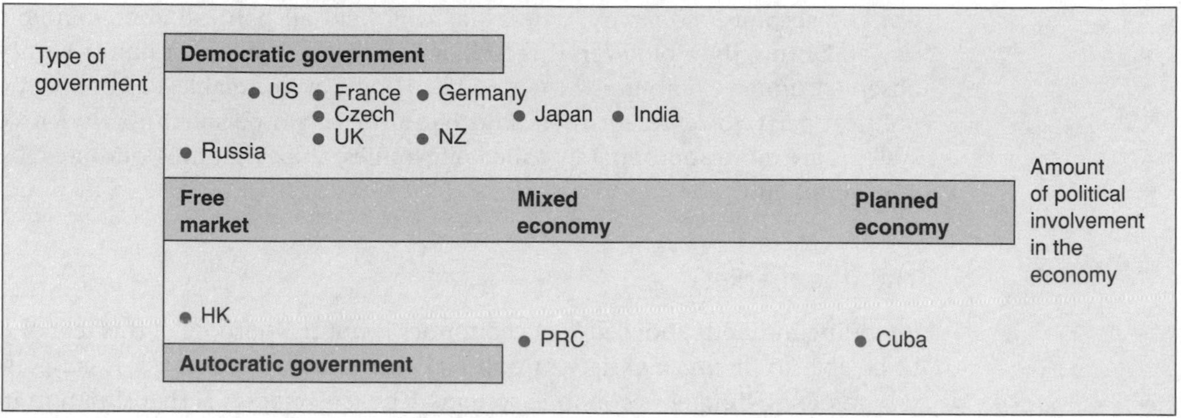

Figure 2.2 Government type and political involvement in the economy

Table 2.11) in relation to one another based on their level of democracy and the level of political interference in the economy. For the sake of this text, this matrix has been completed in a highly subjective and unsubstantiated manner, and indeed countries' positions will alter over time subject to political and economic change. In terms of assessing political and economic risk before entering new markets, organisations should invest in more objective forms of analysis, either done in-company or by external experts. The countries are plotted according to the background information given in Table 2.11.

Check your understanding

Do you understand how the political and economic systems of countries in the former Eastern bloc, like Slovakia, have changed?

Check your understanding by placing Slovakia on the grid in Figure 2.2, both today and before the end of the Cold War.

The economic elements of the external environment

As has been stated, the economic environment faced by organisations is shaped and influenced by the political environment as well as by the economic bodies that are constituents of the external environment. The previous section examined the political elements of the external environment. In this section the role of economic bodies such as banks, stock markets, world money markets, **trading blocs** and bodies is considered.

The local economic environment

Local bank branches

Banks are a key local economic environmental player for companies, as the relationship between a company, big or small, and its bank is a local one

Table 2.11 Country summaries

Cuba	After a Communist revolution over 30 years ago, dictator Fidel Castro has presided over a decaying planned economy. Following the dissolution of the USSR, Cuba's main source of political and economic support, Cuba has found it increasingly difficult to survive under the US trade embargo.
Germany	A federal republic, united finally in 1991, its mixed economy is one of the post-war European success stories, despite the costs of integrating the former Communist East.
Japan	Since the Second World War Japan has been a constitutional monarchy. However, the Liberal Democrats have been elected for most of those 50 years. The original successful Asian tiger economy, its success is also often attributed to the high levels of government intervention in the economy.
India	The largest democracy in the world.
Hong Kong	Directly ruled from London for 99 years, Hong Kong reverted to the sovereignty of the People's Republic of China in 1997. A radical free market, it remains to be seen how this will continue under the 'one country, two systems' plan.
New Zealand	A Westminster system in the Commonwealth, it has seen a Labour government heavily interested in privatisation.
Russia	Since the collapse of the Soviet Union, the Russians have elected their leader for the first time in their history. The emergence of a mafia indicates a lack of regulation in the economy.
People's Republic of China	Controlled by the Chinese Communist Party following 'liberation' in 1949, China has liberalised its economy radically since the late 1980s without relinquishing any political power.
United Kingdom of Great Britain and Northern Ireland	Often called the 'Mother of Parliaments', the UK is a constitutional monarchy without a constitution, and only directly electing one of its two Houses of Parliament. There has been widescale privatisation since the early 1980s.
United States of America	With a written constitution, the Americans directly elect both Houses and their President. The federal system essentially allows for a variety in levels of free-market approach.

between the two organisations. The relationship between a company and its bank is not normally one of national or global importance or influence. Hence a company's relationship with the bank with which it holds a business account will tend to be governed by issues concerning the amount of money in the account, overdraft and loan facilities. *See* Table 2.12.

The local economy

The general state of the local economy also exerts a direct influence on organisations. If the local economy is buoyant, the customer base for products and

Table 2.12 The local economic environment

	Political	Economic	Sociocultural	Technological
Local		• Local bank branches • Local economy		
National				
Global				

service will be wide and profitable. However, wages will be high and employees in short supply from among the local population. In areas with a depressed local economy, there will be little opportunity for selling products or services to people with little disposable income, but the workforce should be cheap and plentiful.

The national economic environment

The main influences on businesses at a national level come from the actions of the country's national bank and stock market (*see* Table 2.13). These two organisations together influence the value of investments held by businesses and individuals and hence affect the amount of cash available in the economy.

Government actions in relation to the economy also obviously have a great influence. The most common forms of taxation are income tax, corporation tax, value added tax (VAT) and duty on imports/exports. VAT is payable on many goods and services and at the time of writing stands at 15 per cent for most goods in the UK. The Conservative government increased the rate of VAT across the board from 8 to 17.5 per cent and also increased the number of items on which VAT is charged. The most opposed introduction of VAT was on domestic fuel, which had been zero rated and was to be charged at 8 per cent. This was not abolished but was reduced to 5 per cent by the Labour government in 1997. Basic food items and children's clothes are zero rated, i.e. VAT is chargeable but it stands at 0 per cent. Food items considered to be luxury items are subject to VAT at the standard rate.

The rate of taxation affects businesses as higher income tax lessens the amount of disposable income that people have available to spend on goods

Table 2.13 The national economic environment

	Political	Economic	Sociocultural	Technological
Local				
National		• Central bank – Bank of England • Stock market – London		
Global				

and services, and VAT makes goods and services more expensive to the consumer than the price set by the manufacturer or service deliverer. Therefore, it is crucial to the standard of living of the individual citizen, to the profitability of private-sector organisations, and to the standard of public services that a balance is achieved between taxation and public spending.

Businesses are effected by corporation tax as the higher the rate, the greater the amount of tax due on any profits made and hence the lower the amount of money available to pay dividends to shareholders and spend on activities such as marketing, product development, pay increases and updating equipment and facilities used to run the business.

Although much of the above is concerned with affecting the economic environment of the country, the decision making behind the management of the economy is essentially political, as it can be political parties' economic strategies that voters find key at the ballot box. Additionally, budgets from opposing political parties often show different approaches towards solving the same problems. Details of the latest budget can be found at the Treasury website – see the weblinks section at the end of this chapter.

The central bank – Bank of England

In the UK the central bank is the Bank of England. In May 1997 the new Labour Chancellor of the Exchequer, Gordon Brown, gave independence in the setting of the base rate of interest to the Bank of England and its Governor Eddie George. This separated out the economic and political decision-making processes concerning interest rates for the first time in the UK's history. Under the previous system, the Chancellor of the Exchequer and the Governor of the Bank of England would meet regularly and jointly agree changes to the base rate of interest. The base rate directly influences businesses and individuals as repayment of overdrafts, loans or mortgages will increase with higher interest rates, hence reducing the amount of activity in the economy. For example, when interest rates are high, businesses spend less on new equipment, advertising and product development and individuals spend less on the goods and services produced by businesses.

The effects of the government handing over decision making on base interest rates to the central bank should be that the influence of short-term political need on economic management is removed. Interest rates, a key economic management tool, should be decided from a purely economic perspective. When a government minister is deciding interest rates, they can be manipulated for political advantage before an election, as Nigel Lawson did when Chancellor of the Exchequer before the 1987 election. The so-called 'Lawson Boom' that he engendered led directly to the recession of the early 1990s. The Bank of England, in contrast, should take only rational, objective decisions about long-term economic strategy. This is in line with other European countries' practice and further prepares the UK for the possibility of entry to the euro at some date in the future.

The London Stock Market

The stock market is where shares of publicly quoted companies are traded. London is an international financial centre.

Company names and share prices are published in all the daily broadsheet newspapers and on the internet. The shares of a company will trade on the stock market at a market price and the price will go up or down depending on the performance of the company and how it is viewed by the City. For example, a company that announces good profits is likely to see a rise in its share price and vice versa. However, good performance can be measured by factors other than profit. Manchester United, a profitable company, had a share price of £1.64 in February 1998; after being beaten 3–2 by Barnsley and knocked out of the FA cup on 25 February 1998, Manchester United shares fell 25p to £1.39. Continued good profits and better performance by the team on the pitch saw the share price climb steadily to £1.52 in June 1998, and to £3.00 in May 2005 at the time of the takeover of the club by Malcolm Glazer.

The value of shares will also be altered by overall movements in the stock market. If the economy is in recession and stagnating, then it is also likely that the stock market has fallen. In November 2008 the FTSE was around 4000; about 12 months previously it had been approaching 7000. Hence share prices were low and in November 2008 the high street retailers were expecting a poor Christmas and started sales at the end of November. The Bank of England sought to stimulate the economy by cutting interest rates to 3 per cent and the Chancellor of the Exchequer cut VAT by 2.5 per cent, but also increased the top rate of income tax to 45 per cent for people earning over £150,000 per annum.

The global economic environment

The global economic environment is shaped by how countries decide to behave economically in relation to each other; for example, countries may decide to group together on a regional basis and confer trade benefits and support on each other. The other economic influence at a global level is the effect of the world money markets. *See* Table 2.14.

Trading blocs and bodies

These are geographic blocs made up of a number of countries that agree to act together in some way with regard to trade and commerce. The countries may, for example, agree to allow special concessions on the taxing and movement of goods within the trading bloc or merely support each other with regard to economic issues.

The European Union

Because of the close association between politics and the economy, it is necessary to mention the European Union again under trading blocs and bodies. The EU's Single European Market came into operation in 1993 and allows free movement of goods between member states. However, the issue of differing rates of taxation in different member states has yet to be dealt with fully. For example, the tax on wine, beer and cigarettes is much lower in France than in

Table 2.14 The global economic environment

	Political	Economic	Sociocultural	Technological
Local				
National				
Global		• Trading blocs and bodies – EU – EFTA – OECD – NAFTA – ASEAN • World money markets • WTO		

the UK and this is clearly shown by the popularity of day trips to France to stock up on cheap drink and cigarettes. The sale of drinks from pubs and retail outlets in the UK has been badly hit, particularly in the south-east of England, with the closest and best access to France. However, day trips to France to stock up on cheaper goods will remain popular until duty rates throughout the EU are harmonised.

The 1991 **Maastricht Treaty on European Union** covers the issues of currency, **immigration** controls and defence policy. It set the timetable for the first round of European monetary union (EMU) that occurred in 1999. The deadline for meeting the necessary economic targets to join the first wave of European monetary union was the end of 1997. The key economic target that countries had to meet was the deficit:GDP (gross domestic product) ratio, which had to be 3 per cent or less. All member states except Greece met this target. However, along with Greece, Denmark, the UK and Sweden did not join the single European currency in the first wave.[18] The expectation is that the euro will generate an area of economic stability with low inflation and low interest rates.

European Free Trade Area

The European Free Trade Area (EFTA) was established in 1960 by the Stockholm Convention. Initially EFTA had seven member states: Austria, Denmark, Norway, Portugal, Sweden, Switzerland and the UK. Eventually some states left EFTA to join the European Union and new states joined EFTA. EFTA currently has four member states – Iceland, Liechtenstein, Norway and Switzerland[19] – and seeks to promote free trade and economic integration by managing the EFTA free trade area, participating in the European Economic Area (EEA), and developing a network of free trade agreements. The European Economic Area was created on 1 January 1994 when the three EFTA states, Iceland, Liechtenstein and Norway, and all EU states combined to create a large free-trade area. The EEA agreement allows free movement of people, goods and capital between participating nations.

Since the end of the Cold War, EFTA has sought to develop relationships with Central and Eastern European countries. This has led to the establishment of free-trade agreements with countries such as the Czech Republic, Poland, Latvia, Lithuania, Estonia, Bulgaria, Romania, Slovakia and Hungary. Currently EFTA is focusing on developing links with other countries, for example Peru, Columbia and Argentina and the South African Customs Union (SACU).[20]

Organisation for Economic Cooperation and Development

The Organisation for Economic Cooperation and Development (OECD) was established in 1961 and is based in Paris (*see* Table 2.15). On 5 June 1947 a speech by George C Marshall, US Secretary of State, gave rise to the post-war European Aid Program, commonly known as the Marshall plan. The view of the US government was that there had to be agreement among some or preferably all European countries as to the aid required and its use to reconstruct Western Europe. Therefore, European and North American countries came

Table 2.15 Members of the OECD

Year of joining	Countries		
1961	• Austria • Denmark • Greece • Italy • Norway • Sweden • UK	• Belgium • France • Iceland • Luxembourg • Portugal • Switzerland • USA	• Canada • Germany • Ireland • Netherlands • Spain • Turkey
1964	• Japan		
1969	• Finland		
1971	• Australia		
1973	• New Zealand		
1994	• Mexico		
1995	• Czech Republic		
1996	• Hungary, Korea, Poland		
2000	• Slovakia		

Source: http://www.oecd.org/pages/0,3417,en_36734052_36761800_1_1_1_1_1,00.html

together to establish the Organisation for European Economic Cooperation (OEEC). Its chief role was to facilitate the planning, allocation and implementation of post-war aid to Western Europe. However, in 1961 the OEEC decided that the reconstruction of post-war Western Europe was complete and sought to convert the OEEC into the OECD. The OECD did not focus on the giving and use of aid but on making the economies of the member countries involved prosper. To this end the policies of the OECD seek to:

- support sustainable economic growth;
- boost employment;
- raise living standards;
- maintain financial stability;
- assist other countries' economic development;
- contribute to growth in world trade.[21]

North American Free Trade Agreement

In 1994 the **North American Free Trade Agreement** (NAFTA) between the governments of Canada, the US and Mexico was established. The principal strands of NAFTA relate to:

- encouraging goodwill and collaboration between NAFTA countries;
- establishment of a larger and more secure market for goods and services produced in NAFTA countries;
- strengthening and sharpening the competitiveness of companies from NAFTA countries in global markets;

- the generation of additional employment opportunities in NAFTA countries;
- the improvement of working conditions and living standards in NAFTA countries;
- the protection and implementation of workers' basic rights.[22]

Trade and the movement of jobs and goods between NAFTA countries are key issues for the countries involved. Many car companies such as Volkswagen and US companies General Motors, Chrysler and Ford all have technological advanced manufacturing facilities in Mexico. These were often set up because wage rates in Mexico are much lower at about 15 per cent of those in the US (*see* entry case study). This has meant there has been growing export sales, and Volkswagen centres worldwide production of the Beetle in Mexico (*see* entry case study). However, in recent years there has been a decline in the sale of small cars, like the Beetle in Mexico, as NAFTA rules mean Mexico has to allow the import of older second-hand US-manufactured cars, which are cheaper and therefore appealing to the Mexican market. However, Mexico is one of the world's larger economies and is also a large exporter, and has established free-trade agreements with the EU, Japan and Mercosur, the South American trade bloc (*see* entry case study).

The Association of South East Asian Nations

The **Association of South East Asian Nations** (ASEAN) was formed in 1967 in Bangkok with five founding members and a further four members joining between 1984 and 1997 (*see* Table 2.16). In July 1997 Burma and Laos were admitted, but Cambodia's entry was postponed due to violence that threatened civil war.[23] Cambodia's entry finally occurred in 1999.

The three main objectives of ASEAN are:

- to promote the economic, social and cultural development of the region through cooperative programmes;
- to safeguard the political and economic stability of the region against big power rivalry;
- to serve as a forum for the resolution of intra-regional differences.[24]

Table 2.16 Members of ASEAN

Year of entry	Countries		
1967	• Indonesia • Singapore	• Malaysia • Thailand	• Philippines
1984	• Brunei		
1995	• Vietnam		
1997	• Laos	• Myanmar (Burma)	
1999	• Cambodia		

Source: http://www.aseansec.org/74.htm

The world money market

The world money market encompasses the world's stock markets and the exchange value of currencies against each other. The main stock markets that make up or have the biggest influence on the world money market are New York, London, Tokyo and Hong Kong. A collapse in one is quite likely to result in a drop in another, with the value of stocks falling and wiping value from the shares of companies.

This was clearly evident in the economic crises of 2008 that saw the major stock markets of London, New York and Tokyo plummet. This also meant that during 2008, currencies such as the pound, euro, yen and yuan all fell against the Americian dollar.

The World Trade Organisation

The **World Trade Organisation** (WTO) is located in Geneva, Switzerland, and officially came into existence on 1 January 1995, replacing its predecessor, the General Agreement on Tariffs and Trade (GATT). The WTO has 153 member countries and 30 observer governments, of which 21 have applied for membership. In administering the rules of trade and helping trade occur, the WTO monitors national policies, cooperates with other international bodies, handles trade disputes and helps provide training and technical assistance for developing economies.

The role of the WTO is summarised as:

- administering the rules of trade between nations;
- helping producers of goods and services, exporters and importers conduct their business.[25]

The biggest change in the WTO in recent years has been the conclusion of China's long-term efforts and negotiations to become a member. China took up its membership of the WTO on 1 January 2002, earning it most favoured nation (MFN) trading status on an immediate and permanent basis.[26] MFN status ensures China's exporters access to US markets. Prior to membership of the WTO, China's MFN status was reviewed annually by the American Congress.

China's drive to join the WTO was been long and slow since it first applied to join GATT in 1987. Consequently in 1997 the thawing of previously frosty political relations between China and the US provided an opportunity for progress on China's entry to the WTO and negotiations took place in Geneva. Final agreement on the terms of China's entry to the WTO was reached on 15 November 1999.

Admittance to the WTO is a significant step towards allowing China's fast-growing economy to face more international competition and allowing foreign exporters and investors access to the country. However, membership requires China to adopt a thorough approach to many complicated issues that establish barriers to trade and commerce. These include the dismantling of investment restrictions, quotas, subsidies and tariffs. China agreed to accept WTO rules, open its economy to the rest of the world and to continue to engage in market-based reforms.

Check your understanding

Do you understand the impact that economic factors in the external environment can have on an organisation like Volkswagen?

Check your understanding by referring to the entry case study, identifying and explaining the economic factors which have made it possible for Volkswagen to manufacture in Mexico.

The sociocultural elements of the external environment

The sociocultural elements of the external environment include the age and structure of a national population, the way a population or society behaves, and elements determining how the culture of a population develops. This section will look at some of these and how businesses and organisations are affected. Greater detail on culture and organisational behaviour can be found in Chapters 5 and 6 respectively.

The local sociocultural environment

Local community and social capital

The local community is part of an organisation's external environment (*see* Table 2.17). The local community may be passive as regards the organisation, or the local community and organisations can have an active influence on

Table 2.17 The local sociocultural environment

	Political	Economic	Sociocultural	Technological
Local			• Local community and social capital	
National				
Global				

each other. For example, a local transport company regularly burns old and broken wooden pallets in its yard and produces a dense black smoke, making the atmosphere unpleasant for people who live in nearby houses with gardens overlooking the firm's yard. This local company has a very direct influence on the quality of life in the local community. The local people may act either individually or collectively and complain to the local council department dealing with pollution. If appropriate action is taken to stop the pollution, this is a very good example of a local firm, its local community and local government affecting and being affected by each other's actions.

There may be other local community influences to which the organisation is subject. A school is a public-sector organisation that interacts significantly with its local community. The community is greatly dependent on how well the school performs due to the personal nature of the service that the school provides. This kind of interdependence is considered in Chapter 3.

Social capital is defined as community spirit and neighbourliness with which people identify. Social capital can take the form of trust which is felt by people living in a neighbourhood. Social capital held by individuals also arises from the number of groups people belong to, such as a local football team, Women's Institute, scouts, or yoga class, and the networks of family and friends with which people interact.[27] Hence people who experience a high level of social capital have good neighbours, see family and friends regularly and belong to social groups and clubs.

The national sociocultural external environment

Demographic change

Demographic change is change in the age and structure of a population. This section considers demographic changes in the population of the UK (*see* Table 2.18). There are three issues which are discussed, namely longevity, immigration and birth rates.

The population of the United Kingdom is currently around 60 million people and estimates are that it will be 75 million people by 2051.[28,29] Longevity, rising immigration and higher birth rates, mainly among migrants, will account for 69 per cent of the population growth.[30]

The number of older people in the United Kingdom has increased: in 1961 there were 16 million people aged over 50 in the UK and by 2021 there will be 22.5 million people, an increase of 40 per cent against an overall population increase of 15 per cent.[31] The 2001 census also highlighted this trend and for the first time, since the first census in 1801, there are now more people aged over 60 than under 16 in the UK's population. The 2001 census also showed there were 1 million people aged over 85 years, five times more than in 1951,[32] and is estimated to grow to around 3 million people by 2031.[33]

Immigration into the United Kingdom had increased largely due to the enlargement of the EU and this has led to an increase in the birth rate. Increasing

Table 2.18 The national sociocultural environment

	Political	Economic	Sociocultural	Technological
Local				
National			• Demographic change • Social change – inequality of income – family and household structure	
Global				

birth rates will clearly add to the population and at the moment the growth in birth rates is significant in the United Kingdom. In the United Kingdom in 2001 the birth rate for UK-born women was 1.5 children each and 2.3 children for non-UK-born women. In 2006 the figures had increased to 1.7 and 2.5 respectively, giving an overall birth rate of 1.8 children per woman.[34] The birth rate needs to be 2.1 children for a country to maintain its population.

Social change

Social change covers the changes and developments in the way societies behave. The changes in society examined in this section are the evolving family and household groups present in UK society and the inequality of income. The role and influence of government are also considered.

Family and household structure in UK society

The demographic changes discussed earlier in this chapter are reflected in changing household structures in the UK. The number of single person households is growing and changes in marriage, divorce and the role of women in the home and at work mean different family structures.

In 2008 the proportion of single person households in the United Kingdom was 28 per cent of all households. Single person households are a diverse group and there are three main types of single person household: single young professional people with very good incomes, divorcees and elderly people.

The greater number of older people in the population and the higher life expectancy of both men and women now results in a growing number of older people living in single person households. This increase is also due to people having always lived in a single person household or the death of a partner or spouse. The average lifetime is 81 years for a woman and 77 years for a man in the UK.

There are various reasons for the growth in the number of single person households and these are discussed below. Traditionally 30 or 40 years ago a young person would have anticipated being single for a short time and remaining in the parental home, before marrying in their mid-twenties and settling down to a lifelong marriage, raising the average 2.4 children and being part of a traditional family unit. Society viewed being single as something undesirable that occurred as a result of misfortune and not an alternative that people chose. Being single was the result of being widowed or divorced because of an unfaithful spouse; indeed, both of these still occur today.

However, today in the twenty-first century there are two general trends regarding young adults and their housing. The first trend is that young adults will get a job and leave home permanently after school or university and will be living independently by their mid-twenties. A proportion of these single young people will be well-off professional people with successful careers and good incomes. Approximately two-thirds of single women and over half of single men are in the ABC1 economic group, with three-quarters of single men and two-thirds of single women in full-time employment.

The other emerging trend is that of so called 'boomerang kids', i.e. children who leave the parental home, often to go to university, only to return and live at home until their late twenties or early thirties, as they are unable to afford to rent or buy their own home. Therefore, the number of adult children living at home has increased significantly since 1993, when 60 per cent of men and 40 per cent of women in their twenties were living at home. In 2008, 80 per cent of men and 50 per cent of women in their twenties were still living at home. Additionally, over the same time period the median age for a first marriage had increased from 26 to 30 years for a man and from 24 to 28 years for a woman.[35]

The number of single person households is increased by marriage and divorce rates and the UK has the highest divorce rate in the EU, with around 35 per cent of marriages ending in divorce, compared with a rate of around 10 per cent in the mid-1970s. This is a consequence of divorce being less shameful and more frequent than 30 or 40 years ago. Between 1970 and 1997 the increased divorce rate, coupled with a 50 per cent fall in the number of first-time marriages, added to the number of single person households. However, in 2006 the divorce rate in the UK had fallen to its lowest level for 22 years and marriage rates were at their lowest level since records began in 1862.[36]

The increase in the single person household in the UK has led to businesses considering their market segments. For example, supermarkets need to cater for single person households, who do not want to buy large packs that contain portions that are unwanted. This is an expensive way to shop, particularly as a pensioner on a budget. There is also an increasing demand for single person household packs of healthy food to be widely available.[37] The young professionals will be big investors in technology, including online, computer and entertainment equipment for the home as well as entertainment outside the home, such as cinemas and gyms.

Further social changes have occurred with regard to the family and the role of women. In 1971 married couples with children comprised 52 per cent of families and 12 per cent of children were born outside marriage. In contrast, by 2007 the figure was 37 per cent of families were married couples with children and 44 per cent of children were born outside marriage.[38] Further social changes in the family include alterations in the role of parents. In 1985 both parents worked in half of all two-parent families with children; the figure was 62 per cent a decade later.

Today fewer people believe that it is a wife and mother's job to look after the home than did so in 1986. However, mothers still spend four times longer than fathers on cooking and housework.[39] The growth in the number of women in the workplace and the resulting greater financial independence of women are due to several factors. First, women are no longer expected to marry and be totally financially dependent on a husband. Since the 1960s there has been improved and increased access to higher and further education, which has meant greater access to better jobs and careers for women. This, coupled with the introduction of legislation in the 1970s covering equality of women in the workplace in terms of equal opportunities and equal pay, has contributed to women's greater role in the workplace.

There are some mixed messages to be observed in the political reactions to social change. In contrast to the moral rhetoric of family values that it espoused at the hustings, the Conservative government in the late 1980s introduced independent taxation for married women for the first time, thereby recognising both the earning potential and the legal status of married women. Nevertheless, in an effort to promote the responsibility of fathers in providing for their children beyond separation and divorce, it also established the Child Support Agency, whose job was to track down and make the errant fathers pay for their children living in one-parent families with their mothers.

Inequality of income in UK society

UK society is one of widening inequality: the well-off have got richer and the less well-off have become poorer. Income inequality has grown rapidly since 1977, fuelled to a large extent by the Conservative governments in power from 1979 to 1997. These governments introduced policies that led to large pay packets and rewards for successful people, in contrast to fewer and increasingly meagre social security benefits for the less well-off, which overall have increased more slowly than wages. Additionally, the wage differences between skilled and unskilled workers has increased, as skilled workers have benefited from technological change and unskilled workers have suffered as a result of the decline in the trade unions.[40] Hence the income distribution gap in the UK is one of the greatest among the industrialised countries of the world.

There are many ways in which government is reacting, as any organisation should, to these changes in the external environment. In terms of the ageing population, government takes the view that more of the burden of social security, healthcare and pensions needs to be provided for privately since the workforce cannot keep up the level of provision traditionally offered by the welfare state when it was introduced. The Blair government was concerned about the widening gap in UK society, and established a Social Exclusion Unit to bring into the mainstream of opportunity and care those who had been excluded for social or systematic reasons, with a view to including more disadvantaged groups in mainstream provision.

This widening inequality is apparent when looking at different areas of the country. In England the problems of poverty, ill health and unemployment are mainly concentrated in cities in the south and the depressed industrial north, with pockets of rural poverty in Cornwall, Kent, Cumbria and Northumbria. London has the highest level of low incomes, about 25 per cent of people, and the south-east the lowest number of people on low incomes at about 18 per cent. In the south, outside of poor inner-city areas, there is generally a higher standard of living, with the problems of unemployment, poverty and ill health occurring less frequently than in impoverished areas. However, the stress of modern living is felt in both the city and the countryside, with fewer people working longer hours. This is illustrated by city workers attending working breakfasts and evening meetings and people in the countryside working longer hours on the land or in the holiday industry for minimal pay.[41]

The global sociocultural environment

Changes in populations at a global level impact on the opportunity for trade and economic development, hence some of the global demographic trends are examined in this section (*see* Table 2.19). In addition, some of the sociocultural issues that affect organisations once they leave their home environment and operate overseas are also considered. Definitions of culture and how it affects individuals and national society are covered in detail in Chapter 5.

Global demographics

There are differing trends in the development of populations in a variety of countries and continents. At a global level these demographic changes will impact on the economic development of different countries and regions in the world.

Europe

The European Union's economic growth rate will potentially shrink to 1.25 per cent a year, due to its ageing population and therefore less productive

Table 2.19 The global sociocultural environment

	Political	Economic	Sociocultural	Technological
Local				
National				
Global			• Global demographics – Europe – Asia – Africa • Cross-cultural issues – Language – Behaviour – Culture shock	

population. This is half the US growth rate of 2.5 per cent per year. One view on tackling the issue of the decline of Europe's economy is to raise the retirement age by five years, significantly increasing pension funding and also increasing productivity, while reducing unemployment.[42] The alternative view to tackling this problem is for Europe to re-examine its current approach to immigration.

It is estimated that without significant policy changes in the EU, Europe's share of world output may decrease from its current 18 per cent to 10 per cent by 2050.[43] This trend is mirrored in Japan, whose share of world output could fall from 8 per cent to 4 per cent. This is in stark contrast to the USA where it is estimated its share of world output could rise from 23 per cent to 26 per cent over the same period.[44] This is attributed to the greater levels of immigration in the US, which brings more workers and increasing fertility rates, as immigrants tend to be young and of childbearing age.[45] This argument that Europe's demographic problem may be helped by immigration is also echoed by the British Venture Capitalist Association (BVCA) which sees at least part of the solution to Europe's demographic problems lying in an enlightened approach to economic migration. The BVCA also points to the 'influx of South American economic migrants' into the US, who will contribute to the expected buoyancy in the US economy.[46]

Asia

Changes in populations at a global level impact on companies and the opportunity for doing business in different countries and regions around the world. For example, significant reductions in fertility rates in Asia during the 1980s resulted in a sizeable reduction in levels of absolute poverty, which is defined as the percentage of a population surviving on less than a dollar a day.[47] The impact of lower fertility rates and the resultant slower population growth is that there is faster economic expansion along with a reduction in poverty.[48] Faster and improved economic expansion is logically due to smaller families having fewer expenses and being able to earn more, which in turn improves the opportunities people have to spend and save.[49] However, it is estimated that around 50 per cent of improvement in economic growth in developing countries arises from a one-off 'demographic window' which occurs when large numbers of working adults support fewer children and older people.[50] Hence, Asian countries will experience population downturns and South Korea, Taiwan and Japan are all experiencing a population downturn and an increasing number of older people in the population.

In Japan the population trend has moved to one of a shrinking population with the birth rate falling to 1.26 children per woman in 2005.[51] However, Japanese people have traditionally experienced longevity, in part due to their traditional diet which is low in saturated fat and high in fish. Therefore, by 2006 life expectancy in Japan was 82 years and 20 per cent of the population were aged over 65, but by 2050 this will have doubled to 40 per cent of the population. China's experience will be similar: today older people represent 7.5 per cent of the population and by 2050 this will have increased to 25 per cent of China's population.[52,53]

Africa

In Africa HIV and AIDS are having an impact on the population and life expectancy and this in turn impacts on economic development. HIV and Aids are forecast to make the populations of the 53 most affected countries 480 million fewer than expected by 2050. The total population of these countries is over 4 billion and the percentage reduction will be 8 per cent by 2050.[54] The impact of HIV and Aids is greatest in Africa, with the population of the 38 most affected countries being 16 million lower in 2000 than otherwise expected. This figure is expected to reach 320 million by 2050, which is 19 per cent or almost one-fifth reduction in the population.[55] In most of these countries high fertility rates will likely result in growing populations; however, Botswana, Lesotho, South Africa and Swaziland are forecast to have lower populations in 2050 than today.[56] This is supported by the projected life expectancy in these countries: in Botswana life expectancy in 2003 was 40 years, against the predicted 68 years without the impact of HIV and Aids; in South Africa, life expectancy was 48 years against the expected 67 years. In 2050, life expectancy in these countries is forecast to be only 56 years.[57]

In conclusion, overall during the next 50 years the world's population is expected to age faster than ever before (*see* Table 2.20, which shows median ages, i.e. the age that divides a population into two halves). During in the same period of time the world's population will grow at an annual rate of 1.2 per cent, giving a net increase of 77 million people every year, with 50 per cent of

Table 2.20 Median ages

	2000 – median age	2050 – median age
Least developed countries	18.1 years	27.1 years
Developing countries	24.1 years	35.7 years
Developed countries	37.3 years	42.5 years
Overall	26.4 years	36.8 years

Source: from UN Population Division Data from 'People, plagues and prosperity', *The Financial Times*, 27 February 2003 (Wolf, M.).

the increase arising from just six countries: India, 21 per cent; China, 12 per cent; Pakistan, 5 per cent; Bangladesh, Nigeria and the USA, 4 per cent each.[58]

Cross-cultural issues

Organisations have to consider political and economic circumstances in other countries when contemplating international business operations. Culture plays an important part in determining how international business is undertaken in different countries and regions of the world. The cross-cultural issues which commonly have to be understood and dealt with when doing business and working abroad are language, behaviour and culture shock.

Language

The most obvious illustration of culture is language. Investing in accurate language assistance when operating in another cultural context is a vital but largely underestimated consideration for organisations assessing the potential costs of international operations. The cost of getting it wrong is often much greater, but is often ignored in short-term decision making. It is only necessary to consider how many misunderstandings occur between native speakers of English who originate from the UK, the USA and Australia to begin to appreciate the difficulties of translating and interpreting other languages. For example, the British lecturer will invigilate an exam, while an American will proctor the exam. While British tourists on holiday in Australia will want to buy flip-flops to wear on the beach, they will be confused when the shop assistant offers a pair of 'thongs' instead.

The back catalogue of language mistranslations and the choice of unfortunate words for products is huge. Volkswagen's multi-passenger vehicle (MPV) suffered when it was introduced to the UK from being called Sharon, a name not associated with the profile of customer to whom it was expected to be sold. Proton, Malaysia's national car manufacturer, did its market research and decided not to introduce its basic model to the UK under its Malaysian name, as 'Saga' is the brand name of products targeted at senior citizens, to whom Proton did not wish to limit sales. The Vauxhall Nova, General Motors' 1980s mini hatchback, was branded Opel Corsa in the rest of Europe because 'Nova', which was meant to have connotations of new, actually translates as 'does not go' in many European languages. The Rolls-Royce Silver Mist had to be renamed for the German-speaking market because *Mist* in German is a colloquial word for excrement.

However, translation or the choice of words meaning other things in different languages is not the only skill required overseas. Interpreting – which is not translating the words, but rather saying the right thing in the target language – is a crucial skill. At a business meeting between British and Chinese businesspeople, when the British host says, 'We hope you have enjoyed your stay in the UK', a direct translation will sound arrogant and rude. Therefore, a skilled interpreter will replace this phrase with the customary 'We are sorry we did not look after you properly', and the courtesy requirements of both sides are fulfilled.

Behaviour

Other types of cross-cultural issues would relate to the consumption of alcohol in Muslim states and of beef in India, where the cow is sacred to Hindus (McDonald's had to substitute a Hindu-friendly version of the burger). How much physical contact or personal space people are customarily allowed is also problematic, as some cultures remain physically very distant from each other, while in others regular touching is commonplace. Again, whether or not physical contact is permissible between the sexes or between people of the same sex is an issue. For example, in many Middle and Far Eastern cultures, any touching between the sexes is unacceptable, while man-to-man handholding and bodily contact are quite normal. This understandably becomes a minefield to the foreign executive. In Japan, blowing one's nose in public is quite taboo, while in China the public expectoration of waste is unsurprising.

Therefore, the behaviour of foreign executives, the design of products and services, and the labelling, packaging and advertising of goods and services must all be subject to intense scrutiny.

Culture shock

The greater the distance between home and host culture, the more likely it is that the host culture will provide elements of everyday life that shock the individual travelling there. From language to food, from individual behaviour to collective customs, culture shock is a real and debilitating influence on the individual businessperson abroad. As it is based in experience, it is difficult to know how culture shock can be dealt with until it has been experienced, since there is still a huge difference between knowing something is going to happen and actually experiencing it. Nevertheless, organisations can invest in pre-departure orientation programmes, training people for overseas postings through visits, access to expatriates who have already lived in that culture and indigenous members of the population. It is essential to consider not only the expatriate executive, but also the relocation and comfort of family members as well.

Check your understanding

Do you understand the sociocultural factors that could impact on an international company like Coca-Cola?

Check your understanding by identifying and explaining sociocultural factors that could impact on Coca-Cola.

The technological elements of the external environment

Technology has an influence on all aspects of business from the very general to the very specific and as such is not split into the local, national and global levels (*see* Table 2.21). To provide a flavour of the impact of technology this section identifies and discusses the impact of technology on business.

The advent of technology has made it easier for people to communicate with each other, whether they operate in the political, economic, social or general business arena. Communications technology takes the form of mobile phones, fax machines, video conferencing, the internet and the world wide web and the key benefit is that staff are contactable all the time while at work and should be able to contact customers and clients without having to return to an office.

Video conferencing is becoming increasingly popular among businesses. Large companies such as British Petroleum (BP) have been using video conferencing since 1983 and have in-house studios in global locations. The greatest benefits of video conferencing are conferred when people in two or more places in different parts of the world use it. SmithKline Beecham has over 30 video conferencing studios worldwide and is able to carry out video conference meetings (see Table 2.22). It is likely that the increased threat of international

Table 2.21 The technological external environment: communications technology

	Political	Economic	Sociocultural	Technological
Local				• mobile phones and faxes • video conferencing • internet and world wide web • manufacturing technology
National				
Global				

Table 2.22 Benefits of video conferencing

- Less time spent travelling to and from meetings, therefore reducing the cost and stress of travelling.
- More people can attend meetings and be called into the meeting at relatively short notice if their knowledge and expertise are required.
- Eye contact and body language can be observed, a clear advantage over phone conferencing.
- Enhancement of teamworking and communication among teams whose work is spread out across the globe.

terrorism and the spread of illnesses such as Avian flu will result in an increased use of video conferencing by organisations seeking to reduce the risks to which their workforce may be exposed.

The internet is an array of interconnected networks to which millions of computers around the world are attached. There are a large number of internet sites that hold information: for example, company sites or the *Financial Times* site. The world wide web (WWW) allows linking of internet sites and research and retrieval tools, hence the WWW and the internet are often seen as one and the same. Search engines such as Google allow searches to be carried out very easily and it is equally easy to repeat and refine any searches that have previously been carried out.[59]

Companies can take up a presence on the internet by setting up a website. This will give a company 24 hours a day, 365 days a year, worldwide exposure on the internet. Companies are able to use their internet presence to advertise their products and services and collect addresses and details from potential customers who visit the site, with a view to e-mailing or posting further information. The internet is equally accessible by both large and small companies, although large companies may have more money to spend on designing a site.

A company that has set up an internet site also has to consider how it is going to persuade people to visit the site. Many companies advertise in the more traditional media, such as the television and press, and include their internet address in the advertisement. An additional method is to be included on search engines so that when users type in a keyword such as books or beer the relevant internet sites are listed. Companies are also able to advertise on search engines by paying to have their logo appear, although costs are high.[60]

Banking and financial services is a good example of an industry where service delivery has been continually altered and modernised since the late 1970s. In banking the most obvious application of technology has occurred in the development of the cashpoint machine. The other main technological development has been in the use of central computer-based systems to hold customer details and account records. These applications of computer technology allow any customer with a passbook or cashpoint card to withdraw money from their bank or building society account anywhere in the country and even overseas. This greater reliance on technology to perform at least some routine tasks has been part of the reason that both banks and building societies have been able to use and train their staff to sell a much wider range of financial services. The development of new ways of delivering banking and financial services has continued to develop and today internet banking is common.

Check your understanding

Do you understand the technological factors that could impact on vacuum manufacturer Dyson, which has moved production from the UK to the Far East?

Check your understanding by identifying and explaining technological factors that could impact on Dyson.

Summary

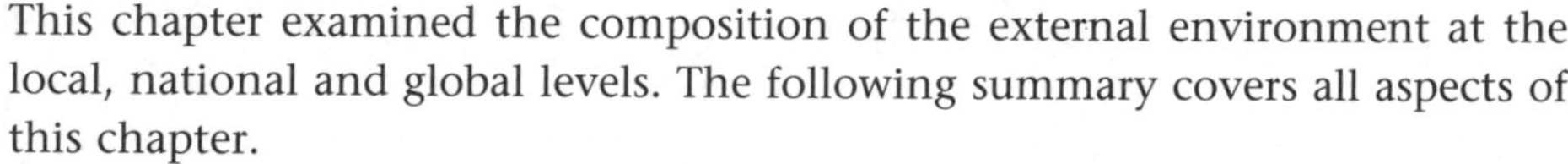

This chapter examined the composition of the external environment at the local, national and global levels. The following summary covers all aspects of this chapter.

1 The local political environment includes local government and national government operating at a local level and local business associations such as Chambers of Commerce. Local government is responsible for regulating private-sector business, for example via trading standards, and for providing a range of public services, e.g. refuse collection and schools. Chambers of Commerce offer their business members access to training and business information on, for example, exporting goods.

2 The national political environment includes national government for the whole UK, Scotland and Wales and national bodies such as the CBI and trade unions. National governments pass legislation, which may impact on business, e.g. health and safety legislation. National governments are responsible for collecting taxation and deciding how it is to be allocated and spent to provide public-sector services such as healthcare and education. Employers' bodies like the CBI and employee organisations such as trade unions (e.g. UNISON) seek to get the best deal for their members in the workplace environment and this may involve lobbying government to pass particular legislation or make a particular decision.

3 The global political environment includes alliances and agreements, such as the special relationship between the UK and the US. Other global factors include international bodies such as the Commonwealth and NATO, which, respectively, play a role in the world economy and the establishment of peace, which is needed to allow economies to flourish.

4 The local economic environment of an organisation will be shaped by its relationship with its bank, which is usually of local significance. The state of the local economy in which a business is located will influence the ease with which labour can be recruited and retained.

5 The national economic environment includes the Bank of England and the stock market. The Bank of England sets the base interest rate, which in turn determines the level of interest businesses and individuals pay on loans, which impacts on the amount of money consumers and industry have to spend, which clearly determines the level of economic activity experienced.

6 The global economic environment includes trading blocs such as the EU and NAFTA, world money markets and the WTO. Trading blocs confer free movement of goods between member states and significant tax concessions on goods imported from member states. For example, goods move freely between EU countries such as France, Germany and the UK. The WTO handles trade negotiations between countries, monitors trade policies and deals with trade disputes.

7 The local sociocultural environment includes the local community and social capital. An organisation's interactions with its local community may impact on the organisation's level of work, particularly if the organisation is, for example, a school. Social capital is defined as community spirit and neighbourliness, and this can either draw communities together or drive them apart.

8 The national sociocultural external environment includes demographic change and social change. Demographic changes are changes in the age and structure of a population. In the UK the key changes centre on longevity, immigration and birth rates. Social change includes development and alterations in the way society behaves. This can include changes to income levels, family and **household structure**.

9 The global sociocultural external environment encompasses change in populations and their impact at a global level on the opportunities for trade and economic development. Such impacts include fertility rates, HIV/Aids, and age of populations, which is higher in the developed world than in the developing world. Also at a global level, the impact of cross-cultural issues, such as language, behaviour and culture shock, can be significant for companies.

10 The impact of technology on organisations occurs at all levels. Improved communications technology allows easier and faster communication between organisations, their employees, customers and potential customers. The use of the internet and the world wide web can allow customers access to an organisation and the products and services it offers, all day, every day.

Chapter objectives and the exit case study

While reading this chapter and engaging in the activities, you should have learned how to apply theory and models and analyse situations. The exit case study and the questions which follow will provide an opportunity to assess how well you have met the relevant chapter objectives relating to specific material covered in the chapter.

Chapter objective	Check you have achieved this by
1 Analyse the external environment of an organisation by using PEST and LoNGPEST, drawing conclusions from the analysis.	answering case study questions 1, 2 and 4.
2 Select the most appropriate data and information sources for undertaking analysis of an organisation's external environment.	answering case study questions 3 and 4.

EXIT CASE STUDY 2.2

Tui slashes number of holiday packages

by Pan Kwan Yuk

Tui Travel has slashed the number of holidays it is offering next summer by 16 per cent as Britons, who have so far been reluctant to forgo their break in the sun, put their suitcases into storage. The group, formed last year from the merger of Germany's Tui and the UK's First Choice, said it was reducing its capacity by 16 per cent from an earlier plan of 9 per cent after booking volumes fell 17 per cent behind the level seen this time last year. The capacity reduction mirrors cuts at rival Thomas Cook, which at the end of September said it would reduce the number of summer holidays for 2009 by 6 per cent after bookings fell by 4 per cent. Peter Long, Tui chief executive, said a worsening economic outlook, further rises in UK unemployment and sustained weakness in the pound against the euro had all contributed to the weaker booking volume.

However, he was careful to stress that the reduction in capacity has helped mitigate this and average selling prices are up 10 per cent on the previous year. 'Unlike retailers, we can constantly tune the level of stock and adapt the number of holidays on sale [to maintain revenue and profit margins],' he said. The company also said it had seen a 'marginal' rise in the cancellations rate, from 6.6 per cent last year to 7.7 per cent. 'The increase is hardly surprising . . . but it is not an alarming figure . . . it is not an area of concern,' he said. Instead, Mr Long believes the collapse of small rival XL in September and the recent wave of consolidation in the sector has left the business well-placed to weather the downturn.

'I can't stand up and say we are just ignoring what is going on in the world, but we have the capability to adapt and trade through,' he said. 'What our customers are saying to us is that their annual summer holiday is important. With everything that is going on it is perhaps even more important that they take that break.' He added that the demise of XL, which left many passengers stranded in their holiday destinations, should lead to a resurgence in package holiday bookings. 'People don't want to take a risk when it comes to their holidays,' he said.

Mr Long's comments came as Tui reported a 43 per cent rise in underlying annual profits and increased its synergy targets as it made better-than-expected progress on integration. The group said it was now targeting annual merger synergy targets of £175m by 2010, an increase of £25m on its previous target. Of that, £15m will come from UK integration and £10m from the overseas businesses.

For the 12 months to September 30, the group swung from a pre-tax profit of £18.4m to a loss of £266.6m, largely as a result of costs related to the merger with First Choice. Stripping out the one-off costs, pre-tax profit rose from £222.8m to £319.7m. Total revenue increased by 9 per cent to £13.9bn and the group is paying a year-end dividend of 6.9p a share, making a total payment for the year of 9.7p, up 16 per cent. This is in contrast to Holidaybreak, the specialist travel company, which on Thursday said it was sharply cutting its final dividend in light of uncertain market conditions. Shares in Holidaybreak fell 4p, or 2.4 per cent, to 163p in afternoon trading, while Tui shares gained $2^1/_2$p, or 1.25 per cent, to $202^1/_2$p.

Source: from 'Tui shashes number of holiday packages', *The Financial Times*, 27 November 2008 (Yuk, P.K.).

Exit case study questions

1 Perform a LoNGPEST analysis of the external environment faced by the holiday industry.

2 Consider your answer to question 1 and comment on how the following types of holidays are affected by the external environment: domestic holidays in the UK; European holidays; or long-haul destinations.

3 Identify further sources of information which would enhance and improve your analysis in question 1.

4 Discuss the advantages and disadvantages of undertaking analysis of the external environment of an organisation or industry.

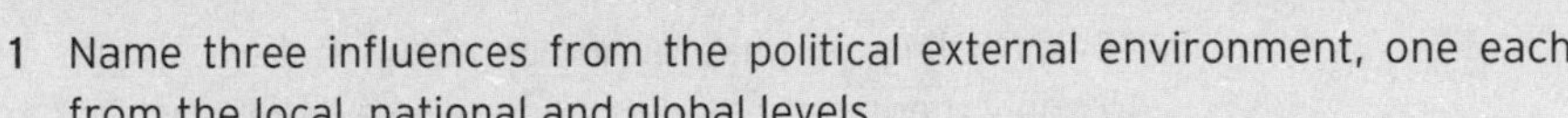

Short-answer questions

1 Name three influences from the political external environment, one each from the local, national and global levels.

2 Name three influences from the economic external environment, one each from the local, national and global levels.

3 Name three influences from the sociocultural external environment, one each from the local, national and global levels.

4 Explain why the influence of technology on an organisation is considered differently from the influence of economic, political and sociocultural factors.

5 Define autocracy.

6 Describe a democracy.

7 List the characteristics of a free market.

8 List the characteristics of a planned economy.

9 List the characteristics of a mixed economy.

10 Explain the function of Chambers of Commerce in the business community.

11 Summarise the role of the IOD and CBI in business.

12 Explain the role of trade unions.

13 Explain the role of NATO in the external environment.

14 Describe the role of the Commonwealth in the external environment.

15 Illustrate the role of the Bank of England in the economy of the UK.

16 Explain the role of the London stock market in the economy of the UK.

17 Indicate the role of the WTO in global trade.

18 Explain the role of NAFTA in North American trade.

19 Explain the role of ASEAN.

20 Explain the role of EFTA and how it differs from the EU.

21 Indicate by example what you understand alliances and agreements to be.

22 Define 'social capital'.

23 What is the main difference in public spending on pensions in the UK and other European countries?

24 Name the six countries with the fastest growing population over the next 50 years.

25 Why, by 2003, had life expectancy fallen in South Africa and Botswana to just 48 years and 40 years respectively?

Chapter objectives and assignment questions

While reading this chapter and engaging in the activities, you should have learned how to apply theory and models and analyse situations. This means you should be able to meet the chapter objectives outlined at the beginning of the chapter. The table below shows which chapter objectives can be tested by the different questions.

Chapter objective	Check you have achieved this by
1 Analyse the external environment of an organisation by using PEST and LoNGPEST, drawing conclusions from the analysis.	answering assignment questions 1 and 3.
2 Select the most appropriate data and information sources for undertaking analysis of an organisation's external environment.	answering assignment questions 1, 2 and 3.
3 Discuss the links between economic and political factors and how this shapes external environments.	answering assignment questions 1 and 3.

Assignment questions

1 Choose *one* of the following organisations: Institute of Directors (IOD), Confederation of British Industry (CBI) or Trades Union Congress (TUC). Identify and collect appropriate information and write an essay of 2000 words that demonstrates and evaluates the influence of your chosen organisation on the individual employee, the workplace and the economy. Comment on the sources of information used.

2 Select two organisations from different industries or sectors and collect relevant and appropriate information. Compare and contrast the impact of technology on your chosen organisations over the past three years and present your findings in a 2000-word report. Comment on the sources of information used.

3 Identify and collect appropriate information and write an essay of 2000 words comparing and contrasting the roles of ASEAN and NAFTA in their home geographic regions. Comment on the sources of information used.

WEBLINKS available at **www.pearsoned.co.uk/capon**

The websites listed here are for international bodies that impact on the external environment of organisations. Websites for UK-based bodies are listed at the end of Chapter 1.

- The following website is for the European Union:
  http://www.europa.eu.int/
- The website for the European Free Trade Area is shown below:
  http://www.efta.int/

- The website of the European Bank for Reconstruction and Development is shown below:
  http://www.ebrd.org/
- The following website is for the Council of Baltic Sea States:
  http://www.cbss.st
- The following website is for the North America Free Trade Association:
  http://www.nafta-sec-alena.org/
- The following website is for the Association of South East Asian Nations:
  http://www.asean.org
- The website for the Commonwealth is shown below:
  http://www.thecommonwealth.org/
- The website for NATO is shown below:
  http://www.nato.int/
- The website of the World Trade Organisation is shown below:
  http://www.wto.org/
- The website of the World Bank Group is shown below:
  http://www.worldbank.org/
- The following website is for the International Monetary Fund:
  http://www.imf.org/
- The website of the Organisation for Economic Cooperation and Development is shown below:
  http://www.oecd.org/
- The Treasury website is shown below:
  http://www.hm-treasury.gov.uk

FURTHER READING

These book chapters all look at the external environments faced by organisations.

- Johnson, G, Scholes, K and Whittington, R (2008) *Exploring Corporate Strategy*, 8th edn, Chapter 2, Harlow: Financial Times Prentice Hall.
- Lynch, R (2006) *Corporate Strategy*, 4th edn, Chapter 3, Harlow: Financial Times Prentice Hall.
- Palmer, A and Hartley, B (2006) *The Business Environment*, 5th edn, Chapters 2, 3, 4 and 5, Maidenhead: McGraw Hill.
- Thompson, J L and Martin, F (2005) *Strategic Management: Awareness, Analysis and Change*, 5th edn, Chapter 4, London: Thomson Learning.
- Worthington, I and Brittion, C (2006) *The Business Environment*, 5th edn, Chapters 3, 4, 5 and 16, Harlow: Financial Times Prentice Hall.

REFERENCES

1 http://www.businesslink.org
2 http://www.bbc.co.uk/politics97/analysis/rozenberg2.shtml
3 Ibid.
4 Ibid.
5 Ibid.
6 Manning, A (1997) 'If it's good enough for everyone else, it's good enough for us', *Independent on Sunday*, 11 May.

7 http://europa.eu/abc/panorama/index_en.htm
8 Barber, L (1997) 'No turning back from brave new Europe', *Financial Times*, 17 July.
9 http://www.cbss.st/history/
10 BBC News (2008) 'Kosovo MPs proclaim independence', 17 February.
11 BBC News (2008) 'Bush salutes Kosovo's independence', 19 February.
12 BBC News (2008) 'UN to transfer powers in Kosovo', 12 June.
13 Ejime, P (1996) Panafrican News Agency (PANA), 'Reconciling Nigeria with the Commonwealth', 23 June.
14 Ejime, P (1997) Panafrican News Agency (PANA), 'Nigeria reassessing Commonwealth membership', 21 August.
15 http://www.thecommonwealth.org/Templates/YearbookHomeInternal.asp?NodeID=138917
16 http://www.thecommonwealth.org/
17 http://www.nato.int/welcome/home.htm
18 *Daily Telegraph*, 28 February 1998.
19 http://www.efta.int/content/about-efta/member-states
20 http://www.efta.int/content/free-trade/fta-countries
21 http://www.oecd.org/pages/0,3417,en_36734052_36734103_1_1_1_1_1,00.html
22 http://www.nafta-sec-alena.org/DefaultSite/index_e.aspx?ArticleID=282
23 Bardacke, T (1997) 'Cambodia rebuffed by Asean', *Financial Times*, 11 July.
24 http://www.aseansec.org/64.htm
25 http://www.wto.org/english/thewto_e/whatis_e/whatis_e.htm
26 Jonquieres, G de and Walker, T (1997) 'New dawn in the east', *Financial Times*, 3 March.
27 http://www.statistics.gov.uk/CCI/nugget.asp?ID=314
28 BBC News (2007) 'Population at least 75m by 2051', 10 October.
29 BBC News (2007) 'Mothers in 30s boost population', 11 December.
30 Ibid.
31 BBC News (2008) 'Minorities set to be US majority', 14 August.
32 Brown, K (2002) 'A lost generation leaves Britain older and calmer', *Financial Times*, 5 October.
33 BBC News 11 December 2007, op. cit.
34 BBC News 11 December 2007, op. cit.
35 Frean, A (2008) 'Return home of the "boomerang kids" stretches parents to limit', *The Times*, 7 February.
36 Batty, D (2007) 'Divorce total lowest for 29 years', *Guardian*, 30 August.
37 http://www.euromonitor.com/One_person_households_Opportunities_for_consumer_goods_companies
38 BBC News (2008) 'One parent families on the rise', 11 April.
39 Jury, L (1998) 'Britions remain true to family values', *Independent*, 7 August.
40 http://www.statistics.gov.uk/cci/nugget.asp?id=332
41 http://www.poverty.org.uk/02/index.shtml
42 Parker, G (2002) 'Brussels warns of ageing population crisis', *Financial Times*, 11 December.
43 Ibid.
44 Ibid.
45 Ibid.
46 Gimbel, F (2003) 'BVCA to call for immigration increase', *Financial Times*, 23 March.
47 Williams, F (2002) 'UN finds link between fertility rate and wealth', *Financial Times*, 3 December.
48 Ibid.
49 Ibid.
50 Ibid.
51 BBC News (2007) 'Japan eyes demographic time bomb', 19 November.
52 BBC News (2007) 'Ageing threatens China's economy', 18 December.
53 BBC News (2006) 'China braced for pensioner boom', 16 October.

54 Wolf, M (2003) 'People, plagues and prosperity', *Financial Times*, 26 February.
55 Ibid.
56 Ibid.
57 Ibid.
58 Ibid.
59 Shankar, B and Sharda, R (1997) 'Obtaining business intelligence on the Internet', *Long Range Planning*, 30(1), February.
60 Bird, J (1996) 'Untangling the web', *Management Today*, March.

CHAPTER 3

The competitive environment

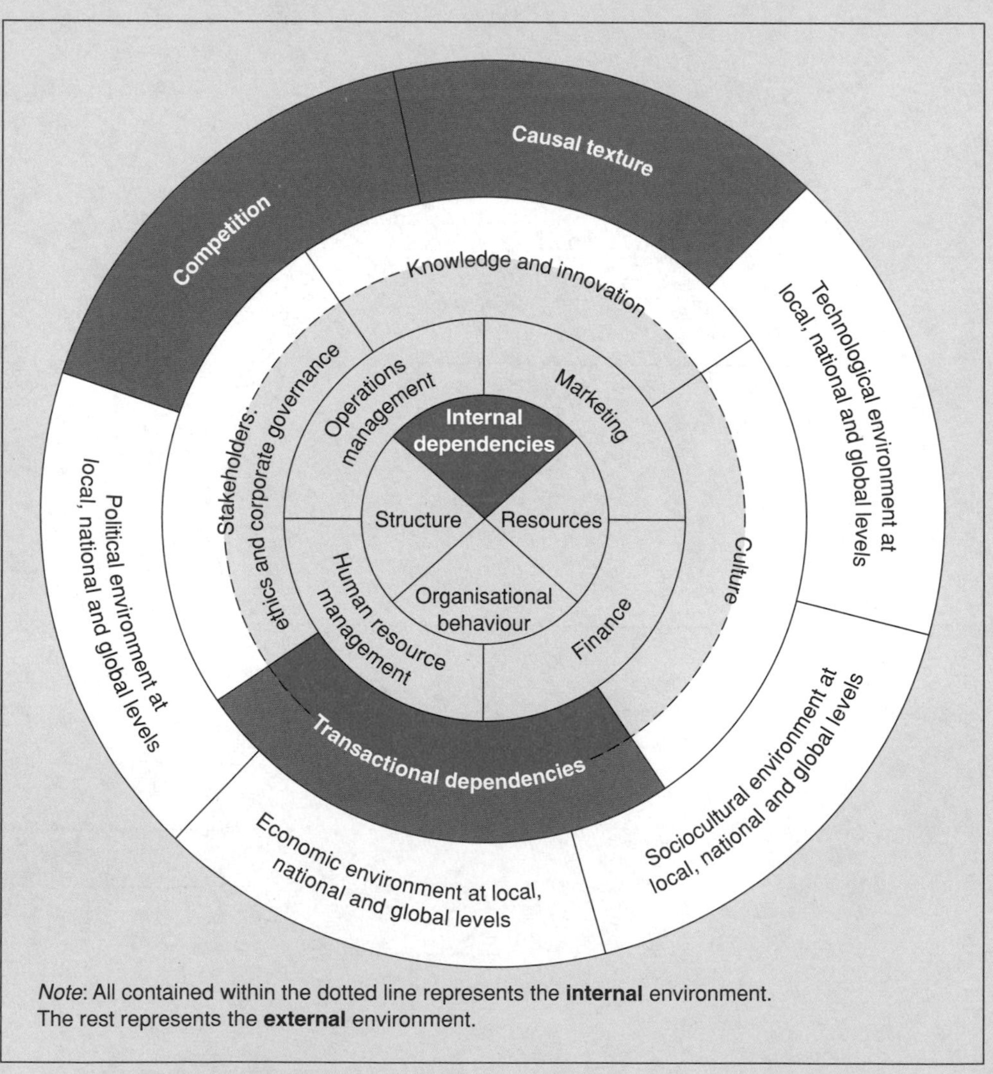

Note: All contained within the dotted line represents the **internal** environment. The rest represents the **external** environment.

Figure 3.1 Business environment model

Chapter objectives

This chapter provides an overview of the regulation of competition in the UK, the competitive environment and competitive strategies. The different regulatory bodies are examined, along with Porter's five forces of competition and competitive strategies.

Therefore, when you have read this chapter and worked through the associated activities you should be able to achieve the objectives specified below.

1 **Explain how competition is regulated and the role of the Competition Commission.**
2 **Discuss the competition faced by a company and use Porter's five forces of competition to support the discussion.**
3 **Identify and explain which competitive strategies are appropriate for companies operating in different types of marketplace.**

This case study examines the regulation of industry and commerce and discusses the Competition Commission's decision regarding BAA's ownership. The Competition Commission has informed BAA that they need to sell three of their seven UK airports. BAA owns and operates Heathrow, Gatwick, Stanstead, Southampton, Glasgow, Edinburgh and Aberdeen airports.

ENTRY CASE STUDY 3.1

Competition watchdog flexes its muscles

FT

by Michael Peel

The sweeping plans to smash BAA's hold on the airport market are the competition watchdog's most aggressive use yet of toughened powers to force companies to sell assets or change the way they do business, lawyers said on Wednesday. Competition experts said the proposals for BAA to sell three of its seven airports showed how an emboldened Competition Commission was willing to use harsh measures against an unusually dominant company. The commission's provisional findings – which BAA's Spanish owner, Ferrovial, could challenge in the courts – are a further sign of greater friction between big companies and more assertive competition authorities.

Rebecca Owen-Howes, a senior associate at the law firm Denton Wilde Sapte, said the proposal to break up BAA was 'hard-hitting' and should make other companies 'prick up their ears'. She said: 'This is the Competition Commission showing it has those powers, and exercising them in quite a dramatic way.'

While competition lawyers had expected trouble for BAA because of its near-monopoly over main airports, some were surprised by a commission verdict that one described as 'damning'. Mark Friend, partner at Allen & Overy, said the BAA investigation showed how the commission was 'willing to take on difficult cases, and is not afraid to put forward what are pretty radical proposals'. The watchdog's provisional findings echo the trenchant tone of its 'emerging thinking' report published in April, which gave the first hints BAA was in for a tough time.

Christopher Clarke, commission inquiry chairman, on Wednesday variously characterised the company as unadventurous, unresponsive to customer needs and slow to share information that airlines needed to make strategic decisions. Mr Clarke gave short shrift to suggestions that the commission might be overreaching itself in its demands for a series of enforced airport sales.

The commission – like its sister body, the Office of Fair Trading – has been bolstered by powers in the 2002 Enterprise Act to give it more independence from government and authority to order businesses to reform. The Office of Fair Trading, which originally referred the BAA probe to the commission, has in the past year come into conflict with big companies over investigations into industries such as banking and supermarkets.

The commission is due to publish its final ruling on BAA early next year, after which the company could take

its case to the independent Competition Appeal Tribunal to try to overturn the findings or simply win breathing space to arrange the airport sales. Few companies have so far gone to the tribunal over the results of commission investigations, although Tesco has launched a closely watched case over the conclusions of the watchdog's grocery industry probe this year.

Quotes

'I've been celebrating all morning. This is the best decision in the history of aviation ever'. Michael O'Leary, chief executive, Ryanair

'Selling a monopoly to a new owner will not help protect the consumer or improve efficiency. Airports need better regulation'. Andy Harrison, chief executive, easyJet

'The ownership structure is secondary, the focus should be on strengthening the regulatory system – that is the way to create the capacity which is most needed'. British Airways

'Any attempt to break up BAA will be resisted'. Steve Turner, Unite national secretary

'BAA should be broken up. We want to see much more competition between our airports'. Theresa Villiers, Conservative shadow transport secretary

'This is a once-in-a-generation opportunity to ensure airports deliver the standard of service that passengers deserve'. Department for Transport

'We will continue to point out to the commission the many areas where we believe its analysis is flawed and its remedies would be disproportionate and counter-productive'. Colin Matthews, chief executive, BAA

Source: from 'Competition watchdog flexes its muscles', *The Financial Times*, 20 August 2008 (Peel, M.).

Introduction

The first two chapters looked at the broad general external environment faced by organisations. This chapter deals with competition, which is an extremely important part of the external environment for organisations. Hence this chapter looks at the competitive environment, its regulation, its relationship to organisations, and strategies for operating in a competitive environment.

The chapter starts by examining the Emery and Trist environmental linkages and this is followed by an overview of the regulation of competition in the United Kingdom, including the utilities. The chapter then goes on to look at the competitive environment using Porter's five forces of competition model. The chapter ends by looking at the competitive strategies organisations can use to help ensure they are effective competitors in whichever type of external and competitive environment they find themselves.

Environmental linkages

Emery and Trist[1] suggest that understanding the environment of organisations depends on a firm grasp of the linkages within an organisation's environment. They identify three types of linkage: from within to within, from outside in and inside out, and outside linkages.

From within to within linkages

From within to within linkages are **internal dependencies** inside the organisation. These internal dependencies can be cooperative or confrontational in nature.

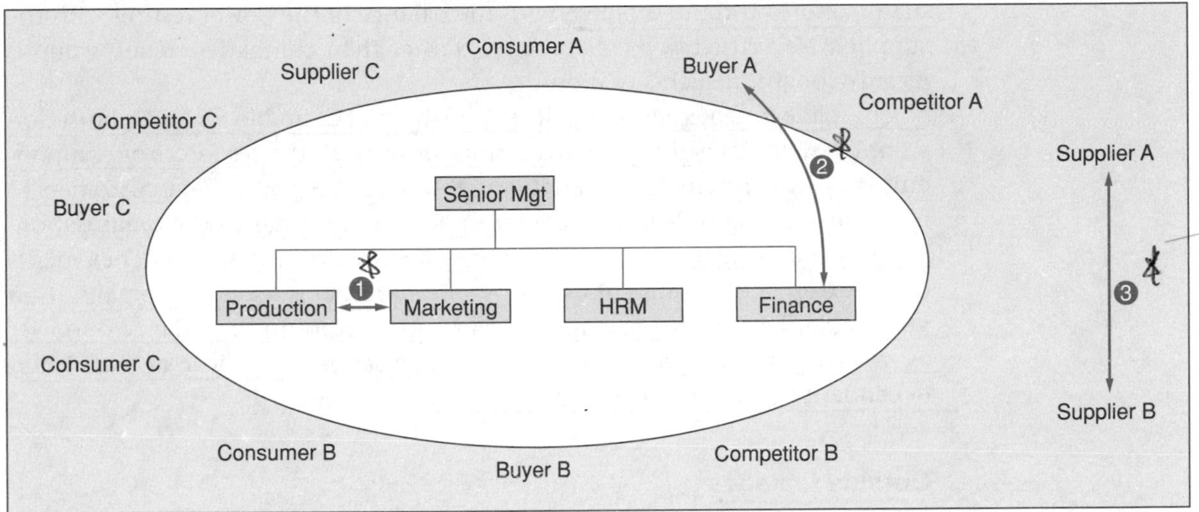

Figure 3.2 Environmental linkages

Source: Based on Emery, F E and Trist, E L (1965) 'The causal texture of organisational environments', *Human Relations*, 18: 21–32.

A cooperative interdependency would be the marketing and production department agreeing to work closely together on developing a new product. A confrontational interdependency would occur if two divisions in an organisation were to disagree on the resources allocated to their divisions – *see* Figure 3.2, link number 1. This type of confrontational interdependency can usually be resolved by an appropriate third party, a more senior employee, for example a supervisor, senior manager or director, depending on the type of confrontation.

From outside in and inside out linkages

From outside in and inside out linkages are called **transactional dependencies**. Transactional dependencies are links in and out of the organisation. In any organisation there are a number of transactions that take place between the organisation and elements of the external environment – *see* Figure 3.2, link number 2. These transactions can be simple or complex, frequent or rare, consistent or one-off. Depending on the kind of transaction, the level of dependence between the organisation and the environmental element will change. Obvious transactional dependencies are those between an organisation and its suppliers, buyers and competitors. The organisation manages such transactional dependencies by negotiation with the other parties involved.

If a manufacturer, such as Nissan, operates a just-in-time production system (*see* Chapter 9), the manufacturer is not keeping stocks of raw materials or component parts. Therefore, the manufacturer is hugely dependent on the suppliers' abilities to provide the resource inputs in an accurate and timely fashion. If the right component does not appear in the correct place on the assembly line at the proper time, the entire production process grinds to a halt. Thus there is a frequent and consistent transactional dependency between the manufacturer and the supplier, with the balance of the power resting with the supplier. Nevertheless, a collaborative, rather than combative, relationship is usually sought in such situations.

Complete independence is neither possible nor desirable for an organisation – not possible since organisations cannot provide all the resources or components they need internally, and not desirable since they must have customers to be in business, and *de facto* these customers are external to the organisation. Too much dependence on one or few suppliers or customers, or other elements of the external environment, is also not desirable, as it leaves the organisation vulnerable. Thus senior managers need to attempt to tip the balance of power as much as possible in favour of their organisation to achieve at least interdependence and at most the upper hand.

Outside linkages

Outside linkages are referred to as **causal textures**. Causal textures are interdependencies outside the organisation in the external environment, which can have an effect on the organisation – *see* Figure 3.2, link number 3. The causal texture in which an organisation operates is called that because there is a cause-and-effect relationship between what elements of the external environment do and how this affects third-party organisations. The simplest example of causal texture would be two suppliers agreeing to fix prices, which is illegal, to the detriment of retail buyers. This causes the cost of supplies to go up for buyers, who in turn increase prices charged to members of the public, which results in lower sales and reduced profits.

This type of linkage or causal texture is difficult for organisations to uncover and manage effectively, so responses to such linkages may be slow and apprehensive. This contributes to an organisation's doubt and uncertainty in managing the external environment. A very clear example of an organisation affected by causal texture is Clan Douglas. This is a manufacturer of luxury cashmere sweaters, based in the Borders area of Scotland, whose biggest market is the US.[2] In March 1999 the US government began a 'banana row' with the EU, with Britain being the most affected European country. The row centred on Britain's favouring of bananas produced by small farmers on Caribbean islands that are former British colonies, as opposed to bananas produced by US companies on plantations in South America. The US viewed this as unfair trade and therefore imposed a 100 per cent import tax on certain luxury goods imported by US companies from Britain and Europe. These goods included cashmere sweaters, which sold for $350, and fountain pens made by Mont Blanc and Watermans, which retailed at $300.[3] The doubling of the price of these goods to over $600 could effectively kill the US retail market and hence put affected manufacturers out of business. Hence a company like Clan Douglas in the Borders would be severely effected by such outside linkages or causal texture. Such companies had absolutely no influence over the banana war, nor could they have been reasonably expected to have anticipated the disagreement.

Check your understanding

Do you understand the three environmental linkages which can impact on an organisation?

Check your understanding by giving one example of your own for each type of environmental linkage.

The competitive environment

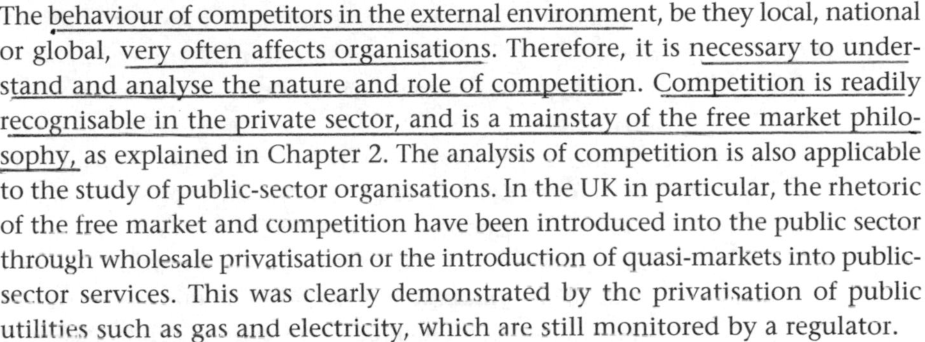

The behaviour of competitors in the external environment, be they local, national or global, very often affects organisations. Therefore, it is necessary to understand and analyse the nature and role of competition. Competition is readily recognisable in the private sector, and is a mainstay of the free market philosophy, as explained in Chapter 2. The analysis of competition is also applicable to the study of public-sector organisations. In the UK in particular, the rhetoric of the free market and competition have been introduced into the public sector through wholesale privatisation or the introduction of quasi-markets into public-sector services. This was clearly demonstrated by the privatisation of public utilities such as gas and electricity, which are still monitored by a regulator.

When examining an organisation's external environment, competition is considered an important element and is therefore analysed in addition to the general external environment, which is examined by LoNGPEST analysis (*see* Chapter 2). The importance of competitors and competition is further illustrated and reinforced in the entry case study, 'Competition watchdog flexes its muscles', which discusses the strong actions taken by the Competition Commission to ensure airpports in the United Kingdom offer competitive service to customers.

The regulation of competition in the UK

The UK economy is a mixed economy, which means that there is some influence and regulation of the competitive behaviour of firms. Some of the regulation of competition is by bodies that may intervene if there is a likelihood of anti-competitive behaviour occurring. These bodies are the **Office of Fair Trading**, the **Competition Commission** (formerly the **Monopolies and Mergers Commission**) and the **Restrictive Practices Court**. The regulation of industry and commerce is illustrated by the entry case study which discusses the Competition Commission's decision regarding BAA's ownership of seven UK airports, namely Heathrow, Gatwick, Stanstead, Southampton, Glasgow, Edinburgh and Aberdeen airports.

Office of Fair Trading

The Office of Fair Trading (OFT) was established in 1973 and is an independent professional organisation which seeks to promote and protect consumer interests and ensure companies compete in a fair and competitive manner. The OFT is accountable to Parliament.

The OFT's activities fall into three areas: enforcement of competition and consumer protection rules, investigation into how markets are working, and communication to explain the benefits of fair competition. The OFT aims to seek out and deter anti-competitive behaviour including cartels. Additionally the OFT will refer mergers and acquisitions that could significantly lessen competition to the Competition Commission. The OFT may investigate markets for specific products or services to ensure that they are working fairly for consumers. Investigations by the OFT can lead to enforcement of the competition rules and legislation or to a recommendation to government. Finally the OFT seeks to ensure that all interested stakeholders, such as businesses and consumers, understand how the competition rules and laws apply to them.

Three key pieces of competition legislation are the **Fair Trading Act 1973**, the **Competition Act 1988** and the **Enterprise Act 2002**. The Fair Trading Act 1973 was introduced to deal with complex and scale monopolies. A scale monopoly exists if one firm has a minimum of 25 per cent market share and a complex monopoly exists if two or more firms together account for more than 25 per cent market share and engage in similar behaviour. The Fair Trading Act is the piece of legislation under which the Director General of Fair Trading, the Utility Regulators and the Secretary of State can refer possible monopoly situations to the Competition Commission for investigation. If the Competition Commission finds that a monopoly situation exists and operates against the public interest, remedies may be imposed and can take the form of behavioural remedies, which is the stopping of particular practices, or structural remedies, which may include closing or divesting specified parts of the business.

The Competition Act 1998 makes anti-competitive agreements, cartels and abuses of a dominant position unlawful from the start and gives the Director General of Fair Trading new powers to stop anti-competitive behaviour from the outset. Competitors and customers who are victims of anti-competitive behaviour are able to seek damages, and perpetrators are liable to financial penalties of up to 10 per cent of UK turnover for up to three years.

The Enterprise Act 2002 came into force in summer 2003 and established the OFT as a corporate body and replaced the Director General of Fair Trading with two separate people, a chairman and chief executive. The main reforms of the Enterprise Act were in the areas of competition measures, consumer protection measures and insolvency reforms. The main changes to competition measures were an increase in criminal sanctions, with up to five years in prison for those convicted of dishonestly operating hardcore cartels, and greater opportunity for victims of cartels to gain redress, including allowing consumer bodies to make claims on behalf of individual consumers.

Consumer protection measures will be increased by the extension of Stop Now Orders to protect consumers from traders who fail to meet their obligations, for example failure to carry out building work to a satisfactory standard. This is complemented by the OFT approving codes of practice which should allow consumers to more easily identify trustworthy traders, for example an honest car repair business. Additionally consumer bodies will be able to make 'super-complaints' about features of a market which they feel harms consumers.

Insolvency reforms include reforming corporate insolvency law such that the process is simplified and streamlined, and the provision of an updated bankruptcy regime with limited restrictions of up to 12 months for those who failed through no fault of their own. In contrast, restrictions on bankrupts who abuse their creditors and the public will range from 2 to 15 years.

Competition Commission

The Competition Commission (CC) was established by the Competition Act 1998 and replaced the Monopolies and Mergers Commission (MMC) on 1 April 1999. The Competition Commission undertakes inquiries referred to it by the other UK competition authorities, including the OFT and other industry regulators, for example OFGEM. The investigations undertaken by the Competition Commission cover three main areas:

- mergers which will result in large companies gaining more than 25 per cent market share and mergers which will result in a significant reduction in competition in UK markets;
- markets where it appears competition is being prevented, restricted or distorted;
- regulated sectors (e.g. the energy sector) where the regulatory system is failing or if there are severe disputes between companies and their regulator.

Source: http://www.competition-commission.org.uk

The investigations each have a decision-making body including at least three independent experts who are supported by specialist staff. If appropriate, the specialist panels for utilities energy, telecommunications, water and newspapers may assist in some of the regulatory inquiries, with newspaper panel members dealing only with newspaper inquiries. Finally, if the outcome of an investigation requires action to correct the anti-competitive situation, then decisions have to be made as to what those actions are to be. The Competition Commission can decide, for example, to prevent a merger going ahead or require the company to sell part of the business. A good example of how the competition commission can act is outlined in the entry case sudy.

Restrictive Practices Court

The Restrictive Practices Court was established in 1956 and controls practices that are presumed to be against the public interest. Restrictive practices can relate to the price of goods, conditions of supply, qualities or descriptions, processes or areas and persons supplied. A case in which the Restrictive Practices Court has ruled is that of over-the-counter medicines. The Office of Fair Trading launched a four-year investigation into the price-fixing agreement for over-the-counter medicines such as aspirin, vitamins and cough and cold remedies. In the 1970s this agreement guaranteed small chemist shops a reasonable profit and living by virtue of an assured profit margin on over-the-counter medicines. However, in the mid-1990s 40 per cent of the market for over-the-counter medicines was held by large supermarket chains. The Office of Fair Trading investigation began when one such supermarket chain, Asda, challenged the protected position of these medicines. In March 1999 the Restrictive Practices Court announced that it would allow the Office of Fair Trading to launch a full-scale hearing into the 30-year-old price-fixing agreement. In January 2003 the OFT recommended removing restrictions on entry to the community pharmacy market, which would include the abolition of the 1970 price-fixing agreement for over-the-counter medicines. This move saves consumers around £30 million a year.

Regulatory bodies for privatised utilities and industries

The privatised utilities in the UK, which immediately after privatisation were not subject to intense competition, are each monitored by a regulator. Regulators exist for telecommunications, gas, electricity, water and rail transport. Their responsibility is to encourage competition and see that customers are not unfairly exploited where there may be only one supplier of a service, such as the supply of water to domestic premises.

Office of Communications

The **Office of Communications** (OFCOM) was established by the Office of Communications Act 2002. OFCOM brought together five existing regulatory bodies: the Independent Television Commission (ITC), the Broadcasting Standards Commission (BSC), the Office of Telecommunications (OFTEL), the Radio Authority (RAu) and the Radio-communications Agency (RA). OFCOM's duties are as follows:[4]

- furthering the interests of consumers in relevant markets;
- securing the optimal use of the electromagnetic spectrum;
- ensuring a wide range of electronic communications service in the UK;
- ensuring the availability of a wide range of television and radio services in the UK;
- protecting the public from offensive or potentially harmful effects of broadcast media;
- safeguarding people from being unfairly treated in television and radio programmes.

Office of Gas and Electricity Markets

The **Office of Gas and Electricity Markets** (OFGEM) replaces the Office of Gas Supply (OFGAS) and the Office of Electricity Regulation (OFFER). OFGEM's powers are provided under the Gas Act 1986, the Electricity Act 1989, the Utilities Act 2000, the Competition Act 1998 and the Enterprise Act 2002 and its main objective is to promote effective competition in the energy market for present and future customers.[5] To achieve this OFGEM seeks to enforce licence obligations, and competition and consumer law to protect customers, for example from rogue doorstep salesmen. OFGEM also plays a major role in regulating the monopoly networks of fuel supply and does so by regulating the wholesale market and prices. OFGEM seeks to ensure that competitive supply arrangements mean competitive prices for customers as well as direct regulation of the prices customers pay for their fuel. Additionally OFGEM seeks to improve the quality of service to customers by encouraging effective long-term investment in the gas and electricity networks in the UK.

Office of Water Supply

The Office of Water Supply (OFWAT) is a government department led by the Director General of Water Services that regulates water supply and pricing to domestic and industrial customers. OFWAT checks that prices for different types of customers – metered or unmetered, large or small, urban or rural – are fair. Generally the prices charged by water companies should reflect the cost of supplying clean water and getting rid of dirty and draining water from homes and premises.[6]

The role of OFWAT is to:

- limit the amount companies can charge customers;
- make sure that companies can carry out their responsibilities under the Water Industry Act 1991;
- protect the standard of service customers receive;
- encourage companies to be more efficient and engage in sustainable development;
- work to encourage competition where appropriate.

OFWAT works closely with two other water regulatory bodies: the Environment Agency, which implements water quality standards in inland waters, estuarial and coastal waters, and the Drinking Water Inspectorate, which regulates standards for drinking water.[7]

Office of Rail Regulation

The **Office of Rail Regulation** (ORR) was established in 2004 under the Railways and Transport Safety Act 2003 and replaced the Office of the Rail Regulator, which had been established under the Railways Act 1993. The key responsibilities of the Office of Rail Regulation are to:[8]

- regulate Network Rail, the owner of the UK's national rail network, ensuring it meets users' needs;
- license operators and set terms for access to the rail network, including implementation of competition legislation;
- ensure compliance with health and safety legislation and develop health and safety policy.

Check your understanding

Do you understand the reasons for regulation of the privatised utilities?

Check your understanding by naming one of the privatised utility regulators and briefly summarising its role and duties.

Assessing the nature of competition

Porter[9] presents a model for examining competition in an industry or sector – *see* Figure 3.3. He argues that five basic forces drive competition in an industry: **competitive rivalry**, **threat of new entrants**, **threat of substitute products or services**, **bargaining power of buyers**, and **bargaining power of suppliers**. These five forces need to be examined and understood if the nature of competition in an industry or sector is to be fully appreciated.

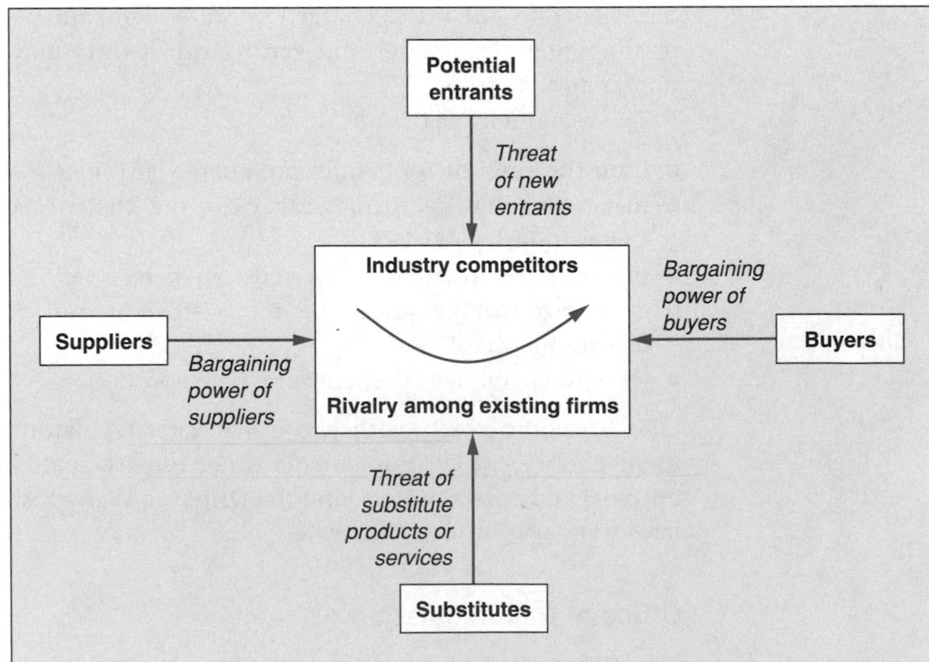

Figure 3.3 The five forces that determine industry profitability

Source: Reprinted with the permission of The Free Press, a division of Simon & Schuster, from *Competitive Advantage: Creating and Sustaining Superior Performance* by Michael E Porter. Copyright © 1985, 1998 by Michael E Porter. All rights reserved.

Competitive rivalry

The first of the five forces examines the nature of competitive rivalry within a particular sector or industry. There are a number of factors affecting how fierce competitive rivalry is in an industry or sector and consequently how difficult the market is for organisations operating there. The key questions to examine concern who the present and potential competitors are, and how intensive the competition is between them. In some industries there are numerous competitor companies, all of a similar size and capacity, all holding comparable market shares and all seeking to dominate the industry. There may be no dominant company or companies within the sector and little to distinguish between the brands and products that are available to the customer. The market itself may be established or mature, with little prospect of major innovation or design surprises. In such an industry or sector, the intensity of competitive rivalry will be very high, as mature companies have to battle to retain market share, sustain **differentiation** and maintain their customer base.

The supermarket industry in the UK is a good illustration of extremely fierce competitive rivalry. Tesco is dominant in terms of market share, but other players all have high profiles and similar market presence. For many customers there is little real difference between the big supermarket chains, with Tesco, Sainsbury's, Morrisons and Asda all offering very similar ranges of products and services. Supermarkets compete ruthlessly and do so by offering an ever-wider range of services, including those complementary to their core business. Supermarkets have opened banks to provide financial services, in addition to a range of ancillary services that are now standard, including dry-cleaning, cafés, clothes stores, recycling collection points and pharmacies.

Threat of new entrants

The second of Porter's five forces is the threat of new entrants to an industry or sector. It is necessary to identify which companies are likely to be able to enter the market in order to compete with existing operators, and to recognise the other markets in which these potential new entrants currently operate. The threat of new entrants will be greatest if an industry is attractive enough to entice them. The attractiveness of an industry depends on there being a sufficient customer base to support the new entrant's business along with existing organisations. High potential profits and low set-up costs make an industry attractive. This gives an attractive combination of low financial risk combined with high potential returns.

In the 1990s the move by Superdrug into the business of retailing up-market perfume and aftershave was undertaken in part to exploit an opportunity for the company to make good profits. The standard profit margin made by an authorised retailer on a bottle of up-market perfume or aftershave is 40 per cent. Hence Superdrug was able to cut its profit margin to, say, 20 per cent and still make an attractive profit. This, combined with the relatively low set-up costs needed to exploit the opportunity, the cost of the perfume and securing supplies, meant it was too good an opportunity for Superdrug to miss.[10]

Threat of substitute products or services

When considering the nature of competition, the alternative products or services available to be purchased require consideration. A substitute product or service provides the same function as the good for which it is a replacement. Straightforward examples of substitute products include tea as a substitute for coffee, or cans and cartons as substitute forms of packaging that have largely replaced glass bottles as containers for milk and soft drinks.

Substitute products or services will be a threat if customers perceive that the alternatives perform a similar or equally good function. The threat from substitutes will be greater if the alternatives provide better value for money. This can be achieved by the substitute being equally good and cheaper or by being equal on price but offering a better product or more added value.

The consumer frenzy that is Christmas shopping provides a vivid example of the exercise of choice and decision making between alternatives or substitute products or services. For the man who is buying a gift for a wife or girlfriend, the initial decision between substitutes is perhaps a choice of a bottle of perfume, a DVD, a new sweater, or a piece of jewellery. If the customer decides on a DVD, there are further decisions to be made. Which film or TV series should they choose? Should it be the latest cinema blockbuster to be released on DVD for the Christmas market? Should it be a Christmas Special DVD for a TV series? Where should it be brought: in a superstore like HMV or Virgin, in WHSmith, or online from Amazon.co.uk? The function of the merchandise purchased is to provide a good Christmas present, hence all of the possibilities mentioned are substitutes for each other and so pose a threat.

Bargaining power of buyers

Earlier in this chapter it was mentioned that organisations have varying degrees of dependence on their customers and suppliers. Porter's five forces of competition model refers to this as the 'bargaining power of buyers and suppliers'. There are two types of buyer: the industrial or commercial buyer who purchases goods on a large scale on behalf of the organisation for whom she or he works, and the individual consumer.

The bargaining power of a commercial buyer depends on a number of factors. If, for example, the threat of substitutes is strong, a number of choices exist and the buyer will exercise their power and shop around to find the best deal and most suitable choice. The bargaining power of the buyer is also strengthened if alternative sources for the supply of a product exist. In this situation the buyer will have the upper hand when negotiating supply and price. In the UK the supermarket sector is a good example of a group of organisations that have high bargaining power as buyers. In purchasing food to sell to the general public the supermarkets purchase in bulk and there are many substitutes and alternative sources of supply for them to capitalise on. Hence they can drive a hard bargain in terms of price and product.

In buying fruit and vegetables, supermarkets require suppliers of products like apples or tomatoes to grow a particular variety, supply fruit of uniform appearance and of a predetermined size. This allows for attractive in-store displays to tempt customers to buy the produce, which is aided by the uniform appearance of the fruit and vegetables, which also limits the amount of handling and rummaging though the goods by customers. If the size of a particular fruit or vegetable is important to the supermarket, that will be specified in the contract with the grower, along with the variety and delivery date. For round fruit and vegetables, size is specified as the circumference in millimetres. For example, in February 1999 Marks & Spencer sold pre-packaged South African plums, labelled as being of the Harry Pickstone variety, size 50/55mm. It should be noted that powerful buyers like supermarkets often work closely with their suppliers in developing new products and the systems for producing them.

The individual consumer is usually much less powerful as a buyer compared with large organisations. The bargaining power of an individual buyer is influenced by factors similar to those for commercial buyers. The strong threat of substitutes and the number of choices available will allow the individual consumer to shop around for the best deal. The city-centre office worker who goes out to buy his/her takeaway lunch every day has a number of choices. They can buy a sandwich, drink and packet of crisps from a city-centre store like Marks & Spencer or Boots, a bakery which is one of a chain, like Greggs, or a coffee shop like Prêt à Manger. Other substitutes are available for the individual consumer to consider, such as a burger, fries and drink from a fast-food outlet like McDonald's or Burger King. Individual consumers are free to exercise choice but have no real power as individuals to negotiate over the price they pay for their lunch.

However, if individual consumers choose to act in unison they may be able to exercise power. For example, in the mid-1990s when the health scare over British beef and BSE erupted, McDonald's faced the prospect of large numbers of its customers acting together and refusing to buy and eat its hamburgers. Therefore it switched from supplies of British beef to supplies of Dutch beef.

Bargaining power of suppliers

The other side of the transactional relationship is the power exerted by suppliers. There are a number of different cases when the bargaining power of suppliers is high. In industries or sectors where there are few possible suppliers, they will be able to exert a good deal of influence on the organisations to which they supply raw materials, components or finished goods for retail. In the supply of highly specialist technology, of highly prized or rare materials where the quantity is low and price is high, the supplier is more powerful as it controls something that is greatly sought after. Thus oil-producing nations have the ability to bring the world to its knees since the most modern industrialised nations are entirely dependent on the supply of crude or refined oil. In some cases, suppliers may not be entirely satisfactory and alternatives may be available, but the cost of switching from one supplier to another is too high in the short term to be affordable, even if, in the long term, the savings would be greater. Hence, where there are few suppliers who cannot be easily substituted, supplier power is high.

In contrast, the suppliers of fragrances to French perfume houses, such as Yves Saint Laurent and Chanel, are family-based firms located in the Grasse area of France and have very low bargaining power. These firms are not paid for the research and product development work they undertake. They receive payment only if they win a contract with a fragrance house, which is issued once the fragrance house is satisfied with the fragrance that has been developed for them. The developers of the fragrances will be competing against other similar firms and they stand a one-in-ten chance of being successful and winning a contract with a perfume house like Chanel. Hence the bargaining power of the fragrance developers as suppliers to the fragrance houses is very low indeed.[11]

Check your understanding

Do you understand the forces driving competition in an industry?

Check your understanding by indicating what gives each of Porter's five forces of competition high power.

Guidelines for assessing competition

In assessing the competitive environment faced by an organisation in a particular industry or sector, it can be useful to consider the following areas in relation to the five forces driving competition.

Competitive rivalry

Identify present and potential competitors in the industry or sector. Assess the intensity of competition between the different organisations. Is this likely to change?

Threat of new entrants

Does a threat of new entry into the industry exist? From which organisations does it arise? Identify the industry in which potential entrants currently operate. Evaluate the likelihood of new entrants coming into the industry.

Threat of substitute products or services

Identify alternative products and services. In what industry are present and potential substitute products located? Assess the likely impact of substitute products and services on the organisation and industry being analysed.

Bargaining power of buyers

Name the buyers of the organisation's products and services. Identify and evaluate any sources of power the buyers have with regard to the organisation being analysed.

Bargaining power of suppliers

Name the suppliers of the organisation's key resources and inputs. Identify and evaluate any sources of power the suppliers have with regard to the organisation being analysed.

Competitive strategies and competitive advantage

In order to operate successfully in an industry or sector where substantial competition is created by the five forces of competition, organisations need to adopt a competitive strategy. They may choose to follow one of Porter's competitive strategies to gain competitive advantage – *see* Figure 3.4. Competitive advantage is gained when an organisation achieves a position in an industry due to cost or differentiation factors, which allows it to make above-average or superior profits. When the supermarket chain Iceland started a home delivery

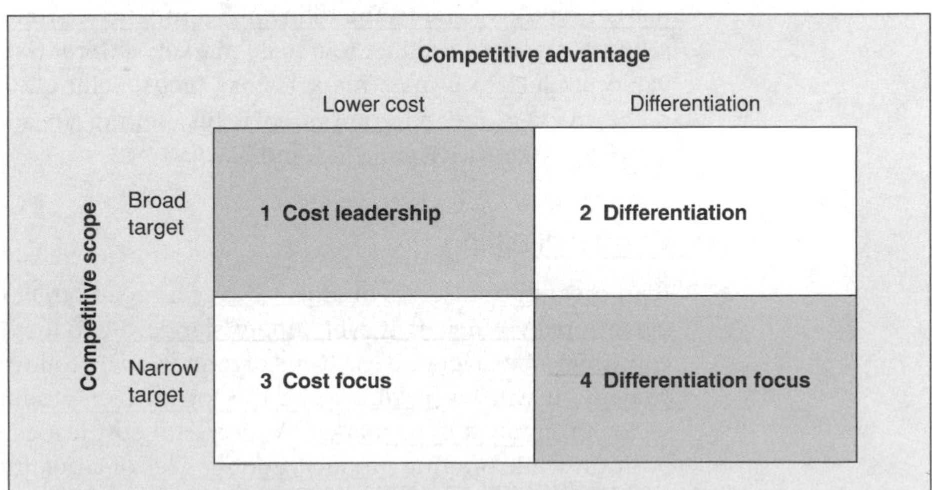

Figure 3.4 Generic strategies

Source: Reprinted with the permission of The Free Press, a division of Simon & Schuster, from *Competitive Advantage: Creating and Sustaining Superior Performance* by Michael E Porter. Copyright © 1985, 1998 by Michael E Porter. All rights reserved.

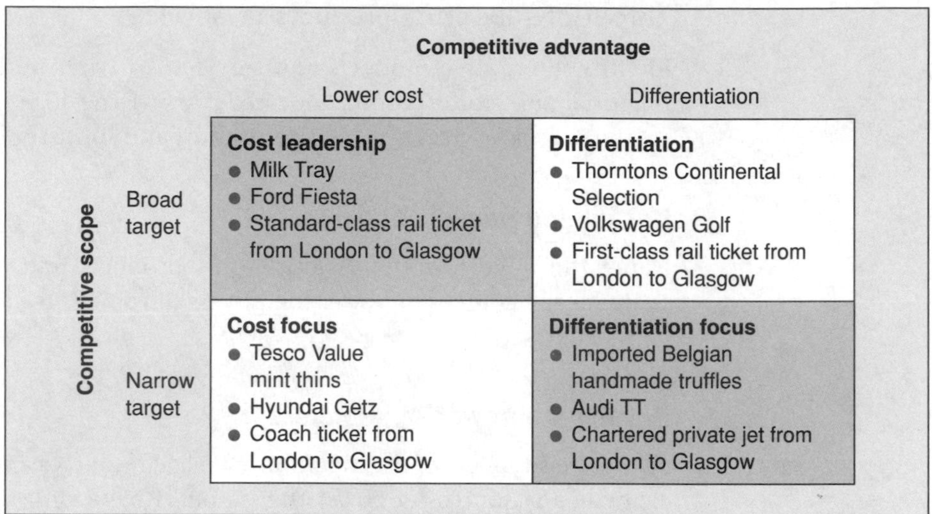

Figure 3.5 Examples of generic strategies

service, which allowed customers to order food shopping from home and have goods delivered direct to their door, it was a source of differentiation that gave the company a competitive advantage over other food retailers, although this advantage has been eroded as its competitors have followed suit.

Porter[12] suggests that there are two decisions that organisations have to make to arrive at a suitable type of competitive strategy. The first is to decide whether competition is to be based on cost or added value. The second is to decide whether a broad target market (mass market) or a narrow target market (niche market) is to be served. Porter suggests that combinations of price and market type give rise to the following competitive strategies: **cost leadership**, selling a standard product to a mass market; **differentiation**, selling an added-value product to a mass market; **cost focus**, selling a low-cost product to a niche market; and **differentiation focus**, selling an added-value product to a niche market (*see* Figures 3.4 and 3.5).

Cost leadership

If an organisation serves or aims to serve a broad target or mass market, to be operationally efficient it will supply standard products or services to many consumers (*see* Figure 3.5). If an organisation is following a cost leadership strategy, it will be seeking to be the lowest-cost producer in its industry or sector to supply a mass market. A successful cost leader will have achieved its position while offering products and services of a quality comparable to those offered by direct competitors. Hence in a mass market there are likely to be a number of key players, and the competitive rivalry could be fierce. However, because of the lack of specialism or high technology, costs for most organisations following a cost leadership strategy are likely to be average, as are profits.

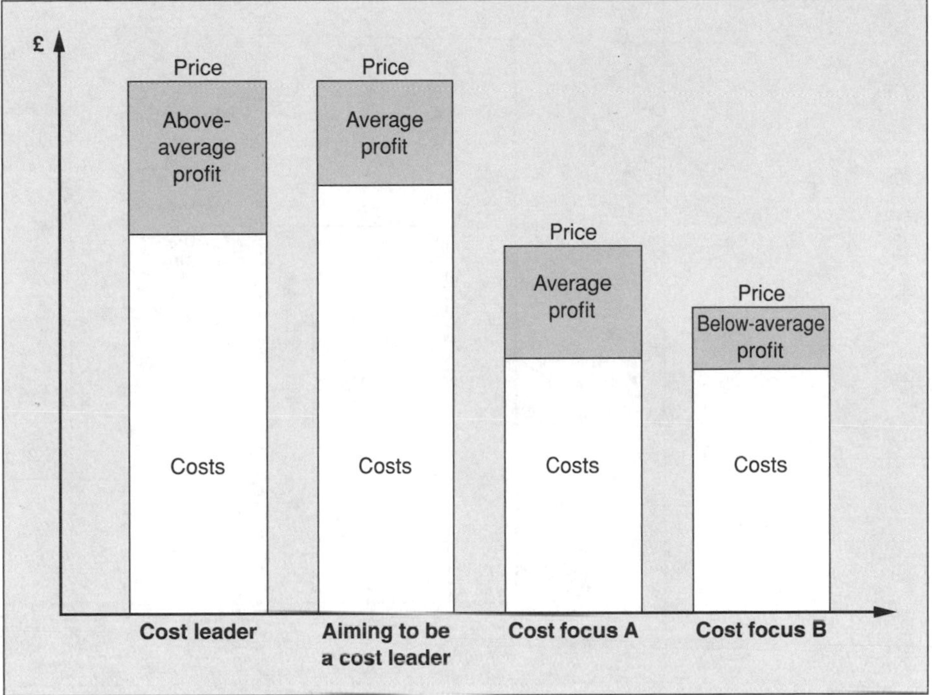

Figure 3.6 Cost, profit and price relationships for cost-based competitive strategies

The successful cost leader that has achieved below-average costs but is selling at an average price will make greater or superior profits – *see* Figure 3.6. It is difficult for any competitor serving a mass market with standard products and services to charge above-average prices, as the competitive rivalry in the mass market prevents individual competitors from raising the price of standard products significantly. Figure 3.5 shows examples of organisations and products that follow a cost leadership strategy.

Differentiation

An organisation following a differentiation strategy perceives that it is still able to serve a broad target market, but by providing a product or service that is different and better – *see* Figure 3.5. A product or service is different and better due to its added value. Added value arises via the addition to the product or service of extra features, or from the better quality of the product or service. The customer needs to be prepared to pay extra for additional features or quality; if this is not the case, the organisation has wasted money in providing the added value. In this situation any superior profit that may have been made as a result of the added value is lost.

In an added-value or differentiated product, costs should be average in areas that do not add value and extra costs incurred only for added value; therefore,

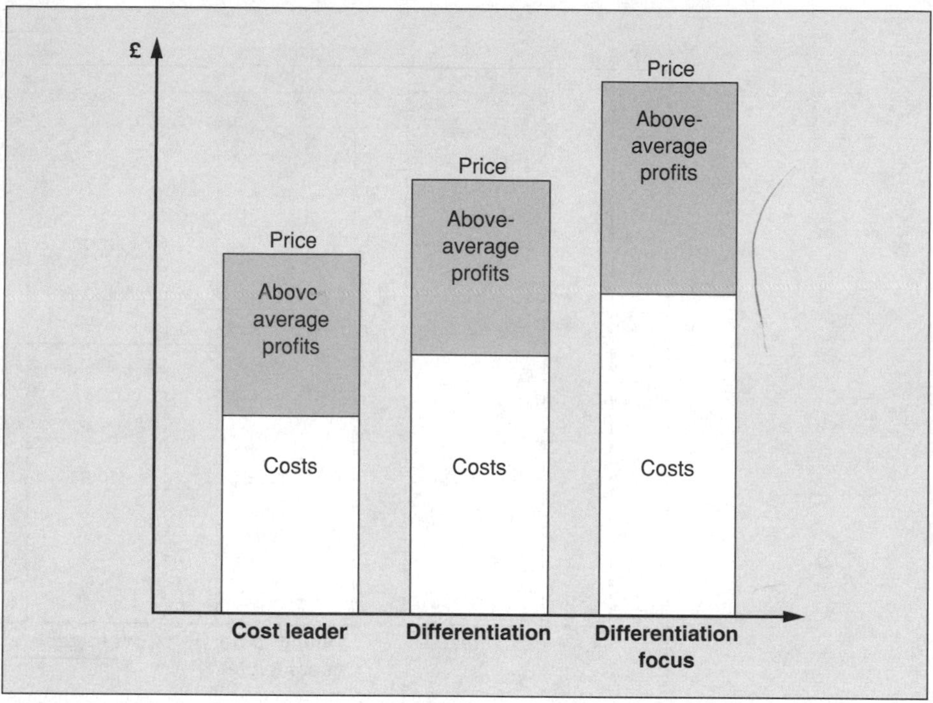

Figure 3.7 Cost, profit and price relationships for differentiation-based competitive strategies

overall costs are higher than average. This allows a higher or premium price to be charged, giving rise to superior profits – *see* Figure 3.7. This can be seen in department stores or supermarkets that have higher-than-average prices but still gain market share because their customers are willing to pay extra for goods they consider to be better, for example House of Fraser or Waitrose.

Added value is not only located in the quality of goods or services. People are prepared to pay extra for packaging and labelling, the image or reputation of the brand, or the lifestyle choices accompanying the use and purchase of certain goods – *see* Figure 3.5. This can be a useful source of competitive advantage, but if people's perception of the company and its offerings changes, there will be a slump in turnover and profits. In the economic downturn that started in 2008 Marks & Spencer experienced just such a slump in its food sales. In July 2008 the company announced it has experienced a fall of around 5 per cent in food sales during the second quarter of the year, while at the same time Aldi and Lidl experienced an increase in market share. Marks & Spencer's customers wanted better value for money and were less willing to pay for perceived added value.

Focus strategies

An organisation employing a focus strategy will centre its efforts on a number of niche market sectors and serve only them, to the exclusion of other broad market segments – *see* Figures 3.4, 3.5 and 3.6. The successful application of a focus strategy rests on there being clear and significant differences between the segments focused on and the other market segments in the industry and the market segments that are focused on being poorly attended to by the competitors serving the broad target market.

Cost focus

The cost focus strategy is followed by organisations aiming for a narrow target market, where customers are very price sensitive – *see* Figure 3.4. Organisations following a cost focus strategy will seek to deliver low-cost and thus low-priced products and services to the market. In order to make profits, costs must be maintained at a minimum through using the lowest-priced raw materials, manufacturing processes, packaging, delivery and advertising. The cost focus strategy allows for average or below-average profits to be made, depending on how well costs are controlled and the level at which prices are set – *see* Figure 3.6.

Differentiation focus

A differentiation focus strategy is used by organisations wishing to serve a narrow target market where consumers are prepared to spend a great deal of money in order to acquire luxury, top-of-the-range goods or services – *see* Figure 3.4. The relationship between costs, prices and profits is shown in Figure 3.7. Examples of products that follow a differentiation focus strategy are shown in Figure 3.5.

Check your understanding

Do you understand Porter's generic competitive strategies?

Check your understanding by indicating which competitive strategy each of the following shops pursues in its food-retailing operations: Harrods, Marks & Spencer, Asda and Lidl.

Choosing a competitive strategy for competitive advantage

The achievement of competitive advantage and hence superior profits is central to the strategy of any organisation. For competitive advantage to be achieved successfully, a company must be clear about which type of competitive strategy is being followed: cost leadership, differentiation, cost focus or differentiation focus. Porter argues that an organisation that tries to follow a combination of competitive strategies, i.e. cost leadership and differentiation, will achieve only average or below-average performance. Hence competitive advantage is not achieved, which Porter calls being 'stuck in the middle'.[13]

However, it is clear from looking at some organisations that it is possible to follow all of Porter's generic competitive strategies and still be successful. For example, British Airways pursues three of Porter's generic strategies by offering a range of different airline tickets: first class (differentiation focus), business class (differentiation), and economy class (cost leadership). The supermarket chain Tesco also follows a variety of Porter's generic competitive strategies. Occasionally supermarkets such as Tesco will display a trolley containing typical weekly groceries just inside the main entrance along with the slogan, 'All this for £24.52'. The groceries will all come from Tesco's value line of products, with the distinctive blue-and-white striped packaging. Clearly a competitive strategy devised to tempt the price-sensitive customer into the store, this is, in Porter's parlance, a cost focus strategy. In contrast, Tesco also follows a differentiation focus strategy and sells a very up-market range of pre-prepared foods called 'Finest', which is clearly designed to appeal to a customer prepared to pay a great deal of money for a meal. Hence it is possible for organisations to follow both cost- and differentiation-based competitive strategies.

Gilbert and Strebel present an alternative view of competitive strategies.[14] They argue that there are two constituents of competitive advantage: lower delivered cost and higher perceived value. However, unlike Porter, Gilbert and Strebel go on to argue that lower delivered cost and higher perceived value can be used together to give a company a superior position in an industry or sector. The essence of their argument is that to achieve competitive advantage a firm must strive to give the highest perceived value for the lowest delivered cost. Examples of organisations that strive to offer such a combination are IKEA and the John Lewis Partnership. IKEA, a chain of Swedish furniture stores, prides itself on offering 'good design at best ever prices'. It achieves this by seeking out and using good design, efficient suppliers, and innovative and rationalised global distribution systems.[15] The commitment of the John Lewis Partnership's retail stores to offering best quality at lowest prices is summarised in its own slogan: 'Never knowingly undersold.' John Lewis offers to refund the difference if a customer finds the same item cheaper elsewhere.

Competitive advantage is achieved by creating 'disequilibrium' between the perceived value of the product and the asking price by increasing the perceived value or reducing the asking price. This alters the terms of competition and could drive competitors out of the market or influence them to offer more perceived value for the same price or the same value for less money. However, Gilbert and Strebel go on to argue that the number of competitive formulas is small, not large. They give two possible reasons for this, the first being that there is an 'internal logic to each business system' that dictates the possible combinations of perceived value and delivered cost that must exist for the whole business system. This number of combinations is clearly finite. The second somewhat obvious reason is that there are only two basic generic competitive strategies: high perceived added value and low delivered cost. Depending on a company's industry position and circumstances, there can exist only variations around these two themes, which must therefore limit the number of competitive formulas.

Further to this, Gilbert and Strebel proceed to suggest that strategic advantage is obtained by the implementation of generic competitive moves in a sequence, such that the implementation of one prepares for the implementation of another, which should of course result in high perceived value for low delivered cost.

Check your understanding

Do you understand that companies may use lower cost and higher perceived value to compete effectively?

Check your understanding by indicating which businesses named below offer lower cost and higher perceived value: Amazon, easyJet, Poundstretcher, Tesco Metro.

Summary

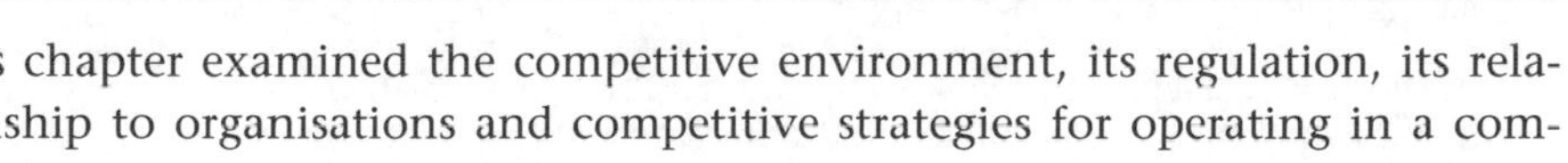

This chapter examined the competitive environment, its regulation, its relationship to organisations and competitive strategies for operating in a competitive environment. The following summary covers all aspects of this chapter.

1 There are three types of environmental linkages: internal dependencies, transactional dependencies and causal texture. Internal dependencies are linkages between different parts of the organisation. Transactional dependencies are linkages between the organisation and its external environment. Causal texture are interdependencies that are completely outside of the organisation and exist only in the external environment.

2 Competition in the UK is regulated by the Office of Fair Trading (OFT), the Competition Commission (CC), the Restrictive Practice Court (RPC) and a host of regulators for privatised utilities, industries and service sectors.

3 Porter's five forces of competition drive competition in an industry. Competitive rivalry is fierce if there are numerous competitors in an industry, markets are mature, with little differentiation and innovation. The threat of new entrants will be high if an industry is attractive, i.e. there are enough customers, profit margins are high and set-up costs low. Substitute products are a threat if they perform the same function as the product or service they replace. A substitute which provides more or is better value for money is a greater threat. Buyers generally are powerful if they have the opportunity to shop around for the best deal and they purchase a significant amount of a product. Suppliers are powerful if there are few suppliers of a good or service, as the buyer is denied the opportunity to shop around for a good deal.

4 According to Porter there are four competitive strategies: cost leadership, selling a standard product to a mass market; differentiation, selling an added-value product to a mass market; cost focus, selling a low-cost product to a niche market; and differentiation focus, selling an added-value product to a niche market.

5 Gilbert and Strebel argue that there are only two constituents of competitive advantage: lower delivered cost and higher perceived value, which can be used in combination to give a company a superior position in an industry or sector.

Chapter objectives and the exit case study

While reading this chapter and engaging in the activities, you should have learned how to apply theory and models and analyse situations. The exit case study and the questions which follow will provide an opportunity to assess how well you have met the relevant chapter objectives relating to specific material covered in the chapter.

Chapter objective	Check you have achieved this by
2 Discuss the competition faced by a company and use Porter's five forces of competition to support the discussion.	answering case study questions 1 and 2.
3 Identify and explain which competitive strategies are appropriate for companies operating in different types of marketplace.	answering case study question 3.

→ EXIT CASE STUDY 3.2

The going gets tough for organic

by Emine Saner

Think back to June last year, when the vast organic food supermarket Whole Foods opened its first UK shop in London, and Britain seemed like a pretty different place. It was two months before the credit crunch bit, and organic food sales were rising each month, fuelled by consumers who had started to care where their food came from and how the way it was grown affected the environment. For some, eating organic had become almost a fashion statement; around the country, farmer's markets were a weekend ritual for eco-conscious shoppers, and expensive organic chains such as Fresh and Wild and Planet Organic were thriving in London and Bristol.

'We have skilled butchers, scratch bakers and even our own store artists! We have chefs, fishmongers, cheese artisans and team members handcrafting fresh foods right in front of our shoppers,' read a Whole Foods press release, breathless with excitement. The chain believed it would change food shopping in the UK the way it had in the US. Words such as 'natural' and 'organic' would be top of every customer's shopping list, regardless of the high prices.

How quickly times change. Last week, the company announced that its six UK stores, five of which operate under the Fresh and Wild label, had lost £9m in a year and it was reconsidering its plan to roll out more stores across the UK. Shoppers complained that its food – six free range eggs for £2.29, a loaf of bread for £1.39 – was just too overpriced; 'I call it "Far and Wide" on account of the number of items it seemingly gets from as far away from England as possible,' says Matthew, who lives near the branch in Stoke Newington, north London. 'I grow my own vegetables so I know what's in season and I do get annoyed when they've flown in veg from other parts of the world. And its prices are absurdly high.' Currently on sale at Fresh and Wild are organic kiwi fruit from New Zealand, at 79p each.

Meanwhile Aldi, which has more than 300 stores across the UK and follows the pile it high, sell it cheap approach to food shopping (no 'cheese artisans' here), says the number of its ABC1 customers (the middle classes, Whole Foods' target customers) has risen by 17% over the past year. And McDonald's is creating 4000 jobs to cope with the increasing demand for cheap fast food. In the current climate, it looks like reckless spending to pay £9 for an organic, free-range chicken when the cost of everything else, from food basics to heating and water, is going up. Expensive, organic food is the middle-class indulgence that even the middle-classes can't seem to afford anymore.

A report from Price-Waterhouse Coopers in May said that 48% of people wouldn't, or couldn't, pay a premium for organic or Fair-trade products. In another survey, 65% of people said they would buy more organic products if they were cheaper. But, according to the Soil Association, the environmental charity that certifies 80% of organic produce, this isn't the whole picture. Annual sales of organic food grew by 26% from 1993 to 2006. This year, it is predicting a more modest 10% growth; but this still, it points out, outstrips the growth in non-organic food. And organic food will start to look more competitively priced as conventionally farmed food – hit by the rocketing cost of fertiliser, pesticides and supermarket distribution costs – becomes more expensive.

Many organic farmers are also feeling the pinch – organic dairy farmers are warning that the increased cost of organic feed may put many out of business – but the squeeze on their livelihoods comes largely from the low prices paid by the supermarkets rather than a dip in demand from consumers. 'Perhaps it is inevitable that we might see some decline in demand among less deeply committed organic consumers, but this is more likely to be a plateau than a reverse,' says Patrick Holden, director of the Soil Association. The market research group Mintel still predicts that by 2012 the organic market will have grown by 44%.

What we are perhaps seeing is a change in the way people approach organic and sustainable eating, and shopping. A survey for Sainsbury's found that 62% of customers are concerned about wasted food and are more likely to use leftovers and cook food from scratch, rather than buy expensive, energy-intensive and over-packaged ready meals. Supermarkets such as Asda are stocking more free range and Freedom Food chicken, while Sainsbury's reported a 60% increase in sales of higher welfare chicken.

While the overpriced organic stores may suffer from the credit crunch, smaller producers are reporting that their organic, locally sourced produce can actually save shoppers money. Last week, Riverford, which delivers 47,000 boxes of organic fruit and vegetables to households in the south-west of England every week, compared its prices with the equivalent organic vegetables from the supermarkets and found its box was cheaper. One of their boxes cost less than Tesco's non-organic equivalents. Growing your own is cheaper still. 'It doesn't make sense to cut back on what it is a very economical way of eating, especially on food where you know where it has come from and you can trust it,' says Guy Watson, the farmer who founded Riverford. He expects growth of around 10% this year. It is, he admits, proving more difficult to get new customers but he believes this has more to do with the 'green' claims of food manufacturers – most of which are rubbish, he says – meaning consumers believe there is more choice out there for sustainable, healthy food. 'We have enthusiastic customers and I don't think that when the bank statement arrives, they will take the organic veg box off their list. I am fundamentally optimistic'.

Source: from 'The going gets tough for organic', *Guardian*, 14 August 2008 (Saner, E.), Copyright Guardian News & Media Ltd. 2008.

Exit case study questions

1 Apply Porter's five forces of competition model to the marketplace for fruit and vegetables and assess the nature of competition faced by the organic food supermarket Whole Foods.

2 How does the launch of a 69p range of fresh fruit and vegetables by Aldi impact on shops like Whole Foods?

3 Which of Porter's competitive strategies applies to each of the following:
 - Marks & Spencer organic avocado pears
 - Sainsbury Basics strawberries
 - Ready prepared fresh fruit salad from Tesco
 - English asparagus from local greengrocers
 - Allotment-grown autumn raspberries in a farmer's market
 - Green grapes from Asda

Short-answer questions

1 Define an internal dependency.
2 Define a transactional dependency.
3 Define causal texture.
4 Name three bodies regulating competition in the UK.
5 Name the two bodies which regulate the rail network in the UK.
6 Name the new regulatory body that was established in 2002.
7 Name the regulatory body which regulates the quality of drinking water.
8 Name Porter's five forces of competition.
9 Specify three factors making an industry attractive to new entrants.
10 List three factors making substitute products or services a threat.
11 Specify three factors strengthening a buyer's power.
12 List three factors strengthening a supplier's power.
13 Which of Porter's generic competitive strategies can be used to target a niche market?
14 Define competitive advantage.
15 According to Porter, how many competitive strategies does a firm need to follow to achieve competitive advantage?

Chapter objectives and assignment questions

While reading this chapter and engaging in the activities, you should have learned how to apply theory and models. This means you should be able to meet the chapter objectives outlined at the beginning of the chapter. The table below shows which chapter objectives can be tested by the different questions.

Chapter objective	Check you have achieved this by
1 Explain how competition is regulated and the role of the Competition Commission.	answering assignment question 1.
2 Discuss the competition faced by a company and use Porter's five forces of competition to support the discussion.	answering assignment questions 2 and 3.
3 Identify and explain which competitive strategies are appropriate for companies operating in different types of marketplace.	answering assignment question 3.

Assignment questions

1 Research the broadcast and communications industry in the United Kingdom for the previous three years. Consider the establishment of OFCOM in 2002. Write a report that:
   - identifies changes in the regulation of the marketplace for the broadcast and communications industry in the United Kingdom;
   - identifies changes in the broadcasting companies and the communications industry;
   - evaluates the effect of these changes on competition in the broadcast and communications industry in the United Kingdom.

2 Consider the universities and colleges in the town or city nearest to where you live. Assess the nature of competition between these colleges and universities by use of Porter's five forces of competition. Determine whether the university or college that you attend is influenced or affected by Emery and Trist's linkages. Present your findings in a 2000-word report.

3 Choose a private-sector industry that delivers a service to members of the public and analyse the competition in the industry by use of Porter's five forces of competition. Select three companies in your chosen industry and discuss the competitive strategies they follow. Present your findings in a 2000-word report.

WEBLINKS available at **www.pearsoned.co.uk/capon**

- These are the weblinks for two important bodies in the regulation of the UK economy:
  Office of Fair Trading (OFT) **http://www.oft.gov.uk**
  Competition Commission (CC) **http://www.competition-commission.org.uk**
- These are the weblinks for the regulatory authorities for some of the privatised sectors:
  Office of Communications **http://www.ofcom.org.uk/**
  Office of Gas and Electricity Markets (OFGEM) **http://www.ofgem.gov.uk**
  Office of Water Services (OFWAT) **http://www.ofwat.gov.uk**
  Office of the Rail Regulator **http://www.rail-reg.gov.uk**
- The following weblink to the Competition Commission's website provides the web addresses for other regulatory bodies in the UK and for overseas regulatory bodies in Europe, North America and Australasia:
  http://www.competition-commission.org.uk/footer/links_and_contacts.htm

FURTHER READING

The following book chapters look at the competitive environment.

- Johnson, G, Scholes, K and Whittington, R (2008) *Exploring Corporate Strategy*, 8th edn, Chapter 2, Harlow: Financial Times Prentice Hall.
- Johnston, R and Clark, G (2008) *Improving Service Delivery*, Chapter 5, Harlow: Financial Times Prentice Hall.

- Lynch, R (2006) *Corporate Strategy*, 4th edn, Chapter 3, Harlow: Financial Times Prentice Hall.
- Palmer, A and Hartley, B (2006) *The Business Environment*, 5th edn, Chapter 10, Maidenhead: McGraw Hill.
- Thompson, J L and Martin, F (2005) *Strategic Management: Awareness, Analysis and Change*, 5th edn, Chapter 4, London: Thomson Learning.
- White, C (2004) *Strategic Management*, Chapter 6, Basingstoke: Palgrave.
- Worthington, I and Brittion, C (2006) *The Business Environment*, 5th edn, Chapter 10, Harlow: Financial Times Prentice Hall.

The following book chapters look at competitive strategy.

- Johnson, G, Scholes, K and Whittington, R (2008) *Exploring Corporate Strategy*, 8th edn, Chapter 6, Harlow: Financial Times Prentice Hall.
- Lynch, R (2006) *Corporate Strategy*, 4th edn, Chapter 13, Harlow: Financial Times Prentice Hall.
- Thompson, J L and Martin, F (2005) *Strategic Management: Awareness, Analysis and Change*, 5th edn, Chapter 6, London: Thomson Learning.
- White, C (2004) *Strategic Management*, Chapter 6, Basingstoke: Palgrave.

The following two readings are Porter's original works on the five forces of competition and competitive strategies respectively.

- Porter, M E (1979) 'How competitive forces shape strategy', *Harvard Business Review*, March/April. Reprinted in Quinn, J B, Mintzberg, H and James, R M (1988) *The Strategy Process*, Hemel Hempstead: Prentice Hall.
- Porter, M E (1985) *Competitive Advantage: Creating and Sustaining Superior Performance*, Basingstoke: MacMillan. Excerpt reprinted in Quinn, J B, Mintzberg, H and James, R M (eds) (1988) *The Strategy Process*, Hemel Hempstead: Prentice Hall.

REFERENCES

1 Emery, F E and Trist, E L (1965) 'The causal texture of organisational environments', *Human Relations*, 18: 21–32.
2 BBC1, *Breakfast News*, 2 March 1999.
3 Edgecliffe-Johnson, A (1999) 'NY trade in luxuries becomes a victim', *Financial Times*, 6/7 March.
4 http://www.ofcom.org.uk/
5 http://www.ofgem.gov.uk
6 http://www.ofwat.gov.uk
7 Ibid.
8 http://www.rail-reg.gov.uk
9 Porter, M E (1985) *Competitive Advantage*, New York: Free Press.
10 Capon, C (2004) *Understanding Organisational Context*, Harlow: Financial Times Prentice Hall.
11 Ibid.
12 Porter, op. cit.
13 Ibid.
14 Gilbert, D and Strebel, P (1988) 'Developing competitive advantage', in Quinn, J B, Mintzberg, H and James, R M (eds) *The Strategy Process*, Harlow: Prentice Hall.
15 IKEA catalogue 98, Inter IKEA Systems BV, 1997.

CHAPTER 4

Inside organisations

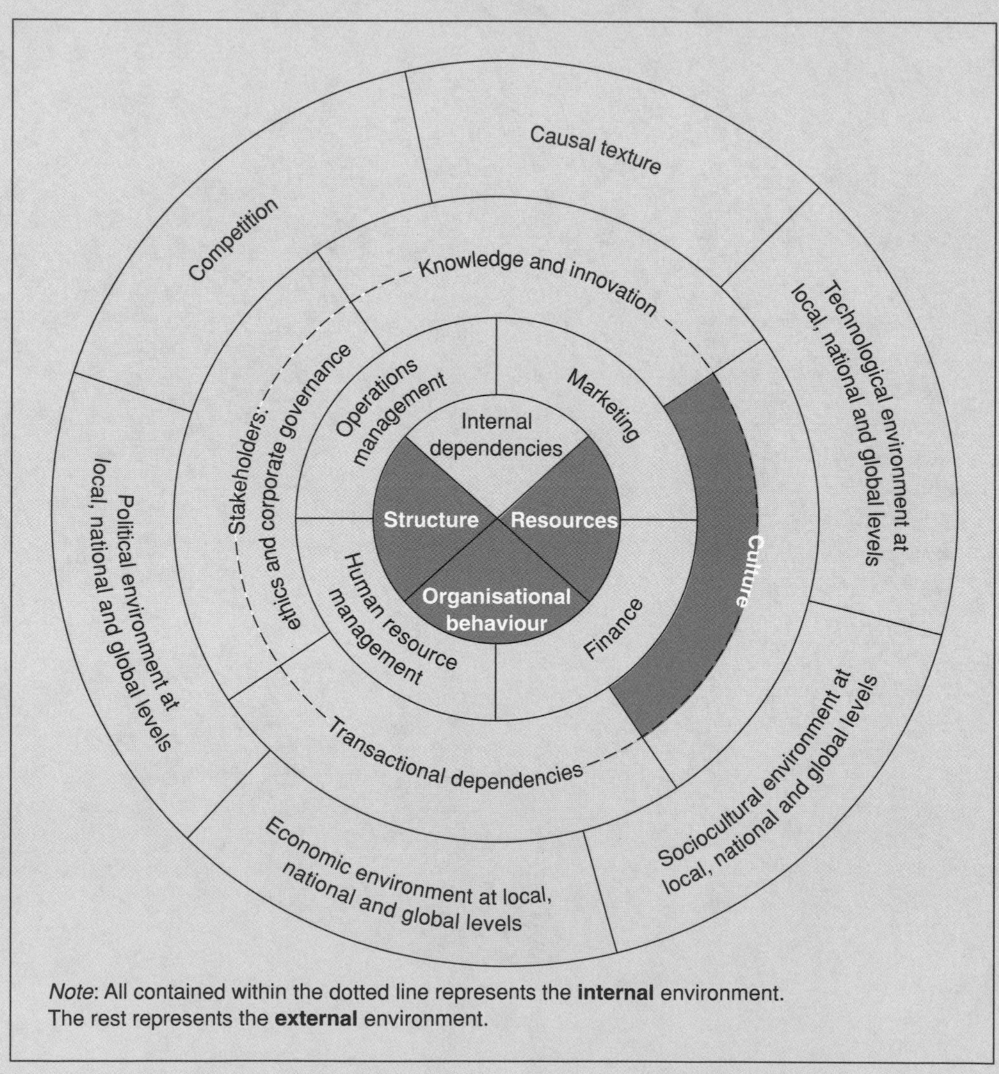

Figure 4.1 Business environment model

Chapter objectives

This chapter provides an overview of the different types of organisation, structure and culture and examines the links between culture, structure and behaviour. The chapter looks at private- and public-sector organisations, the different ownership models, the five generic structures (simple, functional, divisional, holding and matrix) and the Handy cultures (power, role, task and person cultures) and the type of organisation each culture represents.

Therefore, when you have read this chapter and worked through the associated activities you should be able to achieve the objectives specified below.

1 **Define different types of organisation.**
2 **Explain the different ownership models available to businesses.**
3 **Identify and discuss generic organisational structures, their advantages and disadvantages.**
4 **Discuss Handy's cultures and how they apply to organisations.**

This case study examines Lush and the view of one of its founders Mark Constantine on the business structure that should be adopted to ensure Lush retains its ethical approach to consumerism in the long term.

ENTRY CASE STUDY 4.1

Lush chief flags staff control of empire

FT

by Philip Stafford

Mark Constantine, chief executive of Lush, is considering turning the eco-friendly cosmetics chain he co-founded 12 years ago into a John Lewis-style partnership as he considers succession issues. Mr Constantine, 55, is keen to maintain the integrity of the business when he departs and avoid charges of selling out, an issue that dogs all companies riding a wave of ethical consumerism. Although Mr Constantine has no immediate plans for retirement, he said thinking about his succession had begun and that he would prefer Lush to become a partnership in the event of his death. 'But I'm not planning that either!' he joked.

Nevertheless, Mr Constantine has considered an ownership structure on the John Lewis model whereby Lush's 6000 staff worldwide would become partners. An employee trust runs John Lewis and determines its ethics. It has a written constitution that is dedicated to a 'better form of business' not driven by the demands of outside shareholders.

'In an ethical company, the big question is how do you ensure what people bought into isn't syphoned off in the future? It's a big issue for us all,' he said. 'These issues are not normally discussed. What is the business model and how does it exist in the modern world?' He pointed out that listing on the stock market could see principles diluted by future onward sales. It was a criticism levelled at Dame Anita Roddick, founder of the Body Shop, last year when she sold her ethical cosmetics business for £652m to L'Oréal, which tests its products on animals. Green & Blacks faced similar calls when Cadbury Schweppes bought the chocolate maker in 2005.

Lush is best known for its handmade toiletries such as bathbombs made from exotic natural ingredients such as ginger and cardamon. Its ethical stance on cosmetics has been Mr Constantine's key philosophy since he and business partner Liz Bennett founded the business in Poole in 1995.

Last year it ran a campaign in its European Union stores urging customers to sign postcards to MEPs against animal testing and has won awards from the RSPCA and Peta, the animal rights activists, for its work.

Source: from 'Lush chief flags staff control of empire', *The Financial Times*, 23 June 2007 (Stafford, P.).

Introduction

We all live in an increasingly complex and dynamic world in which organisations feature significantly. We work for organisations, we shop at them, we spend our leisure time in them and use them to improve the quality of our life (e.g. schools, doctors and dentists). Some of us even choose to teach about organisations or to study them at college or university.

This chapter looks at **public-sector** and private-sector organisations and some of their elements and features, such as the use of resources, legal structures and organisational cultures and structures. The entry case study for this chapter on Lush illustrates the importance of people and ethics in organisations.

The culture at Lush and other successful companies, such as John Lewis, is often underpinned by good staff and their extensive involvement in the organisation, its management and development. Successful companies depend not only on staff, but also on correctly configuring resources such that they are used efficiently and effectively. For organisations such as the engineering conglomerate Smiths Group[1] this meant reducing head office staff and decentralising decision making to help reduce costs. Equally, managing directors may also cut costs by removing executive 'perks' such as corporate jets, exotic plants and the executive dining room. These approaches are used by corporate leaders to reduce the use of tangible resources and associated costs in their respective organisations with the clear aim of improving the efficiency with which resources are used.

Organisations may also seek to shape intangible resources. The company Happy Computers has its image deeply embedded in its name: 'You can't pick up the phone and say "Happy Computers" with a grumpy voice'.[2] Good managers use resources, including people, money, facilities, buildings, image and reputation to develop successful organisations.

The public and private sectors

Characteristics of the public sector

The public sector consists of enterprises in which the whole or a majority stake is owned by either local or national government, or another publicly owned body established by government. Table 4.1 gives some examples of the more important organisations in the UK that remain in the public sector.

Table 4.1 Public-sector organisations

• National government – ministries and departments – agencies – civil service • DVLA	• NTVLRO • Local government • National Health Service • Armed services • Police forces	• Fire and rescue services • Universities and colleges • State schools • Royal Mail • Post Office

State schools deliver compulsory education free to children in the local area. Traditionally, local schools have been funded from and run by local government. However, in an effort to promote higher standards and to circumvent local authorities where the party in power was opposed to that in central government, the Conservatives introduced a system to allow for schools to opt out of local control and be funded directly by central government.

Some organisations that have been part of the public sector have had a mixed history. Some companies were private, then were nationalised, i.e. taken into public ownership, by previous Labour governments, and are now privately owned again. The largest wave of nationalisations occurred under the first post-war administration when Labour swept into power in the 1945 general election. The railway system in Britain was nationalised after the Second World War and British Rail was formed. This was followed about 40 years later by the privatisation of the railway system in the early 1990s under a Conservative government. This privatisation saw the formation of Railtrack (since replaced by Network Rail) and many train-operating companies. Railtrack was responsible for running and maintaining track, signals and stations. The train-operating companies, of which there are many (e.g. Midland Mainline and Virgin), run train services. The right to operate a train service on a particular route is determined by the train-operating company purchasing the franchise to do so. For example, Midland Mainline runs services between London and Sheffield, while services from London to Glasgow are operated by Virgin on the west coast and National Express on the east coast.

As the public sector is owned and regulated by government itself, it operates in markedly different ways from the private sector. Public-sector organisations tend to provide a service over which they have a monopoly, or certainly most of the responsibility for provision. Public-sector organisations tend to be large and bureaucratic entities, governed by strict rules and procedures that are often prescribed in law.

Market forces

The Conservative governments between 1979 and 1997 believed strongly that the private sector, and competition in particular, had certain advantages over the monopolistic public sector. They believed that market forces and competition could bring better value for money in terms of public expenditure and for private individuals. Many organisations that had been in the public sector since nationalisation were privatised, i.e. sold off to the mass public, in what Prime Minister Margaret Thatcher referred to as the creation of a 'shareholder democracy'. It was felt that a deregulated private sector operating in a free market would be able to provide all the services and products needed at the market price. Examples of privatised organisations are shown in Table 4.2. This also led to considerable one-off cash revenues for the government, which were used in other parts of the government's fiscal policy.

Table 4.2 Privatised organisations

• Deregulated regional and local bus companies	• British Airways
• Regional electricity boards	• British Aerospace
• Regional water boards	• British Rail
• British Telecom	• British Steel
• British Gas	• British Coal

An internal market was introduced to the NHS by the Conservative government in the late 1980s in an attempt to introduce some of the perceived benefits of private-sector operation, such as flexibility of decision making and market forces' effects on cost and pricing strategy. This allowed for general practitioners to become fundholders, deploying funds along with their referral of patients to hospitals, so that the number of referrals to a certain hospital became a key source of revenue. Hospitals, previously run by locally appointed boards on which locally elected councillors held a majority of seats, were able to opt out of this system and establish themselves as independent NHS trusts, directly funded by central government.

Public-sector organisations are sometimes run at a loss to government or are sometimes required to recoup their operating costs through income generation. However, public-sector enterprises rarely operate in order to make a profit.

Characteristics of the private sector

The private sector consists of privately owned companies and businesses. These may be owned by individuals, families or groups, or they may be large organisations that are quoted publicly on the Stock Exchange, with ownership residing in the hands of shareholders. The differences between limited companies and public limited companies are discussed later in this chapter, but for now it is enough to understand that a 'public limited company' has nothing to do with the public sector. Private-sector companies are regulated by laws and regulations introduced by the local, national and global levels of the external political environment.

Some services provided by the public sector also have private-sector providers, including hospitals and schools. Just as 'plcs' are not in the public sector, the term 'public school' refers to privately owned and run schools for which parents pay tuition fees, and not the free state-run counterparts.

As mentioned above, public-sector organisations are sometimes funded partly through their own income-generation activities, but their main source of income is a budget awarded by government from its tax revenues. For example, Passenger Transport Authorities receive money from council tax, collected by local government, but use that money to subsidise bus and rail services which are provided by private-sector companies. Therefore, private-sector organisations seeking to make profits from their business activities actually receive funding from the public sector.

Public and private partnership

The election of the Labour government in 1997 did not see the reversal of privatisation policies or a commitment to renationalise already privatised industries. Further privatisations, such as attempts to privatise the Post Office or the Royal Mail – which had been split into two for this purpose by the Conservatives – have, to date, not been pursued. Instead, the focus became the formation of direct partnerships between the public and private sectors. The Conservatives began this idea with 'Private Finance Initiatives', enabling public-sector organisations to raise money for projects in private money markets, and it has been continued by Labour. For example, private money continues to be available for public bridge- and road-building schemes, schools, hospitals and prisons.

Check your understanding

Do you understand the differences between a private-sector and public-sector organisation?

Check your understanding by describing and giving an example (not mentioned in this text) of both a public- and a private-sector organisation. Can you identify any type of organisation which operates in both the public and private sector?

Organisational resource conversion

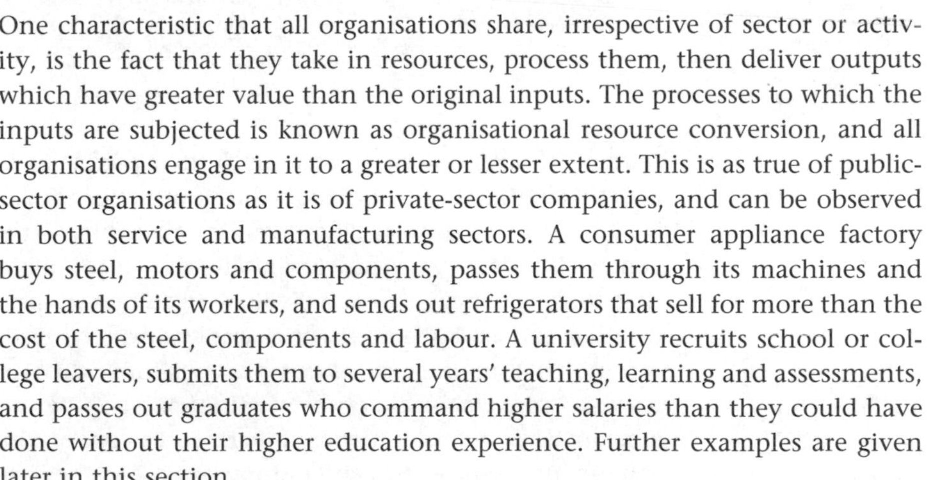

One characteristic that all organisations share, irrespective of sector or activity, is the fact that they take in resources, process them, then deliver outputs which have greater value than the original inputs. The processes to which the inputs are subjected is known as organisational resource conversion, and all organisations engage in it to a greater or lesser extent. This is as true of public-sector organisations as it is of private-sector companies, and can be observed in both service and manufacturing sectors. A consumer appliance factory buys steel, motors and components, passes them through its machines and the hands of its workers, and sends out refrigerators that sell for more than the cost of the steel, components and labour. A university recruits school or college leavers, submits them to several years' teaching, learning and assessments, and passes out graduates who command higher salaries than they could have done without their higher education experience. Further examples are given later in this section.

In examining the resource conversion process, the organisation can be depicted as a chart containing a sequential list of inputs, conversion processes and consequent outputs (*see* Table 4.3). There are also three kinds of inputs, processes and outputs: human, tangible and intangible. These are discussed in detail later in this chapter.

A generic organisational resource conversion chart delineates those activities that all organisations share. The generic chart can be adapted and applied to

Table 4.3 Organisational resource conversion chart

	Resource inputs	Processes	Outputs
Human	• Owners/shareholders • Managers • Employees • Part-timers • Contractors	• Goal setting • Decision making • Planning products and services • Managing functions (including HRM) • Assembling parts • Manufacturing goods • Dealing with customers	• Job satisfaction or dissatisfaction • Salaries and wages • Bonuses • Satisfied or dissatisfied customers
Tangibles	• Money (loans, overdrafts, profits, private capital) • Buildings • Machines and equipment • Raw materials • Components • Energy (gas, water, electricity) • Market research data	• Assembly • Manufacture • Service delivery • Supply • Quality control • Accounting • Distribution • Formal communication systems • Formal information systems	• Products • Services • Waste materials • Waste energy • Effluent • Profit or loss
Intangibles	• Systems • Design • Information • Innovation	• Informal communication • Culture • Corporate memory • Informal information flow	• Professionalism • Happiness • Image and reputation • Innovation

individual organisations according to their particular context. Following this generic chart, the model is applied to four fictional organisational examples.

The chart for any specific organisation contains those elements that are generically applicable to any organisation, such as buildings, as well as elements that apply specifically to an individual organisation's particular sector, activities or other contextual factors. For example, a bakery needs flour and yeast as its raw materials in order to bake bread. Therefore, when using the organisational resource conversion chart to examine closely what any given organisation actually does, an exact model of its resource conversion process must contain generic inputs, processes and outputs as well as the specific elements. Specific elements are those inputs, processes and outputs found only in the individual organisational context.

It must also be recognised that while inputs, processes and outputs can be shown separately in the conversion model, they should not be considered as independent of each other. In the same way that organisations cannot be considered as independent of their external contexts, clear transactional dependencies can be identified between the various cause-and-effect stages of the resource conversion process, i.e. there can be no outputs if there are no conversion processes, and the processes cannot operate without inputs. Initially, however, each stage of the process is considered separately here.

As previously mentioned, resource inputs can be grouped into three categories: human resources (the people in the organisation); **tangible resources** (e.g. machines and money); and **intangible resources** (e.g. information). Both human and financial resources are covered in detail in this book (Chapters 7 and 10 respectively) as internal functional departments of the organisation, each interacting independently and together with elements of the external environment. However, in this chapter money and people are considered as inputs to the organisational resource conversion process.

Human resources

Human resource inputs are obviously key to organisational success, as without people there can be no organisational activity. Despite hierarchical definitions of roles and responsibilities within organisations, which differentiate employer and employee, manager and worker, all make fundamental contributions to the organisation's activity through their efforts. These efforts must be as effective and efficient as possible in order for operational costs to be minimised, while outputs and profits are maximised. Human resources, once input to the organisation, obviously contribute to the conversion processes themselves, regardless of their roles, responsibilities or level in the organisation. Without the right people in the right roles there is little or no possibility of the organisation being able to achieve its goals. Employers or managers have specific roles and responsibilities, which usually include recruiting, managing and supervising the human resources inputs of the organisation. Employees also have specified roles and responsibilities, which usually become more and more defined according to how low down the hierarchy the human resource input is made.

Organisations have to consider what human resource inputs they need to begin, maintain and develop their operations, and how many people are necessary in order to achieve a critical mass for operational efficiency and effectiveness. People in organisations then need to be managed on an ongoing basis in order to ensure that they have the relevant skills at the appropriate level to fulfil the responsibilities their roles require. The numbers of human resources input to the organisation then need to be monitored in order to respond to the changing needs of the operations, i.e. is the organisation growing, shrinking or maintaining its size in reaction to changes in the marketplace? Human resource management, then, is concerned with getting people into the organisation, making sure they can do the jobs they need to do while they are there, and planning for getting them out of the organisation when necessary. Human resource management is covered in Chapter 7.

Tangible resources – finance

Perhaps the most important tangible resource input is money. As with the case of human resources, without money the organisation is totally inoperable. Whether in the private or public sector, all organisations must raise money in order to survive. Financial inputs come from a variety of sources, such as shareholders, banks, profits, budget allocations from head office or reallocation of retained profits. Public sources of financial inputs include grants or allocated budgets from different levels of the state, including local government, or from supranational bodies such as the European Union.

Financial inputs contribute to the organisational resource conversion process in three main ways. First, financial resources fund the acquisition of all other inputs. Money is needed to fund the human resources via their salaries or wages. How much the organisation can afford to pay its employees affects its ability to recruit and retain the people it needs to accomplish its tasks. Motivation is also directly linked to the amount of financial resource devoted to rewarding the efforts of its human resources. In the case of a manufacturing or assembly operation, money purchases the raw materials or component parts necessary to manufacture the organisation's portfolio of products. Additional key inputs to the resource conversion process in a manufacturing organisation include machinery, equipment, and the energy required to operate it, along with the spare parts needed for repair and maintenance. In the service sector, money still funds all other inputs in terms of the service design, physical location of the service delivery and paying for the operation of customer service departments. It also funds the purchasing of external market information, which informs the internal operations of the organisation.

Second, financial resources fund the conversion processes themselves, not only by having paid for the inputs the organisation needs but also by providing the money the conversion processes themselves need. A factory that has purchased its machines needs a healthy cashflow to be able to run them on a daily basis, pay weekly wages or monthly salaries, and provide the money to fund all aspects of operations management, marketing, accounting and quality control that enable it to function. Equally, in the public-sector example of a hospital, money must be found to fund the daily activities of routine surgery, accident and emergency departments, organ transplants and the space for patients to recuperate.

Finally, financial resources are needed in the output stage, to fund the delivery and distribution of the organisation's services or products to its customers in the marketplace, at an appropriate time or location. In addition, sufficient financial resources are required to fund the advertising, sales promotion and marketing of the organisation's products and services, such that the organisation's external image is maintained and developed effectively. Even the disposal of waste products has a financial implication for the organisation.

Tangible resources

The next category of tangible resources to be considered are raw materials or component parts and these are obviously necessary for organisations to make the products or provide the services they offer to the marketplace. Key issues when considering raw materials or component parts are costs and quality, as organisations seek to maximise profits by minimising the cost of inputs, without compromising the quality of the resultant output products and services.

All organisations need premises or buildings, and they must have sufficient equipment in those premises for manufacturing, communications, and health and safety requirements. There are issues here in relation to size of premises, their location – are they near to population centres, motorway networks, sea ports? – and their appropriateness for the required function – are there conversion costs or is it a purpose-built greenfield site?

Slightly less obvious tangible inputs are the resources purchased from the utility companies, e.g. water (including sewage and effluent treatment), gas and electricity, as well as local authority services such as transport infrastructure and refuse collection. These are inevitably key, as organisations cannot function without the input of energy to fuel their machines, and light and heat for their offices. In addition, roads providing access to the organisation for cars and lorries, convenient bus routes, bus stops and other connections for public transport as well as the regular collection and disposal of its waste are vital to ensure the organisation can function efficiently and effectively.

Intangible resources

Finally, there are intangible inputs to organisations, which consist of information and design. Information is essential, enabling an organisation to understand, analyse and react to events in its external environment. The key information inputs that organisations use for this purpose concern the marketplace and competitors. In terms of market information, an organisation needs to know how big the market is, what potential customers are likely to need or want, and how it could provide products or services that meet those needs. In terms of competitor information, an organisation needs to monitor what products or services competitor organisations provide, how much they are charging for these and what share of the market they currently serve. Marketing is considered in more detail in Chapter 8.

Information about the external political and economic environment is equally key for organisations, especially at times of impending significant change such as a general election or national budget. Such information will be used to attempt to anticipate changes in the external environment, hence allowing the organisation to adapt to anything that is likely to have a major effect on it. How well this resource input of information is gathered, analysed and disseminated within the organisation – sending the right information to the right department at the right time – is both a sign and a cause of operational effectiveness. A good information flow demonstrates that an organisation understands and analyses its external environment and ensures that it continues to be able to do so.

The design of an organisation's systems and processes can also be considered as an input to its resource conversion process. The efficient and effective design of the organisation, its internal communication systems, its accounting procedures, the factory layout or the positioning and decoration of its reception area are all manifestations of its interaction with its external environment. The particular conversion processes that add value to the resource inputs vary according to the organisation and the business it is in. Perhaps the most easily understandable resource conversion process is manufacturing, where raw materials such as steel are turned physically into products such as automobiles. Some materials may be subassembled elsewhere, and these components may later be used by another organisation as part of its resource conversion process. In the service sector, planning and executing the delivery of a service counts as a resource conversion process, as this is also concerned with adding value to inputs in order to produce outputs.

In order to contextualise the resource conversion process, four different fictional contexts are given below, showing organisational resource conversion charts for public- and private-sector contexts, in manufacturing and services, and at varying levels of the external environment.

Check your understanding

Do you understand the term 'organisational resource conversion chart'?

Check your understanding by explaining how an organisation is represented by an organisational resource conversion chart.

Little Mester Ltd, surgical steel instrument maker

The example of a self-employed steel instrument maker (or 'Little Mester') in Sheffield shows a very different resource conversion process chart from the generic model (*see* Table 4.4). The context level is largely local, with some quite specific inputs (raw metals), processes (informal quality control) and outputs (development of the toolmaker's craft).

Natpower Ltd, electricity generator

The case of 'Natpower' concerns a private-sector service provider, in this case an electricity generator, in a predominantly national context. Its particular resource conversion chart (*see* Table 4.5) also contains generically applicable elements as well as context-specific items, such as electricity generator plants (input), dealing with electricity distribution companies (process) and the intangible output of safety.

Table 4.4 Organisational resource conversion chart: Little Mester Ltd, surgical steel instrument maker

	Resource inputs	Processes	Outputs
Human	• The owner/ manufacturer (Little Mester) • Suppliers	• All aspects of the business, including planning, manufacturing and selling done by the owner • Providing raw metal and small components	• Job satisfaction • Development of the toolmaker's craft • Wages and profits for the business • Satisfied customers
Tangibles	• Loans, mortgages, overdrafts, sales income, profits • Workshop and home • Machinery • Raw metals • Component parts • Energy	• Supplying metal and components • Manufacture and assembly of tools • Quality control (probably informal – throwing away or recycling mistakes) • Accounting • Delivering products to hospitals • Letters and adverts	• Surgical tools • Waste metal (maybe re-input as recycled raw metal) • Profit or losses
Intangibles	• Very informal systems for monitoring customer needs and reacting to them	• Everything is in the owner's head and hands	• Professionalism • Happiness • Image and reputation • Specialisation

China National State Steel Corporation

Although economic reforms in the late 1980s and 1990s have led to the establishment of both a new private sector and newly privatised industries in China, much of the large-scale means of production remain under state control. Thus the example of the China National State Steel Corporation allows resource conversion at the global level of the external environment to be examined in the context of a public-sector manufacturing environment. Again, there are generic and specific elements in its resource conversion process chart (*see* Table 4.6). A huge, state-owned steel corporation in a country governed by a Communist Party has responsibilities far beyond those of private companies in capitalist countries. The organisation not only has to fulfil the demands of the government's plan for production but also has to provide for all the social welfare needs of its employees and their families, including healthcare, schooling, daily provisions and housing. The environment level would be national, although there are global implications for competition and the international political arena.

Table 4.5 Organisational resource conversion chart: Natpower Ltd, electricity generator

	Resource inputs	Processes	Outputs
Human	• Owners/shareholders • Managers • Full- and part-time workers in electricity generation • Contractors supplying services (e.g. repairs)	• Goal setting • Decision making • Planning for meeting electricity needs • Managing functions • Generating electricity from gas or coal • Dealing with electricity distribution companies	• Job satisfaction or dissatisfaction • Salaries and wages • Bonuses • Satisfied or dissatisfied customers
Tangibles	• Income, profits • Electricity generation plants • Generators and the supply grid • Coal or gas to convert and to power the plant • Data to plan electricity needs • Additional energy from overseas • Legal regulation	• Generating electricity • Quality control • Accounting • Supplying electricity via the grid to electricity supply companies • Formal internal communication systems • Formal internal information systems	• Electricity • Waste (pollution)
Intangibles	• Systems • Design • Information • Innovation	• Informal communication • Culture • Corporate memory • Informal information flow	• Professionalism • Happiness • Image and reputation • Innovation • Safety

Superbuys

A large, shareholder-owned supermarket's resource conversion chart would, again, be fairly standard (*see* Table 4.7). The context would be global and national: global since many products are imported and there are branches overseas; and national as its largest customer base is in the UK. Specific inputs include suppliers of branded and own-label goods, with specific processes including shelf stacking and specific outputs including the image and reputation of the supermarket.

Check your understanding

Do you understand how to construct an organisational resource conversion chart for an organisation with which you are familiar?

Check your understanding by producing an organisational resource conversion chart for your university, college or employer. Remember to include generic and specific items.

Table 4.6 Organisational resource conversion chart: China National State Steel Corporation

	Resource inputs	Processes	Outputs
Human	• Managers • Employees • Families	• Liaising with government departments regarding the five-year economic plan • Operational decision making • Planning products • Managing functions • Manufacturing steel and goods • Dealing with other organisations which use the steel	• Meeting the needs of employees and their families in terms of wages and social welfare
Tangibles	• State funding, sales income • Steel plants all over China • Machines and equipment • Raw materials • Components • Energy (generated on site) • Five-year plan	• Assembly • Manufacture • Supply • Quality control • Budget management • Distribution • Chinese Communist Party (CCP) organisation • Formal communication systems, including propaganda radio • Formal information systems (CCP)	• Fulfilling the five-year plan • Products • Social services (housing, hospitals, schools, shops) • Waste materials • Waste energy • Effluent and pollution • Profit or loss
Intangibles	• Planning, manufacturing and control systems • Product design • State and party information	• Informal communication between workers and families • Culture • Corporate memory • Informal information flows	• Basic standard of living for all • Party control of workers and families

The legal structures of business

The sole trader

A **sole trader** business is owned and administered by one person who is personally liable for all the debts of the business, this being the primary disadvantage of this type of legal structure.[3] The sole trader is the owner of the business, having raised the capital for it from personal funds. The sole trader has direct control over the business and takes all the decisions relating to products and

Table 4.7 Organisational resource conversion chart: Superbuys

	Resource inputs	Processes	Outputs
Human	• Managers • Shop workers • Warehouse workers • Truck drivers • Suppliers of branded and own-label goods	• Goal setting • Decision making (e.g. loyalty cards, banking) • Planning products, services and new stores • Managing functions • Manufacturing own-brand goods • Dealing with customers	• Job satisfaction or dissatisfaction • Salaries and wages • Bonuses • Satisfied customers
Tangibles	• Share capital • Stores, warehouses • Equipment (checkouts, computers, shelving, lighting) • Imports and domestic goods • Energy • Market research data	• Manufacture • Shelf stacking • Supply and distribution • Quality control • Accounting • Formal communication systems • Formal information systems • Enhanced services (loyalty cards, banking, cafés, petrol stations)	• Products • Services • Waste materials • Waste energy • Effluent • Profit or loss
Intangibles	• Systems • Design • Information • Innovation	• Informal communication • Culture • Corporate memory • Informal information flow	• Professionalism • Happiness • Image and reputation • Innovation

services, customers and markets, staff employed and future development. The principal advantage of the sole trader legal structure is that all profits appertain to the owner.[4]

Partnership

A **partnership** is where two or more individuals join together in a business venture with each partner having unlimited liability.[5] Therefore, should the partnership result in debt or bankruptcy, each partner can be held liable for the full amount owed by the partnership. Creditors can either sue each partner in turn or all of the partners jointly for as many of the partners' assets as will pay off their debts. The other option is for the partnership to have limited liability, but limited partnerships are uncommon because only some of the partners can have limited liability, so therefore limited liability is usually established by creating a **limited company** instead of a partnership.[6]

The limited company

A limited company exists as a legal entity in itself, separately from its owners or managers. Therefore, liability for debts is limited to the amount of issued share capital, whether the shares have been sold or not.[7] The shareholders' personal assets cannot be claimed for the payment of business debts to creditors. The creation of a limited company requires the lodging of various documents with the Registrar of Companies, which must include a Memorandum of Association and Articles of Association. If all documentation is satisfactory, a certificate of incorporation is issued, bringing the company into existence as a legal entity.[8]

Check your understanding

Do you understand the different legal structures a business may adopt?

Check your understanding by comparing and contrasting different legal structures which businesses may adopt.

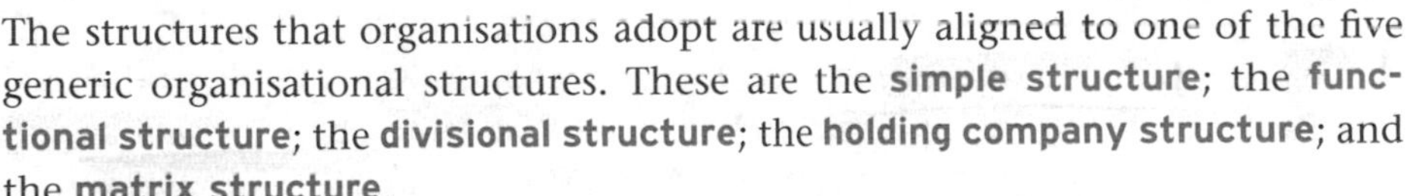

Organisational structures

The structures that organisations adopt are usually aligned to one of the five generic organisational structures. These are the **simple structure**; the **functional structure**; the **divisional structure**; the **holding company structure**; and the **matrix structure**.

The simple and functional organisational structures are centralised structures where all the important and long-term decisions are taken by top management. Top management will determine the rules and procedures that closely govern and direct the jobs and tasks of managers further down the organisation and are responsible for the departments, products, services and markets on a day-to-day basis.

In contrast, the divisional, holding and matrix organisational structures are decentralised, containing divisions/subsidiaries/project teams that have a significant amount of decision-making power and responsibility of their own. Cooperation and coordination between the divisions/subsidiaries/project teams and the board of directors are crucial if the spreading of power and responsibility throughout the structure is to work for the organisation as a whole.

The simple structure

The company that adopts a simple structure (*see* Figure 4.2) is likely to be a small business in the private sector or one in the very early stages of its growth and development. The simple structure is centralised, with all short-, medium- and long-term power and decision-making responsibility resting with the managing director, who is also likely to be the owner of the business. The

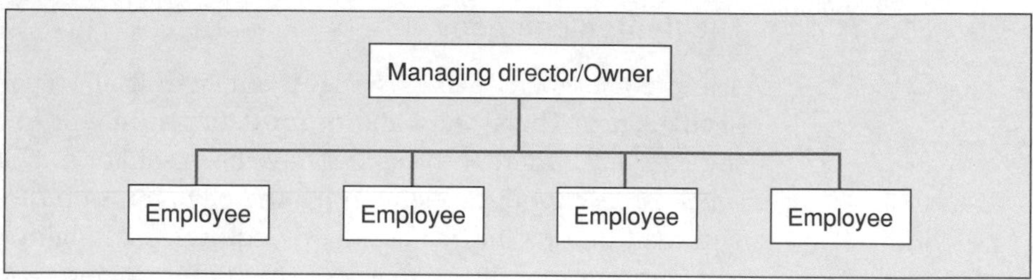

Figure 4.2 The simple structure

managing director/owner controls and oversees all aspects of the company's operations. Therefore, the simple structure is suitable for a small business in the early stages of growth and development, allowing the managing director/owner to have control over the future growth and development of the business. The managing director controls the company as s/he will have a large financial stake in the business, along with expertise relating to the product or service sold by the business and the markets to which it sells. For example, Will Chase, the managing director of Tyrrells Crisps, had the idea to set up a business producing premium crisps, gained the expertise in the US and has overseen the development of his UK business in line with his views. This meant not dealing with retailers such as Tesco, who were seeking to pay what Chase regarded a low price for his premium crisps.

The simple structure becomes less suitable as the business grows. The managing director/owner finds it more and more difficult to control and oversee the greater number of tasks and activities undertaken by a larger and growing business. However, the likelihood also exists that the managing director/owner has the skills, knowledge and abilities to run a small business, but may be lacking some of those necessary to run a larger and growing business. This situation usually requires the business to restructure if it is to survive its growth and increase further in size. Simple structure businesses that grow in size commonly develop functional structures.

The functional structure

The functional structure (*see* Figure 4.3) is rigid and centralised with efficient management control systems, and is common both in companies that have outgrown the simple structure and in well-established public-sector organisations. Such organisations are medium-sized and have a limited range of related products and services delivered to clearly defined and clearly segmented markets. The functional structure also sees the introduction of specialist functional managers who head the different departments, e.g. marketing manager, operations manager, finance manager and human resource manager. In the case of growing private companies, these new managers provide the specialist skills, knowledge and abilities that may have been missing under the simple structure.

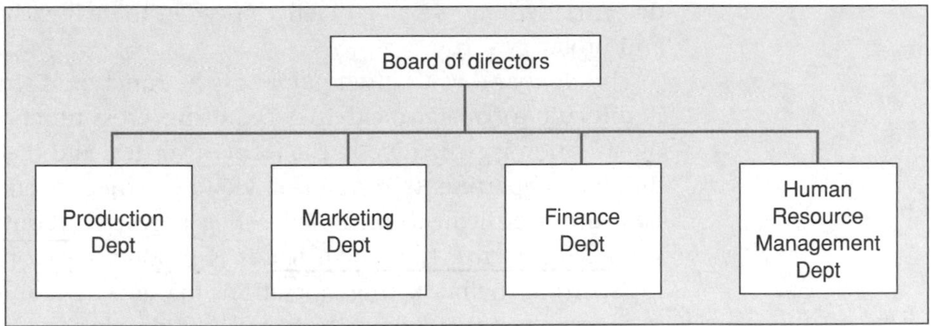

Figure 4.3 The functional structure

The managing director or board of directors will be in close contact with the new departmental heads who run the different departments on a day-to-day basis, hence the lines of communication and information flow within the functional structure are short and vertical. The structuring of the organisation around the different functions or tasks that have to be carried out by its employees results in job roles that are clearly defined and understood by everyone in the organisation. Short-term decision-making power and responsibility tend to rest with the departmental heads, who have to work together with the board of directors to ensure that what is happening at an operational level also reflects and feeds back into the long-term and medium-term decision-making process. Long- and medium-term decision-making power and responsibility, however, rest very much with the board of directors.

One of the reasons why organisations move on from the functional structure is that the organisation starts to diversify its product or service range and no longer has a limited range of related products or services for a clearly defined and clearly segmented market. An organisation that is outgrowing the functional structure is likely to have developed a wider range of products or services that are not so closely related and that sell to more diverse markets. The growth that has led to the need to restructure could have resulted from selling to markets that are more geographically diverse than was the case previously, e.g. the organisation has engaged in international business where before it dealt purely domestically. Another cause of growth could be selling to a wider customer base with more varied needs and wants than the traditional market segment.

When this type of situation arises, the functional structure becomes very stretched and cannot cope well with the increased diversity. The production and marketing managers now have to deal with a diverse range of products and services in a diverse marketplace, whereas in the functional structure there is only one marketing department and one production department to do everything. They are used to dealing with a limited range of closely related products or services and do not necessarily have the resources to service wider ranges or market segments. Thus, in essence, the functional structure has to change in order to cope with growth and diversification. It is the centralised and rigid nature of the functional structure that prevents it from adopting the decentralised and flexible practices needed to deal with more diverse markets and product ranges.

The rigid and centralised nature of the functional structure may also make it difficult to operate activities requiring cross-functional teams. Since the organisation is structured in the form of vertical and hierarchical functions, its different departments have clear views on their operational responsibilities and find it difficult to act outside their perceived remit. A classic example of the need for cross-functional teams is product development, which requires inputs from the marketing, operations management and finance departments in order to research what customers want, develop products or services accordingly, cost their delivery and determine their price. It may be difficult to make this work within the confines of a vertical and hierarchical functional structure, with its clearly defined and understood job roles.

The divisional structure

A company that has adopted a divisional structure (*see* Figure 4.4) contains separate divisions based around individual product lines or services, e.g. a motor manufacturer may have a car division, a truck and van division, and a passenger service vehicle (bus) division. Alternatively, divisions can be based on the geographic areas of the markets served, e.g. Europe, Asia and North America. Organisations may contain a mixture of different types of divisions, with some based on product or service lines and others geographically allocated, e.g. cars, buses, trucks and overseas sales. However, one single division would not usually be based on both product and location, so it is rare to find divisions called 'cars North America' or 'buses Asia'.

The divisional structure is decentralised and, as such, a company with a divisional structure usually offers a wide and diverse range of products and

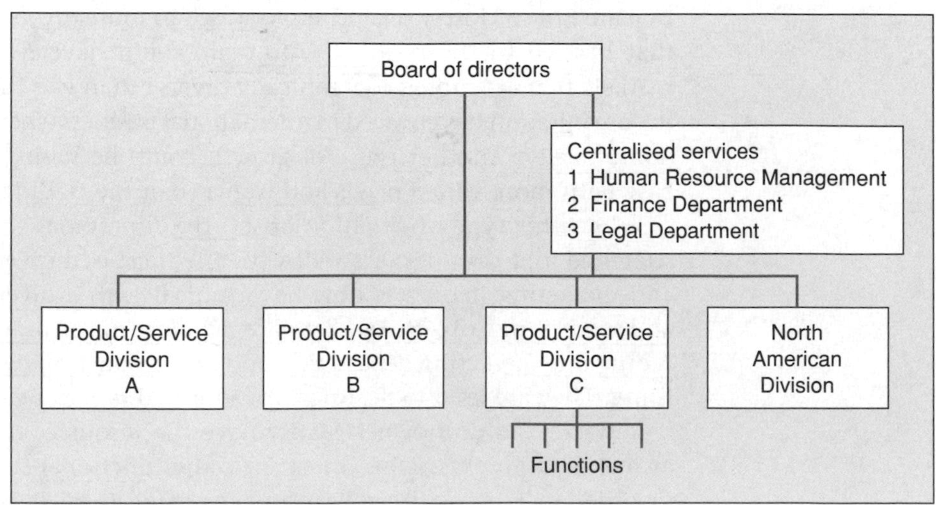

Figure 4.4 The divisional structure

services compared with a company operating with the more rigid and centralised functional structure. The key benefit of a wide and diverse portfolio is the ability to spread risk across a range of activities. Thorntons, the chocolate company, has a divisional structure, with six divisions: Retail, Commercial, Thorntons Direct, Licensing, Franchising and Cafes. The Retail division manages Thorntons's own shops, the Commercial division covers the sale of Thorntons's chocolates in supermarkets and shops such as Asda, and Thorntons Direct is the online business. The Licensing division manages the contracting of the production of Thorntons products such as cakes, biscuits and ice cream and the Franchising division deals with the franchised outlets, including the concessions in Hallmark card shops. Finally Thorntons Cafes is the division responsible for the coffee shops.

Management of this diversity requires the divisional heads or managers to have short-term and medium-term decision-making power and responsibility for the division they manage. This allows the managing director and his/her board of directors to concentrate on long-term planning for the organisation as a whole. However, good communication and working relationships must exist between the divisional heads or managers and the board of directors, as short-, medium- and long-term decision making must all relate to each other and link together if the whole company is to move forward in the same coherent direction.

The divisions in a divisionalised company will be cost centres or profit centres in their own right, having to manage budgets, meet budgetary targets and operate within budgetary constraints. Divisions must also satisfy performance criteria relating to profitability and asset use, with profit margins and return on assets likely to be the key measures applied to individual divisions. The company will aggregate the financial information on each division's performance to produce the overall annual company report and accounts.

The separate divisions within the same organisation have an internal structure of their own. A common structure for individual divisions to adopt is the functional structure because it is suitable for the size and range of activities of a discrete division under the larger divisionalised organisation.

The potential difficulties with the divisional structure relate to the allocation of resources, overall coordination of activities and the cost of running separate divisions. The existence of an element of competition between separate divisions and a very limited resource base may lead to conflict between the divisions, as each separate division vies for the best possible allocation of resources and wants to perform well in the eyes of head office. The diverse range of divisions in a company may also make company-wide coordination demanding. This may be exacerbated if there is duplication of key activities in each division, which makes the cost of running individual divisions high. For example, the presence of a human resource management (HRM) function in each division would be expensive duplication. The activities associated with the HRM function are equally applicable to all people who work for the company, regardless of the division in which they work and, as such, centralisation of HRM activities makes economic and practical sense. With a centralised HRM function for all divisions, one HRM policy for the whole company can be developed and maintained, and every central and divisional employee recruited and measured against the central HRM policy. A different HRM function in each division risks resulting not only in wasteful duplication of effort but also in different HR practices being adopted, thus diluting corporate culture and corporate control.

Other centralised services could include the finance department and there may also be a discrete legal department to interact specifically with the various politico-legal issues at the various levels of the external environment.

Check your understanding

Do you understand which types of organisation adopt the following structures: simple; functional; divisional?

Check your understanding by explaining the similarities and differences between the three structures.

The holding company structure

The holding company structure (*see* Figure 4.5) is usually found in large conglomerates with a parent company acting mainly as an investment company acquiring and divesting smaller subsidiary companies. A company operating as a holding company will usually have a small corporate headquarters from which the parent company will conduct business. This means that central overheads will be low because of the economies of scale that this company-wide coordination achieves. The finance and legal sections are part of the parent company and their purpose is to provide the expertise needed centrally in the acquisition and divestment of subsidiary companies.

The subsidiary companies continue to trade under their own names, with the parent company either wholly owning its subsidiaries or acting as a majority

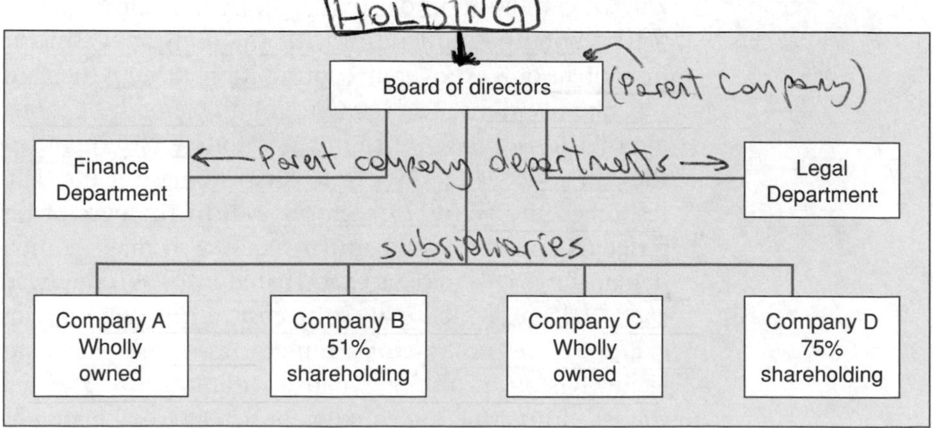

Figure 4.5 The holding company structure

shareholder in them. Subsidiary companies will operate fairly independently of the head office, with all decision-making power and responsibility for their own performance resting with their management. Conglomerates adopting the holding company structure are therefore very decentralised. However, the control systems implemented by head office will tend to centre on the subsidiary companies meeting tight financial targets with regard to profit forecasts, profit margins and return on assets, or risking swift divestment by the holding company.

The ownership of a large number of subsidiary companies in a variety of industries spreads the risk and profit for the parent company as a whole. The use of subsidiary companies to obtain diversity may ease divestment, especially in the light of poor performance, as that performance can be viewed as being ring-fenced in one or more companies and therefore contained.

The main potential disadvantage of the holding company structure relates to the subsidiary companies, which may view themselves as continuously up for sale. This type of situation invokes a high degree of uncertainty, and the likelihood of change can be difficult for the subsidiary companies to manage on a permanent basis. The other potential disadvantage relates to the general fact that diversity is more difficult to coordinate and manage overall than simplicity, and so the holding company management faces a more complex task.

The Arcadia Group, owned by Philip Green and his family, is the UK's largest privately owned clothing retail group[9] and is a good example of a business with a holding company structure. The Arcadia Group owns seven different high-street retailers – Burton, Dorothy Perkins, Evans, Miss Selfridge, Topman, Topshop and Wallis – which all trade as separate businesses under their own name.

The matrix structure

The matrix structure attempts to merge the benefits of **decentralisation** with coordination across all areas of the business. Matrix structures are often used in organisations where there are two distinct and important areas of operation needing to be managed and coordinated in order to deliver the full product or service range. Matrix structures are often found in large multinational companies, educational establishments and small sophisticated service companies.

In a large multinational company (*see* Figure 4.6), the two arms of the matrix structure represent the product or services areas and the geographic areas in which the company operates. The product or service arm is responsible for the production of the product or delivery of the service, while each geographic arm of the matrix is responsible for the advertising, marketing, sales and distribution of those products or services to the end users in the geographic area for which they are responsible. The geographic arm becomes the customer of the product or service arm, as they purchase the product or service they need from them, before selling these on to their geographically defined customer base.

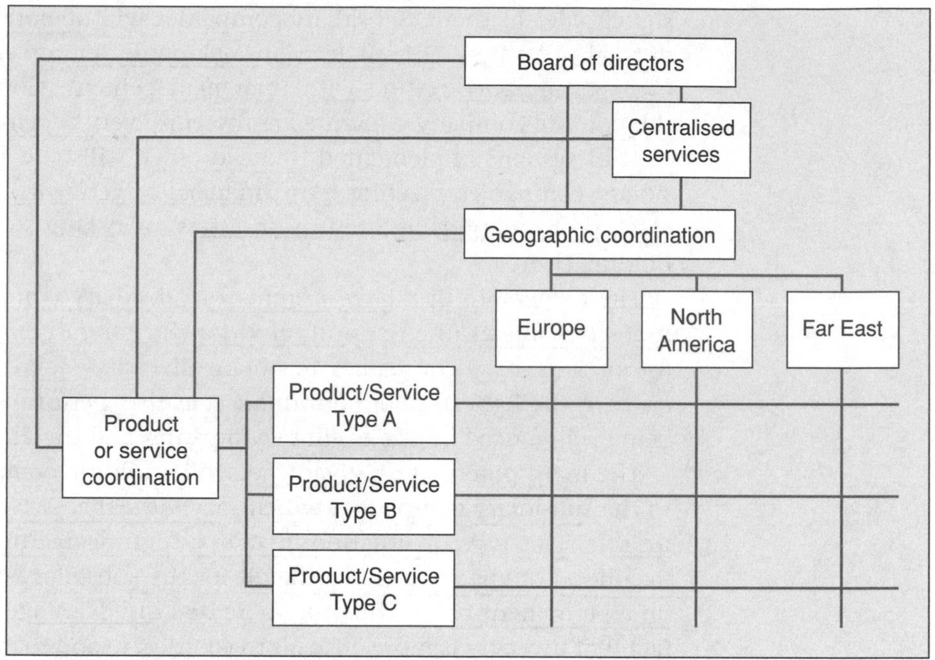

Figure 4.6 The matrix structure: multinational company

The matrix structure in a university business school (*see* Figure 4.7) also has two arms, one responsible for delivering the products – higher education courses – to their internal customer – the other arm of the matrix. This second arm manages course administration and is therefore responsible for delivering the product on to the end users, the students. The internal customers, the course administrators, can be organised in terms of the type of external customer they serve: full-time or part-time students; undergraduates or postgraduates; funded or fee-paying students. Whatever their provenance, each student grouping is enrolled on one of a number of courses or products, e.g. BA (Hons) Business Management, HND Legal Studies and Management, Master of Business Administration or MSc in e-Business.

Within the matrix structure, in order for this arm of the matrix to be able to run its courses and satisfy its external customers, it needs the services of the other arm of the matrix, which represents the staff, usually organised in groups that reflect their academic expertise and the subject they teach. This arm of the matrix is responsible for supplying tutors to classes and for all staff development issues to ensure that individual tutors are competent enough in terms of academic expertise and teaching methodology to deliver the services their internal customers require of them. Hence communication and coordination between the two arms of the matrix should centre on subject groups and the course leaders reaching agreement over who will teach which subject to which classes on which courses, teaching being the main activity occurring in the matrix. The direct contact between people from both arms of the matrix

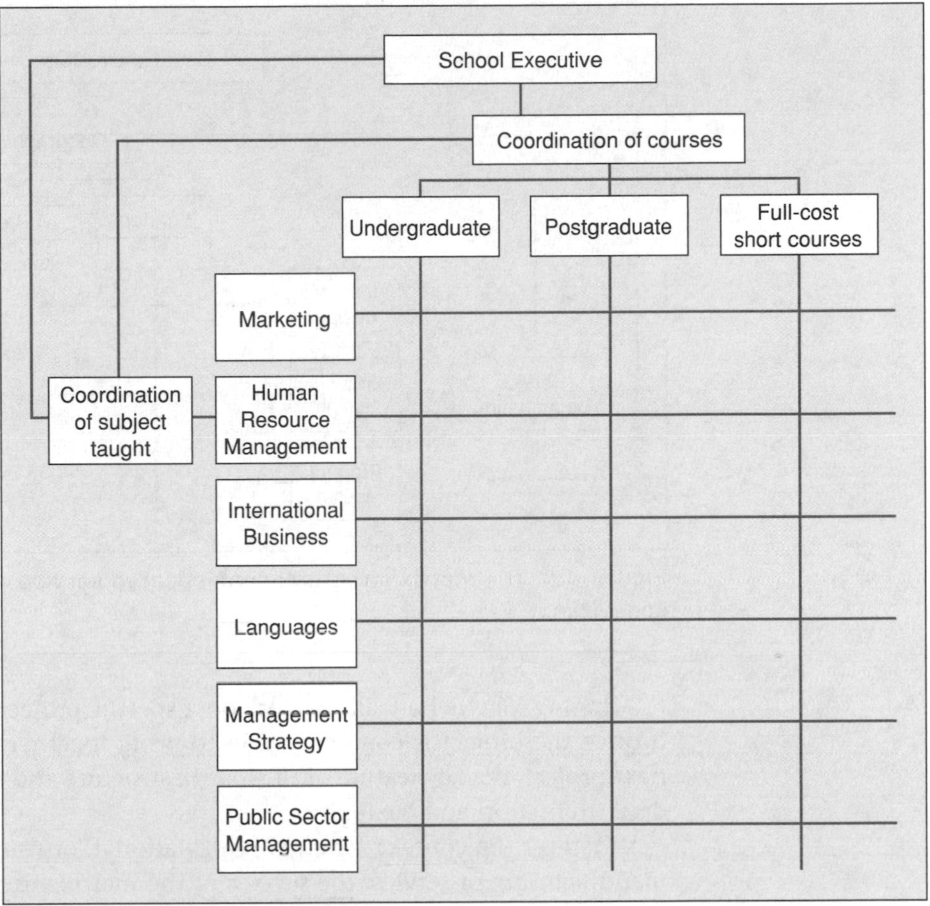

Figure 4.7 The matrix structure: educational establishment – university business school

allows decisions to be made by the staff at the sharp end with direct responsibility for running courses and teaching students, which should avoid hierarchical bureaucracy. Decentralisation of responsibility for decision making to people from both arms of the matrix structure should increase the motivation of the staff involved, provided that job tasks and responsibilities are clear.

A lack of clarity in people's roles, responsibilities and accountability is a potential disadvantage of the matrix structure.

The matrix structure for a small sophisticated service company will contain professional expertise groupings on one arm of the matrix and may contain geographic groupings on the other arm. A design consultancy (*see* Figure 4.8) would operate by having offices in various regions of Britain to handle the accounts and initial enquiries from clients, as well as having design staff working out of that office. The nature of the project from the client would determine whether it could be handled by a team of designers available from the local design staff or whether a team of designers from across the company's different offices would be required.

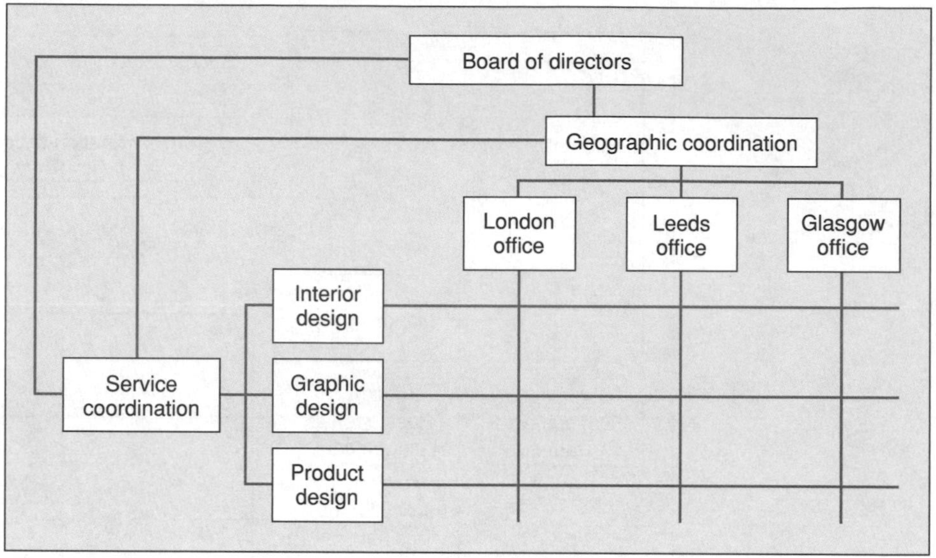

Figure 4.8 The matrix structure: sophisticated service company – design consultancy

Bringing together a team to work on a specific project and then disbanding it once the project is complete, only to bring together another team for the next project, is a key feature of the matrix structure and is able to occur due its decentralisation and flexibility.

Whatever the context, whether multinational, private sector, public sector, manufacturing or service, the success of the matrix structure depends heavily on communication and coordination between the two arms of the matrix for any one product or service in any one market. This requires teams consisting of people from both arms of the matrix to work together well at the points where they meet in the matrix and engage in their internal customer relationship. The quality of the end user or external customer experience depends heavily on the quality of this internal customer relationship between arms of the matrix. Therefore, the main potential difficulty with implementing the matrix structure occurs when people from both arms of the matrix fail to work together and coordination and communication between the two break down, thus impeding decision-making processes and adversely affecting the experience of the external customer or end user of the product or service.

Check your understanding

Do you understand the characteristics of the holding company structure and the matrix structure?

Check your understanding by stating in what type of organisation the holding company and matrix structures may occur. Explain how they may be applied in the stated type of organisation.

Organisational culture and behaviour

The study of culture is a fascinating but complex topic. It is important, since organisations are necessarily filled with people who bring with them the culture they have acquired in society. Culture exists in both the external and internal environments of organisations. Culture in the external environment is dealt with in Chapter 2, as the sociocultural context or the 'S' of LoNGPEST analysis in the model, and in Chapter 5. Here we look at internal organisational culture and examine the implications of the 'chicken and egg' link with organisational structure. There are also clear links between organisational culture and the efficient and effective operation of the four functional areas within the organisation. At all stages in the analysis of organisational environments, the links between culture in society and culture in organisations should be observed to facilitate appropriate decisions concerning the management of the people who work within the organisation.

In order to examine organisational culture, the generic models developed by Handy[10] are used. Handy's observation of and research in organisations led to the isolation of four essential internal cultural models which are considered here.

The power culture

Small, entrepreneurial organisations, where the owner works with few employees, are likely to exhibit the **power culture**. This organisation is a club of intimates, where the colleagues or employees have been chosen by the owner/manager for their similarity to him-/herself. The centre of power, and all crucial decision making, rests with the owner/manager, who either is in personal charge of every aspect of the work or can trust colleagues and employees to do things instinctively the way the owner/manager would have done them him-/herself. This is depicted by the model (*see* Figure 4.9), which resembles a spider at the centre of its web.

The formal structure that most closely echoes the power culture is the simple structure, discussed earlier in this chapter.

The choice of 'cloned' employees can be deliberate or subconscious on the part of the entrepreneur. Whether explicitly sought or not, an internal culture develops that is intimate and comfortable for those on the inside. This creates further issues for anyone different who tries to enter the organisation, and this is possibly the culture that is least open to equal opportunities issues, as the club members do not wish to admit new members not in their likeness. The power culture is exciting because of the risks involved in its operation, as colleagues at the centre of power make decisions in an unauthorised but implicitly supportive environment. They operate the way they think the entrepreneur should, are rewarded and congratulated when they are correct, but risk censure when they inadvertently make a mistake.

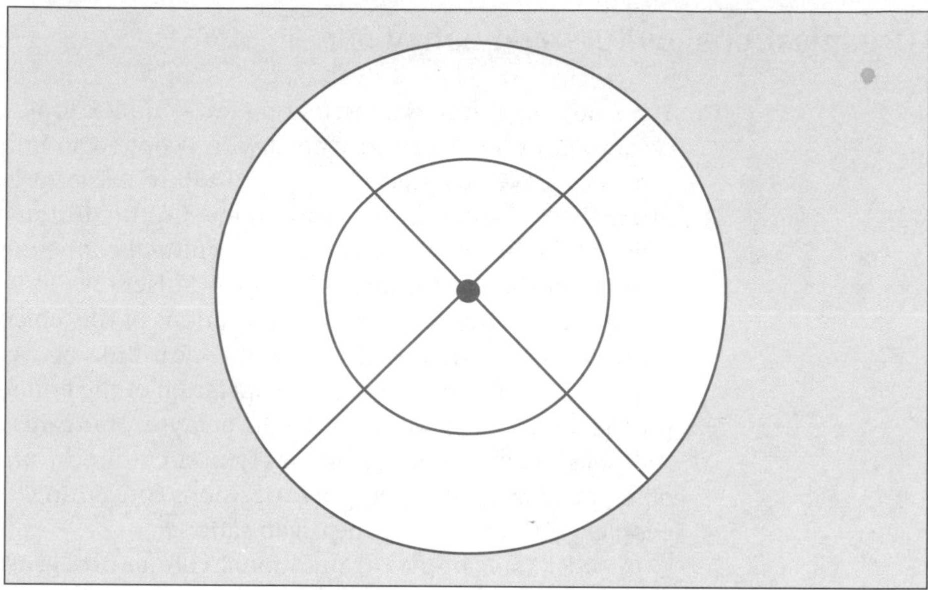

Figure 4.9 The power culture

Source: *Understanding Organizations* by Charles Handy (Penguin Books 1976, Fourth Edition 1993). Copyright Charles Handy 1976, 1981, 1985, 1993. Reproduced by kind permission of Penguin Books Ltd.

Without the leader, the power centre is lost and the club can break down. Should the leader become ill or die, the organisation grieves and can recover from its loss only with difficulty. This illustrates a danger of the club culture, in that the organisation becomes too reliant on the originator and entrepreneur who is all too literally the heart and soul of the organisation.

When the organisation grows, the club becomes too big for all the members to retain their intimacy. Just as the structure changes with growth, developing from simple to functional structure, the culture also alters. The next of Handy's cultures is the **role culture**.

The role culture

The role culture (*see* Figure 4.10) mirrors the functional and **divisional structures** and is evident within more mature and larger organisations with departments, divisions and different geographic areas. The characteristic of the role culture is reflected in everyone in the organisation having a specific job title and description and knowing what it is they are expected to do in their contribution to the organisational mission. Role culture organisations are functional, bureaucratic and highly systematised, with clearly documented, routine procedures and well-organised and efficient operations. Because of their size and the routine nature of their operations, these organisations develop into solid and predictable institutions, which operate the way they do because they have always done things that way. These cultures find an increase in the rate and speed of change a great threat, and are thus not adaptive to change.

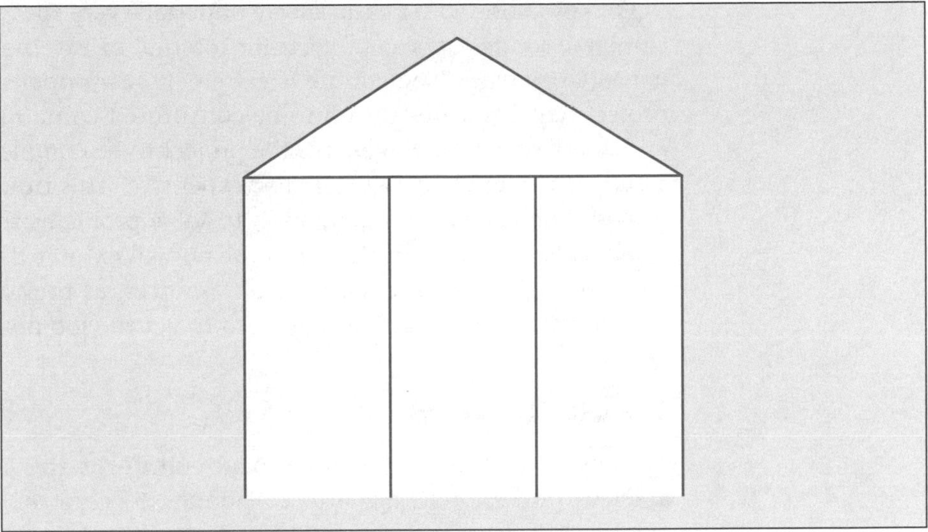

Figure 4.10 The role culture

Source: *Understanding Organizations* by Charles Handy (Penguin Books 1976, Fourth Edition 1993). Copyright Charles Handy 1976, 1981, 1985, 1993. Reproduced by kind permission of Penguin Books Ltd.

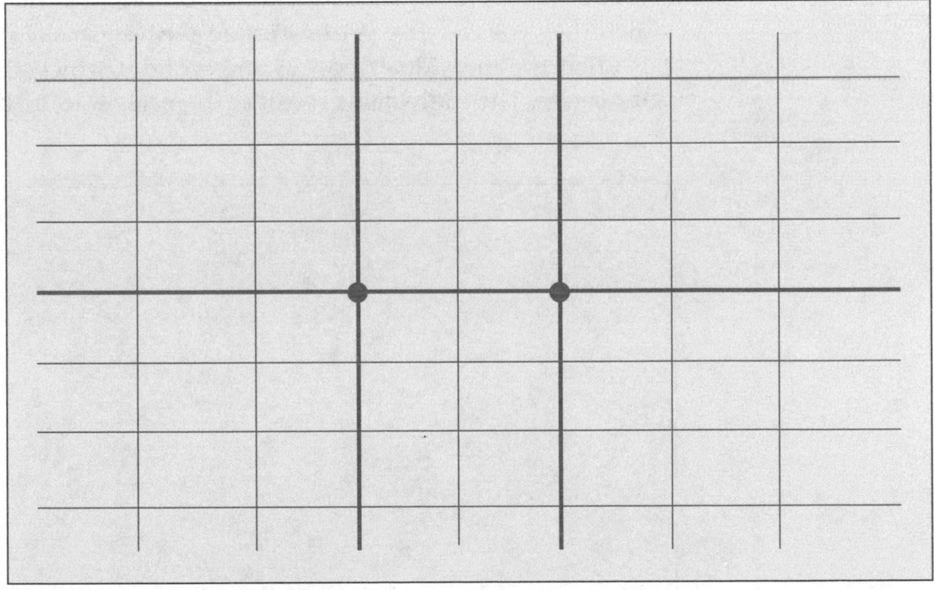

Figure 4.11 The task culture

Source: *Understanding Organizations* by Charles Handy (Penguin Books 1976, Fourth Edition 1993). Copyright Charles Handy 1976, 1981, 1985, 1993. Reproduced by kind permission of Penguin Books Ltd.

The task culture

Handy's **task culture** (*see* Figure 4.11) is more flexible and is often displayed in organisations that frequently undertake work for a variety of customers in a variety of fields. The task culture has close connections with the matrix structure.

Organisations with a task culture undertake very specific problem-solving or troubleshooting tasks as projects for internal or external clients, usually on a consultancy basis. The culture is extremely team oriented, since each task or project requires a fresh team to be constituted containing the required skills and knowledge that will enable the project to be completed successfully. Such a culture is highly flexible, but also expensive. This troubleshooting culture is often brought into an organisation to solve problems that others have found intractable. Members of the project team will exhibit their skills and competence through an extravagant use of resources, as they are used to being able to command anything that they need to get the job done.

The person culture

The fourth of Handy's organisational cultures is the **person culture**, where a set of professionals agree to collaborate to perform a specific service (*see* Figure 4.12). These people could be self-employed, or at least would have little notion of being employees of the organisation in the traditional sense. Rather, they grant the organisation the benefit of their services for which they accept monetary gratitude. They may even avoid the word 'organisation', preferring, as Handy states, terms such as 'practice' to describe the collective activities in which they engage. The person culture centres on the particular professional skills that the individuals possess and without which the organisation could not operate. The individuals consider themselves to be highly valued, unique

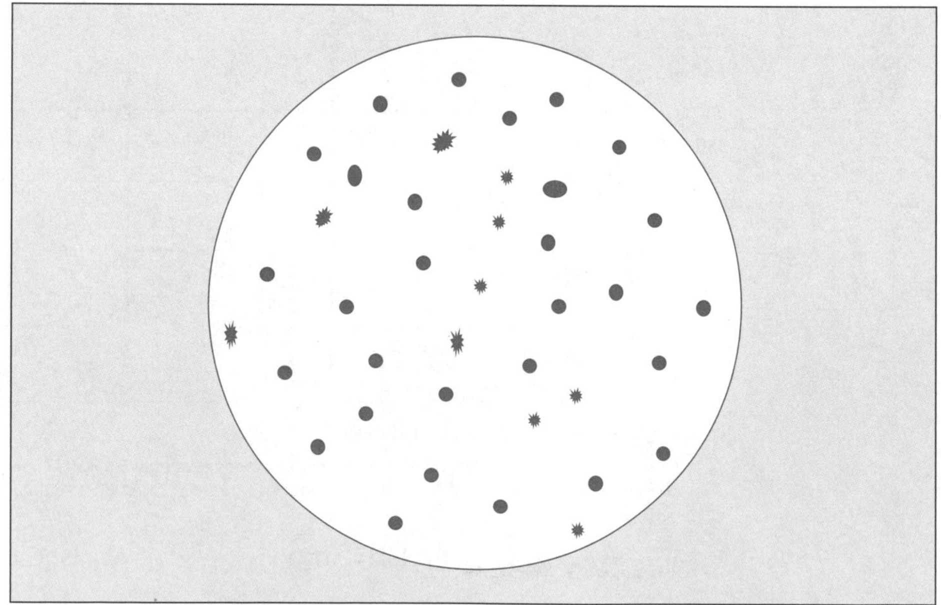

Figure 4.12 The person culture

Source: *Understanding Organizations* by Charles Handy (Penguin Books 1976, Fourth Edition 1993). Copyright Charles Handy 1976, 1981, 1985, 1993. Reproduced by kind permission of Penguin Books Ltd.

and creative. Examples of these person culture professionals would be academics, doctors, solicitors and management consultants.

Check your understanding

Do you understand Handy's definitions of culture?

Check your understanding by defining Handy's four 'cultures' and describing the type of organisation in which each one occurs.

Culture and structure

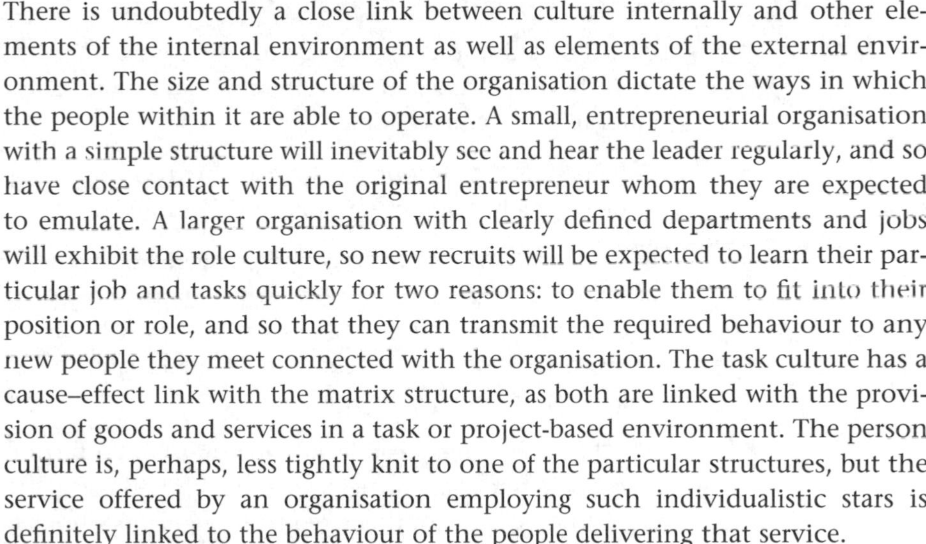

There is undoubtedly a close link between culture internally and other elements of the internal environment as well as elements of the external environment. The size and structure of the organisation dictate the ways in which the people within it are able to operate. A small, entrepreneurial organisation with a simple structure will inevitably see and hear the leader regularly, and so have close contact with the original entrepreneur whom they are expected to emulate. A larger organisation with clearly defined departments and jobs will exhibit the role culture, so new recruits will be expected to learn their particular job and tasks quickly for two reasons: to enable them to fit into their position or role, and so that they can transmit the required behaviour to any new people they meet connected with the organisation. The task culture has a cause–effect link with the matrix structure, as both are linked with the provision of goods and services in a task or project-based environment. The person culture is, perhaps, less tightly knit to one of the particular structures, but the service offered by an organisation employing such individualistic stars is definitely linked to the behaviour of the people delivering that service.

As we will see in Chapter 5, culture in society is generated by us and it also controls us. Whatever their provenance, sociocultural impacts on the human resource inputs to the resource conversion process are key to that organisation's operational abilities. Organisations strive for harmony between the work they have to do, the structure they adopt to make the work possible and the culture of the human resources they employ, so their goals can be achieved. Organisations can be multicultural internally, and may need to be both global in their outlook on business, operating in many markets simultaneously, and local in their sensitivity to the needs and wants of employees and customers in a particular environment. Everyone lives culture, but only the clever are able to manage it.

Check your understanding

Do you understand the relationship between organisational structures and Handy's cultures?

Check your understanding by identifying which structures and cultures most commonly go together.

Summary

This chapter examined different types of organisations, the use of resources by organisations, and the structure and culture of organisations. The following summary covers all aspects of this chapter.

1 Public-sector organisations are owned by local or national government or another publicly owned body. Examples of public-sector organisations include the police, the NHS, colleges and universities.

2 Private-sector organisations are owned by individuals, families or shareholders. Examples of private-sector organisations include Marks & Spencer, HSBC and Cable & Wireless.

3 All organisations take in resources, process them and then deliver outputs which have greater value than the original inputs. This is known as 'organisational resource conversion'.

4 The inputs or resources of an organisation can be grouped into three categories, namely human, tangible and intangible.

5 All organisations have generic or general inputs, processes and outputs. General inputs include employees (human), money (tangible) and information (intangible). Additionally organisations will have specific inputs, e.g. for a university they include lecturers (human), smart boards (tangible) and specialist subject knowledge (intangible).

6 There are three basic legal structures which businesses can adopt. These are the sole trader, a partnership and a limited company. The sole trader business is owned and administered by one person who is personally liable for all the debts of the business. A partnership is where two or more individuals join together in a business venture with each partner having unlimited liability. Therefore, should the partnership result in debt or bankruptcy, each partner can be held liable for the full amount owed by the partnership. The limited company exists as a legal entity in its own right, therefore liability for debts is limited to the amount of issued share capital.

7 There are five generic organisational structures: the simple, functional, divisional, holding and matrix. The simple and functional structures are centralised, with the majority of the power and decision-making responsibility resting with the managing director. The simple structure is found in small businesses selling one or few products. The functional structure is found in organisations which offer a range of related products and services to clearly defined and clearly segmented markets. The divisional structure is decentralised and as such is used by companies offering a wide and diverse range of products and services, compared with companies operating with the more rigid and centralised functional structure. The holding company structure is usually found in large conglomerates with a parent company owning a number of subsidiary

companies. Matrix structures are used in organisations where there are two distinct and important areas of operation needing to be managed and coordinated. Hence matrix structures are often found in large multinational companies, educational establishments and small sophisticated service companies.

8 Culture can be examined by looking at Handy's organisational cultures. The power culture is found in small entrepreneurial organisations, where the owner and employees are members of the 'club', with the owner being the centre of power. In the power culture organisation the simple structure usually occurs. The role culture is found in organisations where everyone has a specific job title and description and knows what it is they are expected to contribute to the organisational mission. The commonly used structures in role culture organisations are the functional and divisional structures. The task culture is commonly found in organisations which undertake team-based problem-solving work. In the task culture organisation the organisational structure is the matrix structure. Finally, the person culture is found in organisations in which a set of professionals agree to collaborate to provide specific services for their clients or customers, i.e. a dentist's practice. Little in the way of a recognised formal structure will exist in such an organisation.

Chapter objectives and the exit case study

While reading this chapter and engaging in the activities, you should have learned how to apply theory and models and analyse situations. The exit case study and the questions which follow will provide an opportunity to assess how well you have met the relevant chapter objectives relating to specific material covered in the chapter.

Chapter objective	Check you have achieved this by
3 Identify and discuss generic organisational structures, their advantages and disadvantages.	answering case study questions 1 and 2.

EXIT CASE STUDY 4.2

Citigroup shakes up operations outside the US

by Peter Thal Larsen and Francesco Guerrera

Citigroup has long grappled with the challenges of managing multiple businesses in many countries around the world. Ever since Citibank adopted – and subsequently abandoned – its famous 'matrix' management structure in the 1970s the bank's executives have debated how to balance cross-border product expertise with local knowledge.

Now Citigroup is once again emphasising the regional. In a wide-ranging shake-up devised by Vikram Pandit, its new chief executive, the bank yesterday announced it was reorganising its operations outside the US into four geographical units, each with its own chief executive.The move comes as Citigroup has continued to add to its senior ranks in London and now has more top global executives in the City than at any other time in its history. Citigroup yesterday said increasing the number of top executives in London would strengthen its 'international perspective and pedigree.' At the same time, Citigroup has split its consumer operations into two divisions – consumer banking and a new division that will bring together all its credit card operations around the world.

While devolving authority and accountability to the regions, Mr Pandit also plans to centralise back-office functions such as human resources and information technology. The move follows an extensive review by Mr Pandit, who is under pressure from shareholders, many of whom argue Citigroup would be worth more if broken up. Citigroup watchers said his move was the latest step in the company's search for a structure that would enable it to harness both its geographical presence and product suite spanning everything from credit cards to derivatives products.

'Some people will say this is change for change's sake. The real issue is not what the matrix is but how they actually go out and engage clients and boost revenues,' a Citigroup watcher said. People close to Mr Pandit said the new regional structure would help to decentralise decisions, eliminate bureaucracy and get closer to clients' needs. It would also mean that executives could be held directly accountable for the financial performance of their region. At the same time, the move to centralise some key back-office functions, such as information technology, would enable Citigroup to slash costs and create synergies across its organisation.

Some Wall Street observers were more sceptical, pointing to some of the problems created by the new structure. In particular, a number of the new regional businesses will be run by executives who have experience of either retail banking or investment banking but not both.

For example, Ajay Banga, the new head of Asia, has a great reputation as a consumer banker but little or no experience of investment banking. Similarly, Bill Mills, who will run Western Europe, the Middle East and Africa, is an investment banker but will take charge of a business that includes branches in Germany as well as Egg, the UK internet bank. George Awad, the highly regarded former GE executive who previously ran Citigroup's consumer banking operations in the region, is expected to move to another job in the organisation. Meanwhile, the appointment of Shirish Apte to a new post of head of Central and Eastern Europe, reporting directly to Mr Pandit and not Mr Mills, could make it harder to coordinate decisions in the European region, especially as Eastern Europe is increasingly becoming integrated with the rest of the continent.

Source: from 'Citigroup shakes up operations outside the US', *The Financial Times*, 1 April 2008 (Larsen, P.T. and Guerrera, F.).

Note: Citigroup's four regions are:
Western Europe, Middle East and Africa
Central and Eastern Europe
Asia Pacific
Mexico and Latin America

Exit case study questions

1. Compare and contrast the possible divisional and matrix structures for Citigroup and illustrate the possible structures for Citigroup with diagrams.
2. Referring to your answer to question 1 identify which advantages and disadvantages of the divisional and matrix structures apply specifically to Citigroup.

s

l organisation'.

ed organisation'.

een organic and external growth?

nal structures.

alised or decentralised?

strengths and weaknesses of the matrix

ised or decentralised?

source conversion'.

ource conversion process chart?

esource inputs? Give one example of each.

culture types.

anisation of the power culture?

evelop a role culture?

rganisations likely to be involved in?

rson culture found?

ment questions

e activities, you should have learned how tions. This means you should be able to ginning of the chapter. The table below by the different questions.

eck you have achieved this by
wering assignment question 1.
wering assignment question 1.
vering assignment questions 2 and 3.
ering assignment question 4.

ree stages of the organ- om the private or public sible to ensure that out- vnership models are most llustrate your answer.

isations in diagrammatic ture on which you have h organisation:
and employing a morning sistants.
ing a range of plants and garden centre is supplied , which also supplies other and. The other gardening r of suppliers. The garden anager, a marketing man- ger.
JK, with offices in Aberdeen, rdiff, Swansea, Nottingham,

res to each of the following tures you have chosen and ch organisation:
ndergraduate BSc students Sc and PhD students under-

ghout the UK, Hong Kong, tly opened a large office in ers consultancy services and business planning.

he role culture. Identify the and role cultures. Comment so on the effects of culture on

pon

e entry case study:

sational structure. Click on

Assignment questions

1 Identify and examine the relationships between the th
isational resource conversion chart. Use examples fr
sector to illustrate your answer. In what ways is it pos
puts are of the highest possible quality? Explain which o
likely to apply to the organisations you have used to

2 Illustrate the structure of each of the following orga
form. Name the type of generic organisational stru
based your structure and explain your choice for ea
- A newsagent's shop in London run by the owner,
paper boy, an evening paper girl and two shop as
- A garden centre on the outskirts of Glasgow sell
gardening equipment to the general public. The
with plants by a commercial nursery attached to i
shops and garden centres in the west of Scotl
equipment is bought in wholesale from a numbe
centre employs 30 people, including a nursery m
ager, an accountant and a human resource man
- A market research company operating across the
Leeds, Southampton, Edinburgh, Manchester, Ca
Glasgow and two offices in London.

3 Apply two of the five generic organisational structu
organisations. Compare and contrast the two stru
comment on which is the more appropriate for ea
- A science department in a university with u
doing full-time three-year degrees and some M
taking postgraduate research qualifications.
- A management consultancy operating throu
Singapore and Malaysia and which has recen
Johannesburg, South Africa. The company off
expertise in the areas of auditing, taxation an

4 Compare and contrast the power culture with
advantages and disadvantages of both the powe
on the link between culture and structure, and al
the organisation's operational abilities.

WEBLINKS available at www.pearsoned.co.uk/ca

- This website is for Lush, the company looked at in th
http://www.lush.com/
- The following site provides an introduction to organ
organisational structures on the table:
http://www.learnmanagement2.com

- The following website shows the organisational structure of the Metropolitan Police of London. Visit the website and click on 'About the met' on the toolbar at the top of the page, then click on 'Structure' in the column on the left-hand-side of the page: **http://www.met.police.uk**

FURTHER READING

These books all contain chapters that look at different aspects of structure.

- Buchanan, D and Huczynski, A (2008) *Organisational Behaviour*, 6th edn, Chapter 14, Harlow: Financial Times Prentice Hall.
- Johnson, G, Scholes, K and Whittington, R (2008) *Exploring Corporate Strategy*, 8th edn, Chapter 12, Harlow: Financial Times Prentice Hall.
- Lynch, R (2006) *Corporate Strategy*, 4th edn, Chapter 16, Harlow: Financial Times Prentice Hall.
- Mullins, L J (2008) *Essentials of Organisational Behaviour*, 2nd edn, Chapter 10, Harlow: Financial Times Prentice Hall.
- Mullins, L J (2007) *Management and Organisational Behaviour*, 8th edn, Chapter 15, Harlow: Financial Times Prentice Hall.
- Palmer, A and Hartley, B (2006) *The Business Environment*, 5th edn, Chapters 6 and 7, Maidenhead: McGraw Hill.
- Thompson, J L and Martin, F (2005) *Strategic Management: Awareness, Analysis and Change*, 5th edn, Chapter 15, London: Thomson Learning.
- White, C (2004) *Strategic Management*, Chapter 12, Basingstoke: Palgrave.
- Worthington, I and Brittion, C (2006) *The Business Environment*, 5th edn, Chapters 2, 7 and 8, Harlow: Financial Times Prentice Hall.

REFERENCES

1. Kavanagh, K and Pfeifer, S (2008) 'Smiths to halve head office staff', *Financial Times*, June 3.
2. Donkin, R (2002) 'Virtuous circle of a two-wheeled wonder', *Financial Times*, October 17.
3. Gore, C, Murray, K and Richardson, B (1992) *Strategic Decision Making*, London: Cassell.
4. Worthington, I and Britton, C (1997) *The Business Environment*, 2nd edn, Harlow: Financial Times Pitman Publishing.
5. Gore et al., op. cit.
6. Worthington and Britton, op. cit.
7. Gore et al., op. cit.
8. Worthington and Britton, op. cit.
9. http://www.arcadiagroup.co.uk
10. Handy, C B (1993) *Understanding Organizations*, 4th edn, London: Penguin.

CHAPTER 5

Culture and organisations

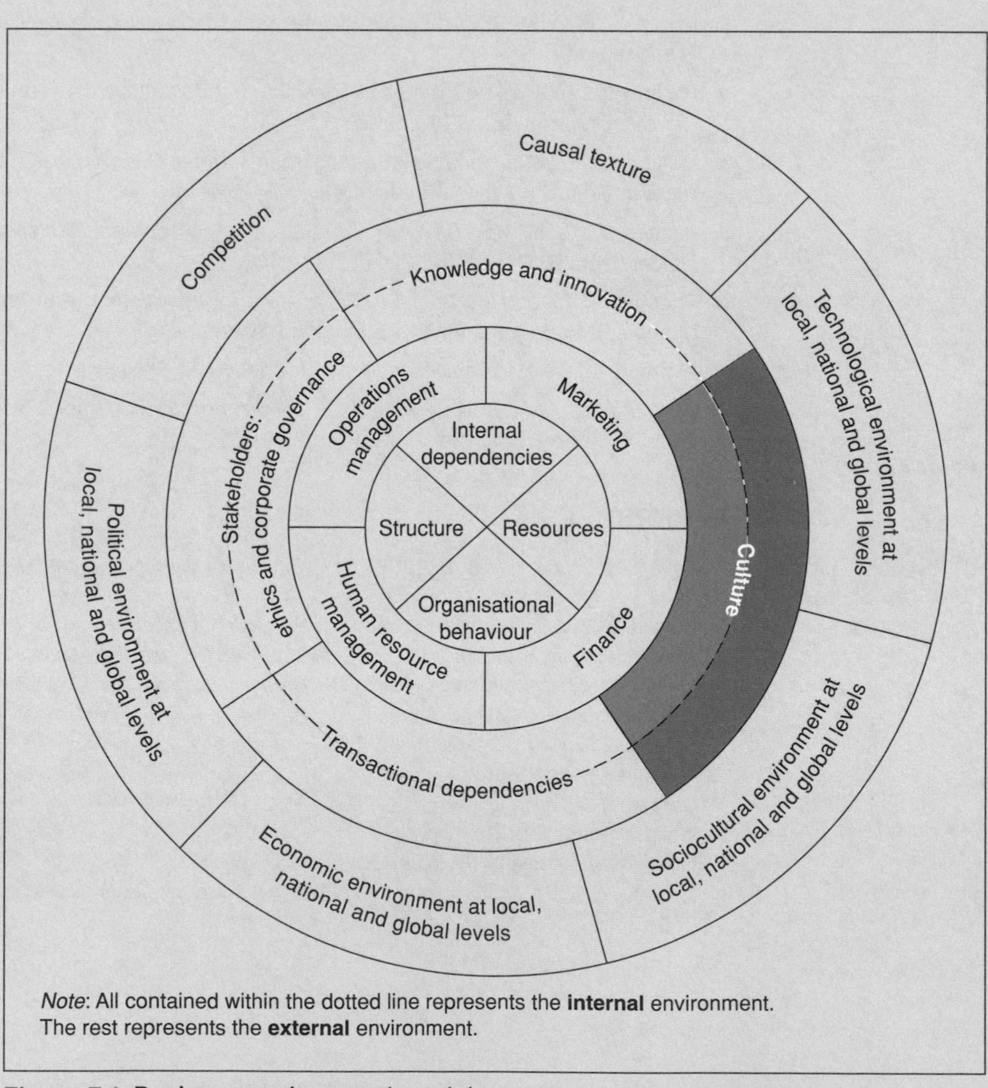

Figure 5.1 Business environment model

Chapter objectives

This chapter provides an overview of individual, national and organisational culture. Culture at the level of the individual is examined. This is followed by the determinants of national culture and organisational culture. Organisational culture is examined by use of the cultural web and Deal and Kennedy's work. Finally, the chapter concludes with a section on managing culture.

Therefore when you have read this chapter and worked through the associated activities you should be able to achieve the objectives specified below.

1 **Define and discuss different types of culture.**

2 **Explain the different approaches to organisational culture.**

3 **Identify and discuss the management of culture.**

This case study summarises the features that have given Microsoft in Europe an open award-winning culture in which people enjoy working and feel comfortable.

→ ENTRY CASE STUDY 5.1

Open culture wins plaudits from staff

The winner of this year's Best Workplace in Europe award for large organisations (those with more than 500 employees) is Microsoft. As reflected in consistently high scores on the Great Place to Work Trust Index survey, the global software company, based near Seattle in the US, excels in maintaining high levels of satisfaction among its 7526 employees, who work in 14 subsidiaries across Europe. This is achieved largely through a loose, informal culture that keeps all employees aligned through a set of core values and various channels of communication.

In their comments for the Trust Index survey, employees noted the culture of openness: 'This is an open organisation that makes you feel at home quickly . . . Higher management is open for a talk when you need advice or feedback . . . They share the goals and results without withholding any information . . . When I just joined, they asked my opinion about what my function should be. They actually did something with my feedback.' Roughly nine out of 10 employees surveyed at Microsoft Netherlands, for example, said they felt that they could 'ask management any reasonable question and get a straight answer'; 95 per cent said that 'management is approachable, easy to talk with' and 91 per cent responded that 'management genuinely seeks and responds to suggestions and ideas'.

Regardless of where they work, Microsoft employees also have fun. The entire company holds a 'Happy Hour' on every second Friday of the month; these events begin with a formal meeting, usually with a presentation by a manager, followed by a chance to eat and drink together. Many of Microsoft's offices have game rooms and lounges, with theatre equipment where employees can pop in and play Xbox video games; employees can also borrow Xboxes to take home with them.

Microsoft also uses its own technological innovations to make its employees' work lives better. Microsoft Netherlands has launched an experimental pilot programme for the company called 'The New World of Work', in which employees helped to redesign their work lives by using the company's IT and mobile devices to make their work lives more flexible.

'Managers and technical experts are freely accessible in many ways,' wrote one European employee. 'You can walk up to their desks, send an instant message, send an e-mail, make a phone call, etc. And their agendas are visible – you can see whether they are available or busy. I've never worked for an organisation as open as this.' Microsoft is also very transparent about its pay model and bonus plans, and encourages a sense of fairness in compensation. All employees are eligible for a bonus, regardless of rank, and everyone is also eligible for stock awards. The company conducts a thorough analysis of pay to ensure there is no difference in the pay between women and men. 'There are equal benefits for all, regardless of position in the company,' wrote one employee comment in the Trust Index survey. *Research by GPTW Europe.*

Source: from 'Open culture wins plaudits from staff', *The Financial Times*, 28 May 2008.

Introduction

The aim of this chapter is to introduce the complex issue of **culture** and its effects on organisational as well as personal efficiency and effectiveness in the workplace. This chapter necessarily combines aspects of a variety of specialisms, each with its own vast literature: sociology, psychology, management development and international business. Here some of the main strands are brought together and interwoven to form a useful framework for the business studies student wanting to examine the impact of culture on the way organisations work.

Culture at different levels of the external environment

Culture at the global level of the external environment

At the global level of the external environment, issues emerge with the interaction of more than one **national culture**. When one leaves one's home country to work, live or even visit abroad, one is faced with different ways of doing things. In Chapter 2, it is mentioned that changes in lifestyle and behaviour can lead to feelings of culture shock, where individuals have to recognise and cope with experiences that are different from those to which they are accustomed. Transferring one's life from Milton Keynes to Tokyo when one is sent off to work in Japan, having grown up in Milton Keynes and never left, is likely to include dealing with culture shock. However, with such a dramatic move we expect things to be different in Tokyo but anticipate we will be able to cope. This may not be the case. The thorough pre-departure orientation of executives posted overseas is one of the key issues in the management of international business operations that can contribute greatly to the success of overseas postings. Nevertheless, it is often overlooked.

Culture at the national level of the external environment

The chapter begins with an illustration of culture in society that aims to explain the concept of culture predominantly at the national level of the external environment. Once an individual's cultural influences from the national level of culture have been identified and analysed, the individual is then furnished with a vocabulary and consciousness that allows them to make coherent comparisons with other nations' cultures, giving that global-level view of cross-cultural issues. National cultural characteristics are adopted by one national grouping and attributed by one nation to others, leading to stereotype and prejudice. National culture, however, belies the fact that within it are local differences between communities, providing a more local perspective to cultural influences on organisations.

Culture at the local level of the external environment

Local cultural issues in the community are complex. The national and local levels of the sociocultural external environment can often intertwine, due to the fact that some people's national characteristics make them the people they are in their local communities. Although we recognise cross-cultural issues between nations, we sometimes do not recognise that equivalent culture shock can occur within the same country. This might have a particular resonance for a full-time student who, at a relatively young age, has left the family for the first time and is attending a higher education course in another part of the country far from home.

As communications, transport and technology have developed in Western industrialised societies in the last 200 years, the provenance of this personal and social identity has changed. A sense of identity used to come from home, family and village, all elements of the local external environment. As society has developed, these local-level sociocultural influences emerge less importantly from influences located at the local level, since personal movement and individual horizons are no longer as limited as they once were. Now, because of the access to travel and communications media, an individual's cultural identity could be said to be much more strongly located at the national level, or has possibly emerged from more global influences, with the strong lifestyle messages emanating from global brands such as Coca-Cola and McDonald's.

Check your understanding

Do you understand the difference between culture at the global, national and local levels of the external environment?

Check your understanding by giving an example of culture at the global, national and local levels of the external enviornment.

Culture inside organisations

It can be seen from the business environment model at the start of this chapter that as well as forming part of the external environment, culture can be identified as existing in the internal environment of the organisation. This chapter therefore also presents models for identifying and analysing internal organisational or corporate culture. Organisations can and do develop their own culture. The open award-winning culture at Microsoft in Europe in which people enjoy working and feel comfortable is summarised in the entry case study for this chapter. **Organisational culture** can emerge as a result of the internal structure of the organisation (*see* Chapter 4) and/or the type of people employed by the organisation.

Where managers identify cultural problems, they may make structural or personnel changes in an attempt to alter the organisational culture and ensure the desired organisational objectives are achieved. Culture can be as explicit or implicit within an organisation as it is in society. Whatever the case, it is vital for the newly recruited employee to understand an organisation's culture if he or she is to learn 'the way we do things around here'. Culture shock can occur within organisations when two whole organisations or sections of organisations are merged and two completely different sets of working practices and behaviours are expected to operate together.

The issues of culture within organisations and culture external to the organisation or in society are brought together in this chapter.

Check your understanding

Do you understand where organisational or corporate culture comes from?

Check your understanding by briefly explaining what may shape organisational culture.

Personal cultural provenance

The topic of culture can begin at the individual level. **Personal cultural provenance** is the origin of an individual's culture. It is another way of saying, 'Where do I get my culture from?' (*see* Figure 5.2). External cultural influences can be identified at a basic level as being the system for understanding and expressing our identity.

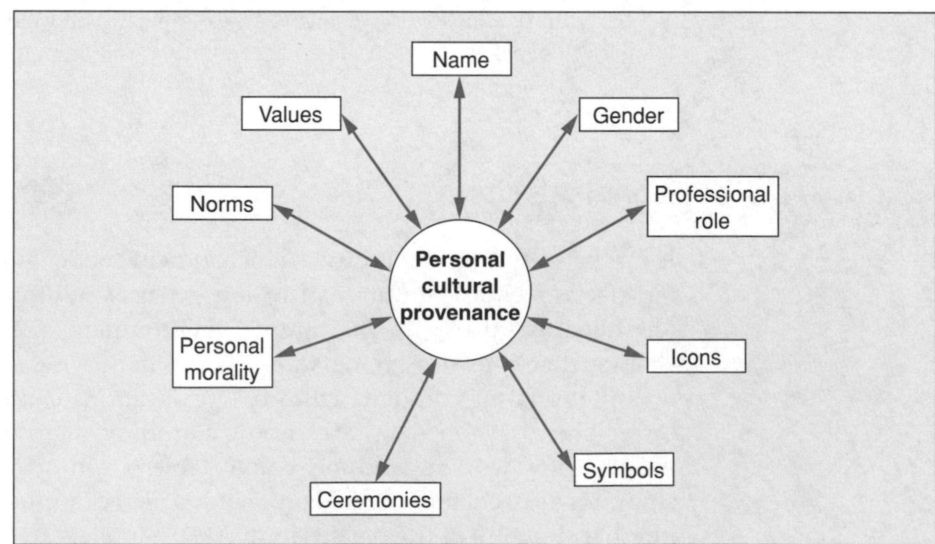

Figure 5.2 Determinants of personal cultural provenance

Identity is a key concept from a sociological perspective, but here we will examine its influence on our sense of who we are, where we come from and how we do things. A first-year university student might identify themselves in all or some of the following ways. These could all be said to be expressions of culture that have their location in sources outside the individual. They are all facets of individual identity that can provide a useful insight to personal cultural provenance.

Name

People respond differently to the question 'Who are you?' according to context. With young people one's own age in an informal setting, it is most probable that the answer would be one of the names given by one's parents, and that the surname or family name would not be given unless specifically asked for later. If people do not use the full name their parents gave them, they use a version of it that they have chosen themselves, e.g. Chris instead of the full Christine or Christopher. Some people prefer to use a new and individual name that they have chosen for themselves. Others have a new name chosen for them by their peers and contemporaries, like a nickname that is a shortened version of their original name, or one based on a particular skill or habit they have, their appearance or their preferences.

Gender

Our gender is a fundamental element of our nature that also determines the cultural experience we have throughout our lives. In whatever ethnic culture we are born, the raising of children conveys clear gender identities and roles, and instils stereotypes and role models from an early age. The simple attribution of qualities or skills to either gender dictates the way a child interacts in society: boys may be discouraged from crying if they are hurt; girls may be taught to cook; boys may learn that fighting in self-defence is 'manly'; girls may be bought dolls to play with. This leads to differences in attitudes towards education as well as variations in treatment of the different genders at school. Ultimately this leads to different expectations of performance and ability in the workplace, and in society in general. Women, for example, bear the brunt of the responsibility for childcare in UK society far more often than fathers. This is a social norm to which most people adhere.

Professional role

When asked 'What do you do?' people identify with their occupation. Despite unemployment statistics, most people have a job and, again, that is a social norm. For the three or four years of full-time undergraduate study, the words 'I'm a student' give many signals as to lifestyle, income bracket now and in the future, level of intelligence, most likely habits and leisure activities and even political affiliations. Replying that one does not have a job can again have many automatic connotations, depending on context: a woman with children who does not work may be praised for having devoted her time to raising the family; a man who has children and no job may be criticised for not providing for them and expecting the state to do it for him.

Icons

A first-year undergraduate who is just beginning to realise how much effort is involved in gaining their higher or further education qualification may respect someone who has already gained the qualification or is at least in the final year. At the same time, many national icons will have resonance. These come in the form of pop and rock stars, actors, television personalities, sports stars and supermodels, with good examples being David and Victoria Beckham. All such icons have influence over culture, as they have a bearing on what we wear, where and how we spend our leisure time, and our attitudes to religion, drugs, politics and a whole host of issues.

Symbols

For many people, an obvious and visible symbol of culture is the clothes they choose to wear. These often make a statement concerning their cultural identity. For example, many students choose to wear jeans and trainers, which are casual and acceptable attire for their relatively informal lifestyle. Other people, including students, may choose to identify more closely with their ethnic background and wear clothing that identifies them as belonging to a particular ethnic culture. In the UK this is often found among people whose families originate from India or Pakistan. Alternatively, people may view their values and professional role as an important part of their cultural identity and choose to symbolise this by wearing smart clothes to work.

Some employers require their employees to identify with the organisation they work for by virtue of the job they do and/or the organisation. For example, hospitals require nursing staff to wear uniforms. This is for two reasons: first, so nursing staff can be easily identified as such; second, because the work nursing staff undertake is sometimes messy and dirty, so a clean, easily washable uniform helps prevent the spread of infection and is preferable to getting one's own clothes dirty. The requirement on nurses to wear uniforms is a long-standing historical example of staff being required to wear clothes that identify them with a particular profession and hospital, since different hospitals often have different coloured uniforms for different types of nurse. Since the 1980s, the idea of a corporate uniform in the UK has caught on with banks, building societies, shops and some restaurants requiring staff to wear corporate uniforms, which identify the individual as working for an organisation with its own organisational culture.

Ceremonies

Most students will attend their graduation ceremony on being awarded their qualification and will enjoy the formal occasion with its mortar board, academic gown and procession before the vice-chancellor of the university to collect their degree certificate bearing the university seal and stamp as proof of the studies they have undertaken. The graduation ceremony marks, in a formal manner, the successful completion of higher education studies, which will in turn influence the professional role one adopts throughout life and hence also an individual's personal cultural provenance.

Personal morality

Cultural influences also give us our innate sense of right and wrong. Thus in our culture it may be wrong to murder, to steal, or for adults to have sex with children. We all agree with this, and those who do not adhere to the code contradict our moral code and our laws, which are the political expression of our moral code. Culture may also express itself in those whom we respect. Therefore, in a free-market or mixed economy, where self-reliance and providing for one's family's material well-being are considered admirable, people who are prudent and work hard all their life are admired. Those who do well for themselves and become 'self-made' by enriching themselves and their families through their own efforts are considered worthy of our respect. Entrepreneurs are admired and ennobled via political honours as people who created wealth for themselves and for the country, and thus have done a public service. Linked to religion, this is embodied in the 'work ethic', where it is seen as a good thing in northern European society to work hard for a living and provide for one's dependants.

Culture also emerges in our system of faith or beliefs, usually through the expression of formal religious belief. Once we have a common system for what we think is right or normal, we then have a language for expressing what we consider to be abnormal. Once we can identify people the same as us, who share our **norms** and **values**, we can then identify those who differ and so do not fit in with our norms and values. This gives rise to another key aspect that culture dictates, which is our moral standards. As we grow we learn society's norms and values, and with this embedded sense of normal and abnormal, right and wrong, we begin to judge the correctness of our own and others' behaviour. Thus the group becomes judgmental, dictating that certain modes of personal action are acceptable while others are not.

An example of this in many societies is the emphasis placed on the family. It is considered the norm, and thus deemed valued and morally correct by the group, for people to form lifelong heterosexual partnerships and to have children within that context. Thus historically the religious and politico-legal systems are designed to support this notion, and marriage, with its accompanying wedding ceremony, marriage certificate and wedding reception, has become the traditional as well as the normal way of demonstrating that this desired legal and social state has been entered into.

Social welfare systems, including pensions, sickness and unemployment benefit, and taxation systems, are also often designed around the notion of a single breadwinner, a dependent adult and dependent children. Backed up by religion, this notion of the nuclear family becomes the moral as well as the social and legal norm. Refer to Chapter 2 for the changing position of the nuclear family in society.

Norms

It is from all the elements in society that affect us as we develop that we obtain our cultural norms and values. Norms are literally ways of behaving or attitudes that are considered to be normal. Norms can be defined as the social rules and guidelines that prescribe behaviour. Furthermore, norms not only affect how an individual behaves but are the shared sense of what a group of individuals thinks is the normal way to behave. Parents begin by teaching them to babies, and children learn them as soon as they come into contact with other children. Thus to behave against the group's norms is abnormal, leading to ostracism.

For many students a key element to take into account when choosing a university is its location and night life. Socialising thus becomes the first-year norm, with the vast majority of first-years going out frequently to pubs, clubs and the students' union with new-found friends and peers. Many town or city-centre pubs and clubs aim to maximise income by cutting entrance and drinks prices on otherwise unpopular nights of the week. They introduce 'student nights', normalising socialising during the week instead of staying in and studying. Late nights and excessive intake of alcohol lead to the inability to rise early the following morning, so missing lectures or seminars becomes a social student norm.

Values

Values are things, people or attitudes that groups of individuals think are important or to be revered or respected. Thus many people might consider that loyalty and honesty between friends, not letting a friend down, not cheating on a boy- or girlfriend or trying to conform to the norms of the peer group are all values that the group would share. Values indicate what society sees as important collectively. While norms may be ways of behaving, values could be qualities that society looks up to.

Thus cultural norms and values contain a variety of elements and attitudes that can be said to come from external influences in society on the individuals who form the group of people constituting that society. These external influences can be formal and explicit, such as the teacher in the classroom rewarding good standards with public praise and a gold star, or punishing bad behaviour with public criticism. Alternatively external influences can be informal and implicit, such as the ways in which children observe adult behaviour and then imitate that, taking their cues from what they perceive around them for the right and wrong way to behave either in the family context or in public.

Check your understanding

Do you understand the determinants of an individual's culture?

Check your understanding by listing the determinants of personal culture and providing an example to illustrate each determinant.

Identifying British culture

The first thing to declare about defining British culture via Hill's[1] determinants of culture (*see* Figure 5.3) is that Britain is not a homogeneous society. It is recognised that there are many cultural groupings populating the British Isles. The United Kingdom of Great Britain and Northern Ireland comprises three countries and one province: England, Wales, Scotland and Northern Ireland. Arguably the Celts in Wales, Scotland and Ireland form the indigenous population of these islands, who suffered Anglo-Saxon, Roman and Norman invasion and conquering as history unfolded. In the twentieth century, there was large-scale immigration from territories within the former Empire and current Commonwealth, making the UK a multiracial society, with large populations whose families originated from the Caribbean, the Indian subcontinent and Hong Kong. Thus any attempt to apply a model such as Hill's to 'British society'

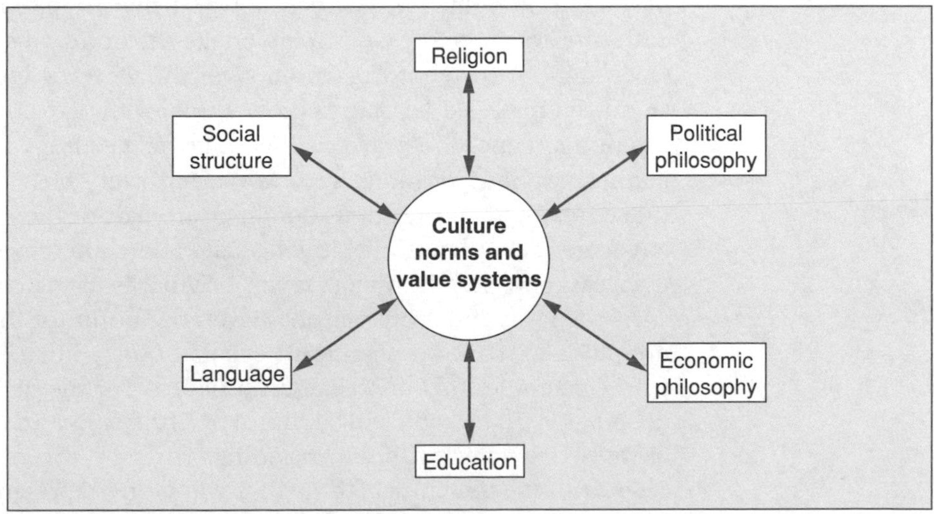

Figure 5.3 The determinants of culture

Source: from *International Business: Competing in the Global Marketplace*, 2nd edition McGraw-Hill Education (Hill, C.W.L. 1994), Reproduced with the permission of The McGraw-Hill Companies.

is liable to be relevant to some British people and irrelevant to others. This supports the notion that the study of culture in society and organisations is extremely complex.[2] Certain elements included in Hill's model (*see* Figure 5.3) may be irrelevant to the individual reader; however, it is expected that one can consider each determinant in relation to one's own personal cultural provenance and arrive at an individual conclusion about how one has been influenced by the acquisition of culture from external influences.

Religion

Many people have some kind of religious faith or have been brought up following the edicts of one of the world's major religions, be it Christianity, Islam, Judaism, Hinduism or Buddhism. The UK has a formal, state religion built into its constitutional monarchy, referred to as an established religion. It is a Protestant Christian religion, divided into churches representing the countries of the Union: England, Scotland, Wales and Northern Ireland. There are many other religions, and a long history of political struggle between the dominant Protestant faith and the previous historically dominant Catholic faith. In addition there are Methodists, Baptists and all the religions of the UK's immigrant communities. However, neither multiculturalism nor ecumenicalism is reflected in the country's political institutions, as the current Queen, who is head of state as well as head of the Anglican churches, has the formal title 'Defender of the Faith', meaning the established church, and not of all the faiths within the country. Prince Charles, heir to the throne, has stated that it is his intention to be enthroned 'Defender of Faith' in an effort to be more inclusive of all Britain's many religions.

Because of the establishment of the church, it is the norm for religion to play a part in all major state occasions. At the coronation of a new monarch, oaths are sworn before God to undertake the duties of sovereign. At the State Opening of Parliament the Queen gives the Queen's Speech, where she reads aloud the intended legislative programme of the government elected to govern in her name, and prayers are said. Royal weddings and state funerals take place in religious locations, such as Westminster Abbey or St Paul's Cathedral. Indeed, these major religious buildings are part of the country's cultural heritage and tourist landscape, linking state and church ever more tightly. There is at least one church in most towns or villages in the country.

At the local and more personal level, the norm for many families (though not all) is to mark the significant events of life – birth, marriage and death – with ceremonies that are religious in nature. For the majority of these people the religion in question will be a form of Christianity. In this tradition, a baby's birth is celebrated with a christening, whereby the new infant is formally inducted into the church through a ceremony representative of the Biblical ritual washing known as baptism. Godparents are appointed to offer spiritual and moral guidance, as well as having the functional role of caring for the children should the parents die. Other religions have their own similar ceremonies to welcome newly born family members, including, in many cultures, ritual circumcision of male babies. Even those who have grown up in a religious tradition but have rejected it still feel the need to celebrate the birth of a child with family and friends through some kind of secular naming ceremony following a recognised pattern, even though the mention of any God is omitted.

Similarly, the pair bonding that marks human relationships is institutionalised in celebrating the joining together of couples through legal marriage and wedding ceremonies. The Christian image of this religious ceremony has become the international symbol for marriage: the white dress of the bride and the church building as a backdrop. In the UK until recently there were only two places licensed to hold legal marriage ceremonies: register offices and churches. This changed in the early 1990s to allow marriages to take place in any suitable venue possessing a licence to hold weddings, which includes venues such as hotels and stately homes.

Finally, it is unusual in the UK to mark the passing of a relative or friend without the involvement of Christianity. Funerals, even if they do not consist of ritual burial of the corpse within consecrated ground such as a churchyard, are 'normally' presided over by a priest who invokes the care of God for the individual who has entered Heaven. This is the case even at municipal crematoria. It should be noted that in the UK at the end of the twentieth century, participation in organised religion on a regular basis was low. Religion also has a significant influence on language, as outlined below.

Politics

The link between culture and nationalism, and by implication politics, has been mentioned above. However, the political system under which we grow up has explicit and implicit effects on our personal cultural norms and values. The UK is a liberal democracy with a largely conservative tradition. While the monarchy's power has been limited over the centuries, and universal suffrage and the rule of Parliament have emerged, this has been achieved with the agreement and deference of the people and not as a result of large-scale popular revolt, apart from the Civil War of 1642–52. Following Oliver Cromwell's short-lived republic, the monarchy was restored in 1660 but severely restricted and subjugated to Parliament from 1688 onwards.

There are traditions that instil in the UK's citizens certain standards of civic behaviour and conduct. We consider democracy to be the norm, and that political life should be conducted with fairness and justice, decisions being made on a majority basis. We expect fair play, equity of access to power and that everyone's views will be taken into account.[3]

Nevertheless, there are some differences in approach to the state's institutions, with particular activist or terrorist factions taking more direct and undemocratic action in an attempt to achieve their goals, for example the terrorist groups in Northern Ireland. On the surface, it seems that the UK's political culture is largely homogeneous and respectful of power and authority. It could be said that the national consensus started to break down at the end of the twentieth century, with votes in favour of devolution from central government in Westminster to regional Parliaments for Scotland, Wales and Northern Ireland. Kingdom writes: 'The geographical, class, gender and racial cracks in the social fascia are only smoothed over with political Polyfilla and concealed beneath unwritten constitutional wallpaper.'[4]

Economics

The UK is a regulated free market, as discussed in Chapter 2. This provides a set of economic norms and values that affect the way people behave and what they consider to be right or wrong behaviour. This was particularly evident in the Western media reporting of the changes in Eastern Europe when the Communist governments lost power and former planned economies introduced free-market reforms. This was reported in many media as the 'normalisation' of their economies, rather than changing from one economic system to another, because now these countries were beginning to do things the way 'we' do and so were now deemed to be normal.

Education

The way in which we are educated (or, in some societies, whether we are educated) affects our comprehension and synthesis of the world around us. The word 'educate' originates from the Latin meaning 'to lead or draw out', and in Western societies the focus for education is to draw out intelligence and understanding that are deemed to be inherent in all. The Western tradition, founded in that of ancient Greece, is to teach people how to think, question, debate and argue their point with philosophical underpinning and supporting individual freedom to differ.

Language

When considering the effects of language on the development of culture,[5] there is a fundamental philosophical aspect to consider that cannot be resolved in this text: does language control thought or does thought control language? If language controls thought, then the way we use our language has some sort of control over the attitudes we hold and the norms and values that underpin our culture. If thought controls language, then the language we use is a symbol of our cultural norms and values.

In fact, when examining British culture it is possible to identify both. Aspects of its historical, political and religious development are evident everywhere in its language. First, the fact that until recent decades all British languages other than English were suppressed is evidence of English colonisation (Wales is now bilingual). Nevertheless, English is itself an impure language, having origins as it does in the Scandinavian languages spoken by the Angles,

German spoken by the Saxons, Latin spoken by the Romans and French spoken by the Norman conquerors. So we have a formal, high-register language full of polysyllabic words of Latin or French origin, reflecting the language of our rulers, while we have more Anglo-Saxon[6] monosyllabic slang and swear words, reflecting the social position of the indigenous peasants. Even the language of food contains class distinctions: beef, mutton and pork for the meat eaten by Norman aristocrats, but ox, sheep and swine for the animals tended by the Anglo-Saxon serfs. Due to this heritage, when inventing words for new technologies English reverts to scholarly words of Latin or Greek origins, while German or Chinese simply use words to describe the function of the new invention. Thus television (which caused a scandal at its coinage for being a hybrid of Greek and Latin) comes from tele ('far') and vision ('sight'), while in German the original word was simply *Fernsehen* ('far seer') and in Chinese it is *dianshi* ('electric sight'). Either of these would seem ridiculous in English.

In UK society, however, it is the way in which an individual uses the English language that says more about them than the mere words being used. As Britain remains a class-oriented society, dialect and accent can be a social advantage or disadvantage, depending on the context. There are different types of English that are taken as the standard or benchmark language: the Queen's English, Oxford English or BBC English. These are in fact not the standard language but are particular class or regional accents that are considered to reflect 'received pronunciation' (RP), or the way we ought to speak. The Queen's English is an aristocratic accent that evolved from her German ancestors, the Hanoverian Georges (I, II, III and IV), whose German accents the English courtiers imitated in order that their sovereign did not feel alien when in England. Oxford English refers to the English exhibited in the dictionaries and grammars written by scholars at one of the UK's oldest universities, a seat of learning that by definition has been invested with the authority to set the national standard. The national broadcaster, the British Broadcasting Corporation (BBC), has changed in its attitude towards accent over its 75 years of broadcasting. In the early days, only the King's English was broadcast across the nation and Empire. In fact, the King was one of the early broadcasters, using the new technology to send messages to his subjects around the world. During the Second World War, broadcaster Wilfred Pickles read the news bulletins and was deemed to have a strong Yorkshire accent for the time, although to the modern listener he sounds as 'posh' as all of his contemporaries. Today, regional accents are commonplace among presenters.

Nevertheless, accent is a passport giving access to different milieux in UK society. If you speak in an accent that sounds upper class, you are immediately accepted by 'posh' people into their society. If you speak colloquially and with a strong regional accent, you are accepted in that part of the country as 'one of us' but may be shunned elsewhere. Some accents have national reputations: Scottish or Yorkshire people sound trustworthy and reassuring; people from Birmingham are widely deemed to be amusing and less intelligent. These language and culture relationships are being used by large companies when selecting locations for national call centres for their direct telephone services. Thus as soon as an individual opens their mouth to speak, those around them make immediate value judgements about social class, profession, education, status, ability and personality.

Social structure

British social structure has changed vastly over the last century. It is now a more fluid, dynamic and **meritocratic** society, with possibilities for social mobility through the classes depending on effort and ability. Up to the end of the Second World War, the British population knew its place in society and did not expect to undergo social change: once an aristocrat, always an aristocrat; once a manual labourer, always a manual labourer. As post-war social attitudes changed, so did traditional attitudes to authority, the family, our elders, and the more disadvantaged members of society such as the poor or the ill.

An aspect of social structure that has changed considerably is the family. Grown-up children move away from home and settle down in other parts of the country or even the world, following economic trends and the necessity to work. This means that they have no help with childcare from their parents, and the parents have no family members to care for them in their old age. This puts pressure on society in terms of providing healthcare for the elderly and childcare for pre-school toddlers. As divorce increases and people marry for the first time later in life, the number of single person households is growing. In 2005 in England there were 7 million one person households compared with 3 million in 1971 and a predicted 9 million single person households in 2021.[7] This affects both the way social structures operate and government reaction to taxation, healthcare provision and education. In addition, the UK at the start of the twenty-first century is a far more informal place than ever before. Attitudes on the part of young people towards their peers and their elders are more **egalitarian** and tolerant than at any time in the past.

Applying Hill's model in a Chinese context

The value of Hill's model (*see* Figure 5.3) is as a framework to help us consider what our culture is and how it affects who we are and how we behave as individuals in society. To aid in this understanding, it is now reapplied to a generic Chinese cultural context.

As part of this it is necessary to examine the issue of what it means to be Chinese and what being foreign means to a Chinese person. In the standard Chinese language the most common name for China is *zhong guo,* meaning 'middle country'. Thus China is the country at the centre of its universe, which equates with many cultures' own view of the world. Logically, everything that is not inside the middle country is outside it, hence the Chinese term for foreigner is *wai guo ren*, literally 'outside country person'. This can be compared to traditional Chinese life, especially in the countryside, where people are immobile and generations live and die in one locale. Anyone not from the same village or town is known as *wai ren* or 'outsider'. It can further be observed that *wa guo ren* is habitually used to mean 'white people'. The traditional image of foreigners for Chinese, often seen in the media, is of a *wai guo ren* with white skin, blond hair and blue eyes. When referring to other races, Chinese will usually specify, for example, 'Japanese', 'black people' or 'Arabs'. In the wider Chinese diaspora the term *wai guo ren* is used to refer to non-Chinese (and specifically white people), irrespective of whether the latter are in China or not.

Chinese remain Chinese and *wa guo ren* (white people) are *wai guo ren* (foreigners) even when nationality is shared or the white people in question are the indigenous population. Chinese never refer to themselves as *wai guo ren*. In contrast, English native speakers use nationality as a determinant, and are comfortable with referring to themselves as 'foreigners' when they are in another country.

After 'Liberation' (the Communist Party takeover in 1949), most foreigners left China, apart from some committed to the revolution's aims. From 1949 to the mid-1980s any foreigners visiting for business or pleasure were closely supervised by cadres of the Foreign Affairs Office to maintain an official filter between the bourgeois, capitalist outsiders and any Chinese people with whom they had contact. Interactions between foreigners and Chinese became carefully crafted and scripted events designed to put both parties as little at ease as possible. During the Cultural Revolution (1966–76), Chinese were persecuted to death for having had contact with foreigners or even for having relatives abroad, thus being culpable in the eyes of the Red Guards of bourgeois rightism and counter-revolution. While recent years have seen the normalisation and humanisation of Sino-foreign relationships, with many Sino-foreign marriages resulting, there is still to some extent a psychological hangover from the fervently anti-foreign dogma of the post-Liberation years that can affect the operational effectiveness of foreign workers in China.

Religion

The main religions affecting social and economic behaviour are Confucianism, Buddhism, Islam and Christianity. Attitudes towards issues of crime and punishment, sex and the family, the position and respect for the aged and how society cares for them can be set by ideological dictate. Buddhism, with its belief in reincarnation, leads the Chinese to be quite fatalistic in their view of the individual's importance in the grand scheme of things. Religious influences are stronger in Chinese societies outside China than within it, where religion has been banned and punished heavily in certain periods since 1949.

Politics

Irrespective of political colour, political systems in most Chinese societies are largely authoritarian, non-democratic or oligopolistic. In mainland China there is no aspect of life on which politics has not had a huge impact at some time during the second half of the twentieth century. It is hard, looking from the perspective of the West, to imagine a society where even the morning delivery of milk could depend on your having demonstrated the correct ideological stance at the workplace's weekly political study meetings. Indeed, the idea of a political study meeting at all in the workplace would seem inappropriate.

Economics

Early entrepreneurs tackled the problem of business with the People's Republic of China (PRC) or 'New China' unaided by source materials, secondary data or effective diplomatic relations. Doing business with the Chinese was a very unfamiliar process and experience, for two main reasons. First, the system, with its interminable bureaucracy, vertical integration and complete lack of flexibility, interspersed with periods of complete economic breakdown due to the supremacy of political dogma, made coping with officialdom difficult for a Western businessperson. Second, the culture, with the uniformly and impossibly inscrutable Chinese people and their unwritten, impregnable, yet unbreakable rules of engagement, led to paralysis through analysis on the part of foreigners interacting with them. Old China hands learned their way around through trial, error, good luck and good judgement.

The Deng era, with burgeoning official foreign trade organs at central and local levels, saw the rapid growth of the number of organisations empowered to deal directly with overseas organisations. Hence new entrants to the marketplace in China have been able to use the services of consultants, 'how to' guides, agencies, information bureaux and government departments to seek the appropriate Chinese opposite number. While the system grows ever more complex as the volume of trade increases and hurdles are undoubtedly still numerous, there are now mechanisms in place to help foreigners understand and manipulate the system in order to meet corporate and individual needs on both sides. Even though there is increasing economic liberalisation, the economic systems in China and elsewhere in Confucian societies have featured interventionist government macroeconomic policies to promote stable and rapid economic growth. It was only after the economic crises of late 1997/early 1998 that this interventionist stance began to be questioned.

Education

Education is highly valued and greatly prized. Parents spend a large amount on ensuring the education of their offspring and their advancement to professional success and social security. This is a legacy from imperial days, where the Mandarins ruling China on the Emperor's behalf were all scholars who had passed rigorous entrance examinations. Confucian teaching also respects and values education and intelligence. The teachings of the ancient Chinese philosopher Confucius left a huge legacy in China, Japan and Korea as well as in Chinese societies in other countries. The tradition of master and pupil is much more didactic, in that the teacher is always right and should be copied and emulated by the student at all times.

The role of and respect for formal education, training and qualifications remains strong in most countries of the Far East. There are clear expectations that families will provide the funding and support for education and the student will put in the hard work necessary to succeed.

Language

Chinese is one language where the written form is not only a tool for communication but an art form as well. Chinese is an ideographic not an alphabetic language, meaning that each word is a picture. Having a good handwriting or calligraphic style is the sign of a good scholar and thus the sign of a good ruler. Otherwise, Chinese is a language of simple structure and ambiguous meaning. Unlike English, the fewer the number of words, the more formal the language being expressed. Thus each word has many meanings and is open to the interpretation of the individual, and many nuances.

Social structure

The regional socialisation process in the Far East is strong and dominant, perhaps much more so than in Europe and North America. Social structures are still rigid and well defined, giving everyone a clear picture of their position and role in society. This fixed view of outsiders, described earlier in this chapter, comes from a cultural source as well as from the fact that the Chinese state classifies the nationality and ethnicity of its citizens automatically at birth. China's 1.2 billion citizens are categorised officially into 56 ethnic groups,[8] 96 per cent of the population being Han Chinese and 4 per cent divided into 55 official ethnic minorities. This is of key importance to the people themselves,[9] as Han Chinese are bound by the 'one child only' population control policy, while ethnic minorities may have two children.

Check your understanding

Do you understand the determinants of national culture?

Check your understanding by listing the determinants of national culture and providing an example to illustrate each determinant.

The determinants of organisational culture

We now move from personal to organisational culture. If an organisation is to function effectively it must develop a coherent culture. This is supported by Deal and Kennedy,[10] who identify two types of culture: strong and weak. The strong culture is highly cohesive and coherent and has a system of informal rules, which indicates to people exactly what is expected of them, so that employees will know how to react and what to do in given situations. In contrast, people operating in a weak culture, one lacking in cohesiveness and coherence, will waste time working out what to do and how to do it.

The entry case study for this chapter indicates how Microsoft has achieved a strong culture with an open approach to the working environment, communication, rewards, benefits and the use of technology to improve the working life of staff.

The Johnson and Scholes cultural web[11] identifies and draws together many aspects of organisational culture: 'The cultural web is a representation of the taken-for-granted assumptions or paradigm of an organisation and the physical manifestations of organisational culture.'[12] The determinants of organisational culture are displayed around the outside of the cultural web and include routines and rituals and power structures (*see* Figure 5.4). The paradigm is the 'taken-for-granted assumptions' concerning the organisation or the perceived characteristics of the organisation and is shown in the centre of the cultural web diagram (*see* Figure 5.4). This section goes on to examine the six determinants of organisational culture. When applying the cultural web to organisations,

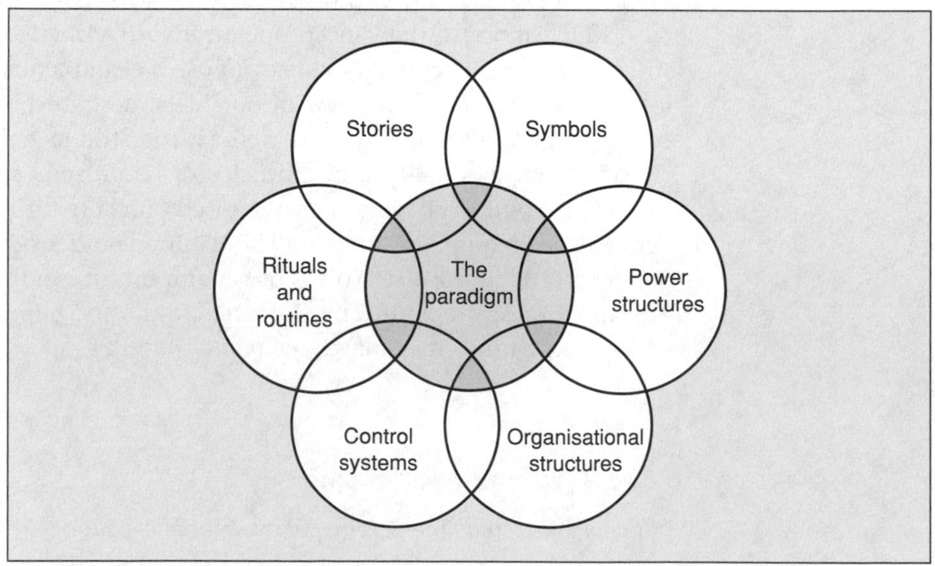

Figure 5.4 The cultural web

Source: Johnson, G and Scholes, K (1999) *Exploring Corporate Strategy*, 5th edn, Prentice Hall Europe.

the determinants should be identified first and then considered when determining the paradigm.

Routines and rituals

Routines (*see* Figure 5.4) are the scheduled and deliberate practices carried out as a matter of course and forming the habits of day-to-day life in an organisation. In normal circumstances routines ensure the smooth running and operation of the organisation. In organisations with a strong culture, routine behaviour is clearly spelt out and allows employees, particularly new employees, to know and understand 'the way we do things around here'. A good example of an organisation where routine is important is a fast-food restaurant such as Burger King and/or a chain restaurant such as Pizza Hut. Here the actions employees have to take in preparing the food and taking orders are explicitly laid down, e.g. frying the french fries for exactly seven minutes or always asking the customer if they would like side orders of garlic bread or salad with their pizza.

Rituals in organisational life are used to reinforce the routines and 'the way things are done around here'. Rituals can be formal events that employees are subjected to such as induction courses, training courses or periodic assessments to ensure an employee's performance is up to scratch and conforming to the routine way of doing things. Rituals may also be more informal in nature, for example the office Christmas party, drinks in the pub on Friday at the end of the working week, or gossiping around the office coffee machine. However, they still promote the common routine of 'the way we do things around here'.

Stories

In any organisation, **stories** will be told by employees to each other, to new recruits who join them and to others outside the organisation. The stories represent the organisation's history and typically highlight significant events and characters in its past. They characteristically focus on the achievements and failures of the organisation and the individuals involved, be they heroes or villains. Stories summarise the meaningful and key aspects of an organisation's past and tell people what counts as acceptable conduct today.

Symbols

The **symbols** present in an organisation can be many and varied and often symbolise someone's position in the organisation or how much that individual is valued by the organisation. Symbols can include titles, office size, company car and salary scales, all indicating the power and value that an individual possesses with respect to an organisation. In long-established organisations like the Civil Service, many symbols will exist and indicate the power and importance of employees. In such organisations there will be a rigid structure, comprising different jobs at different grades with different salaries, with office accommodation directly dependent on job, grade and salary. Individuals with better offices, higher salaries and further up the hierarchy will have greater power and may be perceived to be of greater value to the organisation. In contrast, a newer organisation, such as an architects' practice which has all staff on performance-related pay, all working in an open-plan office, displays a different culture by virtue of the symbols that do or don't exist. The message in such an organisation is that all employees are equally valued and succeed on merit.

Power structures

Power structures evolve in organisations over time and consist of individuals with power who all share a common set of beliefs and values that underpins the way they work together. Membership of the power structure is often determined by seniority and/or length of service in an organisation. Alternatively, power may be based on expertise, with a common source of power being technical expertise that is in short supply and highly valued in the organisation. This may occur particularly in firms where innovation is a key success factor (*see* Chapter 9). This type of power base will be strengthened if there are many valued experts who group together to promote or resist particular issues in the workplace.

Organisational structure

The structure that an organisation adopts will determine where the power exists within it (*see* Chapter 4). For example, in the simple structure the power rests with the owner/manager and in the divisional structure power rests with the board of directors and the divisional managers. The location of power in an organisation will define the power relationships and designate the fundamental linkages between the seats of power and control. Nevertheless, in any formal organisational structure there will exist smaller, more informal structures and networks, which are equally important to the culture of the organisation.

Control systems

The term 'control systems' denotes systems for control, measurement and reward within the organisation. The systems that an organisation puts in place and monitors indicate what is important to it. Control systems include financial control and accounting systems such as cashflow and budgeting, which are systems for regulating expenditure. Measurement systems examine the output of organisations and their efficiency and effectiveness. The output of an organisation can be the amount of product manufactured or the throughput of customers. Efficiency and effectiveness relate to the aspects of time and resources used to produce the final output/throughput (*see* Chapter 9). In some organisations the control of expenditure will be more important than the measurement of output; in others, both will be equally important.

The reward system in an organisation will determine how employees behave with respect to their work and jobs. A reward system that pays for a large volume of work will elicit very different behaviour to a reward system that pays for high-quality work.

Check your understanding

Do you understand the determinants of organisational culture?

Check your understanding by listing the determinants of organisational culture and providing an example to illustrate each determinant.

Deal and Kennedy's organisational cultures

Deal and Kennedy[13] examined hundreds of companies and claim to have identified four generic cultures: **tough-guy macho**, **work hard/play hard**, **bet your company** and **process**. These cultures are defined by two factors in the marketplace: the degree of risk associated with the organisation's activities and the speed at which the organisation and its employees receive feedback on their performance. These cultures are summarised in Figure 5.5. Deal and Kennedy also acknowledge that no organisation will exactly fit one of their four generic cultures and some may not fit any at all.[14] However, they maintain that such a framework is a useful initial step in assisting managers to recognise the culture of their organisation.

Tough-guy macho culture

In organisations exhibiting the tough-guy macho culture, it is customary for staff to take high risks and receive rapid feedback on the effectiveness of their

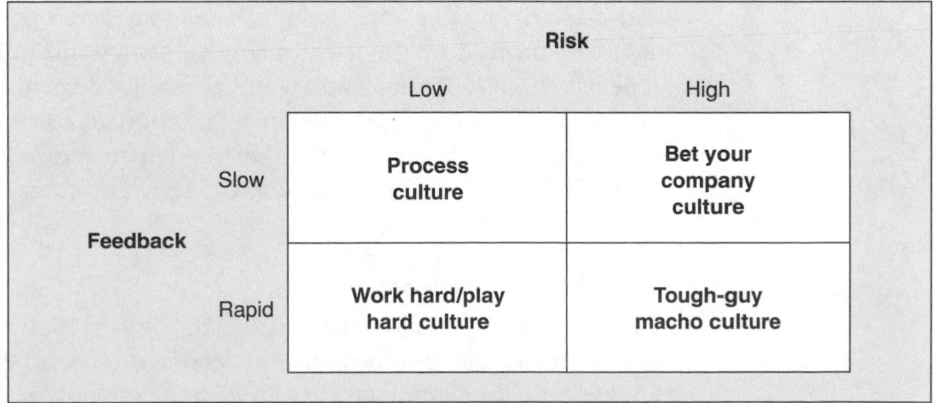

Figure 5.5 Deal and Kennedy's organisational cultures

actions. Deal and Kennedy indicate that police departments, surgeons, management consultants and the entertainment industry may all exhibit a tough-guy macho culture. The key characteristics of this culture are rapid speed and the short-term nature of actions. This results in great pressure being placed on the individual culture to achieve success in the short term. This is often illustrated by such organisations having young staff achieving financial rewards early in life if they are successful.

The consequences of this type of culture are that burn-out is common and failure is harshly condemned, often by dismissal. Those who do succeed and avoid burn-out often do so by taking a tough stance with regard to their work and their colleagues, and pace themselves accordingly. This results in internal rivalries occurring, which in turn produce tension and conflict between staff, which is normally expected in these organisations. An organisation with this type of culture achieves quick returns from its high-risk environment, but it finds it difficult to achieve success via long-term investment. This is due to rapid staff turnover, along with very limited cooperation and tolerance between staff. Hence the creation of an organisation with a strong and cohesive culture is almost impossible if the predominating culture is tough-guy macho.

Work hard/play hard culture

Organisations for which there is low risk and quick feedback on performance are those with a work hard/play hard culture. Sales along with a sense of fun and action are key characteristics of this culture. Typical work hard/play hard organisations include both manufacturing and service companies, such as fast-food and computer companies. In both types of organisation the risks are small; in a service provision organisation failing to sell a single item will not severely damage the salesperson, and in a manufacturing organisation examinations and inspections will ensure that departures from the normal standard of product are minimised.

Quick feedback on performance is easily obtainable in such an organisation, e.g. whether staff have achieved sales or production targets. Hence organisations with a focus on sales and meeting targets are often customer oriented. This may be reinforced by the use of contests, games and rallies that focus on the achievement of individuals and teams of employees and are meant to motivate staff to succeed. There may be an inclination to focus on the sales volume achieved by individuals or teams, at the expense of service/product quality, and thus there is a focus on the short-term rather than the long-term future.

Bet your company culture

The bet your company culture organisation takes high risks and waits a long time for the response to actions and decisions. This is because the investment is huge and long term and the outcome is seen in the long-term future. Examples include the manufacture of aircraft as undertaken by Boeing, or the finding and refining of oil as in British Petroleum. Hence there is an enormous amount of detailed planning that has to take place, evidenced in the ritualistic business meetings that occur. Decision making in this culture focuses on the future and is top down, reinforcing the hierarchical nature of the culture. The person who fares best and survives in this type of culture is the mature worker with a respect for authority and technical ability. They will also possess the skills to operate effectively in a team with similar-minded people and to cope under pressure.

The result of this type of working environment is that many high-quality innovations and scientific discoveries are made. However, innovation and scientific breakthroughs are long-term goals and this makes such companies vulnerable in an economy and to a stock market that are more interested in short-term profit and success. Nevertheless, it could be that companies that innovate are those most needed by Western economies.

Process culture

The process culture is a low-risk and slow-feedback culture. The response to actions and decisions seems to take forever. This type of culture is typically seen in the civil service, public-sector organisations, banks and insurance companies. The lengthy feedback time means that employees focus on how something is done, i.e. the process, rather than the reason for doing it or the outcome. The employees who survive best in such a culture are methodical and punctual. In the process culture there will be significant emphasis on job titles and roles and this will be symbolised by the size of someone's office and the style of office furniture that the rigid, strict and hierarchical organisation will allow that individual. This illustrates one further point concerning the process culture: the position that a person occupies determines the amount of power that individual wields. This is the type of culture in which remaining with the organisation and enduring will be rewarded by long-service awards.

The process culture is most successful if the organisation operates in a predictable and stable environment and is perhaps likely to struggle if asked to react quickly to rapidly changing circumstances, as the organisation lacks the creativity and vision to do so. An alternative view is that such a culture offers a balance to the other three cultures, which all have either high risk and/or rapid feedback.

Check your understanding

Do you understand the different types of culture which may exist in organisations?

Check your understanding by naming the four Deal and Kennedy cultures and briefly summarising their key characteristics.

Understanding and managing culture

An understanding of personal cultural provenance and national culture is important, as it allows managers to develop the cultural awareness that is needed in the world of work in the twenty-first century. This understanding of personal and national culture allows today's employee to appreciate the differing personal and national cultures of employees in a firm in a foreign country or individual consumers in a foreign country. They may have different expectations and different needs and wants (*see* Chapter 8) to those in the home market. Differences in national culture will be reflected in the way that organisations collaborate with one another in the international arena and evaluate the outcome of their activities. The compatibility of national cultures may influence an organisation as to the nationality of a collaborating partner company. The management of corporate or organisational culture is as important as that of individual and national culture and hence has a role to play in the overall management of culture. This is looked at earlier in this chapter.

Managing culture in the international arena

Evaluating success

The way in which organisations evaluate their success or failure can reflect their home country and culture – *see* Figure 5.6. Companies with the USA as their home country are most likely to measure performance on the basis of key quantitative measures such as profit, market share and other key financial benefits. In contrast, Japanese companies evaluate success or failure via skills improvement and how that has strengthened the organisation's strategic position. In European companies a balance between profit and the meeting of social objectives is more often sought.[15] The existence of such variations in the way performance is evaluated can produce difficulties if two collaborating companies have very different expectations regarding how success or failure is

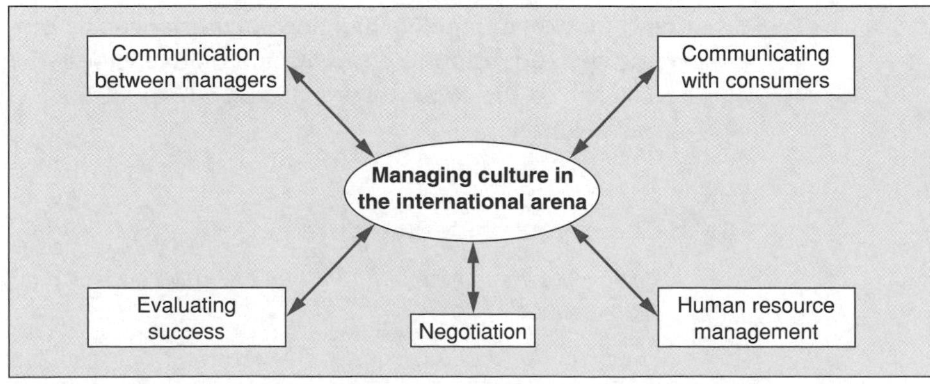

Figure 5.6 Issues for managing culture in the international arena

measured. The most extreme situation would be if one partner viewed the collaboration as a success and the other partner a complete failure.

Problems may also arise from differences in the corporate cultures of collaborating organisations. A collaboration between two companies is unlikely to be successful if the organisations involved have very different corporate cultures and neither is prepared to change. Referring back to Deal and Kennedy's organisational culture types discussed earlier in this chapter, merging an organisation with a tough-guy macho culture (high risk and rapid feedback) with a process culture organisation (low risk and slow feedback) is clearly unlikely to be successful. Hence organisations may agree to collaborate on large long-term projects with each other only once the water has been thoroughly tested by working together successfully on smaller projects, over a significant period of time. Therefore, cultural compatibility is critical to ensuring the consolidation of business relationships.

Communicating with consumers

Consumer buying behaviour is complex and in the international arena there are many potential constraints that the marketer has to overcome to be successful in a foreign country. These include differences in language, taste and attitudes of the target market, as well as variations in government control, media availability and local distribution networks. Hence it is difficult to determine in advance whether new or different products will be accepted by an international or overseas market.

At the start of the twenty-first century there exists a large number of global brands that are familiar to people in many different cultures, such as McDonald's, Kodak and Nokia. However, even successful global brands have experienced difficulties in being accepted. For example, on entering China, Coca-Cola provided shopkeepers with signs in English to advertise the soft drink. This was a mistake, as the Chinese shopkeepers translated the English signs into written Chinese, with the literal Chinese translation being 'Bite the wax tadpole'. This, not surprisingly, held limited appeal for the Chinese and was revised to read 'happiness in the mouth', which is more acceptable and appealing to the target market.[16]

Human resource management

If a manager is posted abroad to manage a subsidiary of a parent company, they are likely to find that they have wide-ranging responsibility for all functions of the business and relations with external stakeholders such as government, the local community, suppliers and customers. Selecting a manager (*see* Chapter 7) to fulfil such a role needs to be done with care. This is because managers with similar profit or cost responsibility at home in the larger parent company are only middle-level management and lack the skills and abilities to perform as a top manager in a foreign environment.[17]

The other type of foreign experience that a manager may encounter is as an international manager who finds him-/herself frequently interacting with very high-level authorities in foreign countries. For example, this may occur when a construction company negotiates with a foreign government for a contract to build major infrastructure projects such as new roads or bridges, or if a company is negotiating to expand current facilities in a foreign country or selling a new, innovative technology. The tasks of an international manager are even more complex than those of subsidiary managers based in one foreign country, as an international manager has to gain trust and build relationships with officials in many foreign countries. Therefore, the international manager will have to deal with the cultures of many countries. Appreciation and understanding of one's personal cultural provenance and national culture are good starting points from which to build a comprehension of the different cultures in which one may work.

Communication between managers

International managers or those interacting on a regular basis with cultures different from that of their home country must ensure that messages between headquarters and subsidiary operations are clearly understood. The advent of technology such as e-mail and faxes makes written communication with people almost anywhere in the world possible in an instant. However, there may be instances when direct contact and verbal communication are preferable to ensure a complex message or idea is correctly understood by its overseas recipients. This is achieved either by international travel, or careful use of the telephone and video conferencing.

It should also be noted that the language of communication may influence how it is received and understood. A manager receiving a message in a non-native language is likely to take longer to read and comprehend it. Equally, a manager working abroad and having to carry out at least some of their work in a second language will take longer for the same reasons and have to work harder than when at home to produce the same quality of work.[18] Therefore, in recruiting overseas managers and international managers, the language part of one's personal cultural provenance is important.

Negotiation

A country's national culture is likely to influence the way managers from that country behave in negotiating contracts with managers from a different national culture. For example, negotiations between the Saudi government and a British company wishing to secure defence contracts will be very different in nature to negotiations between a US and British firm wanting to merge. Hence the type of issue under negotiation and the national culture of negotiators are both likely to influence the nature of the negotiations. In some national cultures it will be normal for individual negotiators to have the power to make decisions, in contrast to other national cultures where referring back to those behind the scenes and head office will all be seen as part of the negotiating process. In some cultures negotiators are required to go through every line of a contract and every possible contingency, in comparison with other negotiators who will be satisfied with a holistic view and understanding of the contract.

The behaviour of the individual negotiators is based on their national culture and this can influence social behaviour in the negotiating process. For example, in some cultures eating and drinking will form part of the negotiating process; in others it will not, or will occur only once a contract has been settled. Equally, some cultures place great importance on punctuality and others do not. Therefore, understanding the national cultures of the different parties involved in negotiations will help those involved discern whether the negotiations are based on their own culture, another party's culture or some hybrid of the different cultures involved.

Managing organisational culture

If the relevance of personal and national culture to business today has been understood, then the same level of perception regarding organisational or corporate culture is required if an individual manager is to work and manage within the context of an organisational culture. The human resource management function is the most powerful of all the four key business functions in influencing the management of organisational culture. For example, the human resource management function will help determine organisational rituals, such as induction courses, training courses and appraisal (*see* earlier in this chapter), as well as cultural symbols such as the allocation of offices, furniture, company cars, job grades, salaries, promotions and dismissals. Hence human resource policies and procedures can have a great influence on an organisation's culture. The outcomes of an attempt to manage culture using the complex influence of human resource policies and procedures are difficult to predict.

If a culture emphasises the importance of teamwork and innovation (*see* the bet your company culture earlier in this chapter) as crucial for success, the managers responsible for culture will want to create one that rewards imaginative and inventive technical behaviour and cooperation and collaboration with others in the workplace. This will mean that rewards, salaries, promotions and bonuses will have to reflect this focus. This may appear to be simple and straightforward, but it is not necessarily so. The lack of simplicity is due to the difficulty in foreseeing the full implications of a specific reward system or promotions policy. There are two main reasons for this: first, the full workings of any policy or procedure are often not determined in enough detail prior to implementation; second, those implementing the system and procedures do not always follow directions to the letter, putting a different interpretation on the policy and procedures and hence producing unexpected outcomes. This variation in interpretation of the policy and procedures compounds the complexities of managing culture in this way.[19]

The role of leadership

The successful management of organisational culture requires the support of top managers, as they play a key role in setting the vision (ideal culture) that the organisation is aiming to adopt. Top management also has responsibility for allocating tasks, activities and resources, and determining the organisational structure, which affects the power structures and control systems in the organisation. Therefore, if human resource policies and procedures, as discussed in the previous section, are to be used in the management of culture, it is essential that top management is involved in the design of human resource policies and procedures as part of its leadership responsibilities.[20]

The role of symbols

Peters[21] recognises a variety of characteristic practices that can enable an executive to influence the culture of their organisation. These include how top executives spend their time, their use of communication and their use of meetings (*see* Figure 5.7). The dominant theme in all these is personal enactment. Managing directors who seek to model an organisation's culture should individually personify the beliefs, values and assumptions that they seek to inspire in others. The same applies to all managers endeavouring to influence employees in the departments or divisions they manage. People generally comprehend a remarkable amount from modelling the conduct of those they respect, particularly if other benefits are derived from doing so. Leaders should seek to maximise the impact of such symbolic actions continually and regularly. Symbolic actions need to be positively reinforced in the shape of praise, money, status and other rewards to champion behaviours in line with the desired culture.

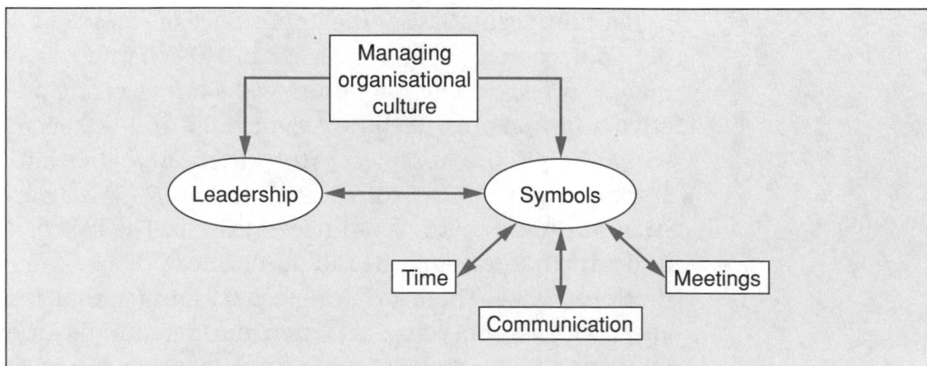

Figure 5.7 Issues for managing organisational culture

The use of time

Senior and middle managers are generally perceptive and sensitive to the activities of their leader and will spend time determining the consequences of what is seen and heard for their current and future careers. Hence a chief executive is able to communicate influential messages to employees through his/her actions.

The use of communication

A good managing director seeks to understand employees and their views on all elements of organisational life, including work activities, colleagues and the marketplace. If a managing director makes a public announcement that quality is the organisation's most pressing problem, employees will listen. If the managing director raises the issue on an ongoing basis and in a memorable fashion by the use of anecdotes and stories, in time people may begin to alter their view of the organisation and the key issues affecting it.

The use of meetings

Organisational leaders enjoy significant authority in determining the key issues, quality, innovation and marketing, which are vital to an organisation and its success. For example, a top manager can communicate the relative importance of an event or meeting by simply turning up, or by turning down an invitation to attend. If a managing director always attends quality meetings but virtually never attends a meeting of the marketing team, the relative importance of quality over marketing is clearly indicated. Accordingly, leaders have the power to convene, postpone and cancel meetings, fashion agendas and influence the manner in which minutes are written up. These devices have a part to play in moulding employees' understanding of what is required of them, what beliefs it is deemed acceptable to hold, and how they are expected to perform their work activities.

Check your understanding

Do you understand which issues are key in managing culture in an international setting?

Check your understanding by identifying and briefly discussing the key issues in managing culture internationally.

Summary

This chapter examined culture at the global, national and local levels of the external environment and the determinants of culture at these different levels. Organisational culture and the management of culture were also examined. The following summary covers all aspects of this chapter.

1 Culture at the global level of the external environment relates to the interaction of at least one national culture with another. Culture at the national level can result from one nation attributing characteristics to another, which can result in stereotyping and prejudice. The national and local levels of culture can be intertwined, as for some people their national characteristics make them the people they are in their local communities.

2 The determinants of personal cultural provenance are name, gender, professional role, icons, symbols, ceremonies, personal morality, norms, values. It is these determinants which define an individual's culture, which in turn makes them the person they are.

3 National culture is determined by religion, politics, economics, education, language, social structure. It is these determinants, their variations and how they are viewed by other nationalities which define a country's national culture.

4 The determinants of organisational culture are presented in the cultural web, which includes routines and rituals, stories, symbols, power structures, organisational structures, control systems. All these determinants will have an impact on the type of place an organisation is to work in. The paradigm consists of the perceived characteristics of an organsiation.

5 Deal and Kennedy identified four possible organisational types. The tough-guy macho culture is where staff take high-risk decisions and receive rapid feedback on the effectiveness of their actions. The work hard/play hard culture is found in organisations in which decisions are routinely low risk and feedback quick, which is often the case in sales-oriented companies. The bet your company culture organisation takes big risks and feedback takes a long time. This is typical of companies which build aircraft or undertake oil exploration. Finally, the process culture is low risk with slow feedback, which is typically found in the civil service and public-sector organisations.

6 How a company manages and behaves in the international arena can be influenced by many factors. The key issues which need to be examined as they are influenced by differing global, national and local cultures include how success is measured, communications with consumers and the marketplace, human resource management, communication with overseas managers (locally based and international managers), and contract negotiations.

7 Managing culture and understanding its relevance to business requires a number of issues to be addressed. These include leadership, the role of symbols, and the use of time, communications and meetings in day-to-day organisational life.

Chapter objectives and the exit case study

While reading this chapter and engaging in the activities, you should have learned how to apply theory and models and analyse situations. The exit case study and the questions which follow will provide an opportunity to assess how well you have met the relevant chapter objectives relating to specific material covered in the chapter.

Chapter objective	Check you have achieved this by
3 Identify and discuss the management of culture.	answering case study questions 1 and 2.

EXIT CASE STUDY 5.2

Mars trades on new healthy image

FT

by Jenny Wiggins

When Pfizer put its Adams chewing gum business up for sale in 2002, Mars took a look at the owner of brands including Trident and Chiclet, but decided against a purchase. 'It's not the sort of habit they wanted to be associated with,' said a consumer industries banker. How times have changed. This week's $23bn acquisition of Wrigley highlights the cultural shift underway at Mars.

With origins in a candy store founded by Frank Mars, an American, just after the turn of the 20th century, Mars has a complicated history. Frank Mars and his son, Forrest, had a difficult relationship, and Forrest left the US in the early 1930s to start his own confectionery business in the UK. From his kitchen in Slough, he invented the Mars bar – based on the Milky Way bar he and his father had developed – and by 1939, Mars was the UK's third-biggest confectionery company.

By the mid-1960s, when Forrest returned to the US to reclaim control of his father's business after a bitter fight with relatives, he had become famous for his secrecy. 'Even in an industry where secrecy and paranoia ruled, Forrest Mars was extreme,' writes Joël Glenn Brenner in her history of Mars and Hershey, *The Emperors of Chocolate*.

In the 21st century, Mars remains something of an enigma. Its executives have traditionally been reluctant to talk to the press, and as a private company, it does not have to disclose its profits and losses, making it hard to understand how well its businesses are performing.

It retains an unusual office culture – everyone has exactly the same size desk, including the managing director who sits in the middle of the group's open-plan rooms. On the walls hang reminders of the company's 'five principles': Quality, Responsibility, Mutuality, Efficiency and Freedom.

However, it is clear that the company feels under pressure to continue playing a leading role in the confectionery industry and to own fast-growing businesses – hence its eagerness to forget any remaining social stigmas attached to chewing gum. One of the reasons that Mars wanted to buy Wrigley was that it can mount a health pitch for the group's gum brands, some of which have American Dental Association approval. Paul Michaels, Mars's global president, said: 'We want to drive more of that.'

Mr Michaels has been at Mars for more than a decade, but is only the third non-family member to run the company. The Mars family began to relinquish some management control between 1999 and 2001, when Benno Hoogendoorn and Peter Cheney became co-presidents – the first non-family executives to hold the top job. Mr Michaels succeeded them as global president in 2004, and also acts as chief executive. Although family members still hold many senior jobs – Valerie Mars, head of corporate development, was one of a 12-person team working on the Wrigley deal – Mars has been bringing in non-family managers. The most recent senior hire was Todd Lachman, who was brought in from Del Monte to run the group's snack business.

Bankers involved in the recent deal between Mars and Wrigley say management at Mars is increasingly professional. 'There is no question it's becoming a more and more sophisticated company,' one banker said. The management changes came amid sluggish sales growth at the group.

In 2005, the group's sales (the bulk of which are in North America and Europe) underperformed the global packaged food market, according to Euromonitor, the research group. This was partly due to declining sales of

Mars's core brands. 'Many of the company's key brands, including Snickers, Mars and M&M's, [were] perceived as increasingly unhealthy in a more health-conscious world,' Euromonitor said. But over the past few years, Mars has sought to change its image. It created a new business unit called 'Mars Nutrition for Health and Wellbeing' and was ahead of other multinational food companies early last year when it announced a self-imposed ban on marketing snack foods and confectionery to children under 12 globally.

It claims to be the first big company in the food industry to get rid of trans-fatty acids from its sweets and chocolates, although it is still in the process of reducing artificial colours. And in September, it emphasised its core confectionery roots by getting rid of the Masterfoods name that it had been using in some parts of the world and bringing its brands together under one name: Mars Inc.

Source: from 'Mars trades on new healthy image', *The Financial Times*, 30 April 2008 (Wiggins, J.).

Exit case study question

1 Apply the cultural web to Mars.

2 Identify the aspects of Mars's cultural web that have changed since 2000. And explain why Mars may have made these changes.

Short-answer questions

1. Define culture at the global level of the external environment.
2. Define culture at the national level of the external environment.
3. Define culture at the local level of the external environment.
4. Define organisational culture.
5. Summarise the impact of symbols on personal cultural provenance.
6. Explain, briefly, the role of norms in determining personal cultural provenance.
7. Name Hill's six determinants of culture.
8. Explain, briefly, the role of religion in determining national culture in your home country.
9. Identify the type of organisation in which a process culture is found.
10. Identify the type of organisation in which a bet your company culture is found.
11. Identify the type of organisation in which a work hard/play hard culture is found.
12. Identify the type of organisation in which a tough-guy macho culture is found.
13. Name six determinants of culture which constitute the cultural web.
14. In determining organisational culture, explain the role of 'stories'.
15. In the cultural web, what do routines and rituals represent?

Chapter objectives and assignment questions

While reading this chapter and engaging in the activities, you should have learned how to apply theory and models and analyse situations. This means you should be able to meet the chapter objectives outlined at the beginning of the chapter. The table below shows which chapter objectives can be tested by the different questions.

Chapter objective	Check you have achieved this by
1 Define and discuss different types of culture.	answering assignment question 1.
2 Explain the different approaches to organisational culture.	answering assignment question 2.
3 Identify and discuss the management of culture.	answering assignment question 3.

Assignment questions

1 Write a 2000-word essay that compares and contrasts the relative importance of personal cultural provenance and national culture to the successful performance of the individual in the workplace.

2 Compare and contrast Handy's cultures (end of Chapter 4) and Deal and Kennedy's organisational cultures. In your opinion, which is a more realistic representation of organisational culture? Justify and explain your answer. Present your response in a 2000-word essay.

3 The university or college you attend is to be privatised and students charged the full fees of around £8000 per annum. Apply Johnson and Scholes' cultural web before and after privatisation. Summarise how the culture of the university or college would have to change if it were to be successful and maintain student quality and numbers in the face of competition. Present your findings in a 2000-word report.

WEBLINKS available online at www.pearsoned.co.uk/capon

- This website provides an overview of corporate culture:
  http://tutor2u.net/business/organisation/culture_more.htm
- This business search engine can provide good articles and information about a range of business and organisational topics, including corporate culture:
  http://www.business.com/
- This website provides some articles about corporate culture:
  http://www.thinkingmanagers.com/business-management/corporate-culture.php

FURTHER READING

These books all contain at least one chapter that discusses culture and changing culture.

- Brown, A (1998) *Organisational Culture*, 2nd edn, Chapters 1 and 2, Harlow: Financial Times Prentice Hall.
- Buchanan, D and Huczynski, A (2008) *Organisational Behaviour*, 6th edn, Chapter 19, Harlow: Financial Times Prentice Hall.
- Burnes, B (2004) *Managing Change*, 4th edn, Chapter 5, Harlow: Financial Times Prentice Hall.
- Deal, T and Kennedy, A (1988) *Corporate Cultures*, London: Penguin Business.
- Johnson, G, Scholes, K and Whittington, R (2008) *Exploring Corporate Strategy*, 8th edn, Chapter 5, Harlow: Financial Times Prentice Hall.
- Martin, J (2005) *Organisational Behaviour*, 3rd edn, Chapter 12, London: Thomson Learning.
- Mullins, L J (2008) *Essentials of Organisational Behaviour*, 2nd edn, Chapter 12, Harlow: Financial Times Prentice Hall.
- Mullins, L J (2007) *Management and Organisational Behaviour*, 8th edn, Chapter 19, Harlow: Financial Times Prentice Hall.
- Thompson, J L and Martin, F (2005) *Strategic Management: Awareness, Analysis and Change*, 5th edn, Chapter 7, London: Thomson Learning.
- Senior, B (2002) *Organisational Change*, 2nd edn, Chapter 4, London: Financial Times Prentice Hall.
- White, C (2004) *Strategic Management*, Chapter 12, Basingstoke: Palgrave.

REFERENCES

1. Hill, C W L (1994) *International Business*, Burr Ridge, IL: Irwin.
2. Hofstede, G (1984) *Culture's Consequences: International Differences in Work Related Values*, London: Sage.
3. Hofstede, G (1980) 'Motivation, leadership and organisation: Do American theories apply abroad?' *Organisational Dynamics*, Summer.
4. Kingdom, J (1991) *Government and Politics in Britain*, Cambridge: Polity Press.
5. Hill, op. cit.
6. Ibid.
7. Mintel Special Report (1996) *Single Person Households*.
8. Hill, op. cit.
9. Ibid.
10. Deal, T and Kennedy, A (1988) *Corporate Cultures*, London: Penguin Business.
11. Johnson, G and Scholes, K (2002) *Exploring Corporate Strategy*, 6th edn, Harlow: Financial Times Prentice Hall.
12. Ibid.
13. Ibid.
14. Ibid.
15. Bleeke, J and Ernst, D (1991) 'The way to win in cross-border alliances', *Harvard Business Review*, quoted in Daniels, J D and Radebaugh, L (1998) *International Business*, 8th edn, Reading, MA: Addison Wesley Longman.
16. Kotler, P, Armstrong, G, Saunders, J and Wong, V (1996) *Principles of Marketing: The European Edition*, Upper Saddle River, NJ: Prentice Hall.

17 Daniels and Radebaugh, op. cit.
18 Ibid.
19 Brown, A (1998) *Organisational Culture*, 2nd edn, London: Financial Times Pitman Publishing.
20 Ibid.
21 Peters, T J (1978) 'Symbols, patterns and settings: An optimistic case for getting things done', *Organizational Dynamics*, 3(23), Autumn, quoted in Brown, op. cit.

CHAPTER 6

Organisational behaviour

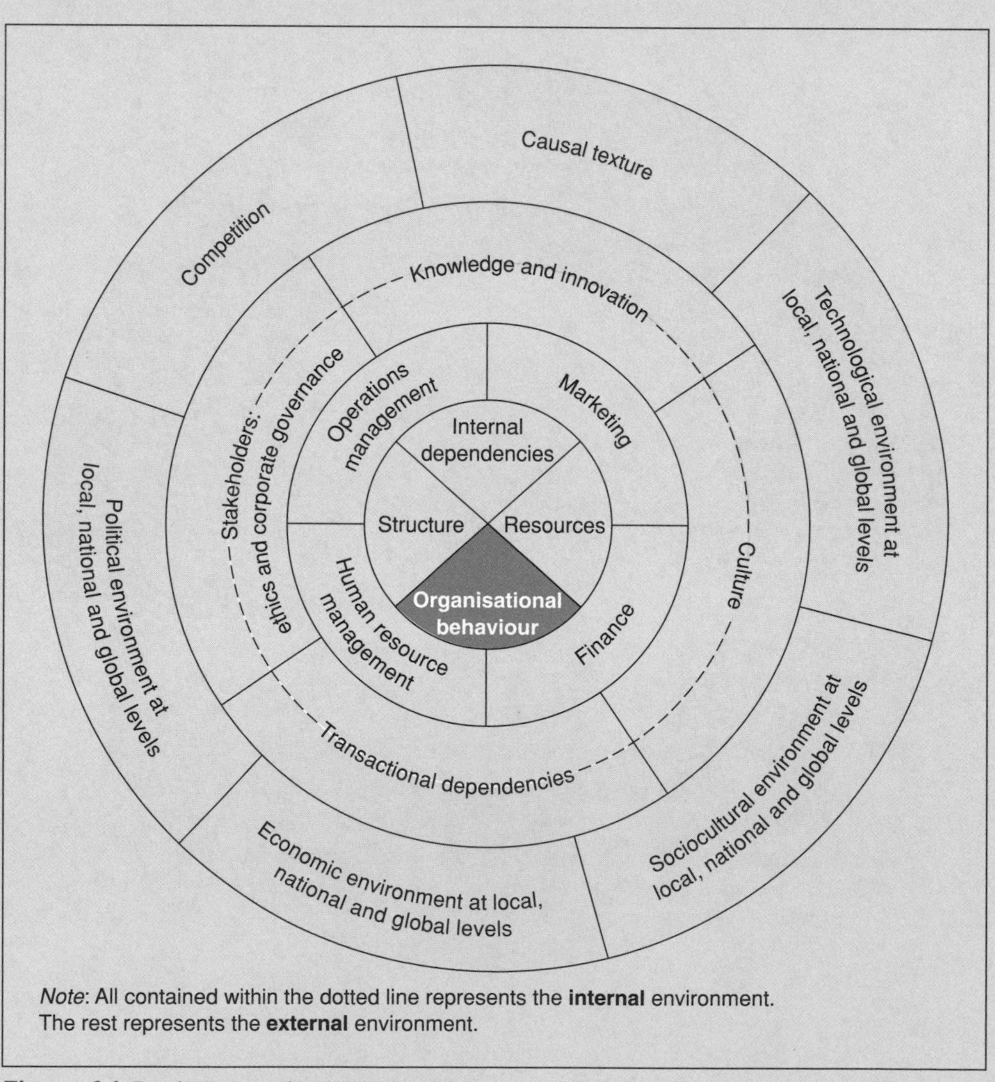

Figure 6.1 Business environment model

Chapter objectives

This chapter provides an overview of some aspects of organisational behaviour. The chapter covers key contributors to the subject such as Taylor, Mayo, Drucker, McGregor and Kanter along with the role of individuals, groups and leaders in organisations.

Therefore, when you have read this chapter and worked through the associated activities you should be able to achieve the objectives specified below.

1 **Explain the contribution of key organisational behaviour writers.**
2 **Summarise the role of the individual in organisations.**
3 **Discuss group membership and development in organisations.**
4 **Identify and explain different types of approach to leadership.**

This case study examines Nelson Mandela and the courage, fortitude and leadership he has shown over a lifetime.

ENTRY CASE STUDY 6.1

Nelson Mandela: Global admiration has drawbacks

by David Blair

Nelson Mandela has not been allowed to rest in retirement. As he turns 90, a few years to himself would be a welcome gift. Even the most jaded and cynical politicians tend to melt in the presence of Nelson Mandela. On the cusp of his 10th decade, this stooping, shuffling man, who can barely walk without a friendly arm to grasp and no longer stands to deliver his speeches, has probably become the most admired human being on Earth.

His visit to London shows yet again the power of his moral authority. No one who has met Mr Mandela can fail to be moved by his aura of principle, courage and stubborn optimism. There is almost a physical charge in the air when that familiar smile flashes across his face and his deep, sonorous and remarkably strong voice holds forth. When he gave a fund-raising banquet this week, it was entirely unsurprising that his fellow diners ranged from Bill Clinton to Pierce Brosnan, from Oprah Winfrey to Gordon Brown.

Yet there are drawbacks to being a living legend. Since he stepped down as South Africa's president in 1999, shortly before his 81st birthday, the world has consistently denied Mr Mandela any chance of a quiet retirement. He has not been allowed any years of peace to round off a singularly tempestuous life.

Mr Mandela, intensely reserved and self-contained, disguises his emotional scars. But this is a man who has buried three of his six children and one of his three wives. His 27 years behind bars, preceded by almost two decades of underground struggle and resistance, effectively destroyed his family life. When his first daughter, Makaziwe, died in infancy in 1945, he was already a central figure in the ANC's Youth League. When his first son, Thembekile, died in a car accident in 1969, Mr Mandela was enduring his seventh year in the cells of Robben Island. Six years after he stepped down as president, another son, Makgatho, died of an Aids-related condition.

Typically, Mr Mandela turned this personal tragedy into a blow against the stigma attached to Aids. Seated in the garden of his home in Houghton, Johannesburg, he challenged a deeply ingrained taboo by quietly and firmly telling the world the cause of his son's death. In tones of repressed sorrow, he added: 'It gives a very bad reflection of members of a family if they do not come out bravely and say "a member of my family has died of Aids".' When asked to pay a personal tribute to Makgatho's memory, however, Mr Mandela's response was tragically revealing. 'My son,' he replied, 'was an attorney' who had enjoyed 'the great honour' of being enrolled by one of South Africa's most senior judges. 'Beyond that,' said Mr Mandela, 'I've nothing else to say.'

The truth was that his relationship with his son had been destroyed. Makgatho went to his grave having

barely known his father. Mr Mandela was leading a general strike on the day Makgatho was born. When the boy was six, his father was charged with treason and endured the longest trial in South Africa's history before being acquitted. Five years later, he was dispatched to Robben Island.

When Mr Mandela became South Africa's first black president in 1994, Makgatho did not attend the inauguration. In his memoirs, Mr Mandela rued that his struggle against apartheid had been 'at the expense of the people I knew best and loved most'. He must have hoped that retirement would give him the chance to pick up the shattered pieces of his personal life. In some ways, this has been so. His third marriage, to Graca Machel, the widow of Mozambique's former president, has been notably happy. His grandchildren and great-grandchildren are ever-present at his spacious, whitewashed home.

Yet the demands on his time remain unrelenting. Some of this is self-generated. In retirement he has established three charitable foundations and made good use of his unrivalled ability to separate hard-nosed businessmen from their cash. He still rises at dawn, but the early-morning walks that were once his constant habit are now beyond him. Zelda la Grange, a formidable Afrikaner, has served as a fearsomely efficient personal secretary since he became president in 1994. She organises his day, fields numerous phone calls from world leaders and copes with an endless flow of visitors.

Old friends believe that Mr Mandela's goodwill has been exploited. 'Nelson is an extremely courteous and warm individual and when anybody asks him to do anything, he always agrees,' said Lord Joffe, the Labour peer who has known Mr Mandela for more than 40 years. 'He wants to please everyone if he can. But then his protectors try to disengage him.' Miss La Grange is the chief protector, along with his wife, Graca. Between them, they try to rescue Mr Mandela from the hordes of well-wishers who beat a path to his door, armed with schemes demanding his involvement.

As a young lawyer, Lord Joffe was on the defence team when Mr Mandela stood trial in 1963, charged with 'acts of sabotage' designed to cause 'violent revolution'. He said of his most famous client: 'He's grown in standing since his retirement and he's now the most outstanding politician of his time.' But this has left precious little time for himself and his family. 'I think everyone in the world wants to meet Nelson Mandela and it's very difficult,' said Lord Joffe.

Now, as he turns 90, no one would deny Mr Mandela's contribution to the world. The question is whether the world can ever return the favour and allow this remarkable human being something that he has never previously enjoyed – a few years to himself. Tragically, it may be too late.

Name: Nelson Rolihlahla Mandela.

Born: 18 July, 1918.

Education: Fort Hare University, Witwatersrand University.

What he says: 'In my country we go to prison first – and then become president.'

What they say about him: 'He has an impish sense of humour. He'll never miss the opportunity to say "I see Joel Joffe over there who sent me to jail for 27 years"' – Lord Joffe, Mandela's defence lawyer.

Source: from 'Nelson Mandela: Global admiration has drawbacks', *Daily Telegraph*, 27 June 2008 (Blair, D.) © Telegraph Media Group Limited 2008.

Introduction

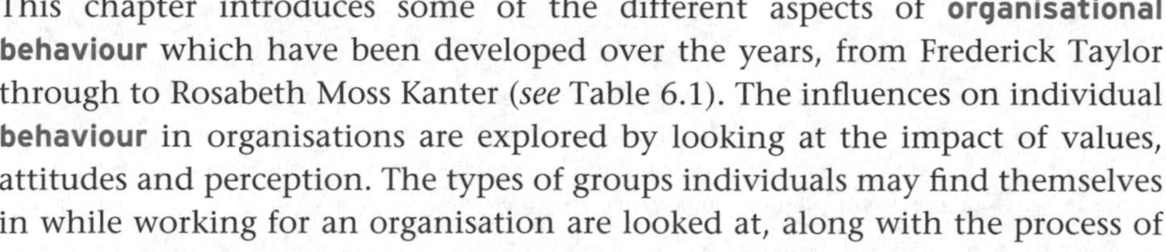

This chapter introduces some of the different aspects of **organisational behaviour** which have been developed over the years, from Frederick Taylor through to Rosabeth Moss Kanter (*see* Table 6.1). The influences on individual **behaviour** in organisations are explored by looking at the impact of values, attitudes and perception. The types of groups individuals may find themselves in while working for an organisation are looked at, along with the process of group development. The final section looks at different types of leadership which are commonly found in organisations.

Table 6.1 Key contributors to organisational behaviour and their work

Frederick Winslow Taylor 1856–1917	Scientific management
Elton Mayo 1880–1949	Hawthorne studies
Peter Drucker 1909–2005	Seven tasks of tomorrow's manager
Douglas McGregor 1906–1964	Theory X and Theory Y
Rosabeth Moss Kanter 1943– Currently Professor of Business Administration at Harvard University, Boston, USA	Innovation in organisations

Approaches to organisational behaviour

There are many approaches to organisational behaviour and this section will look at some of the key contributions to organisational behaviour in the twentieth century (*see* Table 6.1).

Frederick Winslow Taylor

One of the first pioneers to study employees and their management was Frederick Winslow Taylor, who was born in Pennsylvania in 1856, trained as an engineer and died in 1917.[1] Taylor's approach is known as scientific management and he sought to study the performance of individuals in the workplace. Underpinning Taylor's approach was the basic assumption that people dislike work but will undertake it in order to earn a living. Taylor went on to argue that due to this assumed dislike of work, staff need very close supervision as they are not capable of self-management and motivation. Taylor expected that close and fair supervision would be respected and that people would perform their job of repetitive tasks at the required rate and standard, with extra effort gaining greater reward.

Taylor's studies of employees, their management and approach to work took place in factories in the US, such as Midvale Steelworks, Johnson Company and the Bethlehem Iron Company in Pennsylvania. Taylor's approach underpins working practices in organisations today. Think about the approach to work taken by fast-food companies and call centres. It could be argued that Taylor took advantage of people and assumed they were unable to bargain or negotiate on their own behalf. However, in situations where piece-work systems were introduced due to Taylor's approach, staff were able to receive more take-home pay for increased productivity. The counter-argument is that any pay increase was not in proportion to the productivity increase.

Elton Mayo

The human relations school came after scientific management and Taylor. Elton Mayo was born in Adelaide in Australia in 1880 and died in England in 1949. Unlike Taylor, who was an engineer by training, Mayo was a social psychologist. Mayo worked at the University of Queensland from 1911 to 1923, when he left for the US, where finally he worked at Harvard University for over 20 years until 1947.

Mayo's approach contrasted to Taylor's in at least one key way. Unlike Taylor, Mayo took the view that the financial incentive to work was relatively unimportant. Mayo's most well-known study into the workplace was conducted at the Western Electric Company's Hawthorne Works in Chicago, starting in 1927. The project covered around 20,000 people, and used between 75 and 100 researchers over a ten-year period.[2] The Hawthorne studies showed that social factors, such as the relationship between management and in particular the social grouping between staff, can influence the behaviour of employees in an organisation. In a study carried out at Hawthorne, called the Relay Assembly Room Study,[3] a group of women employees were moved to a room which resembled their normal place of work, where they undertook their normal work of assembling small telephone relays. The researchers wanted to examine the impact of the introduction of more rest periods on productivity, e.g. a mid-morning break, a reduction of half an hour in the working day, a move to a five-day working week. The expectation was that some changes, such as the mid-morning break, would help increase productivity and that the move to a five-day working week would reduce productivity. However, the surprising findings were that productivity continued in a gradual upward trend, regardless of the conditions applied to the staff being observed, along with a lower-than-expected rate of absenteeism.

The findings led to the consideration of psychological aspects of the work, as well as the objective alterations to the working environment, such as working hours and lunch breaks. The Hawthorne researchers reached the conclusion that the continued increase in productivity was in part due to the attention paid to the employees by the researchers. The response of the employees to favourable treatment, more breaks, shorter working week and attention from the researchers was to reciprocate by providing the researchers with results the employees perceived they were seeking. This phenomenon was termed the 'Hawthorne effect'.

Peter Drucker

Peter Drucker was born in Vienna in 1909, trained as a lawyer, then worked as a journalist in London between 1933 and 1936, before emigrating to the US in 1937. In 1942 Drucker undertook his first consultancy job for General Motors – where his direct approach to consultancy was not well received. However, Drucker continued to both work as a consultant and look at what constituted

Table 6.2 Drucker's management tasks

Drucker's seven tasks of tomorrow's manager
He or she should: • manage by objectives • take more risks, over a longer time period, and also allow this to happen further down the organisation • take strategic decisions • build an integrated team, in which members are capable of assessing their own performance in relation to common objectives • communicate quickly and clearly and have a motivating influence on staff at all levels such that their participation, in a responsible manner, is obtained • see the organisation as a whole and understand his/her role within it • understand the external environment and the significant factors which impact on the organisation, its products and services, and the sector as a whole.

Source: Summarised from Clutterbuck, D and Crainer, S (1990) *Makers of Management*, London: Papermac Macmillan.

a modern organisation and what the managers should do. Drucker's consultancy work grew and in 1954 his book, *The Practice of Management*, was published, which resulted in management by objectives being high profile in the 1950s and 1960s.[4] In this work Drucker identifies the seven tasks of a manager of 'tomorrow' – *see* Table 6.2.

Douglas McGregor

Douglas McGregor was born in Detroit in 1906 and died in 1964. Like Elton Mayo he was a social psychologist. McGregor was professor of management at Massachusetts Institute of Technology between 1954 and 1964 and is best known for his work *The Human Side of Enterprise*, which presented the arguments for Theory X and Theory Y, which are polar opposites concerning the assumptions managers may make about employees.[5]

Theory X assumes that people dislike work and seek to avoid it at all costs. Hence people need to be controlled, coerced, threatened and punished to achieve an adequate individual contribution to organisational goals. This also supports the assumptions that people prefer to be tightly supervised, with no responsibility and virtually no ambition. A manager making these assumptions about his or her staff will be autocratic, controlling and obsessed with seeking to make uncooperative employees perform. The likelihood is that staff will resent this approach and seek to do as little work as possible, hence reinforcing the original opinion of the manager.

The other extreme is Theory Y in which people regard work as a normal activity and are hence committed to objectives and self-motivated towards their achievement and the associated rewards. Additionally, people will accept and seek out responsibility, and take the opportunity to behave creatively while resolving problems in organisations and developing organisations. Managers adopting such assumptions and views concerning their employees will develop a much more cooperative relationship with their employees.

Rosabeth Moss Kanter

Rosabeth Moss Kanter was born in Cleveland, Ohio in 1943 and is best known for her 1983 book *The Change Masters*, defined in the quote below:

> **literally – the right people in the right place at the right time. The right people are the ones with ideas that move beyond the organisation's established practice, ideas they can form into visions. The right places are the integrative environments that support innovation, encourage the building of coalitions and teams to support and implement visions. The right times are those moments in the flow of organisational history when it is possible to reconstruct reality on the basis of accumulated innovations to shape a more productive and successful future.**
>
> *Source*: Kanter, R M (1983) *The Change Masters*, New York, Simon & Schuster.

The Change Masters examined 115 cases of significant innovation within US companies with the aim of discovering the structures required for change and innovation. According to Kanter, this research showed that organisations have to first put in place systems, practices, cultures and rewards that will encourage and allow people to be enterprising and innovative. In such a culture, the structure must be one of small working teams which are functionally complete for the task being undertaken, and have autonomy at an operational level to allow the team to get things done. Finally Kanter's research showed that *The Change Masters* companies viewed people's problem solving, enterprise skills and ability to innovate as a great strength in which pride was taken.[6]

Check your understanding

Do you understand the key points of some approaches to organisational behaviour?

Check your understanding by matching the statements below with the person whose work they relate to: Rosabeth Moss Kanter, Peter Drucker, Douglas McGregor, Frederick Taylor and Elton Mayo.

(a) People dislike work but will undertake it in order to earn a living.
(b) The continued increase in productivity was in part due to the attention paid to the employees by the researchers.
(c) Managers should take more risks, over a longer time period, and also allow this to happen further down the organisation.
(d) People regard work as a normal activity and are committed to self-motivation and the achievement of objectives.
(e) Companies view people's problem solving, enterprise skills and ability to innovate as strengths in which pride should be taken.

Individuals in organisations

Values

Values are guiding principles which individuals, groups, organisations and society use to determine whether behaviour is acceptable or unacceptable. An understanding of the individual's values will provide a strong indication of their attitudes. Organisations should seek to employ staff whose values correspond with the dominant values of the organisation – if an appropriate match is obtained, the employee's levels of satisfaction and performance are more likely to be high. There are two types of value: terminal and instrumental.[7] Terminal values are desired outcomes, which people and/or organisations seek to achieve. Instrumental values are the types of behaviour preferred by the organisation – *see* Table 6.3.

Terminal values are often indicated in the mission statements which organisations issue, and these in turn inform stakeholders (e.g. customers, employees, suppliers, bankers) of the organisation's stance on, for example, quality, service, innovation and ethics. The aim of this is to ensure that organisational members – staff and managers – understand the standard and type of behaviour required of them in the workplace, which in turn helps determine the organisation's culture (*see* Chapter 5). This also helps ensure that external stakeholders understand the nature of the relationship they can expect with the organisation. For example, customers will expect quality and service in terms of goods, and suppliers will want prompt payment and clear contracts with the organisation.

However, often the most powerful values in an organisation are not written down but are the result of shared norms, beliefs, assumptions and thoughts which staff use to relate to each other and external stakeholders. These shared values inform the response of staff to particular workplace situations or organisational problems. In cultures where terminal and instrumental values are strong and clearly understood by the staff, the behaviour and response of staff will be that which the organisation desires. In contrast, in weak-culture organisations there is greater likelihood that clouded and misunderstood terminal and instrumental values will lead to staff not being able to respond to difficult

Table 6.3 Values in organisations

Organisational values	
Terminal values	**Instrumental values**
• high quality • excellence • innovation • profitability • social responsibility	• being helpful and friendly • hard working • clean and tidy • capable • accurate • creative

situations or responding in an inappropriate manner (*see* Chapter 5). Hence the role of management and leadership needs to include the shaping and clear communication of organisational terminal and instrumental values.

Attitudes

Organisational behaviour includes the study of individuals and their attitudes to their employment. Attitudes to jobs cover a number of areas: job satisfaction, job involvement and organisational commitment.[8] Job involvement is the extent to which an individual identifies with and is involved in their job, while organisational commitment covers the degree to which an employee identifies with the organisation and is loyal to it. Job satisfaction reflects an individual's attitude to their job. A person with a high level of job satisfaction will hold positive views concerning their employment and vice versa.

Job satisfaction is determined by pay, challenges, other rewards, level of support from colleagues and working conditions. People tend to prefer jobs which include a variety of tasks, the opportunity to use and develop skills and abilities, the freedom to manage one's own workload, and the opportunity to receive constructive feedback on job performance. Hence jobs which provide these challenges and opportunities are those most likely to give a high level of job satisfaction.

The US psychologist Frederick Herzberg undertook work on job satisfaction and job dissatisfaction in the 1960s.[9] Herzberg interviewed around 200 Pittsburgh accountants and engineers and asked them to identify occasions on which they felt good about work and occasions on which they felt bad about work. Analysis of the research interviews showed that motivating factors associated with job satisfaction were quite separate from those linked to job dissatisfaction which Herzberg termed 'hygiene factors'. Attention by a company to ensuring the hygiene factors are of a suitable standard to reduce dissatisfaction will not lead to motivation, just an absence of frustration or dissatisfaction. Hence job satisfaction and job dissatisfaction are not exact opposites. Job satisfaction requires the motivating factors or the opportunity to achieve them to be embedded in the organisation.

Job dissatisfaction or frustration can take four major forms: fixation, regression, withdrawal or aggression.[10] Fixation occurs when an individual continually seeks to present the same arguments as discussion or seeks to solve problems using solutions which are known to be inadequate for the current situation. Regression is defined as immature or childish behaviour, including sulking and tantrums, although it can also present as an individual feeling exceptionally low or depressed. Withdrawal occurs when an individual seeks to remove him- or herself from the organisation and can include absenteeism, extended breaks and ultimately success in seeking alternative employment. Hence organisations with high levels of job dissatisfaction or frustration often experience high levels of labour turnover. Finally, the most severe form of behaviour which expresses frustration is aggression, which can range from nasty, unfounded gossip and rumour about the organisation or individuals who are seen as having caused the frustration through to acts of physical aggression – punching a senior manager – or sabotage, e.g. removing computer records or deliberately introducing a virus into the company's computer system.

Perception

Perception is an individual's personal view of the world and definition of reality. Other individuals will hold different views and perceptions concerning the same person, item or situation. Differences in perception can arise from a number of factors which can exist in the perceiver, in the item or individual being perceived, or in the situation in which the perception occurs. The perceiver is influenced by their personal characteristics, which include attitudes, personality, interests, motives, experiences and expectations. Equally, the personal characteristics of individuals being observed will influence what is perceived. A group of very drunk, noisy students in a pub on a Saturday night is likely to be perceived as more disruptive than two drunk old men sitting in the corner of the pub. This example also makes the point that the background or situation in which individuals are observed and their relative relationship to one another influences perception. The same two drunk old men in a pub serving Sunday lunches to mainly family groups would be more likely to be viewed as undesirable in this situation than in the previous one.

People have beliefs, motives and intentions and as a result when observing others will develop explanations for their behaviour. Attribution theory seeks to explain how people judge one another and depends on the meaning attributed to particular behaviour.[11] Judgement is dependent on whether an individual's behaviour is viewed as being internally or externally caused. Internally caused behaviour is seen as being under the control of the individual. The student who misses a 9 a.m. lecture on Thursday could have this behaviour attributed to him/her being out clubbing on Wednesday night, which is student night in the local nightclubs, and oversleeping the following morning. This late behaviour has an internal attribution. However, if the lateness was attributed to the student being caught in an unexpected traffic jam, due to a rush-hour traffic accident, this would be an external attribution. Generally people tend to view the behaviour of others as internally controlled and their own as externally controlled.

The understanding of whether behaviour is caused internally or externally is dependent on three factors: distinctiveness, consensus and consistency. Distinctiveness refers to the degree to which an individual behaves differently in different situations. Is the student who is late for today's 9 a.m. lecture also late for their group project meetings? If the student who was late for the lecture is otherwise normally on time for classes and meetings, then the late behaviour will normally be classed as having high distinctiveness (i.e. the late behaviour is unusual or distinctive for this student) and an external attribution. Alternatively, if the same student is nearly always late for classes and meetings, the late behaviour will more likely be given internal attribution and low distinctiveness – there is nothing unusual or distinctive about this student being late.

Consensus occurs when everyone who is faced with the same or similar situation responds or behaves in the same way. If all students who took the same route to the university missed or were late for the 9 a.m. Thursday lecture, the behaviour shows consensus and would normally be given an external attribution, e.g. the road traffic accident. In contrast, if all students made the 9 a.m. lecture and only our missing student didn't, there is not a consensus of behaviour and the behaviour will likely be given an internal attribution.

Finally, consistency in an individual's behaviour tends to be given an internal attribution, i.e. the missing student always stops out late and oversleeps. In contrast, an individual's actions which are not consistent tend to be given an external attribution, i.e. a student who has not been late for the first ten weeks of the semester but is missing in week 11 is more likely to have this behaviour given an external attribution, e.g. the traffic accident or a late train.

In summary, agreement is low if, for example, a student complains about their lecturer's teaching style and no one else in the class makes the same complaint. Consistency is high if the student has complained about the lecturer and their teaching style throughout the year and distinctiveness is low if the same student has always complained about their lecturers and their teaching styles. The combination of low agreement, high consistency and low distinctiveness leads to an internal attribution of the complaining behaviour. In contrast, agreement is high if many students make the same complaint, as it agrees with or supports the original complaining student's behaviour. Frequent complaints by the original student about this lecturer makes consistency high, and having never complained about a lecturer before, distinctiveness is also high. The combination of high agreement, high consistency and high distinctiveness means the resulting conclusion would most likely be an external attribution of student behaviour, which points to the lecturer being a poor teacher.

Finally, it should be noted that errors of judgement and bias occur with attribution theory, and in general people tend to overestimate the impact of internal factors on behaviour and underestimate the influence of external factors.

Check your understanding

Do you understand the difference between internal and external attribution of behaviour?

Check your understanding by reading the passage below and decide whether Mr and Mrs Smith's behaviour has an internal or external attribution.

> Mr and Mrs Smith eat out about once a week at their local Italian restaurant where the chef always receives lots of compliments from the diners when he comes into the front of the restaurant. Mr and Mrs Smith always compliment the chef if they particularly enjoy his style of cooking and variety of dishes. This is the first time Mr and Mrs Smith have genuinely felt like this about a restaurant's food and they complimented the chef accordingly.

Groups in organisations

A group is two or more people who come together to achieve objectives. Groups can be formal or informal in nature. A formal group is, for example, a department, team or division which is defined by an organisation (e.g. a company, a football team, a charity) and the group will have specific activities and tasks to undertake. The objectives of the formal group will be determined by the organisational goals. Formal groups can be command and/or task groups which are determined by the organisation.[12] Command groups are determined by an organisation's structure, for example a supervisor and his/her team of assembly workers in a TV factory. Task groups are determined by the organisation, but do not depend on the obvious hierarchical relationships that are present in command groups. Task groups come together, like a cross-functional team, to complete a particular job, task or project, and will contain employees from different departments or divisions in the organisation. It should also be noted that command groups are task groups, but task groups are not necessarily command groups as task groups cut across levels and departments in the organisation.

Informal groups are interest groups and friendship groups. People in an interest group may or may not belong to a particular command or task group, but may band together to achieve a common goal. Friendship groupings are formed from people who have a social allegiance. Staff in a friendship group may lunch together in the middle of the working day. Additionally, friendship groups may extend beyond the workplace and be based on a shared or social activity which is not related to work, e.g. gardening, going to the theatre, supporting a particular football team. Friendship and interest groups serve members' social needs and, although informal, do affect the behaviour and performance of individuals in the workplace.

Check your understanding

Do you understand the different types of group which may exist in organisations?

Check your understanding by matching the groups below with group type (group types are command, task, interest and friendship):

(a) A weekend hill walking group.
(b) A managing director and his/her team of senior managers and directors.
(c) A product development team.
(d) A group of workers who are trying to persuade their employer to substitute fringe benefits for extra holidays.

Reasons for group membership

People join groups for a variety of reasons, such as security, affiliation, esteem and task achievement. Group membership can provide individuals with a sense of security and a degree of protection from threats. This underpins the trade union movement, which seeks to give its members protection in the workplace and power in negotiations with employers. In becoming a group member individuals may gain a sense of security concerning their position. However, it is also possible for an individual to feel lost and insecure if the group is large and the individual does not understand their position or role within the group.

People enjoy the interactions that come with group membership and the emotional support it can provide. This interaction and acceptance by the group fulfils an important social need, which can in turn enhance an individual's feeling of esteem and self-worth. Esteem and self-worth provided by group membership also bring recognition by colleagues in the group, important if the nature of the work and achievement is not well understood by those outside the group. Additionally, of course, recognition by those both inside and outside the group can enhance individual and group status.

Group development

Task achievement is one of the key reasons for creating groups. A group may collectively have greater knowledge, skills and abilities to complete the job than any individual acting alone. Hence, in organisations, the use of formal groups to achieve goals can be effective. However, it needs to be recognised that groups and the associated behaviours change over time and this is shown by the five stages of development suggested by Tuckman and Jensen (*see* Table 6.4).[13]

The first stage is one of 'forming' in which group members are finding out about each other, making an impression on each other, seeking structure and direction from a leader, and orientating themselves in relation to the task. At this stage there will be a degree of uncertainty while relationships within the group and ground rules are established. There may also be confusion surrounding the tasks and goals facing the group. Stage 2, storming, is one of conflict in which

Table 6.4 Tuckman and Jensen: the five stages of group development

Stage	Description
Stage 1 Forming	Group members are finding out about each other and orientating themselves in relation to the task.
Stage 2 Storming	This is a stage of conflict in which individuals will jockey for position in the group in terms of leadership, control and priorities.
Stage 3 Norming	The conflict will have been overcome; the group will have gelled and be working cooperatively.
Stage 4 Performing	Builds upon the cohesiveness and cooperation established in stage 3.
Stage 5 Mourning	Is the disbanding of the group because the task is complete.

Source: Summarised from Huczynski, A and Buchanan, D (2001) *Organizational Behaviour*, Harlow: Financial Times Prentice Hall.

individuals will jockey for position in the group in terms of leadership, control, priorities, and goal difference between members. Not surprisingly hostility and conflict will rise to the surface. If the group is to move on to the next stage of 'norming', then the management and resolution of conflict and differences of opinion is critical.

Stage 3, norming, is a much more cohesive stage than stage 2. By stage 3, groups will have moved on to a consensus over leadership, rules, behaviour and tasks. Allocation of tasks will be undertaken with cooperation, as the group has 'gelled' and the conflict of stage 2 has been successfully resolved. Stage 4, performing, builds upon the cohesiveness and cooperation established in stage 3. In a successful group, effective structures, flexibility, openness and a clear understanding of goals and successful performance are required to meet goals to ensure that stage 4 is completed. Less successful groups can become bogged down in the earlier stages and, for example, remain in continual conflict (stage 2) or remain in stage 3, fulfilling roles, but never moving on to completing the tasks and final achievement of objectives (stage 4). Finally, stage 5, mourning, is the disbanding of the group because the task is complete and/or individual members move on to different projects (*see* Table 6.4).

Check your understanding

Do you understand the different stages of group development?

Check your understanding by naming Tuckman and Jensen's stages of group development and matching the behaviours below with the stages you have named:

(a) Group members undertake tasks and activities harmoniously.
(b) Group members tell each other about themselves and their role in the organisation.
(c) Group members talk about the different projects they are going to work on next.
(d) Group members complete tasks and finish the project.
(e) Group members argue about what it is the group should achieve.

Group performance

Group size impacts on the performance of both the individual and the group. In large groups the total resource and effort is greater, but the impact and contribution of an individual is diluted. There are a number of characteristics of large groups and the behaviour of their members. Individuals are most tolerant of authority and very direct leadership in a large group, as group members recognise the difficulties in supervising a large team. Hence usually more formal rules and procedures are used to manage large groups. However, even with clear rules and procedures, large groups usually take longer than small ones to make decisions. It is also likely that job satisfaction in a large group will be less, as individuals have fewer opportunities to participate and receive less attention from the group and its leader. In contrast, in smaller groups individuals are more likely to view their participation as critical and are therefore more likely to involve themselves in the group and its activities. Finally, with large groups, a level of diminishing return is reached in terms of the outcomes of the group, due to the greater difficulties of coordinating and managing a larger group.

The quality of the work undertaken by a group is directly related to the relevance and diversity of members' characteristics, knowledge, skills and abilities. Teams which are composed of members with very similar traits and skills are likely to view a task or problem from a single perspective. This can result in the group being both efficient and effective in terms of completing the task or solving the problem. However, it is also the case that a single-perspective approach lacks critical awareness of the task, problem and possible solutions. Therefore, this leads to the argument that groups with diversity in characteristics, knowledge, skills and abilities are more likely to consider a wider and more innovative range of approaches. This, however, does require that the more diversified characteristics, knowledge, skills and abilities are relevant to the group task – merely increasing the size of the group alone will not improve the group performance.

Roles

The role of a group member can be defined as their expected behaviour in the group. In formal groups in organisations the expected roles can be formally defined via a written job description and via how existing members perform similar roles or jobs. The tasks and activities an individual believes they are required to undertake are known as the perceived role. The expected role and perceived role may overlap or the two roles can diverge greatly. Finally, the enacted role is defined by actual conduct or behaviour of the individual in carrying out their tasks and activities. It is usual for the enacted role to more closely reflect the perceived role than the expected role.

Status

Status is the social worth conferred on an individual due to the position they occupy in the group. Status may be conferred by many factors, either separately or collectively, including title, salary, achievement, seniority and power. Higher status may be conferred on the most experienced or senior member of a group and equally this individual may feel they deserve higher status. However, if it is not also perceived by other group members, the higher status will not be conferred.

Norms

Norms are the rules which define acceptable behaviour, with behaviour not conforming to the norms being unacceptable. Norms help establish consistent behaviour and conduct among the group and can be formal and written or informal and unwritten. Professionals such as doctors and lawyers operate to formal and written codes of conduct, with those who do not conform to the code being 'struck off'.

Hackman defines norms as relating to the actions and situations perceived as important by the group and also as a reflection of the individual personalities in the group and the means by which they regulate behaviour within the group.[14] Norms will usually develop slowly over time, but should the group be under pressure, norms can develop quickly. Norms will apply differently to individual group members, with newer and more junior members expected to conform very closely to all the norms. In contrast, more senior and established group members, who likely enjoy higher status, may be 'exempt' from conforming to particular norms. It is key for group members to publicly comply to norms and adhere to this behaviour. However, group members do not need to privately accept the norms or group behaviour.

Cohesiveness

Cohesiveness is defined as the extent to which group members are attracted to and wish to remain in a group, i.e. how the group sticks together. Group cohesiveness increases if members share goals and the approach to achieving them, with any competition existing outside the group. Hence members of cohesive groups experience higher levels of job satisfaction, with greater and better communications, as the members share values, goals, and an approach to achieving goals. Therefore, hostile and aggressive behaviour by members of cohesive groups is more commonly directed towards those outside the group. This type of behaviour can arise from a feeling of superiority among group members, which leads to the group seeking to reject outsiders.

Generally small groups, with less diversity and more opportunity to interact with all members, are more cohesive. In contrast, large groups with greater diversity, competition between members, dissimilar values and formal rules will experience less cohesion. Cohesive groups, which are strong in terms of value and culture, are likely to be more resistant to change than less cohesive groups. Change which threatens a group's position and existence will be strongly resisted.

Leadership in organisations

Leadership is the ability to influence a group towards the achievement of goals.[15] A person may occupy a leadership role due to their position in the organisation. Normally leadership is associated with the role of manager. However, a leader and manager are not necessarily equivalent, as providing a manager with position and certain rights in an organisation is no guarantee that they will be an effective leader.

Formal leaders are appointed and exist within the formal structure of the organisation. Equally, informal leaders can emerge from outside the formal procedures and structure of the organisation. Both are important and can make a difference in the performance of groups and organisations. A change in leader can enhance the performance of underachieving groups or organisations, while equally, rapid turnover of leaders can be detrimental to performance.

Charismatic leadership

Transactional leaders clarify tasks and roles while motivating their followers or subordinates towards achievement of the group or organisational goals.[16] In contrast, transformational or charismatic leaders will create an organisational culture in which staff will be self-motivating and seek to contribute to the organisation. To achieve this a transformational or charismatic leader will need to be positive and self-confident in their own ability and judgement. The charismatic leader will present a clear vision offering a better future for the group or organisation than the status quo. The charismatic leader also needs to be strongly committed to the vision and prepared to bear personal risk and cost to achieve the vision. A very good example of a charismatic and transformational leader is Nelson Mandela, and his leadership of a country is summarised in the entry case study for this chapter. It therefore normally follows that charismatic leaders are perceived as initiators and managers of change rather than custodians of the status quo. The subject of the entry case study, Nelson Mandela, is a good example of a leader who has great charisma and took great personal risks to see apartheid overcome.

Visionary leadership

Visionary leadership goes beyond charisma.[17] Visionary leadership is the ability to develop the organisation beyond its current situation and to communicate a credible vision for the development in an articulate manner such that it is clearly understood by all relevant stakeholders.

A successful vision needs to offer the organisation and its members an outlook on the future that is a clear and significant improvement on that currently facing the organisation. The organisation and its members need to perceive the vision as challenging yet achievable to retain any motivation to pursue the vision. Effective visionary leaders need to communicate their vision, its objectives and the associated plan of action via oral and written communication such that it can be clearly understood by organisational members at different levels. Additionally, the visionary leader will need to support the vision via their own behaviour in the organisation and be able to extend the vision, its objectives and plan of action beyond the organisation's current situation. This is key as the environments and situations in which organisations find themselves change continually.

Team leadership

Managers who are effective team leaders will trust their team, share information with them and understand intuitively when to intervene and when to withdraw and leave the team to control and manage a situation. Team leaders also have a role to play in developing and managing the team's relationship with the department or organisation in which it is based and with stakeholders, such as other teams in the organisation, customers and suppliers. Additionally, team leaders have a role to play in helping their team resolve problems and conflicts. This includes asking questions which enable the team to structure or talk through problems and conflicts such that there is understanding of the difficulty, and the generation, evaluation and implementation of solutions. If third parties, more or different resources are needed to help resolve the difficulties, the leader has a role to play in negotiating for these with other stakeholders.

A good example of leadership is that offered by Winston Churchill, Britain's Prime Minister during the Second World War. Churchill understood the threat posed by Hitler in the 1930s and this allowed him to have a leading role in taking the Allies to victory. This marks Churchill out as an exceptional leader and one who could be said to have had vision, charisma and excellent team leader abilities.

Summary

This chapter examined approaches to organisational behaviour, individuals, groups and leadership in organisations. The following summary covers all aspects of this chapter.

1 Taylor's basic assumption was that people dislike work but will undertake it in order to earn a living. Close and fair supervision would be required if people were to contribute at the required level to the organisation, although extra effort could be rewarded.

2 Mayo undertook the 'Hawthorne studies' and reached the conclusion that increases in the productivity of a workforce may in part be due to the attention paid to the workers by researchers observing them.

3 Drucker developed the idea of managing by objectives and thought additionally that managers should be strategic, risk takers, delegators, team builders, effective communicators, and should understand the organisation and its environment.

4 McGregor is known for Theory X and Theory Y. Theory X assumes that people cannot be trusted and need to be very highly controlled; hence managers who believe in Theory X will be autocratic. Theory Y assumes people are self-motivated towards achieving objectives and hence managers who believe Theory Y will develop cooperative relationships with their employees.

5 Rosabeth Moss Kanter undertook research which showed that companies which were good at innovation and changing direction greatly value people's problem-solving skills, enterprise and creativity.

6 Values, attitudes and perception all impact on an individual's behaviour in an organisation. Values are guiding principles which individuals, groups,

organisations and society use to determine whether behaviour is acceptable or unacceptable. An understanding of the individual's values will provide a strong indication of their attitudes. Attitudes to jobs cover a number of areas: job satisfaction, job involvement and organisational commitment. Job involvement is the extent to which an individual identifies with and is involved in their job, while organisational commitment covers the degree to which an employee identifies with the organisation and is loyal to it. Job satisfaction reflects an individual's attitude to their job. A person holding a high level of job satisfaction will have positive views concerning their employment and vice versa.

7 Perception is an individual's personal view of the world and definition of reality. Other individuals will hold different views and perceptions concerning the same person, item or situation. Differences in perception can arise from a number of factors which can exist in the perceiver, the item or individual being perceived, or in the situation in which the perception occurs.

8 Groups can be formal or informal. Formal groups can be command or task groups. Command groups depend on a hierarchical relationship in the organisation, i.e. a manager and his/her subordinates. Task groups do not, and will cut across departments and levels in the organisation. Informal groups include interest groups in which members have a common goal and friendship groups are based on social activities.

9 Groups develop through five stages: forming (coming together), storming (roles are established), norming (tasks are undertaken), performing (tasks and the project are completed), and mourning (group disbands and members move on to new projects).

10 Group performance is affected by size, norms, cohesiveness, roles and status of group members. It is likely that job satisfaction is greater in small groups due to more opportunity to contribute. Norms define acceptable behaviour in the group and cohesiveness is the attraction that holds the members together as a group. An individual's expected role in a group may differ from their enacted role and more closely match their perceived role. Status is conferred on individuals in the group by other group members.

11 Leadership is the ability to influence a team towards the achievement of goals. Charismatic leaders create organisational culture in which staff are self-motivating and seek to contribute to the organisation. Visionary leaders have the ability to develop a vision which takes the organisation beyond its current position and to clearly communicate that vision to all stakeholders in the organisation. Effective team leaders are those who trust their team, share information with them and know how to develop the team.

Chapter objectives and the exit case study

While reading this chapter and engaging in the activities, you should have learned how to apply theory and models and analyse situations. The exit case study and the questions which follow will provide an opportunity to assess how well you have met the relevant chapter objectives relating to specific material covered in the chapter.

Chapter objective	Check you have achieved this by
1 Explain the contribution of key organisational behaviour writers.	answering case study questions 1 and 2.

EXIT CASE STUDY 6.2

Final encore for a man of the people

by Jonathan Birchall

Neville Isdell is an imposing figure; more than six feet tall and solidly built, he is often referred to in the media as a former rugby player, a reference to his sporting days at university in South Africa. But as he prepares to step down after four years as chief executive of Coca-Cola, it is a more nuanced biographical detail that he prefers to accentuate. 'My major was sociology; I'm a qualified social worker,' he says. 'I do think it is all about people.'

When he took the helm in June 2004, many of the people at Coke were not very happy. Neither were the board nor the shareholders. Nor were the independent bottlers who mix and distribute Coke, Sprite and the group's other leading brands. The world's biggest soft drink company seemed to have lost its way after the dramatic global expansion in the 1990s under Roberto Goizueta. Sales of sparkling drinks in the US were in decline and its marketing was uninspired. Its strategy was unclear: Coke had lost out to PepsiCo in a battle for Gatorade and had abandoned a botched attempt to launch its Dasani water brand in Europe. There was also a simmering war going on with its independent bottlers over price increases.

The reputation-builder refused to be sidetracked by Olympic protest. Neville Isdell is an advocate of leading by listening. But he shows flashes of deep irritation when talking about the protesters who disrupted this year's Olympic torch relay, of which Coke is the leading international sponsor. 'I am really opposed to what the demonstrators have been doing. And I'm really opposed to the way they have treated the Chinese government as a result. It's the 3 to 4 per cent who try to influence the 96 per cent by utilising a symbol,' he complains, comparing the protests to the 'Killer Coke' campaign by student and labour activists that has led to a number of US campus boycotts of Coke products.

Under Mr Isdell, Coke has adopted a more engaged response to reputational issues. Last year, Coke joined the Business Leaders Initiative on Human Rights, formed a partnership with the WWF on water conservation, and set a goal of 'water neutrality' for its own manufacturing plants. 'If you do those things, the other 96 per cent looks at you in a positive way, they see you in a positive part of society. And the siren song of that 4 per cent doesn't get that resonance.'

Mr Isdell, a former senior bottling executive who turns 65 this month, was enticed out of retirement by a board that wanted a chief executive who knew both sides of the Coke system – meaning both Coca-Cola and the bottlers. He says he had a clear idea about what he wanted to achieve, and how he intended to go about it. 'You don't want to come and do quick fixes. When I accepted I agreed with the board that I was going to set it up for the long term and I believe that I have,' he says.

Within his first month, Mr Isdell made two substantial changes, appointing a new head of human resources who would report directly to him – giving him close control over what he calls 'the people equation' – and creating a new 'bottling investment group' to repair the relationship between the two halves of the business. His next move was to create a shared agreement among Coke's own people about what needed to be done. It was important, he says, to focus on the obvious question of what exactly Coca-Cola was, and what it was not, in spite of a clamour of calls from investors and analysts for action on everything from Coke's assertive board to its lack of non-carbonated beverages.

Before his arrival, he says, Coke had various strategic statements about its purpose. 'But there was [no] coherence to them and . . . there were clearly mixed messages out there.' So in the summer of 2004, 150 of Coke's top

managers were brought together for three days in Miami, for a series of discussions on a new 'manifesto'. In the break-out sessions, Mr Isdell sat listening to people 'pour out what they felt was wrong'. 'That is an important part of the rebuilding process . . . And then you say, "here's what you said is wrong with our business . . . so what are we going to do about it?"'

Mr Isdell's people skills are integral to his management style. He is at pains to put people at their ease, a characteristic shown by his habit of waiting outside the interview room to greet his guests. He can also still deliver an authentic Northern Irish accent, although he left his birthplace for southern Africa at the age of 10. After leaving university, Mr Isdell joined Coke's local bottler in Zambia in 1966, and six years later became general manager of Coca-Cola Bottling of Johannesburg, the largest Coke bottler in Africa. Subsequently, he held positions in Australia, the Philippines and Germany, before moving to Europe and spearheading the expansion of Coke into new markets in India, the Middle East and Eastern Europe and Russia in the 1990s. By the time he retired for the first time in 2001, he was vice-chairman of Coca-Cola HBC, the company's leading European bottler. He was running his own Barbados-based investment company when he was called back by Coke.

Mr Isdell's long history at the company strengthened his resolve to focus on core products. At one break-out session in Miami, managers echoed Wall Street analysts who were suggesting that Coke should try to emulate Pepsi's acquisition of the Frito-Lay snack company, which reduced its dependency on the historically declining fizzy drinks business. 'My reply was simply this: "You're all telling me that we are not running our own business at all well. So why would we buy another business, and think we could run that any better than the people who are there? Unless, you're telling me that we need to get their management to come and run our business." That closed down that debate. That's where you swing it, and they say, "Got it, we're clear".'

The new manifesto, by his own admission, 'is not earth shattering'; it says, for instance, that the company will 'reinvigorate growth . . . by building a portfolio of branded beverages, anchored in our icon, Coca-Cola'. But, he says, 'it does reflect who and what we are'. Armed with $400m in additional spending on marketing and innovation from the board, he helped select Weiden & Kennedy as Coke's new advertising agency – working with Mary Minnick, whom he had brought to Atlanta from Asia in May 2005 to head marketing and innovation. Ms Minnick's proven talents created one of the toughest decisions of the four years – who would become the next chief executive.

Mr Isdell's preference was for Muhtar Kent, rather than Ms Minnick. The two had worked together at the Amatil-Europe bottling subsidiary, building market share in Eastern Europe in the 1990s. However, Mr Kent had left Coke in 1998 after a sale of Amatil shares led to his investigation by Australian regulators for alleged insider trading. But Mr Isdell was convinced of his former colleague's leadership potential and persuaded the board the younger man should return to Coke. In 2006 Mr Kent was appointed chief operating officer and the following year was named international president. Though Ms Minnick subsequently left the company, Mr Isdell says he would have loved her to stay.

As Mr Isdell prepares to stand down, he says that the toughest period came 18 months after he took over, when Wall Street and the media could see no measurable improvements. Then, he said, he focused on keeping people on course, by preparing them for a difficult stage that he argues is part of every turnround effort. 'You know it's working. But most people don't believe it's working . . . That's when people tend to panic, and go back to short termism. And then you have to stick with it . . . [I] talked to everyone a lot about that, just to make sure I kept those people with me.'

Under Mr Isdell, the company has recorded steady international sales growth of more than 4 per cent over the past 12 quarters. And while sales in the US are being depressed by the slowdown in economic demand, he argues that the key carbonated drinks business is 'on track' for better results, supported by initiatives such as new bottle design.

Mr Isdell believes Mr Kent is, like himself, a man with people skills, and describes the UK-educated son of a Turkish diplomat as 'ambassadorial'. 'He's one of the world's great best networkers, and that's what you need in the business that we're in. He's really excellent at that.'

Source: from 'Final encore for a man of the people', *The Financial Times*, 8 June 2008 (Birchall, J.).

Exit case study question

1 Which of Drucker's 'seven tasks of tomorrow's manager' did Neville Isdell undertake while at Coca-Cola? Are there any he didn't undertake and should have?

2 Do you think Drucker's 'seven tasks of tomorrow's manager' are relevant today? Identify any situation in which organisations might use Drucker's seven tasks of tomorrow's manager.

Short-answer questions

1 What was the basic assumption underpinning Taylor's approach to his studies on work and management?

2 Explain the Hawthorne effect.

3 State what, according to Drucker, are the tasks of tomorrow's manager.

4 What is McGregor's Theory Y?

5 What did Rosabeth Moss Kanter study?

6 Identify the following as either terminal or instrumental values for a manufacturing company: world class, cleanliness, precision, customer satisfaction.

7 According to Herzberg, what are 'hygiene' factors?

8 Explain the term 'attribution theory'.

9 Name the different types of group an individual working for an organisation may find themselves a member of.

10 Illustrate the five different stages of group development.

11 Identify the factors which can affect group performance.

12 Explain the different types of leader which may be found in organisations.

Chapter objectives and assignment questions

While reading this chapter and engaging in the activities, you should have learned how to apply theory and models and analyse situations. This means you should be able to meet the chapter objectives outlined at the beginning of the chapter. The table below shows which chapter objectives can be tested by the different questions.

Chapter objective	Check you have achieved this by
1 Explain the contribution of key organisational behaviour writers.	answering assignment question 1.
2 Summarise the role of the individual in organisations.	answering assignment question 2.
3 Discuss group membership and development in organisations.	answering assignment question 3.
4 Identify and explain different types of approach to leadership.	answering assignment question 4.

Assignment questions

1 Undertaking relevant further research, compare and contrast the work of Douglas McGregor and Frederick Herzberg.

2 Consider the individual in an organisation and discuss the relevance of values, attitudes and perception to their role in the workplace.

3 Choose a group of which you are or have recently been a member – it can be at work, college or outside work or college. Identify the type of group it is and your reasons for joining it. Discuss the group's development and evaluate the success of its development and performance.

4 Identify and discuss different approaches to leadership which occur in organisations.

WEBLINKS available at www.pearsoned.co.uk/capon

These weblinks look at unacceptable behaviour in organisations and how it can be dealt with.

- This is the website of arbitration service ACAS:
  http://www.acas.org.uk/
  Click on 'equality'.
  Select 'Bullying and harassment'.
- This is the website of the Trade Union Congress:
  http://www.tuc.org.uk/tuc/rights_bullyatwork.cfm
- This is an American website that looks at unacceptable behaviour in the workplace:
  http://www.workdoctor.com

FURTHER READING

The chapters suggested in the following textbooks cover an introduction to organisational behaviour, perception and teamwork.

- Brooks, I (2006) *Individuals, Groups and Organisations*, 3rd edn, Chapters 1, 2 and 4, Harlow: Financial Times Prentice Hall.
- Buchanan, D and Huczynski, A (2008) *Organisational Behaviour*, 6th edn, Chapters 7 and 11, Harlow: Financial Times Prentice Hall.
- Dick, P and Ellis, S (2006) *Introduction to Organisational Behaviour*, 3rd edn, Chapters 1, 3 and 5, Maidenhead: McGraw Hill.
- Martin, J (2005) *Organisational Behaviour*, 3rd edn, Chapters 1, 3, 6 and 7, London: Thomson Learning.
- Mullins, L J (2008) *Essentials of Organisational Behaviour*, 2nd edn, Chapters 1, 3 and 6, Harlow: Financial Times Prentice Hall.
- Mullins, L J (2007) *Management and Organisational Behaviour*, 8th edn, Chapters 1, 6, 7 and 9, Harlow: Financial Times Prentice Hall.
- Rollinson, D (2008) *Organisational Behaviour and Analysis: An Integrated Approach*, 4th edn, Chapters 1, 4 and 11, Harlow: Financial Times Prentice Hall.

REFERENCES

1 Clutterbuck, D and Crainer, S (1990) *Makers of Management*, London, Papermac Macmillian.
2 Ibid.
3 Ibid.
4 Ibid.
5 Ibid.
6 Ibid.
7 Jones, G R (2001) *Organizational Theory*, New Jersey: Prentice Hall.
8 Robbins, S P (2000) *Essentials of Organizational Behavior*, New Jersey: Prentice Hall.
9 Huczynski, A and Buchanan, D (2001) *Organizational Behaviour*, Harlow: Financial Times Prentice Hall.
10 Tyson, S and Jackson, T (1992) *The Essence of Organizational Behaviour*, Hemel Hempstead: Prentice Hall.
11 Vecchio, R P (2000) *Organizational Behavior*, New Jersey: Prentice Hall.
12 Robbins, op. cit.
13 Tuckman, B C (1965) 'Development sequence in small groups', *Psychological Bulletin*, 36(6), pp 384–99 and Tuckman, B C and Jensen, M A C (1977) 'Stages of small group development revisited', *Group and Organization Studies*, 2(4) pp 419–27 in Huczynski, A and Buchanan, D (2001) *Organizational Behaviour*, Harlow: Financial Times Prentice Hall.
14 Vecchio, op. cit.
15 Robbins, op. cit.
16 Robbins, op. cit.
17 Robbins, op. cit.

CHAPTER 7

Human resource management

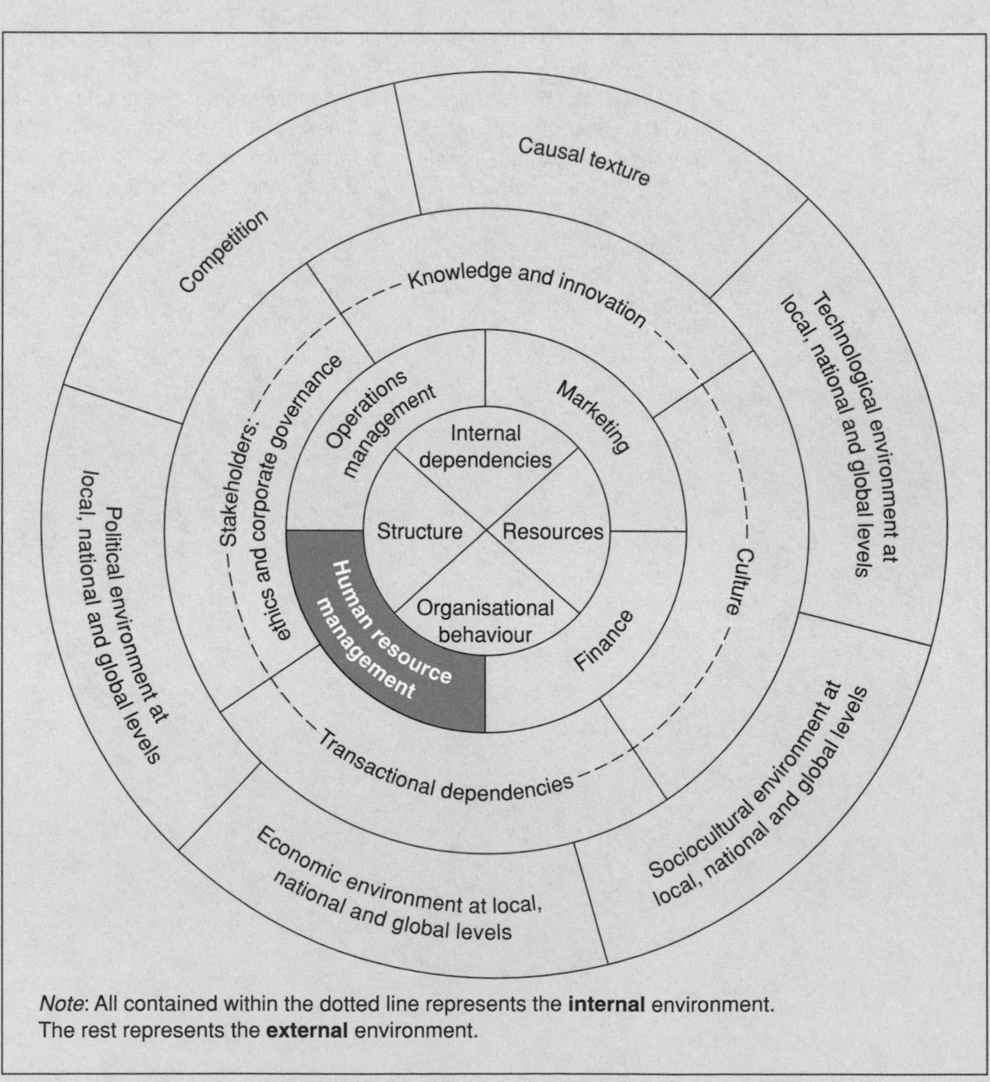

Figure 7.1 Business environment model

Chapter objectives

This chapter provides an overview of external factors that impact on the HR function and also covers the recruitment process, including job analysis, job descriptions, person specification, advertising and assessment of applicants. Therefore, when you have read this chapter and worked through the associated activities you should be able to achieve the objectives specified below.

1 **Identify and discuss external factors that impact on the HR function.**

2 **Summarise the benefits of flexibility in the workforce to an organisation and discuss how it can be achieved.**

3 **Apply the job recruitment process to a vacancy.**

This case study examines the current skills shortage in the Russian power industry and the likelihood that this will continue for some time due to the lower number of highly skilled graduates being produced by the Russian education system. The role of emigration of young Russians to the West and the arrival of immigrants into Russia is also discussed.

ENTRY CASE STUDY 7.1

Skills shortage hits Russian revival

by Stefan Wagstyl and Neil Buckley

Russia's power industry is planning to pour $100bn into modernising the country's creaking electricity network. But it may not find enough engineers for the job.

Faced with serious skills shortages, Unified Energy System, the electricity monopoly, is scouring the globe. It has long hired engineering contractors from old Soviet states, but is now looking in China, the European Union, Turkey and Iran. 'We're worried about labour with so many projects to be developed at the same time,' said Sergei Dubinin, the group's chief financial officer.

Across Russia, employers face similar shortages. Engineers, technicians and commercial managers are in the most demand, with the booming construction industry seeing the biggest difficulties. Peter Aven, head of Alfa-Bank, one of Russia's largest, said labour shortages were 'a real problem'.

The average monthly wage in February was Rbs15,214 ($650, €408, £327) – up 15 per cent in real terms in a year, and a six-fold nominal rise since 2000. But reflecting demand for senior executives, the Hay Group of consultants found last year that managers of big industrial companies had seen annual pay jump 60 per cent in a year to nearly $160,000.

Behind such increases is Russia's average 7 per cent annual economic growth since its 1998 financial crisis. Unemployment has fallen from a peak of 13 per cent to less than 6 per cent, with effective rates in Moscow and some other big cities close to zero. Job agencies in Krasnodar – the southern region covering Sochi, the 2014 Winter Olympics host – report big labour shortages in construction. In the industrial city of Chelyabinsk, 44,226 vacancies were reported in January out of a 1m population. In Murmansk, in the north, fishermen complain that Gazprom, the gas group, is poaching workers for its huge Shtokman offshore project.

Employers worry most about skilled workers. The old Soviet school system, though often delivering high standards, did not prepare students for post-communist times. Reforms after 1991 were hampered by economic upheavals and the emigration of about 1m young Russians to the west. While about 5m legal – and more than 10m illegal – immigrants have arrived in Russia from other parts of the old Soviet Union, they are mostly not of the same educational calibre.

Arkady Dvorkovich, President Vladimir Putin's chief economic adviser, says the answer is investment in education, especially in management and engineering. Education spending has more than doubled from Rbs162bn in 2005 to a budgeted Rbs330bn this year.

Mr Dvorkovich is less concerned about the overall labour market. He says that despite recent increases, Russia's labour productivity is very low – standing at 12

to 15 per cent of developed country standards – and the scope for redeploying labour is huge. 'With increased productivity, we will not have any shortage of labour in the future,' he said.

But others are not so sure. Economists say redeployment requires more flexible labour laws. Also, given Russia's size, poor transport and inadequate housing, people are reluctant to move. Yevgeny Gavrilenkov, chief economist at Troika Dialog, an investment bank, says the government must boost mobility through efficient infrastructure investment.

Such support will be more necessary as the population declines at rates unprecedented among industrialised nations, owing to low birth rates, poor healthcare and high levels of accidents and alcoholism. The working-age population has just passed its post-Soviet peak of 90m – out of a total of 140m – and is forecast to fall to 77m by 2020. The official employment rate is already reasonably high by developed world standards, so the scope for further gains is limited.

At this week's congress of the dominant United Russia party, Boris Gryzlov, its leader, called for policies to boost the population to at least 200m and produce more skilled 'cadres'. 'We've simply got no one to work new equipment,' he said. Only 3m Russians had specialist industrial qualifications, while 12m were unqualified. 'We need those proportions to be reversed.'

Mr Gryzlov appealed for 20m ethnic Russians living outside the country to return home. Russia has long encouraged ethnic Russian immigrants and discouraged others, reflecting widespread anti-foreigner prejudices. But, in practice, millions of illegal migrants from central Asia and the Caucasus work in low-paid jobs.

Last year, the government tightened controls by encouraging illegal residents to register while setting strict quotas for new arrivals. Mr Dvorkovich said: 'Migrants are welcome on the understanding that people must be fully integrated into Russian culture and the Russian economy.'

Demographers say this approach is too cautious for the growing labour needs. Yaroslav Lissovolik, chief economist at Deutsche Bank in Russia, said: 'The needs for labour are so dramatic that the former Soviet Union is probably not big enough. We must go further abroad.'

Source: from 'Skills shortage hits Russian revival', *The Financial Times*, 17 April 2008 (Wagstyl, S. and Buckley, N.).

Introduction

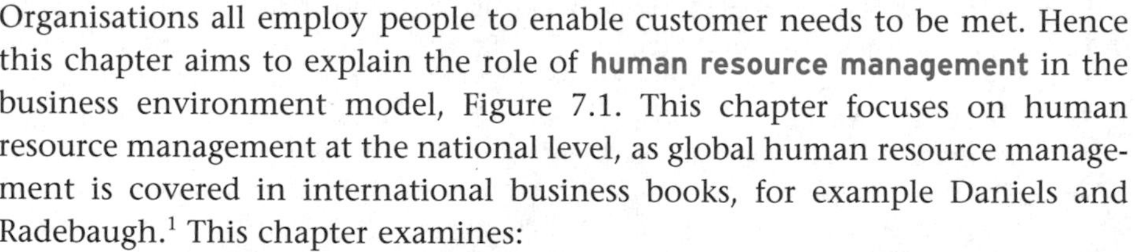

Organisations all employ people to enable customer needs to be met. Hence this chapter aims to explain the role of **human resource management** in the business environment model, Figure 7.1. This chapter focuses on human resource management at the national level, as global human resource management is covered in international business books, for example Daniels and Radebaugh.[1] This chapter examines:

- the role of the human resource management function in organisations;
- the key legislation covering the recruitment and employment of human resources;
- **demographics** and the human resource management function;
- workforce flexibility including the **flexible firm** model;
- the employee recruitment process.

Human resource management

Human resource management is an integrative general management activity that involves examining the organisation's demand for human resources with particular skills and abilities. The entry case study for the chapter discusses the

Russian energy industry where many companies are experiencing a gap between their demand for skilled staff and those available in the labour market. Therefore, HRM includes the training and development of existing staff along with the recruitment of new staff. Alternatively, if the organisation is over-staffed, the issues of redundancy, retirement and non-replacement of staff who leave will all have to be considered. Therefore, the HR department considers both the operational and strategic management of employees and their contribution to the organisation. Issues concerning the number of employees, the skills required and the cost to the organisation of employees with the required skills are of prime importance to the HR department.

The operational role of human resource specialists includes them in offering guidance and support to enable other managers in the organisation to handle their role as managers of human resources. This occurs because the activity of human resource management has become more decentralised as organisations have found a growing need for a more flexible workforce in order to respond more easily to influences and changes in the external environment. Hence the activity of human resource management includes recruitment and selection of appropriate staff, training and development of staff, and the management of the employment relationship, which includes contracts, collective bargaining, reward systems and employee involvement.

The main strategic focus of HRM is the management of human resources utilised by the organisation. The main priority is planning, monitoring and adjusting the number and nature of the organisation's human resources. The argument for this is that the organisation, its objectives and employees' interests are best served by effective overall management, which takes account of employees' skills, abilities and career development needs.

External influences on human resource management

The human resource management function in any organisation is influenced by the external environment. The main external influences currently include legislation, demographics and workforce flexibility. Legislation that affects and influences the human resource management function falls into three categories, shown in Table 7.1, and is discussed later in this chapter. Additionally, the work of the Equality and Human Rights Commission whose role is to tackle discrimination and promote equality in the workplace is covered later in the chapter. The impact of demographics, the flexible firm, and work–life balance along with flexibility are also discussed later in this chapter.

Check your understanding

Do you understand the role of HRM in organisations?

Check your understanding by outlining the activities an HR department could expect to be involved in.

Table 7.1 Employment legislation

Employment legislation	• Contract of Employment Act 1963 • Industrial Relations Act 1971 • Employment (Consolidation) Act 1978 • Employment Acts 1980, 1982 and 1988 • Trade Union Act 1984 • Employment Act 1990 • Trade Union and Labour Relations (Consolidation) Act 1992 • Trade Union Reform and Employment Rights Act 1993 • Employment Rights Act 1996 • Employment Rights (Dispute Resolution) Act 1998 • Employment Relations Act 1999 and 2004 • Employment Act 2002 and 2008
Health and safety at work legislation	• Factories Act 1961 • Offices, Shops and Railway Premises Act 1963 • Fire Precautions Act 1971 • Health and Safety at Work Act 1974 • Health Act 2006
Equalising employment legislation	• Equal Pay Act 1970 • Sex Discrimination Acts 1975 and 1986 • Race Relations Act 1976 • Disability Discrimination Acts 1995 and 2005 • Employment Equality (Sexual Orientation) Regulations 2003 • Employment Equality (Religion or Belief) Regulations 2003 • Equality Act 2006 • Employment Equality (Age) Regulations 2006 • Equality Act (Sexual Orientation) 2007

Employment legislation

The **Contracts of Employment Act 1963** specified, for the first time, that employees should receive the main terms and conditions of their employment in writing. This Act covered the formation, changes to and the ending of the contract of employment. The **Industrial Relations Act 1971** allowed employees, again for the first time, to take their employer to an employment tribunal for unfair dismissal. Both Acts were assimilated in the **Employment Protection (Consolidation) Act 1978**. This Act put into place the condition that an employee must have been in full-time employment for two years or more with an employer before being able to go to an employment tribunal with a case of unfair dismissal.

The Conservatives were in power for a continuous period from 1979 to 1997. During the 1980s Margaret Thatcher and her government embarked on a methodical approach to legislation that reduced the power and rights of both the individual employee and the trade unions. The creation of an economic system that was increasingly free market was one of the aims of the Thatcher government. Consequently, it held the belief that the rights of the individual employee and unions, as established by the 1970s legislation, were obstructive to the establishment of a free-enterprise culture and job creation in the UK economy. Hence a significant amount of employment legislation was passed in the 1980s and some of the key acts are the **Employment Acts of 1980, 1982 and 1988** and the **Trade Union Act 1984**. These four pieces of legislation all diminished the rights of individual employees and unions and expanded the legal regulation of industrial action and trade union activity. This meant there were changes to ballot requirements for calling a strike and nearly all types of secondary industrial action were outlawed – secondary industrial action occurs when employees in one workplace take industrial action in support of employees in another workplace who are in dispute with their employer.

In the 1990s, it was clear that the Tory governments of Margaret Thatcher and later of John Major had won their battle with the trade unions. The **Employment Act 1990** allowed those individuals refused employment due to their lack of membership of a trade union and hence of a closed shop to take the union involved to an employment tribunal, further curtailing the power of the trade unions. This Act also made all forms of secondary industrial action unlawful. The Trade Union and Labour Relations (Consolidation) Act 1992 and the Employment Rights Act 1996 (as amended by the Trade Union Reform and Employment Rights Act 1993 and the Employment Relations Act 1999 respectively) consolidated and replaced previous employment legislation. The 2004 Employment Relations Act builds on the Employment Relations Act 1999 and covers labour law and trade union rights, including the conduct of industrial action ballots.

The Employment Act 2002 is a wide-ranging bill and covers a variety of areas including working parents, the right for time off work for union duties, changes to dispute resolution in the workplace and employment tribunal procedures. The **Employment Act 2008** aims to improve the effectiveness of employment law, increase protection for vulnerable workers and change the law in a number of areas including dispute resolution, unfair dismissal, conciliation by ACAS and implementation of the minimum wage.

Health and safety at work legislation

There are four key Health and Safety at Work Acts, outlined below. These deal with the health and safety of employees at work and were all passed between 1961 and 1974. In addition the smoking legislation in England is examined. These four key Acts were updated in the 1990s by EU Directives. These Directives include regulations covering the implementation of minimum standards for safe use of machines and equipment, lifting heavy loads, using visual display monitors, and health safeguards for employees working with carcinogenic substances such as asbestos. The EU directives also cover the provision and use of protective equipment, lifting equipment, free eye tests, glasses, regular breaks and training. Other health and safety regulations include the Control of Substances Hazardous to Health Regulations 1988, introduced under the 1974 Health and Safety at Work Act. These regulations place a requirement on employers to pay close attention to the manner and the extent to which substances hazardous to health are handled, used and controlled.

Factories Act 1961 and Office, Shops and Railways Act 1963

The **Factories Act 1961** lays down minimum standards in factories regarding cleanliness, workspace, temperature, ventilation, lighting, toilet facilities, clothing, accommodation and first-aid facilities. The **Offices, Shops and Railway Premises Act 1963** extends the same general cover as outlined in the 1961 Act to other work premises. However, there are some small differences in the 1963 Act covering minimum workspace provision and temperature.

Fire Precautions Act 1971

Workplace premises require a fire certificate and the **Fire Precautions Act 1971** allows the fire authorities to impose conditions on the certificate holder, including closure of a building if it does not comply with the conditions. These conditions can cover the means of escape and exit from the premises, instruction and training of employees on how to react in the event of a fire, and limits on the number of people on the premises at any one time.

Health and Safety at Work Act 1974

The **Health and Safety at Work Act 1974** is a comprehensive piece of legislation covering people at work and those who may be at risk from the activities of those engaged in work. It created the Health and Safety Commission and the Health and Safety Executive. The Health and Safety Commission ensured that the Act was implemented correctly and had the power to carry out investigations and enquiries if it appeared the Act was not being adhered to in a workplace and it could also issue codes of best practice and regulation. The Health and Safety Executive was a separate body which assisted in the enforcement of the Health and Safety at Work Act 1974 by undertaking the daily administrative affairs relating to its implementation.

However, in 2008 the Health and Safety Commission and the Health and Safety Executive merged to form a single body, to be called the Health and Safety Executive. The new Health and Safety Executive will continue to be responsible for implementation of health and safety legislation in the workplace, along with the promotion of safe practices in the workplace.[2]

The Health Act 2006

The **Health Act 2006** was implemented in England on 1 July 2007 and meant all employers would have to provide smoke-free workplaces for staff. This act supports the Health and Safety at Work Act 1974 that requires employers to ensure the health and welfare of their staff. The 2006 Act takes account of better understanding of how smoking and passive smoking harm people's health. The legislation also requires appropriate signage using the 'No smoking' symbol to be displayed, indicating that a building or vehicle is smoke free.

The Health Act 2006 requires all workplaces and work vehicles along with enclosed or substantially enclosed public places, e.g. restaurants, bingo halls and shopping malls, to be smoke free. There are a number of exemptions from the law covering hotel bedrooms, care homes, hospices, prisons and offshore installations. The total ban on smoking in residential mental health units in England did not come into force until 1 July 2008; however, this remains controversial and it is being challenged in the European courts. This is in contrast to Scotland where a different view of smoking in residential mental health units has been taken and they are exempted from the smoking ban, with provision in the legislation to review the situation.

Discrimination commissions

The **Equal Opportunities Commission** (EOC), the **Commission for Racial Equality** (CRE) and the **Disability Rights Commission** (DRC) came together as the **Equality and Human Rights Commission** in October 2007.

The Equal Opportunities Commission was originally established by the 1975 Sex Discrimination Act, with the powers to work towards the elimination of discrimination on the grounds of sex or marital status, to promote equality of opportunity for women and men. Additionally the EOC was charged with keeping the **Sex Discrimination Act** (1975) and the **Equal Pay Act** (1970) under review as well as providing legal advice and assistance to people who claim to have been discriminated against.

Today the work on sex discrimination continues under the new Equality and Human Rights Commission and covers a variety of issues impacting on people and the organisations they use and work for, including making public services relevant to the differing needs of men and women and securing comprehensive equality legislation across the UK and Europe. In addition work continues on the obvious sex discrimination issues of: closing the pay gap between men and women; ending sexual harassment at work; and ending male and female stereotypes with the aim of making it easier for parents to balance family and work commitments.

The Commission for Racial Equality was originally established by the Race Relations Act 1976 to tackle racial discrimination and promote racial equality. Additionally, the CRE sought to encourage good relations between people from different racial and ethnic backgrounds and monitored the way the Race Relations Act 1976 worked and advised on possible improvements. This work continues under the new Equality and Human Rights Commission and now includes religious discrimination.

The Disability Rights Commission was established in April 2000 by the Disability Rights Commission Act 1999. The role of the Disability Rights Commission was to work to eliminate discrimination against, and promote equality of opportunity for, disabled people, and promote good practice in these areas as well as advising the government on disability legislation. This work has now been incorporated into the work undertaken by the new Equality and Human Rights Commission.

Equalising employment legislation

Harassment, bullying, direct and indirect discrimination

There are two types of discrimination: direct and indirect and, along with bullying and harassment, these constitute the behaviours which are unlawful. Direct discrimination occurs when workers of a particular sex, race, religion, or ethnic origin are treated less favourably than other workers, for example specifying a female secretary in a job advert when the job could be done equally well by a man. Indirect discrimination arises when a requirement that is not necessary for the job is applied equally to all workers but it is more difficult for one group of workers to comply with by virtue of their sex, race or ethnic origin. For instance, a job advert requiring perfect written English for a manual labourer would discriminate against people of race, ethnic origin or nationality where English is not a first language.

Harassment and bullying are unwanted conduct affecting the dignity of people in the workplace and may be based on age, sex, race, religion, nationality or any other personal characteristic, for example ginger hair. Key to the definition is not what the perpetrator intends by their remarks and actions, but how unwelcome and humiliating the recipient is made to feel. Harassment and bullying can be a one-off act or persistent behaviour over a period of time and includes a variety of behaviours such as shouting, offensive jokes, coercion for sexual favours, graffiti, isolation, and unwanted physical contact.

Sex discrimination legislation

The Sex Discrimination Act 1975 came into force at the same time as the Equal Pay Act 1970, at the end of 1975. This allowed organisations five years to achieve parity of pay between the sexes. The Sex Discrimination Act 1975 promotes the equal treatment of men and women in the areas of recruitment, training, promotion, benefits and dismissal. It also established the Equal Opportunities Commission, whose role was to eliminate discrimination on grounds of sex or marital status, promote equal opportunities between men and women, and monitor the implementation of the Equal Pay Act 1970 and the Sex Discrimination Act 1975.

Genuine occupational qualification allows the recruitment of a particular type of person, if there is a genuine need relating directly to the job. Vacancies in the field of modelling or acting have a genuine occupational qualification, for example a woman to model female clothes. The genuine occupational qualification also applies in the area of recruiting healthcare staff to provide personal care for elderly or infirm patients. However, discriminatory treatment in terms and conditions of employment is not allowed.

The main sexual orientation legislation in the United Kingdom is the 2003 Employment Equality (Sexual Orientation) Regulations and the Equality Act (Sexual Orientation) Regulations 2007. This legislation defines sexual orientations as being heterosexual, homosexual and bisexual. Sexual orientation is not the same as sexual practices and sexual practices such as sadomasochism and paedophilia are not covered by this legislation.[3]

Equal Pay Act 1970

The Equal Pay Act 1970 came into force on 29 December 1975 and promotes equal pay for men and women. It stipulates that a man and woman should receive equal pay if either of the following types of circumstances applies:

- a man and a woman are doing like work; for example, a male shop assistant and a female shop assistant would clearly both be entitled to the same pay;
- a woman can show that she is carrying out work rated as equivalent to that of a man, under the organisation's job evaluation scheme. The woman may have a clerical post in the organisation and the man a technical job; if both jobs score the same points under the job evaluation scheme, then the woman can claim pay equal to that of the man and vice versa.

Proceedings against the British government by the European Commission resulted in the Equal Pay (Amendment) Regulation 1983, which came into force in 1984. This makes it possible to claim equal pay for work that is considered to be of equal value to that done by a member of the opposite sex. Equal value considers the skills, effort and decision-making responsibility involved in carrying out the job and requires no job evaluation scheme to be in operation.

In July 1995 the Conservative government's policy of compulsory competitive tendering was significantly undermined when the Law Lords ruled in favour of 1300 school meals staff employed by North Yorkshire Council. The council had sacked the school meals staff, then re-employed them and reduced their conditions of service by reducing pay from £3.40 to £3.00 per hour, cutting holiday entitlement and abolishing the sick pay scheme. The council carried out these cuts in order to defeat an outside tender for the school meals service. It did so regardless of a 1988 job evaluation scheme that found the work of the school meals staff to be of equal value to that of road sweepers, gardeners and refuse collectors, who were predominantly male. This meant that the school meals staff were discriminated against under the equal pay legislation and entitled to more than £2 million in lost pay and damages.[4]

The 1995 judgment by the Law Lords set a precedent and in July 1996 nearly 2000 school meals staff employed by the old Cleveland County Council won more than £1 million in lost wages and damages at an industrial tribunal. The compensation was for a pay cut introduced to aid the success of Cleveland County Council in compulsory competitive tendering against private firms.[5]

Race and religion discrimination legislation

The Race Relations Act 1976 is similar to the Sex Discrimination Act 1975. It makes it unlawful to discriminate against someone on the grounds of his or her race, colour, nationality or ethnic origin and established the Commission for Racial Equality. In October 2007 the new Equality and Human Rights Commission was established and covers race and religious discrimination along with other discrimination, e.g. sex discrimination. Religious discrimination was made illegal in 2003 and is covered by the Employment Equality (Religion or Belief) Regulations 2003 (SI 2003/1660). This defined religion as 'any religion or religious belief or similar philosophical belief'; however, the requirement for a philosophical belief to be 'similar' was removed by the Equality Act (2006).[6]

The exceptions to the Race Relations Act are similar to those for the Sex Discrimination Act 1975 and include the areas of entertainment, acting, artistic or photographic modelling, specialised restaurants and community or social workers providing personal services to members of a particular racial group. As with the exceptions in sexual discrimination, discriminatory treatment in terms and conditions of employment is not allowed.

Disability discrimination legislation

The **Disability Discrimination Act 1995** defines disability as:

> **a physical or mental impairment which has a substantial and long-term adverse effect on a person's ability to carry out normal day-to-day activities. People who have had a disability, but no longer have one, are covered by the Act.**[7]

Discrimination happens when a disabled person is dealt with less favourably than an able-bodied person due to their disability and this cannot be justified. Employers are not allowed to justify unfavourable treatment of a disabled person if adjustment could be made to overcome the reasons for unfavourable treatment. For example, an employer could not refuse to promote a disabled person because the equipment they had to use could not be accessed, if by rearranging the equipment the disabled person could do the job.

Organisations employing more than 20 people must not discriminate against disabled employees in the areas of recruitment, working conditions or employee benefits – bonuses, promotion, training and dismissal. This covers permanent members of staff, temporary workers and contract workers. However, it does not cover the armed services, police officers, active members of a fire brigade and prison officers, or people working on ships, aircraft or hovercrafts.

The advertising of jobs must not indicate that a person might not get a job because of their disability or because the employer is unwilling to make adjustments. The selection process must not favour people who have no disability, offer jobs on less favourable terms to a disabled person, or refuse employment because of disability.

The **Disability Discrimination Act 2005** generally relates to disability outside employment, although some aspects of the Act do affect employers and employees. The 2005 Act extended the definition of disability to cover people with progressive conditions such as HIV, cancer and multiple sclerosis. In addition, people with mental illness are protected in the same way as people with other disabilities and publishers can now be held liable for publishing discriminatory advertisements.[8]

Age discrimination legislation

Work in the area of age discrimination is undertaken by the new Equality and Human Rights Commission and the main piece of legislation covering age discrimination is the Employment Equality (Age) Regulations 2006. This legislation makes it unlawful to discriminate on the basis of age in the same way that it is unlawful to discriminate on the basis of race, sex, sexual orientation, religion or belief. For example, age criteria should not be used in employment decisions. However, age data on applicants should be gathered in a separate tear-off section on the application form and the data collated, as failure to do so is likely to count against the organisation at any subsequent tribunal hearings. Equally, age must not be used to make judgements about applicants' or employees' ability or fitness. If such a judgement is required, an occupational health adviser or doctor should be consulted. In addition, decisions concerning rewards, training, promotion and redundancy should not be based on age criteria and all requests to work beyond the retirement age of sixty-five should be appropriately considered.

Check your understanding

Do you understand the issues which employment legislation covers?

Check your understanding by naming the Act which:

- allows an employee to take their employer to an industrial tribunal for unfair dismissal;
- requires workplaces to hold a fire certificate;
- led to the establishment of the Disability Rights Commission.

Demographics and human resource management

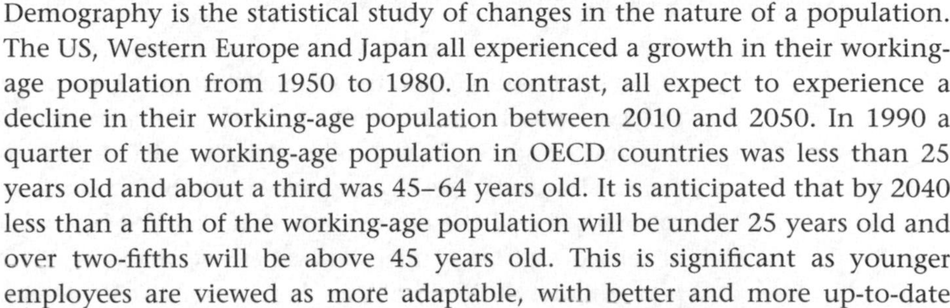

Demography is the statistical study of changes in the nature of a population. The US, Western Europe and Japan all experienced a growth in their working-age population from 1950 to 1980. In contrast, all expect to experience a decline in their working-age population between 2010 and 2050. In 1990 a quarter of the working-age population in OECD countries was less than 25 years old and about a third was 45–64 years old. It is anticipated that by 2040 less than a fifth of the working-age population will be under 25 years old and over two-fifths will be above 45 years old. This is significant as younger employees are viewed as more adaptable, with better and more up-to-date training. Moreover, not all people of working age choose to work: some will be in full-time higher or further education and others, mostly women, may choose to stay at home to care for young children or sick relatives.[9]

From the mid-1970s through to the mid-1990s early retirement was an accepted method of reducing the size of the workforce.[10] Older employees were seen as being more expensive and less flexible. The notion of early retirement has been particularly prevalent in the public sector. The combination of early retirement and reduced numbers of young people in the population means that there is a likelihood of labour shortages in Western Europe, North America and Japan in the early part of the twenty-first century, from 2000 to 2020. The response of organisations to this is the active recruitment of older staff and of migrant labour, who are willing to do low-paid jobs and jobs traditionally taken by younger people. However, the use of migrant labour in low-paid jobs in the United Kingdom will change, as in September 2008 the government announced policies which limit the number of migrants with the skills to do low-paid jobs, for example in the care home sector, food processing and construction industries.[11] The same policies would make migration to the UK easier for people with higher-level skills, for example ballet dancers, civil and chemical engineers, maths and science teachers and skilled chefs earning at least £8.10 per hour.[12]

In the UK the supermarket chain Tesco and the DIY chain B&Q are examples of companies whose employment policies in the past have included the active recruitment of older staff. In the future, retaining and retraining older employees will be a more appealing option for organisations as the competition for skilled younger employees will be increasingly fierce.[13,14] The advantages of an older workforce include the tendency of older people to change jobs and move around the country less frequently than younger people, hence contributing to lower labour turnover.

To attract and retain the required level of skilled labour, lifetime or long-term employment contracts may have to be offered. This will contrast strongly with the period from the 1980s to the early part of the twenty-first century when flexible labour contracts[15] and workforces fashioned on the **flexible firm model**[16] were more common.

The flexible firm

The advent of the flexible workforce owes much to the popularity of downsizing in organisations and the general shift in the economy from manufacturing to service provision. A manufacturer can either employ extra staff to meet peak demand or stock goods produced in a quiet time to meet demand at peak times. However, a service provider is unable to stock products to meet peaks in demand and therefore meets that demand by employing extra part-time or temporary staff. This is less expensive than employing a larger number of permanent full-time staff, as during troughs in demand the extra full-time permanent staff would be inactive. Therefore, downsizing occurs when organisations delayer, i.e. removing layers of employees so that they become structurally flatter, or when organisations reduce the number of core employees and recruit more part-time or subcontracted employees as and when required. The concept of the flexible workforce means organisations operating flexible working patterns to cope with peaks and troughs in demand by redeploying staff across different activities and locations or employing and laying off staff as cheaply as possible.

Classic examples of flexibility in the labour market include retailers taking on extra staff over Christmas; frozen vegetable companies, like Bird's Eye, taking on extra staff during summer months when the vegetables are harvested; restaurants or pubs taking on extra staff on Friday and Saturday evenings when they are busiest; and universities taking on part-time lecturers during an academic year when student over-recruitment has occurred.

The idea of an organisation and its flexible workforce is best summed up by the flexible firm model.[17] This divides employees into three categories: core, peripheral and external. The **core permanent employees** have highly skilled jobs, with relatively good job security and career prospects. These employees are expected to be flexible in terms of their role in the organisation and working location.

The **first peripheral group** are those employees with full-time jobs, not careers. In this group labour turnover is higher than for core employees. Employees in this group often require more vocational skills than core employees. They include supervisors, secretaries, assemblers and administrators.

The **second peripheral group** provides the major component of flexibility in the workforce and includes employees on short-term contracts, part-time employees, term-time employees, job-sharing employees and subsidised trainees. Employees on short-term contracts will hold full-time skilled jobs, for example a software engineer may be employed on a short-term contract to work full time on developing a piece of software for an organisation. In contrast, part-time employees work on a permanent basis for the organisation but only for a fraction of the hours of a full-time employee. For example, a part-time employee may work only mornings or certain days of the week. Term-time employees will work during the school term and will effectively have unpaid leave during school holidays. Job sharing occurs when two people split a job, the pay and rewards between them. This type of arrangement is common among women who wish to work but not for the full working week. Subsidised trainees work for the organisation while learning a trade and/or gaining qualifications. A good example of a subsidised training initiative is the Modern Apprenticeships Scheme, which is accessed via the Learning and Skills Council. Launched in September 1995, a Modern Apprenticeship takes one to three years to complete and involves the apprentice studying for a National Vocational Qualification in an area of craft, technical or junior management skills. The government covers around 25 per cent of the cost to the organisation of employing and training the apprentice.[18]

The final category of staff in the flexible firm model is **external staff**. They can be brought in quickly to meet increased demand and include self-employed consultants, subcontractors and temporary agency staff. The latter may include secretarial staff, administrators and supervisors. The common subcontracted activities are those that are non-core and can be done more cheaply and satisfactorily by contracted staff, such as cleaning, catering, provision of IT support and running the payroll. In contrast, self-employed consultants are used on a project-by-project basis, particularly when the necessary skills are not available in-house.

Flexibility and hours worked

Organisations have been able to develop and create further flexibility in the workforce with the use of other flexible working practices and technology. Variation in the way hours worked are defined and counted can provide organisations with flexibility. Such approaches to flexibility include flexi-time, compressed hours and annual hours. Flexi-time allows staff to choose when they stop and start work. If flexi-time is used in an organisation, then there are usually limits, for example core hours when staff must be present, for instance 10 a.m. to midday and 2 to 4 p.m. Compressed hours are often counted over a week or fortnight. There will not be a reduction in the number of hours worked, but the hours worked will be allocated into fewer and longer blocks of time. For example, the compressed hours arrangement may result in a member of staff working 37.5 hours over 4 days instead of 5 days or 75 hours over 8 or 9 days, instead of 10 days. The annual hours contract defines the number of hours a member staff must work over a year. For example, a university lecturer may be contracted to work 1500 hours a year.

The arrival of technology in the form of broadband, wireless connections, laptops and mobile phones has resulted in employees being able to work anywhere – in hotels, on trains, planes or at home. The ultimate use of technology is in the activity of teleworking or telecommuting. **Telecommuters** work at home, with technology that enables them to receive and send work and messages to their employing organisation. The potential advantages of telecommuting are that it saves commuting time, especially where traffic congestion is common and there are environmental benefits from less driving to and from work. Additionally, telecommuting saves money, as homeworkers spend less money on working clothes and commuting. The organisation also saves money by not having to provide permanent office space for staff; instead, a hot-desking arrangement will usually operate in companies which have a significant number of telecommuters.

However, the potential disadvantages of telecommuting include homeworkers feeling isolated, lonely, overworked and neglected by their work colleagues and the organisation. The danger exists that home and office are the same place and work takes over the home environment; hence, home is no longer an escape from work. The telecommuter also loses the companionship and social side of office life, so augmenting feelings of isolation, loneliness and neglect. The potential benefit of being able to work at any time of the day or night may not materialise for telecommuters as their clients may work only from nine to five. Those involved with high-volume, low-margin work may be reluctant to take time off as they fear loss of business and earnings, leading to feelings of overwork and a lack of work–life balance.

Therefore, companies with telecommuting employees need to manage the potential disadvantages. This can be done by developing a home-working scheme that involves employees working from home but includes regular contact with other telecommuters via technology and occasionally in person at an office or telecentre, where telecommuters may drop in to meet other telecommuters. This provides a social focus for office life and helps to combat feelings of isolation, loneliness and neglect among teleworkers.[19]

The legal position on flexible working in the UK is that any parent of a child under six (set to increase to sixteen in 2009), or eighteen if the child is disabled, or carer of an adult has the right to request flexible working. The organisation is not obliged to grant the request, but must give such a request serious consideration. Reasons for its refusal must be clear and relate to difficulties in operating the business with a flexible arrangement in place. The employee has the right of appeal.

Flexibility and work–life balance

Today many of us live in a 24-hour, 7-day society, with customers often expecting service at a time that suits them, and organisations respond accordingly. Therefore, the issue of work–life balance is important as no member of staff can do a 24/7 job! Hence many people would say that they work long hours, and intensely, and the opportunity to unwind is important for their physical and mental health and the quality of their life and that of their family. It could also be argued that long hours of work have been exacerbated by the growth in technology and teleworking (*see* earlier section).

Work–life balance is important for all types of employees: mothers and fathers with children to care for, adults with another relative for whom they care and people who have no caring commitments. A work–life balance allows employees time to undertake the responsibilities and participate in the activities that are important to them outside the workplace. The benefits of work–life balance include: increased motivation and commitment; higher productivity; improved retention and recruitment of staff; less absenteeism and increased flexibility, which should make it easier to cover absences and holidays.

Organisations are obliged to offer a variety of leave arrangements in the United Kingdom. The annual holiday entitlement is currently 24 days, although this will rise to 28 days, including bank holidays, on 1 April 2009. Maternity leave in the United Kingdom is up to 52 weeks, along with paternity leave and parental leave which can be taken by either parent at any time up to the child's fifth birthday. The law also allows for adoption leave and leave to care for a dependent relative.

Organisations may also encourage work–life balance, providing staff with the opportunity to review their work–life balance on a regular basis, information on health issues, access to health screening programmes, private health insurance and access to onsite or subsidised sports centres and gyms.

Check your understanding

Do you understand the different categories of employees in the flexible firm model?

Check your understanding by placing each of the employees in the appropriate category (core, first peripheral, second peripheral and external). Employees are a part-time university lecturer, an electrical subcontractor, a managing director and his/her secretary.

The employee recruitment process

The recruitment of employees to an organisation is crucial if the organisation is to acquire, retain and maintain the skills and abilities to provide customers with the products and services required in an efficient and effective manner. This also contributes directly to helping the organisation achieve its strategic goals. The development and use of a suitable recruitment procedure allows appropriate applicants to be matched to suitable posts. This should result in employees remaining with the organisation and making efficient and effective contributions to its goals.

The lack of a suitable employee recruitment process or poor implementation of the process may result in initial low recruitment costs. However, a lack of forethought and planning is false economy, resulting in unsuitable employees being recruited. The appointment of over- or under-skilled and qualified employees leads to tasks and activities not being done effectively and employees leaving their jobs relatively soon after taking up employment. This rapid turnover of employees results in the recruitment process being repeated to find a replacement employee and incurring the associated costs: in the areas of defining the job and the type of applicant, reading and shortlisting completed applications, and interviewing shortlisted applicants. There will also be the costs of any advertising undertaken and employment agencies used.

Rapid turnover of employees and associated high recruitment costs can result from a shortage of appropriately skilled labour. Industries in Russia, discussed in the entry case study, are likely to have a high turnover of labour, including engineers, technicians and commercial mangers, due to the rapid growth in industries such as energy and construction. This means companies such as the gas company Gazprom are more likely to poach labour from industries such as fishing to fill some offshore vacancies but will continue to struggle when filling highly skilled and managerial vacancies. Therefore, Russia is seeking to improve labour mobility via investment in infrastructure and housing, in addition to boosting the population from 140 million to 200 million. However, these are long-term solutions and what is needed is a shorter-term solution. This probably lies in good quality education and training of people to increase the number of Russians with specialised technical qualifications from 3 million while decreasing the number of unqualified staff from 12 million. Hence companies can address the shortage of skills on a number of fronts: the recruitment of employees, the use of training and development, the redeployment of existing staff, and the adjustment of work patterns and practices.

The recruitment of employees is one area to consider and build on in any attempt to ease a skills shortage. The advertising of vacancies can be boosted by widening the geographic area of search and increasing the range of advertising media employed. In addition, the advertising effort could be directed towards non-traditional groups of potential employees, for example the nursing profession targeting men and the engineering or construction professions targeting women. Other tactics involve requiring successful applicants recruited in one part of the country to relocate to the organisation's premises in another area where a skills shortage exists. This will be become more probable in Russia if infrastructure and housing improve. The direct approach of offering higher pay and more perks is always available, but expensive. However, the danger of this lies in the vicious circle that can be created when organisations poach skilled staff from each other and drive pay ever upwards. The lowering of entry requirements, such as qualifications and relevant work experience, is another means of reducing a shortage of skills. For example, the Army has on occasion lowered the standard of physical fitness required of recruits and extended the basic training to allow new recruits to attain an acceptable level of physical fitness. Alternatively, for some organisations the use of consultants, subcontractors and agencies could be initiated or extended to reduce a skills shortage.

Another way of handling a shortage of skills is to train existing employees to the required skills level. This will help diminish the skills shortage, although training and acquiring skills can take time and this is not a short-term method. In the entry case study, Russian companies may want to consider employing legal migrant staff and providing training and education to help them operate at the appropriate technical level. However, if the training is ongoing and developmental, it may well help in the retention and increased motivation of existing employees. The hazard of providing appropriate and good training is that well-trained and qualified employees leave for a better job elsewhere, with more pay and perks. One way of stemming a loss of recently skilled employees is to offer opportunities and promotion within the organisation.

An alternative to closing the skills gap by increasing the skills available in the organisation is to reduce the need for skills by altering work practices to accommodate existing skill levels. This includes reducing output, allowing overtime working and adjusting shift patterns, which is particularly practical

Table 7.2 Employee recruitment process

Stage 1	**Assessment of the job** • Job analysis • Job description
Stage 2	**Assessment of the type of applicant required** • Person specification • Key results areas
Stage 3	**Attracting applicants** • Placement of the advertisement • The advertisement
Stage 4	**Assessing applicants** • Assessment of application forms • Assessment of applicants

if it leads to increased productivity and reduced overtime. The skills gap could also be reduced by restructuring and reorganising the workforce and their jobs, which may entail multi-skilling, which in turn may necessitate further training.

Another option for dealing with a lack of skills is to find staff with the required skills from among those already in the organisation and second or promote them into the positions where the skills shortages exist for a temporary or permanent period.

The four stages of the employee recruitment process are looked at in theory (*see* Table 7.2) and in relation to a city-centre café-bar recruiting part-time staff.

Check your understanding

Do you understand how an organisation may reduce a skills gap or shortage?

Check your understanding by identifying three ways to reduce a skills gap or shortage.

Stage 1 – Assessment of the job

Job analysis

This is the first step in the employee recruitment process and involves gaining the correct information relating to the vacant job, as this will allow an accurate **job description** and **person specification** to be drawn up. **Job analysis** normally starts when the current job holder hands in their notice. Information has to be collected in order that the job description for the vacant job is clear and up to date. This is crucial, as the job description and the person specification drawn up from it will be central to the employee recruitment process.

The information collected should cover the areas of the job and its position in the organisation, the tasks and activities the job involves, the responsibilities of the job, and the conditions under which the job is carried out. The current job description is a good initial source of information. Further and more up-

Table 7.3 Job description

1	Identification of the job
2	Summary of the job
3	Content of the job
4	Working conditions
5	Performance standards

to-date information can be gathered by interviewing the current job holder before they leave the organisation and key personnel who surround the vacant job. These key personnel include the manager or supervisor of the current job holder and the latter's peers and subordinates. The utilisation of these sources of information gives a good indication of the tasks that the job involves and the key reporting and working relationships that the job holder must maintain. This information, along with consideration of the organisation's current and future plans and strategy, permits an up-to-date and accurate job description to be compiled.

Job description

The job description defines and outlines the job and covers the areas of the job shown in Table 7.3. In the sections on the job description and personnel specification, all areas are examined and related to the part-time job of a server in a city-centre café-bar, the type of part-time job a full-time student might seek to supplement their student loan.

Identification of the job

This section of the job description sets the job in its organisational context by stating the job title and the location of the job in the organisation. The location is defined by stating which section, department or division the job is situated in and where it will be based. This is important if the organisation has several sites in different geographic locations. The role of the job should also be put in context by outlining which staff the new appointee will be responsible to and how many staff the appointee will be responsible for. Staff with whom the new appointee will be expected to work and liase, both inside and outside the department, are also to be indicated. The city-centre café-bar seeking to recruit part-time staff must identify which position part-time staff are going to occupy. Is the vacancy for a part-time relief manager, part-time bar/serving staff or part-time kitchen staff?

Summary of the job

This segment of the job description examines why the job is done. This is accomplished by stating the overall objectives and purpose of the job, as well as comparing and contrasting it with other jobs in the organisation that are close or similar to it. The resulting differences between the vacant job and any similar jobs must be clearly demonstrated. Finally, the overall objectives and purpose of the job are linked with the overall objectives of the department and organisation. The café-bar recruiting part-time bar/serving staff may summarise such a job as 'welcoming customers and ensuring they receive friendly and accurate service'.

Content of the job

This portion of the job description depicts the content of the job in detail and indicates what is done and how it is done. In writing this, the objectives of the job and why the job is done are also considered closely (*see* previous section).

It is necessary to specify the tasks and activities constituting the job. The main tasks and activities are listed first, followed by those that are secondary. This allows outsiders to the organisation, such as potential applicants, to understand what is involved for the job holder. The people and equipment available and required for carrying out the job tasks and activities are also indicated in this portion of the job description. Issues to consider here are:

- whether the individual does the job single-handed, as part of a team, or perhaps the job requires a mixture of individual and teamwork (the café-bar server is required to work as part of a team);
- whether the job requires physical strength, intelligence, application of individual judgement or a combination of these traits (the café-bar server needs to be of average intelligence);
- whether the organisation provides resources and equipment to enable the job holder to carry out the required tasks and activities (the café-bar server is provided with a uniform of black trousers and purple shirt, which must be kept clean and must always be worn on duty).

Resources provided by the organisation could include access to office equipment such as computers, photocopiers, telephones, faxes and e-mail. Other resources made available to employees to enable them to perform their jobs may include portable personal computers, mobile phones, corporate uniforms, protective clothing, company cars, hand tools, specialised technical equipment and interest-free loans for season tickets.

If the job is for part-time bar/serving staff, the tasks and activities involved would include showing customers to their table, taking orders for food and drinks, serving food and drinks, laying tables, clearing tables, collecting payment, ensuring the customer is happy with the food and drink they have ordered and serving behind the bar. Such part-time bar/serving staff would be responsible to the manager and have to work with the kitchen staff in ensuring that correct orders for food are taken, passed on to kitchen staff and served to the right customer.

Working conditions

This category of the job description looks at the working environment and circumstances of the job. The physical working environment should be reliably

Table 7.4 Performance standards for different jobs

University lecturer in marketing	• 450 hours' class contact per year • Organise and run successful open days to attract potential applicants to the business school • Four publications per academic year
Shop assistant in newsagent's	• 37.5 hours' work per week • Organise correct delivery of morning papers • Pleasant appearance and personality
Computer salesperson	• Generate £15,000 sales per month • Provide relevant customer demonstrations on request • Clean driving licence
Part-time server in café-bar	• 15 hours per week, 1–6 p.m. on Wednesday, 6–11 p.m. on Thursday and Friday • Clean, neat and tidy appearance • Provide friendly and accurate service to customers

portrayed, e.g. a noisy factory, a clean, hygienic factory or an open-plan office. The hours of work and circumstances in which the job is carried out should also be accurately portrayed, particularly if they are unusual; for example, the job may require the job holder to work shifts or travel away from home regularly. The server in a café-bar faces the working conditions of a trendy city-centre café-bar catering for all types of customer. The job is part time, the hours being 1–6 p.m. Wednesday afternoon, and Thursday and Friday evenings, which are very busy, from 6 to 11 p.m.

Performance standards

This part of the job description gives an indication of the normal level of performance or productivity expected from the job holder. This can be expressed in terms of number of hours of work and in terms of meeting the objectives of the job as laid out in the summary of the job. Examples of performance standards for different jobs, including a part-time server in a city-centre café-bar, are shown in Table 7.4.

The job description serves as the basis for the next logical stage in the job recruitment process, the production of a person specification. A person specification is a series of criteria outlining the ideal person for the job. All applicants for the job will be assessed against these criteria.

Check your understanding

Do you understand the importance of performance standards?

Check your understanding by outlining performance standards for a professional football player like Wayne Rooney.

Stage 2 – Assessment of type of applicant required

Person specification

The person specification is derived from the job description by translating the job activities into the specific skills and abilities required to perform the job effectively. Hence the employee recruitment process needs to ensure that the organisation fills vacancies by attracting, recruiting and retaining ideal candidates who possess the skills and abilities required.

The person specification can be drawn up by using a predetermined framework. Frequently used frameworks include **Rodger's seven-point plan**, **Fraser's five-fold grading** system and the key areas identified in a 2003 Industrial Relations Services (IRS) survey. These frameworks are used to draw up criteria that can be employed to assess applicants' suitability for employment – *see* Tables 7.5, 7.6 and 7.7 respectively. The criteria drawn up should be identified as either essential or desirable. The essential criteria are those that applicants must meet if they are to be considered competent to carry out the job. However, in addition to meeting essential criteria, applicants are usually expected to meet some, but not all, desirable criteria.

The key benefit accruing from the use of such criteria is that the areas important to the recruitment decision are clearly defined before the recruitment process takes place, hence ensuring that they are covered and that the

Table 7.5 Rodger's seven-point plan

1	Physical make-up
2	Attainment
3	General intelligence
4	Special aptitudes
5	Interests
6	Disposition
7	Circumstances

Source: Torrington, D and Hill, L (1995) *Personnel Management: HRM in Action*, 3rd edn, Harlow: Prentice Hall.

Table 7.6 Fraser's five-fold grading

1	Impact on others
2	Qualifications or acquired knowledge
3	Innate abilities
4	Motivation
5	Adjustment or emotional balance

Table 7.7 IRS person specification

1	Skills
2	Experience
3	Qualifications
4	Education
5	Personal attributes

Source: Taylor, S (2008) *People Resourcing*, 4th edn, with the permission of the publisher, the Chartered Institute of Personnel and Development, London (www.cipd.co.uk).

interview is divided into focused sections This improves the consistency of the recruitment process and thus the likelihood that all candidates will be treated and assessed fairly. Today many organisations use a diluted version of one of these frameworks. Organisations should use such frameworks carefully as some aspects, such as physical make-up, could be discriminatory and may potentially contravene legislation such as the **Disability Discrimination Act 1995 and 2005**, while the category 'general intelligence' can be difficult to define.

Rodger's seven-point plan

Physical make-up

The physical requirements for effective performance in a job may cover the areas of general health, physical fitness, appearance, manner and voice. For example, the emergency services and armed forces require higher-than-average standards of physical fitness, as do the jobs of physical education teacher and aerobics instructor. Positions in organisations that involve employees in making an impact on others (clients or members of the public) usually require them to be of smart appearance and to possess a pleasant disposition. Alternatively, if the job is in a national call centre and involves frequent contact with clients or customers over the telephone, a pleasant voice will be important. In the case of the student seeking a job as a server in a café-bar, a neat, clean and tidy appearance will be important.

Attainment

This deals with the level of education and experience required for the job to be carried out successfully. The level of education is assessed by considering the qualifications that an applicant has gained. Many jobs will have minimum qualification expectations of applicants. The qualifications sought for particular jobs may include some of the following: minimum number of GCSEs (or equivalents), including English and mathematics, A levels (or equivalents), a degree, a postgraduate qualification, professional, technical or vocational qualifications. For example, the post of marketing assistant in a publishing company specialising in scientific books and journals may require someone with a first degree in science, such as chemistry, biology or physics, and a postgraduate marketing qualification.

The experience required for a job relates to the previous type of employment that suitable applicants are likely to have held. Senior vacancies in most fields of employment will require significant relevant work experience in a similar or related job, whereas posts for new graduates require much less relevant work experience, with the experience limited to that which a new graduate could have acquired via work placement or holiday employment. For example, the post of European sales manager for a chemical company may require a chemistry graduate with a proven track record in European sales and at least five years' sales experience. In contrast, a vacancy for a graduate trainee systems analyst in one of the main high-street banks may specify a computing or mathematics graduate with six or twelve months' commercial experience in systems analysis in a banking environment, gained via a placement or holiday employment.

The student seeking a job as a server in a café-bar is likely to be considered for the job as they will have a good number of GCSEs and A levels (or equivalent), which are the qualifications to get into university or college. The manager of the café-bar may also look for part-time staff who have previous experience in a similar type of job. This may include working in a bar or restaurant, or a job where the applicant has dealt with members of the public, e.g. a Saturday job in a shop. The experience a successful applicant is expected to have should be directly relevant to the vacancy and should not normally exceed a period of five years.

General intelligence

Applicants with an appropriate level of general intelligence will be required if a job is to be undertaken properly, hence the relevant level of general intelligence needs to be looked for in applicants. Jobs requiring complicated work patterns and activities to be picked up quickly will demand a different level of general intelligence when compared with jobs that are repetitive and very routine. Therefore, students seeking a job as a server in a café-bar are likely to be considered because they are expected to possess a good level of general intelligence, which is demonstrated by the fact that they are at university.

Special aptitudes

Special aptitudes are knowledge and skills that are vital for effective performance in the job. Ideally, applicants who already possess or have the propensity to acquire the necessary special aptitudes should be sought. The acquisition of essential knowledge and skills could simply require an applicant to be prepared to adapt or update existing skills and knowledge. The types of knowledge and skills covered by this section of Rodger's seven-point plan are presentation skills, interpersonal skills, telephone skills, numeracy skills, report writing skills, information technology skills and knowledge, and specific job-related knowledge.

The manager of the café-bar may seek part-time employees who already possess some relevant skills. These skills could include waiting on tables, changing a barrel or optic, and working a computerised till.

Interests

The issue being examined in this section of Rodger's seven-point plan is the requirement of the applicant to have any out-of-work activities that support the application for employment. For example, a person playing in a weekend football team could be viewed as more predisposed to being an active team participant who gets on well with colleagues at work.

The manager of the café-bar may look for students who have experience of teamwork from either a sporting or social activity or as part of their studies at university or college. Students undertaking a business studies or catering course at university or college may use this fact to support their application to work part-time in the café-bar.

Disposition

The personal characteristics relevant to the job are considered in this section. If the job requires the successful applicant to work as a member of a team, then the ability to work well with others will be important. Alternatively, if the job is a supervisory or managerial position, then leadership and responsibility will be integral. Other personal characteristics include the ability to cope with pressure and meet tight deadlines and the competence to work on one's own initiative.

The part-time server in the café-bar should be able to get on with customers, work as part of a team and cope with the pressure of a very full bar on Thursday and Friday evenings. Wednesday afternoons are less busy and involve less bar work, but more waiting on tables for people ordering lunch, teas and coffees.

Circumstances

In this section the applicant's ability to conform to the circumstances in which the job has to be undertaken are considered. The circumstances may include shift work, weekend work, working away from home or being on call during evenings, weekends and public holidays. Examples include bus and train drivers working shifts, security guards working during the night and hospital consultants being on call at weekends.

The part-time server in the café-bar has to be able to work Wednesday afternoon 1–6 p.m. and Thursday and Friday evenings 6–11 p.m.

Key results areas

The person specification defines the ideal candidate for the job, but it is becoming more common to also define the **key results** areas expected of the ideal candidate. Therefore, the key results areas are assembled at the same time as the person specification. They declare the important results expected of the job holder. Key results are the outputs and outcomes produced by the job holder and are assessed by use of explicit success criteria. Success criteria express the expected outcomes and outputs in terms of quality, quantity, cost and time. The use of key results areas provides goals for the job holder, with a strong emphasis on outputs and expected results, hence providing a clear basis for appraisal of the job holder.

Check your understanding

Do you understand how to use Rodger's seven-point plan?

Check your understanding by drawing up a person specification for a professional footballer.

Stage 3 – Attracting applicants

Placement of the advertisement

Organisations have to be able to attract potential employees with the required qualifications, work experience, aptitudes and disposition for the vacancy being filled. The success of the organisation in attracting appropriate potential employees depends in part on its selection and use of suitable advertising media and third-party recruitment bodies.

Direct advertising

The interests of the organisation lie in placing advertisements in publications that will circulate among the largest number of suitable potential applicants. The type of publication used will depend on the vacancy being filled. A vacancy for a shop assistant or office cleaner is best advertised in the local press, as these are jobs for which people are unlikely to move into the locality from a long way away. In contrast, suitably qualified applicants for the vacancy of a marketing manager for a multinational company or a university professor are more likely to be attracted from a larger geographic area and therefore such vacancies are advertised at least in the national press or even in international or overseas press.

Local press

The local press in the UK varies depending on the geographic area. For instance, the area of Sheffield and South Yorkshire is served by several local papers including the *Sheffield Star*, the *Yorkshire Post* and the *Barnsley Chronicle*. Large cities also have local papers, many of which are published as evening papers, including the *Evening Times* in Glasgow and the *Evening Standard* in London. The café-bar seeking serving staff would be most likely to use a local paper.

National press

The UK has a number of national broadsheet newspapers published either daily during the week or on a Sunday. Sunday broadsheet newspapers include the *Independent on Sunday*, The *Observer*, the *Sunday Telegraph* and the *Sunday Times*. These advertise senior jobs in a variety of fields.

Daily broadsheet newspapers include *The Times*, the *Financial Times*, The *Independent*, the *Daily Telegraph* and The *Guardian*. A number of these devote a particular day of the week to certain types of job, for example legal jobs are advertised in *The Times* on a Tuesday and The *Guardian* advertises jobs in education on the same day. This approach to advertising vacancies means that a sizeable selection of jobs in a particular field is advertised together on a specific day. The advantage is that individuals seeking employment in a particular field can be guaranteed a good variety of vacancies in that field if they purchase the newspaper on the relevant day. The advantage to the advertising organisation of such an approach is that their vacancy is advertised on a day when a considerable number of individuals seeking vacancies in a particular field are likely to purchase the newspaper.

Trade press

The alternative to advertising in a broadsheet newspaper is to advertise in the industry or trade press, as nearly all professions have at least one such publication. Examples include the *New Scientist* for research scientists and technicians; The *Engineer* for different types of engineering jobs, civil and mechanical; and The *Bookseller* for vacancies in publishing. The key advantages in using the industry or trade press are similar to those for advertising in daily broadsheet newspapers on an appropriate day. In addition, however, interested applicants are perhaps more likely to already be employed in the industry. The industry or trade press is appropriate for unusual or very specific technical jobs, which are not normally advertised extensively in the local or national press. Many have internet sites listing vacancies.

Press websites

Press websites are run in parallel with the job adverts published in the newspapers. Examples include the Guardian's Jobs Unlimited and the jobsite for *The Sentinel*, the local evening paper in Stoke on Trent. Trade publication will also have websites supporting published vacancies. It is usual for employers to pay a fee to be included in both media. Inclusion on the website allows people to search for particular types of vacancy, e.g. administrative, catering or sales. The use of a website to advertise a job also allows a link to be included to the company's website, where more information can be provided, along with the option to submit a job application electronically.

Internal advertising

Other methods of advertising vacancies are equally valid and may be used as an alternative to or in addition to press advertising. Advertising within the organisation itself is relevant if it is large enough that staff in one part of the organisation are unlikely to hear about a vacancy in another part by word of mouth. Such internal advertising also opens up opportunities for skills mixing and development for existing staff. The cost of advertising within the organisation is much less than press advertising, although it reaches a much smaller audience. However, recruiting an employee who already works for the organisation can have advantages in that the applicant will already know about the organisation and its business.

Internal advertising is usually through a vacancies bulletin circulated throughout the organisation to employees, on paper, on a noticeboard or electronically. These media can be accessible to staff only or to staff and the general public. For example, vacancy noticeboards are sometimes located inside supermarkets close to the main public entrance and are used to advertise jobs such as a cashier, on a full- or part-time basis.

Company websites

Company websites can be used to make vacancies available to both existing staff and members of the public. This involves maintaining a vacancies webpage, accessed via the company's website. These are relatively cheap to establish and update and the company can include as much information as they choose about vacancies. This approach probably works best for large organisations that have an established presence in the labour market as they will have a big enough number of hits to attract a good enough number of suitable potential applicants.

Check your understanding

Do you understand the importance of using the correct advertising media?

Check your understanding by saying where you would place an advertisement for the following jobs:

- a shelf stacker at a Waitrose supermarket in London;
- a trainee manager for Waitrose, at various locations around the country;
- a store manager for Waitrose in Southampton.

Third-party advertising

An alternative to the direct advertising of vacancies is to use a third-party organisation to help attract applicants. Third-party organisations bring together applicants seeking work and organisations offering the type of employment sought. Therefore, they often focus on particular types of employment or employees.

Recruitment agencies

There are many recruitment agencies, which either specialise in one particular type of employment, for example accountants or HGV drivers, or operate in a range of fields. The Advance employment agency covers a range of occupations, including office support staff, engineering and technical staff, sales and marketing staff, and hotel and catering staff. Payment is made to place a vacancy with a recruitment agency and in return the agency advertises the vacancy to its clients, monitors responses to the vacancy and performs the preliminary interviews.

Some recruitment agencies may focus on placing senior managers with organisations. The recruitment agency advertises on behalf of organisations seeking to fill managerial posts. They advertise in the press, sometimes not revealing the name of the organisation on whose behalf they are acting. The recruitment agency will carry out the first interviews and produce a shortlist for the client company to assess further. Alternatively, the agency may act on behalf of a client and approach an identified person to assess their interest in the vacancy, which is commonly known as headhunting.

Jobcentres

Government-run Jobcentres are free to advertise in and provide help with shortlisting. The use of Jobcentres is practical when there is a considerable pool of available candidates. Vacancies placed with Jobcentres are made available via the Jobcentre's website, touch-screen television system and telephone service. In addition employers will have a contact within the their local Jobcentre who will work with the employer to fill vacancies with suitable candidates. Advice is also provided on rates of pay, training, equal opportunities and employing people with disabilities and people from overseas.

University employment agency

Universities may set up their own employment agency dealing in part time jobs for students. This type of agency brings together students seeking part-time work and local employers seeking part-time staff. The university agency can refuse to 'advertise' jobs that are likely to result in students being exploited, by offering less than the minimum wage for example.

Schools, colleges and universities

An organisation specifically seeking a school, college or university leaver may use the university, school or college careers service. Schools, colleges and universities employ careers advisers and run careers libraries where brochures, application forms and careers literature are kept for the use of those students about to leave. Organisations supply schools, colleges and universities with brochures, applications forms, industry literature and posters free of charge. If the organisation frequently employs school, college or university leavers, then developing and maintaining a close relationship with schools, colleges or universities may be an appropriate strategy. The schools, colleges or universities may also supply the opportunity for organisations to carry out initial interviews on their premises, hence allowing the visiting organisation to see a number of applicants in one visit.

The advertisement

The cost of advertising vacancies in the press or via a third party such as a recruitment agency varies according to the publication or third party used, length and size of the advert, and duration for which the advert is on display.

Table 7.8 Suggested outline of job vacancy advertisement

Brief details	• Name of the organisation • Line of business – main products/services
Job and duties	• Job title and main tasks – summarised from job description
Key requirements of successful applicant	• Key qualifications, work experience, skills and circumstances – summarised from personnel specification
Salary	• State the salary or salary scale for the job • Tell applicants how to apply, e.g. CV and covering letter or application form

The successful advertising of jobs requires the use of appropriate publications or third parties. This is important, as suitable applicants have to see the advertisement to be attracted to the vacancy. Failure to attract suitable applicants means that the organisation will have squandered time and money on advertising in the wrong place and on dealing with unsuitable applicants.

The information in job advertisements needs to be clear and reliable and to tell potential applicants, in brief terms, what the organisation does, what the job involves and the key requirements looked for in applicants. This allows suitable applicants to assess whether the vacancy is relevant to them and to make an informed judgement about whether to apply or not. It is also usual to indicate the expected salary and how potential applicants should apply for the vacancy. A suggested outline advertisement is shown in Table 7.8.

Stage 4 – Assessing applicants

The assessment of applicants occurs in two steps. The first is an assessment of the applications received, with some being rejected at this juncture. The second step is a further assessment of selected applicants by interviews and aptitude tests, before finally choosing the successful applicant.

Assessment of application forms

The initial sorting of application forms can be a difficult and tedious task, particularly if there has been a large response to the advertising. However, the initial sorting of application forms and shortlisting of candidates for interview needs to be methodically and rationally undertaken. If the sorting process is to be fair and accurate, the staff doing this initial sorting process need to be involved in the recruitment process and fully understand the relevance and use of job descriptions and personnel specifications. A thorough shortlisting process aids in ensuring the accuracy and fairness of the recruitment process and lessens the likelihood of inappropriate applicants being called for interview. Therefore, this initial shortlisting process makes use of the criteria from the person specification, and applicants meeting the essential and some of the desirable criteria are those who will be called for a first interview. Applicants not meeting the essential criteria in the person specification are rejected.

Assessment of applicants

The next step is to assess the shortlisted applicants by interview. There are variations in the interview process: with some vacancies only one interview is required and for other jobs the interview process is in two stages. It is unusual for a candidate to experience more than two interviews for a vacancy. Equally, the number of interviewers can also vary. There are generally two views governing the number of interviewers. One is that an effective interview and discussion can take place only on a one-to-one basis, so candidates meet one interviewer. The other view is that the interview process should be more open, so the interview is carried out and the appointment decision made by a panel of interviewers.

The sequence of events for one- and two-interview vacancies is shown in Table 7.9. In two-interview vacancies aptitude tests and activities are usually taken after the applicant has been selected for a second interview, but prior to that interview being conducted. References should be checked after the selection of the preferred candidate and prior to the confirmation of appointment, as references are used to confirm the interviewers' opinion of the successful applicant.

Interviewing

The job interview is a two-way communication process. It is an opportunity for the interviewer to get to know the candidate and further assess them against the criteria in the person specification. It is also an opportunity for the interviewee to gain a greater insight into the organisation and the work being offered. The interviewer should commence the interview by putting the candidate at ease and outlining the structure of the interview. A possible interview structure is shown in Table 7.10.

Table 7.9 Interviewing applicants

One-interview vacancies	• Interview • Select successful applicant • Check references • Confirm appointment
Two-interview vacancies	• Interview • Select successful applicants for second interviews • Aptitude tests and activities • Second interview • Select successful applicant • Check references • Confirm appointment

Table 7.10 Interview structure

1	Scene setting
2	Application form and person specification
3	Candidate's questions
4	Close the interview

Scene setting

The physical scene or location needs to be appropriate, usually a quiet room away from the disruption of telephones, noise and interruptions. The interviewer should set the scene at the start of the interview and recap on what the job involves and the type of person sought. Information from the job description and person specification can be used to do this.

Application form and person specification

The main body of the interview is structured around the completed application form and the person specification. This allows the information provided on the application form to be tied in with the relevant section of the person specification. For example, qualifications and work experience listed on the application form will link to the attainment section of the person specification. This allows the interviewer to ask the candidate questions about the information provided on their application, while also making sure that the candidate is assessed against the criteria in the person specification.

The questions used in interviews to assess a candidate need to be open ended, as this allows the candidate's reasons for wanting the job to be examined. Open-ended questions give applicants the opportunity to explain the knowledge, skills and experience they have gained and justify how these equip them as suitable for the vacancy. If the candidate provides incomplete answers to the questions, the interviewer should ask follow-up questions and dig for the information required to assess the candidate against the person specification.

Candidate's questions

As previously stated, the interview is an opportunity for the interviewee to gain a greater insight into the organisation and the work being offered. Although having to ask questions may be seen as a nightmare for the nervous applicant, the well-prepared candidate will have researched the company and have a few intelligent questions to ask. Alternatively, from the interviewer's point of view it is always appropriate to give applicants the opportunity to seek any further information they require, as even the best recruitment process may have forgotten something.

Close the interview

The candidate should be thanked for attending the interview and told how to claim any expenses to which they are entitled. Candidates also need to be advised of when they will know the outcome of the interview.

Informing candidates

All candidates who were interviewed need to be informed of the outcome of their interview. The unsuccessful candidates need to be told that they have not succeeded and, if appropriate, why they have not been successful. Equally, the successful candidate needs to be told that they have gained the job. This should be confirmed in writing, along with information on the salary and arrangements for the candidate to start work. A contract of employment should be drawn up and issued to the successful candidate.

Check your understanding

Do you understand the importance of using the 'right' interview process?

Check your understanding by outlining the interview process for:

- a shelf stacker at a Waitrose supermarket in London;
- a trainee manager for Waitrose, at various locations around the country;
- a store manager for Waitrose in Southampton.

Summary

This chapter examined human resource management and some factors in the external environment which impact on HR in organisations. The recruitment process was also discussed. The following summary covers all aspects of this chapter.

1 The activity of human resource management includes recruitment and selection of appropriate staff and management of the employment relationship, which includes contracts, collective bargaining, reward systems and employees' involvement. Therefore, HRM considers the whole picture of staffing in the organisation and takes both the strategic and the operational view of human resource requirements.

2 There is much in the external environment that impacts on organisations, with much coming from legislation. Employment legislation covers employees' rights with respect to contracts of employment, trade unions membership and industrial relations. Health and safety legislation covers the minimum requirement of an employer to ensure the employees work in a safe and secure manner and location. The equalising employment legislation covers the outlawing of discrimination and the promotion of good practice with respect to gender, race, religion, age and disability, covering all aspects of workplace activity.

3 In the UK, organisations are faced with drawing staff from a labour market that has decreasing numbers of younger people and increasing numbers of older people. This is part of the challenge organisations have to deal with in retaining an appropriate number of staff with the required skills and abilities.

4 The flexible firm model divides employees into three categories: core; peripheral and external. Core permanent employees hold the highly skilled jobs in organisations. The first peripheral group are employees with full-time jobs requiring vocational skills. The second peripheral group provides a major component of flexibility for organisations and includes employees on short-term and part-time contracts. External staff can be brought in quickly to meet increased demand. Flexibility in the workplace can also be created via the use of flexible and compressed hours of work, telecommuting and encouraging work–life balance.

5 The employee recruitment process can be broken down into four stages. 'Assessment of the job' covers job analysis and production of an up-to-date job description. The second stage is 'assessment of the type of applicant required' and covers drawing up a person specification and identifying key results or outcomes the job holder is expected to meet. The next stage is 'attracting applicants', which involves drawing up a suitable advertisement and placing it such that appropriate applicants are drawn to the job and organisation. The final stage is 'assessing applicants' and includes an assessment of the applications received and of some of the applicants themselves, via interviews.

Chapter objectives and the exit case study

While reading this chapter and engaging in the activities, you should have learned how to apply theory and models and analyse situations. This means you should be able to meet the chapter objectives outlined at the beginning of the chapter. The table below shows which chapter objectives can be tested by the different questions.

Chapter objective	Check you have achieved this by
2 Summarise the benefits of flexibility in the workforce to an organisation and discuss how it can be achieved.	answering case study question 1.

Recruitment and retention: How to find the best and keep them

by Sarah Murray

The results are striking: on average, the 100 best workplaces in Europe get almost nine job applications a year per staff member and have a voluntary employee turnover of just 7.9 per cent, allowing companies to save money on hiring and training. But while such statistics may be the envy of other companies, defining what exactly it is about a great workplace that contributes to recruitment and retention is not easy.

A big element, in the eyes of employees, is clearly related to the ability to achieve a good work–life balance. Research conducted by Manpower in the UK found that 63 per cent of workers want flexibility and 84 per cent of employers see this as helping retain their best employees.

'Flexibility is particularly important, which may mean giving individuals the opportunity to work the hours that best suit them and the ability to balance work and family needs,' says Barbara Beck, president for Europe, Middle East and Africa at Manpower.

Offering a flexible work schedule also helps companies when it comes to recruitment. Some 73 per cent of people consider the ability to work flexibly a deciding factor when choosing a new job, according to research conducted by Microsoft in partnership with the Chartered Management Institute, Business Link and Management Today. The same study found 52 per cent of workers believed that the ability to work remotely would reduce the stress of their working life.

Microsoft, winner in this year's Best Workplace ranking for the large companies in Europe, is acting on such findings. The company has a pilot programme called 'The New World of Work', in which employees are encouraged to redesign their working lives to make them more flexible with the help of state-of-the-art IT and mobile devices.

Jack Constantinides, a senior human resources executive at Monster, the jobs website, in Europe, also sees technology as a powerful driver. 'With advancements in technology, flexible working in particular has clearly moved up the agenda,' he says.

However, while many companies are recognising and acting on the demand for less rigid work schedules, there is also a growing desire on the part of many job candidates and employees – particularly when it comes to younger workers – to work for companies that are socially and environmentally responsible.

Almost half (47 per cent) of job candidates are more likely to join and stay with a company that addresses its impact on the community and the environment, according to research conducted in 2006 by Mori Research on behalf of Manpower Emea.

'Generation Y is particularly concerned with making sure that its employer of choice is socially responsible, and this might encompass everything from having a low carbon footprint to having responsible labour practices,' says Ms Beck.

Some companies are clearly recognising the power of philanthropic, environmental or community programmes in engaging employees. In the Netherlands, every employee at Samhoud, a global consultancy, spends 5 per cent of his or her time on Vision 21, an initiative bringing together 2,500 people from a variety of backgrounds to create a vision for the future of the Netherlands. Moreover, about 20 per cent of the company's profits are donated to charity.

Fishburn Hedges, the public relations consultancy, gave every staff member an energy-saving light bulb to take home as part of its 'Switch It Off' environmental awareness campaign, while it takes part in the bikes 4 work initiative to promote green commuting. At Yell, the directories company, a recycling scheme run in association with local authorities informs householders about where to dispose of old directories.

But while some companies are clearly leaders in this area, Lesley Uren, chief executive of Jackson Samuel, the UK-based talent management firm, believes others have yet to harness the power of corporate responsibility. 'Organisations have largely come to terms with work–life balance,' she says. 'But I don't think they've made so much progress on the corporate responsibility side in terms of making it part of their processes and using it as a way to engage people.'

Part of the challenge is that corporate responsibility is not something companies can simply tack on to their activities. And with access to information about companies' social and environmental performance freely available on the internet, 'greenwashing' and false claims can be easily detected.

'This generation can spot a fraud a mile off,' says Ms Uren. 'For an organisation to speak about a corporate responsibility agenda and not demonstrate what they're

doing is like putting on a coat that doesn't belong to them. So organisations need to make it meaningful to the work they're doing.'

Despite the attention given to corporate responsibility, Torsten Muth, managing director of Experteer, which provides personalised career services for senior professionals, believes that remuneration remains an essential part of the recruitment process. 'What people are looking for is the salary and package,' he says. 'Then once they are in the process of interviewing, and you can prove you are a company with a corporate responsibility policy, it might make a difference.'

Source: from 'Recruitment and retention: How to find the best and keep them', *The Financial Times*, 28 May 2008 (Murray, S.).

Exit case study question

1 Identify and discuss the forms flexibility in the workplace could take and how it may apply to different jobs. In addition to pay and flexibility, identify the benefits that may be offered to employees by a company aiming to retain good staff.

Short-answer questions

1 Define human resource management.

2 Name the three categories of legislation that most directly influence the human resource management function.

3 Name the piece of legislation which led to the establishment of the Commission for Racial Equality.

4 Which activity was made unlawful in the workplace in England in 2007?

5 Why in most industrialised countries are population demographics likely to influence the human resource management function in the future?

6 Explain why the move to a more flexible labour force has occurred.

7 State the main advantages of telecommuting.

8 State the main disadvantages of telecommuting.

9 Indicate two ways in which an organisation may manage a skills shortage in a particular area.

10 List the four stages of the employee recruitment process.

11 Explain the purpose of the person specification.

12 Name the points in Rodger's seven-point plan for the person specification.

13 Identify one potential difficulty with Rodger's seven-point plan.

14 Give two examples of where each of the following can take place: third-party advertising and direct advertising.

Chapter objectives and assignment questions

While reading this chapter and engaging in the activities, you should have learned how to apply theory and models and analyse situations. This means you should be able to meet the chapter objectives outlined at the beginning of the chapter. The table below shows which chapter objectives can be tested by the different questions.

Chapter objective	Check you have achieved this by
1 Identify and discuss external factors that impact on the HR function.	answering assignment question 1.
3 Apply the job recruitment process to a vacancy.	answering assignment questions 2 and 3.

Assignment questions

1 Identify and discuss which factors in the external environment could impact on an organisation, leaving it with a workforce that is too small and lacking in the required skills and abilities. Explain how the organisation could remedy the situation.

2 Produce a job description for a university lecturer in marketing. Use the job description you have produced to draw up a person specification. Indicate where the job could be advertised and state what information you would include in any advertisement used.

3 Name and explain all the elements of the job recruitment process and discuss which of these elements you consider to be key in terms of ensuring equality of opportunity.

WEBLINKS available at **www.pearsoned.co.uk/capon**

- This site covers equal opportunities, racial equality and disability rights and looks at equality of employment in the workplace and the associated legislation, along with human rights. The website covers the material previously provided by the websites of the Equal Opportunities Commission, Commission for Racial Equality and Disability Rights Commission:
  http://www.equalityhumanrights.com
- This is the site for CIPD that covers all aspects of HR management and provides fact sheets covering good practice in HR:
  http://www.cipd.co.uk/default.cipd
- This site is for the government department Business Enterprise and Regulatory Reform, BERR. Click on 'Employment matters' in the bottom left-hand corner of the home page. This will take you to topics related to employment relations and legislation:
  http://www.berr.gov.uk/

FURTHER READING

The following chapters look at the different aspects of HRM covered in this chapter.

- Armstrong, M (2006) *A Handbook of Human Resource Management Practice*, 10th edn, Chapters 1, 27, 28, 29 and 30, Harlow: Financial Times Prentice Hall.
- Buchanan, D and Huczynski, A (2008) *Organisational Behaviour*, 6th edn, Chapter 20, Harlow: Financial Times Prentice Hall.
- Foot, M and Hook, C (2008) *Introducing Human Resource Management*, Chapters 1, 2, 5, 6, 7 and 8, Harlow: Financial Times Prentice Hall.
- Torrington, D, Hall, L and Taylor, S (2008) *Human Resource Management*, 7th edn, Chapters 1, 7, 8, 22, 23, 24 and 31, Harlow: Financial Times Prentice Hall.

REFERENCES

1 Daniels, J D, Radebaugh, L and Sullivan, D (2008) *International Business*, 12th edn, Reading, MA: Pearson International.
2 http://www.dwp.gov.uk/mediacentre/pressreleases/2008/apr/emp070-010408.asp
3 http://www.cipd.co.uk/subjects/dvsequl/sexdisc/sexdiscrimination.htm?IsSrchRes=1
4 Clement, B (1995) 'Dinner ladies' equal pay win undermines competition law', *Independent*, 7 July.
5 Clement, B (1996) 'Dinner ladies awarded £1m over council's unfair pay cut', *Independent*, 30 July.
6 http://www.cipd.co.uk/subjects/dvsequl/relgdisc/Racereligemplmnt.htm?IsSrchRes=1
7 The Minister for Disabled People (1996) *The Disability Discrimination Act – Employment*, DL 70, October.
8 http://www.cipd.co.uk/subjects/dvsequl/disability/disandemp.htm?IsSrchRes=1
9 Johnson, P (1990) 'Our ageing population – the implications for business and government', *Long Range Planning* 23(2), April.
10 Ibid.
11 Taylor, A (2008) 'OECD criticises low-skilled migrant barriers', *Financial Times*, 10 September.
12 Taylor, A (2008) 'A surprising lack of skilfully sheared sheep', *Financial Times*, 18 September.
13 Johnson, op. cit.
14 *Independent on Sunday*, 29 March 1992.
15 Johnson, op. cit.
16 Atkinson, J (1984) 'Manpower strategies for flexible organisations', *Personnel Management*, August.
17 Ibid.
18 Bolger, A (1997) 'Thoroughly modern training', *Financial Times*, 24 March.
19 Penman, D (1994) 'No workplace like home', *Independent*, 6 June.

CHAPTER 8

Marketing

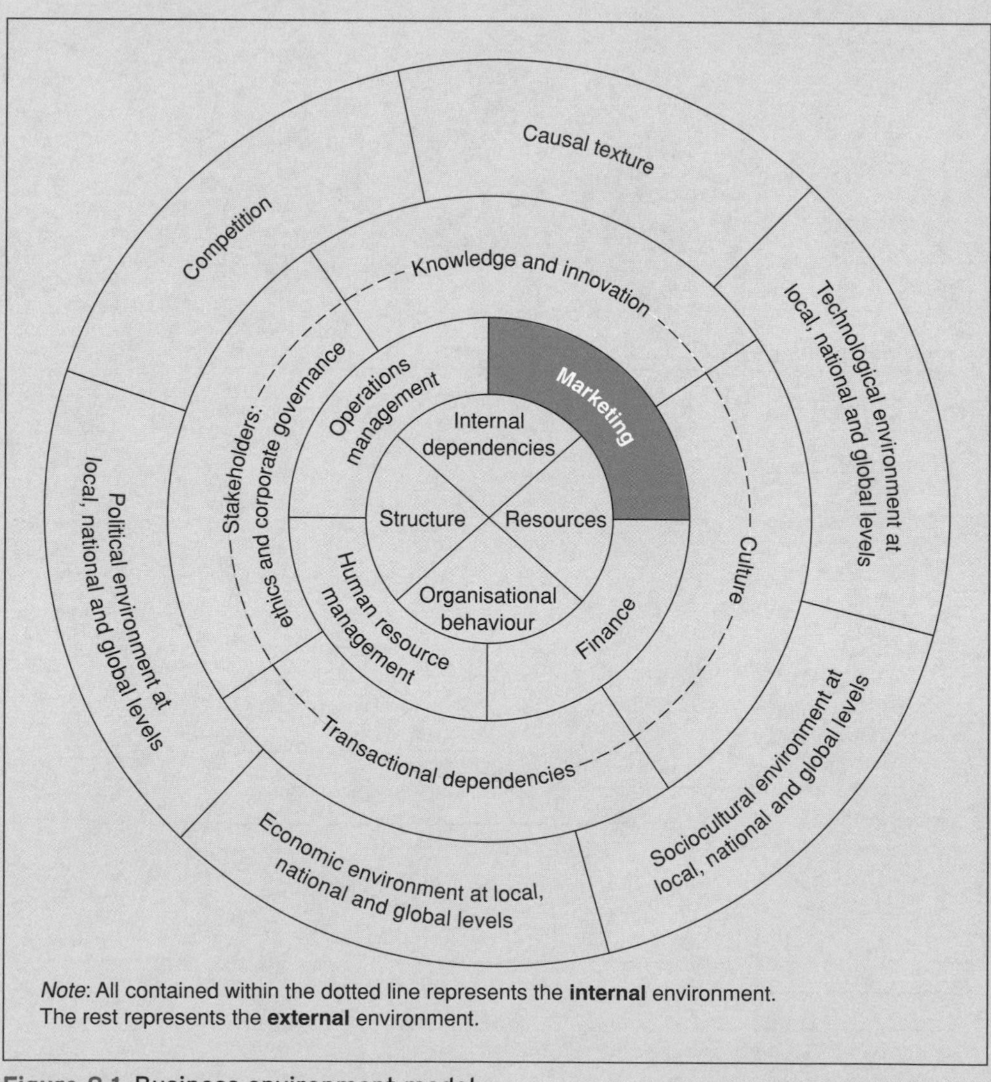

Figure 8.1 Business environment model

Chapter objectives

This chapter provides an overview of the marketing function. The role of marketing in organisations and the range of marketing activities are summarised. This is followed by a look at some key marketing tools, namely the marketing mix, the product life cycle, the customer growth matrix and the BCG matrix.

Therefore, when you have read this chapter and worked through the associated activities you should be able to achieve the objectives specified below.

1 **Define the role of marketing in an organisation.**
2 **Summarise the main marketing activities.**
3 **Apply a range of marketing tools to different products and services.**
4 **Understand the relevance of marketing tools.**

This case study examines Costa Coffee's move into the Russian market and the competition it faces from other well-known Western chains such as Starbucks and McDonald's.

ENTRY CASE STUDY 8.1

Costa aims to stir a coffee revolution in Russia

by Jenny Wiggins

Russia could become the biggest single foreign market for Whitbread-owned Costa Coffee within five years, John Derkach, managing director, said yesterday as the coffee chain opened its first store in Moscow's Pushkin Square.

Costa is the second international coffee chain to enter Russia after Starbucks opened a store in Khimki, a city north-west of Moscow, last year. Costa, a division of hotel and restaurant group Whitbread, made Russia a priority 18 months ago and teamed up with Russian restaurant group Rosinter a year ago in a joint venture.

Costa and Rosinter, which has the licence to the TGI Friday's brand, are investing \$10m (£5m) in the venture and plan to open 200 Costa stores in Russia over the next five years.

Costa is the UK's biggest coffee chain ranked by number of stores, which will top 700 next month. Its global expansion has to date focused on the Middle East, where it has 180 stores, and India, where it has 40 stores. China and India will rival Russia to become Costa's biggest foreign market over the next few years, Mr Derkach said.

Aside from Starbucks, Costa's biggest foreign competitor in Russia will be McDonald's, which has begun opening McCafes in the country. Its key local competitors are the coffee shop chains Coffee House and Shokoladnitsa, which have some 300 stores in total.

Analysts said that Russia appeared to be going through an 'explosive phase' as higher incomes enable people to spend more money on brands.

Food group Kraft said this month it would start making instant coffee in Russia while PepsiCo announced plans to buy Lebedyansky, Russia's biggest juice producer.

Costa plans to keep its Russian stores open late in the evening and to eventually sell coffee mixed with alcohol, as well as offering wine and beer.

Asked whether Costa planned on putting vodka in its coffees, Mr Derkach said: 'I'm not sure coffee and vodka mix terribly well.'

Source: from 'Costa aims to stir a coffee revolution in Russia', *The Financial Times*, 27 March 2008 (Wiggins, J.).

Introduction

This chapter examines the relationship between the **marketing** department and the external and internal environments of organisations. The interactive nature of this relationship will be discussed. Organisations and their context will be examined with the aim of assessing how the external environment dictates the activities of the marketing department, or whether marketers inside organisations are able to exercise their marketing talents to influence the external environment. In addition, how the marketing department relates to other departments in the effort to achieve organisational goals will be examined. Basic **marketing tools** will be presented and these will be applied to practical examples in order to facilitate an understanding of marketing and of how marketing tools play their part in this process.

Marketing

Marketing is considered for two reasons. First, the nature of its activities is such that marketing plays a significant role in the interaction of the organisation and the external environment. Through its **market research** activities, the marketing department is the internal area of the organisation most explicitly required to scan, analyse, monitor and contend with what is going on in the outside world (*see* Chapters 1, 2 and 3). It is therefore the role of marketers to understand the size and nature of the **marketplace**, to know the organisation's customers and to undertake market research into customer requirements. While scanning the external environment, the marketing department will be continually monitoring the activities of competitor organisations and the latest developments in the same or similar fields. These research and monitoring activities are the way in which the marketing department's efforts help ensure that the organisation is first into the market with the products or services to meet its customers' identified needs or wants. Therefore, it could be argued that the marketing department is most aware of the external environment, and of the environmental linkages between the external and internal environments (*see* Chapter 3). Additionally, it also follows that marketing is the department that should be aware of any changes in this relationship and of the effects that these changes may have on the strategic or operational management of the organisation.

Second, it is clear that the marketing department has several roles to play in the relationship between the external and internal environments. It has to identify changes in the external environment and predict the kinds of products or services the outside world requires. In addition, the causal effects of these changes mean that marketing has to manage closely the links between the marketing department and the other departments of the company in order to meet the organisational objectives of satisfying customer wants or needs. Without close collaboration and communication within the organisation, referred to here as **functional convergence**, the marketing department or function will not be able to marshall the tangible, intangible and human resources necessary to achieve organisational objectives. Without functional convergence, the organisation risks wasting organisational energy on internal tension and conflict and not being able to meet the goals it has set itself. Thus this chapter will look closely at the relationship between marketing and the other elements of the internal environment and will draw some conclusions about how the organisation's internal efficiency affects its ability to achieve its business goals.

Defining the marketing concept

A marketing orientation leads organisations to consider the needs and wants of their actual or potential customers before considering what services and/or products to offer. More than this, the marketing concept could be said to be a holistic approach to managing organisations.

Marketing-oriented organisations focus on gearing all their internal activities towards achieving their goals and objectives by satisfying customer needs and wants. Marketing can be likened to a philosophy or a firm set of beliefs. There is a huge literature on and by marketers defining their role in the environment and within the organisation.

Peter Drucker[1] defines marketing as:

> **not only much broader than selling, it is not a specialised activity at all. It encompasses the entire business. It is the whole business seen from the point of view of its final result, that is from the customer's point of view. Concern and responsibility for marketing must therefore permeate all areas of the enterprise.**

This gives an idea of the holistic nature of the marketing concept, dealing as it does with the organisation's activities from the very beginning of product research and planning through to after-sales service and customer comments.

Kotler et al.[2] defined marketing as:

> **a social activity and managerial process by which individuals and groups obtain what they need and want through creating and exchanging products and value with others.**

This introduces the idea of the role of the marketing department as contributing to adding value to the organisation's inputs, an essential element of the resource conversion process (*see* Chapter 4). Kotler goes on to suggest that marketing is the area of a business that identifies and quantifies current unfilled needs and wants, before determining the markets that the organisation can best serve with its current and future products and services. Thus marketing links a society's needs and the organisation's response.

The professional body for marketers in the UK, the Institute of Marketing, in Lancaster and Massingham,[3] identifies the marketing department as 'the management process which identifies, anticipates and supplies customer requirements efficiently and profitably'. This introduces to the marketing concept the notion of prediction and anticipation of **customer needs and wants**. In the realms of innovation and technology, marketers have a role in providing for needs and wants before potential customers know that they could need or want the product or service on offer. Who, for example, in the heyday of the long-playing record could have known that they would be updating their collection to MP3 downloads in the early twenty-first century?

According to the marketing concept, it is the *raison d'être* of the marketing-oriented organisation to allow the marketing department the power and resources to dictate to the organisation's other departments what should be done, for whom and when. This focus is achieved through marketing's research activities, which are the mechanism for identifying customer needs and wants and taking on competitors. Marketing can provide further evidence of how effective it has been in doing this through its customer service and feedback capabilities, closing a circular loop of information and data gathered from the outside world. This is clearly illustrated by the entry case study for this chapter, showing that companies such as Costa Coffee have identified Russia as a growth market for coffee.

Check your understanding

Do you understand the marketing concept?

Check your understanding by explaining the role of marketing in helping organisations achieve their objectives. Use examples where appropriate.

The business environment of marketing

The marketing concept demands that marketing should focus on meeting the wants and needs of customers. Hence the people and resources from all sections of the organisation need to be dedicated to the marketing concept to ensure that the organisation can achieve success. In order to achieve customer satisfaction and success, the marketing concept dictates that any effort in the organisation is wasted if it is not directed towards customer satisfaction and providing the products and services the customer wants or needs. In this, all the organisation's departments need to work together in harmony to achieve organisational objectives. This harmony is referred to as functional convergence, as the internal departments or functions of the organisation must converge their efforts to succeed.

Because the marketing concept deals with the satisfaction of customer needs and wants through organisational activities, it can be seen in organisations' in-house programmes that are focused on achieving 'customer orientation', 'customer satisfaction' or 'customer care'. Hence marketers hold as the tenets of their philosophy the consideration of three basic points:

1 What do customers need or want?
2 How can the organisation meet these needs or wants?
3 How does the organisation make money doing so?

This last point is true not only of private-sector, profit-making enterprises but also of contemporary public-sector or voluntary-sector organisations. In the latter cases, the aim would be to make enough money from products or services to break even or increase activity level rather than making profit for redistribution to owners or shareholders.

This marketing concept demands that the point of the organisation's existence is to try to make or do whatever market research has proved that customers need or want. The organisation needs to have the required resources and technology necessary in order to achieve this. Any organisational resources, whether tangible, intangible or human, that are not focused on meeting the needs and wants of customers are therefore wasted. Although to the business studies student this approach may seem obvious, the opposite attitude may still be found in some organisations, with their approach summed up in the more production- or sales-oriented phrase: 'We make this product because we know how to. Now, who can we find to sell it to?'

An example of this latter approach was the early mass-production pioneer Henry Ford, who famously offered his customers any colour Model 'T' Ford car, as long as it was black – the only colour of car his company made. In the early days of mass production this approach was successful due to the simpler nature of the competitive environment (*see* Chapter 3). This meant that customers and markets were more easily satisfied by the new products that technological advances brought, as the vast majority had never had access to such products before.

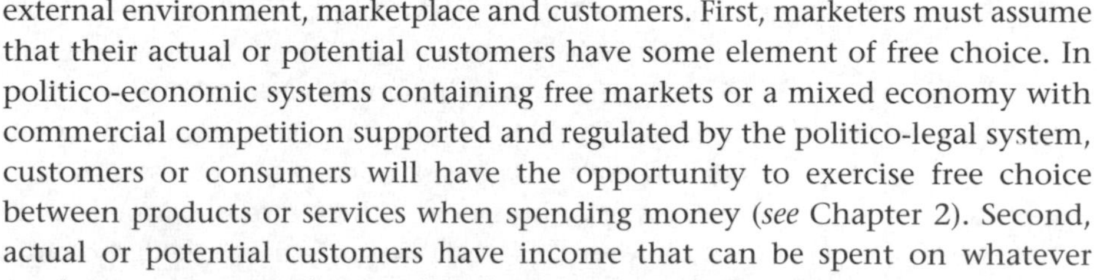

Check your understanding

Do you understand the organisational concept of marketing?

Check your understanding by identifying the role of the marketing department in an organisation.

Marketing assumptions

Underpinning the marketing concept are three basic assumptions about the external environment, marketplace and customers. First, marketers must assume that their actual or potential customers have some element of free choice. In politico-economic systems containing free markets or a mixed economy with commercial competition supported and regulated by the politico-legal system, customers or consumers will have the opportunity to exercise free choice between products or services when spending money (*see* Chapter 2). Second, actual or potential customers have income that can be spent on whatever product or service is being offered. These crucial financial aspects empower customers to follow their needs or wants and make decisions about how to spend their income. Finally, if customers have both disposable income and the freedom to spend it as they wish, it is the job of marketers to persuade them to alter their choice and move from something to which they are loyal or familiar with to something new in the same line. The entry case study to this chapter highlights the efforts that have been made by companies like Starbucks to tempt Russian people to drink Western-style coffee instead of Russian-style tea with which they are familiar.

True marketing orientation could be renamed customer orientation. If organisations are truly marketing or customer oriented, they are achieving the necessary focus of all organisational activities on customer satisfaction. In achieving marketing orientation, the organisation has recognised that the only point of organisational effort is to try to satisfy customer needs and wants through the combination of marketing, finance, human resource and operations management activities. In order to do this, the organisation needs to aim to achieve a level of integration of the efforts of all departments. This is the concept of functional convergence: the cooperation and collaboration of all internal elements of the organisation towards its corporate mission of customer satisfaction. To achieve this, the organisation must understand the needs and wants of the customer.

Needs and wants

It is useful at this stage to consider the difference between customer needs and customer wants, as occasionally marketers will be appealing to a perceived need, but more often they will be focusing marketing activities on appealing to customers' wants or desires. A need is something that cannot be done without, like basic food and water. A want could be said to be something to which someone aspires or which they desire. People need grain and water to survive, but might want to have a variety of grains and vegetables and fruit juice or alcohol to drink.

This difference can be illustrated by using Maslow's hierarchy of needs.[4] This American psychologist defined need at various levels. People all have in common certain basic requirements for food, drink and sleep, referred to by Maslow as 'physiological or basic needs'. In less well-developed countries these needs are the prime concerns of citizens. The family's income is spent on keeping enough food in their stomachs, whether that income be earned through economic activity or handed out in subsidy from the state or from private charity. Once basic physiological needs are met and satisfied, the next priority is to keep a roof over the family's head. Maslow refers to this as 'security or safety needs', which include self-defence and saving for future eventualities.

Once these needs are satisfied, whereby essential life is not threatened by homelessness or hunger and the future is planned for in terms of the upbringing of children and social security for the elderly and sick in the family, less fundamental needs can emerge. Maslow's next level refers to the human proclivity for socialisation activities, e.g. going to the pub, cinema or theme park. Maslow refers to this as 'belonging or affection needs'. From this, natural ambition and aspiration lead to spending surplus income on more luxurious accommodation or better food, or improving social status through acquisition of possessions or land. Maslow calls this 'esteem or ego needs'.

Finally, the pinnacle of Maslow's hierarchy of needs is the stage of self-fulfilment, not only having achieved the fundamentals of basic food and shelter but also being able to obtain things that are desirable for complete fulfilment. Thus the ultimate dream home with all modern conveniences, a top-of-the range sports car, designer-label clothes, regular five-star holidays and eating only in the best restaurants might be the height of aspiration for the successful entrepreneur or lottery winner. Maslow calls this 'self-actualisation'.

However, in July 2008 the Joseph Rowntree Foundation (JRF) published a report, 'A minimum income standard for Britain: What people think',[5] which looked at goods and services required for an acceptable minimum standard of living in Britain. This included food, clothes, accommodation, utilities, fuel, household goods, personal goods and services, transport, social and cultural activities. The survey identified minimum needs in these areas, and did not consider 'wants' or aspirational items. It took the view that needs were more than basic food, clothes and shelter, but that needs included individuals having 'the opportunities and choices necessary to participate in society'.[6] Therefore, needs included allowances for recreational activities, such as cinema visits, meals out, sports and gym use, the cost of celebrating Christmas or similar festival, birthday presents for friends and family and an annual one-week budget holiday in the UK.

Therefore, while organisations can never make customers actually need anything, the job of the marketing department is to tempt potential customers to deploy their financial resources to meet their needs by purchasing Company A's products or services instead of Company B's. For example, in the entry case study to this chapter, Costa Coffee are planning to keep their coffee shops open late into the evening and to sell coffee alongside alcoholic drinks. Hence while marketers cannot create need, they can sometimes make customers want something through their marketing activities. Therefore, the marketing department needs to focus its efforts on appealing to the various needs and wants of the target market. This is why market research (*see* later in this chapter) is important.

Check your understanding

Do you understand the term 'needs and wants'?

Check your understanding by indicating specific needs and wants that customers may have.

The customer

'Customer care', 'customer orientation' and 'customer service' are very much part of the rhetoric of organisations striving for business success in Britain in the twenty-first century. To what extent this orientation is sincere or successful will be examined later in this chapter. In the private sector many truly customer-oriented examples can be cited. Car manufacturers have come a long way since the days of Henry Ford's Model 'T', largely under the influence of the Japanese car manufacturers whose post-war domination of global markets is legendary. Nissan UK Ltd is an example of a marketing-driven car manufacturer. No car going through the factory on the production line in Sunderland has not been ordered by a sales showroom for a customer.

In the UK public sector, service delivery has changed radically since the election of the Thatcher government in 1979. With the introduction of markets in the NHS, education and local government services, public-sector organisations have had to begin considering customer needs and wants in the provision of their services. The university sector also faced radical change in its markets with the expansion of higher education and the introduction of student loans and tuition fees directly payable by students instead of by their local education authority. However, despite having introduced marketing departments, managers and officers, universities have considerable work to do before they could be considered to have a true marketing orientation.

Marketing activities

Put simply, marketing can be said to be the carrying out of business operations to steer the flow of goods and services from manufacturers to consumers. However, it is useful to outline the activities the marketing department undertakes in order to achieve this. There is a temptation to associate marketing with **selling**, but sales is in fact just one of the activities that may be located within the marketing department – *see* Figure 8.2. Housed within the marketing department are likely to be many individual subdepartments, including market research, **product planning and development**, advertising and **sales promotion**, sales, **distribution** and **after-sales customer service**.

This section will examine the marketing department's relationship to the external environment, its activities, and its relationship to other elements of the internal environment of the organisation. In its relationship with the organisation's external environment, the marketing department must seek to answer the following questions:

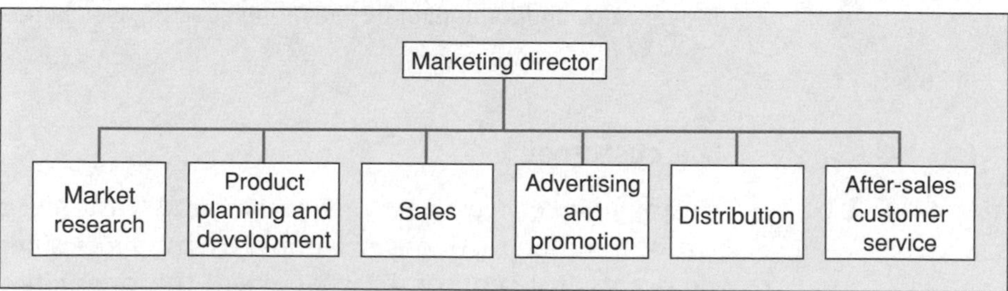

Figure 8.2 Marketing activities

1 Who is in the marketplace and where is the market?
2 What are the changing needs and/or wants of the marketplace?
3 What resource inputs are necessary to meet those needs/wants?
4 How will the organisation make money doing this (even voluntary, public-sector or other not-for-profit organisations have to make their running costs)?

Market research

Having stated at length the importance that the marketing concept places on establishing customer needs or wants, a company will be only as successful as its market research activities. Through market research, organisations can identify who is in the marketplace, where they are located, what they need or want, and how products and services can be developed to meet these identified needs and wants.

Organisations can carry out market research in two basic ways: through generation of **primary data**, or through use of available **secondary data**. The generation of primary data requires the organisation to invest heavily in terms of time, money and people and in the execution of extensive and detailed surveys of current and potential customers through direct contact with them. This may take the form of postal, telephone or online surveys of a database of current customers. Alternatively, the organisation may purchase commercially produced marketing databases of potential customers who fulfil certain criteria in terms of location, income, profession or family composition and then survey them directly.

Market research carried out in the summer of 2008 showed that the supermarkets Asda, Aldi and Lidl had experienced a 0.6 per cent, 0.3 percent and 0.1 percent growth respectively in UK market share between April and June 2008. Marks & Spencer experienced a 4.5 per cent drop in food sales in the same period, while both Tesco and Sainsbury's were struggling to maintain market share.[7]

The advance of technology has assisted organisations in knowing their customers better and contacting them more frequently, as well as increasing the amount and quality of primary data available to help organisations with their market research. The use of itemised bills and customer loyalty cards in supermarkets and shops enables those organisations to build exact customer profiles, and to target the marketing of various products and services at particular customer groups. This technique is called data warehousing and is a growing market research trend in many sectors. A customer identified from the checkout terminal as having begun to buy baby products might be sent details of the supermarket's discount scheme on baby products. Unlike Sainsbury's, Tesco does not offer its loyalty discounts directly at the checkout, but rather mails discount vouchers up to the amount 'saved' on the loyalty card directly to the customer's home address, thus enabling it to include details of other relevant products, services or offers.

Sainsbury's and Tesco have invested large sums in data warehousing to track customer preferences and behaviour, thus providing a rich seam of market research. The speed and sophistication of the technology allow millions of customer records to be searched and processed relatively quickly. This method enables supermarkets to break down their customer base by category of shopper, e.g. young families, thirty-something singles, elderly couples, elderly single people. Thus the supermarket can compare actual shopping habits with a perceived theoretical shopping basket that each average consumer type 'should' be purchasing. This then enables the retailer to tell which products customers do and do not buy from that particular store. This market research can then be used to promote certain products that the customer may be buying elsewhere outside the store. The supermarkets can also tell the frequency of visits and the impact this has on shopping habits. For example, families with young children may shop at the weekend, at which time supermarkets may promote economy brands, bulk-purchase discounts, baby and children's products, including clothes as well as foodstuffs. These efforts are based on information arising from the data and customer records that the supermarket has stored and collated in its data warehouse.

Organisations may also choose to use specialist market research firms to conduct market research for them, particularly when they may not have the skills or resources in-house to devote to carrying out the research themselves. The market research firm may carry out bespoke market research expressly and confidentially for its client, or it may carry out generic market research that is of use to and available to more than one customer. Alternatively, secondary data may be collected and compiled by private market research companies such as Mintel and Euromonitor. This will be topic specific, e.g. retailing of children's clothing, but not specific to any one company. The secondary data will be collected through mailshots to business customers or private households, through cold calling by telephone or in person to business or private addresses, or by in-person interviews on the street. It will then be sold to any interested companies or libraries. There are also publicly available forms of secondary data, including census data and information on social and demographic trends.

Product planning and development

Having gathered the required market research data on customer needs and wants, the next stage in the marketing process is to try to ensure that the organisation is in a position to introduce new products or services designed to meet the needs and wants it has identified. This may seem an obvious and simple stage to achieve, but there are in fact many complex factors to take into account. The organisation may first want to consider how it might meet those needs or wants with its existing products and services, through utilising the marketing tools explained later in this chapter. However, if existing products or services are no longer suitable, the marketing department must clearly work closely with the other departments to achieve a balance between what is required and what can be provided. These internal relationships are dealt with more explicitly in the next section.

In terms of relationships with the external environment, product planning and development are responsible for a number of factors:

- identifying new technology that improves design or production capabilities;
- identifying suitable suppliers of necessary raw materials or components;
- liaising with customer or consumer focus groups at various stages to take into account changes in taste or design.

Product planning and development are included here as part of the marketing department, but considered under the banner of research and development (R&D) and could be equally comfortably located in the operations management department of an organisation. Without close liaison with the operations managers, the marketers' dreams remain dreams. The operations management department must realise the ambitions of the marketing department. Hence, there must be close cooperation between marketing and operations management. This is the functional convergence mentioned before. Functional convergence could be defined as the situation where two or more departments or functions of an organisation work in harmony towards meeting organisational goals and objectives without rivalry or internal competition.

Sales

Once the new product is up and running, there then comes the task of selling it to the people who were identified as needing or wanting it by the market research. However, this is by no means a foregone conclusion. During the market research and product development stages, customers have had time to develop other wants or needs that may supersede those originally identified. Additionally, competitors have had time to enter the market with new products or services. At this stage it is vital to decide on appropriate pricing and marketing strategies to get the finished product or service delivered to the target market at a price it can afford and that also makes money for the organisation. There are different and conflicting approaches to costing and pricing that are covered in Chapter 10.

The marketing-oriented approach to pricing examines what prices the market might support through its market research. If potential customers find a certain price acceptable for certain products, marketers will want their new product's prices to fit in with the public's perception of 'normal' prices. For example, if the range of prices for a box of 48 washing tablets in the supermarket is between £4.89 and £5.29, then any new powder introduced has to be priced within or close to this range in order to be successful. For a higher than normal price to be acceptable to the marketplace, the product has to be differentiated (*see* Chapter 3). This is where the manufacturer relies on additional product features ('Now destroys grease at 30°C'), quality reputation

('Still the market leader') or brand loyalty ('Your favourite washing powder in handy tablet form') to be able to sell the new washing powder.

Therefore, the organisation's challenge is to be able to produce the product and make a profit within this price range, ensuring that all inputs, costs and overheads are covered. While marketing is dictating to the organisation not only what products must be made but also what price the marketplace will stand, the operations management department's reaction can be to state what it is possible to produce and what the cost of this will be. Hence a production-oriented approach to pricing examines the costs of all inputs, including overheads and labour, and then adds profit to this to achieve a sales price. This appears to be a logical approach, even if the resulting price is higher than the market norm for a similar product or service. It is not logical, however, where the ultimate price of the good is higher than the customer is prepared to pay for such a product. Therefore, this is one aspect where the idea of functional convergence might falter.

Salesforce

From the manufacturer's point of view, the typical method for achieving sales is through a salesforce of representatives who are able to travel to or communicate with existing or potential customers with a view to achieving new or continued sales. In addition to staff costs, there is the investment in a fleet of company cars and mobile phones to be considered for an 'on the road' salesforce or the cost of setting up and running a sales processing centre for telephone or online orders. Managing an 'on the road' salesforce, with its quasi-independent status, cut off geographically from the internal culture of the organisation, is a complex issue. There are important concerns covering the quality of information passed between the salesforce in the field and the organisation, as orders must be processed correctly and quickly and organisational developments communicated to sales staff. Equally, motivating and monitoring an office-based salesforce is usually done by monitoring the number of sales made and orders processed in a particular time period, while balancing this close monitoring with good motivation of staff requires skilful management. Office-based and 'on the road' salesforces often work on salary-plus-commission contracts, which can add a motivational incentive to encourage them to meet and/or exceed their targets.

Wholesalers

A large amount of goods are sold not directly to the consumer but through an intermediary such as a wholesaler. This is convenient for the manufacturer as, although reduced profits are made since wholesalers command discounts from manufacturers, they have a simpler task in only selling to centralised wholesalers rather than having to identify and target a variety of customers. Wholesalers need discounts from the manufacturers because they too wish to make a profit from the transactions of buying and selling on to retailers, and they have their own operational costs to consider. The wholesaler requires efficient distribution networks, including appropriate transportation. The wholesaler also removes the need for the manufacturer to keep a large amount of finished goods in stock, as it is the wholesaler who needs the large warehousing capacity, centrally positioned to service a network of retailers.

Companies such Argos and Screwfix both have their own warehouses and distribution centres. In the case of Argos their distribution centres supply their own retail outlets with a wide range of goods from jewellery through to children's toys, and some bigger items, such as furniture, are delivered directly to the customer's home address. Screwfix use their warehouses to store a wide range of DIY tools and goods, which are supplied direct to customers who order either via the phone or online, with the promise of next day delivery. Both Argos and Screwfix seek to make the distribution of their goods as efficient as possible and to do this they will site distribution centres close to major motorways. For example, they both have distribution centres minutes away from one of the UK's major motorways, the M6, in Stafford.

Retailers

The retail trade sells goods to the end user or consumer of the product. In order to be successful in retailing, it is crucial to make correct decisions about a number of factors. Location is a key issue, as the retailer must position itself in the place the consumer would expect or would like to find the goods on offer. Thus city-centre shops are faced with tough decisions when a new out-of-town shopping mall opens, taking trade away from the city-centre location. Do they remain loyal to the city centre? Do they move site into the new environment of the shopping mall? Or do they attempt to make both locations successful?

Department stores in Sheffield are an interesting case in point. Meadowhall opened outside the city in 1992. This had a further significant impact on city-centre shops, given that the economic situation of Sheffield as a whole had not fully recovered from the economic downturn in the 1970s. The department chain House of Fraser initially opened a second store in the Meadowhall complex and kept its city-centre store open. However, after five years of operating two stores, in 1997 it finally closed its town-centre store in favour of the Meadowhall location. Shoppers had demonstrated a preference for visiting the shopping centre-based store over the town-based one. John Lewis, however, remained loyal to the city-centre location with its Cole Brothers store. It resisted the challenge of Meadowhall and retained its band of loyal customers.

Direct selling

Many organisations are avoiding intermediaries such as wholesalers or agents in order to reduce costs and thus prices, hence passing on cost savings to the consumer. In this way, manufacturers or service providers can also increase profit margins by charging the end price directly to the customer rather than selling at a discount to a wholesaler or agent. Examples of organisations now dealing directly with their customers or consumers are home and car insurance services, which sell their services by telephone or via the internet instead of in a shop or office, hence reducing overheads and providing a more customer-oriented service. Customer service is also improved by giving customers access to services at a time convenient to them.

Remote shopping

There is a 'chicken and egg' link between customer orientation and customer demands. As organisations improve their products and services, customers become used to a high level of service and good-quality products. As they become accustomed to better services and products, they demand more and more from the organisations they patronise. One of the manifestations of this is longer opening hours in shops (late-night shopping in city centres, and supermarkets opening 24 hours).

Another trend is the growing popularity of remote shopping. **Remote shopping** refers to shopping by customers in locations other than a retail or sales outlet. Many high street names offer remote shopping in addition to their high street stores. For example Marks & Spencer, Next, Debenhams and Currys all offer website shopping and/or catalogue shopping.

Many retailers now offer more than one way of shopping in an attempt to make it easy for customers to shop with them and to put goods and services more widely on display, i.e. a website is accessible 24 hours a day, every day of the year. Additionally, many other goods and services such as banking, insurance, holidays and cars can be purchased via the web, with companies often offering a good price if the ordering and payment are carried out online. There are also examples of internet shopping being used to promote associated services. For example, Barclaycard has promoted its credit card as being the ideal way to buy Christmas presents without leaving home, by shopping on the internet.

Advertising and promotion

In order to bring new products or services to the attention of the potential market, there has to be advertising and promotion. These, along with sales activities, are the subdepartments most easily associated in the public consciousness with the term 'marketing'. Advertising and promotion are not necessarily the same activities. They are the part of the marketing department responsible for planning strategies to retain existing customers and attract new customers. Advertising and promotion are carried out in a variety of media appropriate to the product or service and to the target audience.

Advertising takes two forms: institutional or product. That is to say, advertisements either promote the company as a whole without focusing on specific products; or they focus on particular products, irrespective of where they are sold. The advertising media most familiar to the general public are print media (newspapers and magazines), broadcast media (television, radio, cinema and the internet), and public spaces, such as roadside billboards and street furniture. The cost of advertising space varies according to the size of audience likely to be reached and the date or time of the advertisements placed.

Many advertisements take on a life of their own quite beyond or apart from the popularity of the product. An example of this is the BT Home Hub advertisements which featured 'Jane and Adam', whose relationship and break-up are featured in adverts for the BT Home Hub. In July 2008 the latest advert in the 'Jane and Adam' series featured Adam working away from home and struggling to talk to Jane over instant messaging using a non-BT router which breaks down, the message being that the BT Home Hub is the most reliable on the market.[8]

Promotion is the way in which the organisation attempts to manipulate the external environment by combining advertising with special offers and particular benefits or service packages intended to attract customers. There are many famous examples of organisations that have failed to match the demand created by special promotions and have come unstuck as a result. In 1994 Hoover seriously underestimated the number of people prepared to purchase a new vacuum cleaner in order to benefit from the offer of free trips to America and the company ended up in the courts having to justify why customers had not benefited from the promised holidays. Advertising and promotion constitute one part of the marketing department that is strictly regulated by law and the Advertising Standards Agency (ASA).

Distribution

After whetting the customer's appetite with advertising and promotion, and potentially making sales to them by remote methods, the next stage in the successful marketing process is ensuring that products or services are physically available to customers who wish to purchase them. The 1998 football World Cup was dogged by problems of ticket distribution. First of all there were the restrictions placed by the French organising authorities on ticket allocations to national football associations to be sold in participating countries. Then they announced that tickets could only be bought over the telephone by customers with an address in France, effectively debarring all non-residents. In order to remedy this situation, they offered an extra allocation of tickets by international telephone over a certain period, only to find the lines so oversubscribed that few callers could get through. This was obviously a clear case of demand outstripping supply, but also one of extremely poor distribution management.

Efficient distribution networks are particularly important for online and mail-order companies. Consumer protection organisations and radio and television programmes are kept particularly busy in the early part of each year investigating complaints from customers who have ordered and paid for goods as Christmas presents that were not delivered in time.

After-sales customer service

The final stage in the holistic customer-oriented package is how customers are dealt with once their purchase has been made. Dealing effectively with follow-up enquiries or complaints is a key indicator of the truly marketing-oriented organisation. This enables organisations to target customers for current or future alternative products or services. Organisations often include aspects of their after-sales service as part of the promotion package, offering money-back guarantees, 24-hour helplines, or free installation or home visits. The standard of this type of service is often the factor enabling customers to judge whether repeat business will be placed with the company or not. The cable communications company that keeps the complaining customer on hold for half an hour before putting them through to 'one of our service operatives' does not demonstrate excellent customer service or good telecommunications equipment.

Privatised utilities have invested heavily in this end of their customer service, which may be partly due to the fact that they have many dissatisfied customers who find service levels below par and prices rising. Partly due to customer service initiatives, and partly due to external regulation, utilities offer *per diem* refunds for any disruption of service in water, electricity or gas, as well as compensation schemes for complaints received.

Check your understanding

Do you understand what each of the activities undertaken by the marketing department involves?

Check your understanding by summarising the key points of each activity carried out by the marketing department.

Relationship to the internal environment

As well as operating on a set of assumptions about potential or actual customers, the marketing concept makes some basic assumptions about the organisation for which the marketing effort is being made. The first of these assumptions is that the organisation is able to be flexible and alter its products and processes in order to meet newly identified customer needs and wants. Having identified customer needs and wants, in theory it should be a simple process for the organisation to plan the production or service delivery required to provide customers with the products or services that they have indicated, via market research, are a need or a want. However, as we will see later in this chapter, the internal culture or structure of the organisation could make this more difficult than might be anticipated.

The second assumption about the organisation is that it is able to react quickly enough to the consumer's perceived needs or wants and redirect the necessary resources away from their current focus towards meeting newly perceived needs and wants in the marketplace. Without the necessary financial resources to purchase new technology or recruit new people, and without the production flexibility to rearrange current production lines to produce the new product lines, the marketing effort is wasted. Again, the marketing department's effort is dependent on the other departments for support and implementation.

The marketers' internal challenge, therefore, is to ensure that their organisations produce only what they have identified as the customers' needs or wants and are flexible enough to react to perceived changes in customer requirements and other external environmental elements. The functional convergence mentioned before is the ultimate goal, i.e. all departments of the organisation work rationally towards meeting the ultimate goal of customer satisfaction. However, this is not always so easy to achieve. With the marketing department's specialist knowledge gained through its market research of the external environment, and with its philosophical conviction of the needs of marketers to take precedence within the organisation, departmental tension can replace functional convergence. Therefore, the relationships that marketing has with the other departments are crucial not only to customer satisfaction but also to the cultural and structural survival of the organisation.

Marketing and operations management

As mentioned previously, the R&D stage is the point at which marketing clearly requires a close and supportive working relationship with operations management, to decide on product or service design and to agree the resource inputs needed. Once resource levels are agreed, operations management can decide costs, and marketing can decide the sales price, thus working towards deciding together how profits can be made within cost and price constraints. Operations management obviously also requires an input into the design of new products and services, to indicate from a practical point of view what can be manufactured technologically and physically.

Marketing and finance

The link between finance and marketing is crucial but is also dependent on the link between marketing and operations management. The finance department is responsible for ensuring that the organisation has enough money to perform all the organisation's activities. Operations management has the responsibility of manufacturing within cost constraints. Marketing must bring the products to market and sell enough of them at a sustainable price to make profits for the organisation.

Marketing and human resource management

If new products and services are being introduced, marketing must keep the human resource management (HRM) department fully informed of developments. The message concerning new products or services must be communicated, as the HRM department needs to know the type of skills and experience that current or new workers will have to possess to be able to deliver the new products or services. HRM will develop its own strategies in order to plan for recruitment and selection of any new staff or to formulate training programmes for existing staff who lack the necessary skills or expertise.

Check your understanding

Do you understand the term 'functional convergence'?

Check your understanding by explaining how functional convergence can occur in organisations. Use examples where appropriate.

Marketing tools

So far this chapter has examined the relationships that the marketing department has with the external and internal environments of the organisation. We have looked at marketing in terms of its responsibility for monitoring changes in customer needs or wants. The marketing department must convince senior management and the other departments that the organisation should be producing new products or delivering new services to meet these perceived changes. Therefore, the marketing department uses an array of tools to monitor elements of the external environment.

Marketing is not only about purely reacting to perceived changes in the external environment. It also has a responsibility to aim to be proactive in relation to the external environment. Thus marketing may aim not only to provide the products or services the customers know they want but also to attempt to influence customer choice by anticipating what customers are likely to need or want in the future and providing it ahead of competitors. For example, as disposable incomes in Russia have grown, many companies, including Starbucks, Costa Coffee and Kraft, have all seen an opportunity to meet a growing customer desire for drinking coffee, both on the go and at home – *see* the entry case study for this chapter.

This proactive stance is to a large degree reliant on assumptions about customers and the organisation. Marketing tools can thus be used both to react to and to influence the marketplace. Some of these basic tools are presented and applied here to a variety of products and services.

The marketing mix

Borden[9] developed the idea of a **marketing mix** to describe the marketing elements that could affect the way a product performed in the marketplace. McCarthy[10] summarised the marketing mix as the four Ps of marketing (*see* Figure 8.3). Today the marketing mix or 4Ps is one of the traditional tools used to manipulate the organisation's relationship with the external environment. The 4Ps are product, price, promotion and place. That is to say, there are four basic ways in which organisations can affect the relationship they have with their customers to increase sales and profitability.

Product

Once the initial investment in research and development has been paid back and resulted in a successfully launched product, it is in the manufacturer's financial interest to recoup as much profit on that investment as possible. Thus the manufacturer will want to make as much of the product for as long as possible with little new investment or alteration in order to keep sales high and reap profits. If sales do begin to decline after a certain time, it is not necessarily inevitable that a brand new product needs to be found straight away. In order to keep sales of the existing product buoyant, it is possible to manipulate certain aspects of that product at little cost in order to offer a newer, fresher and updated product. The clear aim is to continue to attract new customers and/or tempt existing customers to remain loyal and not be attracted by a competitor's product.

Product aspects that may be manipulated include style, performance, quality, branding, packaging and after-sales service. Examples of such product manipulation abound in the washing powder industry. Famous and familiar brands are often relaunched as 'new', 'improved' or as version two or three. While alterations to the basic washing powder have undoubtedly been made

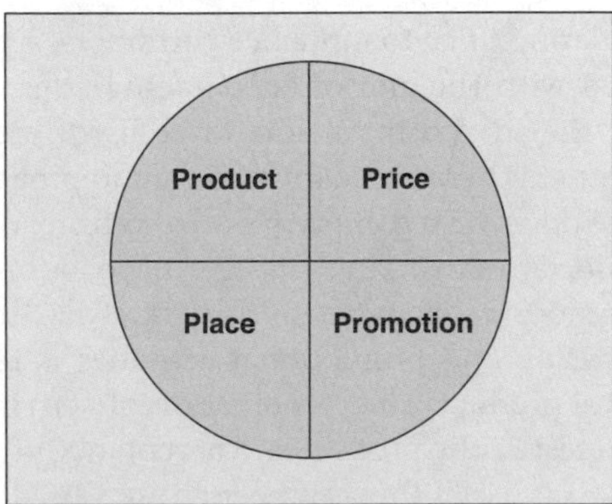

Figure 8.3 The marketing mix

in order that trade description legislation is not infringed by the use of these words, the basic product is still washing powder, with additional features. Altering the product slightly offers the manufacturer the opportunity to make a statement to the marketplace about continual innovation, improvement and customer orientation. Hence this type of manipulation of the product is a reasonably simple yet effective marketing tool. Product manipulation requires cooperation between the marketing and operations management departments.

Price

The second of the four Ps is price, and there are various ways in which organisations can use the price they charge to influence sales. Many fast-food restaurants charge the same price for their products regardless of where in a country they are sold. However, in June 2008 it was reported that McDonald's had appointed consultants to look at the price sensitivity of customers in different parts of the UK. This was done to establish in which areas of the country prices for particular items could be raised by ten to twenty pence in an effort to recoup increasing food costs.[11]

Price can be used not only when introducing new products but also when products are perceived to be near the end of their natural life (*see* the discussion of **product life cycle** in the next section). Special offers and finance deals can be used to affect customers' buying habits. The mass television advertising by furniture companies of lounge and dining room furniture is an excellent example of this. The frequent, prime-time advertisements offer cheaper prices, 'buy now, pay later' deals, 0 per cent finance on hire purchase and long payment terms of 4–5 years. All these are offered in special sales promotions that 'must end Sunday 5 p.m.' and yet seem very similar from week to week. Price manipulation depends on cooperation between the marketing and finance departments.

Promotion

As well as manipulating price to influence customers, a product can be advertised and promoted with the aim of encouraging sales. Decisions have to be made concerning the advertising media to be used: press, magazines, television, radio or internet. There are many different approaches to online promotion, which can be done via a company's own website, on a search engine like Google, or on a social networking site like Bebo. Alongside the advertising decisions, the promotional activity for a product has to be decided. A combination of advertising and promotional activities is required to create and support a successful product. The combination of activities needs to create an awareness and interest in the product and acceptance of it by the marketplace.

The promotional activities that can be used are varied. In supermarkets with loyalty cards, the offer of extra bonus points on certain products or goods entices customers to switch loyalty from one brand to another or to buy products not normally on their shopping list. Magazines are frequently used to offer free samples of cosmetics, chocolate or even books to their readership, in the hope of capturing new and potentially loyal customers. The launch of new products can be heralded by the delivery to target households of free samples, discount vouchers or promotional literature. In 1997 the sponsorship of television programmes was a relatively new activity in the UK following deregulation of broadcast advertising, and is an effective promotional method. Thus Cadbury, 'the nation's favourite' chocolate manufacturer, sponsored *Coronation Street*, one of the leading soap operas for the next ten years until the end of 2007. Television programmes with sponsorship do not explicitly advertise the companies' products in the programme, but the sponsors name usually appears at the start and end of the programme, therefore implicitly linking the company's products in the viewers' minds with the programme. In 2006 the regulator OFCOM (*see* Chapter 3) changed the regulations to allow sponsorship of whole television channels and radio stations, rather than only allowing individual programmes to be sponsored. The rules prohibit the sponsorship of news and current affairs programmes and companies selling products such as alcohol and gambling will not be allowed to sponsor children's programmes.[12]

The importance of an organisation's advertising and promotion activities is clear if a product is a leading brand and the organisation seeks to maintain that position. The importance of good advertising and promotion is heightened if a competing brand advertises heavily and is easily substituted (*see* Chapter 3). Also the advertising and promotion surrounding a product will remind consumers making frequent repeat purchases to buy the same brand of product as before, which is crucial if **customer loyalty** to a brand is low. A product's added value or low cost, which will be important to particular groups of customers, can be emphasised by the use of advertising and promotion, as explained in Chapter 3.

Place

The fourth element of the traditional marketing mix is the location of the interface between customer or consumer and product or service. This links with the issue of distribution, and getting the right amount of product to the right place at the right time is essential. This is fundamental to each stage of the distribution process, whether from manufacturer to wholesaler, wholesaler to retailer, retailer to customer or manufacturer direct to the customer. This is particularly so for those organisations that are reacting to customer demand for more products that can be delivered direct to the home without the need to go out shopping, for example with mail-order or internet shopping.

The manipulation of the place element of the marketing mix can also take place in shops themselves: for example, the simple positioning of special offers at the end of aisles, to ensure maximum exposure to shoppers, with the aim of gaining high turnover for the item on special offer. Supermarkets also use place on a grander scale by frequently changing the position of everyday basket goods by locating them next to more unusual or aspirational goods that shoppers might not purchase on a regular basis. Placing products not normally associated with a particular location is also included. Thus being able to buy Häagen-Dazs ice cream at a Warner Brothers cinema links the two brands in the customer's mind. Similarly, many supermarkets have begun to offer a range of other goods and services, including petrol stations, pharmacies, dry cleaning and photo development, as part of their overall one-stop-shop package.

The extended marketing mix

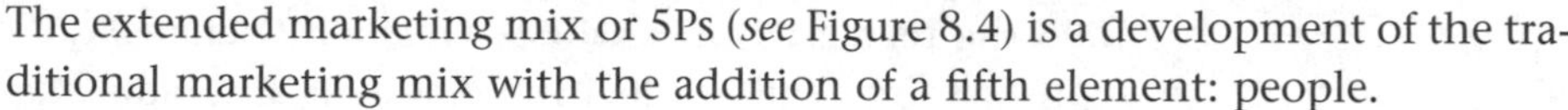

The extended marketing mix or 5Ps (*see* Figure 8.4) is a development of the traditional marketing mix with the addition of a fifth element: people.

People

It is initially difficult to see how marketers could manipulate people in the same way as they could manipulate the other 4Ps, as the latter are internal elements within the direct control of the organisation, whereas people, in terms of customers, are not part of the organisation's internal environment. The people element inside an organisation is constituted by the employees. However, the consideration of people in the marketing mix reflects the importance to successful marketing of both the person who is the customer and the person doing the selling. Interpersonal skills play a large part in achieving a successful relationship between customer and organisation. Hence there is a crucial relationship between the marketing and human resource management departments in ensuring that appropriate staff are recruited to do the selling and marketing. In addition, recognising who customers are and what they want is an explicit part of the people element of the marketing mix.

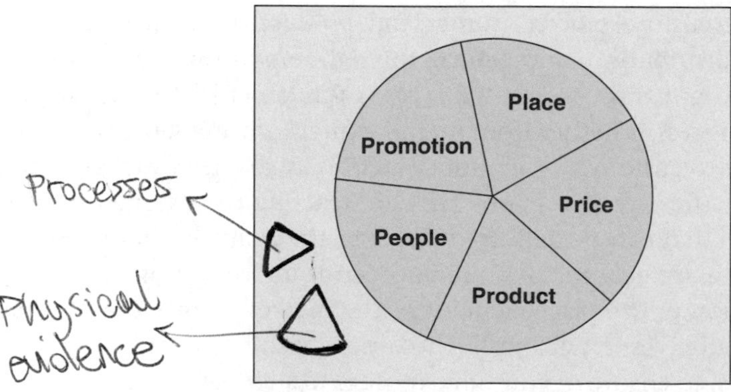

Figure 8.4 The extended marketing mix

Check your understanding

Do you understand the term 'marketing mix'?

Check your understanding by naming and illustrating the components of the marketing mix. Use examples where appropriate.

Product life cycle

The product life cycle is the 'natural' lifespan of a particular product or service and may last for a few short months or many years. For example, a *High School Musical* T-shirt has a life cycle measurable in months or until the next big film hits the cinema screens and its associated merchandise the shops. In contrast, a product like a television set has a product life cycle of many years, due to continued **product development** in the field of television and broadcasting. These developments have included the very first black-and-white television sets that became available in the 1950s, through colour, stereo, digital and high definition (HD) television sets. The development of associated products such as freeview boxes, satellite dishes and cable television have also helped to extend the product life cycle of television sets.

There are five stages in a product life cycle: introduction, growth, maturity, saturation and decline. Companies adopt different strategies for marketing products or services depending on the stage in the life cycle they identify that particular product as having reached. Various products and services will also need varying levels of financial and human resource investment according to the marketing strategy adopted.

Introduction

The introduction stage is self-evidently that stage when a new product or service is launched into the marketplace. The market research and product development have been completed and the product has been designed with its target market in mind. This has meant considerable investment on the part of the organisation with no guaranteed returns, since, until the product is sold, there is no income from it. Thus the sales and profit curves run together at the bottom of the profitability axis in Figure 8.5. It is clear that for new organisations this is the 'make or break' period, as the investment for new products or services is likely to have come from bank loans or other borrowings. For existing organisations the investment for research and development may come from profits earned by other products. This issue is examined under the **Boston Consulting Group matrix** later in this chapter. Research and development will have considered the product and price elements of the marketing mix for the new product or service.

A product in the introduction phase of the product life cycle will have relatively few buyers and those who do purchase the product will buy it to try it.

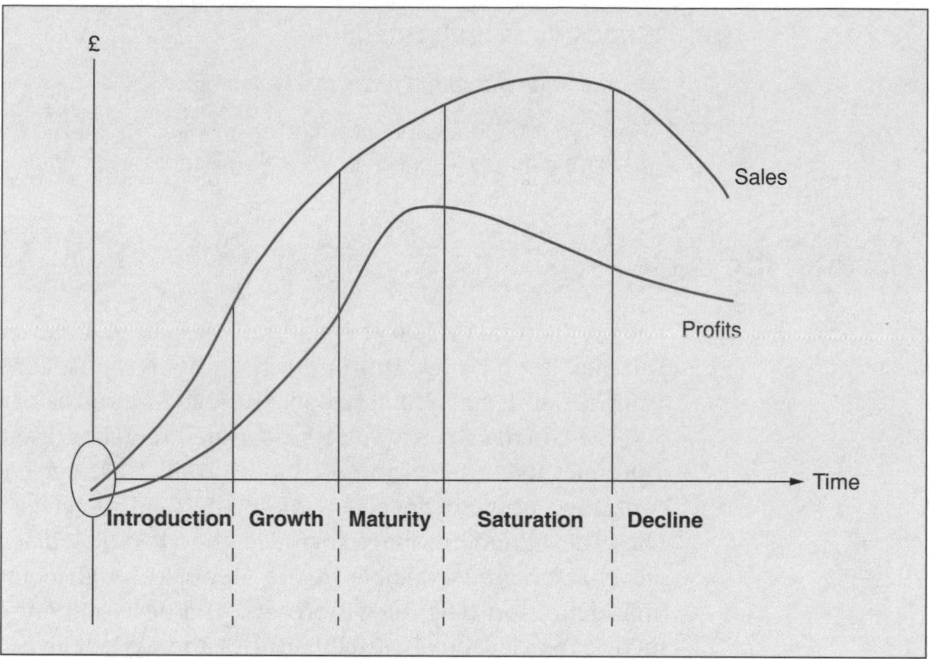

Figure 8.5 The product life cycle

Thus at the introduction stage, promotion of the product is crucial if it is to move on to the growth phase. The introduction of Oreo cookies to the UK market was a case in point. The biscuits have been a long-term success in the US, but have never been sold in Britain. Therefore, their introduction to the UK market relied on successful promotion, since the product, with a price comparable to other biscuits, meant that product and price aspects of the marketing mix were to a large extent unalterable. In television advertisements, Oreo cookies were promoted as a homely product that mothers give their children as a treat with a glass of milk. The television advert shows a small boy demonstrating how to eat Oreo cookies to his dog. The techniques is to separate the two halves of the biscuit, lick the cream from the middle of the biscuit and them dunk the cookie in the glass of milk, hence the Oreo slogan of 'twist, lick, dunk'.[13]

Growth

If the research and development work has been done correctly, a newly launched product will sell well in the early period of its life cycle. Thus sales will rise quite dramatically. However, the profit curve remains relatively low due to the cost of the continued promotion needed to allow sales to grow. Nevertheless, profits are made and market share starts to be accumulated in the growth phase of the product life cycle. The marketing department will use a variety of promotional tools to achieve growth in sales, some of which will include manipulation of other elements of the marketing mix, such as place. For example, a new fragrance could be promoted through a number of locations: the distribution of free samples in fashion magazines; high-profile sales stands in up-market department stores; large advertisements on roadside billboards; as well as television and cinema advertisements.

Maturity

The dramatic growth in sales of a product or service slows down when the maturity stage of the product life cycle is reached. Depending on the type of product and the type of market, the maturity stage may last a long or a short time. A product in the maturity stage still has limited growth, but rapid and significant progress such as that achieved in the growth phase of the product life cycle is unlikely. The maturity stage is where maximum profits are achieved and the outlay required to maintain sales is minimal compared with that in the growth stage – *see* Figure 8.5.

Advertising and promotion of a product in the maturity phase of the product life cycle are aimed at retaining existing customers and persuading others to switch from competitor products. The overall aim is to keep the product at the peak of the maturity stage of the product life cycle for as long as possible as this is when profits peak.

Saturation

The saturation stage of the product life cycle is reached when growth tails off and the market for a product is no longer growing. Nevertheless, sales volume may be kept buoyant and loyal customers retained by price competition and special offers, although this will mean reduced profits – *see* Figure 8.5. These are competitive options that are easy for rivals to replicate. An alternative would be for the marketing department to choose to implement an **extension strategy**. This is discussed briefly in the next section.

Decline

Following the saturation of the marketplace, products eventually lose sales volume through being replaced, in the customers' eyes, by new products introduced by the same organisation or by competitors. A product or service in decline may be withdrawn from the market if it is losing money. Alternatively, it may find a small, loyal, niche market that either breaks even or makes a limited profit for the organisation. An example here is the vinyl LP record. Most people today prefer their music to be on compact disc or downloaded to an MP 3 player; therefore, most music produced today is in those formats. However, there exists a small group of consumers who still buy vinyl LP records, either vinyl buffs or DJs in clubs, so record companies continue to release a certain amount of material on vinyl. The decline of vinyl LPs has been long and slow.

Check your understanding

Do you understand the term 'product life cycle'?

Check your understanding by summarising the key attributes of products in the different stages of the product life cycle. Use examples where appropriate.

Extending the product life cycle

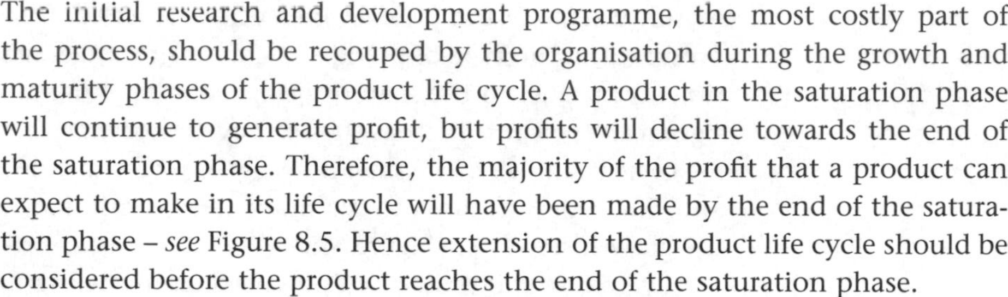

The initial research and development programme, the most costly part of the process, should be recouped by the organisation during the growth and maturity phases of the product life cycle. A product in the saturation phase will continue to generate profit, but profits will decline towards the end of the saturation phase. Therefore, the majority of the profit that a product can expect to make in its life cycle will have been made by the end of the saturation phase – *see* Figure 8.5. Hence extension of the product life cycle should be considered before the product reaches the end of the saturation phase.

There are various methods for accomplishing this. Ansoff[14] summarises four different marketing strategies that organisations may follow and presents them in the Ansoff matrix. The first three strategies, **market penetration**, **market development** and **product development**, can all be used to extend a product's life cycle – *see* Figure 8.6. The fourth, **diversification**, involves changing to a significantly different product.

The customer growth matrix

In following Ansoff's marketing strategies, organisations are seeking to increase the number of sales and/or the number of customers. Jenkins[15] presents four different types of customer growth options that organisations may follow to achieve sales and customer growth – *see* Figure 8.7.

Customer loyalty

Customer loyalty is important and should be developed by organisations because it brings greater profitability.[16] Faithful customers will affect profit directly by purchasing products and services over an extended period of time, and indirectly by telling friends, neighbours and relatives about the benefits and satisfaction they derive from the company's products and services.

The supermarkets in the UK are examples of organisations which attempt to create customer loyalty via their use of so-called 'loyalty cards'. Loyalty to the service provided by the supermarket is created by offering money-off shopping when a certain number of 'loyalty' points have been collected by a customer. The development of loyalty to products involves manipulation of the marketing mix. Alterations may be made to the price at which products or services are being sold, or to promotional activities or distribution locations in order to try to increase sales to existing customers.

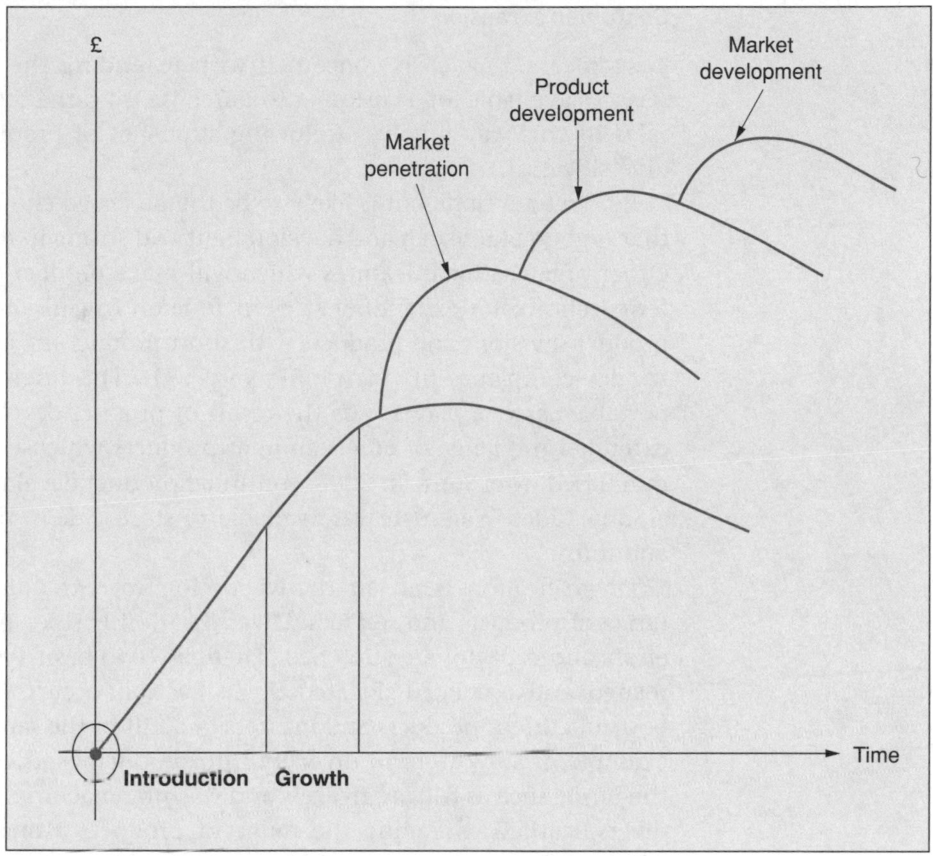

Figure 8.6 Product life cycle and extension strategies

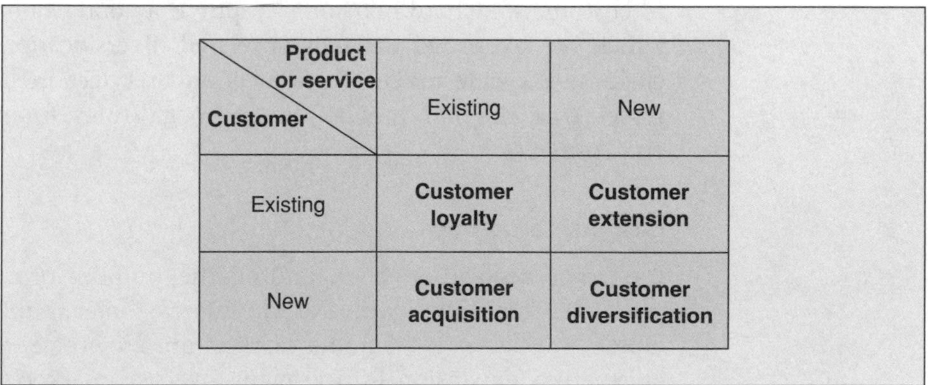

Customer \ Product or service	Existing	New
Existing	**Customer loyalty**	**Customer extension**
New	**Customer acquisition**	**Customer diversification**

Figure 8.7 The customer growth matrix

Source: Jenkins, M (1997), *The Customer Centred Strategy*, Prentice Hall. Reproduced with permission.

Customer extension

Customer extension is concerned with extending the range of products or services available for a customer to purchase from the organisation. Increasing sales in this way involves following strategies of product development and diversification.

Product development is likely to be the preferred choice of the organisation that is good at research and development and strong in the area of innovation. Other organisational features which will make product development the preferred choice for expanding sales include an organisation structured around product divisions and products with short product life cycles. Consumer electronics companies fit this profile very well. The original Sony Walkman, a portable cassette player, was the result of product development by Sony and extended the range of entertainment products which customers traditionally purchased from Sony. In 2008, continual product development at Sony meant a Sony Video Walkman was available to store videos, podcasts, photographs and music.

Diversification is an alternative option for extending the organisation's range of products and services. Diversification is risky, as both organisational effort and capacity are stretched. There are two basic types of diversification: related and unrelated. Related diversification occurs when development is beyond current products and markets but still in the same broad industry. For example, if Sony were to diversify into producing other electronic goods for the home such as fridges, freezers and washing machines, this would be related diversification, extending the range of products available to include white goods but remaining in the broad industry of providing electrical consumer goods. In contrast, unrelated diversification for a company like Sony would be a move into running a rail franchise, which is completely unrelated to electrical consumer goods but still increases the range of products and services available to customers. Richard Branson's empire is a good example of an organisation which has expanded through unrelated diversification and currently offers customers a wide range of products and services including air travel, train travel, cola, cinemas, mobile phones, mega stores, financial services, holidays and cosmetics.

Customer acquisition

Customer acquisition is expanding the number of customers for existing products. This could involve expanding customer numbers in home markets, which will be easiest if home markets are growing in size. If home markets are mature, expansion into growing overseas markets may provide the best opportunity for increasing the number of customers. This was one of the reasons for expansion into China by companies such as Starbucks, Costa Coffee and Kraft, which are seeking to increase the number of customers drinking and buying coffee to drink on the go and at home – *see* the entry case study for this chapter.

Customer acquisition in overseas markets requires the organisation to engage in international business activities such as exporting or internationalising its operations.

- Exporting involves selling existing product ranges, which incur no further development costs, to new customers abroad.
- Internationalising operations involves locating activities overseas, such as manufacturing, distribution and promotion. The benefits of doing this can include overcoming import controls, lower labour costs and lower distribution costs. An organisation may choose to internationalise its operations if the number of customers in a particular geographic market is large and home markets are mature or in decline.

Attempting to increase the number of customers in a static or mature market will be difficult because there will be few or no new customers available – it can be realistically achieved only if customers can be persuaded to switch products or brands. This requires customer loyalty to a competing product or brand to be broken. The only other opportunity for attracting customers in a static or mature market will arise if the market leader becomes complacent and allows performance to slip. Increasing customers while operating in a declining market is possible only if competitors leave the marketplace early and their customers transfer their business to those remaining in the industry. However, it should be noted that seeking to increase customers while operating in a declining market is a short-term option with a limited lifespan.

Organisations may choose to follow a combination or hybrid of customer growth options. An organisation may expand its sales and customer base by following both customer loyalty and customer acquisition options.

Customer diversification

Expanding customer numbers by **customer diversification** is the riskiest of all of Jenkins' options. Customer diversification is achieved if sales are increased by selling a new product or service to new customers. The availability of a new technology or process is usually required if customer diversification is to occur.[17]

The best recent examples of customer diversification are those being achieved through e-commerce by many companies offering products and services over the internet. It is the use of new technology (computers and the internet) which allows services to be offered in an entirely new way. For example, the provision of financial services by many of the high street banks via the internet, bookshop services by companies such as Amazon, and What Car? Online for researching and buying a new car over the internet.

Check your understanding

Do you understand the term 'the customer growth matrix'?

Check your understanding by summarising the attributes of each customer growth option. Use examples where appropriate.

The Boston Consulting Group matrix

Bruce Henderson[18] of the Boston Consulting Group developed seminal work on categorising products in a useful way that then enables the marketing department to decide appropriate strategies for products in different stages of the life cycle. The categories are based on the rate of market growth identified compared with the volume of market share the product has achieved in the marketplace – *see* Figure 8.8. It should be noted that large market share alone will not generate low costs and high margins. The relative comparison of costs and margins to those of competitors is also important (*see* Chapter 3).

Question marks

The question mark is a product located in the introduction stage of its product life cycle that is likely to achieve high market growth but currently holds low market share. If a question mark is to become a star, then high expenditure will be required to promote the product or service such that higher market share is achieved. The funding of a question mark will come from other successful products in the organisation's product range – *see* cash cows below. A product that is a question mark is not necessarily certain to be successful in the future.

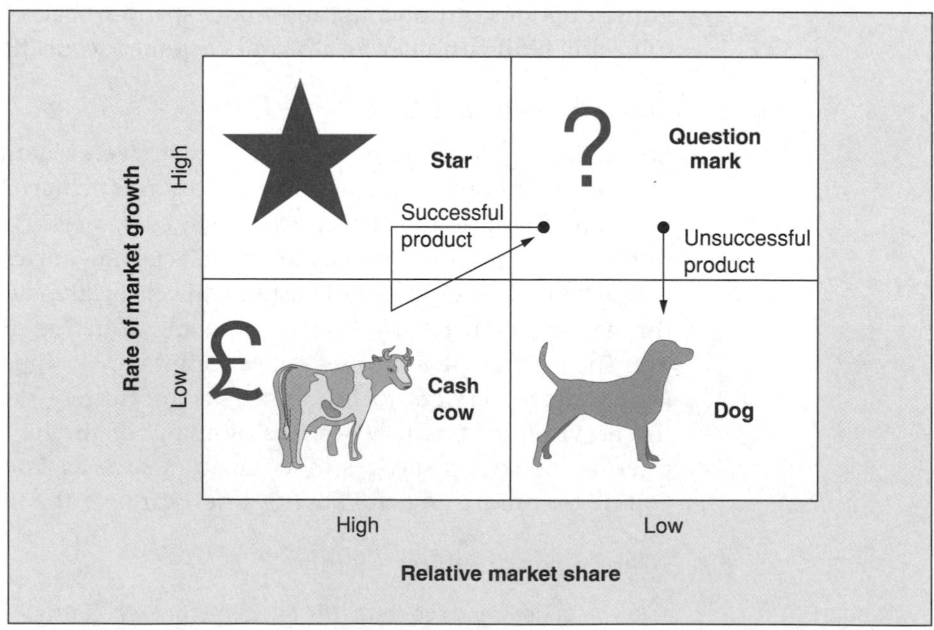

Figure 8.8 The Boston Consulting Group matrix

Source: Henderson, B (1970) *The Product Portfolio*, Boston Consulting Group. The BCG Portfolio Matrix from the Product Portfolio Matrix, © 1970, The Boston Consulting Group.

Stars

The successful question mark will gain market share and become a star. The star product is located in the growth stage of its product life cycle. The market at this stage may still be small in terms of overall sales or size. However, the star has a sizeable portion of overall market share. It is likely that star products will be successful, based on predicted growth in sales and continued domination of the growing market. The successful star product will be on its way to being a cash cow of the future.

Cash cows

The cash cow will be in the maturity or saturation stage of its product life cycle. The rate of market growth will be low, but the volume of market share will be high, as shown in Figure 8.8. Hence sales of the product are at maximum levels, as are profits. Therefore, the cash cow is the bread-and-butter product of the organisation, and its profits provide the finance for research and new product development. The organisation is thus reliant on cash cows and needs to maintain them in its product portfolio.

Dogs

Dogs are products that are definitely in the decline stage of the product life cycle and may have previously been successful cash cows. Dogs have no growth in terms of sales and do not have significant market share. Therefore, the organisation has to decide what to do with its dogs. If the dog product is profitable and has a small but loyal band of consumers still willing to continue purchasing it, then keeping it in the product portfolio is a viable option. Alternatively, the organisation may decide to withdraw the dog from the marketplace. This would be the more viable option if the dog product had become loss making or if the organisation had a substitute product that was a star.

Check your understanding

Do you understand the term 'BCG matrix'?

Check your understanding by summarising the key attributes of products in the different quadrants of the BCG matrix. Use examples where appropriate.

Successful and unsuccessful products

A successful product will move around the Boston Consulting Group matrix in the following order: question mark, star, cash cow, dog. Hence a successful product will at times cost the organisation money and at other times make it money. A product that ceases to be successful may return to the right-hand side of the matrix, moving from being a star or cash cow to being a dog. A product that is never successful will stay on the right-hand side of the matrix (low cash generation) and go from being a question mark directly to being a dog and will never make significant profits for the organisation.

Summary

This chapter examined the concept of the marketing-oriented firm, the marketing activities that organisations carry out today, and some of the best-known marketing tools. The following summary covers all aspects of this chapter.

1 The marketing department of an organisation is that which is best placed to interact with the external environment. The marketing department has to understand and anticipate the products and services its customers require at the present time and in the future.

2 The marketing department in an organisation should ensure that it addresses the following three basic points:

(a) What do customers need or want?
(b) How can the organisation meet these needs or wants?
(c) How does the organisation make money doing so?

3 The marketing department is required to make three basic assumptions concerning its competitive arena. First, customers have disposable income to spend on goods and services. Second, customers have an element of choice when deciding how and where to spend their money. Finally, the marketing department needs to acknowledge that it is its job to persuade the customer to spend that disposable income on the goods and services offered by its company or organisation.

4 There are a number of different activities that the marketing department may undertake, which range from market research through to after-sales service. The marketing activities also include product planning, sales, advertising, promotion and distribution.

5 The organisation should be flexible enough to alter its products and processes to meet newly identified customer needs and wants. This involves the organisation directing resources away from the current focus towards meeting those new needs and wants. This requires functional convergence, i.e. all departments of the organisation working rationally towards meeting the ultimate goal of customer satisfaction.

6 The marketing mix or 4Ps is one of the traditional tools used to manipulate the organisation's relationship with the external environment. Aspects of product, price, promotion and place can all be altered to encourage customers to purchase a particular product.

7 The product life cycle has five stages: introduction, growth, maturity, saturation and decline. Introduction is where sales and profits are low and is the 'make or break' period for the product. In the growth phase sales will increase rapidly, market share starts to be accumulated and profits made. In the maturity phase sales growth still occurs but at a slower rate than in the growth phase and profits reach a peak. In the saturation phase the rate of sales growth starts to slow but sales volume remains buoyant. However, profits will decline as price competition and special offers abound. The decline phase is where a product loses sales volume, profits decline and losses may occur.

8 The customer growth matrix shows four different options that companies can follow to achieve sales and customer growth. These are establishing customer loyalty; customer extension by extending the range of products available to customers; customer acquisition, which involves expanding customer numbers for existing products; and customer diversification, which is selling new products or services to new customers.

9 The Boston Consulting Group matrix groups products based on the rate of market growth and volume of market share. The question mark is a product located in the introduction stage of its life cycle. In turn a successful question mark will gain market share and become a star, which is located in the growth stage of the product life cycle, while continued growth will see a star product become a cash cow. A cash cow product will be in the maturity or saturation stage of the life cycle. Finally, a dog is a product in the decline phase of the product life cycle and may be profitable due to a small band of loyal customers or can be a loss-making product which should be withdrawn from the marketplace.

Chapter objectives and the exit case study

While reading this chapter and engaging in the activities, you should have learned how to apply theory and models and analyse situations. This means you should be able to meet the chapter objectives outlined at the beginning of the chapter. The table below shows which chapter objectives can be tested by the different questions.

Chapter objective	Check you have achieved this by
3 Apply a range of marketing tools to different products and services.	answering case study questions 1 and 2.
4 Understand the relevance of marketing tools.	answering case study questions 3 and 4.

Hot times ahead for curry houses

by Emma Jacobs

When Enam Ali and his family go on holiday to Spain, his wife brings back gifts for their friends and family but he scouts out knick-knacks for his Surrey restaurant, Le Raj. He freely admits that his business preoccupies him. 'Without this restaurant I'd be miserable. I've known my customers for 30 years. I'm like a host every day.'

However, Mr Ali worries for the future of family-run Balti houses and curry restaurants like his. While the more upmarket Indian restaurants such as Rasoi Vineet Bhatia in Chelsea might be thriving, the rising popularity of restaurant chains such as La Strada, which serves pizzas and pasta, or the Gourmet Burger Kitchen is a threat to similarly priced Indian restaurants – even more so as customers start to tighten their belts thanks to the economy's woes. More importantly, staff shortages and rising commodity prices could force many curry houses to close.

So far, most restaurants are resisting passing on the rising price of rice, lentils and energy to customers. Mr Ali, who is chairman of the Bangladesh Caterers Association, which has more than 12,000 members, suggests there are 27,500 job vacancies and says this could mean 12 per cent of restaurants could close.

These fears are shared by the throngs of restaurateurs who last month demonstrated in London's Trafalgar Square to call on the government to relax new visa restrictions for workers from outside the European Union. But it may be that it is the model of family-run businesses that is ripe for change anyway.

Tiffinbites, which runs four restaurants in London as well as a wholesale food business catering to more than 300 companies across the UK, is hoping to take on national chains such as Pizza Express as well as challenging the model of family-run curry houses.

Its solution for staff shortages is to streamline and centralise the cooking operation for all its restaurants and recruit staff locally. Skilled Indian chefs prepare the food in its kitchen in north London before sending it out fast-chilled to the restaurants, while chefs of all nationalities have been trained at the central kitchen's culinary school to make salads, tandoori and naan breads onsite in Tiffinbites' restaurants. Waiting staff are not exclusively Asian.

In the past month, it has launched a nationwide expansion through its franchising programme, hoping to become the first national curry chain. If all goes to plan, 50 new restaurants will be set up across the country by the end of 2009.

Tiffinbites' turnover is £14m, generating profits of £2m. Unusually for the sector it has private equity investment, from Napier Brown Holdings.

Jamal Hirani, chief executive of Tiffinbites, says: 'I have eastern European chefs. Welsh, English people are taught to cook at our culinary school. My best naan bread maker is a Canadian. You have to adapt to the availability of the local workforce.'

Mr Ali disagrees. He does not favour cooking off-site for his restaurant, which last year made a profit of £60,000 on turnover of £150,000; nor does he think the public is ready to see a Pole preparing chicken vindaloo. He is less resistant to recruiting Britons who have been brought up to think curry is their national dish: 'My son's friend, who is English, understands curry, he knows chutney, poppadoms, more than an eastern European. People like to know this is genuine food. Maybe it will change in 10 years – maybe then it won't matter, but it takes time.'

When he started in his family's restaurant 30 years ago, beer was the first item on the menu. 'Half the dishes weren't even curry. We sold chicken Maryland and lots of chicken and chips. Indian restaurants used to be a place [to go] after the pub closed. Now people want an authentic culinary experience,' Mr Ali says.

He is lobbying for a relaxation of immigration rules that require migrants to speak English: 'We need government support to be able to bring skilled chefs into the country from Bangladesh, Pakistan and India. These are not people coming for benefits, they are contributing to the economy. It's not necessary that they speak English; they only need to know names of spices and oil. The immigration service's requirements are so high I'll end up having to recruit a lecturer to work in my kitchen.'

Ranjit Mathrani, chairman of Masala World, which has turnover of almost £20m a year and includes Amaya, a boutique Indian restaurant in Belgravia, Chutney Mary in Chelsea, and Veeraswamy, which is almost 90 years old, as well as the chain Masala Zone (which does not have a central kitchen), also wants the rules relaxed: 'We want people from India for their culinary skills. If someone was setting up a Mexican restaurant in Oslo, would their cook be expected to be fluent in Norwegian?'

Mr Ali also hopes to attract second- and third-generation British Asians into the restaurant business. The BCA established the British Curry Awards in 2005, to celebrate the industry and encourage the younger generation to work in the sector. However, he does not believe chains are the future. 'People come to Indian restaurants for cheaper food but they also like the community feel,' he says.

Mr Hirani disagrees, and says the local community mentality is holding restaurants back. 'Indian restaurants tend to be family-run small businesses. They might have two or three restaurants owned by a cousin or brother. But once they run out of extended family, it's a natural end to their expansion.'

He is ambitious for his company and, as well as attracting private equity investment, he has recruited Maurice Gammell, former chief executive of Harry Ramsden, the fish-and-chip shop chain that started from one outlet near Leeds and was eventually sold to the Wallenberg family, Swedish private investors, as part of a much bigger deal worth £1.8bn, duly noted by Mr Hirani.

Humayun Hussain, editor of *Tandoori Magazine*, a trade title serving the UK Indian food industry, believes the sector is at a crossroads: 'Like many family-run businesses, Indian restaurants have modernised but there is still a long way to go.' Yet he is hopeful for the sector's future: 'Flock wallpaper is dying but not Indian restaurants.'

As Mr Hirani says, 'the popularity of Indian food won't go – it's ingrained in the British psyche. People eat turkey curry on Boxing Day and when they come back from holiday, they run back to eat curry to make them feel at home.'

Family-run kitchens feel the heat as chains aim to leverage costs

Indian restaurants tend to be family-run businesses. But a new breed of curry house entrepreneur, such as Jamal Hirani at Tiffinbites, sees chains as the future.

Nicholas Farhi, retail practice associate director at consultancy OC&C, says that with 30 per cent of the market, chains of any type of cuisine still represent a very small percentage of the 'casual dining' sector, which includes Indian restaurants as well as chains such as Pizza Express.

However, he believes they will grow substantially over the next 10 years and force independents out of the market. Primarily, he says, this is because they are 'increasingly sophisticated about leveraging their fixed cost base to improve profitability. They work hard to get more covers per night than a typical independent and invest some of this higher profit in delivering better value for money to the consumer. Independents don't typically have the commercial savvy to make these kinds of strategic decisions.'

Humayun Hussain, editor of *Tandoori Magazine*, comments that while a chain or a 'high-end restaurant in London, such as the Cinnamon Club [in Westminster], might be attractive to financiers, there aren't that many investors willing to put money into cheaper Indian restaurants'.

Source: from 'Hot times ahead for curry houses', *The Financial Times*, 14 May 2008 (Jacobs, E.).

Exit case study questions

1. Devise a marketing mix, including the fifth P, people, for a traditional Indian restaurant. How does the marketing mix for a traditional Indian restaurant differ from that for Tiffinbites?
2. Identify at least five different types of eating place, e.g. Chinese, and place them on a product life cycle curve. State whether the eating places you have identified are question marks, stars, cash cows or dogs.
3. Consider the extension of the product life cycle and the Jenkins customer growth matrix. Identify and discuss how different eating places may apply these models to help ensure their success.
4. Evaluate the usefulness of marketing models in relation to outlets like restaurants.

Short-answer questions

1 Define marketing concept.

2 State the 4Ps of marketing.

3 Name the fifth P of marketing.

4 In which stage of the product life cycle does a product make most money?

5 In which stage of the product life cycle does a product sell most?

6 In which stage of the product life cycle does a product make virtually no profit and why?

7 Name three strategies that are used to extend the life cycle of a product.

8 In which stage of the product life cycle is a 'star' product located?

9 Name Jenkins' four different types of customer growth options.

10 Product development and diversification are methods for achieving which of Jenkins' customer growth options?

11 List the characteristics of a cash cow product.

12 In what circumstances should a company decide to keep a dog product?

13 Explain the path of an unsuccessful product around the Boston Consulting Group matrix.

Chapter objectives and assignment questions

While reading this chapter and engaging in the activities, you should have learned how to apply theory and models and analyse situations. This means you should be able to meet the chapter objectives outlined at the beginning of the chapter. The table below shows which chapter objectives can be tested by the different questions.

Chapter objective	Check you have achieved this by
1 Define the role of marketing in an organisation.	answering assignment question 1.
2 Summarise the main marketing activities.	answering assignment question 1.
3 Apply a range of marketing tools to different products and services.	answering assignment question 2.
4 Understand the relevance of marketing tools.	answering assignment questions 3 and 4.

Assignment questions

1 You are setting up a small travel company that specialises in outdoor pursuits holidays in the UK. Write a 2000-word report outlining both the marketing and development plans for the venture.

2 Consider your own organisation (employing organisation or university/college). Using the marketing tools discussed in this chapter, analyse the marketing that it undertakes. Use the findings of your analysis to recommend what the organisation should currently be doing in terms of market penetration, product development, market development and diversification. Present your findings in a 2000-word report.

3 Compare and contrast the product life cycle and Boston Consulting Group matrix as marketing tools. Comment on their relevance to marketing departments in the twenty-first century.

4 The 4Ps of marketing were discussed in 1964 by N H Borden in his paper 'The concept of the marketing mix', published in the June issue of the *Journal of Advertising Research*. Critically evaluate its usefulness to today's marketing practitioner.

WEBLINKS available at **www.pearsoned.co.uk/capon**

- This site is a source of advertising and promotion resources: **http://adres.internet.com/**
- This site is a US site for marketing and e-business strategists: **http://www.btobonline.com/**
- This site is about internet marketing: **http://www.marketingtips.com/newsletter/issue11/page1.html**
- This site is about how the market research company Gallup does its work: **http://www.gallup.com/**

FURTHER READING

The following textbook chapters will add to the introduction to marketing provided by this chapter.

- Baines, P, Fill, C and Page, K (2008) *Marketing Principles and Society*, Chapters 1 and 2, Oxford: Oxford University Press.
- Brassington, F and Pettitt, S (2007) *Essentials of Marketing*, Chapter 1, Harlow: Financial Times Prentice Hall.
- Dibb, S, Simkin, L, Pride, W M and Ferrell, O C (2006) *Marketing: Concepts and Strategies*, Chapters 3 and 5, Oxford: Houghton Mifflin.
- Jobber, D (2007) *Principles of Marketing*, Chapters 1–3, Maidenhead: McGraw-Hill.
- Kotler, P, Armstrong, G, Wong, V and Saunders, J (2008) *Principles of Marketing*, Chapters 1 and 4, Harlow: Financial Times Prentice Hall.

The following are all classic marketing journal articles.

- Blois, K J (1989) 'Marketing in five "simple" questions!' *Journal of Marketing Management*, 5(2).
- Doyle, P (1976) 'The realities of the product life-cycle', *Quarterly Review of Marketing*, Summer.
- Keith, R J (1960) 'The marketing revolution', *Journal of Marketing*, January.
- Kotler, P and Levey, S J (1969) 'Broadening the concept of marketing', *Journal of Marketing*, January.
- Levitt, T (1960) 'Marketing myopia', *Harvard Business Review*, July/August.
- Levitt, T (1975) 'Marketing myopia 1975: retrospective commentary', *Harvard Business Review*, September/October.

REFERENCES

1 Drucker, P (1954) *The Practice of Management*, New York: Harper & Row.
2 Kotler, P, Armstrong, G, Saunders, J and Wong, V (1996) *Principles of Marketing*, Hemel Hempstead: Prentice Hall.
3 Lancaster, G and Massingham, L (1988) *Essentials of Marketing*, Maidenhead: McGraw-Hill.
4 Maslow, A H (1943) 'A theory of human motivation', *Psychological Review*, 50.
5 JRF, 1 July 2008, available as freedownload from http://www.jrf.org.uk
6 Ibid.
7 Rigby, E and Birchall, J (2008) 'Asda revels in AB market share increase', *Financial Times*, 14 August.
8 Brownsell, A (2008) 'End of line for BT family?' *Marketing*, 11 July.
9 Borden, N H (1964) 'The concept of the marketing mix', *Journal of Advertising Research*, June, reprinted in (1998) *Management Classics*, 6th edn, Harlow: Allyn & Bacon.
10 McCarthy, E J (1981) *Basic Marketing: A Managerial Approach*, Burr Ridge, Il: Irwin.
11 Wiggins, J (2008) 'Burger chain to vary menu prices by region', *Financial Times*, 14 June.
12 Terazono, E (2006) 'Advertisers allowed to sponsor TV channels', *Financial Times*, 26 October.
13 BBC News (2008) 'Can Oreo win over British biscuit lovers?' 29 January.
14 Ansoff, I (1987) *Corporate Strategy*, London: Penguin Business.
15 Jenkins, M (1997) *The Customer Centred Strategy*, Harlow: Prentice Hall.
16 Ibid.
17 Ibid.
18 Henderson, B (1970) *The Product Portfolio*, Boston: Boston Consulting Group.

CHAPTER 9

Operations management

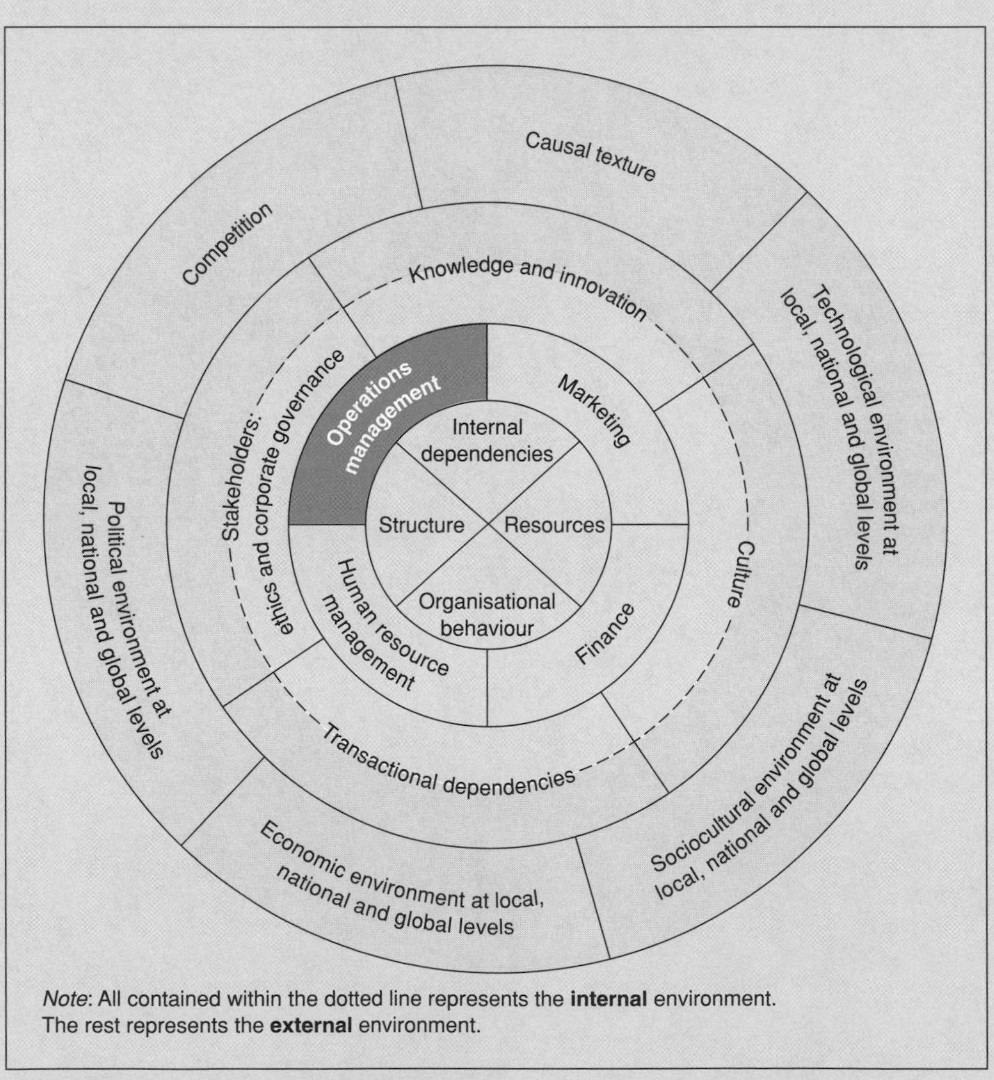

Figure 9.1 Business environment model

Chapter objectives

This chapter aims to provide an overview of the different types of organisation – service, manufacturing, not-for-profit – and the different types of activity they perform. The chapter then looks at the full range of operations management activities and shows how they apply to the different types of organisation.

Therefore, when you have read this chapter and worked through the associated activities you should be able to achieve the objectives specified below.

1 **Define different types and categories of organisation.**
2 **Explain the full range of operations management activities.**
3 **Identify where in organisations the operations management activities apply.**
4 **Determine where in organisations operations management activities need adapting.**

This case study examines a small company, Fudges, which has had mixed fortunes over the years and has sought to improve and adapt its operations with the aim of competing at the top end of the market and working successfully with the big supermarkets.

ENTRY CASE STUDY 9.1

Fingers burnt in a hands-on operation

FT

by Bob Sherwood

It is a perfect symbol of the contradictions inherent in the entrepreneur's attempts to build a national brand with efficient modern production while maintaining an artisan ethos. Fudges has grown from a small west Dorset bread bakery, set up in 1926 by Percy Fudge, into an upmarket cracker and biscuit producer that will turn over £8.5m this year. Its earnings are growing at 33 per cent year on year and it sells its products in nine countries. But twice in the past two decades the business has been on the verge of collapse, and Mr Fudge, his brother Graham and sister-in-law Sue, third-generation owners, have had to mortgage and borrow as much as they could to keep going.

Fudges' focus is now 'all about the brand'. It is one that appeals to modern fashions and sits comfortably on Waitrose shelves. The company stresses its Dorset roots, focuses on the provenance of its ingredients. It sources as much as it can locally, from cheeses to cream, butter and wheat. It does not sound revolutionary now but almost 20 years ago, such practices were far less common. 'It wasn't the vogue then but we had to use our strengths and it was pretty much the only business model open to us,' he says. It has been a hard slog for a man who always swore never to join the family firm. It was a pledge that did not last.

In 1988, with the decline of the farming community that consumed huge amounts of bread and the rise of supermarkets, Fudges' bread bakery business was in trouble. At that time Mr Fudge was teaching modern baking at a college after studying confectionery in Germany and working at large baking businesses across the north of England. He says: 'The question kept coming to me: why aren't you doing something about your own family business?' He took the decision to join his brother, who was already running the family business, and they realised that only fundamental change could save them. They jettisoned bread and began to sell products that could be transported long distances with a good shelf life. Given their West Country heritage, cheddar wafers seemed an apt choice, along with other biscuits and high-quality cakes.

Business began to pick up. With the need for more space, Fudges bought the Dorset Village Bakery for about £600,000 at its current location in Stalbridge in 1998. But the brothers seemed destined to repeat the mistakes of the past by going back to bread. 'It was much

too big a space at the time and we thought we could also turn the ailing bread business around and gradually bring in our biscuits as well,' Mr Fudge recalls. 'But it just haemorrhaged cash. We had raised a lot of capital to buy this place and we just lost huge amounts of money on a day-to-day basis.' The expansion threatened to undo everything the family had done to turn round the business. 'It was really scary – I didn't sleep properly for two years,' Mr Fudge says.

Once again cutting out bread, the company had to compromise its vision and move heavily into supplying 'own label' products for the large retailers. 'It was at the expense of our own wishes and plans but it was just a survival course.' By the third year of the new operation, though, the business was back to meeting its original sales targets and it was then that Mr Fudge decided to push the company's distinctive brand once again.

All of its 80 lines of wafers, crackers, flatbreads, sweet biscuits and seasonal offerings are sourced and marketed to reinforce the high-quality, Dorset country brand. Another brand-building venture has been to link with larger organisations such as Unilever and Tate & Lyle to produce products featuring Marmite, Colman's mustard and golden syrup. 'What we give them is quality and top-end trading. We get an iconic brand to put next to our brand, so there's a symbiosis,' Mr Fudge says. He says the larger companies have been easy to work with because they are divided into smaller product teams. He also insists that being a smaller company is crucial to such a relationship because Fudges' flexibility means it can develop the product and get it to market quickly. It has, for example, just retooled a cutter to change the shape of the Marmite biscuits to resemble the spread's famous tub. 'A bigger company would not have been able to do that because the volume would not have been large enough,' he says.

The competitive advantage of being able to respond quickly with new products is reinforced by Mr Fudge's interest in innovative processes in the bakery, which is full of industrial ovens, long conveyor lines and large bespoke machines. But mechanisation, crucial to controlling costs, cannot be allowed to endanger the traditional, hand-baking image. With a staff of 160, all the mixes are weighed and mixed by hand, as is much of the decorating, dipping in chocolate, packing and marzipan ball rolling. 'We still have to keep the personal involvement,' he says. 'It is crucial to retain quality because to do it all by machine would lose identity – you couldn't guarantee a whole nut on every biscuit, for example – and hand-mixing guarantees every one is perfect. It also makes it very easy to change a mix quickly.'

Running such an operation in the depths of the English countryside, complete with groups of migrant Czech workers is undeniably expensive. Mr Fudge insists that manufacturing in the UK can pay only if a company makes a virtue of it. And, once again, it comes back to the brand. 'We went to China and looked but we are quintessentially English. Sourcing locally and making in China is not particularly clever. We'd lose the market if we moved production abroad.'

Fudges is still 100 per cent owned by the three family members, who maintain a 'great relationship', but the stresses of turning it round have taken their toll – notably the failure of Mr Fudge's two marriages. By the time the company was stable and growing rapidly three years ago, 'as a family, we were weary', he says. A much-expanded professional team resulted, led by Brent Giles, operations director. The company is now moving out of the realms of being simply the Fudge family business. 'Once we got out of the mire, we were in a strong position to say we want to bring in some professional people to take the business beyond what we could do as a family. It will grow because of people now.'

Farewell, squire

You will not find Squires biscuits anywhere on supermarket shelves. But Mr Fudge believes they could have been a household name.

Fudges aims its products at the top-spending 10 per cent of consumers in its market. Following the company's difficulties after taking over Dorset Village Bakery, Mr Fudge devised a plan to target another 5 per cent of the market with a more affordable range in an attempt to increase sales volumes. 'I was trying to be clever after things went wrong here,' he says. 'It was a great idea, and another country-based product. But there were a lot of things wrong.'

The company soon found that creating a second distinct brand was fraught with difficulties. In hindsight, Mr Fudge thinks the company did not have the right infrastructure to make a second identity work. It suffered quality issues with the products and purchasers found it confusing. 'We found we were taking our eye off the ball of Fudges to get this right and there just weren't enough of us to do it then. So we scrapped it after a year.

'But I still like the idea and – if we launched it now in a structured way – we could probably make it work.' So does the company still have the brand stashed away? 'I think we've still got most of the packaging,' he laughs.

Donate and innovate: the approach to supermarkets

Many small food producers are less than complimentary about their dealings with supermarkets. Fudges expend a great deal of effort managing its relationships with the big supermarket chains as a crucial part of its strategy.

Waitrose is its key partner now, but Steve Fudge remembers how difficult it was to break on to the shelves. He says: 'We were desperate to get into Waitrose, we wrote and called but would always be told the buyers weren't interested. Then one day in 1993, we had a phone call and they said "Why haven't we got your products?" We said it wasn't through lack of trying.'

Now the company has drawn up a plan focused on its strategic partners. It supplies supermarkets, which are responsible for 80 per cent of its turnover, with extra support, in-store promotions, and new products before other outlets. It also conducts gap analyses, examines market trends and watches competitors before offering a new product to supermarket buyers.

'It's no good just going to buyers with a product any more,' he says. 'So we have got cuter at it. We try to solve a buyer's problems before he knows he's got them. You have to take the risk away from them.' And though the focus is now on building the Fudges brand, about 40 per cent of turnover still comes from 'own label' products. 'There's always an opportunity to do own-label, but nowadays there needs to be a good reason to do it,' he says. 'So we do a trade-off: if they support Fudges brand, we support them. And we never do exactly the same product for supermarkets. We will donate our innovation in designing just what they need, which is very different from just producing the product.'

Source: from 'Fingers burnt in a hands-on operation', *The Financial Times*, 20 February 2008 (Sherwood, B.).

Introduction

Operations management is the term applied to the activities at the core of any organisation's business and is concerned with the way in which the organisation actually puts into practice what it has set out to do. An organisation will undertake operations to make a product, provide a service or perform a combination of the two. Hence Glaxo manufactures pharmaceuticals; BT provides telecommunications services; and Laura Ashley produces and sells clothes. Accordingly, operations management is concerned with managing the way products are made and/or service delivered, which has a direct connection with how the organisation achieves its objectives. The principles of operations management can be applied to any organisation.

Organisations and operations management

On comparing and contrasting two very different organisations, it would appear that their operations have few similarities. The operations of Glaxo, for example, would seem very unlike the operations of a chip shop run by its self-employed owner. However, closer examination will reveal surprising similarities. Both organisations have to choose the best location, buy raw materials, forecast demand for their products, calculate the required **capacity**, arrange resources to meet demand, use the raw materials to make products, sell the products to customers, manage cashflows and human resources, and seek out reliable suppliers. Both Glaxo and the chip shop want to run an efficient operation, with high **productivity**.

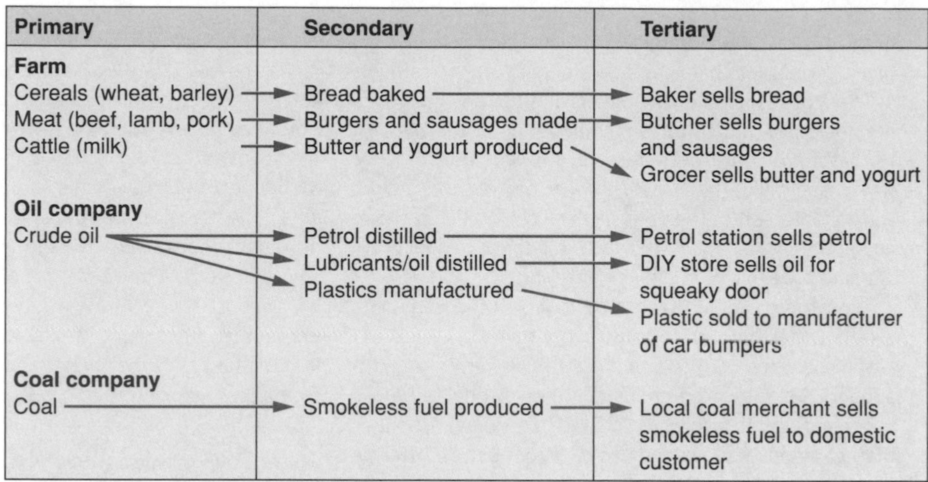

Figure 9.2 Manufacturing and service sectors

There are two basic ways of categorising organisations and the operations they undertake. The first is to consider organisations as belonging to different sectors: primary, secondary or tertiary – *see* Figure 9.2. **Primary-sector organisations** are concerned with producing raw materials and include oil extraction, coal mining, diamond mining and farming to produce food. **Secondary-sector organisations** manufacture and produce goods, often from raw materials produced by primary-sector organisations. **Tertiary-sector organisations** sell goods produced by primary and secondary organisations. The tertiary sector includes service-sector organisations such as banks and social services.

Check your understanding

Do you understand the organisational context of operations management?

Check your understanding by explaining the role of the operations management department in an organisation.

An alternative way of viewing organisations is to consider whether the organisation produces goods, provides a service or delivers a mixture of both, and whether it is a private-sector organisation or not – *see* Figure 9.3 for more details. There are no public-sector/not-for-profit organisations that manufacture. If a public-sector or not-for-profit organisation is to provide a manufactured product, it is most likely that manufactured goods will be made by a subcontractor from the private sector. For example, local councils provide domestic and commercial council tax payers with wheelie bins which are not manufactured by the council but bought in bulk via a negotiated contract from a supplier in the private sector.

	Not-for-profit organisations	Public-sector organisations	Private-sector organisations
Manufacturing			• Pharmaceuticals (GlaxoSmithKline) • Cars (Vauxhall) • Food (Northern Foods)
Manufacturing and service	• Retailing (Oxfam shop/Fairtrade initiatives)	• Housing associations (build and let homes) • Provision of artificial limbs (NHS)	• Restaurant (Pizza Hut) • Retailing (Laura Ashley) • Carpet shop (supply and fit carpet)
Service	• Charities (Red Cross) • Religious organisations (Church of England)	• General practitioner (GP – NHS) • Refuse collection (local council) • Education – schools (LEA)	• Banking (Abbey National) • Telecommunications (BT) • Hotels (Hilton)

Figure 9.3 Manufacturing and service organisations

Operations management

Operations management can be considered from the perspective of the organisation as a resource converter – *see* Chapter 4. It is concerned with forecasting the output required and scheduling the conversion process such that customers' orders are delivered on time. The purchasing and **just-in-time** management of inputs are also crucial if the conversion or operation process is to happen efficiently and effectively. It is these activities, along with a few more, that will be examined in this chapter – *see* Figure 9.4.

The principles of operations management examined in this chapter can be applied to organisations providing a product, service or mixture of both. This section considers the characteristics of all three types of organisation: an organisation delivering a service, with the example of a bank providing

Location	**Product development**	**Forecasting**	**Layout of facilities**
Process and system performance	**Inventory management**	**Material requirements planning**	**Just in time**
Quality	**Scheduling**	**Purchasing**	**Maintenance**

Figure 9.4 Operations management: an overview

financial advice to a customer; a product, with the example of a car company producing a car that has been ordered by a garage for a customer; and a mixture of product and service, a pizza restaurant.

First, we consider the service and product organisations. The most basic difference between a service and a product is that a product is tangible – the car can be touched and driven by the customer – whereas a service is intangible – the financial advice cannot be seen and touched. The latter is delivered by the financial adviser and assimilated by the customer simultaneously and cannot be stored to be repeated another day. This contrasts with a product, which is able to be stored, highlighting the delay between manufacture and consumption. For example, the car is built in the factory and there will be a delay of at least a few days, maybe longer, before it finally reaches the customer who is going to own and drive the car.

The level of contact that occurs between a service provider and customer and a manufacturer and customer is also very different. In delivering a service there is significant contact between the service provider, the financial adviser, and the customer; in contrast, the buyer of a good, such as the purchaser of a car, and its manufacturer are very unlikely to have any contact at all. This is because in providing a service the customer is part of the process of its delivery: the customer has to be there to receive the financial advice. Therefore, the facilities are located close to the customer, e.g. the bank's office will be on the local high street and accessible to the individual receiving the financial advice. In contrast, the customer will not participate in the manufacture of their car and the factory is likely to be located some distance from the end user, maybe even in another country. Finally, in general, services are labour intensive and production is automated.

An organisation that both provides a service and delivers a product will assume characteristics of a service provider and/or a manufacturer. Taking the example of a pizza restaurant, the food is a **tangible product**, but cooking and serving the food are **intangible services**. The food may have been stored in the restaurant's fridge or freezer before being used to produce a pizza. Serving a meal is a service that cannot be stored and indicates the simultaneous nature of service provision: the food is served hot as soon as it has been cooked and is eaten as soon as it is served. Showing the diners where to sit, giving them menus, taking their orders, serving the food and taking payment are all service provision and will therefore involve contact between the waiting staff and customers in the restaurant. In contrast, there will be limited or no contact between diners and the kitchen and cooking staff who produce the pizza. Again, as a service is being provided, the location will be easily accessible to diners: pizza restaurants are on the high street in most towns in the UK. The dining area of the restaurant will be the section of the premises most accessible and used by diners; the storage areas, kitchens and bins will be towards the back of the premises and rarely accessible to customers. A restaurant is one example where providing the service, done by the waiting staff, and production, food preparation and cooking, are both labour intensive.

Check your understanding

Do you understand how operations management can be applicable to both manufacturing and service organisations?

Check your understanding by comparing and contrasting manufacturing and service organisations. Use examples where appropriate.

The examples discussed in the section illustrate that the scope of operations management is wide-ranging and applicable to organisations undertaking different operations. The rest of this chapter goes on to examine the activities of operations management and how they apply to all types of organisations.

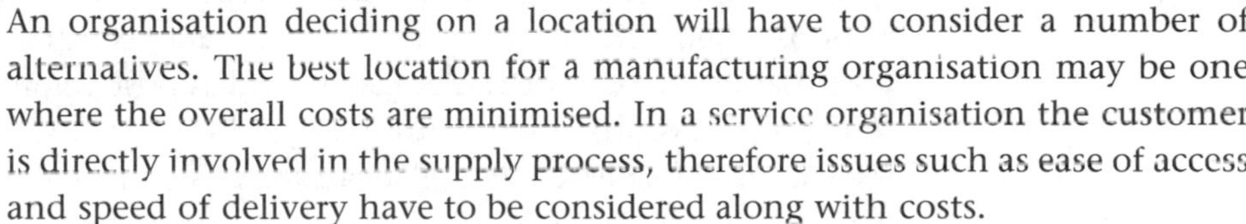

Location

An organisation deciding on a location will have to consider a number of alternatives. The best location for a manufacturing organisation may be one where the overall costs are minimised. In a service organisation the customer is directly involved in the supply process, therefore issues such as ease of access and speed of delivery have to be considered along with costs.

Location strategies

Location can be important for a company in terms of the logistics of its operations. It can make sense to locate similar activities together or close to each other or to be located near customers or major transport networks. In some circumstance the location of a manufacturer can be key to the product name or brand image. For example, champagne must be produced in the Champagne region of France and Stilton cheese can only be produced in the counties of Leicestershire, Nottinghamshire and Derbyshire. The company Fudges in the entry case study relies heavily on its quintessentially English brand image and to support this it chose to manufacture in Dorset in south-west England and has rejected moving production to China.

Naylor[1] identifies three location strategies. The first is **product-based location** and is commonly used by large organisations. A large organisation using this location strategy takes into account that it has different divisions, each responsible for their own product ranges. Therefore, different divisions are likely to occupy separate locations. However, several divisions with similarities may be located on the same site. This separation based on product range allows each division to adopt and utilise the appropriate resources for its business. Locating all divisions in a large organisation together is likely to cause problems of focus and control.

An alternative to the product-based location is the **market-based location**. This strategy reflects the geographic divisions of the organisation and locates facilities in a location convenient to its geographic markets. For example, new supermarkets are usually built close to residential areas in out-of-town locations, which means that they are close to the customers – most customers will not want to travel very far to do supermarket shopping, as it is something that is done fairly frequently, for example every week.

Finally, a **vertically differentiated location** strategy is when separate stages of the supply process are in different locations. Some industries have vertically integrated firms which combine several stages of the manufacturing cycle. Rather than locate the whole operation on one site, location decisions are made for each stage.

Push and pull factors

The decision to relocate is often made by small and medium-sized enterprises (SMEs) for a variety of reasons, which include the need for more space, increase in the scale of operations, and a reduction in unit costs. Larger organisations often relocate if more locations are required.[2] The factors causing organisations to relocate can be categorised as push or pull factors. **Push factors** result from dissatisfaction with existing locations, hence causing the organisation to consider changing location. Push factors originate from a wide variety of issues, some of which are presented below.

1 Current location is inconvenient for current customers and makes providing a good service cumbersome.
2 Competitors have locations that offer competitive advantage.
3 Different facilities are required for changing product/service range.
4 Regulatory authorities impose constraints related to health and safety, effluent disposal or noise.
5 There is a shortage of appropriately skilled labour.
6 The cost of the current site is increasing, for example due to rising rent.

In contrast, rather than pushing an organisation out of an old location, the **pull factors** attract or pull it towards a new location. For instance, an organisation may be pulled to locate in a particular region or country due to the availability of cheap skilled labour. Many consumer electronics companies have located assembly facilities in China as there are educated workers available, requiring wages that are a fraction of those paid in Western economies. Sometimes a combination of factors will pull an organisation to a particular location. The Japanese car companies Nissan and Toyota located in Sunderland and Derby respectively as both labour and government grants were available. The location of the north of England also allowed both companies access to the European market and a location geographically close to mainland Europe, making selling cars in Europe much easier than importing directly from Japan.

Check your understanding

Do you understand why an organisation may choose a particular location?

Check your understanding by explaining the choice of location strategies and indicate factors which may affect that choice.

Product development

Product development and forecasting are both activities that occur early in the operations management process. The commercial evaluation of a new product will include assessing or forecasting likely demand. The process of product development is discussed in this section and forecasting in the next section.

To be successful, an organisation has to manufacture the products that customers desire. Therefore, it must discover the kind of products that customers require and continue to supply them. To do this an organisation has to introduce new products and update or withdraw old products from the market (*see* Chapter 8). The development and introduction of a new product are expensive activities, hence careful planning is essential. The development of the new Apple iPhone will have taken several years and cost several million pounds before it was launched on the market in 2006. There are a number of steps in the product development process, shown in Figure 9.5.

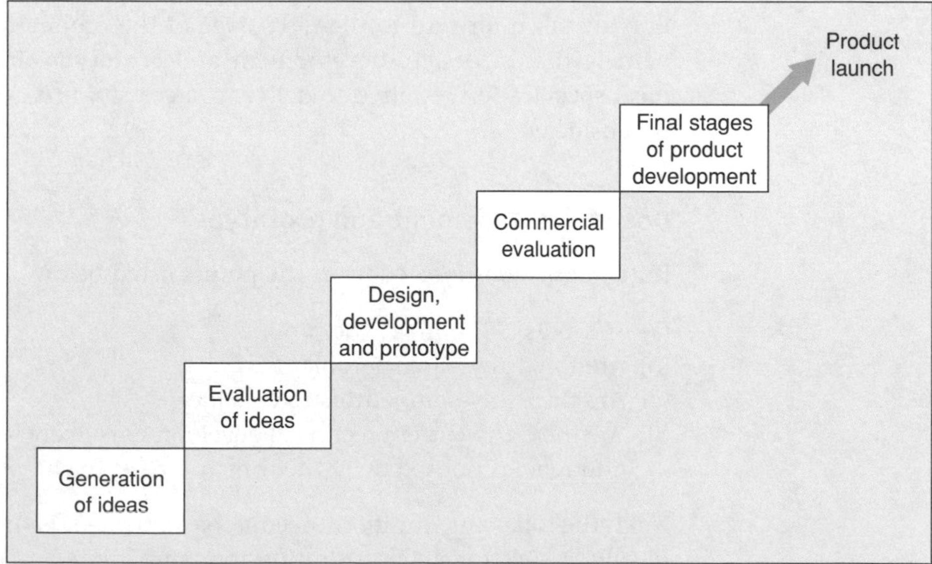

Figure 9.5 Product development process

Generation of ideas

The first step, the generation of ideas, relies on a number of sources of ideas for new products or services. The results of research and development may lead to a new product, for example the drug Viagra. Alternatively, sales staff out in the field may report customer demand for a new product and/or customers themselves may contact the organisation to suggest new products. This is illustrated in the entry case study, as Fudges now develop products and own-label products for supermarkets. The operations management department itself may come up with ideas for new or better products. Finally, the competition may be a source of ideas. Cadbury developed the textured chocolate bar Wispa in the 1980s to compete with the successful Aero bar produced by its main rival at that time, Rowntree.

Evaluation of ideas

The evaluation of all ideas is necessary to filter out those with obvious deficiencies and weaknesses. The sources of deficiency and weakness in an idea for a new product or service can arise from a number of areas. For example, the manufacture of the product may be technically impossible at present. Alternatively, the manufacture of the product may require skills and abilities that the organisation does not possess or the product does not fit into the organisation's current product ranges.

This initial evaluation needs to be done by a team containing a range of people from different areas of the organisation, so that all relevant points of view are considered. Such a team includes representation from marketing, finance and operations. The ideas appraised as worthy of further consideration are taken forward to the next stage of the product development process, namely that of design, development and **prototype**. In that stage the technical specification required to deliver a successful final version of the product is considered.

Design, development and prototype

Initial basic questions concern the points listed below.

(a) Is it possible to make the product?
(b) Are there any patent problems?
(c) Are there any competitors to consider?
(d) Are there any current technical developments likely to overtake the product and render it obsolete by the time it arrives in the marketplace?

Next, the following questions need to be addressed. Is the current design technically feasible for the organisation to manufacture and does the organisation have the necessary technology and skills? Does the new product complement the organisation's current products? The production and testing of a prototype will often help answer such questions.

Commercial evaluation

Products with a satisfactory technical evaluation move on to undergo market and financial evaluation to determine whether the product will make a profit. This studies the market and financial aspects with the aim of determining how well the product will sell. A commercial evaluation will study the competition, the basis on which the new product will compete (*see* Chapter 3), the investment required, the return to be expected, and estimation of the expected sales. The commercial evaluation and the technical evaluation from the previous stage together form the feasibility study for a product. Therefore, on completion of the commercial evaluation some technically valid products will be rejected as they are not commercially valid.

Final stages of product development

The final product development stage sees the feasible product move from a prototype to the form that will be sold to customers. The lessons arising from the technical and commercial evaluation will be used to move from a prototype design to the final design of a product.

For the final version of the product, the design has to be functional (to do the job it has been designed for), attractive (to appeal to customers) and easy to make (to keep down production costs).[3]

Product launch

Finally, the new product is launched into the marketplace and its success depends on a number of factors that customers are likely to consider. First, price: some customers are price sensitive, others are not (*see* Chapter 3). Next, the quality of the product or service: the quality of food purchased from Marks & Spencer is different from that sold in Netto; and a consumer's response to quality is often directly related to their response to price. Accordingly, consumers who are extremely price sensitive will shop at Netto and those who are very quality sensitive will shop at Marks & Spencer. Finally, ease of access for the customer: a home computer that can be taken home from the shop today will sell better than a model for which there is a 10-week waiting list.

The operations management department of an organisation will attempt to simplify and standardise the design of its products. This makes manufacture easier, as fewer components are used. In addition, the manufacturing process contains fewer steps, is cheaper and waste is minimised. The same principles can be applied to the delivery of a service. An organisation delivering a service will seek to reduce the number of steps a customer has to move through and to minimise queuing time.

Check your understanding

Do you understand the different stages of the product development process?

Check your understanding by explaining and illustrating the product development process.
Use examples where appropriate.

Forecasting

Forecasts become effective at some point in the future when a decision is made concerning, for example, demand for a product. Hence forecasts need to be based on the likely conditions in the future. In the example of a company trying to predict demand for a product, conditions such as the amount of disposable income consumers will have and the competition's activity will affect the forecast. For instance, a company manufacturing ice cream making a forecast in December concerning demand for ice cream in the following June, July and August will consider the likely weather conditions and the new varieties of ice cream to be launched by its competitors for the summer.

There are a number of ways in which forecasting can be done. One key criterion for a forecast is the time period in the future that it covers. Long-term forecasting looks ahead over a number of years. The types of projects that will be affected and influenced by long-term forecasts are, for example, capital expenditure projects, such as the building of office blocks or shopping centres. The decision to build a new out-of-town shopping centre will have been influenced by forecasts covering factors such as the number of people likely to visit at different times of the year – Christmas, school holidays and wet Tuesday afternoons in February – the size of the surrounding population, and the distance people will be prepared to travel to get to the shopping centre.

Medium-term forecasts are defined as covering a number of months, from say 3 to 24 months. The types of decision that will be influenced by medium-term forecasts are the launch of new products and fashions. Medium-term forecasts tell retailers and producers which toys will be popular with children in 12 to 18 months' time and what gifts will be in greatest demand from retailers next Christmas, for example. This will depend on what toys are likely to be made fashionable from the latest films, cartoons, TV programmes and bands. Toy manufacturers could easily predict that Harry Potter games, toys and figures would be popular for Christmas 2003, due to the publication of the fifth Harry Potter book, *The Order of the Phoenix*, in the preceding June.

In contrast to long- and medium-term forecasts, short-term forecasts cover a few weeks and often have a direct operational effect on the factory. Returning to the company producing ice cream and expecting a good summer in June, July and August, in the UK a wet summer and a forecast of more rain to come at the end of July, as the schools in England break up for the summer holiday, will have a rapid and direct effect on sales and the amount of ice cream that needs to be produced by the ice-cream factory.

Quantitative forecasting

Forecasting can be either **qualitative** or **quantitative** in nature. Quantitative or numerical forecasting is feasible if the company is already producing the product or providing the service, as historical data already exists concerning the demand for a product or service and the factors affecting demand.

Quantitative data can be used in two ways to forecast future demand. First, **projective** methods examine the patterns of previous demand and extend the pattern into the future. For example, if a shop had purchased 100, 150, 200 and 250 tubs of ice cream over the four weeks of June, it could be projected that demand in the first week of July will be for around 300 tubs. Second, **causal** methods examine the impact of external influences and use them to forecast future demand or activity. The productivity of the ice-cream factory might depend on the bonus rate paid to employees over the busy summer months. In this situation it would be more accurate to use the bonus rate than demand from shops and supermarkets to forecast productivity.

Both projective and causal methods of forecasting depend on accurate data and figures being available. This will not be the case if the company is launching a new product for which no data exists. In this situation it is not possible to use quantitative methods of forecasting, therefore qualitative methods have to be used. Qualitative methods of forecasting rely on the views and opinions of different stakeholder groups.

Qualitative forecasting

There are five commonly used methods of qualitative forecasting:[4] personal insight, **panel consensus**, market surveys, **historical analogy**, and the **Delphi method**.

Personal insight

Personal insight is a frequently used method of forecasting and should be avoided by managers when making critical decisions. Personal insight is simply when a manager who is familiar with the situation produces a forecast based on their own views and opinions. This means the individual's views and opinions are taken into consideration along with their individual prejudices and misconceptions concerning the situation. Hence personal insight is an unreliable method of forecasting.

Panel consensus

The panel consensus is an attempt to dilute the prejudices and misconceptions of an individual. The panel, assuming it is able to talk openly and freely, should produce a more credible agreement. The disadvantages of a panel will occur if the views of the panel members are too wide-ranging to come to a consensus. Also some members of the panel may not perform well in a group and fail to get their views across, hence leaving those who are loudest and most forceful to win through and falsely represent the group.

Market surveys

Market surveys collect data and information from a sample of customers and potential customers. The data and information are analysed and inferences made about the population at large. However, market surveys can be expensive and time-consuming and rely on the following being the case if they are to provide reliable information: a valid sample of customers accurately representing the population, unbiased questions being asked, customers giving honest answers, correct analyses of the answers, and valid conclusions being drawn from the results.

Historical analogy

The product life cycle has periods of introduction, growth, maturity, saturation and decline (*see* Chapter 8). If a new product is being launched, it may be valid for the organisation to assume that demand for the new product will follow the same pattern as that for a similar product already on the market. For example, a publisher launching a new book is able to forecast demand based on the actual demand for a similar book that it published earlier. In the summer of 1999 the publishers of the popular *Harry Potter* children's books correctly forecast that demand for tales of Harry Potter's latest adventures would be very large. This was based on the fact that the previous two volumes of Harry Potter tales had sold extremely well.

Delphi method

This is more formal than the other qualitative methods that have been discussed. The Delphi method follows a well-defined set of procedures in which a number of experts are asked to complete and return a questionnaire by post. The replies from the experts are analysed, the results summarised and posted back to the experts. They are asked to amend their previous replies in light of the summarised results. The replies to the questionnaires are anonymous and the experts do not know who the other experts are. Therefore, the problems of face-to-face discussion, mentioned in the section on panel consensus, are avoided. The amending of replies is repeated several times, up to about six occasions. This should allow a range of opinions to emerge that is narrow enough to aid the decision-making process.

Check your understanding

Do you understand the different types of forecasting available to organisations?

Check your understanding by comparing and contrasting quantitative and qualitative forecasting.

Layout of facilities

Facility layout is concerned with the physical arrangement of resources in the organisation's premises. It covers all types of organisations, for example factories, offices, schools, shops and hospitals. The location of resources and their location with respect to other resources is important – if done well, the flow of work is smooth and efficient; in contrast, poorly laid-out facilities disrupt operations and reduce **efficiency**.

The layout of resources in an organisation therefore has two clearly linked aims: to organise the resources and facilities so that the desired output of product or throughput of customers is achieved using minimum resources, and to ensure that the physical arrangement of resources allows maximum output or throughput. Consequently the layout and design of an organisation's premises should allow operations to run efficiently.

Take the example of retail premises, such as a supermarket like Tesco or Sainsbury's, where the goods are organised in parallel aisles. The layout is designed to allow a steady throughput of customers, even on a busy Saturday morning, and to encourage shoppers to purchase particular items in addition to those they need. For example, staple products such as bread and milk are located around the outside of the store some distance from each other, so the shopper has to walk past aisles of other goods to get to them, hence providing an opportunity for other goods to be promoted to the customer in-store. This includes stocking particular goods on the ends of aisles that customers will see as they search for more staple products.

Layout policies for manufacturing

There are a number of layout policies that manufacturing organisations can follow: the process layout, the product layout, the hybrid layout and the fixed position layout.

Process layout

A **process layout** involves similar equipment and machinery being located together. In a factory manufacturing armchairs and sofas, the process layout would mean all sawing machines would be located in one area, all drilling machines in one area, all equipment used to assemble the frames in another area, and all equipment to upholster the chairs and sofas in another. The process layout works best when a range of products is manufactured on the same general-purpose equipment, as this is less expensive than specialised equipment.

One benefit of the process layout is the ease with which specific orders and variable demand can be met. However, this can mean low **utilisation** rates of the equipment and a high unit cost if the batch size for production is small. Nevertheless, the process layout does allow operations to continue if some equipment is unavailable because of breakdown or planned maintenance. For example, if the upholstery equipment is broken, the factory can continue producing frames. Consequently, the scheduling and controlling of the work in the process layout have to be carefully managed, otherwise queues and backlogs of work can occur, resulting in very large stocks of work in progress. Finally, in the process layout people are grouped together according to their work and skills, which can lead to high morale and productivity. Hence splitting up such groups can be difficult when reorganisation and changes occur.

Product layout

A **product layout** puts together in one location all the equipment required to manufacture one particular product. This forms the basis of a traditional production line, where all machinery is lined up and each unit passes from one piece of equipment to another. A good example of the product layout is the production line in a car plant. The car body moves down the production line, with different bits being added as the car moves along the assembly line, for example the engine, the doors, the seats, the brakes, the lights, the windscreen and windows and the wipers, so at the end of the production line the car is complete. The process uses dedicated equipment that is laid out so that the product can move through in a steady flow.

The production line layout results in a high rate of output and high levels of equipment utilisation and low unit cost. In most production lines the unit cost is further reduced by the use of automation and different methods of **inventory** control, such as JIT – *see* later in this chapter. The implementation of an appropriate system of inventory control will reduce levels of materials, components and work in progress. On a production line, scheduling and controlling operations are easy and it is possible to achieve high and consistent quality.

The disadvantages of the production line layout include the inflexible nature of the operations, as it is difficult to adapt a production line to make another product. For example, adapting a car production line to produce washing machines is impossible without a major refit of the premises. Hence production lines are dedicated and expensive, with failure in one part of the production likely to disrupt the whole line.

Hybrid layout

If neither a product nor process layout is suitable, it is possible to combine them in a **hybrid layout**. For example, this allows a product to be assembled from two components, one being manufactured on a production line and the other in another part of the factory in a job shop using the process layout.

Fixed position layout

A **fixed position layout** occurs when the product is too big or heavy to move, as in shipbuilding, airplane assembly and oil rig construction. All the operations are carried out on one site around the static product. The difficulties of the fixed position layout are that materials, components and workforce all have to be moved on to the site and this will be difficult if there is limited space on site. In the fixed position layout, careful management is required to ensure that the schedule of work is maintained, otherwise completion dates will be in jeopardy. Factors such as weather conditions may also affect operations and completion dates.

Check your understanding

Do you understand why an organisation may choose a particular layout?

Check your understanding by explaining the choice of layouts available to an organisation and indicate factors which may affect that choice.

Process and system performance

All organisations have a finite capacity: a factory can manufacture only so many TV sets in a month, and a school can accept only a finite number of new pupils into Year 1 every September. Therefore, consideration at the design stage of the process system is needed to determine the capacity required in order that products can be made, or services can be offered, to meet the demand of customers.

System capacity involves a significant capital investment, hence careful planning should be undertaken to optimise the utilisation of financial resources and meet demand. This can be crucial, as customers can be lost quickly if a firm's capacity is insufficient to meet demand. Alternatively, under-utilised capacity can be very costly. For example, a local education authority will close down a school if pupil numbers fall significantly, as maintaining school buildings and employing staff are costly activities.

Defining capacity and measuring performance

In theory, an organisation examines the forecast demand for a product and from this determines the capacity needed to satisfy that demand. However, in practice factors other than forecasted demand affect capacity, for example how hard people work, the number of disruptions, the quality of products manufactured and the **effectiveness** of equipment.

Capacity is a basic measure of performance. If a system is operating to capacity, it is producing the maximum amount of a product in a specified time. Decisions concerning capacity are made at the location and process design stage of an organisation's operations management activities. Ideally, an organisation should aim for the capacity of the process to match the forecast demand for products. Mismatches between capacity and demand will result in unsatisfied customers or underutilised resources. If capacity is less than demand, the organisation cannot meet all the demand and it loses potential customers. Alternatively, if capacity is greater than demand, the demand is met but spare capacity and underutilised resources result.

In contrast, if the capacity utilisation hovers around 100 per cent during certain time periods, then on those occasions bottlenecks or queues will occur. A common example of capacity being less than demand is when you are left standing in a long queue in a sandwich bar at lunchtime. You may exercise your consumer choice and go to another sandwich bar with no queues and many staff waiting to serve you. Here capacity is greater than demand, but the cost of paying these under-employed staff will be reflected in your bill.

Utilisation and productivity are directly related to capacity. Utilisation measures the percentage of available capacity that is actually used, and productivity is the quantity manufactured in relation to one or more of the resources used. Take the example of the lunchtime sandwich bar, which makes up sandwiches to order. It has five staff serving at lunchtime and its full capacity is 150 sandwiches per hour. If one member of staff phones in sick with food poisoning on Thursday morning, then utilisation of staff, a key resource in the sandwich bar business, is 4/5 or 80 per cent. If it takes on average two minutes to serve a customer and make up their sandwich to order, then one server has the productivity of 30 sandwiches per hour.

Another measure of how well operations are proceeding is efficiency. Efficiency is the ratio of actual output to possible output, usually expressed as a percentage. Returning to the sandwich shop, where a long-term member of staff and experienced sandwich maker has left and been replaced by a trainee 16-year-old school leaver with no catering experience; on their first day the new staff member can manage to make only 20 sandwiches an hour and is therefore operating at 20/30 or 67 per cent efficiency.

Efficiency should not be confused with effectiveness. Effectiveness is how well an organisation sets and achieves its goals. For example, the sandwich shop may not be 100 per cent efficient while the new member of staff is in training, but it can still remain effective if it achieves its goals of serving sandwiches made from fresh and organic ingredients.

In considering capacity, utilisation, productivity, efficiency and effectiveness, thought should be given to how these measures combine. For example, high productivity is of no use if the quality of products produced is poor or if the finished products remain in a warehouse because there is no demand for them.

Check your understanding

Do you understand the different ways of measuring process and system performance?

Check your understanding by explaining and illustrating the methods for measuring process and system performance. Use examples where appropriate.

Process flow charts

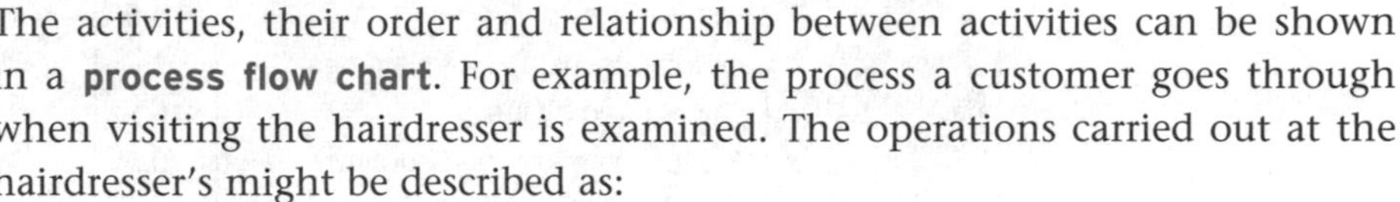

The activities, their order and relationship between activities can be shown in a **process flow chart**. For example, the process a customer goes through when visiting the hairdresser is examined. The operations carried out at the hairdresser's might be described as:

- junior sweeps up hair clippings;
- pay receptionist;
- arrive on time and tell receptionist you've arrived for appointment;
- junior makes you a cup of tea or coffee;
- make next appointment;
- hair is cut by stylist;
- hair is washed by junior;
- you look in mirror and confirm you are happy with haircut;
- wait for stylist to finish cutting previous client's hair;
- sit down and read magazine until called;
- hair is dried by junior.

The following steps are gone through to complete a process flow chart form (*see* Figure 9.6).

Symbol	Activity	Time	Cumulative time	No. of occasions activity can occur in one hour
● ➡ ■ D ▼				
● ➡ ■ D ▼				
● ➡ ■ D ▼				
● ➡ ■ D ▼				
● ➡ ■ D ▼				
● ➡ ■ D ▼				
● ➡ ■ D ▼				
● ➡ ■ D ▼				
● ➡ ■ D ▼				
● ➡ ■ D ▼				

Key: ● Operation ➡ Transport ■ Inspection D Delay ▼ Store

Figure 9.6 A process flow chart

Symbol	Activity	Time (mins)	Cumulative time (mins)	No. of occasions activity can occur in one hour
	Arrive on time and tell receptionist you've arrived for appointment	0.5	00.5	120.0
	Sit down and read magazine until called	20	20.5	003.0
	Junior makes you a cup of coffee	1.5	22.0	040.0
	Hair is washed by junior	8	30.0	007.5
	Wait for stylist to finish cutting last client's hair	5	35.0	012.0
	Hair is cut by stylist	14.5	49.5	004.1
	Junior sweeps up hair clippings	1	50.5	060.0
	Hair is dried by junior	10	60.5	006.0
	You look in mirror and confirm you are happy with haircut	0.5	61.0	120.0
	Pay receptionist	1	62.0	060.0
	Make next appointment	1	63.0	060.0

Key: Operation Transport Inspection Delay Store

Figure 9.7 A process flow chart: visit to hairdresser

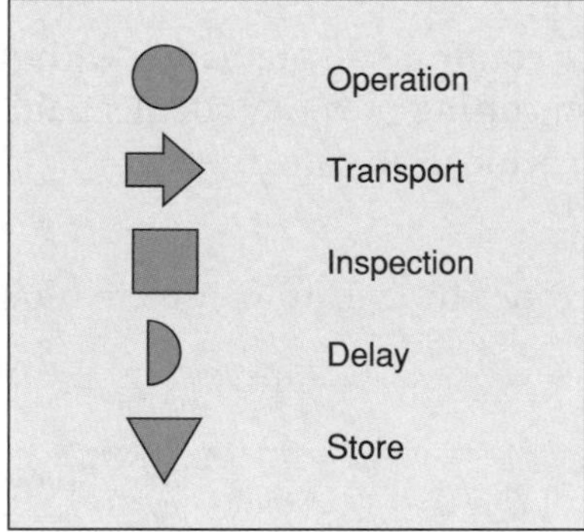

Figure 9.8 Process flow chart symbols

1 Look at the processes and list all the activities in their proper order on the process flow chart. This is shown in the column headed 'activity' in Figure 9.7.
2 Classify each activity using the symbols shown in Figure 9.8. These are shown in the column headed 'symbol' on the process flow chart.
3 Find the time taken for each activity and record it in the column headed 'time'. Also record the 'cumulative time' and the 'number of times an activity can be carried out in one hour'.
4 Summarise the process by adding up the number of each type of activity and the total time.

For the visit to the hairdresser, the following time is spent:

	No.	*Time*
Operations	7	37
Delay	2	25
Transport	1	0.5
Inspection	1	0.5

Drawing up a process flow chart will help answer the following questions:

- What operations are performed?
- What is the sequence of these?
- Which operations cannot be started until others have finished?
- How long does each operation take?
- Is the system being used to full capacity?
- Are products being moved?

Once the process flow chart for a product or service has been drawn up and the basic questions above answered, areas for improvement in the process can be looked for and examined.

In the example of the visit to the hairdresser, finishing the longest activity takes 20 minutes; therefore, at the moment, the maximum number of people that can be processed in one hour is three. However, the longest activity is waiting; therefore, this indicates that the appointments system is one area for improvement. The activity that takes the next longest amount of time is cutting hair and up to four people can be processed by one stylist in one hour. If demand is greater than four haircuts per hour, the number of stylists will need to be increased. An increase in the number of stylists may be needed only on the busiest days, for example Friday and Saturday.

The first three steps give a description of the procedure for drawing up a process flow chart and step four provides some indication of the types of issues looked at if improvement is sought.

Operations management should aim for fewer operations and shorter times, while still ensuring that each operation gives the output required by the customer. If bottlenecks occur, the process and/or equipment need to be adjusted so that the process improves.

Check your understanding

Do you understand how to draw up and use a process flow chart?

Check your understanding by drawing up a process flow chart for a visit to the doctor. Using the process flow chart you have drawn up, indicate where queries may occur in the system which is in place to consult the doctor. How may these realistically be overcome?

Inventory management

All organisations have to use raw materials, components and/or consumables to carry out their operations and meet forecast demand. Insurance companies and council offices use consumables such as pens, printer paper and staples and stock enough to ensure they do not run out of these items. In contrast, a shoe shop such as Clarks will hold stocks of finished goods in the form of pairs of men's, women's and children's shoes in different styles and sizes. Equally, organisations in the manufacturing sector hold **inventory** or stock of different types of items. The inventory can be raw materials, for example paper pulp, wheat, coal and crude oil. Inventory can also be components, for example a car production plant will buy in certain items of inventory in component form, such as tyres, lights and assorted engine parts.

Raw materials and component inventory

Raw materials and components are held as stock by manufacturing companies in case raw materials and components cannot be supplied on demand. Consequently, holding a certain level of inventory allows for production planning to continue. Anticipation of increases in the price of raw materials such as coal, cocoa, crude oil or wheat may mean that organisations choose to purchase larger than normal amounts, possibly via futures contracts. Alternatively, large quantities of raw materials or components may be purchased to take advantage of a lower unit price or reduced transportation costs. For example, coal-fired power stations negotiate rates for the coal they use based on the large amount purchased and its delivery by the trainload.

Work-in-progress inventory

Components and raw materials that have been partly processed by the manufacturing operation have a value to the company and hence are counted as inventory and referred to as work in progress or WIP. There are two points of view on work-in-progress inventory. The first is that if production rates are uneven, work-in-progress inventory ensures that the system always has work to carry out and provides flexibility. The opposite point of view is that work-in-progress inventory merely creates queues and bottlenecks. Consequently the production rate should be balanced, allowing a smooth flow of work right through the process, with no queues.

Finished goods inventory

The final type of inventory is goods that have completed the manufacturing process and are finished goods ready to be passed on to the customer. For many manufacturing organisations the customer is not the end consumer but a manufacturer buying components, for example the car manufacturer buying light fittings, or a distributor of goods, such as a car showroom, acquiring cars to sell.

Retailers such as Marks & Spencer, Next and Debenhams hold an inventory or stock of goods for a variety of reasons. Forecasts for goods are not always completely accurate and the extra inventory allows consumer satisfaction to be met rapidly, rather than the customer purchasing the goods at a competing shop. Alternatively, the distributor may offer a significant discount if finished products are purchased in bulk, hence making it more economic to take advantage of a lower unit price and store what is not needed immediately.

Types of inventory

Inventory can be categorised into two broad types of stock. **Independent demand inventory** is items that are not dependent on other components, i.e. they are finished goods, like cars or shoes. Demand for such goods is directly dependent on consumer demand and to manage this inventory requires the use of forecasts of consumer demand (*see* earlier section on forecasting).

The other category of inventory is **dependent demand inventory**, which covers items or components used in the assembly of a final product. For example, manufacturing a child's tricycle requires three wheels, one frame, one pair of pedals and one saddle. Hence demand for the component parts depends on the demand for the product. This is the dependency and it can be managed using materials requirement planning, discussed below. If 1000 tricycles are to be produced next month, 1000 frames are needed, which in turn means 1000 saddles, 2000 pedals and 3000 wheels.

The cost of holding inventory

Inventory is of value to an organisation and costs money to store. The costs associated with inventory are carrying costs, ordering costs and stockout costs. Inventory carrying costs are the expenses associated with storing stock, borrowing money to purchase the stock, the opportunity costs, the purchase or rental of warehouse premises (which can be expensive if the goods are perishable like food or cut flowers and require refrigerated facilities), insurance, obsolescence and security costs.

Inventory ordering costs

Inventory purchased from an external source incurs the cost of the salary of purchasing staff; preparation and dispatch of the order; salary of accounting staff involved in processing the necessary invoices and making payment; communication including postage, telephone, fax and electronic mail; expediting of the goods if they do not arrive on schedule; and receiving, handling, classifying and inspecting of incoming goods. In summary, inventory ordering costs are the expenses of procurement of the inventory and do not include the cost of purchasing the stock.

Inventory stockout costs

Inventory stockout costs are those costs incurred when inventory is too low to satisfy customer demand. These costs can be difficult to quantify, but include the profit lost on not making a sale and potentially the cost of a client moving all their business to another supplier.

Check your understanding

Do you understand the different types of inventory an organisation may choose to hold and the costs involved?

Check your understanding by explaining the different types of stock an organisation may hold and the possible costs incurred.

Materials requirement planning

The dependent demand inventory system can be managed by use of **materials requirement planning** (MRP). MRP relies on production plans to propose a timetable for when materials orders are required. Consequently the resulting stocks of materials depend directly on a known demand. The alternative is an independent demand inventory system, which means that large enough stocks of materials to cover any probable demand are held.

A hotel coffee shop using an independent demand system would look at the ingredients used last week and ensure that there are enough of the same ingredients in stock to cover likely demand. In contrast, if an MRP system were in use, the number of meals and snacks to be served each day would be assessed and this information used to determine the food required and the time and day of delivery. Hence with an MRP system overall stocks are lower, as only the ingredients and goods needed are ordered and are delivered just before production commences – *see* Figure 9.9. In contrast, with independent demand

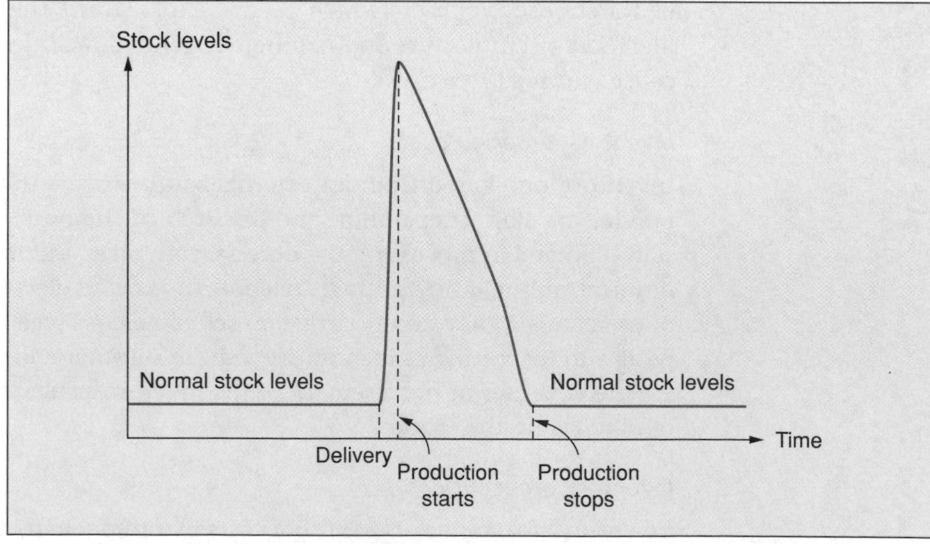

Figure 9.9 Stock levels using MRP

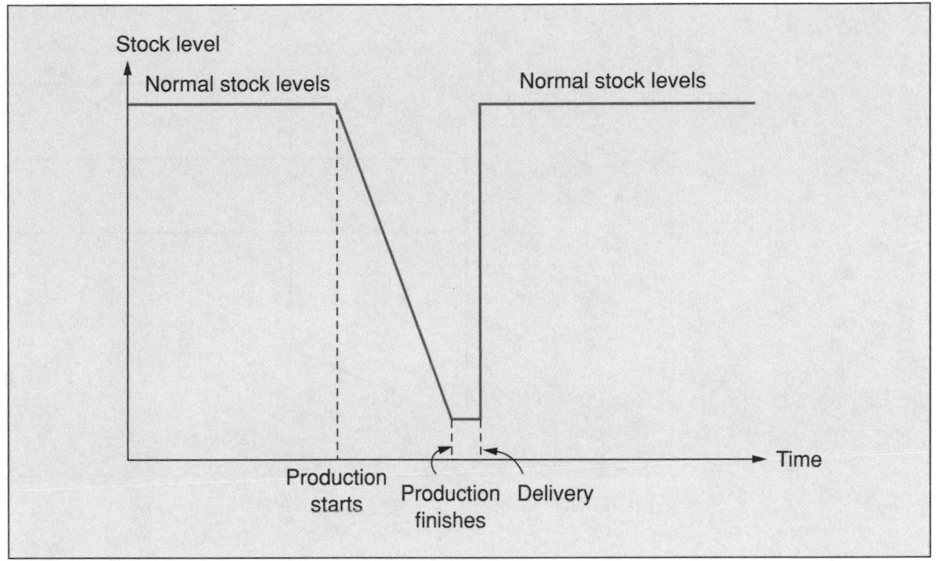

Figure 9.10 Stock levels for an independent demand inventory system

systems the stocks are not related to production plans, so they are kept higher to cover any level of expected demand and are replenished to maintain levels to cover any demand – *see* Figure 9.10.

The MRP procedure

The MRP inventory control system requires a great deal of information about components and products and is therefore computerised. The main information comes from three files:

- master production schedule;
- bill of materials;
- inventory records.

The MRP procedure starts with the master production schedule, which indicates the number of each product to be made in each period. The bill of materials is prepared by the designer or production engineer and is the result of the MRP being broken down to show the materials and components needed to manufacture a product and the order in which they are used. The bill of materials for the desk shown in Figure 9.11 is shown in Figure 9.12. The figures shown in the circles are the numbers needed to make each desk and every item is given a level number that shows where it fits into the process. The finished product is always level 0, with level 1 items used directly to make the level 0 item, the level 2 items used to make the level 1 items and so on.

Closer examination shows that the desktop is made from a wood kit and hardware. The wood kit contains four panels 150cm long, 15cm wide and 2cm thick, two pieces of edging 150cm long, and two short pieces of edging each

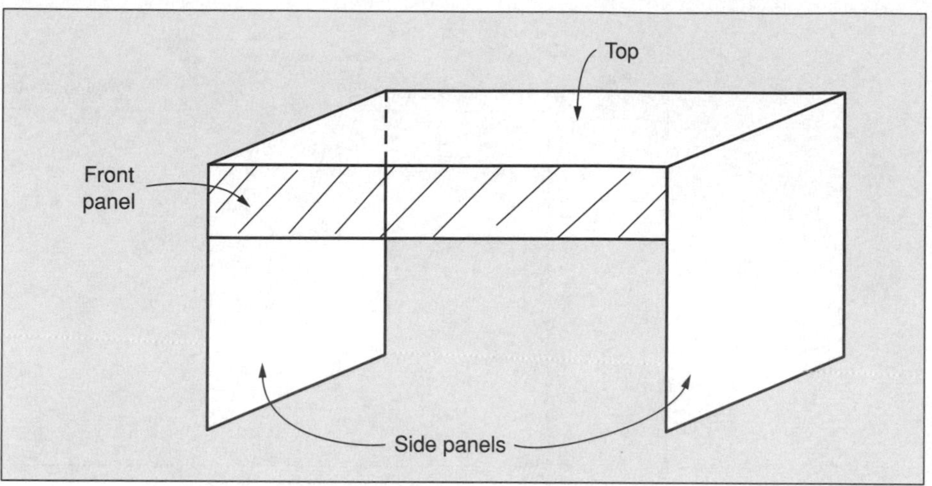

Figure 9.11 Desk

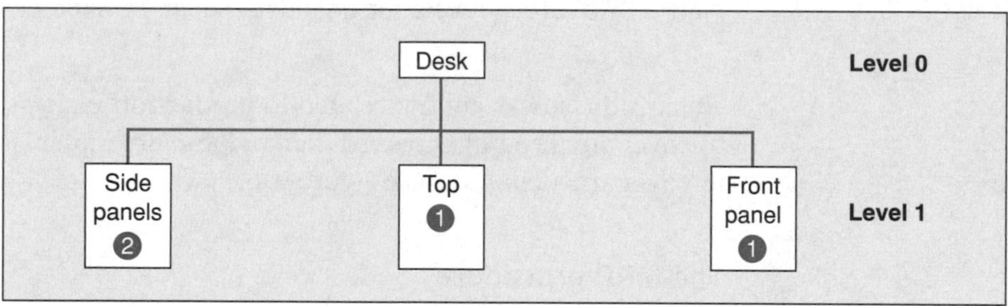

Figure 9.12 Bill of materials for a desk

60cm long. The next level of the bill of materials for the desktop is shown in Figure 9.13. The hardware consists of the tools and machinery required at that stage.

If the master production schedule shows that 100 desks have to be made in December, this means that 100 tops, 200 side panels and 100 front panels have to be available by the beginning of December. These are the gross requirements and the net requirement will have to be determined by examining the inventory records. The stocks of parts that will be available at the start of December should be determined by taking account of current stock and stock on order. If 20 tops, 50 side panels and 10 front panels will be in stock at the start of December, the net requirements that need to be ordered are shown below.

Gross requirements – Current stock/stock on order = Net requirements

Tops	100 – 20 = 80
Side panels	200 – 50 = 150
Front panels	100 – 10 = 90

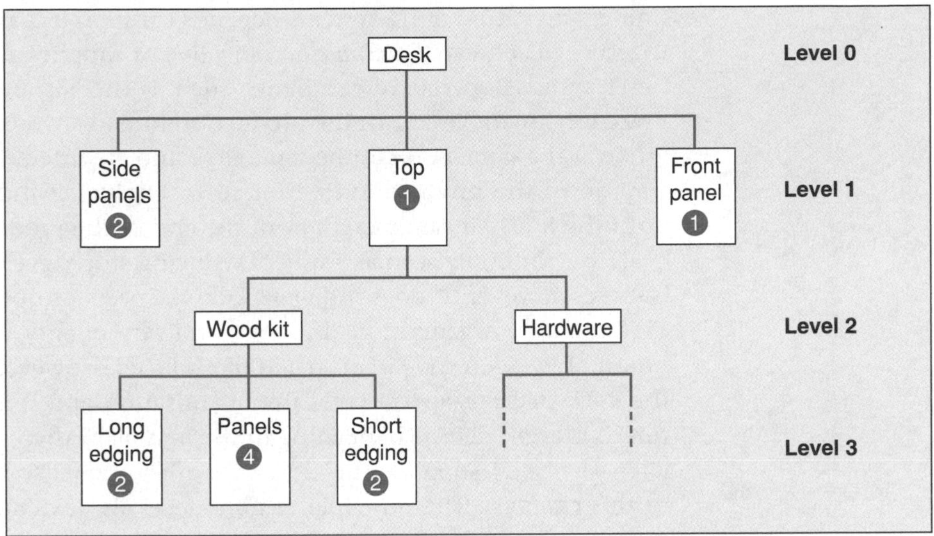

Figure 9.13 Bill of materials for a desk showing details of desktop

Therefore 80 top panels, 150 side panels and 90 front panels need to be ordered, with delivery scheduled for the end of November. For example, if tops take six weeks to arrive (sometimes called lead time) then the order needs to be placed by mid-October at the latest. Information from the supplier also has to be considered when placing the orders, for example if front panels are delivered in batches of 50 only, then 100 front panels will have to be ordered and the extra 10 kept in stock until the next batch of desks is made. Alternatively, the supplier may offer a 15 per cent discount if side panels are purchased in batches of 100. Therefore, careful calculation and consideration have to be given to deciding whether it is worthwhile buying 200 side panels instead of the 150 required. Once the stock and order situations have been clarified, a timetable for production in December can be produced.

Just in time

This chapter has looked at independent inventory demand systems and dependent demand inventory systems, both of which operate with the main aim of managing mismatches between supply and demand for stock. Independent demand inventory systems manage the mismatch by ensuring that stocks are high enough to cover any expected demand. In comparison, dependent demand inventory systems using MRP overcome the stock mismatch by using a master schedule to match the supply of materials approximately to demand. The closer the match of supply to demand, the lower the stock levels needed to cover any mismatches. The just-in-time (JIT) system takes things a stage further and attempts to eliminate the stock mismatch altogether. A just-in-time system is organised so that stock arrives just as it is needed. Accordingly, the immediate nature of JIT systems depends on suppliers and customers working together to achieve the common objective of supplies arriving on time.

JIT systems operate in car plants, such as the Nissan plant in Sunderland. The car body moves down the production line to a work station and the doors arrive at the same point at the same time and are fitted. This is repeated all the way down the production line for seats, engines, windows and other parts, until the finished car emerges from the end of the production line.

JIT is commonly seen as a way of reducing stock levels to zero in the organisation. However, it does influence other aspects of operations management. Traditionally, organisations have set arbitrary quality levels, such as a maximum of two defective items per 100 produced. However, the JIT system takes the view that any defect costs the organisation and it is cheaper in the long run to prevent defects happening in the first place than to pay to correct them later. Hence JIT supports the principles of **total quality management** (*see* later in this chapter). The principle of no defects also extends to the reliability of equipment. The JIT system of supply of materials and components works on the basis of operations being continuous. Hence if a piece of equipment is unreliable and breaks down, managers have to discover why this happened and take action to ensure that this failure does not reoccur. This may include reviewing maintenance procedures and policies (*see* later in this chapter).

Accordingly, JIT is not only a means of reducing inventories but also a way of viewing the whole range of activities in which an operations management department is involved and minimising delays of all kinds, including stock-outs, breakdowns and defects.

Check your understanding

Do you understand the different systems for managing inventory?

Check your understanding by comparing and contrasting MRP and JIT. Use examples where appropriate.

Quality

Quality can be defined as the ability of a product or service to meet and preferably exceed customer expectations. For example, a breathable hillwalking jacket that keeps out the rain and wind and makes the wearer comfortable fulfils its quality expectation, as does a meal in a restaurant to celebrate your birthday if good food, wine and ambience are in evidence. This illustrates the importance of quality. Quality contributes to helping an organisation remain competitive by producing goods and services of the quality demanded by customers. If the quality fails to meet the quality needs and wants of customers, market share and profits will be lost. Hence managers and organisations invest significant effort into quality management, which is concerned with all aspects of product or service quality.

Quality management is affected and influenced by improvements in technology that ensure greater accuracy in the manufacturing processes, resulting in consistently high-quality products. For example, in the entry case study, the marzipan balls placed on Easter simnel cakes are weighed and rolled by a machine giving consistent size and shape, a process that was laborious for staff when done by hand. This consistent quality is used by organisations as a competitive tool to gain competitive advantage (*see* Chapter 3). Therefore, organisations have to pursue the manufacture of high-quality products, as consumers have come to expect them and have become reluctant to tolerate anything less. Hence if the demand for high-quality products is ignored, an organisation will lose out to competitors that can meet customers' quality demands.

Now you can see why organisations must make high-quality products. Any organisation that ignores the demand for high quality will lose out to competitors that can meet customer expectations. Fudges in the entry case study do not ignore the drive for quality and while they have mechanised many processes, some are still done by hand as they add to quality and flexibility. These include mixing ingredients, icing cakes and ensuring a whole nut, not a broken one, is placed on the top of biscuits. Although high quality will not guarantee success for a product, low quality will guarantee failure. There are clear benefits to an organisation from manufacturing high-quality products, such as improved reputation, competitiveness, sales and productivity, along with reduced costs.

The quality of an organisation's products or services can be viewed from two basic points, inside and outside the organisation. The inside or organisational viewpoint of quality is that the performance of a product or service meets its design specifications exactly. The external or customer viewpoint is defined as how well a product or service does the job for which it was purchased. Hence there are two types of quality. The first is designed quality, which is the level of quality designed into a product or service. For example, a Fiesta has a different level of designed quality to an Audi. Second is achieved quality, which illustrates how closely a product achieves the designed quality. For example, at most British mainline railway stations there is a board showing the targets or designed quality for trains running on time, say 97.5 per cent, and alongside these figures the achieved quality, i.e. the actual trains running on time, say 84 per cent. Accordingly, achieved quality is often lower than the designed quality.

Quality costs

The management of quality will both incur and save costs for an organisation. Suppose that a faulty computer games system is sold to a customer buying a Christmas present for their child. The customer complains and the manufacturer arranges for the system to be repaired. However, money could have been saved if the manufacturer had found the fault prior to the games system leaving the factory, and even more money could have been saved by producing a games system that was fault free in the first instance. These costs are known as external failure costs.

There are three other categories of costs associated with quality: design costs, appraisal costs and internal failure costs. Design costs cover the expense of designing a good-quality product. This involves employing appropriate design staff, considering the type and cost of materials, the number of components, the manufacturing time, the ease of production, the amount of automation used, and the skill level required by the workforce. Appraisal costs cover verifying that the designed quality is the same as the achieved quality, which includes quality control costs such as those for sampling and inspecting the goods and work in progress. Finally, internal failure costs cover the cost of any items not meeting the designed quality. This can cover scrapping the item or returning it to an earlier point in the process to be reworked. There is also the cost of the work carried out on the defective item before it was detected. Therefore, defects should ideally be found as early as possible in the process.

Savings are made when a quality system eliminates defective items from the system. For example, if a manufacturer sells goods, 10 per cent of which are defective, and replaces them under guarantee when reported by customers, there is great inefficiency. The inefficiency arises as the manufacturer has to increase production by 10 per cent to cover the faulty goods. A system for dealing with complaining customers and faulty goods also has to be maintained, which incurs costs for the organisation. It is the removal of these inefficiencies that will save money. If the manufacturing process were to eliminate the manufacture of defective goods, productivity would rise by 10 per cent, unit costs would fall, there would be no more customer complaints, and the cost of dealing with them would no longer be incurred.

Total quality management

Total quality management is defined as the whole organisation working together to improve product or service quality. The aim of total quality management is zero defects.

Organisations typically had separate quality control and production departments. These two departments would often have conflicting objectives, with production departments aiming to manufacture products as quickly as possible, and quality control slowing down production by inspecting products, removing defective items and asking for them to be reworked. In this arrangement it is easy for quality control and production to forget that both departments have the overall common objective of customer satisfaction.

Throughout the 1980s and 1990s in the West, quality management and production became integrated into the operations management department. The role of quality staff is to help to ensure that quality is built in, not inspected out. The production and quality staff look for ways of working with each other, customers, marketing staff, engineers and anyone else with a role to play in ensuring high quality.

Check your understanding

Do you understand the importance of quality to an organisation?

Check your understanding by explaining the benefits of 'good' quality and the impact of the costs of quality on the quality of the final product or service which is delivered to the customer. Use examples where appropriate.

Scheduling

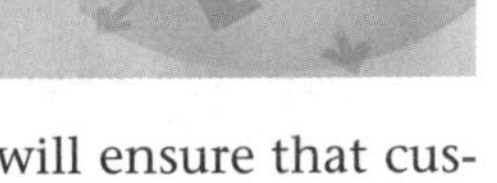

Scheduling involves drawing up a timetable of work that will ensure that customer needs and wants are met. Scheduling is critical in making certain that the utilisation of labour and equipment is optimal and that bottlenecks in the process are avoided. Scheduling generally deals with activities that are normally repetitive and short term in nature. Examples of timetables or schedules are shown in Table 9.1.

Scheduling aims to meet the master production schedule and achieve low costs and high utilisation of equipment. This may appear to be straightforward and easy, but schedules must take account of many different factors. Take the example of drawing up timetables for first-year university students. The availability and requirements of staff, students, subjects and rooms all have to be balanced. The availability of staff and students has to be considered, for instance, as they can be in only one class at a time, and rooms of the right size and type have to be allocated to a subject at a time when both staff member and students can attend. This will be difficult if the number of rooms is limited or if special facilities such as a computer lab, language lab or science lab are required for the class.

There are four different ways for scheduling of services[5] and these are discussed below. Scheduling jobs in services is essentially the same as scheduling in manufacturing, but there are some differences. In service industries the customer is personally involved in the process, often being asked to wait in a queue, so queuing times are critical. Services contrast with manufacturing in that they cannot be produced during quiet times and held in stock for busy times, they have to be provided as required. Hence the capacity of a service

Table 9.1 Examples of schedules

Railways: Railway timetables for trains, drivers, guards, ticket inspectors, catering staff and passengers
Hospitals: Hospital schedules for operations, patients, nurses, surgeons, beds and operating theatres
Chocolate manufacturer: Chocolate manufacturer producing handmade chocolates has a schedule for customer orders, employees, equipment, raw materials delivery (cocoa, butter, cream and flavourings) and delivery of completed orders

process has to be organised to meet peak-time demands and cope with uneven patterns of demand. If there are large differences between peak-time demand and the lowest level of demand, then equipment will have a relatively low utilisation rate. In this situation the employment of staff can be dealt with by employing extra part-timers during the busy period.

First come, first served

First come, first served scheduling is what most of us encounter on a daily basis, for example in the supermarket or queuing for our lunch. It is simple and straightforward: customers are served in the order they arrive.

Fixed schedule system

A **fixed schedule system** arises when a service is delivered to many customers at once. The timetable or schedules are generally known in advance by customers as the information has been made publicly available. Examples include bus, tram, train and airline timetables.

Appointment system

Appointment systems are commonly used by doctors, dentists, lawyers and hairdressers and require the customer to make an advance appointment. The aim of using an appointment system is to ensure the best utilisation of resources and good customer service, such that neither the customer nor practitioner is kept waiting. Problems arise if the appointment systems do not run to schedule, with customers kept waiting beyond their appointed time, or if the customer cancels and the practitioner has to wait for the next appointed customer.

Delayed delivery

The delivery is deliberately delayed in situations when the customer will not be significantly inconvenienced. Dry cleaners are good examples of organisations that delay the delivery to enable them to match capacity and workload. A dry cleaner's that has enough work to operate to full capacity today will still accept clothes for dry cleaning. However, they will not be dealt with until tomorrow and the owner will be told to return the following afternoon or the day after next to collect the clothes. Repair shops such as shoe repairers are also good examples of businesses that operate a **delayed delivery** scheduling system.

Check your understanding

Do you understand the different ways in which an organisation may schedule work?

Check your understanding by explaining and illustrating different scheduling methods. Use examples where appropriate.

Purchasing

The purchasing activity for organisations can be centralised, decentralised or a combination of both. Purchasing the inputs for a company's products is important and may influence the consumer's view of the products manufactured. The entry case study on Fudges clearly illustrates this point, as the use of local suppliers of cheese, cream, butter and wheat helps Fudges achieve its quintessentially country English brand.

Centralised purchasing

Centralised purchasing is when the procurement of all purchased items for the whole organisation is arranged and controlled via one department. This allows bulk buying, which usually means that better prices and service can be obtained from suppliers (*see* Chapter 3). Centralised purchasing also yields a consistent standard and quality of purchased products for the whole organisation, reduced administrative costs, streamlined relations with suppliers, and a reduction in transport costs, since orders are delivered in larger quantities.

Decentralised purchasing

Decentralised purchasing occurs when every division or department of the organisation makes its own purchasing decisions, which is less bureaucratic than a centralised purchasing system. In addition, if the divisions or departments of a large organisation are buying from local suppliers who are responsive to their individual needs, it may be more cost effective than centralised purchasing.

Combination of purchasing functions

If neither a centralised nor a decentralised purchasing system is completely appropriate for the organisation, a combination of centralised and decentralised purchasing may be more suitable. If a combination of systems is used, responsibility for certain items, often of a relatively low value, rests with the decentralised system, which is managed by the division or department. In contrast, the centralised part of the system is used for relatively expensive items and infrequent purchases, such as capital expenditure, which may have to be approved by the board of directors.

Check your understanding

Do you understand the term 'purchasing'?

Check your understanding by explaining the different approaches an organisation may take to buying the resources and inputs it requires. Use examples where appropriate.

Distribution

Distribution is concerned with moving finished goods from the manufacturer to customers. A normal distribution system involves finished goods being moved from the manufacturer's premises to the distributor's warehouse until they are allocated to customers. This type of distribution system allows manufacturers to achieve economies of scale by concentrating operations in central locations, which in turn means that distribution costs are reduced as large orders are moved from manufacturer to wholesaler, rather than small orders being moved directly to retailers or consumers.

This also means that the manufacturer does not need to keep large stocks of finished goods. Wholesalers placing large orders with manufacturers will negotiate a reduced unit price and will also stock a range of goods from many suppliers, hence allowing the retailers a choice of goods. If wholesalers offer short lead times and reliable delivery in addition to a good range of stock, retailers can carry less stock and still offer the consumer a wide range of goods.

Check your understanding

Do you understand the term 'distribution'?

Check your understanding by explaining what is meant by 'distribution'. Use examples where appropriate.

Maintenance

Maintenance activity supports the operations management department by helping ensure that its equipment and facilities are kept in working order. Therefore, an organisation's policy on maintenance is integrated with operations policy. This is important as any unplanned shutdown can have a significant effect on production systems, particularly if other carefully planned systems also support operations, such as a JIT inventory management system, as discussed earlier in this chapter.

Maintenance has two key aims: to reduce both the frequency and impact of failures. The frequency of failure can be reduced by proper installation of the correct equipment along with a programme of preventive maintenance and replacement of items that are wearing out. The impact of maintenance can be lessened by it being planned for quiet times and/or minimising downtime and repair times.

There are two types of maintenance policy: run to breakdown and **preventive maintenance**. If the consequences of failure are limited and the equipment is easily replaceable, run to breakdown is the sensible option. There are two ways to respond to a breakdown: emergency action if the breakdown has serious effects, or corrective action at a point in the future if the impact is limited.

Preventive maintenance is carried out on a planned basis. The intervals between maintenance work are established by experience, manufacturers or external authorities. Inspection is an important part of maintenance, especially for items that are expensive to replace or repair.

Check your understanding

Do you understand the term 'maintenance'?

Check your understanding by explaining the different approaches an organisation can take to keeping its equipment and facilities in working order. Use examples where appropriate.

Summary

This chapter gave an overview of the operations management department of any organisation, product or service, public or private, and examined how operations management activities relate to one another and the other major departments of any organisation. This should have furnished the reader with a broad general knowledge of operations management.

1 Operations management is concerned with managing the way products are made and/or services delivered, which in turn has a direct impact on how well the organisation achieves its objectives. The principles of operations management can be applied to both manufacturing and service organisations.

2 Organisations and operations can be categorised as primary, secondary or tertiary. Primary-sector organisations are concerned with producing raw materials. Secondary-sector organisations manufacture goods. Tertiary-sector organisations sell goods produced by primary and secondary organisations. Tertiary-sector organisations also include service-sector organisations.

3 There are three basic location strategies. First, product-based location, with a company choosing to locate divisions with product similarities close to each other. The next is market-based location, where the company locates its facilities such that they are conveniently placed for the customers. Finally, a vertically differentiated location strategy is when separate stages of the supply process are in different locations.

4 Successful product development helps ensure that an organisation manufactures products that customers desire. The first step is the product development process which covers the generation of ideas, which may come from the salesforce, other staff, customers and competitors. Next, the ideas should be evaluated such that those which are not possible due to technical or skill limitations are not taken forward. The design and development of a prototype should evaluate questions concerning manufacturing, patents, competitors and technical development. The commercial evaluation studies the market

and financial prospects for the product, with the aim of determining how well the product will sell and the amount of profit it will make. Finally, the new product will be launched into the marketplace.

5 Forecasts become effective at some point in the future when a decision is made concerning, for example, demand for a product. Long-term forecasting looks ahead over a number of years, while medium-term forecasting covers periods from 3 to 24 months. In contrast, short-term forecasting covers a few weeks and has an immediate and direct effect on the organisation's operations. Forecasting can be quantitative or qualitative in nature.

6 The layout of resources or facilities in an organisation has two linked aims: first, to organise resources or facilities such that output is achieved using minimum resources and, second, to ensure the maximum throughput is achieved, giving good overall efficiency. The process layout is the grouping together of similar equipment and machinery. The product layout puts together in one location all the equipment required to manufacture one particular product. The fixed position layout occurs when the product is too big or heavy to move, as in shipbuilding.

7 The use of resources in an organisation can be assessed by a number of measures. Capacity is a basic measure of performance and a system is operating to capacity when it is producing the maximum amount of product in a specified time. Capacity is related to utilisation and productivity. Utilisation measures the percentage of available capacity used, while productivity is the quantity manufactured in relation to one or more of the resources used. Efficiency is the ratio of actual output to possible output, usually expressed as a percentage. In contrast, effectiveness is how well an organisation sets and achieves its goals.

8 Process flow charts show the activities performed to manufacture a product or deliver a service, the order they occur in and their relationships. Once a process flow chart has been drawn up for a product or service, it can be used to answer questions concerning the activities, their order, how long they take, and the capacity of the process and its efficiency.

9 All organisations carry inventory in varying forms, including raw materials, components and consumables. Raw materials and component inventory are held by manufacturing organisations to ensure that if supplies of raw materials and components cannot be supplied on demand, production can continue. Components and raw materials which have been partly processed are referred to as work-in-progress inventory. Finished-goods inventory refers to the goods which have completed the manufacturing process and are ready to be passed on to the customer.

10 Inventory can be classified in two ways: independent demand inventory, which is not dependent on other components, i.e. inventory or stock of

finished items, whose demand is directly dependent on consumer demand, and dependent demand inventory, which covers items or components used in the assembly of final products. The costs associated with holding inventory or stock include the carrying costs, the ordering costs and the stockout costs. Dependent demand inventory can be managed by use of materials requirement planning. MRP relies on production plans to propose a timetable for when materials orders are required. Consequently the resulting stocks of materials depend on a known demand.

11 The just-in-time (JIT) inventory system attempts to eliminate stock mismatches between demand and supply. A just-in-time system is organised so that stock arrives just as it is needed. Hence the immediate nature of JIT systems depends on suppliers and customers working together to achieve the common objective of supplies arriving on time.

12 Quality is defined as the ability of a product or service to meet and preferably exceed customer expectations. There are two types of quality, the first being designed quality, which is the level of quality designed into a product or service. The other is achieved quality, which is how closely a product achieves its designed quality.

13 Scheduling involves drawing up a timetable of work which will ensure that customer needs and wants are met. Key aims of scheduling include meeting the master production schedule, along with achieving low costs and a high rate of equipment utilisation. A first come, first served schedule deals with customers served in the order they arrive. A fixed schedule system occurs when a service is delivered to many customers at once, an example being a bus service. The appointment system is where customers are required to make an advance appointment, to enable the service provider to use resources and time efficiently to provide good customer service. This allows the service provider to delay service to closely match capacity and workload.

14 Purchasing in organisations can be centralised, decentralised or a combination of both. Centralised purchasing is when the purchase of all items for the whole organisation is controlled via one department. Decentralised purchasing occurs when each division or department in an organisation makes its own purchasing decisions, which can be less bureaucratic than centralised purchasing.

15 Distribution is the moving of finished goods from manufacturer to distributor. The distributor stores the goods before moving them to the customer. This type of distribution system allows manufacturers to achieve economies of scale by concentrating operations in central locations.

16 Maintenance activities help ensure an organisation's equipment and facilities are kept in working order. Breakdown or unplanned maintenance can have a significant impact on operations and activities such as a JIT inventory system.

Chapter objectives and the exit case study

While reading this chapter and engaging in the activities, you should have learned how to apply theory and models and analyse situations. This means you should be able to meet the chapter objectives outlined at the beginning of the chapter. The table below shows which chapter objectives can be tested by the different questions.

Chapter objective	Check you have achieved this by
4 Determine where in organisations operations management activities need adapting.	answering case study questions 1 and 2.

EXIT CASE STUDY 9.2

Ingredients for success on a plate

by Peter Marsh

Andrew Roper spends as much time as he can with chefs. It's not that he is overly fond of eating but he thinks it only proper that the chief executive of a maker of top-range crockery should get close to the people putting fish on its fine china or water ices on its whiteware.

Achieving a better understanding of customers is one of the changes Mr Roper has introduced during a decade at the head of the 213-year-old, family-owned Churchill China, based in the Potteries area of the Midlands. Hence the company has regular dialogue with experts such as Paul Gayler, head chef at London's Lanesborough hotel, and Nick Vadis, chairman of the Craft Guild of Chefs and head UK chef of Compass, the catering company.

'We have taken on a lot of service disciplines, so you could think of us as less of a pure manufacturer and more as a service company with a manufacturing arm,' says Mr Roper, whose family is the main shareholder in Churchill, even though it has had a stock market listing since 1994. While many other companies in the UK ceramics industry have shrunk or vanished because of low-cost competition, Churchill China has survived – not only by investigating what customers want but also by finding new ideas to help it expand, such as novel designs aimed at restaurants and pubs.

Shrugging off any gloomy thoughts about UK manufacturing in general as it faces the effects of another economic downturn, the 59-year-old Mr Roper is guardedly upbeat about Churchill. 'Even if the sales environment becomes worse during 2008, I feel we are in a better position to withstand weakness in demand than was the case even three years ago,' Mr Roper says. He has, after all, been through a number of economic ups and downs at Churchill since the early 1970s. Indeed, Mr Roper – who was commercial director before he became CEO – thinks an economic slowdown could benefit the company if it brought opportunities for growth by acquisition.

In Churchill's unpretentious Stoke-on-Trent offices, Mr Roper is a cheerful upbeat figure, who points proudly to the gleaming display of the company's latest products. The company traces its origins to Sampson Bridgewood, a pottery business established in the Stoke area in 1795, which Edward Roper, Mr Roper's grandfather, acquired in 1922. Churchill floated on the London stock exchange as a way to put a value on the stakes of family members not involved with the business, as well as to raise money for expansion. But it also wanted 'the challenges' that outside shareholders would bring with their extra scrutiny and questions for senior managers. The company wanted to avoid the problems sometimes experienced by family businesses of becoming complacent and failing to spot new trends, Mr Roper recalls. Overall, the listing was 'a positive step'. Since then Churchill's shares (later transferred to the Aim market for smaller businesses) have hardly set the world on fire. The company's market capitalisation of just over £30m is little changed from the figure when it was floated. More positively, after a calamitous decline in the stock price in the late 1990s – about the time Mr Roper took the helm – the shares have outperformed the broadly based FTSE all-share index by about 300 per cent since the start of 2000. Mr Roper wants to build on this strong run. Part of the plan is for the family gradually to sell some of its stake – by an unspecified amount – to encourage greater liquidity in the shares and so help the stock price.

Churchill ran into financial difficulties in the late 1990s mainly because of the steep rise of sterling against European currencies. In 1999 it reported its only financial loss. Mr Roper took an axe to Churchill's production in its own plants. Employee numbers have fallen from 1600 in 1998 to 650, with most of the losses in manufacturing. But the company has not quit manufacturing altogether. Its only remaining plant in Stoke-on-Trent has the latest high-technology ceramic furnaces and makes every plate, cup and saucer it sells on the professional catering side of the business. About 60 per cent of the company's sales of about £47m last year came from this division and the rest from retailing, a reverse of the split of 10 years earlier.

Items for the professional catering sector are relatively high value, often with a superior standard of finish and made to special shapes and sizes, for hotels, restaurants and institutions such as schools and old people's homes. The company says it is the market leader in this field in the UK, accounting for about a fifth of the £80m-a-year sales to the hospitality sector. Other types of tableware, which Churchill sells directly to consumers via shops – and which are generally both cheaper and subject to more competition – are made by suppliers in countries such as China, India and Colombia. The idea was to concentrate Churchill's manufacturing at its own plant 'on higher-value items, where we feel we have some competitive advantages', says Mr Roper. About 40 per cent of total revenues come from exports. Underlying pre-tax profits, taking into account exceptional items, are expected by the City to have reached about £4m last year, compared with £3.1m in 2006 and £2.6m the year before. The company reports its financial results for last year on April 1.

Through his conversations with chefs, Mr Roper says, Churchill develops ideas on the designs for crockery that will show off chefs' latest concoctions to maximum advantage. For instance, Churchill came up with oblong plates as a way of displaying food as chefs wanted. 'Working with and listening to top professional chefs is fundamental,' says Mr Roper. At nearly a third, a much higher proportion of Churchill's employees work in jobs such as sales, marketing, technical support and product development than a decade ago. It has 22 specialist designers, about three times as many as 20 years ago. 'The sales, marketing and technical people spend far more time than I could ever have imagined [in the late 1990s] checking out what happens to the product in use and asking the customer, professional or otherwise, what they really want next,' he says.

Churchill sells about 7000 items of tableware, twice as many as in 1998, although annual turnover has barely changed. As well as stocking a wider range of items, the company has had to become adroit at switching over products in its overall range. 'On the retail side especially, the life cycle of [designs] is likely to be six months, as opposed to six years a decade ago,' Mr Roper says.

Production overseas, quality control and innovation at home

Churchill China's retreat from most of its UK manufacturing in the past decade has involved the company in a number of strategic changes, including an increased reliance on overseas contractors. On the retail side of the business, aimed at the general consumer, the company uses contractors in low-wage countries.

Source: from 'Ingredients for success on a plate', *The Financial Times*, 26 March 2008 (Marsh, P.).

Exit case study questions

1 Explain how Churchill's operational activities have changed in recent years.

2 Identify some of the key issues for Churchill's operations over the next three years.

Short-answer questions

1 Define operations management.
2 Define primary, secondary and tertiary organisations and give examples of each.
3 Name and briefly describe three different location strategies.
4 Name six stages of the product development process.
5 List five measures of process and system performance.
6 Name two different types of forecasting.
7 Name four different types of layout.
8 Define inventory management.
9 Briefly explain the term 'JIT'.
10 Briefly explain the term 'MRP'.
11 Briefly explain the difference between JIT and MRP.
12 Name four different methods of scheduling.
13 Briefly state the difference between designed quality and achieved quality.
14 Define total quality management.
15 Name two different types of maintenance.

Chapter objectives and assignment questions

While reading this chapter and engaging in the activities, you should have learned how to apply theory and models and analyse situations. This means you should be able to meet the chapter objectives outlined at the beginning of the chapter. The table below shows which chapter objectives can be tested by the different questions.

Chapter objective	Check you have achieved this by
1 Define different types and categories of organisation.	answering assignment question 1.
2 Explain the full range of operations management activities.	answering assignment question 1.
3 Identify where in organisations the operations management activities apply.	answering assignment question 2.
4 Determine where in organisations operations management activities need adapting.	answering assignment question 2.

Assignment questions

1 Choose a manufacturing and a service organisation of your choice. Research your chosen organisations and compare and contrast the operations management procedures they undertake. Present your findings in a 2000-word report.

2 Complete the process flow chart for doing a business studies assignment (Figure 9.14). What mechanisms are there for you to monitor and improve the quality of your work and how effective do you think each one is? What constraints affect the way in which you plan and execute your work?

Order	Activity	Done by whom?	Symbol
	Make rough notes		
	Draw up contingency plan		
	Type up final answers/report		
	Put in correct references		
	Hand report into school office		
	Write questions and assessment criteria/learning outcomes		
	Go to library		
	Collect information		
	Read questions carefully		
	Prepare draft answers to questions		
	Collect information		
	Return feedback and mark for report		
	Buy newspapers		
	Select organisation		
	Mark reports		

Key: ● Operation ◗ Delay ➡ Transport ■ Inspection ▼ Store

Unit leaders
Unit tutors
Students

Figure 9.14 Process flow chart for doing a business studies assignment

WEBLINKS available at www.pearsoned.co.uk/capon

- This is the website of the Health and Safety Executive that deals with the regulation of risk in the workplace:
  http://www.hse.gov.uk/
- This website is concerned with the work of Deming. Click on 'DEN site map' to enter the website, click on Deming Philosophy webpage, click on Deming's 14 points. This looks at methods for quality and improvement in organisations:
  http://www.deming-network.org/

FURTHER READING

The following books all provide an introductory chapter to operations management.

- Barnes, D (2008) *Operations Management: An International Perspective*, Chapters 1 and 4, London: Thomson Learning.
- Greasley, A (2006) *Operations Management*, Chapter 1, Chichester: John Wiley & Sons Ltd.
- Johnston, R and Clark, G (2008) *Improving Service Delivery*, Chapters 1 and 8, Harlow: Financial Times Prentice Hall.
- Naylor, J (2002) *Introduction to Operations Management*, Chapters 1 and 2, Harlow: Financial Times Prentice Hall.

This book provides a good overview of operations management.

- Hill, T (1993) *The Essence of Operations Management*, Harlow: Prentice Hall.

REFERENCES

1 Naylor, J (1996) *Operations Management*, Financial Times Pitman Publishing.
2 Ibid.
3 Waters, D (1996) *Operations Management: Producing Goods and Services*, Addison-Wesley.
4 Ibid.
5 Ibid.

CHAPTER 10

Finance

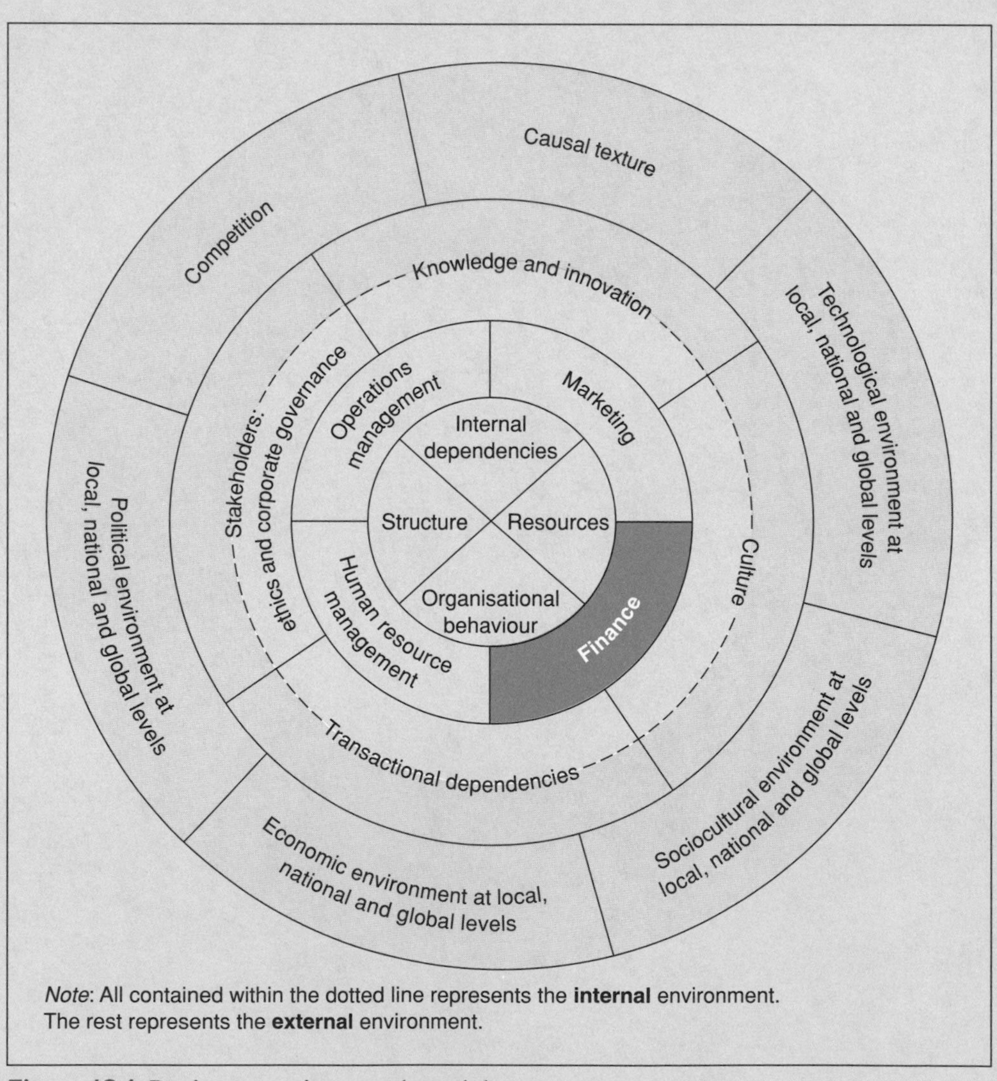

Note: All contained within the dotted line represents the **internal** environment. The rest represents the **external** environment.

Figure 10.1 Business environment model

Chapter objectives

This chapter aims to provide an overview of the finance function, by first looking at the external environment and its financial influences on the organisation. The chapter then goes on to examine the three broad areas of the finance function, namely financial management, management accounting and financial reporting. Finally, how different stakeholders may use financial information is covered.

Therefore, when you have read this chapter and worked through the associated activities you should be able to achieve the objectives specified below.

1 **Discuss the external financial influences that can impact on an organisation.**
2 **Explain the activities of financial management, management accounting and financial reporting.**
3 **Identify and evaluate the different financial stakeholders in an organisation.**

This case study examines Tesco, the largest retailer in the UK, and its reporting of good profits. Tesco has managed to remain profitable in the UK and also grow profitably in its overseas markets, which is important when the UK economy is struggling, as it was in early 2008.

Tesco shrugs off retail clouds

ENTRY CASE STUDY 10.1

by Elizabeth Rigby

Tesco shrugged off concerns of falling consumer confidence as Britain's biggest retail chain reported strong annual profits and insisted it was well placed to weather any downturn. Sir Terry Leahy, chief executive, reassured the markets that Tesco, having lost market share to rivals such as Wm Morrison over Christmas, had sharpened up its promotions, ranges and prices and was winning back business.

The shares responded with their biggest one-day rally in nearly six years, closing 7.3 per cent higher at 419.5p. Underlying sales in the first five weeks of this financial year were up 5 per cent, against 3.5 per cent in the year to February 23, as it began to reverse three consecutive quarters of falling market share. 'That's a very strong rate of growth in this environment. And we're growing market share. And that's a solid start.'

He said he was trimming cutting costs in anticipation of a tough year, but said Tesco was in a strong position to respond to the changing environment. 'I hope there will not be a recession,' said Sir Terry. 'A recession will be harder to manage than a slowdown. It is very difficult to call. We have decided to stop speculating and start dealing with it and trade in the environment you are in.'

Tesco offered comfort on its Fresh & Easy US chain, which has been under intense scrutiny, with Sir Terry insisting that sales were ahead of budget. He also said Tesco was bringing forward the opening of its northern Californian distribution centre. General merchandisers provided a more mixed picture. Burberry, the luxury goods company, beat market expectations, while Debenhams, the UK's largest department store chain, reported falling underlying sales. Both said trade had become much more volatile.

Underlying group profits rose 11.8 per cent to £2.85bn on sales up 11 per cent to £51.8bn. The international business, which will account for 83 per cent of the group's 11.8m sq ft of new space this year, increased sales by 25 per cent to £13.8bn, while trading profits rose 24 per cent to £700m. The UK delivered sales growth of 6.7 per cent to £38bn. Tesco said food price inflation had been 1.2 per cent over the year, but added that it did not expect more inflationary pressure to be passed on to consumers.

Additional reporting by Tom Braithwaite.

Source: from 'Tesco shrugs off retail clouds', *The Financial Times*, 16 April 2008 (Rigby, E.).

Introduction

The resource of money is an important **asset** for nearly all organisations. The financial aims of private-sector organisations will include profit-making objectives. In contrast, for public-sector or charitable organisations the most efficient and effective use of often limited financial resources will be of primary importance.

Therefore, the finance function of a business is concerned with the financing of the organisation, the use of finance by the organisation, and the explanation to interested parties or stakeholders of how the finance has been utilised. The detailed activities undertaken by the finance function will vary in nature from the operational to the strategic and will be influenced by changes in the organisation's external environment. Therefore, the finance function is concerned with **financial management**, **management accounting** and **financial reporting**. We will look at these areas of activity later in this chapter.

External influences on the finance function

The single currency

The 1991 Maastricht Treaty set the timetable for the first round of monetary union to occur in Europe in 1999. The deadline for meeting the necessary economic targets to join the first wave of European monetary union, EMU, was the end of 1997. The key economic target that countries had to meet was the deficit:GDP (gross domestic product) ratio, which had to be 3 per cent or less. All member states except Greece met this target. However, along with Greece, Denmark, the UK and Sweden did not join the single European currency in the first wave in 1999.[1] In June 1998 Robin Cook, British Foreign Secretary, strongly indicated that Britain expected to join the single currency soon after the 2002 general election in the UK; however, by 2008 the timing of a referendum on the UK joining the euro remained unclear.

The single currency is called the euro and is managed by the European Central Bank, based in Frankfurt. The role of the European Central Bank is to maintain the euro as a stable currency, as it is hoped that this will stop price rises caused by devaluing currencies and produce a European economy that is built around low inflation and low interest rates. In the longer term it is expected that such a European economy will attract world trade and international investors keen to be less dependent on the US dollar.

The euro became legal currency for trade and financial markets on 1 January 1999. Coins and notes were introduced in participating countries on 1 January 2002, allowing individuals to be paid in euros, spend euros in shops and pay bills in euros. The two-stage changeover was aimed at allowing organisations to familiarise themselves with the euro and how it would operate. It also gave time for notes to be printed and coins minted. The notes are in denominations of 5, 10, 20, 50, 100, 200 and 500 euros, and the eight euro coins range from 1 cent to 2 euros (200 cents) in value. The circulation of old national currencies and the new euros occurred in parallel for several months after 1 January 2002. During this time organisations displayed the price of goods and services in both euros and a national currency, which along with charts and conversion tables helped the individual consumer to convert from their old national currency to the new euro.

The benefits of the euro for individual consumers include the greater ease with which the price of goods and services can be compared across participating EU member states. Purchasing goods or services from abroad via mail or the internet is less complex and the cost of foreign exchange and exchange rates when visiting different participating EU states no longer exists.

The benefits for organisations in participating countries include a decrease in the number of different-currency bank accounts held, a rationalisation of cash operations and an overall saving in operating costs due to the removal of cash conversion costs and cross-border payments. In contrast, the disadvantages of a single currency arise from the intrinsic risk of the euro as a new currency with no past form and the associated hesitancy that existed while exchange rates were finally established.

The minimum wage

The minimum wage was introduced in the UK in April 1999. The issues and debates surrounding its introduction centred on the level at which it should be set and whether that level should vary for particular groups of people.

The Conservative government abolished the old Wages Councils that set minimum wages in a number of low-paying industries, including, for example, retailing, catering and textiles. It argued that the minimum wage levels set by Wages Councils made employing staff too expensive and hence jobs were lost; this same argument was directed by the Conservatives at the idea of a national minimum wage. However, the Conservatives never proved that discontinuing the Wages Councils *created* jobs. Hence it would appear that their termination had no effect on employment, so the minimum wages set by the Wages Councils could have been an appropriate starting point in establishing a minimum wage level. The minimum wage rates at the time the Wages Councils were disbanded ranged from £2.72 per hour to £3.18 per hour, with an average of about £3 per hour. Revising these rates in line with average earnings growth would have produced a minimum wage rate of £3.85 in October 1998.[2] The minimum wage when it was introduced in April 1999 was £3.60 for an adult employee.

In October 2008 the adult minimum wage increased from £5.52 to £5.73 per hour, an increase of 3.8 per cent. Employers welcomed the increase, which was in line with the increase in average earnings. In contrast union leaders felt that the increase should reflect the 4.1 per cent increase in annual retail price inflation. This means the minimum wage has risen 59 per cent since it was introduced in 1999, more than twice the increase in the retail price index over the same period. This makes the UK minimum wage one of the third highest EU minimum wages and double the minimum wage in the US.[3]

Check your understanding

Do you understand the specific elements of the external environment that affect the finance function?

Check your understanding by discussing the impact of the external environment on the finance department of an organisation.

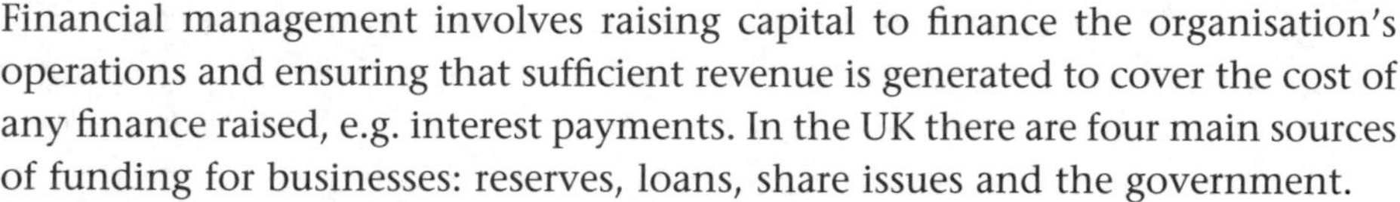

Financial management

Financial management involves raising capital to finance the organisation's operations and ensuring that sufficient revenue is generated to cover the cost of any finance raised, e.g. interest payments. In the UK there are four main sources of funding for businesses: reserves, loans, share issues and the government.

Reserves

Reserves are retained profits from previous years that have not been spent or distributed to **shareholders**. The use of reserves to fund expenditure means that the level of scrutiny to which the organisation's management is subjected is less exacting than if funds were raised from sources external to the company.

Loans

Loans are either **term loans** or **overdrafts** and are commonly provided by banks. Term loans are long term and provide the borrowing organisation with capital in return for repayment of the capital with interest over a number of years, e.g. five or ten. In contrast, overdrafts are short-term loans for 12 months or less and will vary from day to day depending on the amount by which the organisation's current account is overdrawn. However, for many organisations an overdraft will be a 'permanent' source of temporary finance.

Loans are for a definite period and repayable with interest. The amount of interest payable depends on the interest rate charged, which is driven by the base rate of interest set by the Bank of England. The level of risk taken by the lender in lending money to the borrower will be influenced by the security offered against the loan and what the money is to be used for. All these will in turn also influence the interest rate charged on the loan. It is common for long-term loans to be secured against company assets. Securing the loan reduces the risk for the lender and the interest rate for a secured loan will be lower than for an unsecured loan.

The interest payments come out of profits and cannot be reduced by the borrowing business if profits and trading conditions are unfavourable. This contrasts with **dividend payments**, which a company can alter depending on profits and trading conditions. A further characteristic of loans is that they do not carry ownership rights, which is in contrast to **ordinary shares** that do. If a company is unable to meet the loan and interest payments, then the bank or lender may decide to foreclose on the loan and appoint a **receiver** to take day-to-day control of the company. The receiver has to decide whether the business is able to continue trading under its guidance and generate enough cash to pay the bank and other **creditors**, or whether the business should be closed, the assets sold off and the cash generated used to pay the bank and other creditors.

In July 1991 Robert Maxwell used shares in the publicly quoted company Maxwell Communications Corporation (MCC) to secure loans to his own private companies of an estimated £300 million. Earlier in the same year, Maxwell had used shares owned by the pension fund of Mirror Group Newspapers to secure loans to MCC. Much of this was irregular and illegal and on 31 October 1991 the value of shares in MCC started to plummet. Shortly after this, on 5 November, Maxwell died from drowning after going overboard from his yacht near the Canary Islands. This example raises two key issues to bear in mind when accepting assets as security for a loan. First, are the assets being offered as security those the borrower is legally allowed to offer? Maxwell was not legally in a position to offer the shares belonging to the Mirror Group Newspaper pension fund as security, but he did so and they were accepted as security for loans to MCC. Second, will the assets offered as security be of a value equal to that of the loan should the lender have to foreclose on the loan and **liquidate** the security given? The value of MCC shares used as security for loans plummeted in October 1991, leaving the value of the loan security as minimal.

Ordinary shares

Companies issue ordinary shares to raise capital. Once issued, shares can be traded on the **stock market** if a company is listed, where individuals or organisations may buy and sell them. Shareholders will usually fall into one of three categories: the individual investor, institutional shareholders and existing shareholders (**rights issues** are looked at in the next section).

The value of a shareholder's investment in a company will rise or fall depending on how the company itself performs and on how the stock market as a whole performs. For example, on 15 April 2008 Tesco announced profits of £2.84 billion, up 11.8 per cent on the previous year; in light of this announcement Tesco shares rose by 30 pence to close at 419 pence. In contrast, Northern Rock shares plummeted spectacularly due to poor decision making around loans. On 25 January 2007 Northern Rock shares rose 44 pence to stand at £12.08, with the chief executive of Northern Rock stating the bank was aiming to become one of the top three mortgage lenders within 5 years. On 13 September 2007 Northern Rock shares closed down 33 pence at £6.39 amid rumours of a profits warning. In mid-February 2008 Northern Rock shares stood at 90 pence.

Ordinary shares carry ownership rights entitling the holder of the shares to one vote per share owned at annual general meetings and extraordinary general meetings of the company and the right to receive a dividend if the company issues one. Dividends are a distribution of profits to the owners/shareholders of the company and can be raised or lowered as the company sees fit. They are usually expressed in the form of so many pence per share owned. For example, if a company announces a dividend of 17.5p per share, a shareholder owning 200 shares would receive a payment of £35. Most companies seek stability or a slight upward trend in their dividend payments with the aim of keeping shareholders satisfied.

Shareholders are either individual members of the public investing relatively small sums of money (thousands of pounds) in shares or corporate investors with large amounts of money to invest (millions of pounds) for the company or their clients. For the individual small investor, shares are a form of investment that is more risky than keeping savings in a building society or bank, but shares are highly likely to give a better return in the long term than a building society or bank. Corporate investors include insurance companies and pension funds, which invest money to enable them to pay pensions and attractive bonuses on insurance policies to their clients.

In the 1980s individuals were greatly encouraged to become shareholders by the Conservative government of Margaret Thatcher through privatisation offers. Many individuals were new to this type of investing. The companies in which they acquired shares included British Telecom, British Gas, electricity distributors, power generators and British Airways. These flotations were aimed at individual and corporate investors.

Margaret Thatcher's view of Britain's citizens as shareholders continued in the 1990s with privatisations in the financial services industry. In 1997 the insurance company Norwich Union floated on the stock market along with the Halifax, Alliance & Leicester, Woolwich and Northern Rock building societies. These floatations meant that the account and policyholders of those companies received shares in them, hence releasing many millions into the pockets of the individuals who sold the shares they received. Other shareholders viewed the Norwich Union and the building societies as good investments and kept their shares. In light of the 2008 crisis in the banking industry these shares may have proved to be less secure than suggested at flotation.

Rights issues

A rights issue is similar to a share issue but is for existing shareholders only. A rights issue is a way of raising capital that is viewed as less threatening than a share issue, as the shareholder breakdown remains the same. Hence there is no opportunity for another company to build up a stake in the business with the aim of mounting a **hostile takeover bid**. In a rights issue ordinary shareholders are offered new shares in proportion to those they already own. For example, if a shareholder owns 500 shares in a company and the rights issue is a one for ten offer, then the shareholder will be entitled to purchase one new share for every ten already owned, i.e. 50 new shares in total. Rights issue shares are usually offered at a price equal to or below the stock market price to make the investment appear attractive to the shareholders.

If shareholders take up the rights issue by purchasing the shares, the shareholder breakdown remains the same. If the existing shareholders do not buy the new shares and the rights issue is a failure, the shares are offered on the open market by the underwriters and the shareholder profile of the company is likely to change, offering the opportunity for a hostile takeover bid.

A failed rights issue may point to the possibility that the company is not doing well. Therefore, investors should examine closely a company's reasons for undertaking a rights issue. A company using the money raised by a rights issue to expand the business, with the aim of seeing profits, and share price and dividends rise in the future, will be a better investment than a company using the money raised via a rights issue to pay off old debts and avoid business failure.

In early 2008, in light of the 'credit crunch', many banks were looking for ways of strengthening their balance sheet. The options for doing this include selling non-core divisions, reducing dividends, rights issues and restricting loan growth. Despite the rights issue being seen as an unpopular way of strengthening the balance sheet, some banks did appear to consider a rights issue. However, it is difficult to see how a rights issue could be successful in an environment in which the 'credit crunch' was biting. The banks were seeking to strengthen their balance sheets, which had taken severe knocks due to their own decision making around loans and over-exposing themselves when lending money.

In April 2008 Royal Bank of Scotland (RBS) announced a rights issue, which was an eleven for eighteen issue, i.e. eleven new shares for every eighteen already held. The rights issue was to be heavily discounted at 200 pence per share; on the day the rights issue was announced RBS shares closed at 372.5 pence. RBS was seeking to raise £12 billion to improve its capital base, in light of a write-down of £5.9 million linked to the credit crunch and a further significant write-down linked to its acquisition in 2007 of Dutch bank ABN Amro.[4] RBS also considered the sale of its insurance arm for around £5 billion, including Direct Line and Churchill.[5]

Another financial institution, which did go ahead with a rights issue, was the Paris-based Société Générale. Société Générale had lost €4.9 billion when rogue trader Jerome Kerviel was exposed in January 2008. In February 2008 Société Générale announced a €5.5 billion rights issue to help repair the damage of the losses.[6] The rights issue was a one in four offer, which was heavily discounted, with shares offered for a price of €47.5, a reduction of 39 per cent on the previous day's closing price of €77.9. The view was that the rights issue was only worth taking up if speculation of a takeover bid was to be believed. This would make the rights issue a potentially attractive investment, as any outside bidder would be expecting to pay €71 per share.

Venture capitalists

Venture capitalists have a pool of cash, which comes from private investors, or institutions such as pension funds or banks and many are listed in the directory of the British Venture Capital Association. The venture capitalist firm will usually be organised as a limited partnership. Venture capitalists often invest in small, fast-growing companies which find it difficult to raise funds via the stock market, as they are too small and often high risk, although venture capitalists may invest at any stage in the business cycle. The venture capitalist provides a medium- to long-term investment and in return receives a stake in the company. Venture capitalists normally expect to have a management role in running the company and, as well as providing cash, also offer advice, know-how and contacts to aid development of the business. In return for the investment, the venture capitalists will share in the profits and gain capital growth from the investment, which is realised when the venture capitalist sells the stake in the business, once the period of the contract is complete, typically after 5–7 years.[7]

The most well-known example of venture capitalists in the UK is to be seen on the BBC television programme *Dragon's Den*, where budding entrepreneurs pitch their ideas to the venture capitalists. The entrepreneurs will be seeking to negotiate a deal for investment in their business in return for the dragons gaining a stake in the business.

Government

The Department for Business Enterprise and Regulatory Reform (BERR) provides a gateway to information for businesses, including possible sources of funding, which can be accessed via the BERR website which is listed in the weblinks section at the end of this chapter. The BERR website provides access information on how to locate in the UK or expand overseas and, via Business Link (accessed via BERR website), advice on how to start up, run and develop a business.

Business start-ups by young people can seek funding and advice from the Prince's Trust, which seeks to help disadvantaged young people aged 14–30 achieve their goals. Financial help takes the form of low-cost loans of up to £5000, or in special cases grants are available to individuals or groups.[8]

Check your understanding

Do you understand the different ways in which a company can raise money?

Check your understanding by indicating how the following companies could raise money for expansion:

- an established public company, like Tesco;
- an established private company, like Clarks;
- an established small high-tech company;
- a new small business, like Tinytots nursery.

The use of capital raised and leasing assets

Organisations use the **capital** raised to acquire assets. Many organisations are more concerned with using assets than actually owning them and may make the decision to lease rather than purchase assets. The leasing of assets has become more common during the last 20 years. Leasing is one way of acquiring assets without paying the full price. The most commonly leased assets are cars, plant and machinery, and information technology and office equipment. The types of lease used to rent out a particular asset may vary. The common types of leasing arrangement are an operating lease, a finance lease and a sale and leaseback.

An operating lease is a short-term contract in which the supplier of equipment, for example information technology hardware, makes the equipment available to a business. The business will enter into an operating lease and make a series of lease payments to the provider of the equipment. The tax advantages of leasing assets accrue immediately rather than over a number of years, as would be the case with depreciation allowances on purchased assets.

A finance lease is used when suppliers of an expensive item of capital equipment are paid directly in full for the item they have supplied to the company by the financing organisation, e.g. bank, finance house or merchant bank. Therefore, the financing organisation provides the finance and the company makes leasing payments to the financing organisation.

A sale and leaseback is used when a company is concerned with using rather than owning an asset. The key principle here is that the company sells the asset to release the capital tied up in the asset and leases it back. Organisations such as pension funds may purchase a large, expensive fixed asset, like a head office building, and lease it back to a company. Hence the capital is released in the form of cash for the company to spend on other projects, without the upheaval of moving office.

Check your understanding

Do you understand the different types of lease available to companies?

Check your understanding by identifying the sort of lease suitable for:

- a company occupying a large corporate headquarters wishing to reduce the size of its HQ;
- a steel company purchasing a new furnace;
- a print and copy shop wanting to update its equipment.

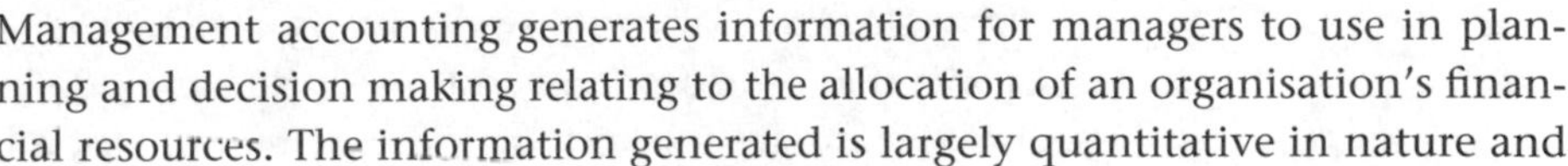

Management accounting

Management accounting generates information for managers to use in planning and decision making relating to the allocation of an organisation's financial resources. The information generated is largely quantitative in nature and is generated by application of management accounting techniques. The type of management accounting techniques examined in this chapter are **costing** and **investment appraisal**.

Costing

Costing involves looking at and defining the costs involved in producing a product or service. How costs are defined influences their use in the techniques of **absorption** and **marginal costing**, which are looked at later in this chapter. The cost of producing a product or service has three elements to it: the costs of materials, labour and overheads. These costs will be **direct** or **indirect** and/or **fixed** or **variable**.

Material and labour costs can be either direct or indirect costs. Direct costs are the expenditure on elements that goes straight into producing the product or service. They include expenditure on raw materials and components and the wages of production staff or front-line service delivery staff. Indirect costs are often called overheads. **Overheads** or indirect costs are the expenses that do not contribute directly to the product or service being produced and therefore cannot be attributed to a particular job. Indirect costs or overheads include indirect labour costs, indirect material costs and indirect expenses. Office cleaners, catering staff and security staff are good examples of indirect labour costs for most organisations. Indirect material costs are the expenditure on cleaning materials, maintenance materials and subsidised food for employees. Indirect expenses are charges for items that have to be met, but that have no direct relationship to the cost of production. Indirect expenses include rent, heating and lighting bills and insurance.

Fixed costs do not change directly in relation to the level of activity or production, but have to be paid out, usually on a short-term basis such as monthly or quarterly. Fixed costs include many of the indirect costs just mentioned such as rent, insurance and maintenance contracts. Variable costs are sometimes called marginal costs. This is quite simply due to the marginal costing technique attributing variable costs only to the units of production/cost. Marginal costing is looked at later in this chapter. Hence variable costs are those that vary in relation to the level of activity or production and include direct labour costs and direct materials costs. **Prime costs** are the sum of direct wages and direct materials (prime costs = direct wages + direct materials).

Absorption costing

The use of absorption costing to provide quotes for jobs takes account of both fixed and variable costs. Absorption costing aims to ensure that all the overhead costs incurred by the business are covered by the revenues it receives. The data generated by absorption costing aims to provide information that can be used to give quotes for jobs. If an accurate quote for a job is to be provided, a correct amount has to be included in the quote to cover the portion of overheads incurred in carrying out the job. This requires a decision to be made on what basis the organisation is going to allocate overheads. Is it going to allocate them on the basis of materials used in jobs, the amount paid in direct wages to complete the job or merely the number of units produced?

There are six methods of absorbing production overheads. These overhead absorption rates (OAR) are outlined in the worked example below. Comment on the calculations being carried out is also provided.

EXAMPLE QUESTION

Absorption costing

(a) Calculate six different overhead absorption rates for Job 03/2014 and indicate the total overhead cost incurred for each OAR.

(b) Using the most appropriate overhead absorption rate, calculate a quote for Job 03/2014.

Production Department – Monthly Costs Report – March 2009

Total cost centre overheads (TCCO)	£60,000
Number of cost units	1600 units
Direct labour hours	5000 hours
Machine hours	4000 hours
Direct wages	£50,000
Direct materials	£40,000
(Prime cost = direct wages + direct materials)	

Job Number 03/2014

Direct material cost	£5000
Direct wages paid (£6.00 per hour)	£3750
Time taken on machine	500 hours
Number of units produced	250 units

Workings, answers and comments – part (a)

1 Cost unit OAR

$$\frac{\text{TCCO}}{\text{Number of cost units}} = \frac{\pounds 60{,}000}{1600} = \pounds 37.50 \text{ overhead per unit}$$

The use of the cost unit OAR means that overheads are charged at a rate of £37.50 per unit supplied. Therefore, the use of the cost unit OAR for Job 03/2014 would result in an overhead charge of £9375 (£37.50 × 250 units produced).

The cost unit OAR is appropriate only if all units of production are the same.

2 Direct labour OAR

$$\frac{\text{TCCO}}{\text{Number of direct labour hours}} = \frac{\pounds 60{,}000}{5000}$$

$$= \pounds 12 \text{ overhead per direct labour hour (DLH)}$$

The use of the direct labour OAR means that overheads are charged at a rate of £12.00 per hour spent directly working on the job. The use of the direct labour OAR for Job 03/2014 is shown in the worked answer for Question (b). This method of absorbing or allocating overheads requires accurate records to be kept regarding the number of direct labour hours worked. However, this absorption rate is particularly suitable if the production department is labour intensive, as there will be a direct relationship between time spent on production and the overheads incurred.

3 Machine hour OAR

$$\frac{\text{TCCO}}{\text{Overhead per machine hour}} = \frac{£60{,}000}{4000} = £15 \text{ overhead per machine hour}$$

The use of the machine hour OAR means that overheads are charged at a rate of £15.00 per hour spent using machines to complete the job. Hence the use of the machine hour OAR for Job 03/2014 would result in an overhead charge of £7500 (£15 × 500 units produced). This method of absorbing or allocating overheads requires accurate records to be kept regarding the number of machine hours used. However, this absorption rate is particularly suitable if the production department is machine intensive, as there will be a direct relationship between machining time and the overheads incurred.

4 Direct wage percentage OAR

$$\frac{\text{TCCO}}{\text{Direct wages}} = \frac{£60{,}000}{£50{,}000} \times 100 = 120\%$$

The use of the direct wage percentage OAR will result in an overhead charge of £1.20 for every £1 of direct wages paid for completion of the job. Consequently, the use of the direct wage percentage OAR for Job 03/2014 results in an overhead charge of £4500 (£3750 × 120 per cent). This overhead absorption rate is in many cases an appropriate OAR as it takes account of rates of pay and the number of hours worked, which usually relate directly to the time a unit takes to produce. However, if there is considerable variation in the rates of pay workers receive, this method of overhead absorption or allocation is much less suitable.

5 Direct material cost percentage OAR

$$\frac{\text{TCCO}}{\text{Direct material cost}} = \frac{£60{,}000}{£40{,}000} \times 100 = 150\%$$

The use of the direct material cost percentage OAR will result in an overhead charge of £1.50 for every £1 of direct material used in the job. The overheads for Job 03/2014 resulting from the use of the direct material cost percentage are £7500 (£5000 × 150 per cent). This overhead absorption rate does not take account of time, i.e. if two jobs take the same amount of time to complete but one job uses more expensive materials, the overhead absorption rates will differ.

6 Prime cost percentage OAR

$$\frac{\text{TCCO}}{\text{Prime costs}} = \frac{£60{,}000}{£90{,}000} \times 100 = 66.7\%$$

The use of the prime cost percentage OAR will result in an overhead charge of £0.67 for every £1 of prime cost for the job. Hence the use of the prime cost percentage OAR will give an overhead charge of £5836.25 (£8750 × 66.7 per cent). This overhead absorption rate combines the downside of both the direct materials OAR and direct wages OAR, without having any benefits of its own.

Workings, answers and comments – part (b)

The next step is to apply one of the overhead absorption rates to Job 03/2014 and calculate a quote or total cost for Job 03/2014. There is considerable variation in the overheads to be charged depending on the overhead absorption rate used, from £9375 with the cost unit OAR down to £4500 with the direct wage OAR. In theory, any of the six overhead absorption rates can be used to provide a quote for a job. However, the company must choose one overhead absorption rate to use in its production department and use it consistently. In most instances the overheads incurred relate to the time a job spends in production, so it is usually best to choose a rate that takes account of time, such as the direct labour hours OAR or the direct machine hours OAR.

The production department in the example has marginally more labour hours (5000 hours) than machine hours (4000 hours), hence the company incurs overhead predominantly to provide labour. Therefore, use of the direct labour hours OAR would be most appropriate and give a total cost of £97,500, as shown in the following calculation.

Job No 03/2014

1 Number of hours worked
= Direct wages paid/hourly rate
= £3750/£6 per hour
= 625 hours worked on Job 03/2014

2 Calculation of overheads
= Number of hours worked × Direct labour OAR
= 625 × £12 (from answer to Q1)
= £7500

3 Calculation of quote for job 03/2014

	£
Direct materials	5000
Direct wages	3750
Prime cost	8750
Overheads	7500
Total Cost	16,250

Check your understanding

Do you understand the six different ways in which production overheads can be absorbed into the costs for a particular job?

Check your understanding by briefly explaining the six different absorption rates.

Marginal costing

Marginal costing is the technique of charging variable costs to the cost of production units. This is a direct contrast with absorption costing where, in addition to variable costs, fixed costs or overheads are charged to cost units by use of one of the overhead absorption rates examined in the previous section.

A key figure in marginal costing is the contribution. This is the difference between sales and variable costs and is a contribution towards fixed costs. Therefore, fixed costs for a period are written off against the contribution for that period to give the final profit or loss for the period. The worked example below demonstrates the calculation of profit and contribution. Contribution can be calculated for one unit or any chosen level of sales.

EXAMPLE QUESTION

Calculation of contribution

A product sells for £75 and has variable costs of £45. During the period ending 31 March 2009 the product sold 3500 units. Fixed costs for the period were £30,000. Calculate the total profit, contribution per unit and contribution for sales of 3500 units.

Working

	per unit	*3500 units*
Selling price	£75	£262,500
less Variable costs	£45	£157,500
Contribution	£30	£105,000
less Fixed cost		£30,000
Profit		£75,000

Answer

Total profit is £75,000, contribution per unit is £30, and contribution for 3500 units is £105,000.

Marginal costing and decision making

Marginal costing can assist in decision making, particularly when deciding:

- which products to manufacture;
- whether to stop production of one or more products;
- whether to accept a special order or contract;
- whether to make or buy a component.

EXAMPLE QUESTION

Which products to manufacture

A company has a choice of manufacturing two out of three products. Indicate which products should be manufactured when each of the following ranking methods is applied to the information given below.

1 Ranking by contribution.
2 Ranking by profit/volume ratio.
3 Ranking by total contribution.

Information provided

	Product A	*Product B*	*Product C*
Selling price per unit	£35	£60	£45
Variable costs per unit			
Materials	£10	£24	£18
Labour	£6	£14	£8
Overheads	£4	£6	£6
Total cost	£20	£44	£32
Contribution per unit	£15	£16	£13

1 Ranking by contribution

Working and comment

This method of deciding which products to manufacture assumes that there are no limits on production resources or sales that can be achieved. Therefore, the amount of the unit contribution can be the decision criterion.

Answer

Products A and B have the highest unit contributions, £15 and £16 respectively, and would therefore be the preferred products for manufacture.

2 Ranking by profit/volume ratio

Working and comment

If the products have a maximum sales income that can be achieved from any of the three products, then the profit/volume ratio can be used to rank the products. If maximum sales of £100,000 could be achieved for each of the three products, the calculation would be

$$\text{Profit/Volume ratio} = \frac{\text{Contribution}}{\text{Selling price per unit}} \times 100$$

$$\text{Product A} = \frac{£15}{£35} \times 100 = 42.9\%$$

$$\text{Product B} = \frac{£16}{£60} \times 100 = 26.7\%$$

$$\text{Product C} = \frac{£13}{£45} \times 100 = 28.9\%$$

→

With sales of £100,000 the contribution from Product A would be £42,900, 42.9 per cent of £100,000; for Product B the contribution would be £26,700, 26.7 per cent of £100,000; and for Product C the contribution would be £28,900, 28.9 per cent of £100,000.

Answer

In this instance the company should choose Products A and C as they make the biggest contributions to fixed costs.

3 Ranking by total contribution

Working and comment

If the maximum sales achievable for each product vary, ranking should be by the total contribution that each product makes to fixed costs. If maximum sales achievable are 5000 units of Product A, or 2500 units of Product B or 3500 of Product C, the following ranking exercise helps establish which products should be produced.

$$\text{Total contribution} = \text{sales units} \times \text{contribution per unit}$$

Product A – Total contribution = 5000 units × £15 = £75,000
Product B – Total contribution = 2500 units × £16 = £40,000
Product C – Total contribution = 3500 units × £13 = £45,500

Answer

Products A and C have the highest total contribution and should therefore be the products manufactured.

EXAMPLE QUESTION

Ceasing manufacture of a product

A company produces a range of three products. The profit and loss account for the period ending 31 March 2009 shows that Product B has made a loss. The managing director suggests that Product B should be dropped as this will not influence sales of the other products. Produce a marginal cost statement for the period ending 31 March 2009 and advise the managing director as regards dropping Product B.

Information provided

Profit and loss account, year ended 31 March 2009

	Product A	*Product B*	*Product C*
Sales	250,000	200,000	140,000
Direct materials	62,500	110,000	32,500
Direct labour	55,000	60,000	40,000
Variable overheads	35,000	12,000	29,000
Fixed overheads	50,000	65,000	30,000
Total costs	202,500	247,000	131,500
Profit/(Loss)	47,500	(47,000)	8,500

Working and comment – marginal cost statement

Marginal cost statement, year ended 31 March 2009

	Product A	*Product B*	*Product C*	*Total*
Sales	250,000	200,000	140,000	590,000
Direct materials	62,500	110,000	32,500	205,000
Direct labour	55,000	60,000	40,000	155,000
Variable overheads	35,000	12,000	29,000	76,000
Total variable costs	152,500	182,000	101,500	436,000
Contribution	97,500	18,000	38,500	154,000
Less total fixed costs				145,000
Profit				9,000

The marginal cost statement above shows that Product B makes a contribution of £18,000 to fixed costs. If the company ceased to manufacture Product B, the contribution of £18,000 would be lost and the company would make a total loss of £9000, calculated in the following way: profit £9000 – Product B contribution £18,000 = –£9000 loss. The general rule is that it is usually expedient to continue with a product that makes a contribution to fixed costs.

Answer

Advise the managing director to continue manufacturing Product B.

EXAMPLE QUESTION

Acceptance of a special order or contract

A company manufactures a product that has variable costs of £15 per unit and a selling price of £19.50. A regular customer asks for an additional 3000 units as well as its normal order, but wants to negotiate a special price of £18 per unit for the additional units. Should the company agree?

Working and comment

In this situation there are clearly issues of customer relationships and the behaviour of competitors, particularly if the additional order is not accepted. However, the financial viewpoint is straightforward. The variable costs of the product are £15, hence any selling price above £15 will give a contribution. Accordingly for financial reasons it is worth accepting the order at the reduced price of £18 per unit. In this case the general rule applies that any product giving a contribution is worth manufacturing.

In contrast it would not make financial sense to sell the product at a price less than variable costs as this would result in a negative contribution. Similarly, if the company could supply the required additional 3000 units at £18 but to do so had to reduce its current sales at £19.50, accepting the additional order would reduce the total contribution and therefore it should not be accepted.

Answer

In this case accept the additional order at a price of £18.

EXAMPLE QUESTION

Making or buying a product

Company CHC can make Component X itself and incur variable costs of £27 per unit or purchase the component from Company RBC for £30 per unit. Which is the best option for Company CHC?

Working and comment

If Company CHC has unused capacity, it makes sense for the component to be produced in-house as the variable cost of £27 per unit is lower than the buying-in price of £30 per unit. It should be noted that fixed costs are omitted from the comparison as they will continue to be paid even when none of the factory facilities is in use. If the company does not have unused capacity and in-house manufacture of the component requires manufacture of another product to be stopped, further analysis is required.

Answer

In this case Company CHC should manufacture the component in-house.

Check your understanding

Do you understand how marginal costing can assist organisations in decision making concerning the purchase and manufacture of goods?

Check your understanding by explaining how marginal costing can be used to help a company decide:

- which products to manufacture;
- whether it should cease the manufacture of particular products;
- whether it should accept a detailed contract to manufacture and supply goods;
- whether it should make or buy in a component.

Investment appraisal

Investment appraisal techniques are used by management to help in making decisions concerning investment in long-term projects and spending capital finance. The application of the investment appraisal methods discussed in this chapter provides quantitative data for use in this type of management decision making. Quantitative data can be useful and pertinent when decisions are being made concerning the investment of capital that an organisation has raised. Hence there is a clear overlap between investment appraisal, an area of management accounting, and the use to which the funds or capital raised are put (*see* section on financial management earlier in this chapter). Capital will be invested in major projects such as the purchase of new equipment or machinery, the acquisition of another company or the development and launch of a new product or service.

Thorough and objective evaluation of an investment opportunity before capital is spent will include assessment of both quantitative and qualitative information. Assessment of any investment opportunity will also include estimating the risk involved in not making the investment and an evaluation of the risk if the project fails. The quantitative assessment of an investment opportunity can be carried out by using any of the investment appraisal methods discussed in this chapter: payback, accounting rate of return, net present value and internal rate of return. An investment represents the commitment of money now for gains or returns in the future, and the quantitative data generated by investment appraisal will help answer the following questions concerning an investment:

1 Will the investment provide an adequate financial return?
2 Is the investment the best alternative from the options the company has available?
3 What is the cost if the project fails?

Payback method

The **payback method** measures the length of time taken for the return on the investment exactly to equal the amount originally invested. Hence where two or more investment proposals are being considered, the one that recovers the original investment in the shortest time is the more acceptable.

EXAMPLE QUESTION

Payback method

Consider each of the three investment opportunities outlined below. Apply the payback method and state which would be the preferred investment.

	Investment A	*Investment B*	*Investment C*
Year 0 original investment	(£20,000)	(£30,000)	(£40,000)
Year 1 net cashflow	£12,000	£8,000	£16,000
Year 2 net cashflow	£6,000	£8,000	£12,000
Year 3 net cashflow	£6,000	£6,000	£10,000
Year 4 net cashflow	£4,000	£6,000	£8,000
Year 5 net cashflow	£4,000	£6,000	£8,000

Example calculation – Payback method – Investment A

Investment A = £20,000

	Cashflow	*Cumulative cashflow*
Year 1 net cashflow	£12,000	£12,000
Year 2 net cashflow	£6,000	£18,000
Year 3 net cashflow	£6,000	£24,000
Year 4 net cashflow	£4,000	£28,000
Year 5 net cashflow	£4,000	£32,000

→

1 The investment has been paid back by the end of Year 3.
2 But exactly when in Year 3 does payback occur?
3 At the end of Year 2 £18,000 has been paid back, leaving £2000 of the original £20,000 investment still to be paid back.
4 The total payback in Year 3 is £6000, therefore the calculation below shows that the £2000 is paid back in the first four months of Year 3.

$$\frac{\text{£2000 (to payback after Year 2)}}{\text{£6000 (Year 3 net cashflow)}} \times 12 \text{ (months in a year)} = \frac{2000}{6000} \times 12 = 4 \text{ months}$$

Therefore, the total payback period is 2 years 4 months.

The payback period for Investments B and C can be calculated in the same way.

	Investment A	*Investment B*	*Investment C*
Payback period	2 years 4 months	4 years 4 months	3 years 3 months

Answer

Hence the preferred investment is A, as this pays back in the shortest time.

Advantages and disadvantages of the payback method

The advantages of the payback method are that the **payback period** is simple to calculate and easy to understand. However, the payback method takes no account of profit, loss and depreciation from the sale of fixed assets, although it does recognise the uncertainty of the future. Therefore, the payback method acknowledges that the sooner the investment is recovered, the smaller the risk involved, and thus uses the earliest cashflows first. If the money is to be invested in a project that is subject to rapid technological change, the project with the most rapid payback and turnaround will be the most favourable.

Further drawbacks of the payback method are that it ignores all cashflow after the payback period and the total life of the project. Other difficulties are that no allowances are made for the lower value of money paid back in the future. The value of money paid back today is more than that of money paid back in the future, i.e. £100 today is worth more than £100 in five years' time. An added problem with the payback method is that profits are disregarded and an investment with a shorter payback period may be selected even if it is less profitable overall than a project that takes longer to pay back. For example, an investment of £5000 will pay back quicker than a £50,000 investment, regardless of the fact that the £50,000 investment may be more profitable in the long run. Another disadvantage is that the payback method relies on estimates of net cash inflows and the timing of their receipt.

Accounting rate of return

The **accounting rate of return (ARR)** expresses the profit generated by an investment or project as a percentage of the capital invested.

$$ARR = \frac{\text{Profit}}{\text{Capital employed}} \times 100$$

In the ARR calculation the net profit before interest and taxation figure is used and averaged over the lifetime of the project. The capital employed can be either the **initial capital employed** or the **average capital employed** over the lifetime of the project. The latter takes into account the residual value of the project at the end of its working life – *see* method 2 below.

Therefore, two methods for carrying out ARR calculations exist:

Method 1

$$ARR = \frac{\text{average net profit per annum}}{\text{initial capital employed}} \times 100$$

Method 2

$$ARR = \frac{\text{average net profit per annum}}{\text{average capital employed*}} \times 100$$

$$\text{*average capital employed} = \frac{\text{initial capital employed + residual value}}{2}$$

The worked example below uses method 2, average capital employed.

EXAMPLE QUESTION

Accounting rate of return

Consider each of the three investment opportunities outlined below. Apply the accounting rate of return (ARR) method and state which would be the preferred investment.

	Investment A	*Investment B*	*Investment C*
Year 0 original investment	(£20,000)	(£30,000)	(£40,000)
Year 1 net profit	£12,000	£8,000	£16,000
Year 2 net profit	£6,000	£8,000	£12,000
Year 3 net profit	£6,000	£6,000	£10,000
Year 4 net profit	£4,000	£6,000	£8,000
Year 5 net profit	£4,000	£6,000	£8,000

Example calculation – accounting rate of return – method 2

	Investment A	*Investment B*	*Investment C*
Total net return	£32,000	£34,000	£54,000
less original investment	£20,000	£30,000	£40,000
Net profit	£12,000	£4,000	£14,000
Years of life	5	5	5
Average profit per annum (profit/years of life)	£2400	£800	£2800
Residual value	£5000	£5000	£7000

→

Average capital employed	$\frac{£20,000 + £5000}{2}$	$\frac{£30,000 + £5000}{2}$	$\frac{£40,000 + £5000}{2}$
	= £12,500	= £17,500	= £22,500
Average rate of return	$\frac{£2400}{£12,500} \times 100$	$\frac{£800}{£17,500} \times 100$	$\frac{£2800}{£22,500} \times 100$
	= 19.2%	= 4.6%	= 12.4%

Answer

Hence the preferred investment is A, as this shows the highest return.

Advantages and disadvantages of the accounting rate of return method

The ARR encompasses the entire life of the project and all expected profits. Its other principal advantage is its comparative simplicity to calculate and understand. However, there are a number of disadvantages relating to this method of investment appraisal. These include the net profit being defined in different ways; for example, should net profit before or after depreciation on the investment be used? Other difficulties include the ARR using profits as a key factor in the calculation, whereas in investment decisions cashflow is the crucial factor. Also the ARR does not make allowances for the different value of money over time, compared with **discounted cashflow methods** (see the next method of investment appraisal to be looked at, net present value). High returns in the early years of an investment have a greater net worth and are easier to predict, but these factors are not taken into account in ARR calculations. Interpretation of the ARR results can be ambiguous as often there will be no indication of what an acceptable ARR would be for a specific project, and, furthermore, different ARRs will be acceptable in different situations.

Finally, the use of residual investment values can substantially affect the ARR calculated. The use of residual values and an average capital employed can make a notable difference in the ARR values for a project. Remember that residual values are difficult to estimate and the difference they can make is illustrated below. The higher the residual value, the lower the ARR.

EXAMPLE

Average net profit per annum = £100,000
Initial capital employed = £300,000
Residual values = £10,000 and £50,000

1 Residual value = £10,000

$$\text{Average capital employed} = \frac{£300,000 + £10,000}{2} = £155,000$$

$$ARR = \frac{£100,000}{£155,000} \times 100$$

$$ARR = 64.5\%$$

2 Residual value = £50,000

$$\text{Average capital employed} = \frac{£300,000 + £50,000}{2} = £175,000$$

$$ARR = \frac{£100,000}{£175,000} \times 100$$

$$ARR = 57.1\%$$

Despite the disadvantages, the ARR method of investment appraisal is suitable if the project is short term and accurate estimates can be made for any residual values to be included in the calculations.

Check your understanding

Do you understand the advantages and disadvantages of payback and accounting rate of return as methods of investment appraisal?

Check your understanding by comparing and contrasting the payback and accounting rate of return methods of investment appraisal.

Net present value

The **net present value (NPV)** method of investment appraisal makes allowances for money received in the future being worth less than if it were received today. Therefore, the NPV method converts future net cashflows into present-day values by discounting the value of money that is expected to be received in the future.

If the discounted net cashflows exceed the original investment then the project could go ahead. When choosing between two or more projects, the project with the highest positive NPV exceeds its original investment by the greatest amount and is usually the preferred project. If the discounted net cashflows are less than the original investment, then the investment should not be allowed to proceed as money will be lost. An acceptable interest rate or rate of return has to be decided on and the discounting factors to be used in the NPV calculation need to be read from a discount table.

In selecting a discounting rate the following need to be considered:

- the rate of interest that the company could obtain if the money were invested outside the business;
- the cost of capital required to make the investment;
- the rate of return (internal) that the company expects to gain on investments.

If the company is to be profitable, then in the long run the rate of return (internal) needs to exceed the external rate that it can earn investing outside the business. The cashflows are multiplied by the discount cashflow value from the discount tables to give the discounted value of future net cashflows. The discounted net cashflows are added up and the original investment subtracted – if the total NPV is positive, the project is acceptable.

EXAMPLE QUESTION

Net present value method

Consider each of the three investment opportunities outlined below. Apply the NPV method of investment appraisal and state which would be the preferred investment. The cost of capital is 8 per cent.

	Investment A	*Investment B*	*Investment C*
Year 0 original investment	(£20,000)	(£30,000)	(£40,000)
Year 1 net cashflow	£10,000	£6,000	£12,000
Year 2 net cashflow	£8,000	£6,000	£12,000
Year 3 net cashflow	£6,000	£6,000	£12,000
Year 4 net cashflow	£4,000	£8,000	£12,000
Year 5 net cashflow	£4,000	£12,000	£12,000

Calculation – net present value

	Investment A			*Investment B*			*Investment C*		
	Cashflow	*DCF 8%*	*Net Cashflow*	*Cashflow*	*DCF 8%*	*Net Cashflow*	*Cashflow*	*DCF 8%*	*Net Cashflow*
Yr 0	(20,000)	1.000	(20,000)	(30,000)	1.000	(30,000)	(40,000)	1.000	(40,000)
Yr 1	10,000	.926	9,260	6,000	.926	5,556	12,000	.926	11,112
Yr 2	8,000	.858	6,864	6,000	.858	5,148	12,000	.858	10,296
Yr 3	6,000	.794	4,764	6,000	.794	4,764	12,000	.794	9,528
Yr 4	4,000	.735	2,940	8,000	.735	5,880	12,000	.735	8,820
Yr 5	4,000	.681	2,724	12,000	.681	8,172	12,000	.681	8,172
			+6,652			–480			+7,928

Answer

Hence the preferred investment is C, as this has the highest positive NPV.

Advantages and disadvantages of the net present value method

The main advantage of the NPV method is that cashflows and hence the relevance of liquidity are both taken account of in the calculations. The other fundamental advantage is that it takes account of the time value of money, unlike the payback and ARR methods. The comparison between projects' NPV values is straightforward and it is easy to judge which is the most profitable project. The disadvantages of the NPV method lie in the difficulty of accurately estimating the initial cost of the project, cash in-flows and the time periods in which cash in-flows will occur.

Internal rate of return

The **internal rate of return (IRR)** method of investment appraisal is similar to the net present value method. The key difference between NPV and IRR is that IRR seeks a discount rate at which the net cash in-flows, when discounted, exactly equal the amount originally invested, i.e. NPV = 0. The initial pieces of information that have to be sought for an IRR calculation are a discount rate giving a positive return or positive NPV, and a discount rate giving a negative NPV. There is no easy way of ascertaining which discount rates will give a positive or negative NPV, except by trial and error coupled with careful judgement.

The IRR is determined by interpolation between the discount rate giving a positive NPV and that giving a negative NPV (*see* guidelines below). The interpolation between the two rates is done by use of the formula shown below. This is not an exact method and the closer together the two discount rates used in the calculation, the more accurate the answer will be.

The formula for calculating the IRR is as follows:

$$\text{IRR} = \text{Positive rate} + \frac{(\text{Positive NPV} \times \text{Difference between discount rates})}{(\text{Range of NPV values})}$$

Guidelines for choosing discounting cashflow rates for IRR calculations

1 You have to find two DCF rates:
   (a) one giving a positive NPV value;
   (b) one giving a negative NPV value.
2 Which DCF rates do you choose?
   (a) Start with a rate of around 10 per cent. If this gives you a *total negative NPV*, then you need to choose a rate that is less than 10 per cent to get a *total positive NPV*, say 5 per cent.
   (b) If the first DCF rate you choose, say 10 per cent, gives you a *positive total NPV*, then the second rate will have to be greater than 10 per cent: you could try 15 per cent.
   (c) The two DCF rates used do not want to be more than 5 per cent apart, although they can of course be less than 5 per cent apart.
3 An alternative to starting with, say, 10 per cent is to start with the DCF rate you may have used in a previous NPV calculation on the same data. To do this the NPV given must be fairly close to zero.

EXAMPLE QUESTION

Internal rate of return method

The company considering each of the three investment opportunities shown below requires a return of at least 10 per cent on all the investments it makes. Using the IRR method of investment appraisal, state which of the three investment opportunities the company should seriously consider.

→

	Investment A	*Investment B*	*Investment C*
Year 0 original investment	(£20,000)	(£30,000)	(£40,000)
Year 1 net cashflow	£10,000	£6,000	£12,000
Year 2 net cashflow	£8,000	£6,000	£12,000
Year 3 net cashflow	£6,000	£6,000	£12,000
Year 4 net cashflow	£4,000	£8,000	£12,000
Year 5 net cashflow	£4,000	£12,000	£12,000

Example calculation – internal rate of return – investment A

	Cashflow	*DCF 22%*	*Net Cashflow*	*Cashflow*	*DCF 23%*	*Net Cashflow*
Year 0	(20,000)	1.000	(20,000)	(20,000)	1.000	(20,000)
Year 1	10,000	0.820	8,200	10,000	0.813	8,130
Year 2	8,000	0.672	5,376	8,000	0.661	5,288
Year 3	6,000	0.551	3,306	6,000	0.537	3,222
Year 4	4,000	0.451	1,804	4,000	0.437	1,748
Year 5	4,000	0.370	1,480	4,000	0.355	1,420
			+166			–192

Internal rate of return = 22% + (166/358 × 1) = 22.464%

Example calculation – internal rate of return – investment B

	Cashflow	*DCF 7%*	*Net Cashflow*	*Cashflow*	*DCF 8%*	*Net Cashflow*
Year 0	(30,000)	1.000	(30,000)	(30,000)	1.000	(30,000)
Year 1	6,000	0.935	5,610	6,000	0.926	5,556
Year 2	6,000	0.873	5,238	6,000	0.857	5,142
Year 3	6,000	0.816	4,896	6,000	0.794	4,764
Year 4	8,000	0.763	6,104	8,000	0.735	5,880
Year 5	12,000	0.713	8,556	12,000	0.681	8,172
			+404			–486

Internal rate of return = 7% + (404/890 × 1) = 7.454%

Example calculation – internal rate of return – investment C

	Cashflow	*DCF 16%*	*Net Cashflow*	*Cashflow*	*DCF 15%*	*Net Cashflow*
Year 0	(40,000)	1.000	(40,000)	(40,000)	1.000	(40,000)
Year 1	12,000	0.862	10,344	12,000	0.870	10,440
Year 2	12,000	0.743	8,916	12,000	0.756	9,072
Year 3	12,000	0.641	7,692	12,000	0.658	7,896
Year 4	12,000	0.552	6,624	12,000	0.572	6,864
Year 5	12,000	0.476	5,712	12,000	0.497	5,964
			–712			+236

Internal rate of return = 15% + (236/948 × 1) = 15.249%

Answer

The investments that should be seriously considered are investments A and C, as both have an IRR of greater than 10 per cent.

Advantages and disadvantages of the internal rate of return method

The two clear advantages of the IRR method are that emphasis is placed on liquidity in the calculation and it results in a clear percentage return required on investment. The IRR is a measure of the intensity of capital use and also gives a return for risks. In the worked example for Investment A, if the cost of capital is 15 per cent and the IRR is 22.464 per cent, the return for the risk is therefore 7.464 per cent, the difference between the two figures (22.464 – 15). In general IRR is a more difficult method to apply than NPV. In most cases IRR and NPV will give the same answer as to acceptance or rejection of an investment, but may vary in ranking, thus possibly leading to different choices.

The disadvantages of the IRR method are that the reasoning behind the calculation is not easy to understand and it is difficult to determine two interest rates to interpolate between. Careful judgement should be exercised when making decisions based on IRR calculations. For example, an IRR of 25 per cent may appear attractive, but if the original investment is only £500, then an IRR of 15 per cent on an original investment of £10,000 would be more sensible.

Check your understanding

Do you understand the similarities and differences between NPV and IRR methods of investment appraisal?

Check your understanding by explaining the use of both NPV and IRR as methods of investment apprasial.

Financial reporting

In the UK companies are obliged by law to produce an annual report and accounts that relate to their financial and business performance. Companies need to ensure their annual report and accounts have been audited and a copy filed with the Registrar of Companies at Companies House in London. The Companies Acts of 1981, 1985 and 1989 specify the layout and format of modern-day published accounts. The published accounts have to contain certain pieces of information to satisfy the legal requirements. The types of information required include information on the directors and their report, **financial statements**, information to clarify the details of the report and accounts, and an **auditor's report**.

The section of the published accounts giving information about the directors is often at the front. In the case of many large well-known companies, e.g. Marks & Spencer or British Aerospace, a photograph of each director is accompanied by a vignette on their career to date and their role on the board. These directors have to produce a report to be included in the published accounts. The report must provide fair comment on the company's performance over the financial year and important events that have occurred since the year-end. Details of transactions involving its own shares by the company must also be included in the directors' report. Comment must also be included on probable future developments that the company is undertaking. In the introductory case study, reporting on Tesco annoucing its 2007/08 profits resulted in the company's share price rising by 30 pence or 7.8 per cent. This is linked directly with the company reporting growth in a struggling UK environment and good growth prospects in its overseas business.

The financial statements that need to be included in published accounts are the profit and loss account, the balance sheet and a cashflow statement. The profit and loss account and the balance sheet are summary statements. The profit and loss account provides a summary of the company's income or sales revenue and expenditure, leaving a profit or loss on the bottom line. This is complemented by the balance sheet, which summarises the company's financial position at the end of the financial year, showing its assets and liabilities. In contrast, the cashflow statement shows in detail how the business has financed its operations. The details included in a cashflow statement are the particulars of how money has been raised – shares, loans or profits – and how the money has been spent – to acquire fixed assets such as buildings and machinery, or to buy current assets such as stock, raw materials and components.

The other sections that need to appear in published accounts are a statement of accounting policies, notes to accounts and statistical information. Notes to accounts provide a large amount of detail relating to the accounts and activities of the company. Some of the details included in the notes are how the operating profit and turnover figures are calculated, how individual asset and liability figures are calculated, loans and interest payments, tax details, paid and proposed dividends, and changes to accounting policies. A complete list can be found in Dyson listed in further reading for this chapter. The statistical information section of the published accounts may compare the current year's financial performance with results from previous years. This can be done by use of the financial ratios for the business over two or more years – *see* Michael Brett's book.[9]

A necessary item in any annual report and accounts is the auditor's report. The auditor should be independent of the directors of the company and a member of one of the chartered professional accounting bodies approved to perform audits. The auditor's report is addressed to the shareholders and should ideally state that the report and accounts provide a true and fair view of the company's activities for the financial year examined. To do this the auditor needs to satisfy him-/herself that the reported assets exist and have been correctly valued in the accounts. The auditor also needs to ensure that the disclosure of liabilities is complete and thorough. The auditor may also inspect data and documents to confirm that entries in the books are genuine, as well as checking the accuracy of the books. Finally, the auditor should check that all benefits are accounted for and have been collected by the proper recipients.

However, the thoroughness of auditing processes has been called into question by the collapse of Enron, the energy trader, in the United States. Arthur Andersen, an 89-year-old company and one of the world's top five accounting firms, signed off Enron's annual report for 2001. Just a few months after this Enron admitted its accounts for 2001 and the previous three years were more or less a work of fiction. Andersen then lost most of its business and 20,000 of its 28,000 employees in the United States. In June 2002 a jury in the US found Andersen guilty of shredding documents relating to Enron. Andersen was considering an appeal.

The annual report and accounts need to give a true and fair view of a company's activities for the financial year examined, as they provide significant information on the company and its activities. Hence a company's annual report and accounts will be of interest to a variety of players who want to know about the business. This will allow concerned parties or financial stakeholders to make informed judgements regarding their role in relation to the company.

Financial stakeholders

The state

The financial information provided determines the level and amount of taxation that a company will pay to the state. At the time of writing, in the UK the current level of corporation tax is 28 per cent and for small businesses it is 21 per cent.

Current and potential investors

The information provided in the annual report and accounts will allow current and potential investors to make informed judgements about future and current investments. For example, in April 2008 Tesco's shareholders would have very likely decided to hold on to their shares in the company, as profits had risen by 11.8 per cent with the company also showing significant growth in its international business. For further details see the introductory case study at the start of this chapter.

Employees

Companies that choose to involve employees in the running of the business may see the disclosure of financial information as an important element of the employees' participation. This is especially so if a profit-sharing or an employee share ownership scheme operates.

Creditors and Banks

These interested parties are concerned with the company's liquidity and need to assess the risk involved in offering credit or loans. The information disclosed in the annual report and accounts will be useful in assessing this risk.

Customers and debtors

Customers and **debtors** are stakeholders who purchase the company's products and services and may find the information disclosed in the annual report and accounts useful in assessing the risk of placing long-term or large orders.

Competitors

Competitors as stakeholders typically find the information provided by the annual report and accounts a practical yardstick against which to measure their own performance. Insights into which directions competitors could be heading may be offered in their annual reports and accounts.

Check your understanding

Do you understand which information is available in a company's annual report and accounts and how different financial stakeholders could use this information?

Check your understanding by explaining how the following people and organisations might use Marks & Spencer's annual report and accounts:

- the John Lewis partnership;
- Mr John Jones who shops at M&S on Sauchiehall Street in Glasgow and is thinking of buying shares in the company;
- the Inland Revenue;
- Mrs Susan Atkin who works at M&S at Meadowhall in Sheffield and owns 1000 shares in the company.

Summary

This chapter examined financial external environmental factors that impact on organisations as well as examining some of the financial activities that organisations routinely undertake. The following summary covers all aspects of this chapter.

1 Financial external environmental factors that have influenced many businesses in the UK are the euro and the minimum wage. The euro was introduced for business transactions in most European countries on 1 January 1999 and coins and notes followed on 1 January 2002. The minimum wage was introduced in the UK in April 1999, when it was £3.60 for adults; by October 2008 it was £5.73. Additionally, the state of the economy and a crisis such as the credit crunch will impact on businesses.

2 Financial management involves the raising and spending of capital finance by an organisation. Sources of capital for a company include its reserves (profits from previous years), borrowing money from a bank, financial institution or, if eligible, an organisation like the Prince's Trust, issuing shares, having a rights issue or seeking government funding.

3 Costing involves looking at and defining the costs involved in producing a product or service. Costs can be defined as fixed or variable. The cost of producing a product or service has three elements to it: the cost of materials, labour and overheads.

4 Absorption costing takes account of both fixed and variable costs, with the aim of ensuring that revenues cover all the overhead costs incurred.

5 Marginal costing allocates variable costs only to the cost of production units. A key figure in marginal costing is the difference between sales and variable costs, which is called contribution. Fixed costs are written off against contribution to give a final profit or loss.

6 The payback method of investment appraisal measures the length of time taken for the return on the investment to exactly equal the amount originally invested.

7 The accounting rate of return (ARR) expresses the profit an investment makes as a percentage of the capital invested. Like the payback method of investment appraisal it is easy to calculate and understand.

8 The net present value (NPV) method of investment appraisal takes account of all returns over the life of the investment and of money received in the future being of less value than that received today.

9 The internal rate of return (IRR) is similar to the NPV method, but seeks a discount rate at which cash inflows, when discounted, exactly equal the amount originally invested, i.e. NPV = 0.

10 Financial reports and accounts contain information on directors and their statement, financial statements (profit and loss account, balance sheet and cashflow statement), information and notes on the financial statements and an auditor's report. The annual report and accounts of a company provide financial stakeholders with information about the company that allows them to make informed decisions concerning their involvement with the company.

Chapter objectives and the exit case study

While reading this chapter and engaging in the activities, you should have learned how to apply theory and models and analyse situations. This means you should be able to meet the chapter objectives outlined at the beginning of the chapter. The table below shows which chapter objectives can be tested by the different questions.

Chapter objective	Check you have achieved this by
1 Discuss the external financial influences that can impact on an organisation.	answering case study questions 1 and 2.
2 Explain the activities of financial management, management accounting and financial reporting.	answering case study question 2.
3 Identify and evaluate the different financial stakeholders in an organisation.	answering case study question 3.

EXIT CASE STUDY 10.2

Minimum wage increases by 3.8%

by Andrew Taylor

The UK minimum wage is to rise by 3.8 per cent from October, in line with an increase in average earnings but slightly lower than prevailing retail price inflation, Prime Minister Gordon Brown announced on Wednesday. The rise in the adult rate, from £5.52 to £5.73 an hour, was welcomed by business leaders who had warned that increases above inflation would cost jobs in vulnerable areas such as hotels, catering and shops. The rate for 18- to 21-year-olds will also rise by 3.7 per cent to £4.77 an hour and by 3.8 per cent to £3.53 an hour for 16- to 17-years-olds. Union leaders, however, accused employers of scare mongering. They said that the rises would not cover increased food and energy bills, with annual retail price inflation currently running at 4.1 per cent.

The adult minimum wage rate has risen by 59 per cent since it was introduced at £3.60 an hour in April 1999 – more than twice the increase in the retail price index over the same period. A study by Eurostat, the European Union's statistical arm, reported last summer that Britain's minimum wage was the third-highest out of 20 EU nations and almost twice the then US federal level. Fears expressed by employers when the minimum wage was introduced, that it would cost 1.7m jobs, however, have proved groundless. John Hutton, business secretary, said on Wednesday that the number of jobs in the economy had risen by 2m since 1999.

Paul Myners, chairman of the Low Pay Commission, which recommended the increases to ministers said: 'Despite many predictions to the contrary, job numbers in the industries most affected by the minimum wage have grown, and grown significantly, over the same period.' Nonetheless, there was relief among employers that the latest rise had not exceeded increases in average earnings, currently running at 3.8 per cent. John Cridland, CBI deputy director-general, said: 'At a time of considerable uncertainty for businesses and with economic growth already slowing, we welcome today's moderate approach.' The Federation of Small Businesses said it was happy with the outcome while Chris Hannant, head of policy at the British Chambers of Commerce, said it was 'reassuring for employers that the national minimum wage will not increase above average earnings'.

Tony Woodley, joint general secretary of Unite, Britain's biggest union, however, complained: 'At a time when inequality is rising up the political agenda and business leaders are awarding themselves record pay rises, the lowest-paid workers continue to slip back. This can not continue.' Dave Prentis, general secretary of Unison, the largest public sector union, said the increase 'fell short of its aim to protect the poor from the constant price rises in essentials like fuel, food and housing. A much more realistic figure would be a minimum wage of £6.75'.

Brendan Barber, TUC general secretary, welcomed the rise. He said: 'The truth is that employers will be able to absorb these sensible increases without too much difficulty.' The Trades Union Congress has called for a rise of up to 29 per cent in the national minimum wage, provoking warnings of possible job losses from business leaders.

Source: from 'Minimum wage increases by 3.8%', *The Financial Times*, 5 March 2008 (Taylor, A.).

Exit case study questions

1 Summarise the situation the trade unions Unite and Unison would like to see as regards the minimum wage.

2 Imagine you were deputy director-general of the Confederation of British Industry, the employers organisation, and summarise the likely view of the CBI as regards the minimum wage.

3 Do you agree with the view of the trade unions Unite and Unison or the likely view of the CBI? Justify your answer. Should organisations consider the views of the trade unions, Unite and Unison, and the CBI? Explain your answer.

Short-answer questions

1. Explain the role of the finance function.
2. Define financial accounting.
3. When did European monetary union occur?
4. When was the national minimum wage introduced in the UK and what level was it set at initially?
5. Name four sources of finance for a company.
6. State the key difference between a share issue and a rights issue.
7. What is a sale and leaseback and when do companies use one?
8. Define management accounting.
9. What is the key difference between absorption and marginal costing?
10. What is the payback method?
11. State the key advantages of the NPV method of investment appraisal.
12. Define financial reporting.
13. Why is an auditors' report necessary in published accounts?
14. Name the three financial statements that must be included in published accounts.
15. What use would a competitor have for a company's published accounts?

Chapter objectives and assignment questions

While reading this chapter and engaging in the activities, you should have learned how to apply theory and models and analyse situations. This means you should be able to meet the chapter objectives outlined at the beginning of the chapter. The table below shows which chapter objectives can be tested by the different questions.

Chapter objective	Check you have achieved this by
1 Discuss the external financial influences that can impact on an organisation.	answering assignment questions 1 and 2.
2 Explain the activities of financial management, management accounting and financial reporting.	answering assignment question 3.
3 Identify and evaluate the different financial stakeholders in an organisation.	answering assignment question 4.

Assignment questions

1 Choose a private-sector organisation. Research and assess the impact of the external financial influences on the organisation's activities. Should such an organisation routinely assess the impact of the external financial influences on its commercial activities? Present your findings in a 2000-word report.

2 Choose a charity or public-sector organisation. Research and assess the impact of the minimum wage on the organisation's activities. In your opinion, is it relevant that a non-commercial organisation routinely assess the impact of financial matters, such as the minimum wage, on itself? Present your findings in a 2000-word report.

3 Discuss the importance of the finance function to both public- and private-sector organisations.

4 Evaluate the impact of the external environment and financial stakeholders on an organisation of your choice. Present your findings in a report, including an executive summary.

WEBLINKS available at **www.pearsoned.co.uk/capon**

- This site contains more about the collapse of Enron and the role of Arthur Andersen. Generally the BBC website is a good source of information about news and business news:
  http://news.bbc.co.uk/1/hi/business/1760107.stm
  http://news.bbc.co.uk/1/hi/business/2047122.stm
- These articles are about the collapse of the financial companies Northern Rock in the UK and Lehman Brothers in the US respectively:
  http://news.bbc.co.uk/1/hi/uk_politics/7258492.stm
  http://news.bbc.co.uk/1/hi/uk/7616996.stm
- This site is for the government Department for Business, Enterprise and Regulatory Reform, BERR. Click on 'Enterprise and Business Support' in the bottom left-hand corner. This will take you to topics related to supporting businesses, including small businesses:
  http://www.berr.gov.uk
- The Treasury website contains information about influences on organisations, including the chancellor's annual budget statement. Visit the home page at the address below and click on 'Budget' on the left-hand side of the screen:
  http://www.hm-treasury.gov.uk/

FURTHER READING

The following chapters cover the aspects of finance looked at in this chapter.

- Brett, M (2003) *How to Read the Financial Pages*, 6th edn, London: Random House Business Books.
- Dyson, J R (2007) *Accounting for Non-Accounting Students*, 7th edn, Chapters 1, 5 and 10, Harlow: Financial Times Prentice Hall.

- Reid, W and Myddelton, D R (2000) *The Meaning of Company Accounts*, 7th edn, Chapter 1, Aldershot: Gower.
- Wood, F and Sangster, A (2008) *Business Accounting: Volume 1*, 11th edn, Chapter 8, Harlow: Financial Times Prentice Hall.
- Wood, F and Sangster, A (2002) *Business Accounting: Volume 2*, 11th edn, Chapters 4 and 6, Harlow: Financial Times Prentice Hall.

REFERENCES

1. Helm, T (1998) 'Rome and Bonn clear the EMU hurdle', *Daily Telegraph*, 28 February.
2. Manning, A (1997) 'If it's good enough for everyone else, it's good enough for us', *Independent on Sunday*, 11 May.
3. Taylor, A (2008) 'Minimum wage increases by 3.8%', *Financial Times*, 5 March.
4. Press Association, (2008) 'RBS announces £12bn rights issue', 22 April.
5. Sibun, J (2008) 'Royal Bank of Scotland investors "will back Sir Fred Goodwin" ', *Daily Telegraph*, 21 April.
6. Hollinger, P (2008) 'Société Générale launches €5.5bn rights issue', *Financial Times*, 11 February.
7. http://www.bvca.co.uk/
8. http://www.princes-trust.org.uk/
9. Brett, M (2003) *How to Read the Financial Pages*, 6th edn, London: Random House Business Books.

CHAPTER 11

Managing knowledge and innovation

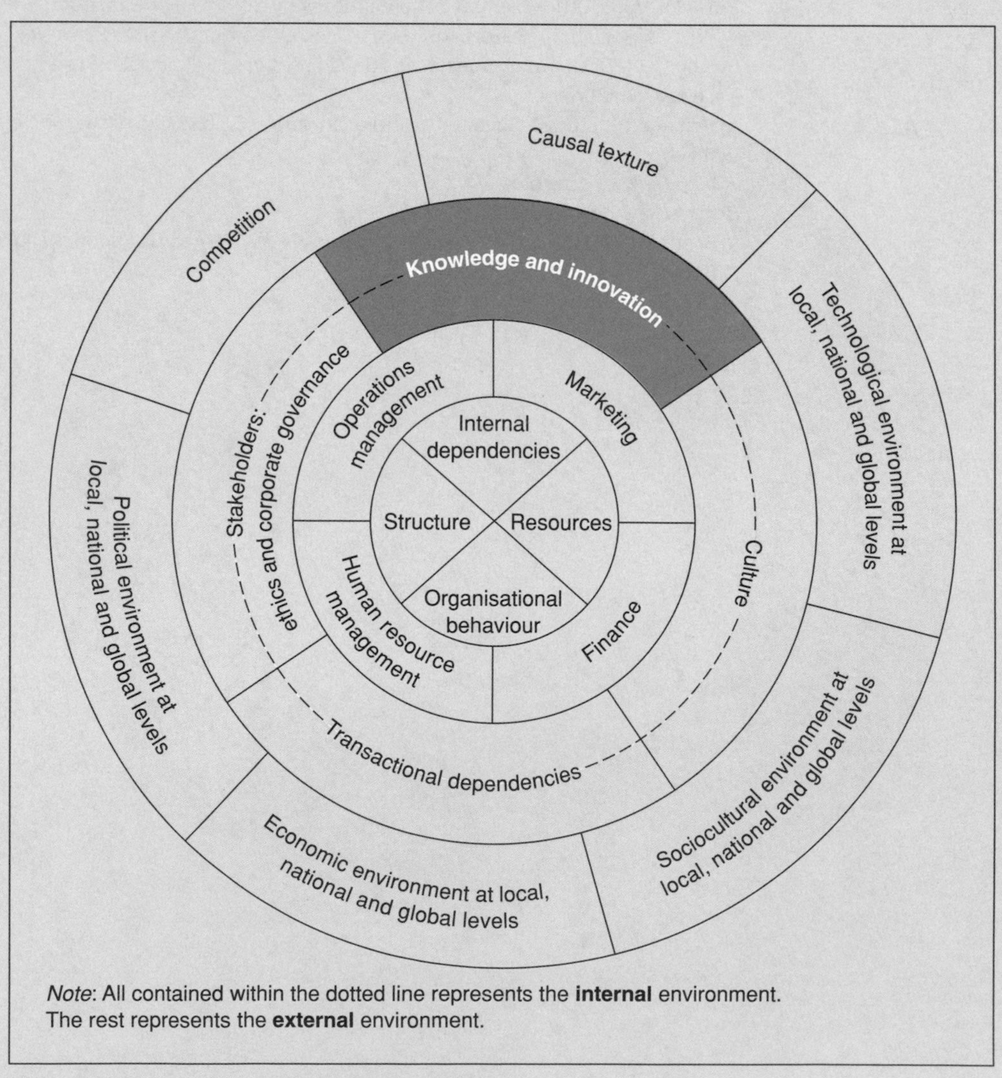

Figure 11.1 Business environment model

Chapter objectives

This chapter provides an overview of knowledge, intellectual capital, innovation and intellectual property and their use by organisations. Knowledge, its creation, and development, and management and protection are all covered.

Therefore, when you have read this chapter and worked through the associated activities you should be able to achieve the objectives specified below.

1. **Define and discuss knowledge, its development and use in organisations.**
2. **Explain intellectual capital and the importance of sharing knowledge among staff members in an organisation.**
3. **Identify and discuss methods for managing and protecting intellectual property.**

ENTRY CASE STUDY 11.1

The brains of the operation

by Rod Newing

The knowledge economy has become a common phrase in discussions of work and management. The shift from jobs based on manual labour towards those based on knowledge is having a fundamental impact on the nature of work. Yet management of work has only recently started to reflect the change.

The World Bank defines the knowledge economy as 'the use of knowledge to produce economic benefits'. In practice, new technologies are as important as human brainpower in creating wealth. The tools of the knowledge economy include empowerment, flexible working, outsourcing, contract manufacturing, innovation, research and development, globalisation, education and skills. This contrasts with labour, land and capital as the traditional factors of production.

Measuring the size of the knowledge economy is difficult. One method is to use the Organisation for Economic Cooperation and Development's definition of knowledge-based industries. These are high to medium technology manufacturing, finance, business services, telecommunications, education and health, which make up 40 per cent of UK gross domestic product. But knowledge is clearly important in all industries. Even low technology manufacturing requires knowledge to design, manufacture, market and sell products.

Another method of measuring the knowledge economy uses the occupational categories of management, professional and associate professionals, including technicians, which account for about 42 per cent of all UK employment. But, again, the measure is flawed because employees outside these categories clearly also use their knowledge, not just their hands.

In truth, it is simplistic to suggest that brainpower can be separated from manual labour and that the knowledge economy is a new economy operating to a new set of economic laws. Ian Brinkley, director of the knowledge economy programme at the Work Foundation, says the knowledge economy is a 'soft' discontinuity from the past, as a growing share of gross domestic product is devoted to knowledge intangibles rather than physical capital. Yet what is clear is that the knowledge economy is releasing work from the age-old constraints. Traditionally, work was based upon manual labour and had to be completed at a set time and in a set place and was closely supervised. This resulted in hierarchical, command and control management styles and employment practices. 'Organisations had a certain amount of work to do and they needed people to do it,' says Peter Thomson, director of the Future Work Forum at Henley Business School. 'They divided the amount of effort needed by 220 days and recruited that number of full-time permanent employees.' Since then, most manual work has been automated and products are becoming increasingly commoditised. Innovation and customer service, particularly in business processes, have taken over from manufacturing efficiency as the main drivers of profit and wealth creation.

'More of people's jobs are involved in receiving and transmitting information and adding value to it,' says Mr

Thompson. 'More of that information is electronic, so we have less need to have people in a fixed location at a fixed time.' This means that work no longer has to be divided into person years, so it can be done by part-timers, job-sharers, contractors, suppliers or remote call centres. The knowledge economy also challenges the concept of compensating people for the time they spend working at a fixed location. Instead, they need to be rewarded for taking responsibility for producing agreed output, in terms of achievements or behaviour, which is more like self-employment. 'It encourages the individual to be more productive,' says Mr Thompson. 'Instead of spending some of their work life sitting at a desk looking busy, they can be out enjoying themselves with their family.' This requires a significant shift in emphasis in the way that organisations and work are managed.

According to Business in the Community, a charity that promotes responsible business, 'knowledge workers are not motivated by command and control structures, nor do such structures facilitate the collaboration from which innovation springs'. They do not see themselves as 'cogs in wheels' but are searching for meaning at work at an individual, organisational and societal level, BITC says in its report, 'Tomorrow's Workplace – Are you fit for the future?' Another report, 'Flexible Working and Performance' from Cranfield School of Management and the charity Working Families, found that flexible workers had higher levels of organisational commitment and some had more job satisfaction.

In the knowledge-intensive telecommunications industry, 80 per cent of BT's employees work flexibly. Some 14,500 are based at home, 5000 work occasionally from home, 40,000 are nomadic, 20,000 are flexible within a building and 20,000 are fixed, usually needing specific equipment. 'The benefits of flexible working are huge,' says Dave Dunbar, head of BT Workstyle, which offers flexible working solutions to external clients. 'It reduces properties, increases productivity, retains the workforce, promotes diversity and reduces the carbon footprint. Organisations must come to grips with it if they are to remain competitive.'

Although embracing the knowledge economy is important for the competitiveness of individual organisations, it also operates at the macro-economic level. Jonathan Kestenbaum, chief executive of the National Endowment for Science, Technology and the Arts, which promotes innovation, points to Finland as an example of an economy that has been transformed. The country suffered after the break up of the Soviet Union, a key customer for its basic industrial products. 'Recovery from severe economic downturn was fast and effective because of its shift to focus on knowledge and innovation,' Mr Kestenbaum says. 'It embraced the internet and communications technology to produce success stories like the Linux operating system and Nokia.'

The BITC report points out that there is keen competition to recruit and retain knowledge workers globally, as they are the ones who create new products, services and business models and manage complex projects and enterprises. Innovation is the lifeline for businesses wishing to grow and compete in the global economy and for public sector bodies pressed to deliver more and better services with limited funding. Skills gaps give knowledge workers huge bargaining power and choice. 'We are in a competitive economy, where almost everything has been commoditised and can be easily replicated at a 10th of the price,' says Mr Kestenbaum. 'Great companies understand the need to create an environment and workplace that capitalises on ideas and maximises the flow of knowledge and information to develop new disruptive products.'

Source: from 'The brains of the operation', *The Financial Times*, 5 November 2008 (Newing, R.).

Introduction

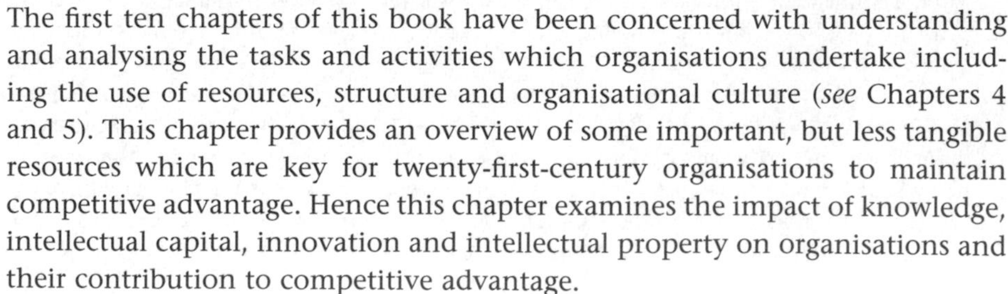

The first ten chapters of this book have been concerned with understanding and analysing the tasks and activities which organisations undertake including the use of resources, structure and organisational culture (*see* Chapters 4 and 5). This chapter provides an overview of some important, but less tangible resources which are key for twenty-first-century organisations to maintain competitive advantage. Hence this chapter examines the impact of knowledge, intellectual capital, innovation and intellectual property on organisations and their contribution to competitive advantage.

It is accepted today that economies in the developed and developing world rely on knowledge and its application in both manufacturing and service organisations (*see* Entry case study). Universities, hospitals, Nokia, Microsoft and Kodak all rely on knowledge in some way or other to deliver products and services to their customers. Therefore, knowledge, its creation and development, along with its communication and transfer throughout the organisation are all examined. The creation and development of knowledge can be an expensive and time-consuming process; therefore, the protection of knowledge is important and hence patents, trademarks, registered designs and copyright are covered.

Knowledge, its creation and development

Knowledge is the information, skills and understanding gained through learning or experience[1] or familiarity gained by experience.[2] Hence knowledge is more than data and information on its own. Knowledge is built up over a period of time from the practices and procedures that occur on a routine basis in the organisation and from contacts, experiences and friendships. Organisations will develop knowledge about stakeholders, such as customers and suppliers (*see* Chapter 12) and new and existing technology that is relevant to the organisation. Therefore, knowledge built up over a period of time is not a static resource but is something that changes and develops along with the organisation.

Tacit and explicit knowledge

There are two types of knowledge, tacit and explicit (*see* Table 11.1). **Explicit knowledge** is recorded and will be in the public arena if it has been published and therefore may be exploited by all the competitors in an industry. Therefore, organisations strive to develop explicit knowledge that is specific to them and seek to protect this knowledge (*see* later section in this chapter). **Tacit knowledge** is rather more vague than explicit knowledge and can be difficult

Table 11.1 Tacit and explicit knowledge

Explicit knowledge	Tacit knowledge
• Patents and legal contracts, e.g. with customers and suppliers.	• Exploiting experience of what has worked in the past developing new brands.
• Development and training programmes for staff.	• Informal networks for placing an order with the company.
• New product development processes, see Figure 9.5.	• The use of informal contacts to identify potential new customers.
• Procedures specified in a franchise manual.	• Practical and unwritten procedures for dealing with dissatisfied customers.

to specify, unclear and unrecorded, but is also valuable to organisations. Tacit knowledge that is analysed, made more specific, clarified and recorded will become explicit knowledge. Both explicit and tacit knowledge can contribute to competitive advantage. Explicit knowledge contributes to organisations as it allows understanding of what the organisation is currently doing and the development of plans and strategy to help in the achievement of competitive advantage. The addition of tacit knowledge can be valuable if it makes a significant contribution to competitive advantage, as it is often difficult for competitors to understand and copy.

Creating knowledge

The pressure to develop and use new and existing knowledge may arise from the organisation's desire to achieve or maintain competitive advantage or from competitive pressures, and the external environment means that the survival of the organisation requires it to use its knowledge to adapt its processes and products.

Using existing knowledge

Existing knowledge can often be the starting point for the creation of new knowledge. It is the development of current knowledge that creates new knowledge and Nonaka and Hirotaka[3] identify four mechanisms for the development of existing explicit and tacit knowledge into new explicit and tacit knowledge, namely; **combination**, **internalisation socialisation** and **externalisation**.

Combination – explicit knowledge to explicit knowledge

Explicit knowledge, which has been previously recorded, can be disseminated around the organisation as explicit knowledge, via an intranet or staff development and training courses or any company-wide communication system.

Internalisation – explicit knowledge to tacit knowledge

Explicit knowledge, in its written form as a book, manual, webpage, can be used as a starting point for informal discussions which develop and share explicit knowledge but in a tacit form, i.e. the discussion and resulting ideas are not recorded.

Socialisation – tacit knowledge to tacit knowledge

Tacit knowledge, which is unwritten, can be disseminated as tacit knowledge via informal meetings and day-to-day informal discussion between staff who work together.

Externalisation – tacit knowledge to explicit knowledge

Organisations could choose to formally record the discussions and ideas that emerge from meetings. This may require several meetings and iterations of the tacit knowledge to take it from a vague idea to clear and structured knowledge. This type of behaviour is an attempt to record knowledge that was previously hidden.

Check your understanding

Do you understand the possible mechanisms for developing existing explicit and tacit knowledge?

Check your understanding by identifying which mechanism is in use in each of the following situations.

1 A training course for new staff explaining how established technology works and is used by the organisation.
2 Discussions about new product ideas, in which notes are taken and ideas formally recorded.
3 An email highlighting the key points from a technical manual which staff working in the organisation need to follow.

Creation of new knowledge

Organisations use and develop existing knowledge as appropriate and this is fine; however, maintaining competitive advantage will usually require the creation and use of new knowledge. New knowledge may come from within the organisation via development work that has been done by the research and development department through to market research. In these situations organisations use their own resources to create new knowledge. The new knowledge may be created by one department, such as research and development, or it may arise from the work of a cross-functional team that contains specialists from a number of areas including, for example, technical and marketing specialists. This type of team would be expected to interact with each other, often, with the aim of developing new approaches and solutions to particular problems, products or projects with which the organisation is involved.

Intellectual capital

Clearly knowledge development and creation are important for organisations seeking to create competitive advantage, which raises the question about the value of knowledge to organisations. Traditionally accounting rules and regulations make it difficult to value knowledge, as only tangible physical assets such as land, plant, raw materials and financial capital appear on a company's balance sheet, while intellectual capital does not. In economies that are increasingly dependent on knowledge, skills and technology (*see* Entry case study) intellectual capital is as important as tangible assets and financial capital. **Intellectual capital** comprises human capital, social capital, organisational capital and customer capital, which all contribute to competitive advantage (*see* Figure 11.2).[4,5]

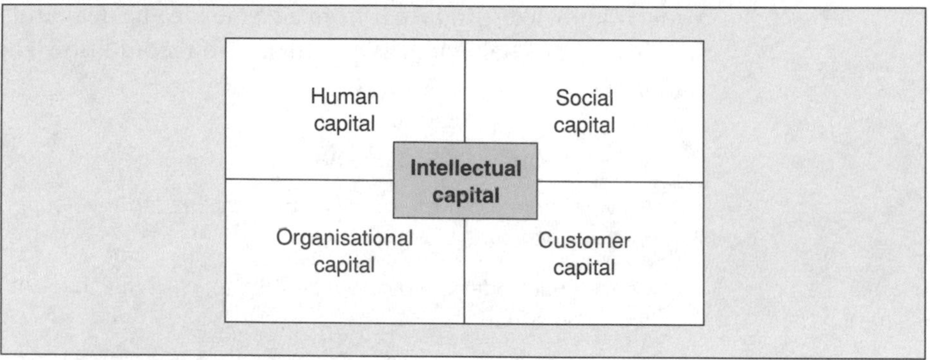

Figure 11.2 Intellectual capital

Human capital arises from the skills, abilities and knowledge of the workforce and their capacity to create value for the business via application of their skills, abilities and knowledge. **Social capital** arises from the formal and informal procedures, structures and networks both inside and outside the organisation which staff are members of and exploit. **Organisational capital** includes explicit knowledge, information systems, market data, production processes and all data, information and solutions provided by IT systems. **Customer capital** comprises the customer base, customer relations and customer potential,[6,7] namely existing customers, the organisation's relationship with existing customers and future customers. It is the balance and combination of these different types of capital and how they are shared and used which is key in helping an organisation achieve competitive advantage. This is the view taken by the learning organisation.

The **learning organisation** will continually refresh its balance of the different types of capital (human, social organisational and customer) around a shared vision for the organisation. Hence the organisation has the potential capacity to regenerate itself from within and for future plans and strategies to emerge. Organisations that behave in this way tend to be dynamic and have flexible structures, e.g. the matrix structure rather than the functional structure (*see* Chapter 4).

In learning organisations managers encourage individuals to use and share their skills, abilities and knowledge within the organisation. The sharing of skills, abilities and knowledge will be via both lateral and vertical relationships; for example, an employee would be equally likely to share knowledge with his/her colleagues, staff and boss. This emphasises the importance of social capital and people not feeling constrained by organisational hierarchies and feeling comfortable in the relevant structures and networks, which means they will learn from others in the same structures and networks. In the learning organisation managers play a facilitative role rather than a directive or prescriptive role. Hence the learning organisation is capable of operating in a changing knowledge-based industry, which reflects the nature of many of the companies in the developed world.

However, organisational learning is not restricted to dynamic organisations and the learning can arise from any organisation continually questioning and challenging their technology and processes to maintain their competitive advantage. Organisations that have taken for granted their technology and processes may review them with a view to regaining lost competitive advantage. The challenge for managers is to recognise the potential benefits of developing a learning organisation and questioning and challenging how things are done.

This has given rise to the field of knowledge management that involves the compilation and dissemination of knowledge throughout the organisation. Therefore, effective knowledge management requires the development of an open knowledge-based organisational culture. Effective knowledge management requires all groups in an organisation to be willing to share their knowledge and expertise. This can be difficult to achieve as some groups of staff, particularly those with a specific highly valued expertise, may regard 'knowledge as power' and be unwilling to share their knowledge. If this is the case, the organisation's culture will need to be very carefully managed (*see* Chapter 5).

Check your understanding

Do you understand the different sorts of capital in organisations?

Check your understanding by identifying the sort of capital being mentioned in each of the following situations.

1 Research scientist develops insulin that can be taken in tablet form.
2 An international conference on managing cholesterol in overweight patients.
3 The NHS.
4 The skills of the research scientist.
5 The library of scientific journals provided by a pharmaceutical company for its scientists to use.

Sharing knowledge

Formal and informal networks for sharing knowledge exist in organisations and professions. These networks may share knowledge via informal meetings and discussions that can be face to face, electronic or via more formal mechanisms such as seminars and conferences. Alternatively knowledge may arise from external bodies which are working with the organisation such as consultants or a university department. In this case ownership of knowledge remains with the external body.

If new knowledge created by the organisation is significant and key to competitive advantage then its full potential needs to be exploited by the organisation and it needs to be disseminated to the right parts of the organisation. If the knowledge is complex its dissemination within the organisation will not be a simple straightforward process. Therefore, knowledge-sharing initiatives need to be carefully thought through if they are to be effective and senior management will need to emphasise the contribution of knowledge to the organisation's financial performance and its impact on gross profits, return on investment, expenses and cost savings. It needs to be clearly understood where the knowledge was created and derived from and which lessons have already been learnt from it.

Staff on the receiving end of the knowledge that is disseminated may not understand the new knowledge or why it has been created and may feel threatened by any new developments. Therefore, the organisation and its managers need to ensure all staff understand what knowledge is used and created by the organisation and how it contributes to the organisation's objectives and competitive advantage. Equally there may be reluctance among staff involved in creating knowledge to share it. This lack of willingness to share knowledge can be tricky if the staff involved consider 'knowledge is power' and openness regarding knowledge a threat to themselves and their position in the organisation. These issues need to be considered if the dissemination of knowledge is to be successful and it could be argued that this should be done as part of the planning process when setting up a team to work on a particular problem, product or project.

The focus of managing knowledge needs to be on the useful and vital knowledge, which needs to be clearly distinguished from what is interesting, as this helps the organisation to avoid drowning in knowledge that is irrelevant to competitive advantage. The focus also needs to be on collating and disseminating both explicit and tacit knowledge equally as both contribute to competitive advantage and it can be easy to focus on the explicit knowledge and largely ignore the tacit knowledge. Knowledge management also needs to consider both the creation of further knowledge and the use of current knowledge in taking the organisation forward. Knowledge and its creation should take the organisation forward; it is not part of a retrospective analysis.

The organisation-wide understanding of knowledge and its role in competitive advantage will be aided by the organisation choosing to adopt an organisational culture which is open when it comes to sharing knowledge. Additionally the organisation's infrastructure and systems need to be fit for purpose and underpin the knowledge and the channels by which it is collated and disseminated. Finally, the culture, systems and infrastructures that are developed and implemented need to enable the recording and dissemination of both explicit and tacit knowledge. The overall aim should be to share best practice across the organisation.

Innovation and moving to the marketplace

Innovation can be an expensive and risky business, which may not pay off, but can often return big rewards when it is successful. Organisations are subject to two types of driver when it comes to innovation, namely market pull and technology push.

Market pull arises from recognising customer needs which identify new market segments or segments of the existing market which are poorly served by current competitors. For example, Canon examined the whole potential market for photocopying and realised that its main competitor, Xerox, focused on the large company market and neglected small and medium-sized companies. Therefore, in the 1980s Canon successfully developed new photocopiers that required little maintenance or repair and hence could be sold to small and medium-sized companies. Canon repeated this type of behaviour more recently by developing a range of small printers-cum-photocopiers for use in the home, which cost around £50. Markets for technology-based products, such as consumer electronics, are often driven by the market; this is market pull, and the market need is met by a company's product development activities (*see* Chapter 8).

Technology push occurs when an innovative product (which may start as a small solution to a particular problem) that the market may not even recognise permeates the marketplace and is taken up by many customers. A good example of this is the Gripple, which was launched in 1988 and developed by a Sheffield-based company as a wiring joining device for use in building and mending wire fences. The Gripple was an innovative product as there was nothing else like it on the market and it did away with the need to twist wire together when joining two pieces. The Gripple was quickly recognised as a time-saving product by the wine industry, which has thousands of wire trellis up which vines grow and the maintenance and repair of these was hugely time-consuming before the advent of the Gripple. Today there are around 500 different Gripple products and variants, including wire tensioners, which are sold in 75 different countries.[8] Initially the Gripple diffused into the vineyard market but the company has continued to look for other markets including the construction industry and the domestic gardening market.[9]

Delivering innovation

Innovation can help a company deliver new products for which a premium price can be charged or new products that offer better value for money, both of which can be effective competitive strategies (*see* Chapter 3). The identification of opportunities for innovation can be sought by questioning current products, markets and competition. Initially evaluation of current products or services may give ideas about possible new offerings. Equally, appraisal of all market segments, including those the organisation serves, may give rise to ideas for redefining current market segments and identify target segments which have previously not be exploited by the organisation. This type of analysis and evaluation helps the company identify market opportunities and ways of achieving and strengthening competitive advantage. Some of the market opportunities identified may, if followed, be an attack on a competitor's weakness and, if this is the case, it should be recognised that retaliation is likely. Hence this should be taken into account before making such a move and consideration given to the extensive resources which will likely be required (*see* Chapter 4) along with the timing of any such competitive moves.

The search for innovative opportunities should be far and wide and take into account PEST/LoNGPEST factors such as legislation, demographics, technology, and customer needs and wants (*see* Chapters 1, 2 and 8). The initial growth of the mobile phone market used technology and shaped customer 'wants' very effectively, resulting in nearly all of us carrying a mobile phone around with us today and often feeling lost if the phone is left at home. Challenging conventional views about products and markets can also lead to new developments (*see* earlier discussion in this chapter on the Gripple).

Innovation can help a company create value and overtake a competitor and as such it is important that the company understands how innovation can be encouraged. Innovation can be the result of careful planning and analysis and this is very much the approach taken by the large pharmaceutical companies. Their innovation is based on years of research, development and testing of new drugs and this clearly suits the highly regulated industry they operate in and the customers they serve. In contrast, media companies such as Google, which are subject to less regulation, often adopt a less prescriptive approach to developing innovative services.

An organisation seeking to use and exploit innovation will generate a culture that encourages innovation. This starts with the managing director and senior managers ensuring innovation is clear in the organisation's objectives and is encouraged and supported at all levels of the organisation. The organisation will need to be flexible and operate with multi-disciplinary teams if new products are to be developed, costed and evaluated, so the structure will likely be flat, so as to avoid being overly bureaucratic.

The innovative process will consider all explicit and tacit knowledge available to the organisation and indeed it may be the least likely tacit knowledge that gives rise to what is ultimately an innovative product. The control systems in such a culture (*see* Chapter 5) will evaluate possible new innovative products and some will go forward for prototype and full market development (*see* Chapter 9). The teams responsible for developing the unsuccessful products should be supported and encouraged and not penalised in any way. They may be the people to have the next profitable bright idea.

Managing intellectual property

The UK Patent Office was set up in 1852 to act as the United Kingdom's sole office for the granting of patents of inventions and in 2007 changed its name to the UK Intellectual Property Office. Knowledge or intellectual property can be protected by patenting, copyright, registered designs and registered trademarks, which are covered by the Intellectual Property Office. Companies can use a combination of ways of protecting their ideas; for example, a product can have both a patent and a registered design, or both copyright and a trademark can be used to protect a company's image.

Patents

A **patent** is a contract between an individual or organisation and the state, which grants a temporary monopoly to the owner of the patent. This enables the patent holder to exploit the invention for up to 20 years in Europe and requires an initial fee to be paid for registering the patent and a further significant fee for its annual renewal.[10] Patents are granted for new products, new manufacturing processes or improvements to existing products or processes which were not previously known. For example, the AstraZeneca's cholesterol-lowering drug Crestor and the Dyson vacuum cleaner and many of its technical features are both patent protected.

Companies that produce a large number of products that are new inventions will have specialist in-house patent agents whose background will combine scientific or engineering knowledge with legal expertise. Large pharmaceutical companies will have in-house patent agents who prepare worldwide patents for the new drugs that are developed and taken to the marketplace. It is this patent protection which allows drug companies to develop expensive new drugs for serious medical conditions and recoup the costs of doing so and make profit during the 20-year monopoly period.

The aim of a government granting patents is to encourage innovation and its commercial application in industry, hence contributing to the economy. Therefore, a patent stops any other individual or organisation from benefiting from the invention; however, the legal prevention of stopping anyone else benefiting from the patent lies with the patent holder, not the state. This is one of disadvantages of the patent system for businesses, as the cost of fighting a patent infringement action through the courts is expensive and time-consuming. It was exactly this disadvantage and large bill that Tate & Lyle faced when, in September 2008, an American judge ruled against Tate & Lyle and in favour of Niutang, which had been accused of breaking patents on the production process for Tate & Lyle's sucralose, sold as the sweetener Splenda.[11,12]

Trademarks

Trademarks indicate which company is providing the goods and services on offer and are often used in industries that are not heavily reliant on invention. Trademarks allow an organisation to differentiate its products and services and indicate to the marketplace the quality, value and origin of the goods and services on offer. Examples of companies that use trademarks include Apple computers, McDonald's, KFC, Mars and NatWest. The importance of trademarks is highlighted as it would be difficult to recognise these companies if their trademarks did not exit. Hence trademarks are often associated with a business's purpose, products, services, image, goodwill and reputation. The ultimate example of the familiarity of a trademark is its incorporation into the language as a verb, for example to hoover is to use a vacuum cleaner (not necessarily a Hoover) and to xerox is to photocopy (maybe on a Canon machine).

The Trademarks Act (1994) covers graphic trademarks, such as logos, as well as other 'trademarks' that up to 1994 had not been regarded as trademarks. The 'new' trademarks 1994 Act opened the possibility of all sorts of marks that would not have previously been registerable and include sounds, smells and containers. For example, manufacturers of expensive perfume and after-shave and Coca-Cola are seeking to register their distinctively shaped and designed bottles. Trademarks need to be distinctive in their own right, i.e. a trademark should not in any way describe the product it relates to. Therefore, the golden arches of McDonald's and the Mars name and the distinctive way it is written on product packaging are good examples of trademarks. The use of the word Mars is allowed as a trademark as it is considered distinctive in relation to chocolate. This is in contrast to the trademarking of the word 'chocolate', as chocolate is a word that other confectionery producers would want to use in describing and marketing their products and therefore it could not be registered as a trademark in relation to confectionery. However, the use of the word chocolate in relation to a range of computers would be acceptable, as its use is distinctive. Finally, trademarks should not seek to deceive or confuse the customers.

Registered designs

Products or designs, which are not inventive and not covered by patent protection, can be covered by registered design legislation. There are three forms of protection: registered design, design right and copyright.

The **registered design** system is for designs with form or aesthetic appeal and therefore it is the outward appearance of the article that is protected, for example its shape, contours, texture and pattern. The design must be new and individual and not remind customers of an existing design. The registered design status is initially granted for 5 years and can be extended, on payment of a fee, every 5 years for up to 25 years. For example the i-Teddy, which was on the BBC television programme *Dragons' Den*, was protected by both registered design and patent and its launch on the marketplace made its inventor, Imran Hakim, a millionaire.

Design right is free and automatic and gives the original creator protection regarding shape or configuration of a product only in the United Kingdom, for a 10- to 15-year period. However, design right does not protect two-dimensional aspects of design, which need to be protected using registered design or copyright and absolute protection applies for only the first 5 years and then other individuals or organisations are entitled to a licence to manufacture products copying the design. The designer Jimmy Choo, best known for shoes, mounted a legal challenge against Marks & Spencer over a £9.50 copy of a satin handbag that bore an uncanny resemblance to a Jimmy Choo £495 silk Cosmo evening bag. Marks & Spencer did not admit responsibility, but removed the bag from sale and reached an undisclosed out-of-court financial settlement with Jimmy Choo.[13]

Copyright

Copyright is recognised by the symbol © and copyright protection is automatic and no formal registration is required. Copyright gives creators of a wide range of work, including literary, musical, artistic and photographic work along with recordings, films and broadcasts, legal rights to control the ways in which their work is exploited. The work must be the author's own work and the result of their intellectual or artistic skill or judgement and be in a tangible form such that it can be communicated or reproduced, for example a book, photograph or film.

In the United Kingdom the copyright for literary, dramatic, written music and artistic works expires 70 years after the death of the author. However, there is one special case under UK copyright legislation: the royalties for H M Barrie's story of *Peter Pan*, which go to Great Ormond Street Hospital for Children in London, commenced in 1937 on the author's death and under the terms of his will. This copyright of *Peter Pan* was due to run out after 70 years at the end of 2007. However, the former UK Prime Minister James Callaghan, encouraged by his wife, was successful in getting the 1988 copyright act altered to ensure that the hospital continues to benefit from UK royalties forever.[14]

In contrast, music recordings only have copyright protection for 50 years from their date of first release in the UK. The singer Cliff Richard and the Who singer Roger Daltrey have campaigned for music recording to be brought into line with other copyright protected work such as literary and artistic works.[15] In 2008 EU proposals were to change the time period for copyright protection for recorded music from 50 years to 95 years. The EU saw no reason to limit the copyright protection to only 50 years for recorded music.[16]

Internet addresses

Recently an American judge ruled that the similarity in characteristics of a trademark and domain name meant that a domain name could be protected in the same way as a trademark.[17] Internet addresses are based on web domains, which are essentially a string of numbers that indicate the web address for a particular website. However, a string of numbers is tricky to remember and hence domain names are assigned, for example pearsoned.co.uk for the publishers Pearson Education and staffs.ac.uk for Staffordshire University act as internet addresses. The internet addresses allow internet users to look up the organisation via a search engine like Google. Therefore, it could be argued that the domain name effectively acts as a trademark.

Check your understanding

Do you understand the various ways in which intellectual property can be protected in the UK?

Check your understanding by identifying how each of the following could be protected in the UK.

1 A Chanel jacket.
2 A new drug for arthritis.
3 A new book, Cheryl Cole's autobiography.
4 A new logo identifying a company and its products.

Counterfeit goods

The protection of intellectual property is important to organisations as they should be the ones to exploit it and benefit from their investment in developing the knowledge or intellectual capital, i.e. human, social, organisational and customer capital. In 2007 the UN reported that counterfeiting goods cost the world's economy £51 billion every year[18] and in doing so it puts people at risk and helps to fund serious crime that is related to drugs and guns. The range of goods counterfeited is vast and includes designer sunglasses, medicines, designer clothes and shoes, DVDs and intellectual property such as computer software. In the UK it is the job of trading standards officers and the police to enforce the legislation, which involves seizing fake goods and prosecuting those trading in them. However, the sale of fake goods happens all over the world, from illegal street traders here in the UK and overseas in places like China through to the online sale of fake goods via retailers such as eBay and Amazon. In 2008 the French luxury goods manufacturer LVMH, which owns Louis Vuitton and Christian Dior, took eBay to court in France and won damages of €41 million for the sale of counterfeit goods. Hermes also took eBay to court and won €20,000 for offering fake bags for sale; eBay plan to appeal.[19]

Summary

This chapter gave an overview of knowledge, intellectual capital, innovation and intellectual property. The creation of knowledge, the components of intellectual capital, the role of innovation and the protecting of intellectual property were discussed. The following summary covers all aspects of this chapter.

1 Knowledge is the information, skills and understanding gained through learning or experience. Explicit knowledge is recorded and will be in the public arena if it has been published and therefore may be exploited by all the competitors in an industry. Tacit knowledge is rather more vague than explicit knowledge and can be difficult to specify, unclear and unrecorded, but is also

valuable to organisations. Both explicit and tacit knowledge can contribute to competitive advantage.

2 Formal and informal networks for sharing knowledge exist in organisations and professions. These networks may share knowledge via informal meetings and discussions, and knowledge may arise from external bodies that are working with the organisation, such as consultants.

3 The focus of managing knowledge needs to be on the useful and vital knowledge, which needs to be clearly distinguished from what is interesting, as this helps the organisation to avoid drowning in knowledge that is irrelevant to competitive advantage.

4 The organisation-wide understanding of knowledge and its role in competitive advantage will be aided by the organisation choosing to adopt an organisational culture which is open when it comes to sharing knowledge. Finally the culture, systems and infrastructures which are developed and implemented need to enable the recording and dissemination of both explicit and tacit knowledge.

5 Intellectual capital comprises human capital, social capital, organisational capital and customer capital, which all contribute to competitive advantage. Human capital arises from the skills, abilities and knowledge of the workforce and their capacity to create value for the business via application of their skills, abilities and knowledge. Social capital arises from the formal and informal procedures, structures and networks both inside and outside the organisation which staff are members of and exploit. Organisational capital includes explicit knowledge, information systems, market data, production processes and all data, information and solutions provided by IT systems. Customer capital comprises the customer base, customer relations and customer potential.

6 The learning organisation continually refreshes the balance of the different types of capital (human, social organisational and customer) around a shared vision for the organisation. Hence the organisation has the potential capacity to regenerate itself from within and for future plans and strategies to emerge. However, organisational learning is not restricted to dynamic organisations and the learning can arise from any organisation continually questioning and challenging their technology and processes.

7 Market pull arises from recognising customer needs which identify new market segments or segments of the existing market which are poorly served by current competitors. Technology push occurs when an innovative product (which may start as a small solution to a particular problem) that the market may not even recognise permeates the marketplace and is taken up by many customers.

8 Innovation can help a company deliver new products for which a premium price can be charged or new products that offer better value for money,

both of which can be effective competitive strategies. The search for innovative opportunities should be far and wide and take into account PEST/LoNGPEST factors such as legislation, demographics, technology, and customer needs and wants. Innovation can help a company create value and overtake a competitor and as such it is important that the company understands how innovation can be encouraged.

9 Knowledge or intellectual property can be protected by patenting, copyright, registered designs and registered trademarks, which are covered by the Intellectual Property Office. A patent is a contract between an individual or organisation and the state, which grants a temporary monopoly to the owner of the patent. Trademarks indicate which company is providing the goods and services on offer and are often used in industries that are not heavily reliant on invention. Recently an American judge ruled that the similarity in characteristics between a trademark and domain name meant that a domain name or web address could be protected in the same way as a trademark. Products or designs, which are not inventive and not covered by patent protection, can be covered by registered design legislation. There are three forms of protection: registered design, design right and copyright.

10 Counterfeit goods cost the world's economy vast amounts of money every year and puts people at risk and helps to fund serious crime that is related to drugs and guns. The range of goods counterfeited is vast and includes designer sunglasses, medicines, designer clothes and shoes, DVDs and intellectual property such as computer software.

Chapter objectives and the exit case study

While reading this chapter and engaging in the activities, you should have learned how to apply theory and models and analyse situations. The exit case study and the questions which follow will provide an opportunity to assess how well you have met the relevant chapter objectives relating to specific material covered in the chapter. The table below shows which chapter objectives can be tested by the different questions.

Chapter objective	Check you have achieved this by
1 Define and discuss knowledge, its development and use in organisations.	answering case study question 1.
2 Explain intellectual capital and the importance of sharing knowledge among staff members in an organisation.	answering case study question 2.

EXIT CASE STUDY 11.2

Help at hand for bringing clients' ideas to market

by Stefan Stern

Consultancies like to talk about solving their clients' problems. Sometimes they may actually do this. Rarer still are the occasions when a consultancy helps the client to develop a new product line or fundamentally different way of doing things.

Everyone wants to see more innovation. But when all is said and done, more is said than done.

The bright ideas and 'Eureka' moments that may spring up in dark corners of the organisation might never make it to the market in a commercially viable form. The thinking may be good, but the execution is lacking.

Clients realise they need to innovate effectively as a matter of urgency. As Martin Smith, head of technology at PA Consulting, says, 'When resources are limited it focuses minds.' PA is entitled to speak with some confidence on this subject as, uniquely among consulting firms, it has a 35-year tradition of working closely with clients via its technology centres, near Cambridge in the UK and in Princeton, New Jersey in the US.

The centres concentrate on hard scientific research and fast-prototyping. They work with several big industrial sectors: pharmaceuticals, for example, developing new delivery systems for drugs: transport, on high-tech timetabling and passenger information systems: and, among others, fast-moving consumer goods (FMCG) companies. PA helped rush the John Smith 'widget' – which uses a tiny gas explosion to create a fuller-bodied beer – to market in a matter of months after rivals Guinness had stolen a march.

'There are broadly two different kinds of companies who work with us,' Mr Smith says. 'We might see a start-up with funding in place that needs the back-up of a "virtual organisation", which we can provide. Or it could be a big corporation, looking for a breakthrough development to come from outside. If you are just talking about extending an existing product line that is not really innovation,' he adds. The people who are still embedded at the business 'know too much' about their world to innovate in a new direction.

Three of PA's recent clients testify to the useful contribution the firm made in their attempts to innovate. Rotork Controls, which makes valve actuators that control the flow of liquids and gases in pipelines, wanted to develop a more creative approach among its engineers, boosting its ability to innovate and develop new products.

'PA's guys were credible in front of our engineers,' says Graham Ogden, Rotork's research and development director.

'They seemed to "walk the talk" – they hadn't just read a book on innovation. What they were saying came from the heart.'

PA ran training sessions in techniques such as brainstorming, ideas clustering, mind mapping, quality function deployment (QFD) and scenario development. These were followed by a series of ideas workshops, which helped Rotork develop hundreds of ideas for new products and services.

Terex, the construction equipment manufacturer, faced a slightly different challenge. As Paul Douglas, its director of product management, explains, new thinking was required to reduce the manufacturing costs of some of its biggest trucks. But 80 per cent of the costs were fixed, and 'you can't re-engineer to get cost down'.

His engineers – 'hard people to impress' – took part in cost management workshops that got them to think differently about their processes. This approach worked, Mr Douglas feels, because the consultants had a solid background in industry – they weren't just 'degree, MBA, consulting' people, he says.

'We came up with a list of short, medium and longer term potential savings, of which 60 per cent came from these workshops. Overall we generated 750 cost-saving ideas. We targeted the 110 short-term and 230 medium-term ideas to give us some rapid cost-reduction at low risk and without any impact on quality.'

So much for heavy industry. At the other end of the scale: imagine a thermometer that is accurate to 0.001 deg C being inserted into the aorta (the main artery from the heart) to pick up early signs of the inflammation that could be the precursor to a heart attack. This is the product, made by Thermocore Medical, which PA has helped bring to the market.

According to John Yianni, company founder, PA managed the coordination of a range of manufacturers, designers and suppliers across Europe (and the US) – which involved leading a roomful of 35 people. It also led the development of the main component, a catheter that is highly innovative. For one thing, it is smaller than previous versions of the device. Secondly, it is easier and quicker to use, thanks to its improved technology.

→

PA produced prototypes throughout the project, to make sure all parties understood how much progress had been made and where they were all heading.

'It was no easy task coordinating all the different players,' Dr Yianni says. The patients' heart attacks were not the only ones that were avoided.

Source: from 'Help at hand for bringing clients' ideas to market', *The Financial Times*, 14 November 2008 (Stern, S.).

Exit case study questions

1 From the case study and your own general knowledge identify the types of organisation and situation in which innovation is likely to occur.

2 Discuss the actions which can be taken to help ensure an innovation makes it to the marketplace. How does PA help this process?

Short-answer questions

1 Define 'knowledge'.

2 Explain the difference between tacit and explicit knowledge.

3 Name and explain the four mechanisms for the development of exsting explicit and tacit knowledge into new explicit and tacit knowledge.

4 Why are formal and informal networks important in organisations?

5 Define human capital.

6 Define social capital.

7 Define organisational capital.

8 Define customer capital.

9 Define intellectual capital.

10 Explain the term 'learning organisation'.

11 Explain 'market pull' and 'technology push'.

12 Briefly summarise the role of innovation for organisations.

13 Define a patent.

14 Define a trademark.

15 Define a design right.

16 Define copyright.

Chapter objectives and assignment questions

While reading this chapter and engaging in the activities, you should have learned how to apply theory and models and analyse situations. This means you should be able to meet the chapter objectives outlined at the beginning of the chapter. The table below shows which chapter objectives can be tested by the different questions.

Chapter objective	Check you have achieved this by
1 Define and discuss knowledge, its development and use in organisations.	answering assignment question 1.
2 Explain intellectual capital and the importance of sharing knowledge among staff members in an organisation.	answering assignment question 1.
3 Identify and discuss methods for managing and protecting intellectual property.	answering assignment question 2.

Assignment questions

1 Choose two organisations. Compare and contrast the type of knowledge they develop and use and the contribution it makes to their competitive advantage.

2 Summarise and discuss the arguments for and against patenting DNA and life forms.

WEBLINKS available at www.pearsoned.co.uk/capon

The websites for this chapter are for some of the key bodies in the UK concerned with innovation and the protection of innovations by the Intellectual Property Office.

- This site is for the Intellectual Property Office, which deal with patents, trademarks and copyright:
  http://www.ipo.gov.uk/
- This is the webpage for the CIPD fact sheet on human capital:
  http://www.cipd.co.uk/subjects/corpstrtgy/hmncapital/humancap.htm?IsSrchRes=1
- The following website is from the government Department for Business, Enterprise and Regulatory Reform:
  http://www.berr.gov.uk/dius/innovation/
- The following website focuses on innovation in the public sector:
  http://www.innovation-unit.co.uk/about-us/about-us/the-innovation-team.html
- The following website is for BT and is about its use of innovation:
  http://www.btplc.com/Innovation/
- The following website is for the Design Council:
  http://www.designcouncil.org.uk/

FURTHER READING

These book chapters look at knowledge and innovation in organisations.

- Johnson, G, Scholes, K and Whittington, R (2008) *Exploring Corporate Strategy*, 8th edn, Chapters 9 and 13, Harlow: Financial Times Prentice Hall.
- Lynch, R (2006) *Corporate Strategy*, 4th edn, Chapter 11, Harlow: Financial Times Prentice Hall.

- Palmer, A and Hartley, B (2006) *The Business Environment*, 5th edn, Chapters 2, 3, 4 and 5, Maidenhead: McGraw-Hill.
- Thompson, J L and Martin, F (2005) *Strategic Management: Awareness, Analysis and Change*, 5th edn, Chapter 4, London: Thomson Learning.
- Trott, P (2008) *Innovation Management and New Product Development*, 4th edn, Chapters 1 and 5, Harlow: Financial Times Prentice Hall.
- Worthington, I and Britton, C (2006) *The Business Environment*, 5th edn, Chapters 3, 4, 5 and 16, Harlow: Financial Times Prentice Hall.

REFERENCES

1 *Dictionary of Contemporary English* (2003) Harlow: Pearson Education Limited.
2 *The Concise Oxford Dictionary* (1982) Oxford: Oxford University Press.
3 Lynch, R (2006) *Corporate Strategy*, 4th edn, Harlow: Financial Times Prentice Hall.
4 http://www.cipd.co.uk/subjects/corpstrtgy/hmncapital/humancap.htm?IsSrchRes=1
5 Lynch, op. cit.
6 CIPD website, op. cit.
7 Lynch, op. cit.
8 http://www.gripple.com/
9 Gripple website, op. cit.
10 http://www.ipo.gov.uk/
11 Hill, A (2008) 'Patents unrewarded', *Financial Times*, 24 September.
12 Urry, M (2008) 'Tate & Lyle hit by sucralose patent ruling', *Financial Times*, 24 September.
13 BBC News (2006) 'M&S caught in copycat design row', 19 November.
14 Allen, K (2007) 'Never ends for Peter Pan', *Guardian*, 28 December.
15 Allen, K (2007) 'Musicians' copyright pleas fall on deaf ears', *Guardian*, 24 July.
16 Gow, D (2008) 'Extend performers' copyright to 95 years, says EU commissioner', *Guardian*, 15 February.
17 Trott, P (2008) *Innovation Management and New Product Development*, 4th edn, Harlow: Financial Times Prentice Hall.
18 BBC News (2007) 'UN warning over counterfeit goods', 30 January.
19 Tait, N (2008) 'eBay ordered to pay €40m to LVMH over counterfeit goods', *Financial Times*, 1 July.

CHAPTER 12

Stakeholders, governance and ethics

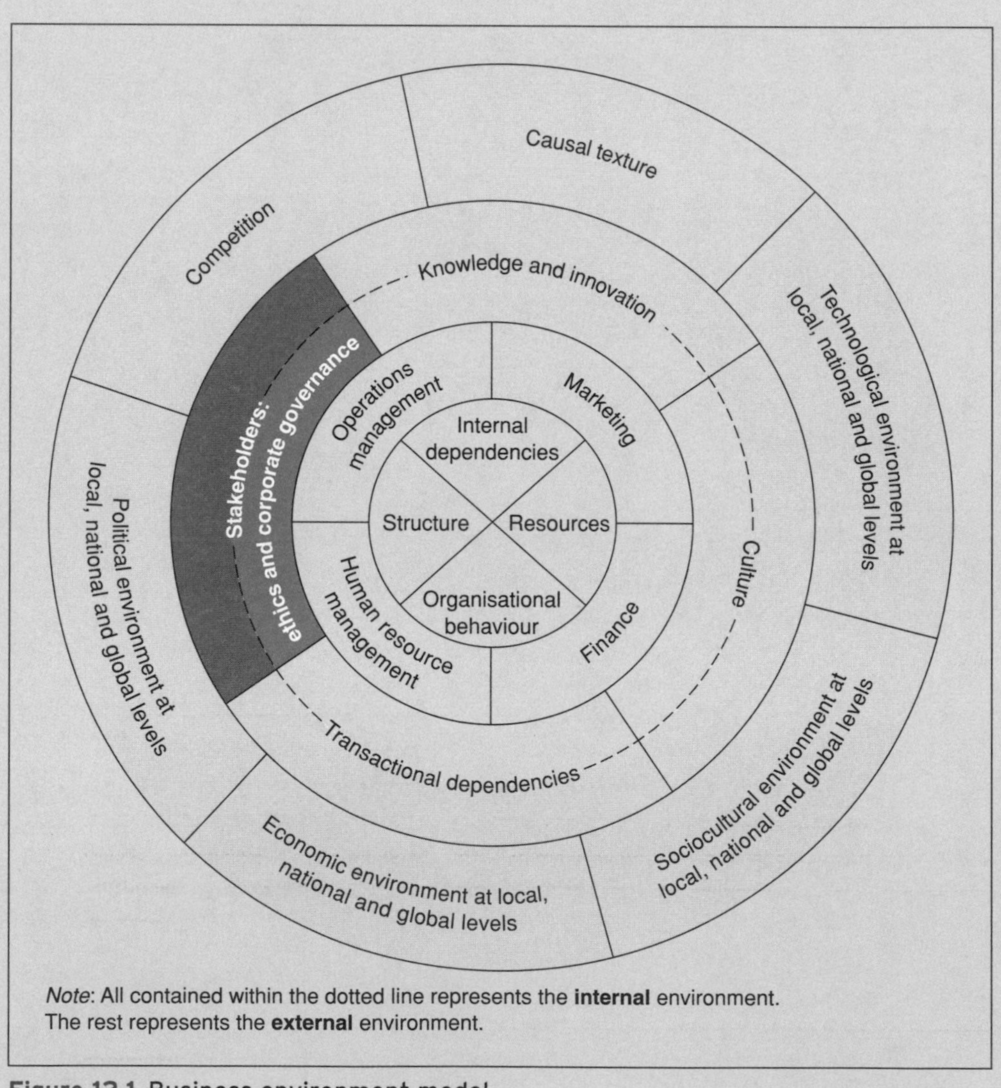

Note: All contained within the dotted line represents the **internal** environment.
The rest represents the **external** environment.

Figure 12.1 Business environment model

Chapter objectives

This chapter provides an overview of stakeholders, **corporate governance**, **ethics** and **corporate social responsibility**. These activities and the role they play in good management of organisations is summarised.

Therefore, when you have read this chapter and worked through the associated activities you should be able to achieve the objectives specified below.

1 **Identify and analyse an organisation's stakeholders.**

2 **Explain and summarise good corporate governance and the key roles involved.**

3 **Discuss ethics and corporate responsibility in relation to a business and its stakeholders.**

This case study examines Marks & Spencer and their decision to combine the roles of chairman and chief executive by appointing Stuart Rose to both positions. This goes against current thinking, which is that good corporate governance is best achieved by separating these two roles.

ENTRY CASE STUDY 12.1

Sir Stuart Rose and the thorny issue of corporate governance

by Tom Braithwaite and Elizabeth Rigby

Sir Stuart Rose has often said he wanted to remain as Marks & Spencer's chief executive until early 2009. In private though, the man responsible for turning round the retail chain's fortunes harboured ambitions towards the chairmanship. Two potential obstacles stood in his path: the UK's Combined Code on corporate governance and Lord Burns, who was only hired as chairman less than two years ago.

Yesterday, both concerns were swept aside as Sir Stuart's wish was granted, with his elevation to the post of executive chairman from June this year. Lord Burns, whose relationship with his chief executive has always been somewhat strained, according to company insiders, will step down, leaving Sir Stuart the task of running the business and the board. 'We want to develop the team,' says Sir Stuart, who along with his board has failed to single out a successor from his executive team over the past couple of years. 'Keeping me and bringing on new people is the best solution. It gives breathing space for me to step back and gives more elbow room around the boardroom.' But the changes have made some shareholders furious. Legal & General Investment Management, which rarely speaks out on corporate governance issues, says it believes strongly in the separation of the chairman and chief executive. 'We believe today's announcement from M&S is unwelcome.' Investors, analysts and other M&S watchers are all mystified about why the company has decided to embark on this route, which is unusual at best and extremely controversial at worst.

Lord Burns says he and Sir Stuart looked at a range of alternatives over the past few months, running from Sir Stuart stepping up to the chairmanship to carrying on in the role as chief executive for a set period beyond 2009. 'He didn't want to carry on as chief executive indefinitely. He wanted a process that signalled an end point at which he would step down and through which we would develop people,' says Lord Burns. 'There was a fear that he might leave in 2009,' he adds. 'The alternative [then] was to begin the process of recruiting someone else immediately. This was going to cause a great deal of uncertainty at this point in the company's development and we thought this was not an attractive option. We wanted to find a way of keeping Stuart Rose in the business.' That the only option of keeping Sir Stuart in the business is to go against the spirit of the Combined Code is a source of concern among shareholders, wary of the concentration of power.

They are also irritated that the company has not managed its succession better, given Sir Stuart's clear statements that he would stay at M&S until 2009. Sir Stuart has been talking about beefing-up his 'bench strength' of executives for some time, but has been unable to translate that potential into a concrete successor. M&S

watchers say this is due in part to the previous management's failure to nurture the next generation of talent. But it also indicates that those with the skills needed to run a business such as M&S are in very short supply.

M&S insiders admit that while the new arrangement is unorthodox, it at least keeps Sir Stuart at the helm during a difficult period. The retailer has not escaped the effects of a worsening British consumer downturn, with trading figures falling to their lowest level in more than two years during Christmas 2007. Meanwhile, the shares are languishing at 375p, having fallen another 3p yesterday. This is half the 750p level hit last summer, when the Sir Stuart Rose revival was in full swing. It is not a legacy that Sir Stuart will wish to leave.

One insider argued that a strong board of non-executives, led by Sir David Michels – who could replace Sir Stuart as chairman, when he steps down in 2011 – would be 'no-one's patsies'. The insider also said that the precise end date to Sir Stuart's tenure provided a safeguard. 'He is not Vladimir Putin.' Sir David admits that while 'no-one likes flouting a rule, sometimes you have to do something a little skew-whiff in the short-term'. 'It is not simply to find the right successor to Stuart Rose,' Sir David adds. 'We believe it is what this company needs in this environment for the next three years. Stuart is the single best person to lead the company.'

Sir Stuart, meanwhile, wants to offer evidence that he is moving ahead with a wider management shake-up as he encourages his would-be successors. Ian Dyson, the finance director, Kate Bostock, head of the clothing operations, and Steven Esom of the food division are all now on the board. Sir Stuart has also added a raft of 30- and 40-something-year-olds to his executive committee, including Clem Constantine, a former Arcadia man, and Steve Rowe, who is replacing outgoing Guy Farrant as director of retail.

Source: from 'Sir Stuart Rose and the thorny issue of corporate governance', *The Financial Times*, 11 March 2008 (Braithwaite, T. and Rigby, E.).

Introduction

This chapter examines stakeholders, corporate governance, ethics and corporate social responsibility. Stakeholders are individuals with an interest in an organisation and are able to influence an organisation to act in their best interests. Ethics and corporate social responsibility are concerned with the standards of conduct that an organisation sets itself in dealing with all relevant associated stakeholders.

Stakeholders and the organisation

Stakeholders are any individuals or a collection of individuals **with an interest** in an organisation. Some stakeholders will be internal to an organisation and others will be external. Internal stakeholders include employees, managers, directors, trade unions and shareholders. External stakeholders include suppliers, customers, competitors, financiers, government and the general public. Various categories of stakeholder will affect or be affected by the organisation in diverse ways, hence stakeholders have different interests or stakes in the organisation. This is shown in Table 12.1.

Stakeholders are also able to influence an organisation to act in their best interests. However, the interests of different stakeholder groups will vary and may even conflict with each other. For example, employees may seek high wages and above-inflation pay rises, while customers would prefer lower prices and lower costs, which are not possible if labour costs are high. The interests

Table 12.1 Stakeholders' power and interest

Internal stakeholders	**Stakeholder interests are:**	**Stakeholder power arises from:**
Employees Managers Directors	• security of employment • wage levels • fringe benefits • responsibility • promotion prospects • working conditions	• job grade or title • position in organisational hierarchy • personal reputation • departmental reputation
Trade unions	• number of union members in the organisation • same as its members (*see* list in box above)	• number of union members • nature of bargaining (local or national)
Shareholders	• profit levels • size of dividend payments • capital growth in share price	• number of shares held
External stakeholders	**Stakeholder interests are:**	**Stakeholder power arises from:**
Suppliers	• size and value of contracts • speed of invoice payment	• location and availability of other suppliers
Customers	• quality of goods and services available • prices and payment terms	• location of other suppliers • quality of goods and services offered by other suppliers • prices and payment terms offered by other suppliers
Competition	• quality of goods and services available • prices and payment terms	• behaviour of other competitors
Financiers	• how promptly repayment of large and short-term loans occurs	• offering better deal (improved quality or better prices and payment terms)
Government	• payment of corporation tax • implementation of legislation (e.g. competition and employment legislation)	• enforcing the legislation via the legal system if necessary

of stakeholders in an organisation and the ways in which **power** is exercised by stakeholders are shown in Table 12.1.

An organisation's stakeholders will be important for an assortment of reasons and to varying degrees; therefore, different stakeholders will respond to the organisation and its behaviour in different ways. Stakeholders whose interests and expectations are met will tend to remain with the organisation. Unsatisfied stakeholders will leave or remain and use their sources of power in an attempt to persuade the organisation to meet their expectations or interests.

Stakeholders who experience a high level of satisfaction with an organisation will tend to demonstrate loyalty and choose to retain their position as stakeholders. For example, employees who feel that their well-paid jobs are secure and offer future prospects are likely to remain with that employer. In contrast, stakeholders who are disappointed with the organisation and its behaviour are more likely to relinquish their stake. The likelihood of an unhappy stakeholder withdrawing their stake in an organisation is increased if better opportunities and potentially greater satisfaction appear to be available by acquiring a similar stake in a different organisation. For example, shareholders in a company who feel that they are not gaining a good enough return on their investment may decide to sell their shares and invest the money in a company that will give a better level of return.

Alternatively, stakeholders who are unhappy with the organisation may decide to remain and attempt to change things. Unsatisfied shareholders may decide to try to influence changes to the organisation's leadership and strategies, with the aim of benefiting in the long run. To achieve this they will have to be able to exert the necessary amount of influence on planning and decision making within the organisation. This requires a suitable combination of authority, determination and ability. It is usually large institutional investors that stand the best chance of being successful with this type of approach, as they have greater power than smaller investors.

Check your understanding

Do you understand the different ways in which stakeholders in an organisation could behave?

Check your understanding by explaining how the following stakeholder might behave:

- a first-year undergraduate student who is very unhappy on their business studies course;
- a teenager who is always happy with the clothes she buys from New Look;
- a finance director who believes the managing director is making poor strategic decisions for the company.

Analysing stakeholders

The analysis of stakeholders involves identifying who they are and considering their power and interest with regard to the organisation. Stakeholders can be identified by brainstorming and are shown on a stakeholder diagram – *see* Figure 12.2. Once identified, the relative power and interest of the stakeholders can be mapped on to a power and interest matrix – *see* Figure 12.3.[1] Additionally, this analysis can be extended to consider the reaction, behaviour and position of stakeholders if a particular strategy or plan were to be implemented by the organisation.

Stakeholders with high power and high interest (category D)

Stakeholders with high power and high interest are key players in the organisation and are often involved in managing the organisation and its future. If

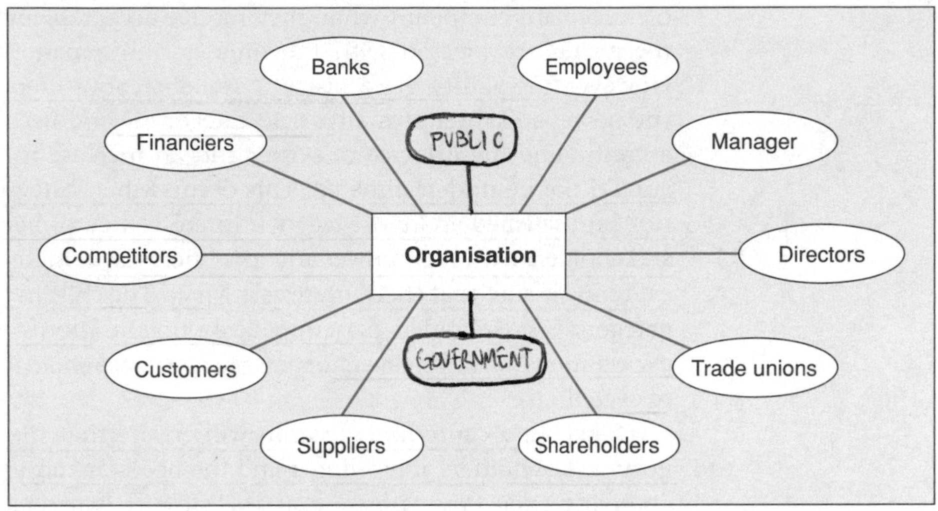

Figure 12.2 Stakeholder diagram

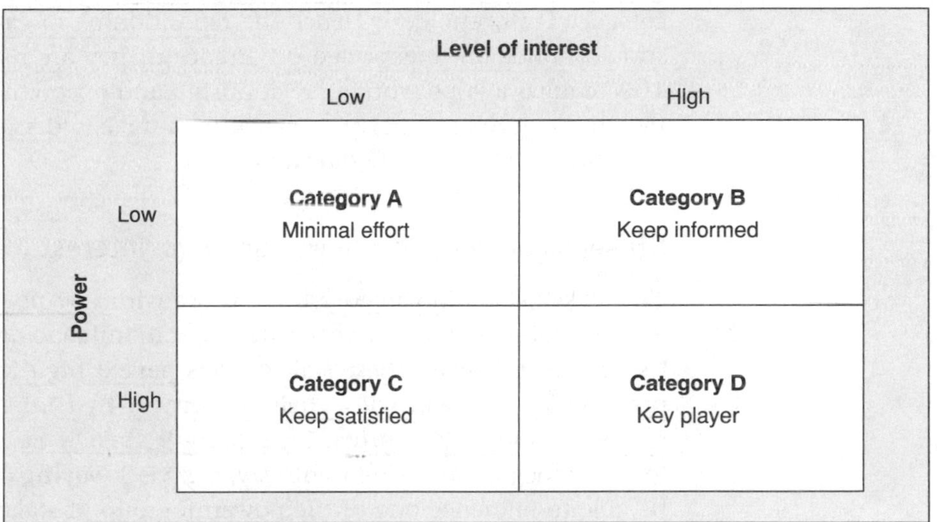

Figure 12.3 Power and interest matrix

Source: Johnson, G and Scholes, K (1999) *Exploring corporate Strategy*, 5th edition, Prentice Hall Europe. Reprinted with permission.

key players are not directly involved in managing the organisation, it is vital that they are given serious consideration in the development of long-term plans and the future direction of the organisation, as they have the power to block proposed plans and implement their own alternative agenda.

Stakeholders with high power and low interest (category C)

Stakeholders with high power and low interest are those who must be kept satisfied, for example institutional shareholders. Institutional shareholders will often remain compliant while they receive acceptable returns on their investment and are pleased with the organisation's management and activities. However, the ability of **category C stakeholders** to reposition themselves on the power and interest matrix into category D and become stakeholders with a continuing high degree of power and an increase in their level of interest should not be underestimated. This occurs when category C stakeholders are not kept satisfied and feel that their interests are not being best served. Hence stakeholders with high power and low interest will increase their level of interest to make sure that their interests are met. The shift in position of unsatisfied category C stakeholders may impede an organisation's plans and prevent the expectations of key players or **category D stakeholders** from being met as expected.

Therefore, a canny organisation will ensure that the expectations of category C stakeholders are well met and the necessary adjustments made to meet changing expectations arising as the current issues facing the organisation change. This helps ensure that category C stakeholders do not feel that their interests are being marginalised at the expense of the interests of key players, category D stakeholders. Hence the repositioning of category C stakeholders should not be an unexpected occurrence if they are managed appropriately. This requires a good working relationship and open channels of communication to be developed between category C stakeholders, the organisation and key players or category D stakeholders.

Stakeholders with low power and high interest (category B)

The stakeholders in category B are those with low power and high interest, who are able to exert relatively little power in influencing the organisation and its actions. However, these stakeholders have a high level of interest in the organisation and will voice their concerns if that interest is not being considered in a suitable manner. If **category B stakeholders** voice their concerns loudly enough and in the right way, e.g. via lobbying or petitions, they may be able to influence one of the powerful group of stakeholders in either category C or D and affect their behaviour. Therefore, organisations need to keep category B stakeholders informed of the organisation's activities and decisions and in doing so convince them that their interests are being taken into account and considered seriously.

Stakeholders with low power and low interest (category A)

Stakeholders with low power and low interest are those in whom the organisation need invest only minimal effort. However, **category A stakeholders** should not be ignored as they may acquire a stake in the organisation by becoming, for example, a customer, supplier or competitor, which will mean an increased level of interest and/or power.

The Automobile Association and its stakeholders

It should be recognised that the position of stakeholders on the power and interest matrix is dynamic and will vary over time according to the current issues that the stakeholders are considering. The situation in which the Automobile Association (AA) found itself during April 1999 provides a good example of an organisation with groups of stakeholders who line up in a certain way due to a particular issue, in this case demutualisation.

The AA was founded in 1905 and by 1999 held around half the motor breakdown market, a market that was experiencing significant change. These changes included the acquisition of Green Flag by Cendant, the entry of the insurance company Direct Line into the market, and the RAC's expected trade sale or flotation. Therefore, in April 1999 the AA considered its options with regard to retaining its mutual status or demutualising. It was rumoured that Ford had informally approached the AA with a takeover offer that would end the latter's mutual status. Other interested bidders were thought to include Centrica and a number of venture capitalists. The then Director-General of the AA, John Maxwell, initiated a strategic review to allow the AA to assess its options. The options available included demutualisation, a joint venture with a suitable partner or takeover by another company. The merchant bank Schroders was advising the AA.

In 1999 the AA had annual sales of around £600 million from its businesses, which included roadside service, publications and driving schools, and its value was estimated to be between £1 billion and £1.5 billion. Pursuit of the demutualisation option and stock market flotation would give each full member of the AA a moderate windfall of £200–250. In 1999 the AA had 9.5 million members, of which 4.3 million were full-paying members who would receive the windfall payouts. However, excluded from the demutualisation windfall were the 1.7 million associate members, including the families of full-paying members who benefit from the association's service. Also excluded were the 3.5 million members who were drivers of fleet cars with AA cover and drivers who received their AA membership as part of a package when purchasing a car.

The AA and stakeholders with high power and high interest (category D)

The key players were the Director-General of the AA and his immediate management team carrying out the strategic review, as well as the full members of the AA – *see* Figure 12.4. John Maxwell and his management team were key players with high power and high interest, as their planning and decision making would determine their future with the AA, the future of the AA, the future of those who worked for the AA, and the future of AA members. The full members would collectively decide whether the AA was to demutualise. They

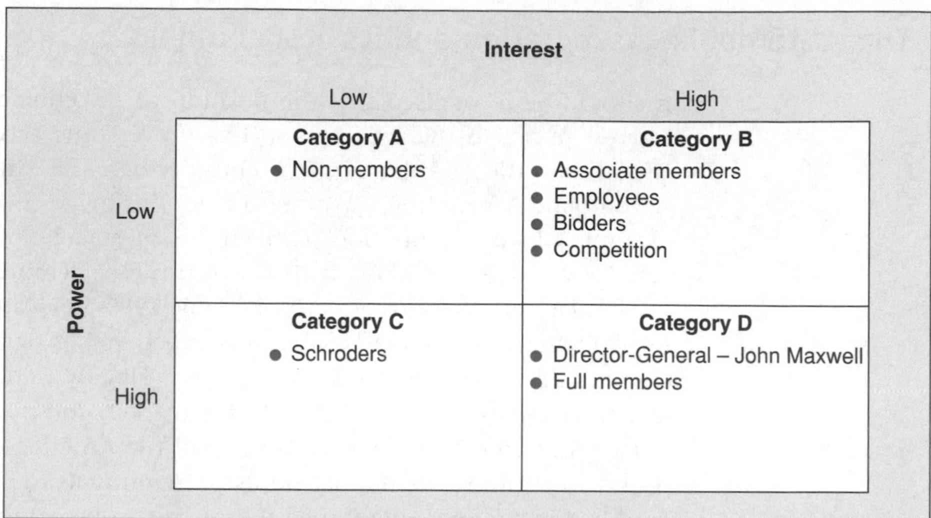

Figure 12.4 Power and interest matrix for the Automobile Association (AA)

might have chosen to support any demutualisation recommendations made by John Maxwell and his team, or to reject them in favour of a bidder, such as Ford, buying the AA. The full members, for example, might have decided this if they were to lose confidence in John Maxwell and his management team and their ability to carry out the demutualisation successfully. Alternatively, full members might have taken the following view, expressed by one of their number in the press in April 1999:

> **I got my membership when I bought a much-loved but temperamental MG Midget. If the AA does choose to demutualise, I would hope they would pay a differential for members who have been with the AA longer. I might vote in favour of the move if they were going to pay me a £300 windfall but the down-side could be that if they become a corporate commercial entity, the cost of its services could soar.**[2]

The AA and stakeholders with high power and low interest (category C)

The merchant bank Schroders was a category C stakeholder, as it had relatively little interest in whether the AA finally decided to demutualise. However, while in the position of corporate adviser to the AA, it was relatively powerful as it was able to advise and potentially influence John Maxwell and his management team.

The AA and stakeholders with low power and high interest (category B)

The category B stakeholders, those with high interest and low power in the demutualisation issue, included associate members and employees. The associate members clearly had a high interest in whether or not the AA decided to demutualise. The primary concerns for associate members were the effect of demutualisation on the services they received and the cost of associate membership. However, as non-voting members, associates had no direct power to influence the outcome of any ballot on demutualisation. Equally, employees had a high interest in the future of the AA and would be concerned as to the effects of demutualisation. Potential effects of demutualisation could have included the AA becoming more competitive and this being achieved via cost cutting and job losses. However, employees had no direct role in the ballot and would ultimately have to accept its outcome.

The **stakeholder matrix** suggests that category B stakeholders, high interest and low power, have to be kept informed, which is true of stakeholder groups such as associate members and employees. In April 1999, the AA kept its members and employees informed by issuing the following statement to the media and via answerphones in its own offices:

> **The AA has always kept an open mind about its structure as it pursues its prime purpose: to serve the best interests of its members. No decisions have been made in this respect.**

However, also with high interest and low power were other stakeholders like potential bidders such as Ford and competitors like Direct Line and Green Flag. These were external stakeholders with a great deal of interest in what the AA would eventually decide to do, as their business and the marketplace in which they operated would be directly influenced by that decision. Any organisation should be aware that any information it releases with the intention of keeping stakeholders such as employees and associate members informed will be in the public arena and therefore available to stakeholders such as competitors and potential bidders.

The AA and stakeholders with low power and low interest (category A)

The category A stakeholders are those with low power and low interest. For the AA, non-members fell into this category. They were unable to receive breakdown services from the organisation and had no influence over its demutualisation decision. However, it should be recognised that stakeholders' power and influence can alter over time. The opportunity of a £200–250 windfall might have encouraged some non-members to become members and move to category D, high interest and high power. This was perfectly possible, as the AA made it clear that it was not closing its doors to new members, nor was it expecting to distinguish between long-term and short-term full members:

> **The AA has no intention of bringing the shutters down on membership. Everyone is as free to join the AA as they were before.**[3]

> **There is no distinction made among full members.**[4]

If the number of new full members joining had been very large and there was no differentiation between new and longer-term members, the value of the windfall paid to full members could have decreased. This could have pushed longer-term full members to seek to lobby or influence John Maxwell and his management team to distinguish between long- and short-term members.

Stakeholder alliances and coalitions

When analysing stakeholders, two points should be noted. First, people and organisations may belong to more than one category of stakeholder. Second, stakeholders and organisations may depend on one another, with the nature of the dependency varying according to the amount of power and/or interest the stakeholder has in the organisation. For example, if the Director-General of the AA favoured demutualisation, he would have depended on the full-time members voting in large enough numbers for the demutualisation proposals. However, he would have needed to recognise that full members might have been subject to influence by associate members, who may have been related to full members, e.g. husband and wife. Similarly, some employees (category B) were also full members of the AA and how they were treated and informed as employees might have influenced their voting behaviour as full members. The employees might have felt that cost cutting and job losses were likely to result from demutualisation. Hence they might have lobbied and sought to influence the voting full members to vote against a change in the AA's structure or to vote for a takeover rather than demutualisation if they thought their best interests would be served in this way. Equally, if associate members were concerned about the service they received and its cost, they might have sought to influence full voting members, which would perhaps have been easy if the full voting members were family members. In addition, associate members and employees might have sought to influence John Maxwell and his management team directly, via letter-writing campaigns and petitions.

Therefore, the arguments in favour of demutualisation had to focus on the benefits for full members (cash windfall and service levels at least maintained, preferably improved in some way), associate members (service levels at least maintained, preferably improved in some way), and employees, particularly those who were also full members (issues of job security and future operation of the AA for employees were crucial).

The members of the AA were balloted in August 1999 on the proposed sale of the AA to Centrica. The result of the ballot was announced in mid-September 1999 and showed 67 per cent of eligible members voted and 96 per cent of them voted in favour of the sale. The sale to Centrica was completed in July 2000 for £1.1 billion.

Check your understanding

Do you understand the nature of stakeholders' power and interest?

Check your understanding by answering the following questions.

(a) A production operative has more power than a senior manager. True or false?
(b) A corporate investor is more powerful than an individual investor. True or false?
(c) The government is usually a stakeholder with low power and low interest in an organisation. True or false?
(d) The interest of a small individual customer is not high. True or false?

Corporate governance

Corporate governance refers to the influence of stakeholders and their exercising of power to control the strategic direction of the organisation. The stakeholders who have the biggest and most important role to play in corporate governance are the key stakeholders, namely the managing director, other directors and senior staff in the organisation. Their role in corporate governance is important as they are able to influence the development and implementation of strategy.

Therefore, corporate governance includes regular monitoring and evaluation of strategy that has been implemented and approval of strategy yet to be implemented. This allows the organisation to adjust and moderate its strategy to ensure the interests of all stakeholders are appropriately met and that one group of stakeholders does not benefit at the expense of another group of stakeholders. For example, good corporate governance would stop directors receiving excessive pay rises at the expense of high prices for customers. The example of directors of utility companies receiving high pay rises, while steeply increasing the price for essentials, such as gas, electricity and water, illustrate poor corporate governance. Equally, at the time of writing, October 2008, the collapse or near collapse of banks, including retail banks around the world, due to their over-ambitious borrowings, must surely call into question the quality of corporate governance at many of these institutions.

Conduct and control

Directors and senior staff are responsible for developing and implementing strategy, meaning they act as agents for other stakeholders. Hence there is a separation of the control of the organisation by the directors and the interests of other stakeholders. Good corporate governance will help ensure that directors do not abuse their power and control to gain benefits at the expense of other stakeholders. In large companies ownership and control are separated, with executive directors managing the business and non-executive directors monitoring management decisions and activity, but having no day-to-day management responsibility for the organisation's operations.

Non-executive directors

The non-executive director will normally hold a senior management job or role in an organisation that has no links to the organisation in which they hold a non-executive directorship. Hence they have no interest whatsoever in the organisation but will have significant senior experience to comment on the decisions and activities of the organisation in their role as a non-executive director.

The appointment of non-executive directors is seen as a way of ensuring that the conduct of the organisation is beyond reproach. It should be noted that organisations appoint their own non-executive directors to undertake the monitoring role. In March 2008 HSBC instituted a boardroom shake-up, which saw three long-serving non-executive directors step down, partly as they had been in office for a long period of time and were no longer considered independent by shareholders. Two new non-executive directors from the software group Oracle and Infosys, an Indian IT services company, replaced them.[5] However, if non-executive directors are of sufficient calibre in their own field and hold tenure for a fixed period time, for example three years, then other stakeholders should be able to have confidence in their independence and good judgement.

The chairman and managing director

Today corporate governance often sees the executive roles of chairman and managing director separated, whereas in the past the chairman and managing director were often the same person. The chairman, the most senior person in the organisation, often focuses on the organisation's relationship with powerful external stakeholders such as financiers, governments and shareholders.

In contrast the managing director, the most senior manager in the organisation, will be responsible for running the organisation and ensuring its operations are efficient and effective. This means a critical part of the managing director's role are the relationships with internal stakeholders, such as other directors, managers, staff and trade unions, and the transactional relationships (*see* Chapter 3) with external stakeholders, such as suppliers, that effect the running of the organisation. An organisation which chooses not to follow this accepted approach to corporate governance is Marks & Spencer, as illustrated when it appointed Stuart Rose as executive chairman while he continued to hold his chief executive role – *see* Entry case study 12.1.

Small companies that cannot afford to separate the roles of chairman and managing director may choose to undertake corporate governance by monitoring decisions and activities via a series of committees which each have responsibility for specific areas of the organisation, e.g. pay and remuneration.

Corporate governance and information

Important to good corporate governance is how senior staff exercise their power in making information available for inspection by other stakeholders. However, this can be fraught with difficulty due to the limitations of the information. On occasions the full picture may not be given and some commercially sensitive information will not be made available outside the organisation, nor will it be fully circulated within the organisation. For example, the annual report and accounts made available to shareholders and the public is limited to what the organisation chooses to tell its shareholders, although it is audited to say it is a true and fair representation of the business at that point in time. In contrast, the main board will have access to very full information, and it is important that this is used correctly when making decisions and informing other stakeholders. The role of the non-executive director is key in ensuring full disclosure of relevant issues. This is why the independence and good character of non-executive directors are important.

In the UK there have been several commissions on standards and corporate governance that have produced reports; for example, the Cadbury, Greenbury and Hampel reports. In the US, corrupt corporate behaviour resulted in the Sarbanes-Oxley Act (2002). This Act makes it essential for all companies operating in the US, including overseas companies, to keep an audit trail of all decisions taken by the company. This has involved companies in setting up new, expensive and time-consuming procedures for documenting decisions.

Check your understanding

Do you understand the different roles involved in good corporate governance?

Check your understanding by summarising the role of each of the following members of senior management in corporate governance.

(a) The chairman.
(b) The managing director.
(c) The non-executive director.

Ethics and corporate social responsibility

Ethics and **corporate social responsibility** are standards of conduct that an organisation sets itself in dealing with both the internal and external environments and all associated stakeholders – *see* Table 12.2. Ethics are the basic standards by which organisations conduct business and include honesty, health and safety, and corrupt practice. In contrast, corporate social responsibility covers a wider range of issues, which will vary from organisation to organisation, but could include climate change, global poverty, charitable and political donations. For example, was it right that Bernie Ecclestone, chairman of

Table 12.2 Ethical and corporate social responsibility issues

Ethical issues	Corporate social responsibility issues
• Honesty in dealing with workforce, suppliers and customers • Health and safety of workforce • Doing business in countries with tyrannical regimes • Corrupt practice, espionage and bribery	• Climate change and sustainability in business • Global poverty • Charitable and political donations • Provision of education and healthcare for workforce and their families

Formula One motor racing made a political donation of cash to the Labour Party around the same time that the Labour government in power exempted Formula One from a ban on tobacco advertising and sponsorship? This should illustrate that in reality both ethics and corporate social responsibility are interrelated and most organisations accept that ethics and corporate social responsibility influence how they conduct business.

Organisations need to accept that ethics that are present in society need to be conformed to and may be legally enforceable, for example health and safety legislation. The behaviour of an organisation can also include being responsible with regard to other issues that are not legally enforceable, for example being carbon neutral. An organisation may choose to serve its own interests by behaving professionally and ethically with respect to its stakeholders, such as its workers, suppliers and customers. This is done in the belief that such stakeholders value ethical and professional behaviour and will be loyal to and remain with the organisation (*see* earlier section of this chapter). This approach means the organisation exercises good judgement in regard to its behaviour and hence decreases the likelihood of inappropriate behaviour and the resulting bad publicity.

Any organisation needs to consider how far beyond the legal minimum it wishes to go with regard to ethical and responsible behaviour. An organisation may choose to have a number of policies that it implements, covering a range of issues, for example environmental sustainability, work–life balance, dealing with suppliers. In contrast, it may choose to have no such policies and leave the management of these issues with the individual mangers who make decisions on behalf of the organisation. Underpinning the decisions taken regarding ethical and responsible behaviour will be the consideration of cost. The cost of developing any ethical policy will be evaluated against the advantages of implementing it and the disadvantages of not implementing it. The organisation may also want to consider if it has a responsibility beyond the legal minimum towards stakeholders who may benefit from the implementation of corporate social responsibility policies. For example, a company may choose to pay staff more than a minimum amount and provide education for the children of staff, particularly if the company is operating in a developing country where education may not be easily available and free. Companies may also take the view that it will benefit if its workforce enjoys good health, and provide health clinics or private medical insurance as appropriate.

Occasionally companies may undertake or find themselves caught up in allegations of bribery and corruption. In July 2008 an employee of the German company Siemens was found guilty on 49 counts of breach of trust; he was fined and given a two-year suspended sentence. He stated he was acting on the orders of more senior staff and indeed several other witnesses at his trial implied senior managers knew the extent of the bribery taking place. Siemens is alleged to have bribed corporate customers all over the world in a bid to win contracts. The allegation is that this was done by channelling up to €1.3 billion via a series of false companies and slush funds.[6,7] Equally, it is also possible for a company to find itself linked to allegations of bribery, which are unknown to it. This happened to Tesco in Turkey: an entrepreneur who sold Tesco land with commercial planning consents in place was accused of bribery in relation to the planning consents he gained for the land before selling to Tesco.[8]

Whistle-blowing

Whistle-blowing is the release of confidential corporate information to an external third party. The third party may be the media, although a conversation with a colleague, friend or family member, in which corporate information and concerns are revealed, can be whistle-blowing. This applies even if the third party, e.g. a friend, was unaware that confidential information was being revealed to them. In the United Kingdom, the Public Interest Disclosure Act 1998 (PIDA) allows for the whistle-blower to loose the protection of the law if it comes to light that they voiced their concerns with a third party before raising their concerns via the organisation's formal internal procedures and are dismissed. Therefore, whistle-blowing is not an action to be undertaken lightly. Whistle-blowers often suffer personal damage, such as losing their job and finding it difficult to find alternative employment, especially in the same industry, which in turn leads to stressful financial and emotional hardship, which will be felt by the whole family of the whistle-blower.

This raises the question, 'why whistle-blow?' The simple answer is to prevent a tragedy. There are examples of tragedies, such as the Piper-Alpha oil-rig disaster in the North Sea, the *Herald of Free Enterprise* ferry disaster at Zeebrugge and the Clapham railway crash outside London. In such tragedies employees raised concerns before the tragedy occurred and had these concerns been acted upon the tragedy in question might have been avoided. Hence such tragedies are predictable and occur due to the failure to listen to and act on the concerns of employees, along with poor practice, control and checks. In some instances employee concerns may have been unreported due to the authoritarian nature of management.

In 1987 the Townsend Thoresen ferry the *Herald of Free Enterprise* capsized 100 yards from the shore as it left Zeebrugge harbour in Belgium due to its bow doors being left open. This resulted in the death of 193 people.

On five occasions prior to the capsizing of the *Herald of Free Enterprise*, staff had raised their concern about ships leaving port with their bow doors open, but they were not acted upon. The suggestion was made that lights should be fitted to the bridge to indicate whether or not the bow doors were closed. This suggestion was described as 'sensible' and likely to have prevented the disaster by the final report.[9] The fitting of lights would have allowed the captain and staff on the bridge taking the ship to sea to know if the bow doors were closed. The concerns had been reported, but not been conveyed to the top management, as they were lost in middle management.

Is whistle-blowing justified?

As discussed earlier in this section, the consequences of whistle-blowing and getting it wrong can be harmful for both the whistle-blower and the organisation. Hence there have been some attempts to draw up conditions and criteria, which if met make whistle-blowing justifiable. De George[10] is one such author and he argues that there are six such conditions, and that whistle-blowing is justifiable if the overall effects are likely to be positive. De George argues that that the first three conditions (*see* Table 12.3) make whistle-blowing allowable, but not obligatory. However, if conditions 4 and 5 can also be met, then the whistle-blowing becomes a far more compelling option. Hence, without these conditions being met it is very difficult to justify whistle-blowing and it is likely the result will be harmful for both whistle-blower and organisation.

DeGeorge also argues that the whistle-blower, in meeting these criteria, should avoid confrontation and look for effective ways to resolve the issues. The whistle-blower should also be sure their claims are justifiable, and seeking the support of professional colleagues can be helpful here, as can support from management if possible. Before whistle-blowing and probably resigning,

Table 12.3 De George's conditions for whistle-blowing

1 Product possesses the potential to do serious harm to members of the public.

2 Concerned employee should report all the facts to their immediate superiors.

3 If the immediate superiors fail to act effectively, then more senior managers, including directors, should be approached and all available internal channels should be exhausted.

4 The whistle-blower should have documentary evidence that will convince the impartial external observer that the product posses a serious danger.

5 The whistle-blower must believe appropriate changes will be implemented as a result of their whistle-blowing and prevent serious harm.

6 The whistle-blower must be acting in good faith, without malice or vindictiveness.

Source: Fisher, C. and Lovell, A. (2003) Business Ethics and Value, FT/Prentice Hall.

make sure all the formal internal procedures have been exhausted. The act of whistle-blowing should be one of last resort.[11]

Summary

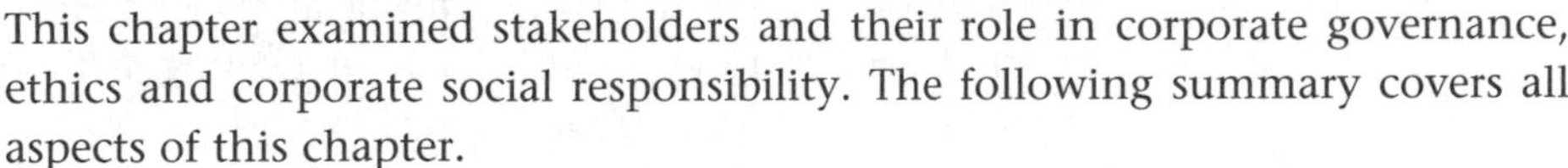

This chapter examined stakeholders and their role in corporate governance, ethics and corporate social responsibility. The following summary covers all aspects of this chapter.

1 Stakeholders are individuals or groups who have an interest in an organisation. Different stakeholders have varying levels of power and interest in an organisation.

2 Stakeholders whose interests are satisfied by an organisation will remain with it. In contrast, those stakeholders who are dissatisfied will seek to leave the organisation or they may chose to remain and try to change things.

3 Stakeholder relative power and interest can be mapped on to a power and interest matrix. Additionally, this analysis can be extended to consider the reaction, behaviour and position of stakeholders if a particular strategy or plan were to be implemented.

4 Category D stakeholders, those with high power and high interest, are key players, such as the managing director. Category C stakeholders are those with high power and low interest, an example being a corporate shareholder in a company. Individual customers and employees often fall into category B, having low power and high interest. Those stakeholders in which the organisation has minimal interest are category A, low power and low interest.

5 Different categories of stakeholders may not always act individually – they may form coalitions with another category of stakeholders. For example, individual employees (usually category B) may band together and try to influence category C stakeholders who have high power, unlike themselves.

6 Corporate governance refers to the influence of stakeholders and their exercising of power to control the strategic direction of the organisation. The key stakeholders who have the biggest and most important role to play in corporate governance are the managing director, other directors and senior staff in the organisation. In good corporate governance the roles of chairman and managing director are normally separated.

7 Corporate governance includes regular monitoring and evaluation of strategy that has been implemented and approval of strategy yet to be implemented. This allows the organisation to adjust and moderate its strategy to ensure the interests of all stakeholders are appropriately met and that one group of stakeholders does not benefit at the expense of another group of stakeholders.

8 Ethics are the basic standards by which organisations conduct business and include honesty, health and safety, and corrupt practice. In contrast, corporate social responsibility covers a wider range of issues, which will vary from organisation to organisation, but could include climate change, global poverty, and charitable and political donations.

9 Therefore, ethics and corporate social responsibility are standards of conduct that an organisation sets itself in dealing with both the internal and external environments. Hence in reality both ethics and corporate responsibility are interrelated and most organisations accept that ethics and corporate social responsibility influence how they conduct business.

10 Whistle-blowing is the release of confidential corporate information to an external third party. The consequences of whistle-blowing and getting it wrong can be harmful for both the whistle-blower and the organisation. Hence there have been some attempts to draw up conditions and criteria which, if met, make whistle-blowing justifiable. De George is one such author and he argues that there are six such conditions (*see* Table 12.3) and that whistle-blowing is justifiable if the overall effects are likely to be positive.

Chapter objectives and the exit case study

While reading this chapter and engaging in the activities, you should have learned how to apply theory and models and analyse situations. This means you should be able to meet the chapter objectives outlined at the beginning of the chapter. The table below shows which chapter objectives can be tested by the different questions.

Chapter objective	Check you have achieved this by
1 Identify and analyse an organisation's stakeholders.	answering case study questions 1 and 2.

EXIT CASE STUDY 12.2

No help for charities in Iceland plight

by Jim Pickard and Tom Braithwaite

Scores of charities came away empty-handed on Friday after seeking emergency compensation from the Treasury for the potential loss of millions of pounds left on deposit in failed Icelandic banks. In the latest twist to this week's Icelandic saga, the National Council for Voluntary Organisations suggested that charities could lose up to £120m deposited in Iceland's banks. But after talks with government on Friday, the NCVO was blunt about the help offered: 'None,' said a representative. That figure takes the total of public sector cash in Icelandic banks up to nearly £1bn, including at least £800m from councils, £40m from Transport for London, £30m from the Metropolitan Police and £2m from NHS foundation trusts.

The nationalisation of three Icelandic banks this week – Glitnir, Landsbanki and Kaupthing – has prompted wider fears about the safety of an estimated £6bn of retail deposits from 300,000 British citizens and an unknown quantity of business savings. As UK Treasury officials flew into Iceland on Friday to discuss a solution to the crisis – talks begin on Saturday – Gordon Brown pledged to do 'everything in our power to get this money returned'.

The UK government was talking to Icelandic authorities and taking legal action to secure investments at risk, the prime minister said.

On Wednesday, the UK put Kaupthing Singer & Friedlander into administration, prompting the nationalisation of parent company Kaupthing in Iceland. It also froze an estimated £4bn of Landsbanki assets in the UK using anti-terror laws, to the fury of Icelandic authorities. That action was questioned by Shami Chakrabarti, director of pressure group Liberty, who said: 'This may not be an abuse of "terror laws" but it certainly demonstrates the way that very broad security measures are sneaked into such legislation for creative use later on.'

Mr Brown authorised the move after failing to receive assurances that UK citizens would receive compensation from Icelandic authorities. As political leaders in Reykjavik and London stepped up their war of words, some drew comparisons with the 'Cod Wars' of the 1970s. On Friday 10 Downing Street complained that the Icelanders had withheld information and indicated preferential treatment for domestic creditors. But the rhetoric was toned down a notch, with Mr Brown hailing 'strong bilateral relations' between the two countries and his spokesman predicting 'cooperative' talks.

The NCVO has identified seven charities with £30m at risk but estimates the total investment of UK charities at risk to be more than £120m. Among those hit was Cats Protection, with £11.2m of deposits in Kaupthing Singer & Friedlander. Separately, the National Housing Federation is seeking to establish how many housing associations have been hit.

Councils were forced to defend themselves against accusations of naivety after leaving their money in Icelandic banks – despite warnings of financial instability. They said the banks had reasonable credit ratings when they made the deposits. Landsbanki, in particular, had huge numbers of British depositors who invested £4.6bn through its 'Icesave' internet bank, which had customers across Europe.

It is hoped most of the money can be recovered from the sale of the bank's assets. If not, Treasury officials had hoped to secure £2.2bn from Iceland's depositor compensation scheme – up to £16,000 per account – though this is now the subject of wrangling between the two countries. Of the remainder, £1.4bn could come from the UK's Financial Services Compensation Scheme – which covers up to £50,000 per account – with the rest from the government. But with insufficient money in the FSCS, public cash could be needed to cover the gap until Landsbanki's assets are sold.

Icesave house purchasers face completion problems. Savers hoping to buy a home with their Icesave savings may find themselves unable to complete the deal, with consequences for property chains, Alice Ross reports.

David Pedrick, 31, an accountant, and his wife Hayley, 28, are in the process of buying their first house but the money they need to pay the deposit is in an Icesave account. The couple, currently renting in Surbiton, Surrey, said they had decided to buy as house prices have fallen so much they can now buy a larger place in their price range. The house they are looking to buy, also in Surbiton, is at an agreed price of £243,500. The couple have £24,000 saved for their 10 per cent deposit. Some £6,000 is with NatWest but a further £18,000 is now locked away in Icesave. 'You almost take it as a personal offence as you're only two weeks away from buying your first house,' said Mr Pedrick. They are hoping to exchange contracts within three weeks, which is likely to mean they will not have the cash to pay the deposit. 'If we don't have the money, we're considering personal loans or we might even start phoning friends and family,' said Mr Pedrick.

But Ray Boulger, senior technical manager at John Charcol, warned that with no clarity on how long Icesave customers have to wait, this could mean hefty loan repayments. Mr and Mrs Pedrick are safe as they have not exchanged contracts yet. But for those who have, the consequences could be serious. Lawyers warn that people who cannot complete on a property transaction could be sued.

Source: from 'No help for charities in Iceland plight, *The Financial Times*, 10 October 2008 (Pickard, J. and Braithwaite, T.).

Exit case study questions

1 Identify the stakeholders in Icesave and comment on the likelihood of the different stakeholders getting their money back.

2 What lessons are to be learned from the Icesave experience with regard to investing money as a large organisation and as an individual?

Short-answer questions

1 Define a stakeholder.
2 Define a key player.
3 Identify a stakeholder in an organisation and their source of interest.
4 Identify a stakeholder in an organisation and their source of power.
5 Briefly summarise the expected behaviour of satisfied stakeholders in an organisation.
6 Briefly summarise the expected behaviour of unsatisfied stakeholders in an organisation.
7 What should organisations seek to do with stakeholders who have high power and low interest?
8 What should organisations seek to do with stakeholders who have low power and high interest?
9 What should organisations seek to do with stakeholders who have low power and low interest?
10 Define corporate governance.
11 Explain the differing roles of chairman, managing director and non-executive director.
12 Explain the difference between ethics and corporate social responsibility.
13 How are ethics and corporate social responsibility linked?
14 Summarise the role of ethics and corporate social responsibility in managing stakeholders.
15 Define whistle-blowing.
16 List the six conditions that make whistle-blowing justifiable.
17 Explain how the whistle-blower could ensure they have met the criteria listed in response to question 16.

Chapter objectives and assignment questions

While reading this chapter and engaging in the activities, you should have learned how to apply theory and models and analyse situations. This means you should be able to meet the chapter objectives outlined at the beginning of the chapter. The table below shows which chapter objectives can be tested by the different questions.

Chapter objective	Check you have achieved this by
1 Identify and analyse an organisation's stakeholders.	answering assignment question 1.
2 Explain and summarise good corporate governance and the key roles involved.	answering assignment question 2.
3 Discuss ethics and corporate responsibility in relation to a business and its stakeholders.	answering assignment question 3.

Assignment questions

1. Choose and research an organisation. Identify all its stakeholders and plot them on a power and interest matrix. Comment on how and why you think the power and interest of the stakeholders will change in the next 12 months and the next five years. How does this analysis help you understand the organisation's environment?
2. Choose any two organisations and discuss the similarities and differences in their approaches to corporate governance.
3. Identify two organisations, one with sound ethical behaviour and corporate social responsibility and one with a poor record on ethics and corporate social responsibility. Compare and contrast these two organisations and their behaviour.

WEBLINKS available at **www.pearsoned.co.uk/capon**

- The website below looks at the National Grid and its stakeholders:
  http://www.nationalgrid.com/uk/social&environment/stakeholders.asp
- The website below is for the UK Shareholders Association – shareholders are important stakeholders in organisations:
  http://www.uksa.org.uk/
- The two websites listed below are for Monsanto, a company that produces genetically modified crops. Ethical issues concerning genetically modified food are often debated:
  http://www.monsanto.com/monsanto/
  http://www.monsanto.co.uk/
- This is the CIPD webpage for whistle-blowing:
  http://www.cipd.co.uk/subjects/empreltns/whistleblw/whistle.htm
- This is the Health and Safety Executive webpage for whistle-blowing:
  http://www.hse.gov.uk/workers/whistleblowing.htm
- This is a government page on whistle-blowing:
  http://www.direct.gov.uk/en/employment/resolvingworkplacedisputes/index.htm

FURTHER READING

The following chapters all look at aspects of the material covered in this chapter.

- Fisher, C and Lovell, A (2008) *Business Ethics and Values*, 3rd edn, Chapters 6 and 9, Harlow: Financial Times Prentice Hall.
- Johnson, G, Scholes, K and Whittington, R (2008) *Exploring Corporate Strategy*, 8th edn, Chapter 4, Harlow: Financial Times Prentice Hall.
- Lynch, R (2006) *Corporate Strategy*, 4th edn, Chapter 10, Harlow: Financial Times Prentice Hall.
- Martin, J (2005) *Organisational Behaviour*, 3rd edn, Chapter 12, London: Thomson Learning.
- Palmer, A and Hartley, B (2006) *The Business Environment*, 5th edn, Chapter 9, Maidenhead: McGraw-Hill.
- Torrington, D, Hall, L and Taylor, S (2008) *Human Resource Management*, 7th edn, Chapter 30, Harlow: Financial Times Prentice Hall.
- Worthington, I and Britton, C (2006) *The Business Environment*, 5th edn, Chapter 17, Harlow: Financial Times Prentice Hall.

REFERENCES

1 Johnson, G, Scholes, K and Whittington, R (2008) *Exploring Corporate Strategy*, 8th edn, Harlow: Financial Times Prentice Hall.
2 Jagger, S (1999) 'AA ponders its road to the future', *Daily Telegraph*, 24 April.
3 Ibid.
4 Ibid.
5 Larsen, P T and Burgess, K (2008) 'Board shake-up after criticisms over corporate governance', *Financial Times*, 4 March.
6 Schafer, D (2008) 'Siemens enters crunch week in long running bribery scandal', *Financial Times*, 28 July.
7 Schafer, D (2008) 'Former Siemens executive found guilty over bribery schemes role', *Financial Times*, 29 July.
8 Barker, A T and Braithwaite, T (2008) 'Tesco pulled into bribery case over Turkish site', *Financial Times*, 15 August.
9 http://www.maib.gov.uk/publications/investigation_reports/herald_of_free_enterprise.cfm
10 De George, R T (1999) *Business Ethics*, 5th edn, Englewood Cliffs, NJ: Prentice Hall.
11 Ibid.

Glossary

Absorption costing is a costing technique which ensures that all the overhead costs incurred by the business are covered by the revenues it receives.

Accounting rate of return (ARR) expresses the profit generated by an investment or project as a percentage of the capital invested.

Advertising is undertaken by organisations to attract new customers or retain existing customers. Advertising takes place in a variety of places: on TV, on radio, in the cinema, on the web, in the press. Firms usually have to pay to advertise in any of these media.

After-sales customer service is provided by organisations to support customers who have purchased and are using their products and services. Common examples include repair and maintenance services.

Appointment systems are schedules by which organisations see customers to enable resources to be used efficiently such that neither the customers nor practitioners are kept waiting.

Assets are things which companies own, such as buildings and stock.

Association of South East Asian Nations (ASEAN) is the trading bloc which encompasses many countries located in the Far East.

Auditor's report appears in the annual report and accounts and is addressed to the shareholders and should ideally state that the report and accounts, including the financial statements, provide a true and fair view of the company's activities.

Average capital employed over the lifetime of a project takes into account the residual value of the project at the end of its working life.

Bargaining power of buyers is where the industrial or commercial buyer is powerful if the threat of substitutes is strong, giving rise to a number of choices that allow the buyer to shop around. The individual consumer is usually much less powerful as a buyer compared with large organisations but is still influenced by factors similar to those for commercial buyers.

Bargaining power of suppliers is high in industries or sectors where there are few possible suppliers and they can exert a good deal of influence on the organisations to which they supply goods.

Behaviour defines things people do that can be observed.

Bet your company cultures occur in organisation which take high risks and wait a long time for the response to their decisions.

Boston Consulting Group matrix is one of the marketing tools which can be used to examine the range of products and product types an organisation offers. The idea is that a balanced portfolio is best.

Capacity is a measure of performance, and if a system is operating to capacity, it is producing the maximum amount of product over a specified time period.

Capital is money which a company raises to acquire assets and comes from sources such as bank loans, retained profits and shares.

Category A stakeholders have low power and low interest in the organisation and are those in whom the organisation need invest only minimal effort.

Category B stakeholders are those with low power and high interest, who are able to exert relatively little power in influencing the organisation and its actions. However, these stakeholders have a high level of interest in the organisation and will voice their concerns if that interest is not being considered in a suitable manner.

Category C stakeholders have high power and low interest in the organisation and should be kept satisfied as they have the ability to reposition themselves on the power and interest matrix into category D. This occurs when category C stakeholders are not kept satisfied and feel that their interests are not being best served.

Category D stakeholders are key players and hold high power and high interest in the organisation and are often involved in managing the organisation and its future and have the power to block proposed plans and implement their own alternative agenda.

Causal methods of forecasting examine the impact of external influences and use them to forecast future demand or activity.

Causal textures are outside linkages or interdependencies that are entirely in the organisation's external environment.

Centralisation is the concentration of decision-making responsibility in the hands of managers at the top of an organisation.

Charismatic leaders will create an organisational culture in which staff will be self-motivating and seek to contribute to the organisation.

Cohesiveness is defined as the extent to which group members are attracted to and wish to remain in a group.

Combination is the process for transferring explicit knowledge around an organisation as via an intranet or staff development and training course or any company-wide communication system.

Command groups are determined by an organisation's hierarchy and structure.

Competitive rivalry in an industry or sector concerns who the present and potential competitors are, and how intensive the competition is between them.

Copyright is recognised by the symbol © and copyright protection is automatic and no formal registration is required. Copyright gives creators of a wide range of work, including literary, musical, artistic and photographic work, along with recordings, films and broadcasts, legal rights to control the ways in which their work is exploited.

Core permanent employees have highly skilled jobs, with relatively good job security and career prospects.

Corporate governance refers to the influence of stakeholders and their exercising of power to control the strategic direction of the organisation. The stakeholders who have the biggest and most important role to play in corporate governance are the key stakeholders, namely the managing director, other directors and senior staff in the organisation.

Corporate social responsibility covers a wider range of issues, which will vary from organisation to organisation, but could include climate change, global poverty, and charitable and political donations.

Cost focus is serving a narrow target market, where customers are very price sensitive and the company will deliver low-cost and thus low-priced products and services to the market.

Cost leadership is seeking to be the lowest-cost producer in the industry or sector to supply a mass market.

Costing involves looking at and defining the costs involved in producing a product or service.

Creditors are individuals or companies to which a firm owes money.

Culture – *see* local culture, national culture, global culture, organisational culture and personal cultural provenance.

Customer acquisition is expanding the number of customers for existing products.

Customer capital comprises the customer base, customer relations and customer potential.

Customer diversification is achieved by increasing sales of a new product or service to new customers.

Customer extension is concerned with extending the range of products or services available for a customer to purchase from the organisation.

Customer loyalty is the behaviour customers exhibit when they make frequent repeat purchases of a brand.

Customer needs and wants – the needs are those things customers must have; wants are those things which customers would like to have.

Debtors are individuals or other companies that owe a firm money.

Decentralisation is the dispersal of decision-making responsibility to operational managers.

Delayed delivery scheduling system occurs when the customer will not be inconvenienced by delivery of a service being delayed, e.g. a dry cleaners.

Delphi method follows a well-defined set of procedures in which experts are asked to complete and return a questionnaire. The results are summarised and the experts asked to amend their replies in light of the summarised results. This avoids problems of face-to-face discussion.

Demographic change is change in the age and structure of a population.

Demographics/Demography is the statistical study of changes in the nature of a population.

Dependent demand inventory covers items or components used in the assembly of a final product.

Design right is free and automatic and gives the original creator protection regarding shape or configuration of a product only in the United Kingdom, for a 10- to 15-year period.

Differentiation is serving a broad target market, but by providing a product or service that is different and better due to its added value.

Differentiation focus is serving a narrow target market where consumers are prepared to spend a great deal of money in order to acquire luxury, top-of-the-range goods or services.

Direct costs are the expenditure on elements that go straight into producing the product or service, e.g. raw materials.

Discounted cashflow methods of investment appraisal take account of returns in later years being worth less than returns in the early years of a project.

Distribution is the method by which goods and services are delivered to customers.

Diversification is using new products to move into a new market, in which the company has not previously operated.

Dividend payments are the share of profits paid out to the shareholders of a business.

Divisional structures contain separate divisions based around individual product lines or based on the geographic areas of the markets served. The divisional structure is found in diversified organisations.

Drivers of change are influences inside or outside of the organisation that can be a source of change.

Economic influences on organisations include the impact of banks, stock markets and trading blocs.

Effectiveness is how well an organisation sets and achieves its goals.

Efficiency is the ratio of actual output to possible output, usually expressed as a percentage.

Egalitarian describes the principle of equal rights for all.

Ethics are the basic standards by which organisations conduct business and include honesty, health and safety, and corrupt practice.

European Union (EU) is a trading bloc which encompasses virtually all the countries of Western Europe, with countries from Eastern Europe due to start joining.

Explicit knowledge is recorded and will be in the public arena if it has been published and therefore may be exploited by all the competitors in an industry.

Extension strategy is a plan for lengthening the life cycle of a product or service.

External environment is the big wide world in which organisations operate. It encompasses the broad general environment, the competitive environment and the marketplace.

External staff are those brought in quickly to meet increased demand and include self-employed consultants, subcontractors and temporary agency staff.

Externalisation is the process for transferring tacit knowledge to explicit knowledge. Organisations could choose to formally record the discussions and ideas that emerge from meetings. This may require several meetings and iterations of the tacit knowledge to take it from a vague idea to clear and structured knowledge. This is an attempt to record knowledge that was previously hidden.

Financial management is the raising of capital to finance an organisation's operations and its careful use.

Financial reporting is allowing shareholders and other stakeholders in a company to know how it is performing. This is done by issuing an annual report and accounts.

Financial statements are found in a company's annual report and accounts and include balance sheets, profit and loss accounts and cashflow statements.

First come, first served scheduling is simple and straightforward: customers are served in the order they arrive.

First peripheral group are those employees with full-time jobs, not careers. Employees in this group often require more vocational skills than core employees.

Fixed costs do not change directly in relation to the level of productivity, but have to be paid on a regular basis, e.g. rent and insurance.

Fixed position layouts are used when the product is too big or heavy to move, as in shipbuilding, airplane assembly and oil rig construction. All the operations are carried out on one site around the static product.

Fixed schedule system arises when a service is delivered to many customers at once. The timetable or schedules are generally known in advance by customers as the information has been made publicly available. Examples include bus, tram, train and airline timetables.

Flexible firm model divides employees into three categories: core, peripheral and external.

Force field analysis is the analysis of the impact of driving forces on restraining forces when an organisation is undergoing change.

Forming is a group coming together and finding out about each other.

Fraser's five-fold grading can be used to produce a person specification and covers the areas of impact on others, qualifications or acquired knowledge, innate abilities, motivation, adjustment or emotional balance.

Free market occurs where there is little or no regulation of commercial activity by government.

Friendship groups are formed by people who have a common social interest.

Functional convergence is the close collaboration and communication within and between departments in an organisation which helps ensure objectives are met.

Functional structures are common in both companies that have outgrown the simple structure and in well-established public-sector organisations. The organisation will be structured around the tasks and activities to be carried out.

Global culture emerges from the way in which national cultures interact with each other. The challenge for global organisations is to operate in a way which spans a variety of national cultures.

Global level is anything beyond the local and national levels of the external environment.

Hawthorne studies were Elton Mayo's work which showed that social factors, such as the relationship between management and in particular the social grouping between staff, can influence the behaviour of employees in an organisation.

Heroes, according to Deal and Kennedy, are high achievers in organisations who personify the organisation's cultural values and hence provide an explicit role model for employees.

Historical analogy occurs when an organisation assumes that the sales pattern for a new product will be similar to that for a product already on the market.

Holding company structures are usually found in large industrial conglomerates with a parent company acting mainly as an investment company acquiring and divesting smaller subsidiary companies.

Hostile takeover bid is the buying of a majority shareholding in a company with the aim of becoming the new owners against the wishes of all or some of the current owners or shareholders.

Human capital arises from the skills, abilities and knowledge of the workforce and their capacity to create value for the business via application of their skills, abilities and knowledge.

Human resource management includes recruitment and selection of appropriate staff and management of the employment relationship, which includes contracts, collective bargaining, reward systems and employee involvement, and considers the strategic and operational view of human resource requirements.

Hybrid layout occurs when a product is assembled from two components, one being manufactured on a production line and the other in another part of the factory in a job shop using the process layout.

Immigration occurs when a person enters a new country with the intent of settling there on a permanent basis.

Independent demand inventory comprises items that are not dependent on other components, i.e. they are finished goods, like cars or shoes. Demand for such goods is directly dependent on consumer demand.

Indirect costs do not contribute directly to the product or service being produced, e.g. security staff. Indirect costs are often called overheads.

Initial capital employed is the money available at the start of a project and takes no account of residual values at the end of the life of the project.

Innovation in organisations, according to Rosabeth Moss Kanter, is best achieved by organisations first putting in place systems, practices, cultures and rewards that will encourage and allow people to be enterprising and innovative.

Instrumental values are the types of behaviour preferred by the organisation, for example hard working, accurate and creative.

Intangible resources include things like brand image and information.

Intangible services are those things which organisations provide but which customers cannot see or touch, e.g. financial advice.

Intellectual capital comprises human capital, social capital, organisational capital and customer capital, which all contribute to competitive advantage.

Interest is what stakeholders seek from an organisation, for example employees have an interest in the wages an organisation pays.

Interest groups are people who band together to achieve a common goal.

Internal dependencies are from within to within linkages or internal dependencies inside the organisation.

Internal rate of return measures the discount rate at which future net cash in-flows, when discounted, exactly equal the amount originally invested, i.e. NPV = 0.

Internalisation is the process for transferring explicit knowledge into tacit knowledge. Explicit knowledge in a written form can be used as starting point for informal discussions which develop and share explicit knowledge but in a tacit form, i.e. the discussion and resulting ideas are not recorded.

Inventory or stock are different types of items held by an organisation and include raw materials, components, work in progress and finished goods.

Investment appraisal techniques are used by management to help in making decisions concerning investment in long-term projects and spending capital finance.

Job analysis is the first step in the employee recruitment process and involves gaining the correct information relating to the vacant job, to allow an accurate job description and person specification to be drawn up.

Job description defines and outlines the job. It includes identification of the job, summary of the job, content of the job, working conditions and performance standards.

Just-in-time systems attempt to eliminate stock mismatches and the system is organised so that stock arrives just as it is needed.

Key results are the outputs and outcomes produced by the job holder and declare the important results expected of the job holder. They are assessed by use of explicit success criteria. Success criteria express the expected outcomes and outputs in terms of quality, quantity, cost and time.

Key success factors are those things the organisation must do to satisfactorily meet the needs and expectations of its customers and other stakeholders.

Knowledge is the information, skills and understanding gained through learning or experience.

Leadership is the ability to influence a group towards the achievement of goals.

Learning organisations continually refresh their balance of different types of capital (human, social, organisational and customer) around a shared vision for the organisation.

Limited companies exist as individual legal entities, separate from the owners or managers. Therefore, liability for debts is limited to the amount of issued share capital, whether the shares have been sold or not.

Liquidate is to turn into cash, usually done by selling assets.

Local culture could be defined as the type of place a village, town or city is, and the strength of identity that individuals from a place feel for it.

Local level of the external environment is the immediate town, city or region in which an organisation operates.

LoNGPEST is analysis of the PEST factors at the local, national and global levels of the external environment.

Maastricht Treaty on European Union covers the issues of currency, immigration controls and defence policy.

Management accounting generates information for managers to use in planning and decision making relating to the allocation of an organisation's financial resources.

Marginal costing is a costing technique of charging variable costs to the production units.

Market development occurs if an organisation manages to sell its existing products and services in new marketplaces.

Market penetration occurs if an organisation manages to sell more of its existing products and services to existing customers.

Market pull arises from recognising customer needs which identify new market segments or segments of the existing market which are poorly served by current competitors.

Market research is the way by which companies identify who is in the marketplace, their location, and their needs and wants.

Market survey is a collection of data and information from a sample of customers and potential customers. The data and information are analysed and inferences made about the population at large.

Market-based location is when an organisation locates its facilities in a place which is convenient for its geographic markets.

Marketing is the identification and meeting of customer needs and wants.

Marketing era for an organisation is when it gears all its activities towards achieving the goals and objectives associated with satisfying customer needs and wants.

Marketing mix describes the marketing elements that could affect the way a product performs in the marketplace. They are product, price, promotion and place.

Marketing tools are frameworks or models which can be used to conceptualise or think about a firm's markets, products and customers. Examples of marketing tools include the product life cycle and the Boston Consulting Group matrix.

Marketplace is where the company's products are sold and can be defined by types of customer and/or location.

Materials requirement planning (MRP) relies on production plans to propose a timetable for when material orders are required. Consequently the resulting stocks of materials depend directly on a known demand.

Matrix structures attempt to merge the benefits of decentralisation with coordination across all areas of the business and are often used in organisations where there are two distinct and important areas of operation needing to be managed and coordinated in order to deliver the full product range.

Meritocratic describes government by persons selected according to merit in competition.

Mixed economy occurs where there is some regulation to protect businesses, consumers and employees.

Mourning is the disbanding of the group and members moving on to their next project.

Moving to a new level involves finding solutions to the organisation's difficulties and implementing them successfully, such that old working practices are no longer followed.

National culture can result from one nation attributing characteristics to another, which can result in stereotyping and prejudice. National culture needs to take account of differences in the groups and communities which all contribute to national culture.

National level of the external environment is the home country with which an organisation identifies.

Net present value (NPV) method of investment appraisal converts future net cashflows into present-day values by discounting the value of money that is expected to be received in the future.

Norming is when the group cooperates, and tasks are allocated and undertaken.

Norms are the rules that define acceptable behaviour, with behaviour not conforming to the norms being unacceptable.

North American Free Trade Agreement (NAFTA) is a trading bloc made up of Canada, the US and Mexico.

Ordinary shares are issued by companies to raise capital and are commonly traded on the stock market.

Organisational behaviour is the study of the performance of individuals and groups in different structures and cultures within the workplace.

Organisational capital includes explicit knowledge, information systems, market data, production processes and all data, information and solutions provided by IT systems.

Organisational culture results from the organisation's structure, employees and their behaviour, and the type of power and control present.

Overdrafts are short-term loans for 12 months or less and will vary from day to day depending on the amount by which the organisation's current account is overdrawn.

Overheads are costs which do not directly contribute to the product or service offered by the organisation.

Panel consensus is the gathering of consumer views on a product via groups, with the aim of reducing prejudices and misconceptions of the individual.

Partnerships are where two or more individuals join together in a business venture with each partner having unlimited liability.

Patents are contracts between individuals or organisations and the state, which grants a temporary monopoly to the owner of the patent.

Payback method measures the length of time taken for the return on an investment exactly to equal the amount originally invested.

Payback period is the length of time taken for the return on an investment exactly to equal the amount originally invested.

Perception is an individual's personal view of the world and definition of reality.

Performing is when the group completes tasks and objectives are achieved.

Person cultures are found in organisations where a set of professionals agree to collaborate to perform a specific service. These people could be self-employed, or at least would have little notion of being employees of an organisation in the traditional sense.

Person specification is derived from the job description by translating the job activities into the specific skills and abilities required to perform the job effectively.

Personal cultural provenance makes an individual the person they are and is determined by things such as name, gender, profession, icons, symbols, ceremonies, personal morality, norms and values.

PEST analysis is the examining of political, economic, sociocultural and technological categories into which external influences on the organisation can be placed.

Planned economies occur where production and other aspects of the economy are planned by central government.

Political influences on organisations encompass both legislation and industry regulations.

Power is the pressure a stakeholder is able to bring to bear to persuade an organisation to act in a particular way. For example, shareholders with many shares have greater power than those with only a few.

Power cultures are found in small, entrepreneurial organisations, where the owner works with few employees, with the centre of power, and all crucial decision making, resting with the owner/manager.

Power structures evolve in organisations over time and consist of individuals with power, who all share a common set of beliefs and values that underpins the way they work together.

Preventive maintenance is carried out on a planned basis, with the intervals between maintenance inspections established by experience, manufacturers or external authorities, and can be critical for items that are expensive to replace or repair.

Primary data is collected directly from people and organisations via questionnaires or surveys before being analysed to reach conclusions concerning the issues covered in the questionnaire or survey.

Primary-sector organisations are concerned with producing raw materials and include oil extraction, coal mining, diamond mining and farming to produce food.

Prime costs are the sum of direct wages and direct materials (prime costs = direct wages + direct materials).

Process cultures occur in organisations which take low-risk decisions, with feedback being slow.

Process flow charts show the order of and relationship between activities performed to make a product or deliver a service.

Process layout involves similar equipment and machinery being located together, as the processes they are used for are closely related.

Product development occurs when updated or new products and services are produced and sold to existing customers.

Product layout puts together in one location all the equipment required to manufacture one particular product and is the basis of a traditional production line.

Product life cycle is one of the marketing tools. The product life cycle can be used to examine the sales and profits a product or service is making, relative to the length of time in the marketplace.

Product planning and development covers identifying new technology which the company could use, new suppliers and opportunities to liaise with customers concerning new products.

Product-based location is used by large organisations with different divisions each responsible for their own product ranges located close to each other but separately, hence allowing each division to use appropriate resources for its own area of business.

Production era occurred when organisations viewed their customers as a plentiful and captive supply of people who were happy to buy whatever firms produced.

Productivity is the quantity manufactured in relation to one or more resources used.

Projective methods of forecasting examine the patterns of previous demand and extend the pattern into the future.

Prototype is the first version of a new product, which will be tried with a few consumers as part of the market research process before being modified to give a final version which is launched on to the marketplace.

Public-sector organisations are owned and regulated by government at either local or national level.

Pull factors attract or pull an organisation towards a new location, e.g. the availability of cheap skilled labour.

Push factors result from dissatisfaction with existing locations, hence causing the organisation to consider changing location.

Qualitative forecasting is that which is non-numerical and relies on people's views and opinions.

Quantitative forecasting is numerical and is feasible if the company is already producing the product or providing the service, as historical data will already exist concerning the demand for a product or service.

Receiver is a company or individual called in, often by the bank, to decide whether a failing business has any chance of survival and generating enough cash to pay its creditors or whether it should be shut down, assets sold off and as many creditors paid as possible.

Registered design is for designs with form or aesthetic appeal and therefore it is the outward appearance of the article that is protected, e.g. its shape, contours, texture and pattern. The design must be new and individual and not remind customers of an existing design.

Remote shopping occurs when customers purchase goods or services in a location other than a retail outlet, e.g. on the internet or via a catalogue.

Reserves are retained profits from previous years that have not been spent or distributed to shareholders.

Restrictive Practices Court was established in 1956 and controls practices that are presumed to be against the public interest. Restrictive practices can relate to the price of goods, conditions of supply, qualities or descriptions, processes or areas and persons supplied.

Rights issues are share issues for existing shareholders only.

Rituals in organisational life are used to reinforce the routines and 'the way things are done around here'.

Rodger's seven-point plan can be used to produce a person specification and covers the areas of physical make-up, attainment, general intelligence, special aptitudes, interests, disposition and circumstances.

Role cultures are found in mature and large organisations with departments, in which everyone will have a specific job title and description and know how they are expected to contribute to the organisational mission.

Sales era was when firms did not consider the actual needs or wants of customers, but concentrated on persuading customers to buy their products rather than those of competitors.

Sales promotion is the activity firms undertake to persuade customers to buy their products or services. Examples include free samples and money-off vouchers.

Scientific management was Frederick Winslow Taylor's work and he sought to study the performance of individuals in the workplace. Underpinning Taylor's approach was the basic assumption that people dislike work but will undertake it in order to earn a living. Taylor went on to argue that due to this assumed dislike of work, staff need very close supervision, as they are not capable of self-management and motivation.

Second peripheral group includes employees on short-term contracts, part-time employees, job-sharing employees and subsidised trainees.

Secondary data has already been collected and analysed and presented in written form, ready for people to use.

Secondary-sector organisations manufacture and produce goods, often from raw materials produced by primary-sector organisations.

Selling is part of the process by which organisations persuade customers to purchase their goods and services.

Seven tasks of tomorrow's manager is Peter Drucker's work. He identifies the seven tasks of tomorrow's manager, namely: manage by objectives; take more risks, over a longer time period; take strategic decisions; build an integrated team; communicate quickly and clearly and be motivating; see the organisation as a whole and their own role within it; understand the external environment.

Shamans, according to Deal and Kennedy, are outside consultants who can be useful in helping the people affected by cultural change in an organisation span the gap between the two different organisational cultures.

Shareholders are the owners of a business as they hold or own shares.

Simple structures are adopted by small businesses in the private sector, which may be established businesses or in the very early stages of growth and development. The organisation is structured around the owner/manager.

Social capital arises from the formal and informal procedures, structures and networks both inside and outside the organisation which staff are members of and exploit.

Social change is change in the way people behave and live their lives, including the changing nature of decisions relating to marriage, divorce and children.

Socialisation is the process for transferring tacit knowledge around an organisation via informal meetings and day-to-day informal discussion between staff who work together.

Sociocultural influences on organisations include changes in the age, structure and behaviour of populations.

Sole trader businesses are owned and administered by one person who is personally liable for all the debts of the business.

Stakeholder matrix is used to plot the varying levels of power and interest which stakeholders have in an organisation.

Stakeholders are any individuals or a collection of individuals with an interest in an organisation and will hold varying degrees of power.

Status is the social worth conferred on an individual due to the position they occupy in the group.

Stock market is where a company's shares are traded. The UK stock market is in London.

Stories in organisational life represent the organisation's history and typically highlight significant events and characters in its past.

Storming is when group members jockey for position and roles in the group are established.

Substitute products or services provide the same function as the goods they replace. A straightforward example is coach travel being a substitute for rail travel.

Symbols present in an organisation can be many and varied and often symbolise someone's position in the organisation or how much that individual is valued by the organisation.

Tacit knowledge is rather more vague than explicit knowledge and can be difficult to specify, unclear and unrecorded, but it is also valuable to organisations.

Tangible products are those which customers can see and touch.

Tangible resources are physical resources and include things like machines and money.

Task cultures are flexible and often found in organisations that frequently undertake work for a variety of customers, which will involve a team with the required skills and knowledge undertaking very specific problem-solving or troubleshooting tasks as projects.

Task groups are determined by the organisation, but do not depend on the hierarchical relationships that are present in command groups.

Technological influences include the impact of computers, software, communications technology and electronic media.

Technology push occurs when an innovative product (which may start as a small solution to a particular problem) that the market may not even recognise permeates the marketplace and is taken up by many customers.

Telecommuters/teleworkers work at home, with technology that enables them to receive and send work and messages to their employing organisation.

Term loans are long term and provide the borrowing organisation with capital in return for repayment of the capital with interest over a number of years, e.g. five or ten.

Terminal values are desired outcomes, which people and/or organisations seek to achieve, for example quality, service, innovation and ethics.

Tertiary-sector organisations sell goods produced by primary and secondary organisations. The tertiary sector includes service-sector organisations such as banks and social services.

Theory X is Douglas McGregor's work and assumes that people dislike work and seek to avoid it at all costs. Hence people need to be controlled, coerced, threatened and punished to achieve an adequate individual contribution to organisational goals. This also supports the assumptions that people prefer to be tightly supervised, with no responsibility and virtually no ambition.

Theory Y is Douglas McGregor's work and assumes people regard work as a normal activity and are hence committed to objectives and self-motivated towards their achievement and the associated rewards. Additionally, people will accept and seek out responsibility, and take the opportunity to behave creatively while resolving problems in organisations and developing organisations.

Threat of new entrants will be greatest if an industry is attractive enough to entice them. Attractive industries have high potential profits and low set-up costs.

Total quality management is defined as the whole organisation working together to improve product or service quality. The aim of total quality management is zero defects.

Tough-guy macho cultures occur in organisations which take high-risk decisions and receive rapid feedback on the effectiveness of their actions.

Trademarks indicate which company is providing the goods and services on offer and are often used in industries that are not heavily reliant on invention.

Trading blocs are made up of a number of countries that agree to cooperate with regard to trade and commerce.

Transactional dependencies are from outside in and inside out linkages or links in and out of the organisation, i.e. between the internal environment and the external environment.

Transactional leaders clarify tasks and roles while motivating their followers or subordinates towards achievement of the group or organisational goals.

Unfreezing process occurs when old behaviour in organisations becomes regarded as unsuitable and ceases, so that attitudes and behaviour can start to change.

Utilisation measures the percentage of available capacity that is actually used.

Values are things, people or attitudes that groups of individuals think are important or to be revered or respected.

Variable costs are those which vary in relation to the level of productivity and include direct labour costs and direct materials costs.

Vertically differentiated location strategy occurs when separate stages of the manufacturing and supply process are in different locations.

Visionary leaders develop the organisation beyond its current situation and are able to communicate a credible vision for the development of the organisation in an articulate manner such that it is clearly understood by all relevant stakeholders.

Whistle-blowing is the release of confidential corporate information to an external third party. The third party may be the media, although a conversation with a colleague or friend in which corporate information and concerns are revealed can be whistle-blowing. This applies even if the third party, e.g. a friend, was unaware that confidential information was being revealed to them.

Work hard/play hard cultures occur in organisations which take low-risk decisions and receive quick feedback on their performance.

World Trade Organisation (WTO) is the international organisation which deals with the rules and regulations of trade between nations.

Index